96 —

D1565068

# Lifespan Development and the Brain

This book focuses on the developmental analysis of brain-culture-environment dynamics and argues that this dynamic is interactive and reciprocal: brain and culture co-determine each other. As a whole, this book refutes any unidirectional conception of the brain-culture dynamic, as each is influenced by and modifies the other. To capture the ubiquitous reach and significance of the mutually dependent and co-productive brain-culture system, the metaphor of biocultural co-constructivism is invoked. Distinguished researchers from cognitive neuroscience, cognitive psychology, and developmental psychology review the evidence in their respective fields. A special focus of the book is its coverage of the entire human lifespan.

Paul B. Baltes is noted for his theoretical and empirical work in developmental psychology and the interdisciplinary study of human aging. Aside from multiple honorary doctorates and election to academies, he has received numerous awards, including the International Psychology Award of the American Psychological Association, the Lifetime Achievement Award of the German Psychological Society, and the Aristotle Prize of the European Federation of Psychological Associations.

Patricia A. Reuter-Lorenz is known for her research on the neuropsychological mechanisms of attention and working memory, in particular through her work with special patient populations, functional brain imaging, and normal human aging. She is co-founder of the Cognitive Neuroscience Society, has served on its governing board since its inception, and serves on the editorial boards of leading journals in the field.

Frank Rösler is recognized for his research on biological correlates of cognitive processes, in particular memory, learning, imagery, language, and neural plasticity. He has received several awards, including the Max-Planck/Humboldt prize for international cooperation, and he has been elected as full member to two academies of sciences in Germany.

# Lifespan Development and the Brain

## The Perspective of Biocultural Co-Constructivism

Edited by

**PAUL B. BALTES**
*Max Planck Institute for Human Development, Berlin, Germany*

**PATRICIA A. REUTER-LORENZ**
*University of Michigan, Ann Arbor, Michigan*

**FRANK RÖSLER**
*Philipps-University, Marburg, Germany*

CAMBRIDGE
UNIVERSITY PRESS

CAMBRIDGE UNIVERSITY PRESS
Cambridge, New York, Melbourne, Madrid, Cape Town, Singapore, São Paulo, Delhi

Cambridge University Press
32 Avenue of the Americas, New York, NY 10013-2473, USA

www.cambridge.org
Information on this title: www.cambridge.org/9780521844949

First published 2006
Reprinted 2007

Printed in the United States of America

*A catalog record for this publication is available from the British Library.*

*Library of Congress Cataloging in Publication Data*

Lifespan development and the brain: the perspective of biocultural co-constructivism/
edited by Paul B. Baltes, Patricia A. Reuter-Lorenz, Frank Rösler.
    p.  cm.
Includes bibliographical references and index.
ISBN-13: 978-0-521-84494-9 (hardback)
ISBN-10: 0-521-84494-0 (hardback)
1. Brain – Growth.   2. Culture.   I. Baltes, Paul B.   II. Title.
QP376.L565   2006
612.8′2 – dc22                                                            2006000773

ISBN   978-0-521-84494-9 hardback

# Contents

*List of Contributors*                                                    *page* ix

*Preface and Acknowledgments*                                                  xiii
*Paul B. Baltes, Patricia A. Reuter-Lorenz, and Frank Rösler*

PART ONE. SETTING THE STAGE ACROSS THE AGES
OF THE LIFESPAN

1. Prologue: Biocultural Co-Constructivism as a Theoretical
   Metascript                                                                    3
   *Paul B. Baltes, Frank Rösler, and Patricia A. Reuter-Lorenz*

2. Biocultural Co-Construction of Lifespan Development                          40
   *Shu-Chen Li*

PART TWO. NEURONAL PLASTICITY AND BIOCULTURAL
CO-CONSTRUCTION: MICROSTRUCTURE MEETS THE
EXPERIENTIAL ENVIRONMENT

3. Neurobehavioral Development in the Context of Biocultural
   Co-Constructivism                                                            61
   *Charles A. Nelson*

4. Adult Neurogenesis                                                           82
   *Gerd Kempermann*

PART THREE. NEURONAL PLASTICITY AND BIOCULTURAL
CO-CONSTRUCTION: ATYPICAL BRAIN ARCHITECTURES

5. Sensory Input–Based Adaptation and Brain Architecture                       111
   *Maurice Ptito and Sébastien Desgent*

6. Blindness: A Source and Case of Neuronal Plasticity                         134
   *Brigitte Röder*

PART FOUR. BIOCULTURAL CO-CONSTRUCTION: SPECIFIC
FUNCTIONS AND DOMAINS

7. Language Acquisition: Biological Versus Cultural
   Implications for Brain Structure                                    161
   *Angela D. Friederici and Shirley-Ann Rüschemeyer*

8. Reading, Writing, and Arithmetic in the Brain: Neural
   Specialization for Acquired Functions                              183
   *Thad A. Polk and J. Paul Hamilton*

9. Emotion, Learning, and the Brain: From Classical
   Conditioning to Cultural Bias                                      200
   *Elizabeth A. Phelps*

10. The Musical Mind: Neural Tuning and
    the Aesthetic Experience                                          217
    *Oliver Vitouch*

PART FIVE. PLASTICITY AND BIOCULTURAL CO-CONSTRUCTION IN
LATER LIFE

11. Influences of Biological and Self-Initiated Factors on Brain
    and Cognition in Adulthood and Aging                              239
    *Lars Nyberg and Lars Bäckman*

12. The Aging Mind and Brain: Implications of Enduring
    Plasticity for Behavioral and Cultural Change                     255
    *Patricia A. Reuter-Lorenz and Joseph A. Mikels*

PART SIX. BIOCULTURAL CO-CONSTRUCTION: FROM MICRO- TO
MACROENVIRONMENTS IN LARGER CULTURAL CONTEXTS

13. Characteristics of Illiterate and Literate Cognitive Processing:
    Implications of Brain–Behavior Co-Constructivism                  279
    *Karl Magnus Petersson and Alexandra Reis*

14. The Influence of Work and Occupation on
    Brain Development                                                 306
    *Neil Charness*

15. The Influence of Organized Violence and Terror on Brain
    and Mind: A Co-Constructive Perspective                           326
    *Thomas Elbert, Brigitte Rockstroh, Iris-Tatjana Kolassa,
    Maggie Schauer, and Frank Neuner*

16. Co-Constructing Human Engineering Technologies in Old
    Age: Lifespan Psychology as a Conceptual Foundation              350
    *Ulman Lindenberger and Martin Lövdén*

# Contents

PART SEVEN. EPILOGUE

17. Letters on Nature and Nurture                          379
     Onur Güntürkün

Author Index                                              399
Subject Index                                             416

# Contributors

**Paul B. Baltes** Director, Max Planck International Research Network on Aging, Max Planck Institute for Human Development, Berlin, and Distinguished Professor of Psychology, University of Virginia, Charlottesville, USA

**Lars Bäckman** Professor of Psychology, Aging Research Center, Karolinska Institute, Stockholm, Sweden

**Neil Charness** Professor of Psychology, Department of Psychology and Pepper Institute on Aging and Public Policy, Florida State University, Tallahassee, USA

**Sébastien Desgent** Doctoral Candidate in Neurosciences, Department of Physiology and School of Optometry, University of Montreal, Canada

**Thomas Elbert** Professor and Chair of Clinical Psychology and Neuropsychology, University of Konstanz, Germany

**Angela D. Friederici** Director, Max Planck Institute for Human Cognitive and Brain Sciences, Leipzig, and Honorary Professor at the Universities of Leipzig (Psychology) and Potsdam (Linguistics) and Charité University Medicine, Berlin, Germany

**Onur Güntürkün** Professor of Biopsychology, Institute of Cognitive Neuroscience, Ruhr-University, Bochum, Germany

**J. Paul Hamilton** Postdoctoral Fellow, Stanford Mood and Anxiety Disorders Laboratory, Stanford University, Palo Alto, California, USA

**Gerd Kempermann** MD, Head of Neuronal Stem Cells Research Group, Max Delbrück Center for Molecular Medicine (MDC), Berlin-Buch, Germany

**Iris-Tatjana Kolassa** Research Scientist, Department of Psychology, University of Konstanz, Germany

**Shu-Chen Li** Senior Research Scientist, Center for Lifespan Psychology, Max Planck Institute for Human Development, Berlin, Germany

**Ulman Lindenberger** Director, Center for Lifespan Psychology, Max Planck Institute for Human Development, Berlin, and Honorary Professor of Psychology, Free University, Berlin, and Humboldt University, Berlin, and Professor of Psychology, Saarland University, Saarbrücken, Germany

**Martin Lövdén** International Research Fellow, Center for Lifespan Psychology, Max Planck Institute for Human Development, Berlin, Germany

**Joseph A. Mikels** Postdoctoral Fellow, Department of Psychology, Stanford University, Palo Alto, California, USA

**Charles A. Nelson** Professor of Pediatrics, Harvard Medical School, Richard David Scott Chair in Pediatric Developmental Medicine Research, Developmental Medicine Center Laboratory of Cognitive Neuroscience, Boston, Massachusetts, USA

**Frank Neuner** Junior Professor of Clinical Psychology and Psychotherapy, University of Konstanz, Germany

**Lars Nyberg** Professor of Neuroscience, Umeå University, Sweden

**Karl Magnus Petersson** Postdoctoral Fellow, F. C. Donders Centre for Cognitive Neuroimaging, Radboud University Nijmegen, Netherlands

**Elizabeth A. Phelps** Professor of Psychology and Neural Science, New York University, USA

**Thad A. Polk** Associate Professor of Psychology, University of Michigan, Ann Arbor, USA

**Maurice Ptito** Harlan Sanders Professor of Visual Science, School of Optometry, University of Montreal, Canada

**Alexandra Reis** Associate Professor of Biological and Behavioral Psychology, Neuropsychology, and Cognitive Psychology, University of Algarve, Faro, Portugal

**Patricia A. Reuter-Lorenz** Professor of Psychology, University of Michigan, Ann Arbor, USA

**Brigitte Rockstroh** Professor and Chair of Clinical Psychology, University of Konstanz, Germany

**Brigitte Röder** Professor of Biological Psychology and Neuropsychology, University of Hamburg, Germany

**Frank Rösler** Professor for Experimental and Biological Psychology, Philipps-University, Marburg, Germany

**Shirley-Ann Rüschemeyer** Postdoctoral Fellow, Max Planck Institute for Human Cognitive and Brain Sciences, Leipzig, Germany

**Maggie Schauer** Director of the Psychological Research Clinic for Refugees, University of Konstanz, Germany

**Oliver Vitouch** Professor and Chair of Cognitive Psychology, University of Klagenfurt, Austria

# Preface and Acknowledgments

As described in Chapter 1, this book is the outgrowth of the desire to generate a theoretical orientation in which simple models of unidirectional determinism in regard to human behavior and human development, whether gene, brain, behavior, or culture driven, are laid to rest. A vibrant counterdose of interactionism seemed especially necessary in light of recent public discussions in Germany, much stimulated by noted neuroscientists, about the unquestionable dominance of the brain in the determination of behavior and individual action. We believed that this seeming movement toward reductionistic determinism, stemming in part from the justifiable excitement associated with new methods of neuroscience, was cause for concern. Of course, there were many important forerunners to our general theoretical orientation. Nonetheless, we judged that strengthening a more dynamic and interactionist conception of the nature of human behavior and the role of culture in co-constructing the brain and behavior was the call of the times.

Our first step was to have discussions among the three editors and a few close colleagues, such as Ulman Lindenberger and Shu-Chen Li. Subsequently, we planned a conference to examine the basic rationale and enrich its conceptual framework. Specifically, the goal was to bring noted scholars together, who, as a collective, would be prepared to activate and orchestrate a position where the various participating elements – the genome, the brain, behavior, the physical environment, and culture – were seen as somewhat independent agents that influence each other in pervasive, deep, and cumulative ways. To counteract the seeming movement toward a stronger dose of brain determinism, we also believed it necessary to compensate by creating a new metaphor: biocultural co-constructivism was the result of these deliberations. The field chosen to illustrate this position was human development across the lifespan. We are grateful to each chapter author, who, through his or her participation in the conference and contribution to this volume, endeavored to reach into the heart of the biocultural co-constructivism metaphor or metascript and to illustrate its relevance to his or her respective specialization.

Preparation of this book was aided by many who deserve much of the credit but none of the blame. First, there was the generous financial support of the Max Planck Institute for Human Development in Berlin, Germany. Second, there was the outstanding infrastructure of that institute and its longstanding connection to an enticing conference center in Dölln, a city north of Berlin. Then, there were the individuals who bring such activities to life and permit scientists to engage in their intellectual agendas.

Foremost was Dr. Julia Delius, who functioned as conference coordinator, ably assisted by Amy Michele. Dr. Delius was also the editorial assistant who led the book editors through the initial stages of the review process and supervised submission of the final book manuscript. This book owes much to the care and collegial atmosphere she created. In the final steps of the editorial process, Amy Michele rose to the occasion, becoming Dr. Delius's competent and committed substitute. In addition, Anke Schepers and Annette Brose provided excellent secretarial and technical support. They deserve our heartfelt gratitude.

Our review process included not only outside reviewers, but also the charge that each chapter author participated in commenting on two or three chapters written by his or her colleagues. We are grateful for this special engagement, and we thank the original chapter authors for their willingness to consider the input. Undoubtedly, because of this cooperative spirit, many, if not all, chapters reached new heights of clarity and cogency.

Considering the complexity of the topic, it is not surprising that such a book cannot offer a definite and comprehensive account. Biocultural co-constructivism is in the making, and it is practiced in rather different areas of the bio-, behavioral, and social sciences. Thus, this book is selective. Other lines of scholarship, and perhaps even more advanced models of treating the topic, could have been included.

Despite these limitations, we are hopeful that the book offers new insights, an attractive counteroffer to simple biological determinism, and a good selection of what current biocultural co-constructivism has to offer. May it age well, less on the dusty shelves of libraries or in rarely accessed computer files, but rather on the handy desks and in the lively minds of active scholars.

Paul B. Baltes
Patricia A. Reuter-Lorenz
Frank Rösler

# Lifespan Development and the Brain

# PART ONE

# SETTING THE STAGE ACROSS THE AGES OF THE LIFESPAN

1

# Prologue: Biocultural Co-Constructivism as a Theoretical Metascript

Paul B. Baltes, Frank Rösler, and
Patricia A. Reuter-Lorenz

The main objective of this book is to advance research and theory in the study of brain–culture relationships. Contentwise, our primary arena is the study of human behavior, in general, and human development, in particular. When speaking of human development, we refer to the view that human development is a lifelong process, extending from conception into old age. When we speak of culture in this context, we use it in its most general sense and mean to include all aspects of the environment – physical, material, social, and symbolic.

On the one hand, we note the already existing and recently strengthened connections between researchers and scholars in the neuro, behavioral, social, and cultural sciences that give testimony to a new level of "interdisiplinarity." It is increasingly recognized that such collaborative work, aimed at a more explicit treatment of the brain–culture interface, is necessary to better understand the interactive systems that shape the human mind and its development.

On the other hand, we also suggest that there are lacunae or misunderstandings in recognizing the full reciprocal nature of the brain–culture interaction. One example is the occasionally high emphasis that brain researchers place on brain determinism. A similar one-sidedness exists among some social scientists when they engage themselves in demonstrating the exclusive role of social-cultural environmental conditions. To counteract such lacunae or one-sided perspectives, we introduce a new "metatheoretical" paradigm as a guiding principle. This is the principle of *developmental biocultural co-constructivism*. In principle, it states that brain and culture are in a continuous, interdependent, co-productive transaction and reciprocal determination. This was true for the interplay between genetic and cultural evolution, continues to be true for modern-day human behavior, and applies to all stages of human life from conception to death. In our view, this concept, if accepted and practiced as a guiding theoretical paradigm, will facilitate a deeper recognition of the

3

brain–culture interface, counteract discipline-bound biases, reduce misunderstandings, and, above all, suggest new lines of inquiry.

In the following, we begin by describing in more detail the background that resulted in this book, as well as why we think that introducing a new concept is helpful in directing the field to the kind of full-fledged collaboration that in our view is necessary to capture the brain–culture dynamic. Then we make an attempt to formalize the co-construction hypothesis at the level of individual learning. By this, we want to explicate how endogenous and exogenous factors co-construct in a highly dynamic manner both the functional-structural architecture of the brain and the environment of an acting organism. We conclude with a characterization of the individual chapters. In describing the chapters, we make an effort to highlight their special contributions to understanding the brain–culture relationship.

## BACKGROUND OF THE VOLUME

The origins of this volume lie not only in recent developments signaling a rapprochement among the neurosciences, the behavioral sciences, and the social sciences in the study of behavior in general and human development in specific (Lerner, 2002; Li, 2003; Magnusson, 1996; Tomasello, 1999), but perhaps more significantly in the nature of the public and scientific discussions that arose since the 1990s in connection with new imaging methods to study the brain. The surge of the neurosciences as the foundation of human development appeared to us as so rapid and seductive, especially when presented to the public and in the media, that despite the parallel evolution of collaborative interdisciplinarity, we were faced with a revival of reductionist biological determinism of mind and behavior – this time focused on the brain rather than on genetics. Such an all-too-biology-based determinism was strengthened by the emergence of molecular genetics and associated findings linking specific genes to specific pathologies. For some molecular biologists and brain scientists, genes and brains seemed to hold the potential for unidirectional and all-encompassing causality and determination of mind and behavior.

What seemingly was often overlooked in this debate is that the brain itself is a dependent variable, something that is co-shaped by experience and culture, something that does not operate within an environmental vacuum, but that at any moment is subject to environmental constraints and affordances. The same, of course, applies in principle to modes of thought that place the environment into the driver's seat of development, as some proponents of environmental behaviorism attempted to teach us during the twentieth century.

Certainly, this characterization of the impact of the recent advent of neuroscience is an oversimplification of the intellectual dialectics within the scholarly community. Most certainly, and this is especially true for researchers with a developmental orientation, whether evolutionary or ontogenetic, there were and are researchers who understand the vexations of the problem, who did not and do not forget the historical lessons learned from the nature–nurture debate, including the extremes of both sides, such as full-blown environmentalism or geneticism, and who do promote in their work the important role that reciprocity and interactional processes – between genes, brain, nonbrain bodily states, experience, behavior, physical environment, and culture – play in the evolution, ontogeny, and production of behavior.

We already mentioned the special role of developmental scholars in the recognition of the reciprocal effects in the nature–nurture and brain–behavior–culture dynamic. This is not surprising. Developmental researchers focus not only on the proximal, but also on the distal antecedents of change (Baltes, Reese, & Nesselroade, 1977); therefore, they are immediately confronted with the question of the interplay between nature and nurture and between brain and culture. On the one hand, in this spirit, the arguments for explicit recognition of reciprocity and interactional processes evolved from groundbreaking work over the last decades in evolutionary theory and the role of cultural evolution (e.g., Durham, 1991; Ehrlich & Feldman, 2003; Jablonka & Lamb, 2001). On the other hand, a similar scientific evolution occurred in the ontogenetic developmental sciences. Here, it was argued that the process of ontogenetic development requires the joint (distal as well as proximal) action of genes, brain, material environment, culture, and behavior (e.g., Baltes, Reese, & Lipsitt, 1980; Baltes & Singer, 2001; Bronfenbrenner & Ceci, 1994; Cole, 1996; Gottlieb, Wahlsten, & Lickliter 1998; Greenfield, 2000; Greenough & Black, 1992; Li, 2003; Magnusson, 1996; Nelson, 2000; Quartz & Sejnowski, 1997; Singer, 2003; Staudinger & Lindenberger, 2003; Tomasello, 1999). The kind of categories used to describe the internal and external forces and dynamics varied, but the thrust of the argument was always similar, namely, to treat the determining system as interactive and reciprocal, over time and across space (context).

Yet, we as editors and organizers of a preparatory conference – although with different degrees of conviction and rationales – believed that, to move the field forward and to not lose the insights of the past, more needed to be done to counteract the seemingly overemphasized position of biological factors, if not of unidirectional biology- or brain-based determinism. Even if our evaluative and chagrined view of the new Zeitgeist was out of proportion, we believed that having another chance to articulate the issues and promote constructive dialogue across theoretical orientations seemed enough reason to bring together brain- and culture-oriented scholars. We were convinced that the new paradigm of human development demanded a full-fledged view of the principles of collaboration between biological and cultural systems.

We hoped for a more firmly based dialogue, not only between the respective scholars and specialized fields, but also in support of the notion that human behavior itself is inherently the outcome of a "dialogue" among and "co-production" of genes, brain, and culture. To achieve such a goal, we also believed that exploring a new concept, if not a new metaphor, would be beneficial. We were looking for a metaphor that would consolidate and solidify the intellectual position that brain, behavior, and culture are a reciprocal and interactive system of influences, mechanisms, and outcomes, with each being affected by the other – in the past, the present, and the future; at all levels of analysis from the molecular to the molar to the social-cultural; and for each of the two major dimensions of human development – the evolutionary and the ontogenetic (Baltes, Lindenberger, & Staudinger, 1998, in press; Baltes & Singer, 2001; Jablonka & Lamb, 2005; Li, 2003). As described in this chapter, our suggestion for such a new metascript, if not metaphor, is the term *biocultural co-constructivism*.

## ON THE ROLE OF METAPHORS

Here is the place where a brief detour to the notion of metaphor may be helpful, although we immediately concede that our own choice of metaphor by the criteria of metaphors that follow is not optimal. There is much debate about the specific meaning of metaphors and their varying role in communicating knowledge, generating knowledge, and crystallizing a particular theoretical orientation (Lambourn, 2001); the sum evidence seems to have tilted in the direction of the perspective that metaphors and other language-based, short-hand concepts play a powerful role in the shaping of a field, including (1) the ways in which research questions are asked; (2) how they are conceptualized on a general level of analysis; (3) what and how data are generated; and (4) how results are interpreted, mentally represented, and communicated.

In recent history, the book by Lakoff and Johnson (1980), *Metaphors We Live By*, has become a kind of classic, illustrating the endemic nature of metaphor in everyday understanding, as well as its usefulness in generating and maintaining a given body of knowledge. In psychology, Leary's (1990) work, *Metaphors in the History of Psychology*, is a persuasive example, as is the book by Sternberg (1990) entitled *Metaphors of Mind: Conceptions of the Nature of Intelligence*.

What are metaphors? The concept carries a variety of meanings (Lambourn, 2001). One of the seemingly agreed-on commonalities is that metaphors often involve other modes of representation than language, such as visualization. Another is that metaphors involve a process of comparison or a crystallized characterization at a higher level of conception. The "other" used for comparison or characterization can take many forms.

It can be a word or operation from everyday life, a model, or a concept from another field of study. Importantly, metaphors are short-hand for communicating something larger about the ways and means of the object or phenomenon under consideration. "Intelligence functions like a computer" would be an example (see Sternberg, 1990, for other examples). If such a metaphor of intelligence is deemed to be persuasive, research into intelligence is likely to follow the concepts and methods of computer systems and technology. One ensuing example would be to consider intelligence as composed by two components – hardware and software.

In this spirit, we proceeded to ask whether the field under consideration, the study of lifespan human development, or even behavior in general, is remiss in not having the kind of metaphor that would protect us from all-too-simple principles of biology or brain-based determinism. Although the risk of one-sidedness concerns, of course, both sides – the biological-neuronal and the cultural-social – we believed that at the present time, protection against the bias of brain-based unidirectional determinism is the more important goal. To repeat our starting point – the excitement and enthusiasm about the new evidence generated by modern genetics and functional and structural measures of the brain, in which we share, seemed to have pushed many researchers into a position that did not sufficiently reflect the conceptual achievements of the past, namely, the recognition that there are complex and truly reciprocal interactions and influences between genes, brain, behavior, and culture.

## FROM INTERACTIONISM OVER CONSTRUCTIVISM TO BIOCULTURAL CO-CONSTRUCTIVISM

For quite a few years now, interactionism has been in style. But how far does this concept take us? The situation in the field linking environmental-cultural to genetic-neurobiological factors is not unlike the conceptual history of the nature–nurture debate (Ehrlich & Feldman, 2003; Lerner, 2002; Singer, 2003). In this instance, researchers introduced the concept of interactionism to highlight that nature and nurture interact in reciprocal ways. Some may think, therefore, that the term interactionism should be sufficient to clarify that nature and nurture, genes and environment, brain and behavior, and brain and culture influence each other. However, for others, although this is definitely a step in the right direction, it may not be sufficient to communicate a state where such interactions alter the factors of nature and nurture themselves.

Thus, in our view the concept of interaction, although pointing in the right direction, is underspecified and not sufficiently robust. Depending on one's conceptual predilection, the meaning of interactionism can be tilted in one way or another. For instance, one often raised question is whether the interactions are conceived of as "weak" or "strong." The more reciprocity, nonlinearity, and *emergent properties* are involved, the more the conceptual core of interaction is considered as being strong rather than weak. In other words, does the concept of interaction communicate with sufficient clarity that the sources, nature and nurture, are not mere passive and additive recipients of input from each other, but that the developmental outcome is one of shared and *collaborative production,* including *reciprocal modification,* and which under some conditions involves qualitatively new states whose emergence cannot be fully predicted from either of the two sources alone? The emergence of species in biological evolution is one example of a *developmental qualitative innovation*; the emergence of intentionality in human evolution and formal logical thought in cognitive ontogeny of children is another. A further example is the role of "collective memory" systems and their impact in defining human identity and constructions of past history (Assmann, 2006).

As a consequence, we join in the argument that the use of the term "interaction" alone is not sufficient and that additional qualification is necessary. In this spirit, we have witnessed the emergence of additional concepts that credit both genes and cultures, and brain and behavior, with being agents and producers of novel phenomena that are not in the core of the influences themselves. Making this point resulted in espousing notions such as *co-evolution* for the case of evolutionary development and *constructivism* for the case of ontogenesis.

Yet, in discussions with esteemed colleagues, we continued to be impressed that neither concept, co-evolution and constructivism, was sufficiently known across the isles of the forum, nor did they seem to carry with firmness the whole message that we were after, namely, that brain and culture are independent sources and full-fledged partners and reciprocal modifiers. In other words, they not only work together in the production of the brain, behavior, and culture, but they also change, "develop," and influence each other in an ongoing fashion – in the past, the present, and the future. Perhaps we were overly sensitive and not sufficiently cognizant of the state of affairs. However, we believe that it continues to be worthwhile to look for a concept that would not permit priority to be allocated to one or the other, but that by its very nature would give equal standing to both the brain and the environment. Our primary focus is on creating a metaphorical language that would make such perspectives a key and unalterable mode of thinking.

Thus, as we were pondering a title for this book and the possibility of promoting a robust concept for our favored orientation, we deemed three interrelated aspects essential. First, the concept should permit the separate identification of biological and environmental factors as sources of influence. Second, the concept should be unequivocal about the premise that each factor is an independent partner that, in collaboration with the other, produces the brain, the behavior, and the human environment. Third, the concept should be unequivocal and not permit deviations from the underlying framework, at whatever level of analysis. No term would suffice that would not satisfy these three postulates.

This is a tall order, and we are not necessarily happy with the semantic elegance of the term that emerged. The result was the concept of *"biocultural co-constructivism."* We claim no theoretical originality with this concept. There were and are important forerunners (Durham, 1991; Ehrlich & Feldman, 2003; Gottlieb, Wahlsten, & Lickliter, 1998; Quartz & Sejnowski, 1997; Tomasello, 1999). Moreover, we do not believe that the concept is easily digested or that it represents a new theory. At best, it is a theoretical or metatheoretical orientation. We are also not overly excited about the visualization and memory strength of the metaphor. If, for instance, there is a visualization component in the concept of biocultural co-constructivism, it is language of architecture and construction (see also Baltes, 1997, for a discussion of the concept of the biocultural architecture of the life course). Understanding that nature and nurture have been co-constructing partners of brain, behavior, and culture is an essential component of what we want to communicate as firm knowledge about human development in evolution and ontogeny.

In the spirit of the heuristic role of metaphors, we only argue that having the metaphor of "biocultural co-constructivism" protects us from an unintended bias or even seeming ignorance. The brain itself is the result of such co-construction, as is behavior, as is culture. Of course, similar arguments can be advanced with other concepts. More recently, for instance, we found that Jablonka and Lamb (2005; see also Baltes et al., 1998; Li, 2003) advanced similar lines of thought by focusing on the concept of "levels of analysis" and different forms of "inheritance" (genetic, epigenetic, behavioral, and symbolic) to more fully understand questions of co-evolution and ontogeny. We are fully prepared to accept such alternative forms of making the argument that we assume under the metaphorical concept of biocultural co-constructivism.

CONCEPT OF PLASTICITY AS ILLUSTRATION

In the developmental sciences, there is one concept that has repeatedly spurred the notion of interactionism and reciprocal modifiability. It is the concept of plasticity (e.g., Baltes et al., 1980; Cotman, 1985; Lerner, 1984, Magnusson, 1996). Arguably, plasticity is the concept most emphasized, at least by developmental and cultural scholars, to highlight the momentary and long-term modifiability of brain, behavior, and culture in association with internal and external conditions of life. Among neuroscientists, for instance, one speaks of experience- or learning-dependent brain development, among behavioral and social scientists of the many and rather varied phenotypes that can result from different compositions of factors of nature and nurture. The concept of epigenetic inheritance, defined, for instance, by Jablonka and Lamb (2001) as "the transmission from one generation to the next of structural and functional variations that do not depend on genetic differences," is another illustration, this one advanced primarily in neurobiological and genetic-anthropological circles. In a similar spirit, comparative cultural and lifespan developmental research conducted by social scientists is assumed to demonstrate the wide range of manifestations that genetically similar, if not identical, individuals can express if living in different cultural contexts, at different stages of life, or in different generations within a given culture (Assmann, 2006; Baltes et al., 1998, 2006; Dannefer, 2003; Schaie, 2005; Settersten, 2005; Valsiner & Lawrence, 1997).

The focus on plasticity, then, highlights the search for the developmental potentialities of brain, behavior, and culture, including their boundary conditions. To prevent a possible misunderstanding, note that plasticity does not refer to complete or arbitrary malleability and constructability of brain, behavior, and culture. Rather, it denotes that behavior is always simultaneously open and constrained (Hagen & Hammerstein, 2005). For developmentalists, the search for the conditions and ranges of plasticity is fundamental to their raison d'être. The concept implies that developmental outcomes are not fixed, but modifiable, and although such modifiability does not necessarily involve each component (genome, brain, behavior, environment), it at least suggests that if modifiability exists, there must be antecedent, correlated, or consequent changes in some of them.

Following are some historical observations. Although in modern times the concept of plasticity seems rooted primarily in neurobiology (e.g., Cotman, 1985; Gottlieb, 1982; Gottlieb et al., 1998; Lerner, 1984; Li, 2003), it has a counterpart place in psychology (e.g., Baltes & Schaie, 1976; Baltes & Singer, 2001; Lindenberger & Baltes, 1999; Tetens, 1777). The meanings attached to the concepts of plasticity are varying. However, the primary emphasis on modifiability and constructability seems to be shared by whatever scientific discipline is using the terms. This meaning of modifiability and constructability can be found in rather early forerunners, predating the fields of evolutionary biology and neuroscience. For Germans, the two-volume work of the philosopher-psychologist Tetens written more than 200 years ago (Tetens, 1777) is the historical masterpiece.

In the following, we explore how the concept of plasticity can be used to present the case of biocultural co-constructivism at a general level of analysis. To this end, we speak of at least three kinds of plasticity: neurobiological, behavioral, and societal or cultural. We suggest that understanding on a general and perhaps metalevel of analysis the existence of these three kinds of plasticity and their dynamic interactions is critical to avoid unnecessary restrictive biases in one direction or the other, and to advancing and explicating the metaphorical notion of biocultural co-constructivism. The

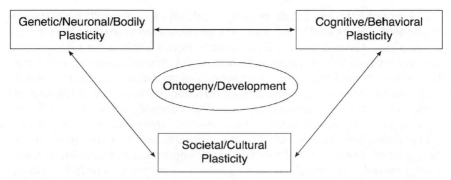

FIGURE 1.1. Biocultural co-constructivism in lifespan development: multidisciplinary concepts of plasticity as foundation (for further explanation, see also Baltes et al., 1998, 2006; Li, 2003).

different kinds of plasticity are interrelated, they are collaborative partners that over time and across contexts co-constructed the evolution and ontogeny of human behavior.

Figure 1.1 summarizes the general approach. Note that the concepts identified are not on the same level of analysis nor do they involve the same phenomena (Li, 2001). Here, the focus is on ontogenesis, that is, individual development from conception to old age. Furthermore, note that the basic assumption for each concept is the occurrence of a designed or naturally occurring change (alteration) in developmental conditions that set the stage and express plasticity, whether biochemical, experiential, physical-environmental, or societal in nature and composition. Such changes in the make-up of the genome and culture, and associated conditions of life and living, are necessary to understand the determining factors of plasticity, at whatever level of analysis. In the conceptual approach outlined here, the study of such changing developmental conditions is always intrinsically tied to changes in the biological, behavioral, and environmental conditions. The challenge is to identify such changes and to interrelate them to capture their joint operation at different levels of analysis and with varying dimensions of proximal and distal causality (Baltes et al., 1998; Li, 2003; Li, Lindenberger, & Sikström, 2001).

If one were to expand this categorization of plasticity in the direction of related "interactive" mechanisms that produce plasticity-based individual and societal development over time, the terms of "inheritance" that evolved within anthropological evolutionary thinking, such as genetic, epigenetic, cultural, and symbolic inheritance (Durham, 1991; Jablonka & Lamb, 2005), would come in handy. The multiple inheritance approach is one way to explicate biocultural co-construction; the use of learning principles would be another, one that appears especially useful for the case of ontogeny.

As shown in Figure 1.1, there are several ways to define plasticity (Baltes et al., 2006; Li, 2003). Their differentiation is not the primary focus of this book, although individual chapters are aimed at such specification. On a general level, *genetic and neuronal plasticity* involves identifying potentialities on the level of genetic expression and neuronal development, including structural features of the brain and other parts of the body. In fact, it is worthwhile to consider whether this category of plasticity should be extended to include nonneuronal parts of the body such as muscles and organs. *Behavioral plasticity* involves modifiability and the study of the range of psychological characteristics and functions, associated for instance with research on rates, levels, and forms of learning. *Societal plasticity* involves differences in social contexts and environments on the macrolevel of environmental input. Examples are comparative studies of societies or within-society group comparisons involving gender, social class, ethnicity, or migration. Another distinction useful for communicating this mode of thinking about societal plasticity is to speak of the opportunity and constraint structures of culture and societal conditions.

Because the notion of introducing the concept of plasticity as a guiding concept or metaphor in the social and cultural sciences is new, we offer some further observations on the concept of societal plasticity. The social and cultural comparative approach (Mayer, 2003; Settersten, 2005) is inherently based on the assumption that humans share in their original potentialities (interindividual differences and specific exceptions notwithstanding) and that social-cultural patterns of influences unfold human potentialities and elicit different outcomes in differentiating and cumulative ways (Cole, 1996; Valsiner & Lawrence, 1997). In accounts of such variation in outcomes from similar starting points, both agentic and reactive psychological and sociological mechanisms are involved, as are factors associated with the physical and human-made environment (Brandtstädter & Lerner, 1999; Heckhausen, 1998). Although many social scientists give the impression that they view societal plasticity as the dominant factor in accounting for interindividual and societal differences in human behavior and societal institutions, this is not necessarily so.

As we present this view on societal plasticity, one feature of this approach strikes us as especially relevant and important for the more neuroscience-oriented scholar to appreciate. Although the biological sciences and perhaps also the behavioral sciences have identified or developed a "holistic" taxonomy of the "world" of their systems of influences and mechanisms – for example, charting the genome or specifying a theory of schedules or types of learning – the social and cultural sciences are still struggling to identify a holistic account of their world of influences in terms of structural identities or mechanisms (Assmann, 2006; Bronfenbrenner, 2001; Cole, 1996; Dannefer, 2003; Heckhausen, 1998, Sternberg, 2004, Tomasello, 1999). Certainly, and aside from physical aspects of the environment, concepts such as norms, social incentives, theories of sanctions, patterns of socialization, levels of social support, social stereotypes, or collective memories, are eminently important. However, it seems to many that these concepts exhibit less comprehensiveness and coherence in their "structural" components and process characteristics than is certainly true for the genome. It is an open question whether this lack of a firm social science theory of the environment is intrinsic to all matters of human-social production or whether this simply reflects the relative youth of a field. Likely, one factor is that in modern-culture times, the change dynamic of cultural factors is much more rapid and pervasive than that of the genome. The genome has a longer history than culture, and as a whole, it is much slower in its transformations because mechanisms of changes in biogenetic inheritance have a longer time span than factors and processes of culture (see also Durham, 1991; Jablonka & Lamb, 2001, 2005; Li, 2003).

Returning to our argument for a change in the metaphorical language that guides the study of brain, behavior, and culture, we argue that expanding the concept of plasticity from the biogenetic over the behavioral to the societal and cultural in its broadest sense highlights the fact that all entities involved in the development and manifestation of brain, behavior, and culture are deeply interwoven and influence each other in cumulative ways. These influences can be more than influences of modulation, they include co-productive and mutually changing influences with qualitative, emergent consequences.

In this context, these reciprocal systems are not always in synchrony or simply matters of amount. The "collaboration" between the factors that emerge from the various sources can be facilitative or interfering. The facilitative and collaborative effect pattern between genetic and environmental factors is in the center of much work. Less frequent is the argument for mutual interference. For example, if it were true, as evolutionary psychologists suggest, that much of human behavior is guided by biogenetic factors resulting from the operation of dominance and reproductive fitness, it has become a challenge in the evolution of culture not only to exploit the potentials of dominance and reproductive fitness, such as effective mating and parenting, but also to regulate the extreme effects of such evolution-based predispositions, for instance, through mechanisms of cultural control or redirection. In this vein, the cultural anthropologist Gehlen (1956) argued that one of the important functions of culture is compensation for the "deficient biological" state of the human organisms. Similarly, there can be a mismatch between evolution- and culture-based forms of information processing involving, for instance, modern culture-based modes of problem solving, such as logical reasoning dealing with mathematical concepts of proportions or percentages (e.g., Gigerenzer, Todd, & the ABC Research Group, 1999).

These examples illustrate the important role of theory development that is specific to the questions at hand. Of special importance are questions of how levels of analysis – for instance, the evolutionary and the ontogenetic – can be interrelated, how it is possible to identify the interplay between distal and proximal causality, and how evolution and ontogeny interact in generating new aspects of the genome and culture (e.g., Ehrlich & Feldman, 2003; Li, 2003; Tomasello, 1999). In general, the more the biological species *Homo sapiens* generated its own culture, the more it moved in the direction of intentional-agentic and society-based (including technology) forms of production and biocultural collaboration. In the following, we suggest, as an additional example of illustration, one general frame that we consider helpful in understanding the system of influences that the metaphor of biocultural co-constructivism is meant to articulate and explore. It focuses on the experimental and cognitive psychologist's longtime favorite, learning and memory.

## AN ATTEMPT TO FORMALIZE THE CO-CONSTRUCTION HYPOTHESIS AT THE LEVEL OF INDIVIDUAL LEARNING

The previous discussion of plasticity – written primarily from the point of view of the developmental sciences and especially lifespan psychology – has stressed once more that there is neither a structural nor a functional invariance of behavior, of the brain, or of the (cultural) environment. All three aspects are in a constant flux, irrespective of whether one considers a macro- or a microlevel of observation. In the following, we add a frame to these observations that emerges primarily from a cognitive neuroscience perspective.

Change is continuous but relative. Of course, on an intermediate scale of observation, invariances can be inferred. In some sense, the environment in which an organism behaves is highly stable, and behavior itself also has many reliable facets. If this would not be the case, we would not be able to interact successfully with the environment or with social partners. These interactions being purposeful and intentional can occur only if there is some stability of the relevant input and output variables. However, these stabilities are abstractions and only comprise a medium temporal window. Extending the temporal window to years, decades, or the lifespan immediately reveals that all the presumed invariances are relative – the environment into which one was born will no longer be the same when one has reached the age of 30, 50, or 70, and this holds true even if an individual stayed all these years in the very same neighborhood – buildings will have been replaced by new ones; the technical environment will be completely modified (think of communication aids today versus 30 years ago); the content of media – books, films, music, and so on – will be different; and last but not least, the social partners will have changed or will be different as well.

In the same manner as the environment changes over a longer period of time, behavior also changes. Such behavioral changes do not only concern superficial aspects of how an individual dresses or how he or she communicates, but also concern values or personality traits (consider how intelligence – its crystallized and fluid constituents (Li et al., 2004) – or attitudes – political and personal – change over the lifespan (Baltes et al., 1998; Caspi, Roberts, & Shiner, 2005). Likewise, if one narrows the temporal window to minutes or seconds, it becomes evident that both behavior and the environment are also subject to continuous changes. The stimulus situation to which an organism is exposed is permanently changing (think of the light and temperature conditions that depend on whether a cloud covers the sun for a minute, or think of all the subtle changes within the visual field or the auditory perceptual space that occur because other living organisms pass by, approach, or move away). The behaving organism is constantly adapting to these changes (e.g., eye movements follow the bird that passes by; the muscle system becomes more or less active, depending on the temperature conditions; the attentional focus is moved from one location in the visual field to another). Basically, this idea of a permanently adapting organism that acts in a continuously changing world is captured by dynamics systems theory (e.g., Amaral, Díaz-Guilera, Moreira, Goldberger, & Lipsitz, 2004; Molenaar, Huizenga, & Nesselroade, 2003; Port & van Gelder, 1995).

These changes in environment and behavior of an organism are reflected by changes on the biological level within the organism; the just mentioned fluctuations of behavior and environment are mirrored by fluctuating activation patterns in the brain and in various other, more or less brain-independent servosystems of the organism (e.g., the cardiac system, the digestive system, the immune system). These activation patterns and their moment-by-moment changes are a joint function of both the current input conditions and the currently prevailing mental and functional states of the body (Beer, 2000). To avoid misunderstandings, the input conditions include all sensory inputs of the main sensory systems (vision, audition, somatosensation, taste, and smell), whether consciously or nonconsciously processed, and all sensory inputs within the intestines. The mental and functional state conditions include all memory traces and all genetically preestablished conditions of the central nervous system (CNS), but also the momentary set points of the autonomous nervous system, of the muscular system, of hormonal levels, and so on.

Because these physiological activation patterns are dependent both on the structural and functional features of the CNS (and the organism as a whole) and on the momentary input of the environment to the sense organs,

16         *Paul B. Baltes, Frank Rösler, and Patricia A. Reuter-Lorenz*

they can be seen as the common code into which both causes of behavior – the environmental and the intraorganismic antecedent conditions – become manifest. Information from the environment is transformed into neural activity by the sense organs and organism-inherent information due to the genome and the learning history of an individual is expressed in the very same code. Of course, this code not only comprises action potentials of neurons, but also all activation indices known so far have to be taken into account, like postsynaptic potentials, transmitter levels at synapses, hormone levels that influence gross synaptic activity in cell assemblies of the brain or in peripheral ganglia, and so on. These signals contribute to the "neural code" that, on the one side, reflects the current environmental input patterns, and on the other the genetic constituent and the learning history of an individual.

Whereas Figure 1.1 attempts to present the biocultural co-constructivist notion on a general level of concepts and processes, Figure 1.2 is an attempt to achieve an equivalent by a formal analysis of microgenetic processes closer to the usual process analyses of experimental cognitive psychological or cognitive neuroscience analysis. When attempting such a formal analysis, we can say that behavior and its related mental and environmental

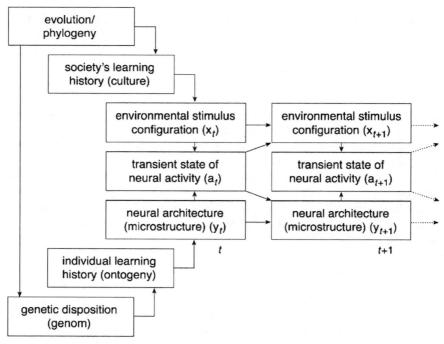

FIGURE 1.2. Formalization of the co-construction hypothesis on the level of microgenesis of brain–environment–behavior transactions.

states correspond to biological activity patterns, which can be summarized as a vector of electrical, biochemical, and other indices $(a_t)$. A particular biological activity pattern at time $t$ that corresponds to this vector $(a_t)$ is a function of the microstructure of the system at time $t$ $(y_t)$ and of the environmental stimulus configuration $(x_t)$. So, the momentary activity pattern is the cross-product of these two vectors (Eq. 1):

$$a_t = f(x_t \times y_t) \tag{1}$$

The individual learning history is engraved in the neuronal architecture (i.e., the currently prevailing microstructure depends on the individual learning history), and of course, this in turn depends on the genome. As mentioned, there are invariances of functional anatomy, but these invariances are relative. Due to the potential of neural plasticity, there is substantial variability in the structural-functional organization (e.g., in dendritic arborization and synaptic connectivity) (Quartz & Sejnowski, 1997). Thus, the genome determines the prevailing microstructure only partially. As argued convincingly, for example, by Gottlieb (2002), even the expression of genes must be seen as a function of both the genetic code and the currently prevailing inner- and extraorganismic environment. Of course, plasticity and gene expression varies over the lifespan. There are critical windows during which the influence of the environment on gene expression and on the plastic changes of the brain are much more substantial than during other epochs. This is the case, in particular, during early development. Nevertheless, the potential for plastic changes persists during the whole lifespan until old age. Otherwise, learning that finds its expression in structural changes of the nervous system could not take place at all (see Chapters 4 to 6, this volume).

On the other side, the current stimulus configuration depends on the society's (learning) history and on cultural and social progress. As the individual learning history depends on the genome, the cultural societal learning history likewise depends on the far-reaching roots of mankind – phylogeny (e.g., Dunbar, 2003). This is the state of affairs at time $t$.

The complexity and the interrelatedness of these factors becomes apparent, if one moves one step further, from time $t$ to time $t + 1$. Now, there is a new transient state of neural activity, which again is a function of the stimulus configuration and of the neural structure at that time (Eq. 2):

$$a_{t+1} = f(x_{t+1} \times y_{t+1}) \tag{2}$$

However, to understand this new activity pattern, one has to consider that the system and the environment are plastic and, therefore, that the functional structure of the system does change with each and any activity pattern. In other words, each activity pattern that prevails at time $t$ leaves its traces in the system (due to various learning mechanisms). Thus, it has to be assumed that the microstructure of the system at $t + 1$ is itself a function of the previous structure *and* the previous activity pattern (Eq. 3):

$$y_{t+1} = h(a_t \times y_t) \tag{3}$$

Likewise, the environmental stimulus configuration is also a function of both the previous stimulus configuration *and* its changes, which are due to the interacting organism (i.e., the new stimulus configuration is in part determined by the previous neural activity pattern) (Eq. 4):

$$x_{t+1} = g(a_t \times x_t) \tag{4}$$

To make this dynamic aspect of the interaction more vivid, think of an individual hammering a nail into the wall. With each stroke of the hammer, the environment will be changed – the nail will be moved a little more into the wall ($a_t$ affects $x_{t+1}$) – and this new stimulus configuration feeds back onto the organism via the sense organs. Thus, $x_{t+1}$ influences the momentary activity pattern of the CNS ($a_{t+1}$), and as a result, the output muscle system may be adjusted to apply the proper force to the next stroke ($a_{t+2}$) and so on (e.g., see Kelso, 1995, and Thelen & Smith, 1994, for more elaborate accounts of the dynamic interaction between organism and environment during complex motor behavior and the development of movement patterns).

So, by considering all mutual influences (i.e., by inserting [Eqs. 3 and 4] into [Eq. 2]), it becomes apparent that the activity state *a* of the organism at $t + 1$, which corresponds to a particular behavior ($b_{t+1}$) or a mental state ($m_{t+1}$), is a function of two recursive functions (Eq. 5). The equation and the figure reveal that behavior and mental states (the center boxes in Fig. 1.2) are indeed a co-construction of the biology (vectors *y*, lower boxes in Fig. 1.2) and culture (vectors *x*, upper boxes in Fig. 1.2). So, Equation 5 expresses in a formal and direct manner the biocultural co-construction idea:

$$b_{t+1} \equiv m_{t+1} \equiv a_{t+1} = f[g(a_t \times x_t) \times h(a_t \times y_t)] \tag{5}$$

Moreover, the two recursive functions *g* and *h* comprise proximate and distant causes of behavior, respectively. Due to the continuous interactions, the continuous structural changes of the system (caused by its everlasting learning-dependent plasticity), and the continuous changes of the environment (caused by social and cultural change), it is evident that events long ago can have an influence on the current activity state of the organism, as do the more recent, proximate events. This holds true for the memory trace that was engraved in early childhood or yesterday as for an historical event that took place several hundred years ago or a political decision that happened this morning. The historical and political event, if documented, can be read or will be perceived through some of the media, and the memory trace may be triggered by such information or by any other stimulus, as it has been so convincingly described on the introspective level by Marcel Proust in his monumental œuvre *A la recherche du temps perdu.*

Due to this intimate relationship between physiological and environmental changes and its mutual expression in the activity states (neural and nonneural) of the organism, it seems questionable to distinguish firmly between hardware and software as far as the human brain is concerned. Rather, brain function as it becomes manifest in behavior or subjective experience is insolvably tied to the ever-changing structure of the nervous system and the ever-changing outer world (Clark, 1999; Markman & Dietrich, 2000). Moreover, on the level of neural plasticity, effects due to proximate causes, as they are studied in experimental and biological psychology, become indistinguishable from effects that are due to more distant causes, as they are studied in developmental or lifespan psychology.

## THE SCOPE OF THE VOLUME

The subject of the book, then, is the question, "to what extent does the brain determine our culture and its diversity?", its inverse, "to what extent does culture influence the brain?" and their interactive joining, "how do they collaborate?" The topic is approached within the framework of human development from birth to old age and by examining the role that societal institutions play in the organization of this interactive system.

The topic was first discussed at a conference (August 2003) sponsored by the Center of Lifespan Psychology of the Max Planck Institute for Human Development and organized by the three co-editors. At that conference, the organizers and the authors of this book explored the possibility of using the conference as a forum from which to develop a written product. The goal was not a publication of conference proceedings, but rather a book that would go beyond the conference presentations to include input from sources outside the conference, and consider further input from the lively discussions at the conference. It was also decided to prepare texts with a high degree of interdisciplinary readability and openness so nonexperts would benefit. Definitely, the goal was to stimulate transdisciplinary discourse among the neurosciences, the social sciences, and the behavioral sciences.

The contributing neuroscientists, experimental psychologists, and developmental psychologists were expected to take a stand from their respective research fields – not for the generally accepted thesis that the genome and the environment interact with one another (interactionism) – but rather, as outlined previously, for the more provocative perspective that the brain itself is a joint construction of biological predisposition and cultural reality (co-constructivism), and that this is particularly valid over the life course of the individual. How does a specific environment and the life experiences embedded in it change the neuroanatomical structures and functional organization of the brain? What consequences arise for the behavior implemented by the brain and, further, for the society in which the behavior takes place? Finally, how does the environment that has been changed by this behavior in turn affect the neuroanatomical and functional architecture of the brain?

It was also emphasized that this position of developmental biocultural co-constructivism would be exemplified by reference to two streams of interaction: the evolutionary and the ontogenetic. Ontogenetic lifespan development was seen as an exemplar. It is during lifespan development that the sequential and cumulative principles of biocultural co-construction are instantiated. A focus on lifespan development would also permit showing how the principles of biocultural co-construction may change in their interactional system over time, including age differences in the role of nature–nurture dynamics and the role of interindividual differences due to differences in genomes and environments.

The consensus emerging from the 17 chapters is unambiguous. There is ample evidence for biocultural co-construction in evolution and ontogeny. Aspects of societal plasticity, its physical environment, culture, and learning experiences belong to the most important determinants of the development and organization of the brain's functional architecture. The anatomical and functional architecture of the brain is neither established genetically nor fixed at birth. Instead, the system has an extraordinary plasticity; its formation reacts in response to the structure and influence of its environment. At the same time, culture deeply depends on the brain as an essential component of production. Cultural entities are human-made and therefore brain dependent, but during ontogeny, they exist independently of the developing individual brain. At the same time, the fundamental existence and plasticity of the works and teaching principles of culture, largely mediated through humans and cultural products such as the reading and writing of texts and viewing of media, offer a system of continued and stable input into brain development. Brain and culture are co-producing partners. Each of them, as well as their changes in structure and function, depends on the other and operates as a co-modifier.

This book has been organized so the theme of biocultural co-construction is developed progressively from the microstructural to the macrostructural levels, and from early to late ontogenetic development. In addition, the chapters are organized by domains and functions, as well as by typical versus atypical conditions and contexts of life.

The substantive chapters of the book begin with a comprehensive and tour-de-force chapter on the conceptual, historical, and interdisciplinary basis of biocultural co-constructivism prepared by Shu-Chen Li. In Chapter 2, entitled "Biocultural Co-Construction of Lifespan Development," Li uses earlier writings, including her own (Li, 2001, 2003), to articulate the empirical and theoretical reasons for advancing a concept of biocultural co-constructivism. She also highlights why a lifespan approach to human development requires such an orientation (see also Baltes & Singer, 2001; Baltes, Staudinger, & Lindenberger, 1999; Staudinger & Lindenberger, 2003) and why this field, especially if considered in the larger frameworks of the behavioral and social science of human development, offers a substantive arena where the interacting, recursive, and reciprocally modifying processes between environment, behavioral, and brain development find ample evidence in research. Each of many lines of work, whether neuroscientific, cognitive, behavioral, social, or societal in origin, point to the important role of interactional, reciprocal, time-cumulative, and co-modifying influences and mechanisms.

From Li's chapter, it is also evident that both developmental time windows – the evolutionary and the ontogenetic – are important. Evolutionary processes have produced brains and environments that already reflect the operation of biocultural co-construction, including diversity in the form of interindividual differences. As individuals move through their lives, these biocultural predispositions not only undergo maturational-contextual and experience-dependent influences, but also include forms of co-determination that are novel due to changes in the goals and contexts of the culturally constructed life course, as well as age-related changes in behavioral and neuronal plasticity. Putting these biocultural co-construction components together in a new form of intellectual agenda and organization is the task of the future. This volume takes a few steps in that direction. Its focus is less on comprehensiveness than on power through illustration.

Four chapters focus on neural plasticity. Chapters 3 and 4 concentrate on the more normative (i.e., the ages of life such as childhood and adulthood), whereas Chapters 5 and 6 focus on atypicality and deviations from the biologically and culturally constituted norm. As mentioned already, a focus on neural plasticity exemplifies the principle that genome- and brain-based plasticity are not only a fact of the biological system, but also that environments are necessary conditions for the expression of biogenetic potential. The neuroscientific approaches that are prominent, particularly in the first chapters, reveal to the reader the microstructural manifestations of co-constructivism, as well as their dependency on larger conditions of environmental structures in which such more specific manifestations are grounded. For humans, the cultural conditions of the environment are as important to brain development as the presence of oxygen. Strictly speaking, brain-based plasticity without such environmental feedback and activating contexts does not exist.

Charles A. Nelson begins Chapter 3, "Neurobehavioral Development in the Context of Biocultural Co-Constructivism," with a persuasive brief historical account of the difficulties involved in linking the fields of behavioral development and brain development. His argument is that our knowledge of the brain would be best grounded in knowledge of child development, and conversely, that knowledge of child development could be vastly improved were we to explicate the neural mechanisms that underlie behavioral development. Yet, for a complexity of pragmatic and institutional reasons (e.g., professional separatism or insularity, the discipline-centeredness of individual research careers, the challenge of organizing and identifying the typical experiential matrix of children), this desirable state of affairs is less advanced than the power of the argument would suggest.

Nelson leads the reader through a series of exemplary lines of inquiry and offers a number of suggestions for how one might think about and study the relations among brain, culture, and development. He also explores how in future research the notion of culture might be incorporated into neural substrate and how such remodeled brains might lead to changes in behavior. One of his arguments is that behavioral scientists need to specify more carefully the specific cultural elements and experiences that constitute the typical environment of children, to translate these into specific behaviors, and to study their effects on brain development and vice versa. Areas covered in Nelson's chapter include sensory and perceptual development (e.g., pattern perception, face perception), cognitive development (e.g., speech perception, language acquisition, role of early childhood education) and socioemotional development (e.g., discrimination of facial expressions of emotions, attachment).

In each area, Nelson reports research highlights, including findings from the Bucharest Early Intervention Project, that illustrate the biocultural co-constructivist nexus. For instance, he reviews the work of Greenough and colleagues on experience-dependent effects on synaptic growth and stabilizing organization, on the role of environmental input and timing in these developments, and on how such work needs to consider varying forms of effect patterns, such as the difference between two kinds of activity-dependent changes: experience-expectant that are common to all members of the species, and experience-dependent that are unique to individual members. When extending such views to the life course as a whole, he raises the question of whether the "developing" brain is more plastic than the "developed" brain. A similar perspective can be applied to the biocultural counterpart, that is, the cultural environment. In fact, there are arguments in the lifespan literature that there is a systematic change in the lifespan profile of the biology–culture interface, with social-cultural plasticity having its strongest impact (especially regarding the individualized, experience-dependent kind) in early and middle adulthood.

Gerd Kempermann extends this perspective in Chapter 4, "Adult Neurogenesis." This chapter is especially important because it was believed for quite some time that adult neurogenesis was nonexistent, that is, that the basic neuronal architecture of the brain was fixed by late childhood. Although conceding that adult neurogenesis is small compared with the vast numbers of neurons in our brains developed before adulthood, Kempermann highlights the theoretical and empirical significance of the demonstration of adult neurogenesis and speculates that new neurons, fewer as they are, may serve important functions in learning and memory processes. He also alludes to the possibility that the frequency and spectrum of adult neurogenesis may be subject to optimizing interventions. The chapter exemplifies that throughout life, brain development is activity- and experience-dependent, and therefore, culture-dependent, and, most important, it never ends.

Chapter 5, "Sensory Input-Based Adaptation and Brain Architecture," by Maurice Ptito and Sébastien Desgent moves beyond usual conditions of lifespan development and opens our eyes to the significance of biocultural co-constructivism in the case of atypicalities, regardless of whether due to genetic deviations or development-relevant events in life history such as accidents or diseases associated with brain dysfunction. The authors of this chapter review work, much of their own, signaling the principle of multi- functionality of brain regions. Specifically, Ptito and Desgent show that the brain region of the visual cortex can also gradually be recruited to process other sensory modalities, namely, learning a discrimination task using tac- tile senses – in this case, stimulation of the tongue with an alphanumerical display. Moreover, in the rewiring studies performed by the same author, a full reorganization of functions was achieved in hamsters by connecting afferents from the retina to what is known as the auditory cortex. After recovering from surgery, these animals successfully performed visual dis- crimination tasks with their "auditory" cortex. This proves a remarkable plasticity of the functional architecture of the brain.

In Chapter 6, "Blindness: A Source and Case of Neuronal Plasticity," Brigitte Röder continues this line of argument involving multifunctionality of brain regions, which is seen as an exemplar of the principle of biocul- tural co-construction. Specifically, massive reorganization of the functional architecture of the brain can also be found in persons that became blind as the result of an accident or a degenerative illness in which the retina is no longer sensitive to light. Röder summarizes a series of systematic studies on how brain functions change if the visual input is missing from birth or gets lost due to an accident later in life. Her studies provide clear evidence that brain regions no longer needed for sight can take on other information processing functions. The area of the brain typically known as the visual cortex in sighted persons is activated systematically in blind persons by higher cognitive activities (e.g., when they hear a message or when they handle haptic information in working memory). These activations are sys- tematically related to task difficulty, suggesting that they are functionally specific. Moreover, Röder could show that some functions (e.g., spatiotem- poral discriminations of tactile information) are much better developed in congenitally blind than in sighted or late blind people. This suggests not only a full adaptation to special input conditions in the early blind, but also that some functions seem to be shaped by other modalities within critical periods during development (in the late blind).

Chapters 7 to 10 deal with evidence of biocultural co-construction in several functions and domains: language, reading-writing-arithmetic, emotion, and musical experience. Although in Chapters 7 and 8 on language and reading-writing-arithmetic, respectively, it seems immediately obvious that cultural constructions are involved, the case has been less elaborated for the domains of emotion and the musical mind (see Chapters 9 and 10, respectively).

In Chapter 7, "Language Acquisition: Biological Versus Cultural Implications for Brain Structure," Angela D. Friederici and Shirley-Ann Rüschemeyer use language as the vehicle through which cultural experience can penetrate and shape brain organization during early development and likewise illustrate the reciprocity between the changed brain and its influence on the environment. This chapter is also persuasive in demonstrating degrees of co-modification. On the one hand, cross-linguistic data suggest that the same brain areas, functionally identified to be specific for syntax, semantics, and phonology, are active in participants across languages. On the other hand, comparisons between first and second language processing reveal differences with respect to the recruitment of the different subcomponents. In other words, although native language processing seems to be similar across different languages, the strategies used to process a nonnative language appear to be different. Thus, in biocultural co-construction, we are not dealing with a fully open system, but the degree of co-constructability varies markedly depending on the functions involved, the age of the developing individual, and the degree to which evolution, culture, and science have produced the kind of knowledge and instrumentarium necessary to engage in co-construction (see also Hagen & Hammerstein, 2005).

Thad A. Polk and J. Paul Hamilton's Chapter 8, "Reading, Writing, and Arithmetic in the Brain: Neural Specialization for Acquired Functions," describes a fundamental mechanism through which environmental contingencies can influence the architecture and functioning of the brain. This mechanism operates across the lifespan, and Polk's empirical work exposes in the adult brain the consequences of both evolution- and ontogenesis-based functional modularity. Thus, their chapter continues the argument that there is large variation in the degree to which co-construction can be operative with some functional modularity being largely innately predetermined, whereas others have been shown to have a strong dose of experience-dependent neural modularity associated with ontogenetic life histories of experience.

Evidence is reviewed from three domains: reading, writing, and arithmetic. Among others, they report a study on U.S. postal workers that sorted mail going to Canada. In Canada, the postal code consists of a combination of letters and numbers (e.g., Toronto is M5S 1A1). Neuroimaging studies have shown that different brain regions are involved in processing numbers as opposed to letters; however, in the postal workers who had dealt with these letter-number combinations on a daily basis while sorting the mail there was less differentiation in the categorical separation of letters and numbers. Moreover, Polk and Hamilton report case and neuroimaging studies of neurological patients, suggesting that the brains of educated adults do include neural modules dedicated to culture-based systematic instruction.

Chapter 9, "Emotion, Learning, and the Brain: From Classical Conditioning to Cultural Bias," by Elizabeth A. Phelps extends the reach of illustrating the biocultural co-constructivism notion to another topic that traditionally has been in the forefront of more biologically based conceptions, the structure and function of emotions. In line with an experience- and culture-dependence perspective, Phelps examines basic mechanisms of emotional learning, how these shape brain and behavior, and how different types of emotional learning may be related to the expression of cultural stereotypes. By highlighting the significance of facial displays of emotion and facial clues about racial origins, this work has crucial implications for delineating the mechanisms of cultural-biological reciprocity. The chapter also highlights where the biocultural approach needs more specification, for instance, regarding the degree and timing of the construction involved, or the relative role of evolution- or ontogeny-based forces. For instance, although cultural knowledge and some forms of social communication may be uniquely human characteristics, how emotional value is expressed in these domains seems to rely on more basic mechanisms that are shared across species.

In Chapter 10, "The Musical Mind: Neural Tuning and the Aesthetic Experience," Oliver Vitouch provides another example of how the genome-based maturation of the brain and environment-based forces of experience, including systematic training, result in an altered brain, altered aesthetic experiences, and altered environments (e.g., novel forms of musical productions). He explores the effects of "innate" musical predispositions and the effects of musical training, and in so doing, offers provocative ideas about the interplay of evolution, culture, and biology. Vitouch argues that musical training is a model case for neural and behavioral-experiential plasticity, with extended perceptual and motor skills having their morphological and functional imprints on the neocortex. This is true not only for the sensory-motor skills in the more narrow sense, but also for more refined forms of aesthetic experience – from the early development of absolute pitch to macroscopic changes in cortical specialization to strong experiences with music and their supposed substrates.

Again, more specificity is called for in the co-productive process. For instance, the relative weighting differs, depending on which aspects of the musical experience and which time windows in development are considered. When it comes to the aesthetic level, the generation and experience of music seems to be one of the peaks of the relatively speaking more powerful role of culture in the process of biocultural co-construction. This includes the favorite structures of musical experience that shape the preferences of a given generation.

Chapter 11 by Lars Nyberg and Lars Bäckman, entitled "Influences of Biological and Self-Initiated Factors on Brain and Cognition in Adulthood and Aging," and Chapter 12 by Patricia A. Reuter-Lorenz and Joseph Mikels, entitled "The Aging Mind and Brain: Implications of Enduring Plasticity for Behavioral and Cultural Change," return to the topics of the ages of life and to those later ages of life where, in the past, largely because of negative images of aging, the notion of biocultural co-construction and associated plasticity was the least represented.

The general topic of these chapters is cognitive aging. In the history of research on human development, aging was seen as the state of life that is most defined by biologically based conceptions of decline. Although as early as the 1970s behavioral intervention studies had demonstrated the powerful role of experience-based interventions, especially in research on cognitive training and the use of optimizing and compensatory mechanisms (e.g., Bäckman & Dixon, 1992; Baltes & Labouvie, 1973; Baltes & Lindenberger, 1988; Willis, 1987), the more recent advent of methods of neuroimaging provided a new impetus. Both chapters wrestle with the new debates that are emerging in the face of evidence for later life compensatory reorganization on the neuronal level, while offering new insights into the levels and range of functioning, where co-constructive processes may be relevant and how they may be relevant.

More specifically, in Chapter 11, Nyberg and Bäckman focus on deficits in age-related plasticity of memory function, including interindividual differences, and on the neural and behavioral conditions that operate as modifiers. They draw a distinction between two categories of individual difference factors that influence memory functioning. The first category concerns biological factors that impose constraints and predispose the aging brain toward cognitive decline. The second category includes a heterogenous collection of factors that are "self-initiated," such as lifestyles and cognitive practice, and offer possibilities rather than imposing constraints. Both categories are subject to co-constructive principles, although of a different kind. The first is likely more strongly attached to biology-based genetic and medical interventions, the second likely more strongly tied to cultural programs of support and stimulation that provide the context or prompt self-initiated behavior. In fact, when considering the concept chosen by the authors, self-initiated factors are located in a given person, but their manifestation carries a strong dose of culture that offers the resources for developing and expressing self-initiation. Thus, it becomes obvious that self-initiated factors are intimately associated with the culture-based opportunities and constraints. As individuals, we do not invent the full instrumentarium of self-initiation on the spot during ontogenesis, rather its basic structure is very dependent on what culture has to offer. In this vein, the kind of cognitive training research reported by Nyberg and Bäckman, especially if combined with methods of cognitive neuroscience, seems like an area of choice to demonstrate instances and mechanisms of biocultural co-construction.

Chapter 12 by Reuter-Lorenz and Mikels reviews some of the same evidence and points in the same direction, that is, the combinatorial use of neuroscience and behavioral methods to identify the scope and mechanisms of biocultural co-construction in cognitive aging. It further identifies the many possibilities that may emerge as societies develop novel forms of biological intervention, as well as a new culture of old age and associated programs of experience-dependent forms of cognitive mastery in the face of biology-based decline. Selective and compensatory behavior strategies, such as the ones identified in Chapter 11 (and in related models of successful aging [Baltes & Baltes, 1990]), have also been observed on the more general neurobiological level. The potential for new learning, although to a lesser degree, persists well into the later decades of life. Reuter-Lorenz and Mikels point to the far-reaching implications of the work presented.

On the one hand, then, this chapter yields a deeper understanding of the limitations that biological aging imposes on cognitive function. For example, when functional magnetic resonance imaging (fMRI) is used to measure brain activity during certain memory tasks, activity is seen only in limited areas of the left hemisphere in young persons, whereas in older persons it is seen in larger areas of both hemispheres. The older brain apparently needs to mobilize greater resources to accomplish the same task. On the other hand, the work exemplifies how the human mind and brain respond adaptively to the loss of cognitive plasticity associated with the biological aging process. Thus, in line with the anthropological tradition of viewing the development of culture as a compensation for biological deficits of *Homo sapiens* (Baltes, 1997; Gehlen, 1956), neurobiological limits on the one hand and the brain's functional plasticity on the other hand can definitely serve as a catalyst for development. A culture can be supportive of adaptive aging, for example, by providing not only aids that help compensate for the reduction in sensory performance (e.g., eyeglasses or hearing aids), but also ones that counteract limitations in cognitive resources. In this spirit, neurocognitive investigations of the reciprocity between culture, mind, and brain reveal new avenues to influence and shape neural processes that underlie mental fitness in the golden years. These ideas underscore the importance of embracing a dynamic view of the individual as an agent situated in a world that interacts to bring about reciprocal change at multiple levels of neural, behavioral, social, and cultural organization.

Chapters 13 to 16 take the biocultural co-constructivist metaphor from more microgenetic and individual-level perspectives (areas usually more familiar to neuro- and behavioral scientists) to a higher level of aggregation, and reach into topics of societal structures and collective functioning as interactive minds (Baltes & Staudinger, 1996). The series of chapters as a whole call for efforts to decompose or rerepresent the larger cultural context by concepts and mechanisms that explicate why much of what we see in the "typical" or "specialized" brain is the result of culture at large and of more individualized (Greenfield, 2000) cultural practices. They highlight that physical, social, and cultural environments can be characterized by structures that organize experience-dependent activities at a broad level of organization across time and space (context). In our assessment, such a development-generative structure of influences approach is more obvious for the genome, especially in light of recent efforts to chart the genome as a whole. Thus, regarding the genome and its expression, there exists a highly differentiated structural theory of elements, their location, and their expressive mechanisms and interdynamics.

A relatively advanced theory of structure and associated mechanisms is not available for the counterpart of the biocultural co-construction process, the physical and cultural environment. However, lack of adequate theory and method for the physical, behavioral, and cultural mapping of the macroenvironment is not an argument against its existence. Consider, for instance, the vast evidence on human development that has been accumulated for effects of gender, social class, education, or ethnicity. Similarly, the experiential structure and function of families, schools, the work environment, leisure, and the media have all been shown to result in long-term consequences involving brain–behavior–environment interactions (e.g., Dannefer, 2003; Li, 2003; Settersten, 2005).

Neuroscientists think less in such macrocontextual or macrosocietal modes. Therefore, we found it especially important to add a section to the book where neuroscientists are invited to think more explicitly than is true so far about how such macro-environmental conditions shape the structure and function of the brain. If one does not recognize this possibility one is tempted as a neuroscientist to assume the "normal" population of brains to be fully due to biological maturation rather than include a solid dose of cultural shaping. We need to emphasize, however, that the chapters in this section are also novel for behavioral scientists. These chapters are innovative in the true sense; they have few forerunners.

Chapters 13 and 14, the first two chapters of this section, open the macrolevel approach to structuring the environment by two major themes that are central to Western society – education and work. With this approach, the biocultural co-construction principle is extended to environments and associated learning processes that govern large parts of an individual's life in modern societies.

In Chapter 13, "Characteristics of Illiterate and Literate Cognitive Processing: Implications of Brain–Behavior Co-Constructivism," Karl Magnus Petersson and Alexandra Reis examine one of the most stunning human advances in cultural history, the ability to read and its consequences on modern child development. By comparing, with a natural quasiexperimental design, children with different degrees of formal education, they offer a potentially groundbreaking glimpse of brain-based alterations that result from educational experience or the lack thereof. Their findings are based on a comparison of otherwise comparable (in their level of intelligence) literate and illiterate inhabitants of a Portuguese village. These behavioral and functional neuroimaging data indicate that learning a written language, and more generally, formal education, modulates cognitive functions both in terms of behavior and in terms of the structural and functional organization of the human brain.

Taken together, such and similar data provide strong support for the idea that the functional architecture of the brain is co-constructed by literacy and formal education, which in turn change the brain's capacity to interact with its environment. The domains to be considered can be easily extended to other aspects of the contemporary culture ranging from processes of emotional child rearing to questions of computer literacy. Thus, the individual "acquires" a brain that makes him or her able to participate in, interact with, and actively contribute to the process of cultural construction and transmission in new and lasting ways. In this vein, it is easy to view such work as fundamental to the argument that in human evolution the power of new forms of inheritance and transmission (epigenetic, behavioral, symbolic) take center stage (Durham, 1991; Jablonka & Lamb, 2005).

In Chapter 14, "The Influence of Work and Occupation on Brain Development," Neil Charness takes a similarly broad perspective on another major context of life. He examines how the activity and nature of work itself modifies the mind and brain in reciprocal and cumulative ways. Despite the important role of work in the life course of individuals (e.g., Schooler, Mulatu, & Oates, 1999), Charness notes that there has been relatively little research on the role of work in co-producing brain functioning and brain development.

Findings are reviewed that deal with the impact of work on physical and psychological functioning, including their correlates and consequences on the functional architecture of the brain. Very much in line with work on cognitive training and the demonstration of cognitive plasticity on the neuronal and behavioral level, findings on professional specialization and expertise-related phenomena are equally impressive. The emphasis is on identifying the mechanisms by which occupations influence the development and maintenance of brain structures across the life span and how brain and culture share a common developmental history.

Moreover, societal and cultural influences on the development of occupational niches and their training requirements are discussed, as well as how these may account for the co-evolution of cultures and their occupations. One example is the so-called Flynn effect, the historical increase in average IQ during the twentieth century. It is a reasonable assumption that this effect involved a co-construction of brain and culture. Moreover, as Schaie (2005) showed in his long-term study of human intelligence, such an effect is not general, but specific to abilities. There are abilities where the historical change in the United States was negative, such as in the psychometric factor of numerical ability, and others where the change was positive, such as in the psychometric ability of vocabulary. Such examples illustrate the wide range of research opportunities that the biocultural co-constructivist approach suggests for future work on lifespan intelligence (see also Sternberg, 2004).

In Chapter 15, "The Influence of Organized Violence and Terror on Brain and Mind: A Co-Constructive Perspective," Thomas Elbert, Brigitte Rockstroh, Iris-Tatjana Kolassa, Maggie Schauer, and Frank Neuner illustrate the principle of the co-construction of brain and culture by reference to extreme life circumstances, that is, traumatic events, and the concept of posttraumatic stress disorder. This model of stress effects on the brain's structure and function with concomitant alterations of the mind (i.e., in memory, affect regulation, fear network), as well as effects on the social environment with concomitant and reciprocal alterations of societal conditions (i.e., context of terror, violence, anxiety, and fear), offers a platform to investigate hypotheses of biocultural co-construction over ontogenetic and historical time, including the study of individual and collective cycles of violence, psychopathology, and other forms of dysfunction and social disadvantage.

Specifically, using behavioral, cognitive, and neuroimaging research with people who have been traumatized by life-threatening experiences, such as the victims of civil wars, deprivation, and torture, the authors have studied refugees in Germany and war victims in crises regions such as the Balkans and Somalia. In their work, Elbert and his colleagues demonstrate that traumatic events massively change the brain's structure and function. For instance, with memory paradigms and neuroimaging techniques (fMRI), they show that due to such traumatic experiences the organization and functioning of these persons' brains are changed (in part, seemingly irreversible). Often, such changes correspond to brain functioning of persons typically classified as being pathological, based on psychiatric diagnoses. What is especially impressive in this line of inquiry is the possibility that such effects are long lasting, general, and stable. They are long lasting because they involve a triangulated developmental coalition of brain, behavior, and environment conditions, both at the level of the individual and at the level of interactive minds involving the population as whole. In some sense, the observations of Elbert's group relate directly to Chapter 3 and Nelson's observations of institutionalized children in the Bucharest Early Intervention Projects. Nelson also provided strong evidence that severe social and behavioral deficits will inevitably result if appropriate environmental cues are missing during critical periods of childhood development.

Although, as the authors concede, this line of inquiry is in the making and not yet tested in its full complexity, this chapter is another powerful illustration of how a biocultural co-constructive perspective moves research into new arenas, in this instance, how societal conflicts and civil war-affected communities provide a background for the study of the reciprocal and mutually modifying interaction of brain, mind, and culture. One perspective that the authors use to illustrate the ontogenetic and generation-linking impact of high-frequency or collective traumatic experiences and their impact on the brain is the script of "violence breeds violence." For reasons of the brain–mind–environment co-constructive triangulation, the authors speculate that "abused and neglected children would become tomorrow's murderers and perpetrators of other crimes of violence." Solely in sub-Saharan Africa, the authors write, more than ten countries are currently affected by civil wars, many of them having lasted for decades. Because of the bioculturally constructed brain–behavior–environment matrix, the effects of these experiences may last for decades and affect many dimensions and, therefore, represent a source for "development in the reverse."

In Chapter 16, "Co-Constructing Human Engineering Technologies in Old Age: Lifespan Psychology as a Conceptual Foundation," by Ulman Lindenberger and Martin Lövdén, the lens is focused on another major component of social change that affects lifespan development: technological conditions of life. On the surface, this chapter deals with one stage of life, old age. However, the implications of the chapter reach beyond this stage. Old age is a model case for a larger topic for biocultural analysis – the role of technology in optimizing human development and compensating for deficits and weaknesses. In doing so, the authors embrace the potential and limitations of plasticity and adaptive reorganization that occur in adulthood and later life. In addition, they describe how intelligent human engineering technologies will alter the aging of future generations by reducing cognitive resource demands through personalized external cuing and support structures. The result is a new form of the brain–behavior–environment system, a form that involves novel adaptations of each component involved.

The authors proceed from discussing lifespan development as the orchestration of three interacting processes: selection, optimization, and compensation (Baltes, 1997). Within this framework, they highlight three criteria by which advances in the brain–mind–environment matrix may be evaluated: marginal gain for the individual, person specificity and adaptability, and conjoint consideration of distal and proximal frames of evaluation. As empirical demonstrations, studies are reported that illustrate the resulting new levels and forms of plasticity through human engineering-based interventions in such areas as spatial navigation, sensory/sensorimotor functioning, or the aging of memory functioning. In each case, research demonstrates that it is possible to improve functioning with ensuing consequences on the functional architecture of the brain, as measured by neural indicators, and on the mind, as measured by behavioral performance indicators. These results are important, particularly because many brain scientists underestimate the power of how the brain can be "developed" beyond childhood through experiential and technological factors.

The biocultural co-construction of the brain is a lifelong process. Likely, it is also a process where the degree of individualization, that is, person-specific expressions of the brain and behavior system, becomes stronger and stronger as individuals age (Baltes et al., 1999; Greenfield, 2000). Chapter 16 opens an important avenue to understand such processes of general and individualized lifespan trajectories that reflect the co-construction of the brain and the environment. Thus, this chapter illustrates that the future, including that of old age, is not simply something that we enter, but also something that can benefit from individual and collective co-construction of biological and environmental systems.

In the concluding epilogue, Chapter 17, entitled "Letters on Nature and Nurture," the biobehavioral developmentalist Onur Güntürkün uses an imaginary exchange of letters between two conference participants, Hakan and Maxim, to offer us a finely shaped view both of his own far-reaching scholarship and of the comparative and integrative perspectives that guided an exciting concluding discussion at the conference that served as a preparatory forum for this book. With these insightful letters, Güntürkün reflects with historical wisdom, intellectual sharpness, and refined humor on the foundational perspectives of the biocultural co-constructive framework. In the letters, we find a characterization of the "dual" origin of human development, that is, the genetic and the evolution-based background that assembles the brain and the organized system of experiences that shape the brain into its final status. On the one hand, he highlights the advantages that may have come from a separate, dialectical emphasis on biological nativism versus developmental environmentalism. On the other hand, he argues that genetic predisposition and environmentally dependent learning processes interact continuously at every neural and mental entity, from cortical development to social customs. As he writes, "Not a single territory of our mind is outside the scope of this interaction." The same line of argument, of course, applies not only to the brain, but also to the co-construction of the physical and cultural environment.

When appreciating his insightful integrative and comparative commentary, we see three goals in Güntürkün's epilogue: (1) to exemplify, (2) to emphasize the relative weights by which culture and biology contribute to the co-construction of the brain, and (3) to demand more clarification of the evolutionary and ontogenetic mechanisms involved. The message is clear. Güntürkün challenges his colleagues to advance their thinking beyond the territory covered in this book and inquire more deeply into the foundational mechanisms (such as they are associated, e.g., with principles of genetic, epigenetic, behavioral, and cultural inheritance) that govern the process of biocultural co-construction. True to the task, the epilogue is a stimulating invitation for what needs to follow if the metaphor of biocultural co-construction can be expected to be more than a one-time, short-lived advent. Güntürkün's concluding sentence symbolizes this challenge: "Is this really all we can say? Or are new discoveries ahead of us?" We can only add: "Perhaps not new discoveries, but a more firmly grounded insight in the co-constructive game of biology and culture across the lifespan."

## CONCLUSION AND FURTHER AVENUES

Biocultural co-constructivism, the question of the mutual interactions and the reciprocal as well as the co-modifying influences of two equal partners – brain and culture – has many facets, as will become apparent in the chapters in this volume. Even though much has not yet been studied, the fundamental principle that a recursive, multiplicative linkage of cultural and biological variables jointly affect the evolution, as well as the ontogenesis of human behavior and culture, appears to be indisputable. Even the provocative idea of conceiving the brain as a "dependent variable," as a product of behavior and culture, to even out the present imbalance between the neuroscience and the behavioral social science approaches, has its proponents.

Biocultural co-construction by definition is an interactive and collaborative term. Nevertheless, because part of our original motivation was to counteract the seeming reemergence of more simplistic brain-to-behavior determinism models, it may be permitted to ask the more unidirectional question of experiential and environmental dependency of the brain development during ontogenesis. How far can the influence of the environment and life experiences on the brain reach? This issue about the "range of plasticity" is touched in many of the contributions. Certainly, it includes functional reorganization of the brain at the neuronal level and local extension of brain regions. Definitely, it also includes the development of neurons, although likely to a lesser degree as individuals become older. Much less likely are fundamental changes in the regional-anatomical structure of the brain. At the same time, it must be acknowledged that the present anatomy of the brain is influenced not only by evolutionarily determined factors, but also by those factors presently existing in environmental and behavioral structures. Thus, one cannot exclude the possibility that the anatomy of the brain that seemed so unchangeable in traditional neuroscientific thinking derives a part of its stability from the similarly rigid and well-organized conditions in the physical and social environment and their cumulative and adaptive influence on the early childhood development of the brain.

Although the chapters collected here present many pieces of the evolving co-construction puzzle, the contributions also make it clear how little of the entire territory has been investigated to date. In our view, this seems especially true for the question of macrostructural environmental factors. So far, less progress in the structural mapping of the physical and cultural environment has been made than for the genome and the brain. However, this is a challenge to the spectrum of disciplines involved in charting this course. It is a necessary course to bring the notion of biocultural co-constructivism to fruition and represents an invitation to the social scientists to join the enterprise.

This invitation for more collaboration, especially between the social sciences and the neurosciences, suggests one concluding frame of observations, a few hints at scholarly connections to other lines of inquiry that are not in the center of this book. We have emphasized several times that this volume has as its primary objective the search for a metascript or metaphor that helps us prevent unidirectional and simple deterministic conceptions of the gene–brain–behavior–culture dynamics. In addition, we have restricted the treatments of the topic to the context of lifespan development. Although we continue to believe that such an approach has its strengths, it also has its limitation because it does not address in any degree of depth other dimensions of the dynamics, for instance, relevant questions of epistemology and the specifics of the mechanisms that are involved. In a way, the coverage is more illustrative than explanatory.

Therefore, we realert the reader to the need for juxtaposing, interrelating, and integrating this volume with relevant developments, for instance, in the philosophy of the brain–mind interface or more specific treatments of the brain and cultures as emergent systems during evolution and ontogeny. This is an extraordinary rich and challenging field, whose seeding and harvesting, although still in the making, has reached a new level of interdisciplinary specificity and collaboration. It ranges from work in philosophy (e.g., Clark & Chalmers, 1998) over long-standing traditions in evolutionary anthropology or psychology (e.g., Barkow, Cosmides, & Tooby, 1992; Cavallis-Sforza & Feldman, 1973; Durham, 1991; Ehrlich & Feldman, 2003; Gärdenfors, 2003; Jablonka & Lamb, 2001, 2005; Odling-Smee, Laland, & Feldman, 2003; Tomasello, 1999; Vandermeer, 2004), new conceptions of the concept of development and the nature–nurture interface (e.g., Bronfenbrenner, 2001; Gottlieb et al., 1998; Greenfield, 2000; Singer, 2003), cultural dimensions of basic psychological structures and mechanisms (e.g., Cole, 1996; Nisbett, Peng, Choi, & Norenzayan, 2001; Sternberg, 2004; Tomasello, 1999), neuroscientific efforts at capturing specific brain-based mechanisms in culturally relevant maladaptive behavior (e.g., Cicchetti, 2002; Karmiloff-Smith & Clark, 1993), to work that highlights the problems of levels of analyses and their integration in a co-constructivist perspective (Baltes, 1997; Baltes et al., 2006; Li, 2003; Nesselroade, 2002; Quartz, 1999).

The objective of this volume, although directly and indirectly benefiting from and promoting these lines of inquiry, is more modest. From the point of view of the editors, if we have succeeded in alerting human development scholars and researchers in the behavioral sciences to this intellectual architecture and in providing them with some conceptual and experimental-empirical keys to open the relevant doors and chambers, we will be happy. If, in addition, the concept of developmental and biocultural co-constructivism were to play a guiding "metaphorical" or "metascript" role in future efforts at organizing our basic thinking about the gene–brain–behavior–culture dynamic, that would be icing on the cake.

## References

Amaral, L. A. N., Díaz-Guilera, A., Moreira, A. A., Goldberger, A. L., & Lipsitz, L. A. (2004). Emergence of complex dynamics in a simple model of signaling networks. *Proceedings of the National Academy of Sciences (USA), 101*, 15551–15555.

Assmann, A. (2006). Memory, individual and collective. In R. E. Goodin & C. Tilly (Eds.), The Oxford handbook of contextual political analysis (pp. 210–224). Oxford: UP 2006.

Bäckman, L., & Dixon, R. A. (1992). Psychological compensation: A theoretical framework. *Psychological Bulletin, 112,* 1–25.

Baltes, P. B. (1997). On the incomplete architecture of human ontogeny: Selection, optimization, and compensation as foundation of developmental theory. *American Psychologist, 52,* 366–380.

Baltes, P. B., & Baltes, M. M. (1990). Psychological perspectives on successful aging: The model of selective optimization with compensation. In P. B. Baltes & M. M. Baltes (Eds.), *Successful aging: Perspectives from the behavioral sciences* (pp. 1–34). Cambridge, UK: Cambridge University Press.

Baltes, P. B., & Labouvie, G. V. (1973). Adult development of intellectual performance: Description, explanation, and modification. In C. Eisdorfer & M. P. Lawton (Eds.), *The psychology of adult development and aging* (pp. 157–219). Washington, DC: American Psychological Association.

Baltes, P. B., & Lindenberger, U. (1988). On the range of cognitive plasticity in old age as a function of experience: 15 years of intervention research. *Behavior Therapy, 19,* 283–300.

Baltes, P. B., Lindenberger, U., & Staudinger, U. M. (1998). Life-span theory in developmental psychology. In R. M. Lerner (Ed.), *Handbook of child psychology:*

*Vol. 1. Theoretical models of human development* (5th ed., pp. 1029–1143). New York: Wiley.

Baltes, P. B., Lindenberger, U., & Staudinger, U. M. (2006). Lifespan theory in developmental psychology. In R. M. Lerner (Ed.), *Theoretical models of human development: Vol. 1. Handbook of child psychology* (6th ed., pp. 569–664). New York: Wiley.

Baltes, P. B., Reese, H. W., & Lipsitt, L. P. (1980). Life-span developmental psychology. *Annual Review of Psychology, 31*, 65–110.

Baltes, P. B., Reese, H. W., & Nesselroade, J. R. (1977). *Life-span developmental psychology: Introduction to research methods.* Monterey, CA: Brooks/Cole.

Baltes, P. B., & Schaie, K. W. (1976). On the plasticity of intelligence in adulthood and old age: Where Horn and Donaldson fail. *American Psychologist, 31*, 720–725.

Baltes, P. B., & Singer, T. (2001). Plasticity and the ageing mind: An exemplar of the bio-cultural orchestration of brain and behaviour. *European Review, 9*, 59–76.

Baltes, P. B., & Staudinger, U. M. (Eds.). (1996). *Interactive minds: Life-span perspectives on the social foundation of cognition.* Cambridge, UK: Cambridge University Press.

Baltes, P. B., Staudinger, U. M., & Lindenberger, U. (1999). Lifespan psychology: Theory and application to intellectual functioning. *Annual Review of Psychology, 50*, 471–507.

Barkow, J. H., Cosmides, L., & Tooby, J. (Eds.). (1992). *The adapted mind: Evolutionary psychology and the generation of culture.* New York: Oxford University Press.

Beer, R. D. (2000). Dynamical approaches to cognitive science. *Trends in Cognitive Sciences, 4* (3), 91–99.

Brandtstädter, J., & Lerner, R. M. (Eds.). (1999). *Action and self development: Theory and research through the life span.* Thousand Oaks, CA: Sage.

Bronfenbrenner, U. (2001). Bioecological theory of human development. In N. J. Smelser & P. B. Baltes (Eds.), *International encyclopedia of the social and behavioral sciences* (pp. 6963–6970). Oxford, UK: Elsevier.

Bronfenbrenner, U., & Ceci, S. J. (1994). Nature–nuture reconceptualized in developmental perspective: A bioecological model. *Psychological Review, 101*, 568–586.

Caspi, A., Roberts, B. W., & Shiner, R. L. (2005). Personality development: Stability and change. *Annual Review of Psychology, 56*, 453–484.

Cavallis-Sforza, L. L., & Feldman, M. W. (1973). Cultural versus biological inheritance: Phenotypic transmission from parents to children (A theory of the effect of parental phenotypes on children's phenotypes). *American Journal of Human Genetics, 25*, 618–637.

Cicchetti, D. (2002). The impact of social experiences on neurobiological systems: Illustration from a constructivist view of child maltreatment. *Cognitive Development, 17* (3–4), 1407–1428.

Clark, A. (1999). An embodied cognitive science? *Trends in Cognitive Science, 3*, 345–351.

Clark, A., & Chalmers, D. J. (1998). The extended mind. *Analysis, 58*, 10–23.

Cole, M. (1996). Interacting minds in a life-span perspective: A cultural/historical approach to culture and cognitive development. In P. B. Baltes & U. M. Staudinger (Eds.), *Interactive minds: Life-span perspectives on the social foundation of cognition* (pp. 59–87). New York: Cambridge University Press.

Cotman, C. W. (Ed.). (1985). *Synaptic plasticity.* New York: Guilford.

Dannefer, D. (2003). Cumulative advantage/disadvantage and the life course: Cross-fertilizing age and social science theory. *Journals of Gerontology, 58b*, S327–S337.

Dunbar, R. I. M. (2003). The social brain: Mind, language, and society in evolutionary perspective. *Annual Review of Anthropology, 32*, 163–181.

Durham, W. H. (1991). *Coevolution: Genes, culture and human diversity.* Stanford, CA: Stanford University Press.

Ehrlich, P., & Feldman, M. W. (2003). Genes and cultures: What creates our behavioral phenome? *Current Anthropology, 44* (1), 87–107.

Gärdenfors, P. (2003). *How homo became sapiens: On the evolution of the thinking.* Oxford, UK: Oxford University Press.

Gehlen, A. (1956). *Urmensch und Spätkultur.* Bonn: Athenäum.

Gigerenzer, G., Todd, P. M., & the ABC Research Group (Eds.). (1999). *Simple heuristics that make us smart.* New York: Oxford University Press.

Gottlieb, G. (1982). *Individual development and evolution: The genesis of novel behavior.* New York: Oxford University Press.

Gottlieb, G. (2002). Developmental-behavioral initiation of evolutionary change. *Psychological Review, 109* (2), 211–218.

Gottlieb, G., Wahlsten, D., & Lickliter, R. (1998). The significance of biology for human development: A developmental psychobiological systems view. In R. M. Lerner (Ed.), *Handbook of child psychology: Vol. 1. Theoretical models of human development* (5th ed., pp. 233–273). New York: Wiley.

Greenfield, S. (2000). *The private life of the brain.* New York: Penguin Press.

Greenough, W. T., & Black, J. E. (1992). Induction of brain structure by experience: Substrates for cognitive development. In M. R. Gunnar & C. A. Nelson (Eds.), *Minnesota symposium on child psychology: Vol. 24. Developmental behavioral neuroscience* (pp. 155–200). Hillsdale, NJ: Erlbaum.

Hagen, E. H., & Hammerstein, P. (2005). Evolutionary biology and the strategic view of ontogeny: Genetic strategies provide robustness and flexibility in the life course. *Research in Human Development, 2* (1), 87–101.

Heckhausen, J. (1998). *Developmental regulation in adulthood: Age normative and sociostructural constraints as adaptive challenges.* New York: Cambridge University Press.

Jablonka, E., & Lamb, M. J. (2001). Epigenetic inheritance. In N. J. Smelser & P. B. Baltes (Eds.), *International encyclopedia of the social and behavioral sciences* (pp. 4706–4710). Oxford, UK: Elsevier.

Jablonka, E., & Lamb, M. J. (2005). *Evolution in four dimensions: Genetic, epigenetic, behavioral, and symbolic variation in the history of life.* Cambridge, MA: MIT Press.

Karmiloff-Smith, A., & Clark, A. (1993). What's special about the human mind/brain? A reply to Abrahamsen, Bechtel, Dennett, Plunkett, Scutt & O'Hara. *Mind & Language, 8* (3), 569–581.

Kelso, S. (1995). *Dynamic patterns.* Cambridge, MA: MIT Press.

Lakoff, G., & Johnson, M. (1980). *Metaphors we live by.* Chicago: University of Chicago Press.

Lambourn, D. (2001). Metaphor and its role in social thought. In N. J. Smelser & P. B. Baltes (Eds.), *International encyclopedia of the social and behavioral sciences* (pp. 9728–9743). Oxford, UK: Elsevier.

38     *Paul B. Baltes, Frank Rösler, and Patricia A. Reuter-Lorenz*

Leary, D. E. (Ed.). (1990). *Metaphors in the history of psychology.* Cambridge, UK: Cambridge University Press.

Lerner, R. M. (1984). *On the nature of human plasticity.* Cambridge, UK: Cambridge University Press.

Lerner, R. M. (2002). *Concepts and theories of human development* (3rd ed.). Mahwah, NJ: Erlbaum.

Li, S.-C. (2001). Aging mind: Facets and levels of analysis. In N. J. Smelser & P. B. Baltes (Eds.), *International encyclopedia of the social and behavioral sciences* (pp. 310–317). Oxford, UK: Elsevier.

Li, S.-C. (2003). Biocultural orchestration of developmental plasticity across levels: The interplay of biology and culture in shaping the mind and behavior across the life span. *Psychological Bulletin, 129* (2), 171–194.

Li, S.-C., Lindenberger, U., Hommel, B., Aschersleben, G., Prinz, W., & Baltes, P. B. (2004). Transformations in the couplings among intellectual abilities and constituent cognitive processes across the life span. *Psychological Science, 15* (3), 155–163.

Li, S.-C., Lindenberger, U., & Sikström, S. (2001). Aging cognition: From neuromodulation to representation. *Trends in Cognitive Sciences, 5,* 479–486.

Lindenberger, U., & Baltes, P. B. (1999). Die Entwicklungspsychologie der Lebensspanne (Lifespan-Psychologie): Johann Nicolaus Tetens (1736–1807) zu ehren. *Zeitschrift für Psychologie, 207,* 299–323.

Magnusson, D. (Ed.). (1996). *The life-span development of individuals: Behavioral, neurobiological and psychosocial perspectives: A synthesis.* Cambridge, UK: Cambridge University Press.

Markman, A. B., & Dietrich, E. (2000). Extending the classical view of representation. *Trends in Cognitive Sciences, 4,* 470–475.

Mayer, K. U. (2003). The sociology of the life course and lifespan psychology: Diverging or converging pathways? In U. M. Staudinger & U. Lindenberger (Eds.), *Understanding human development: Dialogues with lifespan psychology* (pp. 463–481). Boston: Kluwer Academic.

Molenaar, P. C. M., Huizenga, H. M., & Nesselroade, J. R. (2003). The relationship between the structure of inter-individual and intra-individual variability: A theoretical and empirical vindication of developmental systems theory. In U. M. Staudinger & U. Lindenberger (Eds.), *Understanding human development: Dialogues with lifespan psychology* (pp. 339–360). Boston: Kluwer Academic.

Nelson, C. A. (2000). Neural plasticity and human development: The role of early experience in sculpting memory systems. *Developmental Science, 3,* 115–136.

Nesselroade, J. R. (2002). Elaborating the differential in differential psychology. *Multivariate Behavioral Research, 37,* 543–561.

Nisbett, R. E., Peng, K., Choi, I., & Norenzayan, A. (2001). Culture and systems of thought: Holistic versus analytic cognition. *Psychological Review, 108,* 291–310.

Odling-Smee, F. J., Laland, K. N., & Feldman, M. (2003). *Niche construction: The neglected process in evolution.* Princeton, NJ: Princeton University Press.

Port, R., & van Gelder, T. (Eds.). (1995). *Mind as motion: Dynamics, behavior, and cognition.* Cambridge, MA: MIT Press.

Quartz, S. (1999). The constructivist brain. *Trends in Cognitive Science, 3,* 48–57.

Quartz, S. R., & Sejnowski, T. J. (1997). The neural basis of cognitive development: A constructivist manifesto. *Behavioral and Brain Science, 20,* 537–596.

Schaie, K. W. (2005). *Developmental influences on intelligence: The Seattle Longitudinal Study.* New York: Oxford University Press.

Schooler, C., Mulatu, M. S., & Oates, G. (1999). The continuing effects of substantively complex work on the intellectual functioning of older workers. *Psychology and Aging, 14,* 483–506.

Settersten, R. A., Jr. (2005). Toward a stronger partnership between life-course sociology and life-span psychology. *Research in Human Development, 2* (1/2), 25–41.

Singer, W. (2003). The nature–nurture problem revisited. In U. M. Staudinger & U. Lindenberger (Eds.), *Understandung human development: Dialogues with lifespan psychology* (pp. 437–447). Boston: Kluwer Academic.

Staudinger, U. M., & Lindenberger, U. (Eds.). (2003). *Understanding human development: Dialogues with lifespan psychology.* Dordrecht, The Netherlands: Kluwer Academic.

Sternberg, R. (1990). *Metaphors of mind: Conceptions of the nature of intelligence.* New York: Cambridge University Press.

Sternberg, R. (2004). Culture and intelligence. *American Psychologist, 59,* 325–338.

Tetens, J. N. (1777). *Philosophische Versuche über die menschliche Natur und ihre Entwicklung.* Leipzig, Germany: Weidmanns Erben und Reich.

Thelen, E., & Smith, L. (1994). *A dynamic systems approach to the development of cognition and action.* Cambridge, MA: MIT Press.

Tomasello, M. (1999). *The cultural origins of human cognition.* Cambridge, MA: Harvard University Press.

Valsiner, J., & Lawrence, J. A. (1997). Human development in culture across the lifespan. In J. W. Berry, P. R. Dasen, & T. S. Saraswathi (Eds.), *Handbook of cross-cultural psychology* (Vol. 2, pp. 69–106). Boston: Allyn & Bacon.

Vandermeer, J. (2004, January 23). Evolution: The importance of a constructivist view. *Science,* 472–474.

Willis, S. L. (1987). Cognitive training and everyday competence. In K. W. Schaie & C. Eisdorfer (Eds.), *Annual review of gerontology and geriatrics* (Vol. 7, pp. 159–188). New York: Springer.

2

# Biocultural Co-Construction
# of Lifespan Development

Shu-Chen Li

ABSTRACT

*Neuroscientists have long recognized that the brain is an open, adaptive system and that the organism's experiences are environmentally contextualized. However, the proposition that sociocultural contexts may exert reciprocal influences on neurobiological mechanisms is rarely considered and could not be empirically explored until very recently. This chapter reviews an emerging trend of interdisciplinary research aimed at exploring the effects of sociocultural influences on human brain functioning. Viewed through the lens of a cross-level biocultural co-constructive framework, human development is co-constructed by biology and culture through a series of reciprocal interactions between developmental processes and plasticity at different levels.*

> "Mental exercise facilitates a greater development of . . . the nervous collaterals in the part of the brain in use. In this way, preexisting connections between groups of cells could be reinforced . . . "
>
> (Ramón y Cajal, 1894, Croonian lecture to the Royal Society).

INTRODUCTION

For more than a century, neuroscientists have been interested in how neural mechanisms implement mental experiences and how experiences may exert reciprocal influences on the neurobiological substrates of the mind. Ramón y Cajal enunciated what today is known as the "activity-dependent synaptic plasticity and memory hypothesis." Since the formulation and discoveries of synaptic processes of memory and learning, a great variety of neurochemical mechanisms involved in tuning synaptic efficacy have been identified (see Bliss, Collingridge, & Morris, 2003, for a recent review). As Rosenzweig (1996) gathered in his seminal review, animal research conducted in the second half of the twentieth century showed that differential

40

experience (or training) provided by environments with varying levels of complexity could alter brain neurochemistry, anatomy, and electrophysiology to varying degrees, indicating brain plasticity at these various levels.

The functional effects of various aspects of neuronal plasticity on behavior and cognition during development (e.g., Greenough & Black, 1992) and aging (e.g., Mohammed et al., 1993) have attracted much research attention. Furthermore, aside from the predominant emphasis of experiential influences on neuronal plasticity, recent studies have also started to investigate experiential influences on nonneuronal changes, such as experience-induced plasticity of astrocytes, myelination, and cerebrovasculature. In summary, current evidence indicates that, in response to different types (or aspects) of experiences (e.g., activity, learning, or task demands), the brain exhibits multiple forms of plasticity, allowing its processes to adapt to different forms of experiential tunings at various levels.

### From Complex Environment Paradigms in Animal Research to Socioculturally Constructed Experiential Contexts in Humans

The complex environment housing paradigm was developed in the late 1940s and early 1950s by Hebb (1949) and his associates. Since the first use of this paradigm as a method for studying neural plasticity in the mid-1960s, research on neural plasticity has recognized that the brain is an open, adaptive system and that the organism's experiences are contextualized by environmental characteristics. More rarely considered, however, is the proposition that sociocultural contexts may also exert reciprocal influences on neurobiological mechanisms. It is quite understandable that hitherto such a proposition has been atypical for neuroscientists to consider empirically. Lacking techniques for studying brain functioning in vivo in humans during most of the twentieth century, the relevance of social and, particularly, cultural contexts for animal studies is not only minimal, but also hard to define. Therefore, the research has been investigating the effects of empirically more tractable aspects of environment, such as the relative complexity and space of the animal's home cage and simple proxies of social interactions as defined by group size or amount of handling (see Rosenzweig, 1996, for a review).

One could also argue that experience *is* the proximal channel through which the influences of external contexts are mediated (see Chapter 3). Therefore, it may be more practical to consider experience-dependent neural plasticity, instead of contemplating the influences of some macro contexts, such as socioculturally constructed experiential contexts. Indeed, contextual influences interact with neurobiological processes through the organism's behavioral and cognitive experiences. However, environmental complexity simulated in laboratories is typically below the level of complexity in natural settings. This is particularly true for research on human brain functioning, given that human behavioral, emotional, and cognitive experiences are embedded in socioculturally constructed experiential contexts. The complexity and diversity of human experiential context are way beyond the proxies of environmental complexity and social interaction that animal studies have considered. Furthermore, in humans, cultural resources that have accumulated through cultural evolution (Tomasello, 1999) and ongoing social dynamics in contemporary societies structure the modal experiences the individuals experience (e.g., Cole, 1999). For instance, socioculturally based knowledge, such as the knowledge of language and numerical systems, is learned by individuals through parent–child interaction and formal schooling. Basic skills of reading, writing, computing, and professional skills, as well as other areas of expertise, are also acquired and exercised through different life periods in socioculturally constructed contexts.

The case of socioculturally structured contextual influence can perhaps be more clearly illustrated with respect to the occupational contexts within cultures. Different types of occupations impose job-related stimulus and demand characteristics on the individuals' daily working contexts (see Chapter 14). At the behavioral level, longitudinal studies have demonstrated reciprocal effects between the complexity of the occupational contexts and intellectual functioning in older adults (e.g., Schooler & Mulatu, 2004). Moreover, there are also great sociocultural diversities in contemporary societies that give rise to a wide range of differential experiences for individuals developing, going through adult life, and aging in these divergent experiential contexts. At the cognitive and behavioral level, a series of recent cross-cultural studies have demonstrated that different cultures foster different cognitive styles that, in turn, may affect the basic perceptual, cognitive (e.g., Kitayama, Duffy, Kawamura, & Larsen, 2003; Nisbett, Peng, Choi, & Norenzayan, 2001), and social attributional (Miyamoto & Kitayama, 2002) processes. With the arrival of a range of neuroimaging techniques to study human brain functioning, it has now become possible to start exploring the influences of sociocultural contexts on brain plasticity at different levels.

This brief review selectively focuses on an emerging trend of interdisciplinary research that investigates sociocultural influences on brain development and functioning across the lifespan. The chapter begins with a brief overview of recent co-constructive views of brain development and functioning, along with evidence of developmental plasticity at the evolutionary, behavioral and cognitive, neural, and genetic levels. Findings showing neural plasticity across different life periods are then highlighted. Although only limited evidence is available, three selective sets of recent findings are reviewed to demonstrate the influences of social context, culture-specific language environment, and expertise on brain functioning. In the concluding section, some potential future research directions are considered.

## CO-CONSTRUCTIVE VIEWS OF BRAIN DEVELOPMENT AND FUNCTIONING

> The brain's capacity to produce and combine mental objects, to remember them, and to communicate them is seen most vividly in humans. *Mental representations are propagated in different coded forms from one individual to another and perpetuate themselves through generations, without requiring any sort of genetic mutation.* . . . Writing leaves an impression on the brain, but where? Our lack of knowledge here does not allow us much room for speculation. We might expect that many areas are involved. . . . But neurological data are often hard to interpret; moreover, experimentation is difficult, if not impossible. Nevertheless, *the diversity of human culture provides fantastically rich material.* . . .
>
> (Changeux, 1985, pp. 241, 244; italics added)

Co-constructivism (or the related interactionism per se) is not new. Conceptions of environmental, cultural, and behavioral factors interacting with the biological inheritance of human development have long philosophical traditions. For instance, at the level of individual ontogeny, in the late eighteenth century Tetens assigned extraordinary plasticity to human nature, thus stipulating opportunities for environmental, cultural, and individual regulation during lifespan development. At the evolutionary phylogenetic level, in the late nineteenth century St. George Jackson Mivart suggested that behavioral changes and adaptation precede and affect natural selection. Modern behavioral researchers of human development have also been sensitive to the interplay between biology and various aspects of developmental contexts. Conceptually, there is the consensus that individual ontogeny is hierarchically organized within an open developmental system with multiple levels of contexts, from micro to macro. Developmental phenomena, thus, need to be investigated by jointly considering the reciprocal interactions between endogenous (e.g., genetic and neurobiological) and exogenous (e.g., sociocultural and environmental) processes at various levels (e.g., Baltes, 1987; Bronfenbrenner & Ceci, 1994; Gottlieb, 1998; Magnusson, 1988). Advocating the necessity and benefits of integrating sociocultural influences into neurobiological research does not stem only from the viewpoint of behavioral researchers. In the field of neurobiology, as expressed in the previous quote, Changeux (1985) saw the possibility of "cultural imprint" (p. 241) and stressed the importance of integrating cultural influences into neuroscience research nearly 20 years ago.

## Developmental Plasticity at Different Levels and Recent Co-Constructive Views

> . . . Recent work in neuroscience, robotics, and psychology . . . stresses the unexpected intimacy of brain, body, and world and invites us to attend to

the structure and dynamics of extended adaptive systems.... While it needs to be handled with some caution, I believe there is much to be learned from this broader vision. *The mind itself, if such a vision is correct, is best understood as the activity of an essentially situated brain: a brain at home in its proper bodily, cultural, and environmental niche.*

(Clark, 2001, p. 257; italics added)

More active interdisciplinary theoretical and empirical endeavors aimed at investigating the influences of socioculturally constructed experiential contexts on brain development and functioning did not begin until more recently. The previous quote by Clark (2001) is a good example of an emerging trend of interdisciplinary research that seeks to understand brain development and functioning as adaptations to broader experiential contexts. Contrary to the nativist view of innate and encapsulated genetic and neurobiological processes, there is a clear reemerging Zeitgeist across various subfields of life and developmental sciences of co-constructive conceptions that are accompanied by much recent empirical support for developmental plasticity at different levels. These conceptions and evidence of developmental plasticity across various levels have been integrated in a recent metatheoretical framework of development that advocates that brain and cognitive development be considered as continual biocultural co-construction of neurocognitive representations across the lifespan (Li, 2003). As schematically shown in Figure 2.1, an integral whole of biocultural influences on lifespan brain and behavioral development is implemented through reciprocal interactive processes and developmental plasticity that are simultaneously embedded within three time scales (i.e., phylogenetic, ontogenetic, and microgenetic times) encompassing multiple levels (i.e., sociocultural, behavioral, cognitive, neurobiological, and

**Biocultural Co-Construction of Lifespan Brain and Behavioral Development**
**Implemented Through Reciprocal Interactive Processes and Developmental Plasticity Across Levels**

Social Situational Contexts
and
Individual Cognition and Behavior
(involving behavioral and cognitive plasticity)

Culture–Gene Co-Evolution
(involving cultural and evolutionary plasticity)

Genetic and Neuronal Epigenesis
(involving genetic and neural plasticity)

FIGURE 2.1. Schematic diagram of the cross-level dynamic biocultural co-constructive framework of development, showing that concerted biocultural influences are implemented through interconnected interactive processes and developmental plasticity across various levels. (Adapted with permission from Li, 2003; copyright © by the American Psychological Association.)

genetic). Individual ontogeny throughout life is seen as a dynamic process that is cumulatively traced out by moment-to-moment experiences and activities taking place through interactions across the behavioral, cognitive, and neurobiological levels on the microgenetic time scale. These moment-to-moment microgenetic events are couched within (1) the proximal developmental context involving culturally embedded social interactions and situations on the lifespan ontogenetic time scale and (2) the distal context of culture–gene co-evolution occurring on the long-term phylogenetic time scale. In the following, co-constructive notions and evidence of developmental plasticity at the various levels are reviewed.

## Evolutionary Plasticity

Recently, it has been argued both on empirical and theoretical grounds that genetic programs and brain organization reflect the sociocultural basis of evolution. The conventional co-evolutionary theory has been extended by postulating a set of mediating mechanisms called "niche construction" to relate biological evolution and cultural changes to each other (Laland, Odling-Smee, & Feldman, 2000). Central to the concept of niche construction is the capacity of organisms and individuals to modify and construct the sources of natural selection in their environment via (1) learning- and experience-dependent processes during individual ontogeny and (2) processes of cultural change on another scale. For instance, the dairy farming culture selects for adult lactose tolerance and leads to populations in dairy farming societies with a higher percentage (i.e., more than 90%) of lactose absorbers in comparison to the percentage of lactose absorbers (i.e., less than 20%) in societies without dairy faming (Aoki, 1986). A more recent study found evidence in support of gene–culture co-evolution between cattle milk protein genes and human lactose genes. The geographic patterns of variation in genes encoding the most important milk proteins in 70 native European cattle breeds showed substantial geographic coincidence with present-day lactose tolerance in Europeans. The diversity in cattle milk genes is higher in North Central Europe than in Southern Europe and the Near East, and, correspondingly, lactose tolerance is higher in northern Europeans (Beja-Pereira et al., 2003). Consider a different example regarding brain evolution: Dunbar (1993) proposed that the biological evolution of brain encephalization was, in part, driven by the increase of social group size and the emergence of language as a more efficient means for handling complex social interactions.

## Behavioral and Cognitive Plasticity

As for developmental plasticity at the behavior and cognitive levels, various theories in the field of developmental psychology have emphasized the malleability of behavior and cognition by contextualized experiential factors. For instance, sociocultural contextual approaches (e.g., Cole, 1999; Gauvain, 1995) have focused more specifically on cultural influences affecting these social interactions and their subsequent mediated effects on individual development. In a related but different vein, rather than focusing on cultural influences at a higher level, the relationship contextual approach (e.g., Reis, Collins, & Berscheid, 2000) examines fine-grained details (e.g., emotional and cognitive aspects) of different types of interpersonal relationships and their impact on child development. Still others focus on the linguistic environment as a main facet of culture-specific social interactions in an individual's proximal developmental context (e.g., Nelson, 1996). Cross-cultural studies on parenting style (Bornstein, Tal, & Tamis-LeMonda, 1991) found that differential emphases on interpersonal versus object orientation that were mediated through parent–child interactions in the Japanese and American cultures, respectively, affected the types of games and languages at which the toddlers in these two societies performed well. It has also been suggested that the differential emphases of holistic versus analytical thinking in the East Asian and Western cultures, respectively, are associated with individuals' causal attribution processes (Nisbett et al., 2001). As for cognitive plasticity across the lifespan, memory training studies showed that older adults (ages 60 to 80) still displayed a fair amount of cognitive plasticity in improving their memory performance after training (Baltes & Kliegl, 1992) and that in very old age (i.e., age 80 years and older) marginal cognitive plasticity is still preserved (Singer, Lindenberger, & Baltes, 2003).

## Neural Plasticity

At the neuronal level of analysis, building on evidence showing experiential influences on synaptic numbers, axonal arborization, and dendritic arborization, as well as neurocomputational studies exploring learning and activity-dependent representational complexity, Quartz and Sejnowski (1997) proposed *"neural constructivism"* to consider representational features of the synaptic connections as built from dynamic interactions between neural growth mechanisms and environmentally derived neural activity. On a related theme, but at the level of cortical functional specification during development, Kingsbury, Lettman, and Finlay (2002), unlike most previous studies focusing primarily on intrinsic factors (e.g., the expressions of molecular markers) in cortical specialization, recently advocated that cortical specialization, particularly specification involving later layers of the cortical plate (e.g., layers IV, II/III), is the result of interactions between intrinsic factors and extrinsic input (e.g., somatosensory thalamic input). Similarly, to emphasize that brain development and functioning are co-constructed by contextualized experiences and neural processes, instead of speaking about "experience-dependent" neural plasticity, some researchers now prefer the term "experience-induced" neural plasticity, which more clearly indicates the active, constructivist role of experiential contexts (e.g., Greenough & Black, 1992; see Chapter 3).

## Genetic Plasticity

As to developmental plasticity at the genetic level, there is a recent shift from the traditional view of unidirectional gene → protein information flow to a probabilistic epigenetic framework emphasizing bidirectional interactions among genes, neuronal activity, behavior, and environment (Gottlieb, 1998). At this level, behavior-initiated evolutionary change also highlights that behaviors play active roles, instead of simply being the outcomes determined by genetic processes. For instance, it has been suggested that behavioral changes incurred during development could instigate genetic changes if transgenerational rearing conditions were relatively stable (Gottlieb, 2002).

## Cortical Plasticity Across the Lifespan

One important but less emphasized aspect of the evidence on plasticity is that neural plasticity occurs even after maturation, beyond infancy and early childhood (see Nelson, 2000, for a review; cf. Chapter 4). As to plasticity during early development, accumulating data suggest that the functional specialization of the neocortex is established through subsequent epigenetic interactions with the immediate experiential context (Changeux, 1985; Johnson, 2001). Thus, experiential influences leave traces in developing brains, capturing cumulative developmental effects acquired through the individual's moment-to-moment activities and experiences. For instance, it recently has been demonstrated that face processing is less localized or specialized (i.e., not as differentiated) in infants than in adults. In infants, face processing involves both left and right ventral visual pathways, whereas in adults face processing primarily involves the right ventral visual pathway. Although adult brain activity shows specific sensitivity to upright human faces, no such sensitivity for face orientation is observed in young infants (e.g., de Haan, Pascalis, & Johnson, 2002).

As to plasticity after maturation, there is also increasing evidence for cortical and cognitive plasticity extending beyond the developing brain to other periods of the lifespan (see summary in Table 2.1). Many recent data show that the adult brain can also adaptively change its structural and functional organization in response to accumulated developmental history reflecting daily experiences and aging. For instance, Maguire et al. (2000) found that the brain region involved in storing spatial representation of the environment (i.e., posterior hippocampi) was significantly larger in adults who had had extensive navigation experience than in age controls. As for functional plasticity during aging, a series of recent neuroimaging studies found evidence for reorganization of cortical functions in old age. In comparison to the more clearly lateralized cortical information processing in young adults, people in their 60s and beyond showed bilateralized (bihemispheric) activity during memory retrieval and during both verbal and spatial working memory processing (see Cabeza, 2002; Reuter-Lorenz,

TABLE 2.1. *Experiential and Life History-Dependent Cortical Plasticity Across the Lifespan*

| Lifespan Period | Studies |
|---|---|
| **Childhood** | |
| • Early bilinguals (<7 yr) show overlapping cortical activation for native and second language, whereas late bilinguals do not. | Neville & Bavelier (1998) |
| • Individuals who learn to play string instruments early show enlarged cortical representation of the left playing hand. | Elbert et al. (1995) |
| • Language-specific memory traces develop in infants at 12 months. | Cheour et al. (1998) |
| **Adulthood** | |
| • Individuals who are blind develop larger sensorimotor representation corresponding to the Braille reading finger. There is evidence of recruiting the visual cortex for tactile information processing. | Hamilton & Pascual-Leone (1998) |
| • The size of posterior hippocampi is enlarged in individuals such as taxi drivers who rely heavily on navigation skills in daily activities. | Maguire et al. (2000) |
| • Extensive training of complex finger motor sequences increase the extent of primary motor cortex activation, suggesting slowly evolving, long-term, experience-dependent reorganization of the adult primary motor cortex. | Karni et al. (1995) |
| **Old Age** | |
| • Aging increases bilateral cortical activation in various cognitive processes, indicating aging-related functional reorganization in the brain. | For a review, see Reuter-Lorenz (2002) and Cabeza (2002) |
| • Although brain aging is associated with loss in white and gray matter density, physical trainings that increases aerobic fitness reduces brain tissue loss. | Colcombe et al. (2003) |
| • Enriched environment induces neurogenesis in the hippocampus of old rats and improves memory performance. | Kempermann, Kuhn, & Gage (1997) |
| • Enriched environment restores aging-related decrease of synaptophysin content in old rats by enhanced packing density of synaptic vesicles in synapses. | Nakamura, Kobajashi, Ohashi, & Ando (1999); Saito et al. (1994) |

*Note:* All data are from humans, except two sets of results, as indicated in the table. Adapted with permission from Li (2003); copyright © by the American Psychological Association.

2002, for a review). It has been suggested that these data might indicate that the aging brain can "recruit" cortical areas in both hemispheres to compensate for neurocognitive decline during aging. As to structural plasticity in old age, neuroscience's century-old dogma that there is no addition of new neurons in the adult mammalian brain has also recently been revised. There is now evidence showing that increased environmental complexity stimulates the growth of new hippocampal neurons (i.e., neurogenesis) in the adult brains of various species, such as birds, rats, and humans (see Gross, 2000, for a review). There are also recent data showing that physical exercise training that increases aerobic fitness reduces aging-related loss in gray and white matter density (Colcombe et al., 2003).

In summary, sociocultural influences could have effects on the brain's structural and functional organization through early experiential "tuning" of synaptic connections and functional circuitry. In addition, although less flexible than in the early part of development, marked cortical plasticity is still evident throughout most of the adult lifespan, in terms of both structural and functional plasticity. This opens up possibilities for cultural and experiential influences to be intimately integrated into the individual's cumulative developmental history. This developmental history reflects life-long adaptations to both ongoing life experiences couched in the respective sociocultural context and lifespan developmental change in the efficacy and integrity of the brain itself.

## INITIAL EVIDENCE OF BIOCULTURAL CO-CONSTRUCTION OF NEUROCOGNITIVE FUNCTIONING

As the interdisciplinary research on biocultural co-construction of lifespan neurocognitive development is still at a very early, developing stage, available studies are limited. Nevertheless, three sets of selective findings reviewed in this section demonstrate particularly the reciprocal influences of social contexts, culture-specific language environment, and expertise training.

### Co-Evolution of Language, Social Group Size, and Brain Encephalization

Focusing predominantly on the human phylogenetic scale, Dunbar (1993) showed that group size covaries with relative neocortical volume in non-human primates. This led to the proposal that the brain's encephalization is not driven by the cognitive demands of tool making, but rather by an intricate co-evolving process between the growth in social group size and the development of language as a more efficient method for social bonding. More recent data comparing the complexity of social structure in New World and Old World monkeys in part also supported this proposal. Clark,

Mitra, and Wang (2001) found that the neocortical volume of Old World monkeys, as well as some orders of New World monkeys with more complex social structure (resembling that of Old World monkeys), is larger than that of New World monkeys with less complex social structure. The subsequent effect on the level of individual ontogeny was for language to become part of the socially inherited, species-specific cultural resources different societies use to support the individuals' interactions with each other and with the environment. Indeed, the linguistic relativity theory (Whorf, 1956) contends that human understanding of the world is, in part, constructed through language.

Brain encephalization is also correlated with the extended juvenile period in primates and humans, possibly also arising from social selection pressures involved in managing complex and dynamic social environments (Bjorklund & Pellegrini, 2000; Joffe, 1997). The extended juvenile period in humans, in turn, allows an extended amount of time and opportunities for intergenerational social interactions, operating in conjunction with language and other cultural resources to influence brain and cognitive development.

## Culture-Specific Language Environment
## and Cortical Language Processing

Culture-specific language differences do not only affect language processing at the perceptual and cognitive levels. Recent findings indicate a dynamic shift in cortical organization over the course of language acquisition. For instance, the time course of the changes and the degree of experience-dependent changes vary with different aspects of language. Event-related potential (ERP) data indicate that at 20 months, when children are typically speaking in single-word utterances, open-class words (i.e., words conveying referential meaning) and closed-class words (i.e., words providing structural and grammatical information) elicit similar patterns of brain activity. At 28 to 30 months of age, when children typically begin to speak in short phrases, ERPs to open- and closed-class words reveal different patterns of brain activity. By 3 years of age, when most children speak in sentences and use closed-class words appropriately like adults, ERPs start to display a left hemisphere asymmetry similar to adults (Neville & Mills, 1997). In a related vein, neuroimaging data indicate strong left-hemisphere activation for the native language in bilinguals. Whereas early bilinguals (second language learned before 7 years of age) showed overlapping areas of cortical activation for native and second language (e.g., Kim, Relkin, Lee, & Hirsch, 1997), late bilinguals showed completely independent or less overlapping activation (see Neville & Bavelier, 1998, for a review).

Although language processing depends on a system of neural networks primarily located in the left hemisphere, within the common system, however, there is room for the progressive developmental history of learning and using languages that differ in their orthographical mapping complexity to leave its trace at the cortical level. In comparison to the Italian language, English orthography is rather inconsistent, with complicated mappings of letters to sounds. In the English language, there are more than 1,000 ways of representing 40 sounds (phonemes), whereas in the Italian language 33 graphemes are sufficient to represent 25 phonemes. Paulesu and colleagues (2000) recently found that Italian readers showed greater activation in the left superior temporal regions associated with phoneme processing, whereas English readers showed greater activations, particularly for nonwords, in the left posterior inferior temporal gyrus and anterior frontal gyrus, areas associated with word retrieval during both reading and naming tasks. These data seem to suggest that acquiring the rather complex orthographical mapping of the English language impels the English readers to invoke additional neurocognitive mechanisms involving word retrieval from semantic memory while reading.

In addition, other culture- and society-based symbolic tools could also affect cognitive processing. At the neurobiological level, there is evidence for dissociated digit and letter processing, with the area of left inferior occipitotemporal cortex responding significantly more during a letter recognition task than during a digit recognition task. Interestingly, recent evidence showed that even a rather nonsalient aspect of cultural practice, that is, what postal codes are composed of, affects the individual's letter and digit processing (see Chapter 8). In comparison to their fellow postal workers who do not sort mail, mail sorters who daily sort outgoing mail to Canada, which has postal codes that are a mixture of both digits and letters (e.g., V6K 2E8), show less behavioral evidence for segregated letter and digit processing. An intriguing question is whether the behavioral findings observed in this case can also be found at the level of cortical processing.

## Expertise and Training-Induced Neural Plasticity

Besides language, there is also evidence showing that acquiring other expertise such as music or navigation skills leads to experience-induced cortical functional reorganization. It was found that cortical representations of the fingers of the left playing hands of string players were larger than those of the right hands, which hold the bow. This was particularly true for individuals who started playing the instrument early in life (Elbert, Pantev, Wienbruch, Rockstroh, & Taub, 1995). Another more recent neuroimaging study compared expert musicians with nonmusicians and found that while listening to J. S. Bach's *Italian Concerto*, nonmusicians who were not familiar with classical music showed activity primarily in the secondary auditory association area in the right temporal cortex. The musicians, however, also showed activities in the auditory association area in the left temporal cortex and in the left posterior dorsolateral prefrontal cortex, the brain regions associated with language processing and working memory functions, respectively (Ohnishi et al., 2001).

Outside the domain of music, Maguire et al. (2000) found that, given their extensive navigation experience, London taxi drivers' posterior hippocampi, a region of the brain involved in storing spatial representation of the environment, were significantly larger in comparison to same-age individuals who did not have as much navigation experience. Furthermore, in a comparison among drivers, the number of years spent as a taxi driver correlated positively with hippocampal volume. These data indicate that the adult brain still possesses functional plasticity, which allows the posterior hippocampus to expand regionally to accommodate elaboration of environmental spatial representation in individuals who rely heavily on their navigation skills and who have achieved a high level of navigation expertise in a particular environment.

## FUTURE RESEARCH DIRECTIONS AND CONCLUSION

Currently, findings regarding sociocultural influences on lifespan neurocognitive development are still very limited and leave many gaps between the different levels of analyses. Nevertheless, emerging co-constructive views and empirical evidence of developmental plasticity at various levels, as reviewed in this chapter, indicate that there are at least gradually increasing possibilities for bridging these gaps. Given neural plasticity that responds to lifespan developmental changes in the integrity of the brain itself and lifelong adaptations to ongoing life experiences couched in the individual's own respective sociocultural context, future research studying neurocognitive processes will need to focus less on the commonly used localization approach, mainly analyzing regional activation differences as a function of task conditions. Instead, lifespan changes and individual differences in brain–behavior mapping need to be considered more explicitly (Li & Lindenberger, 2002). For instance, instead of assuming that cortical regions and circuitry associated with particular functionalities in normal adults are very similar, if not identical, to those in developing children or old adults, lifespan changes in brain–behavior mapping need to be investigated and taken into account (e.g., Cabeza, 2002; Reuter-Lorenz, 2002; Schlaggar et al., 2002; Thomas & Karmiloff-Smith, 2002).

Furthermore, given the highly interactive nature of neurocognitive processes, which involve constant information exchanges with the experiential contexts, future research needs to more explicitly consider information exchanges between the individual and the context, and how such interactions may affect the functional aspects of neurocognitive processing. For instance, in addition to studying neural substrates of social cognition

(Adolphs, 2001), the ways in which dynamic, online social interactions may affect functional circuitry involved in different aspects of social cognition could also be of interest.

So far, we have only focused on findings showing adaptive neural plasticity induced by supportive sociocultural contexts. However, plasticity can be a two-edged sword. Thus, at the applied level, there is also a need to investigate the maladaptive effects of neural plasticity couched in changing societies where subjective social isolation (loneliness) increases for individuals of all ages (Cacioppo, Hawkley, & Berntson, 2003) or in dysfunctional social contexts that cause individuals highly stressful experiences or even trauma (e.g., Nelson & Carver, 1998). In addition, applied research on providing technological supports to assist individuals with limited neurocognitive capacity to better maintain the flow of information exchange between them and their experiential contexts is also important (see also Chapter 16).

In conclusion, the existing empirical evidence of developmental plasticity at different levels presents a warning against the "pure reductionist approach" to the genetic and neuronal bases of mind and behavior that ignores the influences from cultural, experiential, and cumulative developmental contexts. The reason is clear: genetic activities and neural mechanisms themselves possess remarkable plasticity awaiting sociocultural contexts to exert reciprocal influences on them and to be the "co-authors" of mind and behavior. People are more than mere biological organisms; the human mind and behavior need to be understood by situating them properly within a brain in a body that lives in an eventful world abounding with objects and people. Indeed, the brain offers the necessary biophysical reality for individual cognition and action; it alone, however, is not sufficient to engender the mind or behavior. The very processes for personalizing the biological faculty of the mind take place throughout lifespan development within environmental and sociocultural contexts, which entail intimate dynamic exchanges between nature and nurture.

ACKNOWLEDGMENTS

The author thanks her colleagues at the Max Planck Institute for Human Development and the anonymous reviewers for helpful comments on a previous version of this chapter.

**References**

Adolphs, R. (2001). The neurobiology of social cognition. *Current Opinion in Neurobiology, 11*, 231–239.

Aoki, K. (1986). A stochastic model of gene-culture coevolution suggested by the "culture historical hypothesis" for the evolution of adult lactose absorption in humans. *Proceedings of the National Academy of Sciences (USA), 83*, 2929–2933.

Baltes, P. B. (1987). Theoretical propositions of life-span developmental psychology: On the dynamics between growth and decline. *Developmental Psychology, 23,* 611–626.

Baltes, P. B., & Kliegl, R. (1992). Further testing of the limits of cognitive plasticity: Negative age differences in a mnemonic skill are robust. *Developmental Psychology, 28,* 121–125.

Beja-Pereira, A., Luikart, G., England, P. R., Bradley, D. G., Jann, O. C., Bertorelle, G., et al. (2003). Gene–culture coevolution between cattle milk protein genes and human lactase genes. *Nature Genetics, 35,* 311–313.

Bjorklund, D. F., & Pellegrini, A. D. (2000). Child development and evolutionary psychology. *Child Development, 71,* 1687–1708.

Bliss, T. V. P., Collingridge, G. L., & Morris, R. G. M. (Eds.). (2003). Long-term potentiation: Enhancing neuroscience for 30 years. *Philosophical Transactions: Biological Sciences, 358,* 607–829.

Bornstein, M. H., Tal, J., & Tamis-LeMonda, C. S. (1991). Parenting in crosscultural perspective: The United States, France, and Japan. In M. H. Bornstein (Ed.), *Cultural approaches to parenting* (pp. 69–90). Hillsdale, NJ: Erlbaum.

Bronfenbrenner, U., & Ceci, S. J. (1994). Nature–nurture reconceptualized in developmental perspective: A bioecological model. *Psychological Review, 101,* 568–586.

Cabeza, R. (2002). Hemispheric asymmetry reduction in older adults: The HAROLD model. *Psychology and Aging, 17,* 85–100.

Cacioppo, J. T., Hawkley, L. C., & Berntson, G. G. (2003). The anatomy of loneliness. *Current Directions in Psychological Sciences, 12,* 71–78.

Changeux, J.-P. (1985). *Neuronal man.* New York: Oxford University Press.

Cheour, M., Ceponiene, R., Lehtokoski, A., Luuk, A., Allik, J., Alho, K., & Näätänen, R. (1998). Development of language-specific phoneme representations in the infant brain. *Nature Neuroscience, 1,* 351–353.

Clark, A. (2001). Where brain, body, and world collide. In G. M. Edelman & J.-P. Changeux (Eds.), *The brain* (pp. 257–280). London: Transaction.

Clark, D. A., Mitra, P. P., & Wang, S. S. H. (2001). Scalable architecture in mammalian brains. *Nature, 411,* 189–193.

Colcombe, S. J., Erickson, K.-I., Raz, N., Webb, A. G., Cohen, N. J., McAuley, E., & Kramer, A. F. (2003). Aerobic fitness reduces brain tissue loss in aging humans. *Journal of Gerontology: Medical Sciences, 58A,* M176–M180.

Cole, M. (1999). Culture in development. In M. H. Bornstein & M. E. Lamb (Eds.), *Developmental psychology: An advanced textbook* (pp. 73–123). Mahwah, NJ: Erlbaum.

de Haan, M., Pascalis, O., & Johnson, M. H. (2002). Specialization of neural mechanisms underlying face recognition in human infants. *Journal of Cognitive Neuroscience, 14,* 199–209.

Dunbar, R. (1993). Co-evolution of neocortical size, group size, and language in humans. *Behavioral and Brain Sciences, 16,* 681–735.

Elbert, T., Pantev, C., Wienbruch, C., Rockstroh, B., & Taub, E. (1995). Increased cortical representation of the fingers of the left hand in string players. *Science, 270,* 305–307.

Gauvain, M. (1995). Thinking in niches: Sociocultural influences on cognitive development. *Human Development, 38,* 24–45.

Gottlieb, G. (1998). Normally occurring environmental and behavioral influences of gene activity: From central dogma to probabilistic epigenesis. *Psychological Review, 105,* 792–802.

Gottlieb, G. (2002). Developmental-behavioral initiation of evolutionary change. *Psychological Review, 109,* 211–218.

Greenough, W. T., & Black, J. E. (1992). Induction of brain structure by experience: Substrates for cognitive development. In M. R. Gunnar & C. A. Nelson (Eds.), *Developmental behavioral neuroscience* (Minnesota Symposia on Child Psychology, Vol. 24, pp. 155–200). Hillsdale, NJ: Erlbaum.

Gross, C. G. (2000). Neurogenesis in the adult brain: Death of a dogma. *Nature Reviews Neuroscience, 1,* 67–73.

Hamilton, R. H., & Pascual-Leone, A. (1998). Cortical plasticity associated with Braille learning. *Trends in Cognitive Sciences, 2,* 168–174.

Hebb, D. O. (1949). *The organization of behavior: A neuropsychological theory.* New York: Wiley.

Joffe, T. H. (1997). Social pressures have selected for an extended juvenile period in primates. *Journal of Human Evolution, 32,* 593–605.

Johnson, M. H. (2001). Functional brain development in humans. *Nature Review Neuroscience, 2,* 475–483.

Karni, A., Meyer, G., Jezzard, P., Adams, M. M., Turner, R., & Ungerleider, L. G. (1995). Functional MRI evidence for adult motor cortex plasticity during motor skill learning. *Nature, 377,* 155–158.

Kempermann, G., Kuhn, H. G., & Gage, F. H. (1997). More hippocampal neurons in adult mice living in an enriched environment. *Nature, 386,* 493–495.

Kim, K. H. S., Relkin, N. R., Lee, K. M., & Hirsch, J. (1997). Distinct cortical areas associated with native and second languages. *Nature, 388,* 171–174.

Kingsbury, M. A., Lettman, N. A., & Finlay, B. L. (2002). Reduction of early thalamic input alters adult corticocortical connectivity. *Developmental Brain Research, 138,* 35–43.

Kitayama, S., Duffy, S., Kawamura, T., & Larsen, J. T. (2003). Perceiving an object and its context in different cultures: A cultural look at New Look. *Psychological Science, 14,* 201–206.

Laland, K. N., Odling-Smee, J., & Feldman, M. W. (2000). Niche construction, biological evolution, and cultural change. *Behavioral and Brain Sciences, 23,* 131–175.

Li, S.-C. (2003). Biocultural orchestration of developmental plasticity across levels: The interplay of biology and culture in shaping the mind and behavior across the life span. *Psychological Bulletin, 129,* 171–194.

Li, S.-C., & Lindenberger, U. (2002). Co-constructed functionality instead of functional normality: Dynamic biocultural co-construction of brain–behaviour mappings. *Behavioral and Brain Sciences, 25,* 761–762.

Magnusson, D. (1988). *Individual development from an interactional perspective: A longitudinal study.* Hillsdale, NJ: Erlbaum.

Maguire, E. A., Gadian, D. G., Johnsrude, I. S., Good, C. D., Ashburner, J., Frackowiak, R. S. J., & Frith, C. D. (2000). Navigation-related structural change in the hippocampi of taxi drivers. *Proceedings of the National Academy of Sciences (USA), 97,* 4398–4403.

Miyamoto, Y., & Kitayama, S. (2002). Cultural variation in correspondence bias: The critical role of attitude diagnosticity of socially constrained behavior. *Journal of Personality and Social Psychology, 83*, 1239–1248.

Mohammed, A. H., Henriksson, B. G., Soderström, S., Ebendal, T., Olsson, T., & Seckl, J. R. (1993). Environmental influences on the central nervous system and their implications for the aging rat. *Behavioural Brain Research, 23*, 182–191.

Nakamura, H., Kobajashi, S., Ohashi, Y., & Ando, S. (1999). Age-changes of brain synapses and synaptic plasticity in response to an enriched environment. *Journal of Neuroscience Research, 56*, 307–315.

Nelson, C. A. (2000). Neural plasticity and human development: The role of early experience in sculpting memory systems. *Developmental Science, 3*, 115–136.

Nelson, C. A., & Carver, L. J. (1998). The effects of stress and trauma on brain and memory: A view from developmental cognitive neuroscience. *Developmental Psychopathology, 10*, 793–809.

Nelson, K. (1996). *Language in cognitive development.* Cambridge, UK: Cambridge University Press.

Neville, H. J., & Bavelier, D. (1998). Neural organization and plasticity of language. *Current Opinion in Neurobiology, 8*, 254–258.

Neville, H. J., & Mills, D. (1997). Epigenesis of language. *Mental Retardation & Developmental Disabilities Research Reviews, 3*, 282–292.

Nisbett, R. E., Peng, K., Choi, I., & Norenzayan, A. (2001). Culture and systems of thought: Holistic versus analytic cognition. *Psychological Review, 108*, 291–310.

Ohnishi, T., Matsuda, H., Asada, T., Hirakata, M., Nishikawa, M., Katoh, A., & Imabayashi, E. (2001). Functional anatomy of musical perception in musicians. *Cerebral Cortex, 11*, 754–760.

Paulesu, E., McCrory, E., Fazio, F., Menoncello, L., Brunswick, N., Cappa, S. F., et al. (2000). A cultural effect on brain function. *Nature Neuroscience, 3*, 91–96.

Quartz, S. R., & Sejnowski, T. J. (1997). The neural basis of cognitive development: A constructivist manifesto. *Behavioral and Brain Science, 20*, 537–596.

Reis, H. T., Collins, W. A., & Berscheid, E. (2000). The relationship context of human behavior and development. *Psychological Bulletin, 126*, 844–872.

Reuter-Lorenz, P. A. (2002). New visions of the aging mind and brain. *Trends in Cognitive Sciences, 6*, 394–400.

Rosenzweig, M. R. (1996). Aspects of the search for neural mechanisms of memory. *Annual Review of Psychology, 47*, 1–32.

Saito, S., Kobajashi, S., Ohashi, Y., Igarashi, M., Komiya, Y., & Ando, S. (1994). Decreased synaptic density in aged brains and its prevention by rearing under enriched environment as revealed by synaptophysin contents. *Journal of Neuroscience Research, 39*, 57–62.

Schlaggar, B. L., Brown, T. T., Lugar, H. M., Visscher, K. M., Miezin, F. M., & Petersen, S. E. (2002). Functional neuroanatomical differences between adults and school-age children in the processing of single words. *Science, 296*, 1476–1479.

Schooler, C., & Mulatu, M. S. (2004). Occupational self-direction, intellectual functioning, and self-directed orientation in older workers: Findings and implications for individuals and societies. *American Journal of Sociology, 110*, 161–197.

Singer, T., Lindenberger, U., & Baltes, P. B. (2003). Plasticity of memory for new learning in very old age: A story of major loss? *Psychology and Aging, 18*, 306–318.

Thomas, M., & Karmiloff-Smith, A. (2002). Are developmental disorders like cases of adult brain damage? Implications from connectionist modelling. *Behavioral and Brain Sciences, 25*, 772–787.

Tomasello, M. (1999). *The cultural origins of human cognition.* Cambridge, MA: Harvard University Press.

Whorf, B. (1956). *Language, thought, and reality.* Cambridge, MA: MIT Press.

# NEURONAL PLASTICITY AND BIOCULTURAL CO-CONSTRUCTION: MICROSTRUCTURE MEETS THE EXPERIENTIAL ENVIRONMENT

# 3

## Neurobehavioral Development in the Context of Biocultural Co-Constructivism

Charles A. Nelson

ABSTRACT

*Biocultural co-constructivism is a concept new to the field of developmental neuroscience, and thus there is no precedent for modeling how cultural processes are incorporated into the developing or developed brain. In this chapter, I offer a number of suggestions for how one might think about and study the relations among brain, culture, and development. I begin by providing a brief overview of brain development, followed by a discussion of neural plasticity. I conclude by speculating as to how culture might be incorporated into neural substrate, and subsequently and conversely, how such a remodeled brain might lead to changes in behavior.*

BACKGROUND

In 1997, Bloom and I published a paper in which we lamented the lack of communication among those studying behavioral development and those studying brain development (Nelson & Bloom, 1997). We argued that the impressive advances being made on both fronts – brain and behavioral development – and our knowledge of children in general would expand exponentially if there was greater cross-fertilization across disciplines. We illustrated a few examples, emphasizing most how advances in brain imaging and in our knowledge of neural plasticity may ultimately come to revolutionize our thinking about brain–behavior relations.

The arguments in favor of studying "neurobehavioral" development are as true today as when Bloom and I first proposed this in 1997. I still contend that our knowledge of the developing brain would best be grounded in knowledge of child development, and conversely, that our knowledge of child development could be vastly improved were we to explicate the neural mechanisms that underlie behavioral development. Thus, for example, rather than constrain ourselves to describing the cascade of cellular and physiological changes that occur during the time an immature brain is engaged in learning, why not attempt to insert this mechanistic view into a real live child? Similarly, why stop at describing the changes in memory capacity across the first years of life if such changes could also be well grounded in developmental neurobiology? Might our view of child development benefit most if we could not only describe changes in behavior across age, but also elucidate the biological mechanisms underlying such changes?

Yet, despite growing interest in interdisciplinary work in child development, there remains only a relatively small cadre of investigators working at this juncture of disciplines (see Nelson, 2003a). Why is this? Simply put, there is a long history of insularity among disciplines, even disciplines that have things in common (e.g., an interest in development). Overcoming such history is surely possible, but it will likely require the training of a new generation of scientists. A second reason pertains to the long, arduous training necessary to become an expert in *either* child development or developmental neurobiology. In the United States, a typical developmental psychology or neuroscience Ph.D. student requires 5 years to complete a degree, followed by several years of postdoctoral training. To be well trained in both disciplines typically requires not so much more time to degree completion, but rather (1) more time devoted to coursework (e.g., 3 full years vs. 1.5–2), and (2) some compromise in the amount of research that can be performed (generally due to additional time devoted to coursework, method acquisition, etc.). A third reason often cited for the paucity of interdisciplinary work pertains to the levels of analysis each discipline employs. Thus, most developmental psychologists are used to working at the level of behavioral systems, whereas most developmental neuroscientists work at a much more molecular level. How to traverse the boundaries between, say, molecular biology and behavior is not always clear. As a result, the neuroscientist typically develops a much more mechanistic approach to development, whereas the psychologist works at a more descriptive level.

There is one additional conundrum that delays further acquisition of knowledge of neurobehavioral development that must be mentioned because it is germane to the topic of this volume. Specifically, many developmental neuroscientists are keenly interested in modeling how experience-induced changes in brain physiology, anatomy, and function take place, but they look to psychologists for help in understanding the specific experiences that exist in the typical child's environment; after all, how can one model the effects of experience on brain if the experience in question is not well defined? Here, many psychologists respond by arguing that the precision with which one can assess discrete experiences and manipulate such experiences is very limited. Thus, for example, one cannot (1) measure every element of a child's environment or interaction with the environment, or (2) randomly assign children to different rearing conditions (although I cite an exception later in this chapter) and observe the effects on brain and behavior.

How is this relevant to biocultural co-constructivism? In brief, if our ability to model how the structure of experience works its way into the structure of the brain is limited for the reasons previously cited, how will it be possible to understand how *culture* affects brain and, conversely, how brain development affects culture? For example, it is currently very challenging to describe experience-based changes in brain function because of the difficulty in describing these experiences in precise spatial and temporal terms (i.e., what the specific experience is and the timing of this experience). If we assume that at least at some level culture represents a collection of diverse current and historical experiences, it becomes even more challenging to model the effects of culture on brain and of brain on culture (it is this bidirectionality that I view as "biocultural co-constructivism"). Why? Simply because to examine the effects of culture on brain one needs to state precisely what *elements* of culture are of interest, translate these elements into specific and possibly discrete behaviors, and then examine the effects on brain. If one is interested in the far more challenging issue of understanding the effects of brain development on culture, it is once again necessary to establish linkages between specific biological events and specific experiences. Finally, if culture is *more* than the collection of discrete experiences, it is absolutely essential for those studying culture to define precisely what constitutes a cultural experience in order for the neuroscientist to model its effect on brain.

For the purposes of this chapter, I assume that the way culture gets into the brain is through the same mechanisms that experience in general gets into the brain. This assumption should retain its validity, regardless of whether culture is simply a collection of experiences or is something more entirely. I would therefore contend that a starting place to understanding biocultural co-constructivism would be to examine what is currently known about experiential effects on brain development. I begin by drawing on examples from sensory and perceptual development, and then move to cognitive, and finally, to social-emotional development. To understand how experience influences brain development, however, it is necessary first to provide a brief tutorial on neural development.

## INTRODUCTION TO BRAIN DEVELOPMENT

Extensive and multiple reviews of this topic exist, and thus I provide only a brief overview (see Levitt, 2003; Monk, Webb, & Nelson, 2001; Nelson, 2002; Nelson, Thomas, & de Haan, 2006; Webb, Monk, & Nelson, 2001). A graphic overview of human brain development can be seen in Figure 3.1, and a more detailed representation is shown in Table 3.1.

Brain development is typically believed to begin with the formation and then closure of the neural tube, events that occur between roughly the third and fourth prenatal weeks. Essentially, the dorsal side of the ectodermal layer of the embryo thickens and then, once a longitudinal axis appears,

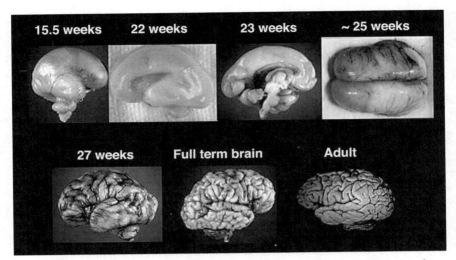

FIGURE 3.1. Superficial/anatomical view of the developing brain, ranging from 15.5 weeks' gestation through term. The adult brain is provided as a reference. (Adapted from http://medstat.med.utah.edu.)

begins to fold over onto itself to form first a groove and then a tube. After the uppermost and lowermost ends of the tube have closed, cells trapped inside the tube eventually give rise to the central nervous system, whereas those trapped between the outside of the tube and the ectodermal wall give rise to the autonomic nervous system. When this phase (referred to as neurulation) has been completed, there is a massive proliferation of immature brain cells (both neuronal and glial precursors). Starting at around the sixth prenatal week and continuing through at least the third trimester, the cortex itself forms in an inside-out fashion by way of migrating neurons. Eventually, the cortex comes to have six layers, along with columns of related cells (e.g., ocular dominance columns). When a cell has completed its migratory journey (keeping in mind that there are thousands of cells migrating in wave after wave of migratory movement), it is in a position to differentiate and develop processes (axons and dendrites). Of course, not all cells differentiate; indeed, it has been estimated that 40% to 60% of all neurons die, a normative, highly regularized process referred to as apoptosis (programmed cell death). However, assuming a cell has not died, many such cells go on to develop axons and dendrites, and many of these go on to develop synapses (a process referred to as synaptogenesis). Throughout all areas of the cortex, there is an initial overproduction of synapses followed by a retraction. In the human brain, the peak of overproduction and retraction varies by area. For example, synapses peak between 4 and 6 postnatal months in the visual cortex, followed by a gradual retraction to adult numbers by 4 to 6 years. In contrast, synapses in the middle frontal

TABLE 3.1. *Timeline of Developmental Events*

| Developmental Event | Timeline | Overview of Developmental Event |
|---|---|---|
| Neurulation | 8–24 Prenatal days | • Cells differentiate into one of three layers – endoderm, mesoderm, and ectoderm – which then form the various organs in the body.<br>• The neural tube (from which the CNS is derived) develops from the ectoderm cells; the neural crest (from which the ANS is derived) lies between the ectodermal wall and the neural tube. |
| Neuronal migration | 6–24 Prenatal weeks | • Neurons migrate at the ventricular zone along radial glial cells to the cerebral cortex.<br>• The neurons migrate in an inside-out manner, with later generations of cells migrating through previously developed cells.<br>• The cortex develops into six layers. |
| Synaptogenesis | 3rd Trimester–adolescence | • Neurons migrate into the cortical plate, and extend apical and basilar dendrites.<br>• Chemical signals guide the developing dendrites toward their final location, where synapses are formed with projections from subcortical structures.<br>• These connections are strengthened through neuronal activity, and connections with very little activity are pruned. |
| Postnatal neurogenesis | Birth–adulthood | • The development of new cells in several brain regions, including<br>  • dentate gyrus of the hippocampus<br>  • olfactory bulb<br>  • possibly cingulate gyrus; regions of parietal cortex |
| Myelination | 3rd Trimester–middle age | • Neurons are enclosed in a myelin sheath, resulting in an increased speed of action potentials. |
| Gyrification | 3rd Trimester–adulthood | • The smooth tissue of the brain folds to form gyri and sulci. |
| Structural development of prefrontal cortex | Birth–late adulthood | • The prefrontal cortex is the last structure to undergo gyrification during uterine life.<br>• The synaptic density reaches its peak at 12 months; however, myelination of this structure continues into adulthood. |
| Neurochemical development of prefrontal cortex | Uterine life–adolescence | • All major neurotransmitter systems undergo initial development during uterine life and are present at birth.<br>• Although it is not well studied in humans, it is believed that most neurotransmitter systems do not reach full maturity until adulthood. |

ANS, autonomic nervous system; CNS, central nervous system.

*Source:* From White, T., & Nelson, C. A. (2005). Neurobiological development during childhood and adolescence. In R. Findling & S. C. Schulz (Eds.), *Juvenile-onset schizophrenia: Assessment, neurobiology, and treatment.* Baltimore: Johns Hopkins University Press2005, pp. 61–62, Table 3.1. © 2005 [Copyright Holder]. Adapted with permission of The Johns Hopkins University Press.

gyrus of the prefrontal cortex reach their peak at about 12 postnatal months, but adult numbers are not obtained until mid- to late adolescence. Finally, once axons have been formed, the process of myelination can begin. Like synaptogenesis, myelination varies by area, with axons in many of the sensory and motor regions beginning to myelinate during the last trimester, whereas some of the association areas of the cortex (notably, the frontal association cortex) are not fully myelinated until sometime between the first and second decades of life.

The final dimension of brain development worth mentioning concerns the relatively new area of postnatal neurogenesis (cf. Chapter 4). As alluded to previously, it has long been believed that we are born with all the neurons we will ever have, with the exception of cells in the olfactory bulb. However, more recently it has been discovered that in the dentate gyrus of the hippocampus, and possibly in regions of the prefrontal and parietal cortices, new cells are made on a regular basis, in some cases through middle age. Moreover, the degree of neurogenesis, at least in the dentate, appears experience dependent; for example, rats housed in complex environments where there are cognitive challenges tend to upregulate the birth of new cells, whereas rats exposed to stress tend to downregulate neurogenesis (for a recent review, see Gould & Gross, 2002).

Overall, brain development is a long process that has its origins early in prenatal life and continues postnatally. Although the basic architecture of the brain exists by the time a child is 2 to 3 years old, there is considerable refinement in brain structure, function, and physiology for another two decades – as anyone who is familiar with child development will attest.

The overview provided in this section may lead one to think that brain development is largely controlled by genetics. Although this is indeed true for many aspects of prenatal brain development, as the next section illustrates, experience exerts profound effects on the developing brain, both pre- and postnatally. It is to this topic that I next direct my attention.

## INFLUENCE OF EXPERIENCE ON BRAIN DEVELOPMENT

Experience is not something that simply happens to the brain; rather, experience is the product of an ongoing, reciprocal interaction between the environment and the brain. Moreover, experience has typically been defined by the properties of the environment in which an individual lives, such as one's linguistic or cultural environment. Finally, experience is not only a function of the environment per se, but it is also the result of a complex, bidirectional interaction between that environment and the developing brain, with one's genetic make-up playing an important role in regulating some aspects of the relation between brain and experience.

The argument put forth in the previous section, although reasonable, is not easy to study, at least in the human. An example from the rodent literature, however, nicely illustrates these points. Francis, Szegda, Campbell,

Martin, and Insel (2003) cross-fostered two strains of mice with one another. One strain was cross-fostered prenatally (in which hours-old embryos from one strain were implanted in the mothers of the other strain) or postnatally (in which newborn pups from one strain were placed with the mothers of the other strain) or both. The offspring of two noncross-fostered strains served as controls, and all animals were tested at 3 months of age. The control animals differed reliably from one another on a number of dimensions, such as exploratory behavior and spatial learning. Animals that had been cross-fostered prenatally *or* postnatally did not exert any phenotypic effects. However, mice that had been prenatally *and* postnatally cross-fostered exhibited the same behavioral phenotype as the adopted strain, despite differing genetically from the adopted strain. The fact that mice that had been cross-fostered prenatally did not show this effect supported the contention that the effects of the combined cross-fostering must be due to nongenetic factors, and the powerful role of experience on gene expression.

Naturally, a study such as this would be impossible to conduct in humans, but it does reinforce the point that there is a complex and symbiotic relation between brain and experience. This point resurfaces later in my discussion of culture.

## Models of Experience–Brain Relations

Perhaps the most elegant models of experience-dependent changes in brain development come from the work of William Greenough. He and his colleagues (e.g., Black, Jones, Nelson, & Greenough, 1998; Greenough, Black, & Wallace, 1987) suggest that the overproduction of synapses serves a useful purpose: to capture experience, thereby confirming and/or stabilizing a particular synaptic circuit. Two types of activity-dependent changes have been proposed: those that are common to all members of the species (experience expectant) or those that are unique to the individual (experience dependent). In the former, it is assumed that rather than genetically code for the development of a particular function, genes provide only a rough sketch pad on which experience writes. Importantly, such experiences must be common to all members of the species for development to proceed normally and for the brain to be organized correctly. Embedded in this model is the assumption that the timing of specific experiences is critical; that is, if a particular experience comes along too late or too early, the brain may not be wired correctly and thus a particular function may not develop normally.

Experience-dependent plasticity is unique to the individual and does not assume that timing is essential for normal development to occur. As elaborated in this section, the most common example of experience-dependent changes in brain function is learning.

There is one additional caveat to discuss about brain plasticity before continuing that pertains to developmental versus adult plasticity. This distinction is nontrivial, but by the same token, difficult to articulate. Most superficially, we are concerned with experience-driven changes in brain and brain function that occur during the most rapid period of development – undoubtedly, the first few years of life, with a tapering off that continues until the end of adolescence – versus those that occur once the brain has attained adult status. Of course, on further inspection, this becomes problematic because the transition between "childhood" and "adulthood" clearly represents a continuous function. Moreover, given recent evidence that some areas of the brain continue to make new neurons through at least middle age, how do we incorporate this into the dichotomy of developmental versus adult plasticity? Nevertheless, the overarching issue concerns whether the *developing* brain is more plastic (or differentially plastic) than the *developed* brain. Because this debate is still being hotly debated, I avoid a direct confrontation in this chapter; instead, in the sections that follow, I primarily talk about domains of plasticity rather than the timing of plasticity, although periodic references to timing issues are sprinkled throughout the chapter.

### Visual Development

DEPTH PERCEPTION. It has long been known that stereoscopic depth perception (which refers to the ability of the brain to fuse the slightly disparate images each eye receives) is made possible by the development of ocular dominance columns, which represent the connections between each eye and layer IV of the visual cortex. If the two eyes are not properly aligned, thereby preventing them from converging correctly on a distant target (as occurs in the ocular disorder *strabismus*, cf. Chapter 5), then the regions of the brain that support normal stereoscopic depth perception fail to develop normally. If this situation is not corrected by the time the number of synapses in the visual cortex reaches adult values (approximately ages 4 to 6; see earlier sections), the child will not develop normal stereoscopic vision. The result is not only poor stereoscopic vision, but also the possibility of poor vision in general in one eye. Clearly, then, these data point to the importance of experience-expectant changes in brain development. Specifically, if we assume a certain veridicality in the visual world (e.g., access to patterned light information), and we assume further that the fundamental components of the visual system are intact (e.g., there is no strabismus), then vision should develop normally.

PATTERN PERCEPTION. Yet another example of activity-dependent changes in brain function can be found in recent work on congenital cataracts.[1] For example, drawing on longitudinal data, Maurer, Lewis,

---

[1] A cataract is an opacity that covers the eye, which, if dense enough, may permit only light perception but no pattern perception. In the studies reviewed in this section, the assumption is that pattern vision was dramatically limited in these patients.

Brent, and Levin (1999) reported that among infants born with cataracts that are removed and replaced by new lenses within months of birth, even just a few *minutes* of visual experience lead to a rapid change in visual acuity. Not unexpectedly, the longer the cataracts are left, reducing the amount of time for exposure to a normal visual world to occur, the less favorable the outcome.

There is an important qualifier to this basic finding: specifically, although most visual functions undergo dramatic improvements following early cataract removal, some aspects of *face* processing remain impaired for years. Thus, here there is the suggestion of a fairly narrowly defined sensitive period for one aspect of visual function – face processing – to which I next direct my attention.

FACE PERCEPTION. There is now extensive evidence to support the notion that experience makes a powerful contribution to the ability to process faces (for recent reviews, see Nelson, 2001, 2003b; Scott & Nelson, 2004). First, for example, we know that adults have difficulty discriminating inverted faces, a phenomenon that appears to emerge by about 4 months of age (Fagan, 1972). This inversion effect is typically attributed to the fact that we have extensive experience seeing faces upright and virtually no experience seeing them upside down; thus, it is experience with the former that accounts for poorer performance in processing or recognizing inverted faces. Second, there is the well-known "other race" effect, in which adults, more so than children, find it easier to recognize faces from their own race (see Chance, Turner, & Goldstein, 1982; O'Toole, Deffenbacher, Valentin, & Abdi, 1994). Third, as previously discussed, Maurer and colleagues (1999) reported that children born with cataracts go on to develop very good visual functions in general once the cataracts are removed, although subtle deficits in face recognition persist. These findings have been interpreted to suggest that exposure to normal faces during a sensitive period of development is crucial for normal face processing skills to develop in full later.

Fourth, perhaps the strongest evidence for the role of experience in the development of face processing comes from the findings that both monkeys and human adults are better at recognizing faces from their own species (Pascalis & Bachevalier, 1999). For example, work from my lab and that of my collaborators (e.g., Pascalis, de Haan, & Nelson, 2002) has reported that in the first 6 months of life infants are quite good at discriminating both human and monkey faces, but by 9 months infants behave more like adults: they can discriminate two human faces but have a very difficult time discriminating two monkey faces. Work is currently underway to examine whether this perceptual window can be kept open by exposing infants to monkey faces between 6 and 9 months, but suffice to say, these data support the view that cortical specialization for face processing is driven by experience with faces. Presumably, this process reflects an experience-expectant system versus an experience-dependent system (see Nelson, 2001, for elaboration).

A final bit of evidence to support the experience-driven nature of face processing comes from the child maltreatment literature. For example, maltreated children *generally* perform more poorly on emotion recognition tasks than do nonmaltreated children (Camras, Grow, & Ribordy, 1983; Camras et al., 1988); however, Pollak and Kistler (2002) reported that *abused* children show greater sensitivity to angry expressions than do nonabused children. This pattern of findings has been interpreted as supporting the view that experience with facial emotion greatly influences the development of the ability to recognize emotion.

Collectively, most higher forms of vision are not only dependent on postnatal experience, but this dependency occurs within a relatively narrow period of time – and when it comes to face processing, a *very* narrow period of time (perhaps the first few months of life).

## Speech and Language Development

There are a number of elements of language development that can be considered in the context of experience-induced (or experience-sensitive) changes in brain development.

SPEECH PERCEPTION. It has been known for some time that unilingual adults have great difficulty discriminating speech contrasts from their non-native language. For example, English-speaking adults who have not been exposed to such languages as Swedish, Thai, or Japanese experience great difficulty in discriminating speech contrasts from these languages. This stands in contrast to a highly developed ability to discriminate speech contrasts from one's native language (in this example, English). A number of authors have demonstrated that some time in the second half year of life the infant's ability to discriminate phonemes from languages to which they are not exposed diminishes greatly (for review, see Werker & Vouloumanos, 2001). Thus, although a 6-month-old infant raised in an English-speaking home may be able to discriminate contrasts from English, as well as those from Swedish or Thai, by 12 months of age, such infants become more like English-speaking adults. In other words, normative development involves the loss of the ability to discriminate contrasts from their nonnative language. These data have been interpreted to suggest that the speech system remains open to experience for a certain period of time, but if experience in a particular domain (e.g., hearing speech contrasts in different languages) is not forthcoming, the window begins to close early in life (similar, perhaps, to what happens in face perception, as discussed previously). Again, this represents an example of an experience-expectant model.

Importantly, Kuhl, Tsao, and Liu (2003) reported that if before 12 months of age infants are given additional experience with speech sounds in a nonnative language, they are able to retain this ability. These data provide confirmation for the perceptual narrowing hypothesis discussed earlier; specifically, the normal progression of speech perception is one in which certain discriminatory abilities are lost, *unless experience with nonnative languages occurs during a sensitive period of development.*

### Second Language Acquisition/Neural Representation of Language

Throughout the 1980s and 1990s, as our neuroimaging tools began to be refined, there were early reports that the neural representation of second languages differed from first languages. However, we now know that this general observation requires qualification (cf. Chapter 7).

Dehaene and colleagues (1997) reported that the neural representation of a second language is identical to that of a first language *if* the individual is truly bilingual. However, if the mastery of the second language is not as strong as the first, then the functional neuroanatomy is different. Because the majority of the bilinguals studied in this work acquired their second language at an early age, the initial conclusion was that the second language needed to be learned early in life in order to share the same neural representation as the first language. This does not appear to be the case, however. These same authors (see Perani et al., 1998) asked whether it was the *age* at which the second language was acquired that was the critical variable, or rather, the subject's *proficiency* in speaking this language. In this study, the age at which the second language had been mastered was covaried against the proficiency of speaking this language. The authors observed that it was the mastery of the language that proved most important. Thus, regardless of when the second language was acquired, speaking this language proficiently (i.e., as well as the first language) led to shared neural representation for both languages. Similar findings have recently been obtained with individuals who are congenitally deaf and who are proficient in sign language; thus, the areas of the brain involved in signing are the same as those of hearing speakers using spoken language (see Petitto et al., 2000). Collectively, these findings raise doubts about a strict sensitive period for acquiring some elements of a second language (or at least raise the possibility of a broadly tuned sensitive period).

It is important to note that the issue of shared neural representation for multiple languages should not be confused with the issue of speaking a second language without an accent. Thus, individuals who acquire a second language before the age of 10 years are far more likely to speak that language without an accent than those who acquire that language after the age of 10 (e.g., Johnson & Newport, 1989).

## Cognitive Development

The field of cognitive development has a long tradition within developmental psychology. Interestingly, the vast majority of this literature is rich in description of changes in cognition that unfold over time, and in positing various cognitive mechanisms that underlie such change (e.g., models proposed by Piaget). However, relatively little attention has been paid to the neural underpinnings of cognitive development (for recent reviews, see Johnson, 1998; de Haan & Johnson, 2003; Nelson & Luciana, 2001) and to how experience influences these mechanisms (e.g., in the context of memory, see Nelson, 2000). A major exception to this observation occurs in the context of early intervention programs designed to boost intellectual functioning in children living in poverty.

### *Experience and the Brain: Some Background*

In 1947, Hebb reported having reared rats in his home as pets. Upon testing in the Hebb-Williams maze, it was reported that these home-reared rats scored better than laboratory-reared rats (Hebb & Williams, 1946). Hebb concluded that *"the richer experience of the pet group during development made them better able to profit by new experiences at maturity"* (Hebb, 1949, p. 299; italics in original). And so was ushered in the movement to examine how experience affects cognition.

In a series of studies conducted in the 1960s at the University of California at Berkeley, scientists began to report rather dramatic changes in the rodent brain based on exposure to so-called "enriched" experience (as Greenough notes, a more appropriate descriptor would be "complex" because enrichment is a term relative to the typical impoverished environment in which most rats live). These changes included increased cortical activity of the neurotransmitter acetylcholine, greater efficiency of synaptic transmission, and successful problem solving in rats (for a recent review, see Curtis & Nelson, 2003).

This early work was extended by Greenough and colleagues, who fine-tuned the experimental paradigm. Moreover, they reported changes at multiple levels of the nervous system ("genes to behavior"). Most relevant to this chapter is how these data were eventually transformed into programs in the United States designed to boost children's intellectual development, which brings us to our next topic – the effects of early experience on cognitive development.

### *Environmental Enrichment for Humans: Early Childhood Education and Enrichment*

As discussed by Curtis and Nelson (2003), early childhood enrichment programs such as Head Start were intended to provide children from disadvantaged households with "enriched" (relative to their home life) cognitive and linguistic experiences to level the playing field with children coming from more economically able households (Zigler & Valentine, 1979). On the whole, outcome studies of Head Start have shown initial IQ gains followed by subsequent declines (Lazar, Darlington, Murray,

Royce, & Snipper, 1982). Other more recently developed and methodologically rigorous preschool intervention programs, such as Abecedarian, have
attempted to boost cognitive and social development in high-risk young
children (e.g., Ramey & Ramey, 1998). For example, the curriculum was
targeted at multiple developmental domains, and included work in cognitive, motor, language, and social skills. In terms of IQ, by the time children
reached the age of 3, the average IQ scores of the intervention and control groups were, respectively, 101 and 84, whereas by age 12, the mean
IQ of both groups had dropped, with the intervention and control groups
attaining, respectively, mean IQs of 93 and 88. By age 15, there was a nearly
5-point IQ score difference in favor of the intervention group.

Farran (2000) and Barnett (1996) have both elegantly summarized the
collective effects of various early intervention programs, and offer the following conclusions. First, all programs raise child IQ during the children's
enrollment in the program, with the largest IQ gains seen in children from
programs that began in infancy (Farran, 2000). Second, with the exception
of the Abecedarian project, IQ effects are nonexistent by or before age 12. As
Curtis & Nelson, 2003 noted, *"... it is important to remember that animal studies of enrichment, which generally employ enrichment that is all-encompassing
for the organism and is not aimed at specific behaviors, show a pervasive, generalized impact on the brain and learning ability. Thus, specific narrow effects, such
as increase in IQ, may not be reasonably expected from preschool programs that
provide broad-based enrichment"* (Curtis & Nelson, 2003, p. 472). Of course,
an additional point worth noting is that if we assume the diminished IQ
among children living in poverty is due to some level of deprivation, it
should not be entirely surprising that elevated IQs due to early enrichment would eventually abate. After all, children spend considerably more
time at home than at school, and thus, the deprivation effects inherent
in the home environment may eventually overwhelm the effects of early
enrichment.[2]

Overall, it is clear that the effects of early intervention on intellectual
function among children living in impoverished circumstances are modest
at best. The reasons for such modesty are many, and include (1) the global
measures used to assess intellectual function, (2) the broad targets of the
intervention (i.e., the lack of precision in the specific "enriching" experiences), and (3) the failure to consider the child's genetic potential, which
may influence the ceiling of intellectual ability. Given the sophistication
with which we now conceive of specific cognitive abilities, along with our

---

[2] An alternative view worth considering would be that a "bolus" of early experience serves
to inoculate a child against the effects of deprivation. As attractive as this concept is, however, the data fail to support this view when it comes to IQ. However, perhaps this model
applies to domains of social-emotional functioning; for example, in the Abecedarian project,
children in the treatment group were less likely to drop out of high school and to become
pregnant as teenagers.

knowledge of the neural circuitry that underlies such abilities, it would seem important in future research to examine whether specific intellectual abilities in children living in typical (i.e., nonimpoverished) environments can be enriched by specific experiences.

### Social-Emotional Development

As has been the case in perceptual and cognitive development, the most common way to examine the role of experience on social-emotional development has been to examine the effects of being reared under conditions of deprivation. It has long been known, for example, that early deprivation can have profound effects on a variety of aspects of development. For example, in a recent review of this literature, Gunnar (2001) reported that the long-term sequelae of children experiencing early institutionalization and concomitant deprivation include deficits in social-emotional functioning and in executive functions. However, despite the lengthy history of studying postinstitutionalized children, there are few if any studies that have (1) examined the effects of institutionalization on brain and behavioral development, and (2) shown, using a randomized, case-control design, the efficacy of early intervention in ameliorating the effects of early deprivation. These limitations of previous studies have recently been addressed in a large-scale project based in Bucharest, Romania, entitled the Bucharest Early Intervention Project (BEIP).

The goal of this project was to assess the effects of early institutionalization on a host of neural and behavioral functions, and to determine if a specific intervention – in this case, high-quality foster care – could ameliorate the expected negative sequelae of the deprivation that is inherent in institutional settings. Three groups of children served as participants in this study. One group included children living in six different institutions throughout Bucharest (IG). A second group consisted of children who were initially placed in these same orphanages, but who, following a baseline assessment, were randomly assigned to live in foster care especially created under the auspices of this project (FCG).[3] A third group was comprised

---

[3] There are three ethical issues pertaining to this study that are worth mentioning. First, prior to the onset of this study, there was no formal foster care system in Bucharest. Accordingly, we were required to develop our own foster care system. The limits on this system were essentially the number of families we could identify who were willing to have a child placed in their care. This totaled about 75 families. Second, we also agreed at the outset that no child placed in foster care would be returned to institutional care once our study ended. This guarantee was made possible by working closely with the Romanian child protection authorities and a nongovernmental organization (SERA Romania), both of which were committed to keeping children in foster care, or when possible, placing children in adoptive families. Third, we also agreed at the outset that any child living in the institution would be reunited with his or her biological family or be placed in state-run foster care should that opportunity present itself. Indeed, by year 3 of our study, nearly half the children in our institutionalized group had left the institution for family care of one sort or another.

of children living with their biological families in the greater Bucharest community (NIG).

### Procedures and Measures

Without going into great detail (see Zeanah et al., 2003), our baseline and follow-up measures centered on the following domains: physical development, language, social functioning/social-emotional development, a careful characterization of the caregiving environment, cognition, temperament, attachment, brain function, problem behaviors, and competencies. Follow-up data were taken when children turned 9, 18, 30, 42, and 54 months.

Although the focus of this section is on social-emotional development, our findings from other domains merit brief attention. Thus, we found that children in our IG were remarkably delayed in all measures of physical growth and development. Thus, their height-for-age, weight-for-age, and head circumference all clustered around the twentieth to twenty-fifth percentile. Importantly, among our FCG, our height and weight (but not head circumference) measures moved closer to the population norm the longer infants stayed in foster care. Not surprisingly, children in the IG and NIG remained approximately level across time. In terms of language development, at baseline the IG's overall language quotient was at about 65 (with 100 being the mean); however, for measures of comprehension and production, the IG infants performed at about the tenth percentile, respectively. In contrast, the overall language quotient among our NIG infants was about 110, and they scored at the seventieth and sixtieth percentiles, respectively, on language comprehension and production. Importantly, foster care appears to have been remarkably effective in ameliorating much of this language delay. For example, among the infants placed in foster care before 26 months, catch-up growth in language amounted to approximately 3 raw score units per month; for those placed after 26 months, the rate of change was about 1 raw score unit per month. Needless to say, the language of both IG and NIG children remained relatively flat during follow-up visits. Finally, in terms of cognitive development, we found that at baseline the average developmental quotient of our IG infants was about 65, whereas among our NIG the value was about 103. Follow-up data have not yet been examined (for elaboration, see Smyke et al., 2004).

Let me now turn to a discussion of the effects of early deprivation on social-emotional development. Although we have just begun to skim the surface of our data, suffice it to say, preliminary inspection of the baseline attachment data (here, we employed the Strange Situation Procedure) reveals profound attachment difficulties among our IG infants. For example, whereas 100% of our NIG infants fall into the A, B, C, and D classification categories, only approximately 5% of our IG infants do so. Within the IG group, roughly 10% of the infants are classified as nonattached, and almost 30% show attachment behavior with severe abnormalities.

Interestingly, among our NIG infants, nearly 75% are classified as "B" babies, or as securely attached (for elaboration, see Zeanah et al., 2004). Thus far, we have not examined our follow-up data.

Aside from attachment, we have also examined in our baseline data the frequency of behavior problems, based on caregiver report. Here, we observe a substantial difference in mastery behavior, such that the IG is scoring lower on most measures of competence than the FCG or NIG.

A critical dimension of social-emotional functioning concerns the ability to decode and recognize facial expressions of emotion. Specifically, based on the hypothesis that infants reared in institutional settings receive impoverished exposure to social-communicative facial signals, we predicted that IG infants would show deficits in discriminating facial expressions of emotion. Surprisingly, our preliminary look at the baseline findings reveals that our IG and NIG infants are performing comparably on our emotion discrimination task, when evaluated behaviorally or electrophysiologically. Thus, based on preferential-looking measures, certain expression pairings are easily discriminated (e.g., happy vs. fearful, sad vs. fearful), whereas others are not (e.g., neutral vs. fearful; for elaboration, see Nelson, Parker, Guthrie, & the BEIP Core Group, in press). Consistent with our behavioral study of emotion recognition, our IG and NIG infants did not differ from one another when it came to electrophysiological evidence of discriminating facial expressions of emotion (Parker, Nelson, & the BEIP Core Group, 2005).

Collectively, attachment behavior and behavior problems generally appear greatly affected by early institutionalization, whereas the ability to discriminate facial expressions of emotion seems largely spared.

CONCLUSION

When surveyed as a whole, it is clear that experience can exert powerful effects on multiple domains of brain–behavioral development. With that broad statement in mind, it is important to consider the following when modeling experience-based effects.

First, we need to be very precise in defining the specific experience to which a child is exposed. To a neuroscientist, the success of modeling experience-based brain effects depends to a great degree on the precision with which the behavior in question is defined and described. Once such specificity is attained, it becomes possible to peer inside the brain to examine where and how this experience exerts its effects. This will prove absolutely crucial as interest in examining the effects of culture on brain increases. It is not enough to say, for example, that a child's "language environment" or "cultural milieu" affect a child's brain development – rather, it is imperative to talk in precise terms about specific language or cultural experiences.

Second, we must be precise in demarcating the timing and duration of the experience. Given how rapidly both brain and behavioral development unfold over the first two decades of life, we need to know *when* and *for how long* a brain is exposed to a specific experience. For example, it is entirely possible that a very positive or a very negative experience may exert little effect on the brain if it is of very short duration (although see points 3 and 4 next). Conversely, an experience of very short duration might derail development if it occurs at the wrong time (such an example was provided earlier in this chapter when discussing the effects of early visual deprivation on face recognition).

Third, we must consider the domain of brain function when modeling experience-based brain effects. As discussed earlier in this chapter, visual experience is likely to have an effect on brain development for a relatively brief period of time (e.g., the first few years of life), whereas cognitive experience could affect brain function through the entire lifespan. Collectively, we must be careful in specifying the precise experience to which a child was exposed, the duration of exposure, and the domain of that exposure (which partially overlaps with the nature of the experience).

Finally, we must have a clear understanding of developmental status of brain when exposed to specific experiences. Thus, after specifying the experience, the timing of the experience, and the domain of brain function, we need to consider where the brain is in its development when these three factors interact.

It is important at this juncture to address whether the principles for modeling experiential effects on brain apply equally to cultural effects on brain. As very much a nonexpert when it comes to biocultural co-constructivism, this is not an easy question to address. As alluded to earlier, one perspective is that culture represents nothing more than the collection of experiences. To examine the effects of culture on brain, then, one need "only" deconstruct culture into its constituent parts. Examples might include differences in language, differences in child rearing practices, differences in intellectual stimulation, and so on. An alternative perspective, however, is that culture is far more than the sum of its parts, which strikes me as far more likely. Thus, one cannot simply deconstruct culture into discrete experiences because the reassembly of such experiences would likely not add up to the original model. If this is the case, modeling cultural effects on brain function and brain development will prove much more difficult than modeling experiential effects on brain function and brain development. One approach to this challenge may be to identify differences in some core function across cultures, much as one attempts to identify core deficits in neurodevelopmental disorders (e.g., autism). Having established such cores, one can sort subjects into appropriate groupings, and then identify the key ways in which participants differ from one another (e.g., the use of social praise to reinforce children's behavior, the sensitivity with which one responds to children's needs). Next, one can design tasks sensitive to detecting such differences, while examining brain function.

Of course, a critical issue with this approach is the ability to identify the core "functions" of individual cultures; undoubtedly, as is the case with gender differences, many more similarities will be observed than differences. Still, assuming consistent differences are observed, then one can treat those differences as one would treat discrete experiences. Thus, for example, at what age are children first exposed to these differences, what happens when one is deprived of such exposure, and what neural circuits are likely involved in incorporating these "experiences?"

This view is undoubtedly naïve. What will only make matters worse is the inability to develop animal models of cultural differences. Nevertheless, it is surely true that culture affects brain in ways that must bear at least some similarity to the way experience affects brain. Modeling cultural effects, however, is surely going to be more challenging than modeling experiential effects, and that is challenging enough when it comes to cognitive and social-emotional behaviors.

What about the reciprocal effects of changes in brain on culture? Again, they are unknown, but undoubtedly this would be the mechanism of cultural transmission. Thus, once the brain has been altered by some cultural experience, the possessor of that brain would interact differently with his or her environment, which would perpetuate and/or reinforce the existing cultural milieu.

The speculation of cultural effects on brain, and conversely, the effects of brain on culture, are offered with a great degree of circumspection, recognizing both my lack of knowledge and that of the field of neurodevelopment. Where I hope I have succeeded, however, is in laying down the groundwork for future queries in this domain by describing in more general terms experiential effects on brain and behavioral development.

ACKNOWLEDGMENTS

This chapter was made possible by grants from the National Institutes of Health (2R01NS329976) and from the John D. and Catherine T. MacArthur Foundation (through their support of a research network on Early Experience and Brain Development). The author wants to thank Lisa Benz for editorial assistance.

**References**

Barnett, W. S. (1996). Long-term effects of early childhood programs on cognitive and school outcomes. *Future Children, 5,* 25–50.
Black, J. E., Jones, T. A., Nelson, C. A., & Greenough, W. T. (1998). Neuronal plasticity and the developing brain. In N. E. Alessi, J. T. Coyle, S. I. Harrison, & S. Eth (Eds.), *Handbook of child and adolescent psychiatry: Vol. 6. Basic psychiatric science and treatment* (pp. 31–53). New York: Wiley.

Camras, L. A., Grow, J. G., & Ribordy, S. C. (1983). Recognition of emotional expression by abused children. *Journal of Clinical Child Psychology, 12* (3), 325–328.

Camras, L. A., Ribordy, S., Hill, J., Martino, S., Spacarelli, S., & Stefani, R. (1988). Recognition and posing of emotional expressions by abused children and their mothers. *Developmental Psychology, 24* (6), 776–781.

Chance, J. E., Turner, A. L., & Goldstein, A. G. (1982). Development of differential recognition for own- and other-race faces. *Journal of Psychology, 112,* 29–37.

Curtis, J. W., & Nelson, C. A. (2003). Toward building a better brain: Neurobehavioral outcomes, mechanisms, and processes of environmental enrichment. In S. Luthar (Ed.), *Resilience and vulnerability: Adaptation in the context of childhood adversities* (pp. 463–488). London: Cambridge University Press.

de Haan, M., & Johnson, M. H. (2003). *The cognitive neuroscience of development.* London: Psychology Press.

Dehaene, S., Dupoux, E., Mehler, J., Cohen, L., Paulesu, E., Perani, D., et al. (1997). Anatomical variability in the cortical representation of first and second language. *Neuroreport, 8,* 3809–3815.

Fagan, J. F. (1972). Infants' recognition memory for faces. *Journal of Experimental Child Psychology, 14* (3), 453–476.

Farran, D. C. (2000). Another decade of intervention for children who are low income or disabled: What do we know now? In J. P. Shonkoff & S. J. Meisels (Eds.), *Handbook of early childhood intervention* (2nd ed., pp. 510–548). Cambridge, UK: Cambridge University Press.

Francis, D. D., Szegda, K., Campbell, G., Martin, W. D., & Insel, T. R. (2003). Epigenetic sources of behavioral differences in mice. *Nature Neuroscience, 6,* 445–448.

Gould, E., & Gross, C. G. (2002). Neurogenesis in adult mammals: Some progress and problems. *Journal of Neuroscience, 22,* 619–623.

Greenough, W. T., Black, J. E., & Wallace, C. S. (1987). Experience and brain development. *Child Development, 58* (3), 539–559.

Gunnar, M. R. (2001). Effects of early deprivation: Findings from orphanage-reared infants and children. In C. A. Nelson & M. Luciana (Eds.), *Handbook of developmental cognitive neuroscience* (pp. 617–629). Cambridge, MA: MIT Press.

Hebb, D. O. (1949). *The organization of behavior: A neuropsychological theory.* New York: Wiley.

Hebb, D. O., & Williams, K. (1946). A method of rating animal intelligence. *Journal of General Psychology, 34,* 59–65.

Johnson, J. S., & Newport, E. L. (1989). Critical period effects in second language learning on the production of English consonants. *Cognitive Psychology, 21,* 60–99.

Johnson, M. H. (1998). The neural basis of cognitive development. In W. Damon (Series Ed.), D. Kuhn & R. S. Siegler (Vol. Eds.), *Handbook of child psychology: Vol. 2. Cognition, perception, and language* (5th ed., pp. 1–49). New York: Wiley.

Kuhl, P. K., Tsao, F. M., & Liu, H. M. (2003). Foreign-language experience in infancy: Effects of short-term exposure and social interaction on phonetic learning. *Proceedings of the National Academy of Sciences (USA), 100,* 9096–9101.

Lazar, I., Darlington, R., Murray, H., Royce, J., & Snipper, A. (1982). Lasting effects of early education: A report from the Consortium for Longitudinal Studies. *Monographs of the Society for Research in Child Development, 47* (2/3, Serial No. 195).

Levitt, P. (2003). Structural and functional maturation of the developing primate brain. *Journal of Pediatrics, 143* (Suppl. 4), S35–S45.

Maurer, D., Lewis, T. L., Brent, H. P., & Levin, A. V. (1999). Rapid improvement in the acuity of infants after visual input. *Science, 286*, 108–110.

Monk, C. S., Webb, S. J., & Nelson, C. A. (2001). Prenatal neurobiological development: Molecular mechanisms and anatomical change. *Developmental Neuropsychology, 19*, 211–236.

Nelson, C. A. (2000). Neural plasticity and human development: The role of early experience in sculpting memory systems. *Developmental Science, 3*, 115–130.

Nelson, C. A. (2001). The development and neural bases of face recognition. *Infant and Child Development, 10*, 3–18.

Nelson, C. A. (2002). Neural development and life-long plasticity. In R. M. Lerner, F. Jacobs, & D. Wetlieb (Eds.), *Promoting positive child, adolescent, and family development: Handbook of program and policy interventions* (pp. 31–60). Thousand Oaks, CA: Sage.

Nelson, C. A. (2003a). *Gray matters: A neuroconstructivist account of cognitive development.* Master lecture delivered at the Society for Research in Child Development, Tampa, FL.

Nelson, C. A. (2003b). The development of face recognition reflects an experience-expectant and activity-dependent process. In O. Pascalis & A. Slater (Eds.), *The development of face processing in infancy and early childhood: Current perspectives* (pp. 79–97). Hauppauge, NY: Nova Science Publishers.

Nelson, C. A., & Bloom, F. E. (1997). Child development and neuroscience. *Child Development, 68*, 970–987.

Nelson, C. A., & Luciana, M. (Eds.). (2001). *Handbook of developmental cognitive neuroscience.* Cambridge, MA: MIT Press.

Nelson, C. A., Parker, S. W., Guthrie, D., & the BEIP Core Group (in press). The discrimination of facial expressions by typically developing infants and infants experiencing early institutional care. *Infant Behavior and Development.*

Nelson, C. A., Thomas, K. M., & de Haan, M. (2006). Neural bases of cognitive development. In W. Damon (Series Ed.), R. M. Lerner, D. Kuhn, & R. S. Siegler (Vol. Eds.), *Handbook of child psychology: Vol. 2. Cognition, perception, and language* (6th ed.). New York: Wiley.

O'Toole, A. J., Deffenbacher, K. A., Valentin, D., & Abdi, H. (1994). Structural aspects of face recognition and the other-race effect. *Memory and Cognition, 22* (2), 208–224.

Parker, S. W., Nelson, C. A., & the BEIP Core Group (2005). The impact of early institutional rearing on the ability to discriminate facial expressions of emotion: An event-related potential study. *Child Development, 76*, 54–72.

Pascalis, O., & Bachevalier, J. (1999). Neonatal aspiration lesions of the hippocampal formation impair visual recognition memory when assessed by paired-comparison task but not by delayed nonmatching-to-sample task. *Hippocampus, 9* (6), 609–616.

Pascalis, O., de Haan, M., & Nelson, C. A. (2002). Is face processing species-specific during the first year of life? *Science, 296*, 1321–1323.

Perani, D., Paulesu, E., Galles, N. S., Dupoux, E., Dehaene, S., Bettinardi, V., et al. (1998). The bilingual brain: Proficiency and age of acquisition of the second language. *Brain, 121*, 1841–1852.

Petitto, L. A., Zatorre, R. J., Gauna, K., Nikeiski, E. J., Dostie, D., & Evans, A. C. (2000). Speech-like cerebral activity in profoundly deaf people processing signed languages: Implications for the neural basis of human language. *Proceedings of the National Academy of Sciences (USA)*, 97 (25), 13961–13966.

Pollak, S. D., & Kistler, D. J. (2002). Early experience is associated with the development of categorical representations for facial expressions of emotion. *Proceedings of the National Academy of Sciences (USA)*, 99 (13), 9072–9076.

Ramey, C. T., & Ramey, S. L. (1998). Early intervention and early experience. *American Psychologist*, 53 (2), 109–120.

Scott, L., & Nelson, C. A. (2004). The developmental neurobiology of face processing. In B. J. Casey (Ed.), *Developmental psychobiology* (Review of Psychiatry Series, Vol. 23, pp. 29–68). Arlington, VA: American Psychiatric Publishing.

Smyke, A. T., Koga, S. F. M., Johnson, D. E., Zeanah, C. H., & the BEIP Core Group. (2004). *The caregiving context in institution reared and family reared infants and toddlers in Romania. Child Development*, 76, 1015–1028.

Webb, S. J., Monk, C. S., & Nelson, C. A. (2001). Mechanisms of postnatal neurobiological development in the prefrontal cortex and the hippocampal region: Implications for human development. *Developmental Neuropsychology*, 19, 147–171.

Werker, J. F., & Vouloumanos, A. (2001). Speech and language processing in infancy: A neurocognitive approach. In C. A. Nelson & M. Luciana (Eds.), *Handbook of developmental cognitive neuroscience* (pp. 269–280). Cambridge, MA: MIT Press.

White, T., & Nelson, C. A. (2005). Neurobiological development during childhood and adolescence. In R. Findling & S. C. Schulz (Eds.), *Juvenile-onset schizophrenia: Assessment, neurobiology, and treatment* (pp. 59–83). Baltimore: The Johns Hopkins University Press.

Zeanah, C. H., Nelson, C. A., Fox, N. A., Smyke, A. T., Marshall, P., Parker, S. W., & Koga, S. (2003). The effects of institutionalization on brain and behavioral development: The Bucharest Early Intervention Project. *Development and Psychopathology*, 15, 885–907.

Zeanah, C. H., Smyke, A. T., Koga, S., Carlson, E., & the BEIP Core Group. (2005). *Attachment in institutionalized and community children in Romania. Child Development*, 76, 1015–1028.

Zigler, E., & Valentine, J. (Eds.). (1979). *Project Head Start: A legacy of the war on poverty.* New York: Free Press.

# 4

# Adult Neurogenesis

## Gerd Kempermann

ABSTRACT

*Contrary to widely held belief, a small number of new neurons are generated in the adult brain and even in the aging brain. Although this adult neurogenesis is minute compared with the vast number of neurons in our brains, and although adult neurogenesis does not lead to substantial regeneration in cases of neuronal loss, the new neurons may serve an important function in learning and memory processes. Adult neurogenesis is neuronal development in nucleo and is controlled by genetic and environmental factors. It exemplifies that, throughout life, brain development is activity and experience dependent, and, more important, that it never ends.*

INTRODUCTION

"Adult neurogenesis" is the generation of new nerve cells in the adult brain (Fig. 4.1), a process that was long believed to be impossible, although it occurs in both nonhuman primates (Gould et al., 1999) and humans (Eriksson et al., 1998). Today, adult neurogenesis has become a prime topic in biomedical research because of its implications for the treatment of neurodegenerative disorders and essentially all diseases that involve a loss of nerve cells (neurons). Because it is the stem cells residing in the adult brain from which new neurons originate in adult neurogenesis, many researchers believe that we might learn from adult neurogenesis how to "grow" stem cells into new neurons for transplantation – in cases of Parkinson's disease, for example (Bjorklund & Lindvall, 2000). Despite promising first clinical experiences with neural transplantation, this may remain a utopian idea for a long time, but some more general aspects of research on adult neurogenesis are even more intriguing and closer to present-day real life.

We normally tend to limit our understanding of "development" to the intrauterine building of our body and mind, and its growth and shaping

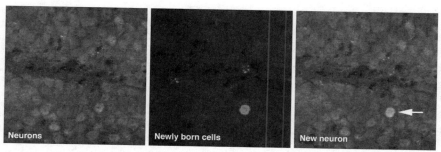

FIGURE 4.1. Adult neurogenesis. In the left image, nerve cells (neurons) are visualized with an immunological method. The middle panel shows the same area of a brain section in which another staining technique identifies newly generated cells. The cells have incorporated a specific marker at the time when they underwent division many weeks earlier. In the third panel, the two other panels are merged. Thereby, it becomes obvious that the cell with the arrow is a new neuron: evidence of neurogenesis.

after birth. Most people would probably intuitively say that their "development" ended after puberty. Pessimists and misanthropes might add that after the age of 25 it was all decay. Although aging might in fact mean losses, this overly negative view has never been truly fitting. With the discovery of adult neurogenesis, it was found that the brain, which was believed to be "hard-wired" by the time of puberty, undergoes continuous and incessant changes, even at the level of the neurons. Development never ends. In the case of other organs such as skin, blood, and intestines, this was long known and did not have too much influence on our image of ourselves. However, the brain is the seat of our cognitive powers: "Mind is what the brain does," as a famous but rather superficial saying goes. We need our brains for everything that makes us human. The death of the brain has consequently become a justifiable definition of a person's end. Persistent development in the brain therefore has the potential to challenge many concepts of how the brain "does" the mind.

## NEW NEURONS IN THE ADULT BRAIN

Adult neurogenesis is nothing special for a lizard. When the lizard's tail is lost to the grip of a predator or curious boy, it can regrow, including that part of the central nervous system running through it, the lower spinal cord. In mammals, adult neurogenesis was long believed to be impossible. Only in the 1960s did Joseph Altman publish the first reports on adult neurogenesis in rodents (Altman, 1969; Altman & Das, 1965). He identified single new cells as neurons in the hippocampus and later in the olfactory system. These are in fact the only two neurogenic regions of the adult mammalian brain. At that time, however, the findings were taken largely as a curiosity or as an atavism special to rodents and other "lower" mammals. Further research was not conducted by other scientists until the late 1970s, when more information was reported by two research groups. Michael Kaplan confirmed and extended Altman's data by using electronmicroscopy to prove that the new cells were indeed neurons (Kaplan & Hinds, 1977); also, in the early 1980s, Maxwell Cowan and colleagues showed that new neurons are added to the hippocampus and do not replace older cells (Crespo, Stanfield, & Cowan, 1986). A hallmark study by Stanfield and Trice (1988) finally demonstrated that the new hippocampal neurons send out their processes appropriately to hippocampal subregion CA3 and thus presumably make proper functional connections. The stage was clearly set, but for the scientific mainstream the whole phenomenon apparently still seemed suspect. Then, Fernando Nottebohm from Rockefeller University dazzled the scientific world with his report that in canary birds, neurogenesis in the brain centers responsible for song learning is correlated to the time of the year when the birds have to learn their songs (Goldman & Nottebohm, 1983). In contrast to other songbird species, canaries have to learn new songs every year. This research showed adult neurogenesis in an entirely new light. Although evolutionarily humans are not as closely related to birds as they are to rodents, songbirds share one highly unusual feature with humans – vocal learning – which might be why this finding captured the imagination. Most species have an inborn vocal repertoire; that is, no dog has to learn how to bark. But humans, songbirds, and dolphins have to learn their vocalizations.

In 1994, Nottebohm and colleagues also showed that neurogenesis in the hippocampus of chickadees, a food-caching bird species that has to remember the location of food storage sites to survive the long winters, was correlated to the seasons in which the animals had to learn the new storage locations (Barnea & Nottebohm, 1994).

Surprisingly, these suggestive findings did not immediately lead to the search for learning-dependent adult neurogenesis in the hippocampus of rodents. However, Elizabeth Gould, Heather Cameron, and Bruce McEwen, also from Rockefeller University, began to wonder whether diminished adult hippocampal neurogenesis might be somehow involved in the hippocampal damage that is seen under prolonged stress and chronically elevated blood levels of cortisol (Cameron & Gould, 1994; Cameron, Woolley, McEwen, & Gould, 1993). Their rediscovery of adult hippocampal neurogenesis of rodents in the context of stress research, complemented by a clear demonstration that neurogenesis can be downregulated, finally evoked the broad interest that adult neurogenesis attracts today. Another important reason for the rising interest in adult neurogenesis was that Brent Reynolds and Sam Weiss (1992) from Calgary reported that the adult mammalian brain contains neural stem cells.

## STEM CELLS AND PRECURSOR CELLS IN THE ADULT BRAIN

One of the reasons adult neurogenesis had been considered to be impossible for so long is that neurons cannot divide, and in fact, this knowledge still holds true. Neurons are postmitotic cells, that is, they are terminally "after division" (mitosis) and cannot successfully reenter the cell cycle. Many other cell types remain proliferative throughout life. In particular, the cells specialized for cellular reconstitution are highly proliferative. These cells are called stem cells. Stem cells of the skin produce new epithelial cells to replace the losses on the outermost layer of skin cells, where our body's interface with the abrasive outside world requires continuous repair. Stem cells of the bone marrow replace our short-lived blood cells, as do intestinal stem cells for the mucosal lining of our guts. The brain was considered to be hard-wired after puberty and not to contain stem cells. The circular logic even went so far as to suggest that there was no need for stem cells in the adult brain because, on principle, neurons could not be replaced like gut, blood, and skin cells due to their complex and delicate integration into the fixed neuronal networks of the brain. Although the latter thought has some truth to it and might, in fact, explain why the brain cannot make too much use of the regenerative potential of its stem cells, the conclusion that this would causally explain the absence of stem cells and any adult neurogenesis in the brain was clearly overdrawn.

Stem cells are cells that embody the openness of the genome. All body cells (except the red blood cells that do not have a nucleus) carry identical genomic information. Cells differ not in their genome but in what part of their genome they transcribe into proteins. Stem cells can make wider use of their genomic information than other cells and can develop into many different cell types. This ability is called multipotency. It is an interaction with their environment that determines how their potential is realized. The fertilized egg as the ultimate stem cell has the potential to generate an entire organism. Through development, the width of this potency becomes increasingly limited. Embryonic stem cells are called pluripotent; they can make all tissue types of the body, but no complete organism. The stem cells that are found in the adult brain and other organs are called multipotent: they generate only the cell type of that one organ (Fig. 4.2).

As a second characteristic, stem cells are programmed to self-renew, that is, to divide and produce exact copies of themselves (Weissman, Anderson, & Gage, 2001). This makes stem cells "eternal." They can persist in an otherwise differentiated organism and provide the potential for regeneration. To do so, stem cells spin off cells that start differentiation into specific cell types. In adult neurogenesis, multipotent neural stem cells that exist in the brain lifelong give rise to neurons and the other main type of brain cells, glia cells (Gage, 2000).

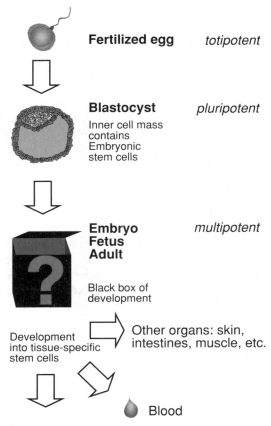

Fertilized egg    *totipotent*

**Blastocyst**    *pluripotent*
Inner cell mass
contains
Embryonic
stem cells

**Embryo**    *multipotent*
**Fetus**
**Adult**

Black box of
development

Development          Other organs: skin,
into tissue-specific  intestines, muscle, etc.
stem cells

Blood

Brain

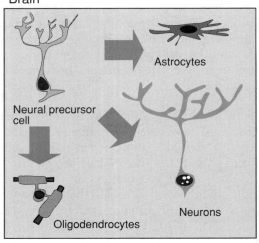

Astrocytes

Neural precursor
cell

Oligodendrocytes                Neurons

We have thus far used the term "stem cell" because of its wide acceptance, but in many situations "precursor cell" is actually preferable. Scientifically, "stem cell" is reserved for a group of cells that fulfills a strict definition of "unlimited self-renewal plus multipotency." Precursor cell, in contrast, is another term encompassing stem cells, but with less narrow defining criteria. It is thus often used as a generic label, when no conclusions about the exact nature of the cells in question are justifiable, even if the cells obviously show a certain degree of "stemness," that is, some self-renewal and a developmental potential.

Adult neurogenesis is limited to the two neurogenic regions, the hippocampus and the olfactory system, and does not normally occur in the rest of the brain. Surprisingly, however, the main prerequisite for adult neurogenesis, the existence of neuronal stem cells from which the new neurons could develop, is not restricted to these privileged regions. Apparently, stem cells can be found almost everywhere in the brain (Palmer, Markakis, Willhoite, Safar, & Gage, 1999). Thus, it seems that the brain possesses but does not use its potential to make new neurons, except in a few distinct circumstances. There are, in fact, reports about a limited regenerative neurogenesis in otherwise nonneurogenic regions (Arvidsson, Collin, Kirik, Kokaia, & Lindvall, 2002; Magavi, Leavitt, & Macklis, 2000). An interaction between the stem cells and their local microenvironment has to occur to allow adult neurogenesis. If one were to understand this interaction, this might indeed provide a novel therapeutic strategy by tapping endogenous resources for regeneration in neurodegenerative disorders.

The discovery of stem cells in the brain leads to a reconsideration of these prevailing assumptions. If both stem cells and adult neurogenesis can be found in the adult brain, we might also have to reevaluate our thoughts about the statics of brain structure in general. Other scientific

---

FIGURE 4.2. Stem cells. Stem cells are those cells with the greatest potential. The ultimate stem cell is the fertilized egg. It is totipotent because an entire living organism can originate from it. Over the course of development, the potential of the stem cells that are found in the organism becomes increasingly more restricted. In embryonic stem cells, found in the inner cell mass of the blastocyst stage, we find pluripotency: all cell types of an organism, but not the complete organism itself, can develop from these cells. Later in development, one finds tissue-specific stem cells. They are specialized to provide the regenerative potential in many body tissues such as skin, blood, intestines, and others. Only since 1992 do we know that the adult brain also contains stem cells that can produce new neurons. Neurogenesis originating from these neural stem cells, however, occurs only in two privileged "neurogenic" regions. Neural stem cells produce the three major cell classes of the brain: the neurons and two types of so-called glia cells – astrocytes, which provide the optimal environment for neurons, and oligodendrocytes, which insulate the nerve fibers.

insights into how "plastic" the brain is have long led to similar conclusions (e.g., Cotman, 1985; Greenough & Black, 1992). Stem cells and adult neurogenesis have brought a new aspect into research on brain plasticity. We return to this thought later.

## NEURONAL DEVELOPMENT IN THE ADULT BRAIN

Adult neurogenesis is nothing other than neuronal development under the conditions of the adult brain. Generally, these conditions are unfriendly, if not outright hostile, to neurogenesis. Adult neurogenesis is consequently exquisitely rare in the adult brain. It normally occurs only in the two regions mentioned, and even there it shows a steep, age-dependent decline. Given that we have billions of nerve cells, the hundreds of thousands of new neurons that adult neurogenesis adds to the hippocampus and the olfactory system are only good for a minute change. In rodents, hippocampal neurogenesis also pales against the comparatively high number of new neurons in the olfactory bulb. In humans, it might be the other way around (Sanai et al., 2004). This could have species-dependent causes. Rodents, like dogs, heavily rely on their olfactory sense to get their picture of the world. Adult hippocampal neurogenesis has also been shown for humans (Eriksson et al., 1998), and we rely on our hippocampus for learning and memory processes as much as rodents do, if not more. We do not, however, require our olfactory sense as much as mice, rats, and dogs. This might explain why adult olfactory neurogenesis does not persist in the human brain as late into adulthood and senescence as adult hippocampal neurogenesis does.

It seems that there is something particular about these two privileged regions that makes neurogenesis useful, even if it does not add bulk neurons and seems to fail miserably in successfully compensating pathological neuron losses. The functional contribution of the new neurons might, however, be qualitative rather than quantitative. Adult hippocampal neurogenesis occurs at only one particular spot within the hippocampal circuitry, in a structure called the dentate gyrus. This is the first of three relay stations and processing units within the hippocampus (Fig. 4.3). Information that is supposed to be learned has to pass through these three stations. The hippocampal entry structure, of which the dentate gyrus is part, is a relative bottleneck in the neuronal network of the hippocampal formation. Consequently, a small number of new neurons can make a big difference here. A few thousand new neurons in the cortex with its billions of cells would seem lost; added to a structure that in a rodent only has 300,000 neurons in the first place, they provide for a substantial structural change.

The brain goes through a considerable amount of trouble to maintain the potential of adult neurogenesis in the hippocampus – although this way of phrasing a simple observation makes it very questionable from

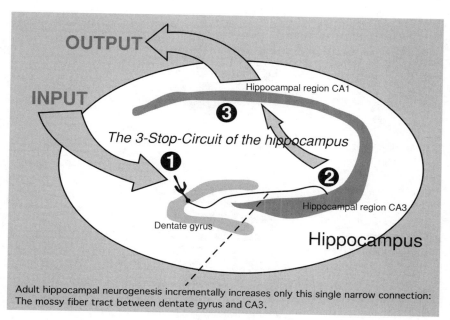

FIGURE 4.3. The hippocampus. Adult neurogenesis is found in the hippocampus, a brain structure centrally involved in learning and memory. Essentially, the hippocampus has a very simple structure with three relay stations. New neurons add new connections only between the first and the second station. The hypothesis is that adult neurogenesis allows optimization of the network of the hippocampus to make it more efficient in coping with the levels of complexity and novelty that are frequently encountered by an individual. Because the hippocampus is involved in the transition of contents into long-term storage and is thus called the "gateway to memory," we have called our hypothesis the theory of "new gatekeepers at the gateway to memory."

the perspective of evolutionary theory, which abhors teleological thinking. Nevertheless, permitting adult neurogenesis requires a machinery that is otherwise characteristic of embryonic development and does not have a general purpose in the adult brain. Precursor cells taken from the neurogenic region of the adult hippocampus and placed into the nonneurogenic cortex do not become neurons, although they might survive and although they would turn into new neurons if they were placed into the other neurogenic region of the brain, the olfactory bulb. This shows that neurogenesis is not so much an intrinsic property of precursor cells, but is very much dependent on a permissive environment. Development is a constant interaction of the precursor cells and their progeny with their environment. The cells unfold their potential only if the environment permits or actively induces it.

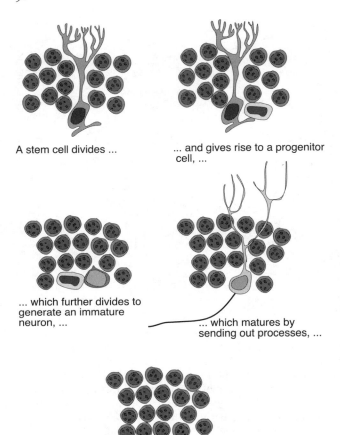

A stem cell divides ...

... and gives rise to a progenitor cell, ...

... which further divides to generate an immature neuron, ...

... which matures by sending out processes, ...

... and finally becomes indistinguishable from the surrounding other neurons.

FIGURE 4.4. Schematic rendering of adult neurogenesis in the hippocampus. Neuronal development is a process, not an event. It proceeds through many identifiable stages, all of which can be regulated in an interaction between genes and environment. Note, that all neurons, not just the new ones, have processes. They are only omitted to make the drawing clearer.

Neuronal development begins with the division of a stem cell (Fig. 4.4). The stem cell gives rise to progenitor cells, which are a second class of cells besides the stem cells under the umbrella of "precursor cells." Progenitor cells show reduced self-renewal and a restricted developmental potential, sometimes to only one cell type, but they can proliferate massively. They dramatically expand the number of cells that later can become new neurons. Stem cells only divide rarely and replenish the pool of progenitor cells. The progenitor cells are also migratory cells; they move away from the site of their initial division. While on the move, the cells continue to divide. After two or three divisions, the progenitor cells may exit from the cell cycle and begin to express neuronal markers (i.e., proteins that are characteristic of neurons). This early phase of neuronal differentiation is also characterized by massive cell death. Only selected cells survive. It is not clear how this selection works, but it seems that all immature neurons first seek functional contacts. Only those that make useful connections are recruited for further development into mature neurons. This would be a process similar to that in embryonic development. The genome does not carry enough information – by orders of magnitude – to predetermine all contacts of all neurons; only the general architecture is determined. The rest of the process is "Darwinian." A random connectivity is built up by many more neurons than ultimately necessary, followed by a selection of those connections that "make sense" and are used, while the other cells are eliminated again. Regulation of development therefore not only consists of building new structures, but also of destroying them. Birth and death are subtly balanced.

The essence of neuronal function is communication. Neurons send out two types of cell processes, the neurites. One type of neurite is called the dendrite; antenna-like, it picks up signals from other neurons. Neurons also usually have one outgoing neurite, the axon, which projects to other neurons and provides the output. The contact points between neurons are called synapses. After leaving the cell cycle and becoming postmitotic, new neurons have to establish contacts by extending their axon and dendrites and forming synapses. This step requires intricate regulation and is a race against the opposing force of cell death, which eliminates all cells that did not make successful connections. In those cells that are selected and do survive, more signs of neuronal maturation appear over the following weeks. The tree of dendrites is continuously reshaped, more synapses form and are eliminated, and the response that the neurons show on electrical stimulation (which can be done directly under experimental conditions) becomes increasingly more indistinguishable from the neighboring older neurons. If the hippocampus is stimulated by an appropriate behavioral stimulus, especially in a learning situation, the new neurons begin to respond like older cells. Once the new neurons are really integrated into the circuit, they will stay lifelong. Adult neurogenesis, at least in the hippocampus, is cumulative. There is no neuronal turnover as the new cells are added to the dentate gyrus; they do not replace older cells (Crespo et al., 1986). Cell death and elimination occur before the neurons reach maturity and normally not afterward.

Adult neurogenesis provides ample opportunities for regulation on the level of stem and progenitor cells, on the level of migration and survival, on the level of neurite elongation and synapse formation, and on the level of differentiation and maturation (Kempermann, Kuhn, & Gage, 1997a). A genetic program determines the sequence of these events, but external influences make this process unfold. Adult neurogenesis is an in-a-nutshell example of how genes and environment interact in the formation of biological complexity. Nowhere else is development as clearly contrasted to a nondeveloping cellular background as in adult neurogenesis. Besides being a fascinating research topic of its own, adult hippocampal neurogenesis can also serve as a wonderful model of how genes and environment build and shape the brain.

## NATURE AND NURTURE: GENES AND ENVIRONMENT

Literary figures such as Rudyard Kipling's Mowgli, and real fates such as Kaspar Hauser and the wild boy of Aveyron in France, who was brought up by wolves like Romulus and Remus, are profoundly fascinating because they embody the fundamental question of how we become what we are. If mind is what the brain does, then the "becoming" of our brain is at the core of biocultural co-constructivism. Adult neurogenesis has been given a chapter within this book because it shows that the brain- and mind-forming forces of nature and nurture remain active throughout life.

If we say that we are something "by birth," this is a simplification. Interaction of a growing child with the outside world begins within the mother's womb and never stops until life ends. From a biological point of view, the nature–nurture question can be phrased as the relative contribution of genes and environment to the realization of human life. Both genes and environment act from the very first moment of fertilization. Every other cell in the body will be derived from the fertilized egg. However, this will occur only if very particular environmental conditions are met. Not all fertilizations lead to successful pregnancies. New neurons from neural stem cells in the adult brain similarly require their appropriate niche. On a fundamental level, the same rules apply: a potential has to be realized.

As this book readily demonstrates, the dichotomy of nature and nurture is a severe simplification anyway. In the ideologically strong-opinioned 1960s and 1970s, the theory was even often referred to as the nature *versus* nurture theory; at that time an interaction between nature and nurture was not even part of the equation. Today, we know that the interaction is almost everything. Development is inseparably nature *and* nurture at every single moment of our lives. As much as this applies to the development of the entire organism, it is mirrored in smaller-scale developments within the body. Adult neurogenesis is a particularly intriguing example of such development because it occurs in a cellular environment that is otherwise relatively stable and even opposed to change.

A classical construct in the theoretical neurosciences is the stability-plasticity dilemma. The ability to adjust a neuronal network to new situations has to be balanced with the stability of the network. There would be no gain in being able to learn new things efficiently and quickly if an ever-changing structure of the brain, as the price for this ability, would consequently not allow the learned information to be stored permanently. In fact, it was long believed that adult neurogenesis was impossible because stability was assumed to have the highest priority for the adult brain. There is, however, much more plasticity in the adult brain than was believed, and adult neurogenesis is the most surprising example of this.

As mentioned, our genome does not carry enough information to realize an organism to its fullest extent. But the genome contains the necessary information to build the parts and to initiate a still rather miraculous process of self-assembly, which can be considered the pivotal biological aspect of life. This developmental process, however, is never independent of environment. Environment, in this sense, is not only the green nature around us and our social and cultural contexts, but also essentially everything outside the genome. This might be an unusual definition, but it explains the difficulties with a strict dichotomy of nature and nurture. Nurture encompasses everything that is influencing the processes of life by acting on the genome, not just the education of the "completed" organism. This range of influence is vast and makes one wonder how people can seriously believe that clones could ever become exact copies of their "parent."

However, there is no doubt that much of what we are is laid out and determined in our genes. But how much? The sequencing of the human genome has been hailed a fundamental breakthrough because we should now be able to "read the book of life." But with less than 30,000, the number of genes turned out to be surprisingly low. Life is parsimonious: it uses only four nucleotides to code for twenty amino acids that make up the 30,000 primary gene products, which then, however, are modified, spliced, shortened, and combined in so many ways that they can generate hundred thousands of proteins. The same gene, although it always codes for the "same" protein because the sequence of its nucleotides does not change, can thereby ultimately exert many different "meanings" in many different contexts. In addition, even one identical protein can do very different things at different places in the body and at different times of development. Chrystallins, for example, the transparent structural proteins that give form to the lens of the eye, lead a double life in other organs as chaperone molecules protecting other proteins against degradation.

Although the genome is identical in every cell in the body, dependent on the course of its development, its position in the body, its functional state, its health, and many other potential factors, only a subset of genes is active. The proteome, the entirety of all proteins of a cell in a given state of activity, is by orders of magnitude harder to decipher than the genome. Other than the genome, it is continuously in flux. The ultimate meaning of a gene is thus context specific in both space and time. How this is accomplished remains one of the great scientific mysteries. The genome carries a potential that has to be realized as dependent on extragenetic factors, subsumed under nurture or environment.

Evidently, this also applies to neural stem cells and adult neurogenesis. In fact, for researchers it provides one of the most direct opportunities to study the unfolding of a developmental potential and the contributions of genes and environment to the many different steps that together are "development."

## BRAIN PLASTICITY

Plasticity is how the brain adapts its structure when we use it, not the wear and tear, but those changes for the better that cause some local or general functional improvements. The relationship between structure and function is thus bidirectional. Although the term "plasticity" has many implications and although plasticity can also fail in that it, for example, might produce aberrant connections in the epileptic brain, the most prominent use of plasticity is in the context of learning. Learning is more than just the plain acquisition of new information and skills; it is a fundamental aspect of life. In some very profound (and not just proverbial) sense, life is continuous learning. We might intuitively find it difficult to apply the word "learning" to all living things, including invertebrates or even bacteria and plants, but quite a bit of the biology of learning and memory relevant to humans was first discovered in the sea snail aplysia and the nematode *Caenorhabditis elegans*. Some of the most fundamental mechanisms of learning are evolutionarily highly conserved.

In the second half of the twentieth century, the concept of structural brain plasticity fundamentally changed our views of the brain. The brain was long considered to be a rather static organ, hard-wired to perform a challenging computing task that would have been fatally sensitive to any changes in the underlying "hardware." It was the time of the so-called "No new neurons!" dogma, ascribed to Santiago Ramón y Cajal, the father of modern neurobiology. He is famously quoted with the sentence "In the brain everything can die, nothing regenerate." The phrase appears in many reviews on adult neurogenesis because it captures a misperception that even today is widely encountered.

But even in his lifetime, Ramón y Cajal qualified his pessimistic statement because he had discovered signs of regeneration in the brain. He found that axons and dendrites could recover after injury. In fact, we know today that their exact shape is permanently changing, even under normal function. On the level of entire cells, the brain is much more static than it is on the level of synapses and neurites, but the assumption that there were no exceptions to the "no new neurons" rule turned out to be wrong. Other cell types in the brain had long been found to be highly plastic; however, their relevance to brain function had been underestimated. Glial cells were initially described as "nervenkitt," the substance that fills the gaps between the nerve cells. Neurons, in contrast, were considered the "noble elements of the brain," in the language of Ramón y Cajal. Glial cells, but not the noble neurons, were known to be as proletarian as to renew throughout life.

Even when adult neurogenesis was finally discovered, it soon turned out to be the exception, not the rule. The old, rather pessimistic "no new neurons" views were not so far off after all. The brain does regenerate poorly, and one of the reasons for this is that it cannot replace lost nerve cells. This is why many neurodegenerative disorders are chronic and incurable. Nonetheless, from the research over the last 30 years, the important conclusion is that adult neurogenesis is possible. This is more than an academically interesting proof of principle with few implications outside the ivory tower. It turns a number of widely held concepts upside down about how the brain works and how it can react to the world.

## GENES AND ENVIRONMENT IN THE REGULATION OF ADULT NEUROGENESIS

To study a complex interaction such as that of genes and environment, it is useful to control for one of the variables and study the resulting changes in the other. Laboratory mice are inbred and, as such, are as close to a genetic clone as one can get with conventional breeding. Although even between humans who are not inbred, interindividual genomic differences are less than a promille (every thousandth nucleotide is different), the greater genetic homogeneity in inbred mice provides an important advantage for researchers because it allows genetic influences to be kept constant. Biological research is often hampered by difficulties in adequately measuring a phenotype. If one has only one individual at hand to study, the unknown variance in the measurement dramatically reduces the accuracy of the conclusions that can be drawn from that one measure. In inbred mice, one finds more than one individual with identical genetic make-up. These mice can thus be used to study the effects of environmental changes on adult neurogenesis by keeping the influence of the background genes constant. In addition, one can use different strains of mice to compare the influence of genes when the environment is kept constant.

When these strategies were applied to study adult neurogenesis, it was found that adult neurogenesis differs considerably between strains of mice, despite their close relationship (Kempermann et al., 1997a). This was true not only for the total number of new neurons, but also for quantitative measures of single stages of neuronal development. The number of the dividing cells, grossly representing the number of precursor cells, for example, differed considerably (Kempermann & Gage, 2002). The relationship between cell proliferation and the net number of new neurons was also not linear between strains, and the survival rate also differed. In addition, strains showed different ratios of the numbers of new neurons to new glial cells. Relatively small genetic differences thus influenced adult neurogenesis on many levels of neuronal development. The mouse strains with more neurogenesis did not possess the one "neurogenesis gene" that the other strains did not have. Rather, the many genes involved in adult neurogenesis were the same, but they showed tiny differences that made the gene products unequally effective in their function (so-called polymorphisms).

To make matters even more complicated, these overtly "neurogenic" genes do not have to differ between strains to result in differences in the number of new neurons. It may well be that other genes not directly related to adult neurogenesis nevertheless influence the microenvironment of the cells at the different stages of neuronal development and thus have indirect effects. In other words, the list of genes that are "somehow" involved in adult neurogenesis is quite large and can grow almost indefinitely, depending on what is counted as relevant. An important goal for developmental biologists is to understand the patterns of gene expression that determine a particular step of development and to identify the most relevant genes, that is, those key genes that have the largest and most direct influence.

Because the range and spectrum of external influences is generally much larger in adulthood than in utero, where the immediate outer world is the mother's womb, adult neurogenesis surpasses embryonic brain development in the modulating effects of environment and experience on the already complex genetic program of neuronal development.

The classical experimental model to study environmental effects is the "enriched environment," a paradigm systematically developed by Mark Rosenzweig from the University of California at Berkeley in the late 1950s and early 1960s (Rosenzweig & Bennett, 1996). Conceptually, this pioneering work was preceded by Donald Hebb, who is most famous for formulating the theory of the synaptic basis of learning in 1949 (Hebb, 1949). Two years earlier, Hebb had reported how rodents reared as pets showed better learning and memory than their littermates living in standard laboratory housing (Hebb, 1947).

In Rosenzweig's definition, an enriched environment is the "combination of inanimate and social stimulation" (Rosenzweig & Bennett, 1996). The animals are offered a larger cage, toys with which to play, a larger group for social interaction, and changing items within the cage (e.g., a rearrangeable tunnel system). Compared with mice or rats kept in the rather Spartan standard housing, animals living in enriched environments show numerous differences, many of them related to the brain.

In 1997, my colleagues and I showed that mice living in an enriched environment also have increased adult hippocampal neurogenesis (Kempermann, Kuhn, & Gage, 1997b). The mice living in the enriched

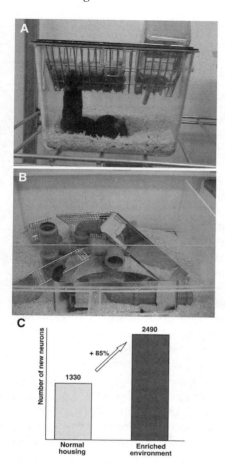

FIGURE 4.5. The experimental paradigm of environmental enrichment. (A) Normal laboratory housing for mice is rather Spartan. (B) In contrast, an enriched environment consists of a larger cage with more animals, toys, and rearrangeable tunnel systems. (C) Living in an enriched environment induces neurogenesis in the adult hippocampus, in this experiment increasing it by a factor of 1.8. This study showed that experience of environmental complexity and novelty can have structural consequences in the adult brain (Kempermann et al., 1997b).

environment had more new neurons than their littermates in standard cages (Fig. 4.5). Because the experiment was done with mice in young adulthood, when baseline levels of adult neurogenesis were still very high, the increase even led to a measurable increase in the total number of neurons in the dentate gyrus. This demonstrated that, in the adult brain and in direct response to stimuli from the outer world, substantial growth of a brain structure highly relevant for cognition can be found.

An interesting detail of this finding was that the proliferation of the putative precursor cells in the dentate gyrus was not changed in these mice. In this sense, the progenitor cells were not reached by the neurogenic stimulus. Precursor cell division was not induced; instead regulation seemed to occur in the survival of the newly generated neurons. More of the progeny of the dividing precursor cells survived in mice living in an enriched environment. This is in accordance with the theory of neuronal development in the adult already mentioned: new neurons are recruited from a much larger pool of immature neurons produced by the dividing precursor cells.

The mouse strain 129 is a mouse strain with very low constitutive levels of adult neurogenesis. When exposed to an enriched environment, however, the induction of adult neurogenesis in the 129 mice was much stronger than in strain C57, a strain with high levels of adult neurogenesis (Kempermann, Brandon, & Gage, 1998). The mechanism by which the similar net result was achieved, however, differed between the two strains. In 129 mice, exposure to an enriched environment also induced precursor cell divisions, in addition to the survival-promoting effect already mentioned. Consequently, the genetic background determines not only the baseline level of adult neurogenesis, but also *how* adult neurogenesis is regulated. The finding confirmed that different stages of neuronal development in the adult are regulated separately, if not independently.

The C57 mice, however, also showed a strong induction of precursor cell proliferation when a running wheel was placed in their cage (Van Praag, Kempermann, & Gage, 1999). Running is a natural behavior for mice, and they make heavy use of this offer. Granted, there is not much else to do in a laboratory cage, but the point is that the mice were not forced to run, rather they just had access to the running wheel. They ran about 5 to 8 km per night (rodents are night-active). This physical stimulus led to a strong increase in both precursor cell proliferation and the resulting production of new neurons. Although this finding might seem surprising, given the fact that running is not a particularly "hippocampal behavior," the result fits well with other observations. Some are quite speculative: for example, ambulating and thinking are closely related for many people (not only in some of the novels by Thomas Bernhard, such as *Walking*, where walking and thinking unite; Bernhard, 1971). The repetitive act of walking seems to prepare a mind-set particularly well-suited for "thinking." Animal studies support this link. Clinical observations, too, speak in favor of the relevance of physical activity for cognition. The effects of physical therapy in rehabilitation go beyond bodily fitness; they also influence mood and cognition. Epidemiological studies suggest that people who are physically active run a somewhat lower risk of neurodegenerative disorders such as Alzheimer's and Parkinson's disease (Wilson et al., 2002). The biology underlying these observations is poorly understood, but our and other researchers' data indicate that precursor cells in the adult brain and adult neurogenesis may play a role in maintaining and rebuilding aspects of cognitive health. Even in nonneurogenic regions, physical activity can induce cell proliferation and genesis, although no new neurons are born (Ehninger & Kempermann, 2003). There are, of course, limits in studying "biocultural co-constructivism" in mice, but limits in humans are even stricter. We know that adult neurogenesis occurs in humans, but for obvious reasons it cannot be studied directly. Sophisticated magnetic resonance tomography (MRT) studies at least allowed first glimpses into cellular plasticity in the adult living human brain. A now famous study by Richard Frackowiak showed that London taxi drivers, a professional group with high demands on their hippocampal function of spatial navigation, had larger hippocampi than matched control subjects (Maguire et al., 2000). Intriguingly, there was even a correlation between the time spent as a taxi driver and the volume of the hippocampus, indicating that it is not simply the case that people with larger hippocampi tend to become taxi drivers. Arne May from Regensburg University also demonstrated that in individuals who had picked up juggling for the first time in their lives, the size of a part of the visual cortex, a region prominently involved in keeping balls in the air, increased (Draganski et al., 2004). Physical fitness, too, has measurable effects on brain morphology (Churchill et al., 2002; Colcombe et al., 2004). These reports do not claim that adult neurogenesis or other consequences of precursor cell activity were underlying their findings, but they clearly support the evolving concepts of structural activity-dependent plasticity in the adult brain.

ADULT NEUROGENESIS AND LEARNING

When adult neurogenesis was first discovered, the fact that it was found in the hippocampus, a brain region that is required for learning, led many people to the idea that the new neurons might serve as some sort of memory sticks. However, very much unlike a computer, the brain is a living processor of information. The brain is not the hardware on which the "mind" software runs. In the brain, form follows function in a very fundamental sense. It would be surprising enough if a computer were to upgrade its processor while running. We know that changes in the hardware are problematic, so we usually buy a new system when the old one has reached its limits, instead of rebuilding the processing unit. In a way, that is what the brain is permanently doing. Whereas the general architecture of the brain remains rather constant and is not obviously altered in response to functional demands, the deeper we delve on the microscopic scale, the more flux we see. Chemically, there is hardly any constancy. Memories are not laid down as proteins and shelved as individual pieces in the depths of the brain's storage areas. Memories are not even stored in individual nerve cells, much less in only new neurons. Instead, information is stored in functional states that neuronal networks can acquire. Memory appears to be the probability for groups of neurons to fire together. The billions of neurons in the brain are connected by an incredibly high number of contacts. An indefinite number of excitation states can be inscribed into such networks. "Remembering" in such a concept means that some of the neurons that are active become stimulated by some cue ("association"). Due to their shared participation in the excitation pattern standing for a particular memory content, the neurons are able to activate the entire pattern. The idea of memories as such patterns would, for example, explain why many memories are so fragile and why some memories can be awakened by some highly unlikely cue. "Wild associations" are common parts of otherwise very unrelated network states.

The hippocampus has an important function in preparing information for storage. It seems to compress the data and attach hidden tags to it that allow the information to be organized in space and time. Intriguingly, it is at this bottleneck position of the hippocampus, where all information that is to be stored must be processed, that we find adult neurogenesis (Fig. 4.3). Strictly speaking, not all information requires hippocampal processing – only "declarative" memory does. For humans, declarative contents are those that can be "declared" or put into words. In contrast, procedural learning, such as riding your bicycle or brushing your teeth, are difficult to put into words but are learned by imitation and doing. Procedural learning is independent of the hippocampus. Declarative memory also exists in animals: spatial memory, for example, can also be measured in rodents and is highly hippocampus dependent.

In Alzheimer patients, for example, the hippocampus is affected early in the illness. Consequently, one of the classical early symptoms is a loss of spatial orientation. The patients are found lost in an environment in which they may have lived for many years. Spatial orientation is one example of putting information into a coordinate system. The hippocampus is also necessary to keep track of the temporal dimension. This form of memory is called "episodic" memory, and it is a prerequisite for consciously experienced history. Although rodents do not have consciousness as humans do, this does not exclude the possibility that they may have something like episodic memory (Day, Langston, & Morris, 2003). Although all mammals have a hippocampus and need it, in essence, for similar functions, the hippocampus is nonetheless a brain structure that is deeply involved in profoundly human cognition. Knowledge about the extent and particular details of adult hippocampal neurogenesis in humans is scant, but the perspective of facing a biological mechanism underlying plasticity of a brain region co-responsible for "what makes us human" rightfully draws the particular interest and fascination of researchers and the public alike.

How can a few new neurons make a meaningful difference? The hippocampus is called "the gateway to memory" because it is involved in preparing information for storage. This is a simplification because the hippocampus probably has many different functions in the context of learning and memory. However, irrespective of its additional possible roles (e.g., in retrieving stored information), one very prominent task of the hippocampus is the "consolidation" of memory, in other words, the preparation of certain types of information for long-term storage. This processing consists of (1) compressing the data (analogous to a .jpeg file of your digital camera images), that is, a so-called orthogonalization or transformation of the data in such a way as not to interfere with other sets of data that are processed before or afterward, and (2) making annotations to the information, that is, orienting them in spatial and temporal coordinates and assigning an emotional value to them. The latter is particularly important: as everybody knows who has studied for an exam, it is much harder to learn things we are bored by than those we deem essential. The phone number of our new date will stick in mind more easily than Euler's number (2.7182818245 . . . ). In matters of life and death, we learn in one shot; one does not have to touch the electric fence twice.

For some reason, it seems that the dentate gyrus – which manages a considerable part of all these functions – should be as small as possible, but, of course, as large as necessary for optimal performance. Adding new neurons to the dentate gyrus allows its size to be increased in response to the actual level of cognitive challenges that are experienced. We have called this idea the "new gatekeepers at the gateway to memory" theory (Kempermann, 2002; Kempermann & Wiskott, 2004). It is consistent with the finding that adult neurogenesis decreases with increasing age without a parallel decrease in learning abilities. If new neurons were memory chips, old animals learning new tasks would require as many new neurons as younger ones, but, in general, old animals learn much better than their extremely low rate of adult hippocampal neurogenesis would predict. Exposure to a challenging environment induces adult hippocampal neurogenesis and so do more specific learning stimuli, but the many weeks it takes for a new neuron to develop and mature make it impossible for the new cell to contribute to solving the cognitive task that once triggered its generation. Adult neurogenesis is an investment for the future. The hippocampus becomes better prepared, but not overprepared, for future tasks. Just enough new neurons are added to maintain a dentate gyrus that is as sleek as possible. Nevertheless, the mammalian hippocampus grows with age: in a mouse's first year of life, the dentate gyrus grows by about 50% (Boss, Peterson, & Cowan, 1985). In older age when there is less neurogenesis, the increase plateaus, but old mice do not require as much neurogenesis. They "have seen it all" and need only few new neurons to adjust their hippocampus for new levels of complexity and novelty of the environment. If really challenged, however, the old hippocampus seems to mobilize its entire potential for neurogenesis. The relative induction (but not the absolute amount) of adult neurogenesis in old mice experiencing complexity for the first time can be much larger than in young animals (Kempermann, Kuhn, & Gage, 1998).

Comparing baseline adult neurogenesis and the ability to learn a task highly dependent on the hippocampus showed that the genetically determined rate of adult neurogenesis correlates well with the ability to acquire the task, but not with the level of performance once the test has been learned (Kempermann & Gage, 2002). This makes sense in the light of the new gatekeeper theory. The hippocampus is involved in storing information, but information is not physically stored in the hippocampus. The site of long-term memory storage is the cortex, which does not show adult neurogenesis. Adult hippocampal neurogenesis thus does not upgrade the hard-drive (in an ill-fitted computer analogy), but streamlines the processing unit by strategically inserting a small number of relevant new neurons. This improvement is made possible by lifelong neuronal development regulated in an activity-dependent way.

## ADULT NEUROGENESIS IN THE AGING BRAIN

Research on adult neurogenesis also adds a new facet to emerging concepts of successful aging. Activity-dependent regulation of brain plasticity seems to suggest that the individual holds the key to maintaining his or her brain in a functional state for as long as possible. The old phrase "use it or lose it" has gained a new meaning in the age of cellular neural plasticity and adult neurogenesis. Although this idea is extremely simplistic, it nevertheless reflects a correct impression. Brain structure responds to activity, and the brain can be trained to show structural and, in turn, cognitive consequences.

What is not known is how large and how relevant the possible contribution of activity-dependent neural plasticity to mental health actually is. Although physically active individuals have a decreased risk of developing dementia, the reduction is only moderate. Too many other factors contribute to cognitive aging to make, say, Nordic walking and language classes the silver bullets of successful cognitive aging. Except for very general statements such as "sports and cognitive activity cannot do harm, why not engage in them," it is difficult to give concrete advice based on the present experimental evidence. This, though, is likely to change if the current speed of development is any indicator of future discoveries in the field. On a conceptual level, adult neurogenesis and cellular plasticity bring an important, often neglected aspect into research on aging. If brain development does not end and even neurons continue to be generated in an activity-dependent manner throughout life, then this can be seen as a prominent aspect of growth and positive impulse – rather than only decay and slow-down – in the biology of the aging brain.

As mentioned, however, the rate of adult neurogenesis decreases with increasing age (Kuhn, Dickinson-Anson, & Gage, 1996). Old mice have only very low levels of adult neurogenesis (Cameron & McKay, 1999), but when they were exposed to an enriched environment, the induction of adult neurogenesis in old mice was, in relative terms, much larger than in young mice (Kempermann, Gast, & Gage, 2002). It seems that in old animals that had never before experienced a challenging environment, the hippocampus tried to recruit as many new neurons as possible to cope with the novel stimuli. When the mice entered an enriched environment only for the second half of their lives, after a comparatively boring youth and middle age in regular laboratory cages, the results were even more astounding.

Like many other cells, the granule cell neurons of the dentate gyrus accumulate the age pigment lipofuscin as they age. This accumulation can be taken as a measure of biological aging. Mice that were spending the second year of their 2-year life in an enriched environment had significantly less lipofuscin deposits in their hippocampus. They also performed much better in tests of hippocampus-dependent learning. Adult neurogenesis was at a five-fold higher level than in controls living in standard cages (Kempermann et al., 2002). This was an effect of chronic exposure, not an acute upregulation. In a way, the enriched environment animals had retained a hippocampus that corresponded to a younger age. The finding thus added some new insights as to why activity is "good for the brain."

A new hypothesis has connected a failure of adult hippocampal neurogenesis to explaining the pathogenesis of major depression (D'Sa & Duman, 2002; Jacobs, Praag, & Gage, 2000; Kempermann & Kronenberg, 2003). Not only do patients with chronic depression have a reduced hippocampal volume, but also all known antidepressants induce adult hippocampal neurogenesis. In an animal model, the behavioral effects of the antidepressant even disappeared when adult neurogenesis had been blocked (Santarelli et al., 2003). The neurogenesis hypothesis of major depression has received widespread interest and rightfully so because it is one of the first cellular theories to explain a mysterious mental disease. Many questions remain open, but the theory has already sparked a number of very interesting experiments. Even if the hypothesis ultimately turns out to be wrong, it will have generated much useful insight into brain plasticity.

We have previously argued that the neurogenesis hypothesis of major depression should be seen in the larger context of a plasticity hypothesis (Kempermann & Kronenberg, 2003). Chronic failure of the brain to adjust its structure to the demands of a challenging life (what constitutes these challenges can differ vastly among individuals) might make the individual susceptible to situations in which compensation is no longer possible. In the case of depression, adult neurogenesis might be the most prominent aspect of a relevant disturbance in cellular plasticity. Given the role of the hippocampus in attributing emotional coloring to information to be learned, thereby determining how well it will be learned, if at all, it is conceivable that not only cognitive, but also at least part of the affective symptoms of major depression could be explained by dysfunction of adult neurogenesis. In principle, one can also apply such a concept to other mental disorders such as schizophrenia.

These considerations of adult neurogenesis and cellular plasticity in the context of mental disease draw particular attention because of the socio-economic impact of these disorders and the burden they impose on the patients. This, however, is only the flip side of a broader view that incorporates the insight of brain plasticity in general, and neural stem cell biology and adult neurogenesis in particular, into novel thoughts about aging in the absence of brain pathology.

If a failure of adult neurogenesis can lead to complex cognitive disorders, then this will tell us much about the contribution of these processes to normal brain function. The risk of dementia increases with older age, and the contribution of adult neurogenesis to the maintenance of hippocampal function might in fact play an important role in the pathogenesis of some forms of cognitive decline. However, this implies that persistent, lifelong brain development normally works against such decline. This is a fundamentally different view than seeing the brain in a constantly progressing deterioration after the age of 25.

The idea of continuous development confronts some common misunderstandings about the general nature of aging and allows us to see aging in a different light. In this chapter, we discuss the regulation of adult hippocampal neurogenesis as a key example of the effects of genes and environment, nature and nurture, or biocultural co-constructivism in the adult brain. The central message is that brain development never ends. In a brain region centrally involved in the cognitive processes underlying many essentially human traits, new neurons are being born throughout life in an activity-dependent manner.

## References

Altman, J. (1969). Autoradiographic and histological studies of postnatal neurogenesis: IV. Cell proliferation and migration in the anterior forebrain, with special reference to persisting neurogenesis in the olfactory bulb. *Journal of Comparative Neurology, 137* (4), 433–457.

Altman, J., & Das, G. D. (1965). Autoradiographic and histologic evidence of postnatal neurogenesis in rats. *Journal of Comparative Neurology, 124,* 319–335.

Arvidsson, A., Collin, T., Kirik, D., Kokaia, Z., & Lindvall, O. (2002). Neuronal replacement from endogenous precursors in the adult brain after stroke. *Nature Medicine, 8* (9), 963–970.

Barnea, A., & Nottebohm, F. (1994). Seasonal recruitment of hippocampal neurons in adult free-ranging black-capped chickadees. *Proceedings of the National Academy of Sciences (USA)*, 91, 11217–11221.

Bernhard, T. (1971). Gehen. Frankfurt: Suhrkamp. (in English: *Three Novellas: Amras, Playing Watten, Walking*, P. Janse, K. Northcott, & B. Evenson, Trans. Chicago: University of Chicago Press, 2003. Available: http://www.conjunctions.com/archives/c31-tb.htm)

Bjorklund, A., & Lindvall, O. (2000). Cell replacement therapies for central nervous system disorders. *Nature Neuroscience*, 3 (6), 537–544.

Boss, B. D., Peterson, G. M., & Cowan, W. M. (1985). On the number of neurons in the dentate gyrus of the rat. *Brain Research*, 338 (1), 144–150.

Cameron, H. A., & Gould, E. (1994). Adult neurogenesis is regulated by adrenal steroids in the dentate gyrus. *Neuroscience*, 61 (2), 203–209.

Cameron, H. A., & McKay, R. D. (1999). Restoring production of hippocampal neurons in old age. *Nature Neuroscience*, 2 (10), 894–897.

Cameron, H. A., Woolley, C. S., McEwen, B. S., & Gould, E. (1993). Differentiation of newly born neurons and glia in the dentate gyrus of the adult rat. *Neuroscience*, 56 (2), 337–344.

Churchill, J. D., Galvez, R., Colcombe, S., Swain, R. A., Kramer, A. F., & Greenough, W. T. (2002). Exercise, experience and the aging brain. *Neurobiology of Aging*, 23 (5), 941–955.

Colcombe, S. J., Kramer, A. F., Erickson, K. I., Scalf, P., McAuley, E., Cohen, N. J., et al. (2004). Cardiovascular fitness, cortical plasticity, and aging. *Proceedings of National Academy of Sciences (USA)*, 101, 3316–3321.

Cotman, C. W. (1985). *Synaptic plasticity*. New York: Guilford.

Crespo, D., Stanfield, B. B., & Cowan, W. M. (1986). Evidence that late-generated granule cells do not simply replace earlier formed neurons in the rat dentate gyrus. *Experimental Brain Research*, 62 (3), 541–548.

D'Sa, C., & Duman, R. S. (2002). Antidepressants and neuroplasticity. *Bipolar Disorders*, 4 (3), 183–194.

Day, M., Langston, R., & Morris, R. G. (2003). Glutamate-receptor-mediated encoding and retrieval of paired-associate learning. *Nature*, 424 (6945), 205–209.

Draganski, B., Gaser, C., Busch, V., Schuierer, G., Bogdahn, U., & May, A. (2004). Neuroplasticity: Changes in grey matter induced by training. *Nature*, 427 (6972), 311–312.

Ehninger, D., & Kempermann, G. (2003). Regional effects of wheel running and environmental enrichment on cell genesis and microglia proliferation in the adult murine neocortex. *Cerebral Cortex*, 13 (8), 845–851.

Eriksson, P. S., Perfilieva, E., Björk-Eriksson, T., Alborn, A. M., Nordborg, C., Peterson, D. A., et al. (1998). Neurogenesis in the adult human hippocampus. *Nature Medicine*, 4, 1313–1317.

Gage, F. H. (2000). Mammalian neural stem cells. *Science*, 287 (5457), 1433–1438.

Goldman, S. A., & Nottebohm, F. (1983). Neuronal production, migration and differentiation in a vocal control nucleus of the adult female canary brain. *Proceedings of the National Academy of Sciences (USA)*, 80, 2390–2394.

Gould, E., Reeves, A. J., Fallah, M., Tanapat, P., Gross, C. G., & Fuchs, E. (1999). Hippocampal neurogenesis in adult old world primates. *Proceedings of the National Academy of Sciences (USA)*, 96, 5263–5267.

Greenough, W. T., & Black, J. E. (1992). Induction of brain structure by experience: Substrates for cognitive development. In M. R. Gunnar & C. A. Nelson (Eds.), *Developmental behavioral neuroscience* (Minnesota Symposia on Child Psychology, Vol. 24, pp. 155–200). Hillsdale, NJ: Erlbaum.

Hebb, D. O. (1947). The effects of early experience on problem-solving at maturity. *American Psychologist, 2,* 306–307.

Hebb, D. O. (1949). *The organization of behavior.* New York: Wiley.

Jacobs, B. L., Praag, H., & Gage, F. H. (2000). Adult brain neurogenesis and psychiatry: A novel theory of depression. *Molecular Psychiatry, 5* (3), 262–269.

Kaplan, M. S., & Hinds, J. W. (1977). Neurogenesis in the adult rat: Electron microscopic analysis of light radioautographs. *Science, 197* (4308), 1092–1094.

Kempermann, G. (2002). Why new neurons? Possible functions for adult hippocampal neurogenesis. *Journal of Neuroscience, 22* (3), 635–638.

Kempermann, G., Brandon, E. P., & Gage, F. H. (1998). Environmental stimulation of 129/SvJ mice results in increased cell proliferation and neurogenesis in the adult dentate gyrus. *Current Biology, 8,* 939–942.

Kempermann, G., & Gage, F. H. (2002). Genetic determinants of adult hippocampal neurogenesis correlate with acquisition, but not probe trial performance in the water maze task. *European Journal of Neuroscience, 16,* 129–136.

Kempermann, G., Gast, D., & Gage, F. H. (2002). Neuroplasticity in old age: Sustained fivefold induction of hippocampal neurogenesis by long-term environmental enrichment. *Annals of Neurology, 52* (2), 135–143.

Kempermann, G., & Kronenberg, G. (2003). Depressed new neurons? Adult hippocampal neurogenesis and a cellular plasticity hypothesis of major depression. *Biological Psychiatry, 54,* 499–503.

Kempermann, G., Kuhn, H. G., & Gage, F. H. (1997a). Genetic influence on neurogenesis in the dentate gyrus of adult mice. *Proceedings of the National Academy of Sciences (USA), 94,* 10409–10414.

Kempermann, G., Kuhn, H. G., & Gage, F. H. (1997b). More hippocampal neurons in adult mice living in an enriched environment. *Nature, 386,* 493–495.

Kempermann, G., Kuhn, H. G., & Gage, F. H. (1998). Experience-induced neurogenesis in the senescent dentate gyrus. *Journal of Neuroscience, 18* (9), 3206–3212.

Kempermann, G., & Wiskott, L. (2004). What is the functional role of new neurons in the adult dentate gyrus? In F. H. Gage, A. Björklund, A. Prochiantz, & Y. Christen (Eds.), *Stem cells in the nervous system: Functional and clinical implications* (pp. 57–65). Berlin: Springer.

Kuhn, H. G., Dickinson-Anson, H., & Gage, F. H. (1996). Neurogenesis in the dentate gyrus of the adult rat: Age-related decrease of neuronal progenitor proliferation. *Journal of Neuroscience, 16* (6), 2027–2033.

Magavi, S., Leavitt, B., & Macklis, J. (2000). Induction of neurogenesis in the neocortex of adult mice. *Nature, 405,* 951–955.

Maguire, E. A., Gadian, D. G., Johnsrude, I. S., Good, C. D., Ashburner, J., Frackowiak, R. S., et al. (2000). Navigation-related structural change in the hippocampi of taxi drivers. *Proceedings of the National Academy of Sciences (USA), 97,* 4398–4403.

Palmer, T. D., Markakis, E. A., Willhoite, A. R., Safar, F., & Gage, F. H. (1999). Fibroblast growth factor-2 activates a latent neurogenic program in neural stem cells from diverse regions of the adult CNS. *Journal of Neuroscience, 19* (19), 8487–8497.

Reynolds, B. A., & Weiss, S. (1992). Generation of neurons and astrocytes from isolated cells of the adult mammalian central nervous system. *Science, 255* (5052), 1707–1710.

Rosenzweig, M. R., & Bennett, E. L. (1996). Psychobiology of plasticity: Effects of training and experience on brain and behavior. *Behavioral Brain Research, 78* (1), 57–65.

Sanai, N., Tramontin, A. D., Quinones-Hinojosa, A., Barbaro, N. M., Gupta, N., Kunwar, S., et al. (2004). Unique astrocyte ribbon in adult human brain contains neural stem cells but lacks chain migration. *Nature, 427* (6976), 740–744.

Santarelli, L., Saxe, M., Gross, C., Surget, A., Battaglia, F., Dulawa, S., et al. (2003). Requirement of hippocampal neurogenesis for the behavioral effects of antidepressants. *Science, 301* (5634), 805–809.

Stanfield, B. B., & Trice, J. E. (1988). Evidence that granule cells generated in the dentate gyrus of adult rats extend axonal projections. *Experimental Brain Research, 72* (2), 399–406.

Van Praag, H., Kempermann, G., & Gage, F. H. (1999). Running increases cell proliferation and neurogenesis in the adult mouse dentate gyrus. *Nature Neuroscience, 2* (3), 266–270.

Weissman, I. L., Anderson, D. J., & Gage, F. (2001). Stem and progenitor cells: Origins, phenotypes, lineage commitments, and transdifferentiations. *Annual Review of Cell and Developmental Biology, 17*, 387–403.

Wilson, R. S., Mendes De Leon, C. F., Barnes, L. L., Schneider, J. A., Bienias, J. L., Evans, D. A., et al. (2002). Participation in cognitively stimulating activities and risk of incident Alzheimer disease. *JAMA, 287* (6), 742–748.

# NEURONAL PLASTICITY AND BIOCULTURAL CO-CONSTRUCTION: ATYPICAL BRAIN ARCHITECTURES

# 5

## Sensory Input-Based Adaptation
## and Brain Architecture

Maurice Ptito and Sébastien Desgent

ABSTRACT

*It is well established that brain development depends on the interaction between the basic components of the nervous system (nature) and the environment (nurture). This interaction, however, relies on a number of rules that could modify not only the organization of neural systems, but also their function. In this chapter, we report results on the plasticity of the visual system in animal and human models, using a variety of methodological approaches. In particular, we describe major findings regarding plasticity that result from modifications of the visual input through lesions in the various stages of the visual pathway (peripheral and central). Possible mechanisms for such neural reorganization are also discussed.*

### NATURE VERSUS NURTURE: ENVIRONMENTAL EFFECTS
### ON BRAIN PLASTICITY

One of the oldest issues in modern psychology and biology concerns the nature versus nurture conundrum. Miscellaneous inquiries have been explored in this topic, such as "to what extent can genetic dispositions endow behaviors?" and "to what degree can the environment shape these?" It is well established that brain development depends on the interaction between the basic components of the nervous system (nature) and the stimulating environment (nurture). However, this interaction relies on a number of rules that could modify not only the organization of neural systems, but also their function. As we consider the main principles of evolution, we focus on the characteristics of the brain that are inheritable. Indeed, several features of cortical organization that are genetically mediated and highly constrained in evolution are invariant across mammals, including humans; for example, the gross anatomical positioning of the various cortical areas occupies the same topographic distribution. One of the most studied parts of the brain in that respect is the mammalian visual system. In the following, we review some studies, including our own, on the visual systems of animal and human models relating to the *nature–nurture* debate. We show, using behavioral, anatomical, physiological, and brain imaging evidence, how the brain reacts to abnormal environmental inputs resulting from sensory deprivation or injuries in either the peripheral organ (the eye) or the central processor (the visual cortices).

Early experience plays a key role in the social and personal functional phenotypes that emerge in an individual. Some features of cortical organization can vary with changes in peripheral morphology and with the patterned environmental activity associated with it. These features include the whole surface of a particular sensory area, the size and shape of the cortical field, the details of the internal organization of this same field, and some aspects of thalamocortical and corticocortical connectivity (Krubitzer & Kahn, 2003). Thus, the normal development of the nervous system can be altered either experimentally or by anomalies. It is then possible to modify, fine-tune, and adapt those "blueprints" of harmonious development to changes in nurture background. This adaptation phenomenon is called brain plasticity and refers to the lifelong changes in the brain structure that accompany experience (experience-dependent plasticity). This concept suggests that the brain is pliable, like plastic, and can be molded into different forms in response to the environment, which includes stimulus deprivation, peripheral and central injury, or abnormal gene expression and regulation. Hence, plastic changes across brain systems and related behaviors seem to vary as a function of time and the nature of the changes in experience.

ENVIRONMENTAL MODIFICATION-INDUCED PLASTICITY

**Rearing Conditions**

During early postnatal development, visual cortical connections are highly plastic. They consolidate progressively and become less modifiable by experience, parallel to visual function maturation. For example, the absence of visual experience from birth (dark rearing) prevents this maturation. In particular, visual connections do not consolidate, remaining plastic well after the normal critical period, and visual acuity does not develop. Recently, it became clear that environmental enrichment and exercise (large cages with running wheels and toys) have strong effects on the plasticity of neural connections (see Chapter 4). In fact, development of the visual cortex is strongly influenced by visual experience during short periods of postnatal development called critical periods. During these intermissions of heightened plasticity, experience can produce permanent and extensive modifications of cortical organization. Environmental enrichment has been

**A**

**B**

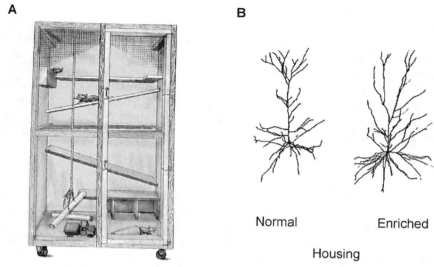

Normal           Enriched

Housing

FIGURE 5.1. Influences of enriched housing. (A) An example of an enriched housing apparatus. (B) In complex housing environments, neurons develop more elaborate neurites and more dendritic space for synapses. (Adapted from Johansson & Belichenko, 2002.)

shown to produce several changes in brain anatomy, for example, neurons in rats raised in an enriched and complex housing environment are more elaborate and possess about 25% more dendritic space for synapses (Fig. 5.1). Their cortical thickness increases, gene expression is elevated, and the oligodendrocyte-to-neuron ratio is higher compared with other rats raised in normal conditions of captivity (Johansson & Belichenko, 2002; Rampon & Tsien, 2000). Neurophysiological properties of sensory neurons can also be enhanced by enrichment of the environment. In cats reared in enriched environments, for example, primary visual cortex neurons show sharper orientation tuning and are able to resolve higher spatial frequencies compared with kittens reared in standard conditions (Beaulieu & Cynader, 1990). Similar changes are also noted in the primary somatosensory cortex of the rat, whereby environmental enrichment narrows the neurons' receptive fields and sharpens topographic organization (Coq & Xerri, 1998). The shaping of visual cortical organization and responses can also be modified by stripe-rearing an animal in an environment with one single orientation. In this situation, nonselective cells acquire a preference for the orientation present in the environment or shift their orientation preference toward the experienced orientation (Blakemore & Cooper, 1971). More recently, optical imaging studies carried out on kittens reared in striped cylinders providing a single orientation environment showed that the representation of the experienced orientation occupied a larger part of the cortical surface than all other orientations. It was also found that cells that responded maximally to the experienced orientation and those preferring other orientations all exhibited a similar sharpness of tuning, and the overall responsiveness did not vary across the cortical surface. These results demonstrate that visual experience plays an important instructive role for neurons and causes a shift in their orientation preference toward the experienced direction (Sengpiel & Kind, 2002). Hence, enrichment or distortion of the environment does result in morphological and physiological changes in sensory and motor cortices, mostly in the young, but also in adults.

## Visual Deprivation

Sensory areas of the cortex are characterized by specific inputs, processing networks, and outputs whose synergy enable those areas to play a particular role in behavior. Studies on visual deprivation, pioneered by Hubel and Wiesel in the early 1960s, had considerable impact on our knowledge of the development of the visual cortex. Suturing the lid of one eye during the critical period reduces the number of cells activated by the deprived eye and also the size of its corresponding ocular dominance column in the primary visual cortex (V1; Fig. 5.2). In 1965, Wiesel and Hubel proposed that ocular dominance plasticity reflects dynamic competitive interactions between the two eyes for synaptic space. Their experiments demonstrated ocular dominance plasticity for the first time, whereby the open or untreated eye dominated the visual cortex both physiologically and anatomically. This concept was firmly established by the finding that binocular deprivation was far less detrimental to the response properties, in particular the binocularity, of neurons in area V1 than a similar period of monocular deprivation. It is generally accepted that experience shapes the development and the maintenance of visual cortical circuits through activity-dependent mechanisms that seem to follow Hebb's principle. Activity in not only the presynaptic axons, but also the targeted cells, has a role in regulating the outcome of this competition. If one eye is deprived of patterned vision during the critical period, there is an irreversible reduction of visually driven activity in the visual cortex through the deprived eye, which is reflected by a shift in the ocular dominance distribution of cortical neurons in favor of the nondeprived eye (Berardi, Pizzorusso, & Maffei, 2000; Berardi, Pizzorusso, Ratto, & Maffei, 2003).

Until recently, it was believed that the mechanisms of ocular dominance column formation and maintenance were similar. This view requires that axons from the two eyes are initially overlapped in the cortex and segregate subsequently due to correlated activity in one eye and uncorrelated activity between the two eyes. These correlations, however, seem to depend more on cortical than on retinal inputs because ablating the cortex abolishes the correlations, whereas enucleation does not. We also know that

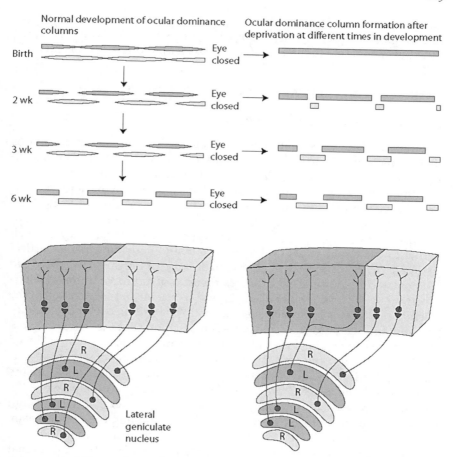

FIGURE 5.2. Effects of eye deprivation on the formation of ocular dominance columns in kittens. Deprivation of the right eye (R) at birth is critical because only axons from the nondeprived eye survive. However, eye closure at 2, 3, and 6 weeks has a gradually decreasing effect because ocular dominance columns have become more segregated with time. Bottom drawings show that altering the input from the right eye (R) induces a more widespread arborization of the geniculate axons from the left eye (L) in primary visual cortex. (Adapted from Wiesel & Hubel, 1965.)

ocular dominance columns form very early in life, when thalamic retinal projections (axons from the lateral geniculate nucleus [LGN]) initially grow into the primary visual cortex. This emphasizes that early development of ocular dominance projections appears to follow an intrinsic developmental program, and it would seem unlikely that activity instructs their formation. Available evidence suggests that specific molecules related to left and right eye brain regions, yet to be isolated, have a key role in setting up at least an initial scaffold of terminals in the primary visual cortex. An instructive role for patterned activity in shaping the cortical columns is also indicated by experiments that involve animal models with induced strabismus.

PERIPHERAL MANIPULATION-INDUCED PLASTICITY

## Eye Misalignment and Central Repercussions

Congenital strabismus in humans or surgically induced ocular deviations in animals results in amblyopia, a decrease in the visual acuity of the deviated eye. Strabismic amblyopia is generally attributed to abnormal interocular interactions. During development, visual afferents of the deprived and normal eye compete for synaptic space on their subcortical and cortical terminal targets. At the cortical level, the competition for control over synaptic space favors the normal eye at the expense of the deviated eye, which shows lower visual acuity and a reduced ability in driving visual cortical neurons (reviewed in Ptito et al., 1995). Because of the imbalance between the deviated and normal eyes, the striate cortex of esotropic animals is characterized by the loss of binocular cells and by the virtual segregation of the afferent projections from each eye that result in a shift in ocular dominance distribution (see Ptito et al., 1995). It seems that most of the deficits in spatial vision occurring in strabismic amblyopia are related to the unbalanced interocular interactions that, in the course of development, favor the normal over the deviated eye. Several attempts have been made to reduce the amblyopia of the affected eye by decreasing the competition between the eyes through restriction of visual inputs to the ipsilateral cortex through chiasmatomy. This procedure, performed by sectioning the optic chiasm, releases the deviated eye from the inhibitory influence of the other eye. Results obtained on split-chiasm preparations, for example, indicate that the deviated eye can indeed benefit from such a segregation of inputs, but only at the cellular level (Di Stefano, Ptito, Quessy, Lepore, & Guillemot, 1995). Neurons in the primary visual cortex can be driven by the deviated eye (Fig. 5.3); however, certain changes in cortical topography occur, as indicated by the anomalous positioning of the receptive fields. These plastic changes seem to be age dependent because the restoration of visual responsiveness occurs only after neonatal chiasmatectomy. This improved effectiveness of the deviated eye to drive visual cortical neurons is not paralleled by an improved visual acuity, as demonstrated in behavioral studies on similar preparations. Assessment of visual acuity performed in binocular and monocular viewing (Ptito et al., 1995) indicates that the visual acuity of strabismic cats with an optic chiasma section deteriorated, compared with otherwise intact strabismic cats.

These results underline the limits of brain plasticity and emphasize the dichotomy between brain reorganization and recovery of function. In fact,

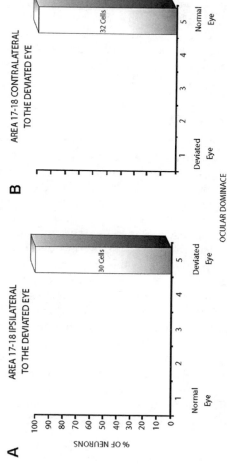

FIGURE 5.3. Effects of strabismus in cats. Ocular dominance distribution of cells recorded in area 17–18 of both hemispheres (ipsilateral (A) and controlateral (B)) in esotropic split-chiasm cats. Note that the deviated, supposedly blind eye is able to drive cells in the visual cortex of both hemispheres.

118 Maurice Ptito and Sébastien Desgent

the perturbation of the temporal retina following strabismus is even more devastating behaviorally when the transection of the chiasma is added to it, despite some kind of anatomical reorganization having occurred. We believe that the simultaneous induction of esotropia and chiasmatomy during the critical period of plasticity modify the internal retinal connections of the deviated eye. The branching pattern of individual ganglion cell axons may be perturbed, and the axonal sprouting may lead to inappropriate horizontal connections such that some ganglion cells in the area centralis, formerly belonging to the nasal retina, would convey information through the remaining ipsilateral pathway. These new "aberrant" projections might be physiologically functional in their ability to drive visual cortical neurons but not strong enough to trigger behavioral improvement of visual acuity (Di Stefano et al., 1995).

## Effects of Retinal Lesions on Plasticity

If the retina is partially lesioned, visual cortex neurons with receptive fields (RFs) in the damaged zone move into the area surrounding the peripheral scotoma (Chino, 1999; see also Dreher, Burke, & Calford, 2001). This reorganization occurs almost immediately, and the RF expands and consolidates within the next few months. Neurons with new RFs ultimately build up normal selectivity for spatial frequency and orientation, although their size remains larger and their response rate is lower than normal. Interestingly, these plastic changes are suppressed if the second eye is enucleated or a corresponding lesion is performed in the other eye. Hence, the cortical map reorganization after monocular retinal lesions requires experience-dependent plasticity and may be involved in the perceptual filling of blind spots due to retinal lesions in early life. This reorganization, although less intense, is also present in the adult brain after retinal injuries. Plasticity in the visual cortex declines with age, but the adult cortex still responds to experience with plastic changes, as shown by the effects of retinal lesions and dark rearing; however, the extent of plasticity is age dependent, being stronger in the young. For example, monocular deprivation or strabismus in adults produces no effect, and recovery from trauma such as amblyopia is also very limited once the critical periods have terminated.

## Intermodal Plasticity Following Natural Deprivations or Enucleations

Sensory deprivation can result from a natural event, such as the lack of differentiation of cochlear nerve cells or ganglion cells in the retina, as in early deafness or blindness or from traumatic events (see Chapter 6). It can also result from surgical intrusions (i.e., enucleations) or pauperization of sensory stimulation, as in dark rearing (Bavelier & Neville, 2002; Toldi, Feher, & Wolff, 1996). Sometimes, the failure of one sensory input to grab the information present in the environment causes changes in the function of the corresponding sensory cortical area. This area can therefore be driven by the remaining or intact sensory inputs. Such intermodal connections result from a phenomenon called cross-modal plasticity. Early studies done by Rebillard, Carlier, Rebillard, and Pujol (1977) reported that the primary auditory cortex can be driven by visual stimuli in congenitally deaf cats. Such results confirmed that experience and sensory inputs have a central role in specifying the functional architecture of the brain regions to which they project. Studies on natural models of cross-modal plasticity such as the mole rat (*Spalax ehrenbergi*), which is born with microphthalmia, have shown that auditive stimulations can drive cells in the primary visual cortex (Bronchti et al., 2002). Visual deprivation also leads to cross-modal reorganization because in visually deprived cats, rats, or mice, cells in the primary visual cortex can be driven by somatosensory or auditory inputs (Toldi, Farkas, & Volgyi, 1994).

Binocular and monocular enucleations have been good models to study cross-modal plasticity. Enucleation in newborn rats results in better maze performance mediated by somatosensory perception with intact whiskers, as well as a concomitant change in the size and angular sensitivity of the receptive fields of the primary barrel cortex (Toldi et al., 1994). Recent studies performed by Izraeli and colleagues (2002) on neonatal Syrian hamsters have shown that bilateral enucleation results in auditory activation by visual targets and in a more vigorous behavioral response to noise than found in controls. Similar results have been found in congenitally enucleated opossums (Krubitzer & Kahn, 2003), where a large degree of phenotypic variability in cortical organization can be accomplished only by decreasing or modifying sensory inputs. Hence, peripheral innervation plays a large role in the organization of the neocortex because cortical territories usually involved in visual processing are invaded by the auditory and somatosensory system.

## Studies on Blindness: Perceptual Training-Induced Plasticity

As we have just seen, the visual cortex is capable of rewiring to accommodate abnormal visual inputs. However, in cases where visual inputs are not possible, such as in congenital blindness, the brain must readapt to compensate for the loss of vision (see Chapter 6). Blind people thus have to rely on other sensory modalities (i.e., audition and touch) to be able to function and appreciate the visual world. It is a common belief that in blind people the senses of hearing and touch are more developed than in sighted people, due most probably to training-induced plasticity. Processing "visual information" through touch has been a major contribution of the Braille method, which enables the blind to read and write. It has been shown, for example, that a certain degree of plasticity occurs in the brain of trained Braille readers, in the sense that the cortical somatic and motor areas representing the reading index finger are larger (Pascual-Leone & Torres, 1993). Interestingly, the visual cortex of the congenitally blind is not only active, but also shows a supranormal metabolism measured with positron emission tomography (PET) with radioactively labeled glucose at rest (De Volder et al., 1997). This indicates that this cortex is available and can be recruited for tactile or auditory information. In fact, several studies using a variety of brain investigation tools such as PET, functional magnetic resonance imaging (fMRI), event-related potentials, and magnetoencephalography to examine proficient Braille readers all concur on the activation of the visual cortex (Kujala, Alho, & Näätänen, 2000; Sadato et al., 1998). Moreover, transient inactivation of this area by transcranial magnetic stimulation significantly impairs Braille reading accuracy in terms of reading speed and fluency (Cohen et al., 1997). These results argue for cross-modal sensory plasticity in the absence of visual input at birth. It is then possible that the deprived visual cortex contributes to a finer perception of auditory or somatosensory functions. Some have called for multimodal integration, whereby a given unimodal cluster of neurons would recruit neighboring neurons responsive to more than one sensory modality (see Röder, Stock, Bien, Neville, & Rösler, 2002). For example, in visually deprived cats, the visual portion of a multimodal area located along the ectosylvian sulcus is recruited by auditory and somatosensory modalities. Moreover, these deprived animals are better than normal animals at localizing sound sources presented in rear and lateral positions (reviewed in Rauschecker, 1995). Similar results have been obtained in congenitally blind humans who also show superior localization skills and demonstrate a more pronounced N2 wave over posterior brain regions (Röder et al., 2002). They also demonstrate superior spatial and memory functions (see Chapter 6). Additional recent studies using the tongue as an input organ confirmed that cross-modal plasticity does occur in congenitally blind people. More recently, our laboratory has been using a device coined a "tongue display unit" that transforms a visual image taken by a camera into electrotactile pulses applied on the tongue through a grid (Kupers & Ptito, 2004). Congenitally blind subjects are able to identify geometric shapes (Bach-y-Rita, Kaczmarek, Tyler, & Garcia-Lara, 1998), detect motion, and learn an orientation discrimination task. Interestingly enough, PET scans performed before and after training in both blind and blindfolded controls show activation of the visual cortex only in the blind and only after the task has been learned (Fig. 5.4). These results indicate that the recruiting of the visual cortex in the blind depends on training. Our hamster studies on the "rewired" retinofugal projections following central lesions are pertinent to the cross-modal plasticity hypothesis and are described in the following section.

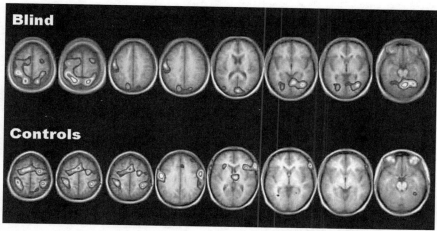

FIGURE 5.4. PET results after training in blind and normal blindfolded controls. Blind subjects activated large parts of the occipital cortex during the orientation detection task, whereas regional cerebral blood flow increases in controls were restricted to parietal and frontal areas.

## BEYOND THE RETINA: CENTRAL LESIONS AND THE MODIFICATION OF RETINOFUGAL PROJECTIONS

The mammalian cerebral cortex is composed of a multitude of different areas that are each specialized for a unique purpose. It is still unclear whether the activity pattern and the modality of sensory inputs to cortex play an important role in the development of cortical regionalization. How does a particular area of cortex develop and gain its own functional capacities? Studies thus far have had difficulty separating the "blueprint" aspects of developmental programs from those that are influenced by environmental changes. A different approach to examine this problem comes from the so-called "rewiring" studies carried out on ferrets (reviewed in Lyckman & Sur, 2002) and hamsters (Ptito, Giguere, Boire, Frost, & Casanova, 2001). These experiments supply important evidence that several aspects of cortical development and functions are crucially influenced by the type of input and experience.

If brain damage occurs during development, abnormal neuronal connectivity patterns can be produced. It is thus possible to induce, by lesioning central retinal targets, the formation of new and permanent retinofugal projections into nonvisual thalamic sites such as the auditory nucleus (M. Ptito et al., 2001; Fig. 5.5a). These surgically induced retinal projections are retinotopically organized and make functional synapses. Neurons in the somatosensory cortex of animals with ectopic retinal projections have

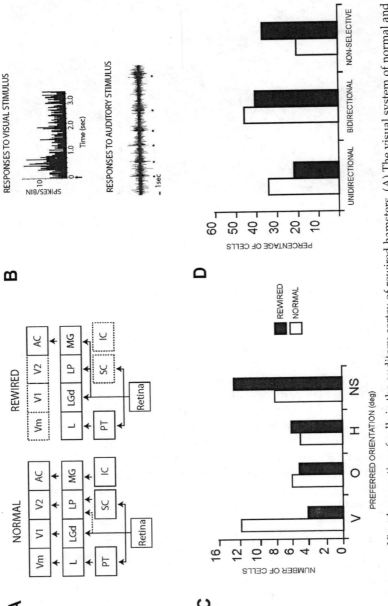

FIGURE 5.5. Visual properties of cells in the auditory cortex of rewired hamsters. (A) The visual system of normal and rewired hamsters (Vm, medial visual cortex; V1, primary visual cortex; V2, secondary visual cortex; AC, auditory cortex; L, lateral nucleus of the thalamus; LGd, lateral geniculate nucleus pars dorsalis; LP, lateral posterior nucleus; MG, medial geniculate nucleus; PT, pretectum; SC, superior colliculus; IC, inferior colliculus). Examples of receptive field properties: (B) a bimodal neuron (auditivovisual), (C) orientation, and (D) direction selectivity.

visual response properties similar to those of neurons in the primary visual cortex of normal animals. Ferrets have retinofugal projections to the auditory thalamus, but no visual cortex appears to perceive light stimuli as visuals (von Melchner, Pallas, & Sur, 2000). The question of parallelism between a different brain organization (produced by lesions) and a behavioral recovery is still being debated, although recent experiments both in rewired ferrets and hamsters seem to indicate a large degree of recovery in visual functions (reviewed in M. Ptito et al., 2001). For example, hamsters with robust and permanent projections to the auditory thalamus nucleus (medial geniculate nucleus) and no visual system exhibit visual responses in their auditory cortex. Single neurons respond to visual stimuli, and some of them respond equally well to auditory stimuli (Fig. 5.5b). Moreover, those cells that respond to visual stimuli show orientation selectivity (Fig. 5.5c), as well as motion and direction sensitivity (Fig. 5.5d). These receptive field properties compare favorably with those obtained from cells in the visual cortex of normal hamsters.

At the behavioral level, rewired hamsters can learn visual discrimination tasks as well as normal ones, and a lesion of the auditory cortex abolishes this function (Fig. 5.6; Frost, Boire, Gingras, & Ptito, 2000). In fact, rewired hamsters with auditory cortex lesions exhibit cortical blindness similar to nonrewired hamsters with visual cortex lesions. These results provide strong evidence for sensory substitution, where a given sensory modality acquires the functional properties of a missing one. This is reminiscent of recent data obtained with congenitally blind subjects in whom the visual cortex was found to be active during Braille reading (reviewed in Röder & Rösler, 2003) or during an orientation discrimination task using the tongue as a medium (Kupers & Ptito, 2004).

## CORTICAL LESIONS IN HUMANS AND MONKEYS

In the preceding sections, we have shown that modifications of the input structures and alterations of the retino-recipient subcortical structures lead to a rearrangement of brain architecture. These altered brain structures can process sensory information and lead, in some instances, to quasinormal behavioral functions. Recovery from large cortical lesions associated with brain plasticity is still unclear. It remains an utmost challenge in understanding human patients who are brain damaged, particularly those with lesions restricted to the primary visual cortex (area $V_1$) and those with massive lesions that include all visual cortical areas of one cerebral hemisphere (as in hemispherectomy). For example, selective lesions of visual cortical areas yield to a specific loss in visual function: lesions of area $V_4$ induce a loss of color vision, and lesions of area $V_5$ (medial temporal cortex [MT]) specifically alter motion perception, leaving form perception intact (Kolb & Whishaw, 2001; Zeki, 1991).

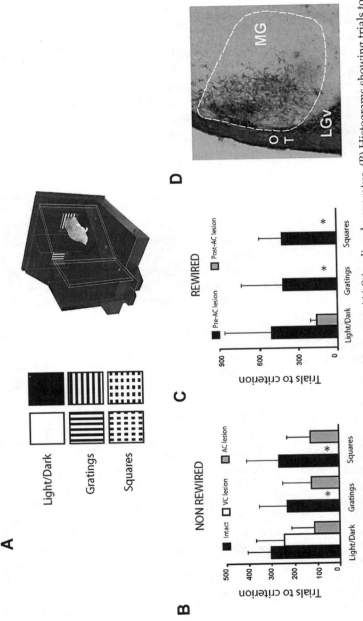

FIGURE 5.6. Visually guided behavior of rewired hamsters. (A) Stimuli and apparatus. (B) Histograms showing trials to criterion on the visual discrimination tasks in nonrewired hamsters before and after ablation of visual cortices (VCs) and auditory (ACs) cortices. (C) Behavior of rewired hamsters before and after AC lesions. (D) Video micrograph showing retino-MG projections in rewired hamsters (OT, optic tract; MG, medial geniculate nucleus; LGv, ventral lateral geniculate nucleus).

## Lesions of Area V1

Destruction of area V1, however, has more devastating effects, such as cortical blindness, which results in the loss of the visual field contralateral to the lesion (homonymous hemianopia). Spontaneous recovery of vision has been reported only in cases of congenital developmental anomaly of both occipital lobes (Ptito, Dalby, & Gjedde, 1999), and plastic changes in the visual pathways found using brain imaging techniques were associated with such visual recovery (Ptito, Johanssen, Faubert, & Gjedde, 1999). In the adult lesioned brain, no recovery of vision has ever been reported in the blind hemifield, although evidence has been accumulating that hemianopic human subjects and monkeys possess wide-ranging residual visual capacities in the blind part of their visual field (see Ptito, Fortin, & Ptito, 2001, for a review). For example, in a forced-choice paradigm where subjects were asked to respond to stimuli presented in their blind field, performance was always above chance levels, although subjects consistently denied having seen the stimulus. This lack of acknowledged awareness has been termed "blindsight" (Weiskrantz, Warrington, Sanders, & Marshall, 1974) and has received considerable attention. The visual abilities reported are far ranging, and include target detection and localization by eye movement or manual pointing, movement detection and direction, as well as relative velocity discrimination, stimulus orientation, and in some cases wavelength discrimination (reviewed in A. Ptito et al., 2001). These residual functions have been ascribed to the extrastriate cortices of the lesioned hemisphere that have been spared by the primary visual cortex damage and maintain "normal" anatomical connections with their subcortical targets (see Weiskrantz, 2004, for a review). By using hemispherectomy patients, it is possible to study the neural mechanisms subserving blindsight because all visual cortical areas of one hemisphere have been surgically removed. This is a unique model for studying the plasticity of the visual system and, in particular, the contribution of the remaining hemisphere through a rewiring of the subcortical visual pathways.

## Hemispherectomy in Human Patients

Hemispherectomy refers to a surgical procedure whereby an entire or large part of a cerebral hemisphere is removed (Fig. 5.7a). It is usually performed as a last resort for the treatment of intractable epilepsy. Hemispherectomized patients rarely show blindsight because they are usually aware of the presence of the stimulus presented in their blind hemifield (maybe similar to type 2 blindsight, see Cowey, 2004). In some instances, however, these patients are able to show the traditional blindsight (type 1). In a non–forced-choice situation (the subject was asked to respond to stimuli presented in the intact hemifield only), for instance, we showed

**A**

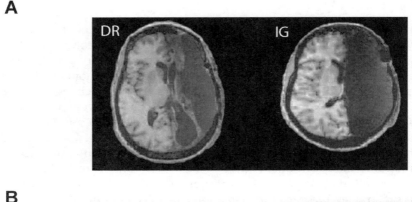

**B**

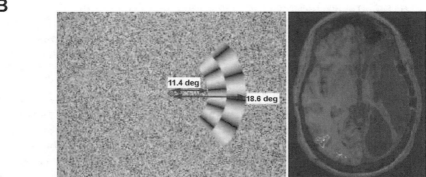

FIGURE 5.7. Contribution of the remaining hemisphere following hemispherectomy in humans. (A) Magnetic resonance axial images showing the extent of right hemisphere similar cortical ablations in two patients (DR and IG). (B) Stimulation of the blind hemifield with a moving grating following cerebral hemispherectomy results in significant activation foci in V5 (area MT), V3, and V3A of the remaining hemisphere.

that a stimulus in the blind hemifield can influence the subject's response (measured by reaction time) to a stimulus in the intact field. Although none of the patients were aware of the stimuli, their reaction times were faster when a second flash was simultaneously presented in their blind hemifield, indicating a spatial summation effect (Tomaiuolo, Ptito, Marzi, Paus, & Ptito, 1997).

To directly investigate the neural pathways involved in blindsight, we (Bittar, Ptito, Faubert, Dumoulin, & Ptito, 1999) performed fMRI on these same patients following stimulation of the intact hemifield. We found activations in the same sites as the controls in the contralateral hemisphere: areas V1–V2 (primary visual cortex), V3–V3A (associative visual cortex),

VP (lingual gyrus), and V5 (middle temporal gyrus). Stimulation of the blind hemifield, however, produced activations in the ipsilateral occipital lobe, namely, in extrastriate areas V3/V3A and V5 (Fig. 5.7b). These results are consistent with the hypothesis that the remaining hemisphere does play a role in the processing of information presented in the blind hemifield; however, using brain imaging techniques, we failed to highlight the subcortical structures used by the visual information to reach the intact remaining hemisphere. This prompted us to study a monkey model of human hemispherectomy.

Hemispherectomized monkeys show a remarkable behavioral recovery, most notably in sensory and motor behaviors (A. Ptito et al., 2001). Responses to noxious stimuli could be elicited on the deafferented limbs, and responses to visual stimuli could be elicited at 45 degrees into the blind hemifield (Fig. 5.8a) in early hemispherectomized monkeys, but not in adult lesioned ones. These results are reminiscent of what has been observed in our hemispherectomized patients, namely, the improvement in motor and somaesthetic functions (Olausson et al., 2001) and visual perimetry (Fendrich, Wessinger, & Gazzaniga, 2001; A. Ptito et al., 2001). Because the removed hemisphere can no longer control the contralateral hemibody, one has to invoke a massive reorganization of the brain for the behavioral recovery to occur. It thus seems that all motor and sensory functions assumed by the removed hemisphere have been transferred to the remaining intact hemisphere, allowing for the near normal behavior of our lesioned subjects. The visual pathways following hemispherectomy are still preserved. (1) The retina of the blind hemifield is far from being depleted of retinal ganglion cells (RGCs), and there is no evidence of any loss of photoreceptors. RGC loss is circumscribed to the foveal and parafoveal regions, whereas the periphery remains normal (Herbin, Boire, Theoret, & Ptito, 1999). (2) The remaining RGCs send their axons to the LGN ipsilateral to the ablated hemisphere. Although this structure has undergone massive degeneration, it continues to receive laminar eye-specific retinal input (Boire, Theoret, Herbin, Casanova, & Ptito, 2000; Fig. 5.8b). The LGN cell population appears to be made mainly of only residual interneurons, from which no outside projections emerge, indicating that the residual retinal projections arrive at a dead-end situation. The contribution of this thalamic relay to visual recovery is limited. (3) However, retinal input is maintained to both superior colliculi (SC) and shows a near normal distribution pattern. The SC ipsilateral to the cortical ablation has a volume reduction of 28.2% and a moderate cell loss (Boire, Theoret, & Ptito, 2001; Fig. 5.8c). The small reduction in volume and cell number, unaltered distribution pattern of oxidative metabolism, and presence of retinal terminals in the SC ipsilateral to the cortical ablation suggest that this structure maintains visual processing capabilities (cf. Boire et al., 2001, for a review).

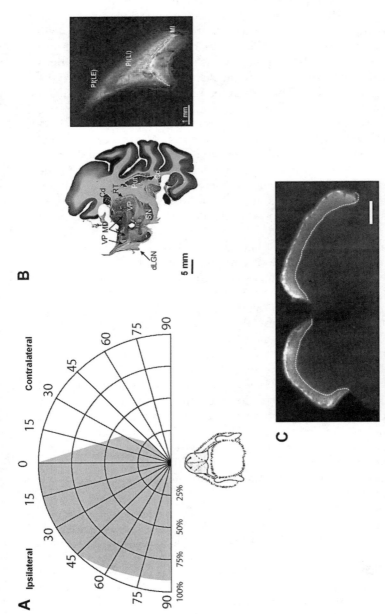

FIGURE 5.8. Hemispherectomy studies in monkeys. (A) Visual perimetry in monkeys. The responses to a novel stimulus are plotted with respect to the position where the target was presented. (B) Coronal section through the thalamus in an early hemispherectomized monkey. Note the reduction in the volume of the lateral geniculate nucleus pars dorsalis (dLGN) ipsilateral to the lesion (indicated by the arrow). Inset shows horseradish peroxydase-labeled retinal projections in dLGN of the same monkey. The dotted line indicates the border between parvocellular and magnocellular layers. (C) Photomicrograph showing retinal projections in the superior colliculi in early hemispherectomized monkey (scale bar, 1 mm).

These animal results suggest that hemispherectomy performed at an early age induces neural changes that could account for the residual behavioral functions observed in both monkeys and human patients. They are also consistent with the possibility that the remaining hemisphere plays a role in the mediation of many residual abilities, such as motor and sensory (vision, somesthesis) behaviors. Our results on hemispherectomized humans and monkeys lead us to propose the following neural substrate to explain visual residual functions: information entering the blind hemifield is processed by the photoreceptors (still in place) and transmitted to the ipsilateral LGN and SC. Because the LGN is devoid of projection neurons, its contribution to relay information to the cortex is null; however, retinal projections to the ipsilateral SC are maintained and show metabolic activity. Information from the ipsilateral SC is funneled to the contralateral SC via the intertectal commissure. From the contralateral SC, the information goes to the pulvinar on the same side, and from there, on to the visual cortical areas of the remaining hemisphere.

CONCLUSION

In this review, we show that sensory experience, loss of sensory receptors, or central traumas result in profound changes in the structure and function of the central nervous system, typically demonstrated by a reorganization of the projection maps in the sensory cortices. The repercussions of localized injury of the cerebral cortex in young brains differ from the repercussions triggered by equivalent damage in the mature brain. In the young brain, some distant neurons are more vulnerable to the lesion, whereas others survive and expand their projections to bypass damaged and degenerated structures. The net result is that neural processes and behaviors are spared (Payne & Lomber, 2002). Vision is critical for the functional and structural maturation of connections in the mammalian visual system. Early in development, internally generated spontaneous activity shapes circuits based on genetic estimates of the initial configuration of connections necessary for function and survival (genetic nature). With maturation of the sensory organs, the developing brain relies less on natural activity and gradually more on sensory experience (environmental nurturing). The sequential grouping of spontaneously generated and experience-dependent neural activity gives the brain an ongoing capability to adapt to dynamically changing inputs during growth and throughout life.

This molding or remolding of cortical response features may mirror changes in synaptic efficacy, local neuronal connectivity, gene expression, and intrinsic cellular mechanisms. Without visual experience and neuronal activity to stimulate or alter the strength of synaptic connection and gene expression, the normal response properties of the visual cells will not develop. Even if we now know that sensory-based activity can greatly influence the development and maturity of the visual cortical networks, the cellular and molecular mechanisms that control the experience-dependent plasticity, coupled with functional recovery, are still unclear. More recent studies, however, point to several potential molecular intra- and extracellular cues that could participate in these plastic processes.

## Molecular Basis of Experience-Related Plasticity

The first modifications induced by experience in visual cortical circuits are likely to be changes in synaptic efficacy. Cellular mechanisms of learning have initially been studied in the hippocampus, in which this synaptic effectiveness has been shown to depend on two mechanisms called long-term potentiation (LTP) and long-term depression (LTD). Both forms are also found in the visual cortex, and one type of LTP is only found during the critical period. Briefly, these mechanisms are used by the presynaptic cell to store information about the history of its activity in the form of residual $Ca^{2+}$ in its terminals. The storage of this biochemical information in the neuron, after a brief period of activity, leads to a strengthening of the synaptic connectivity for many minutes (see Berardi et al., 2003, for a review). LTP and LTD are closely linked to the function of N-d-methylaspartate (NMDA) receptors. The involvement of these receptors in developmental visual cortical plasticity was suggested initially by the observation that blocking them eliminates the effects of monocular deprivation or dark rearing. Their characteristic of being both transmitter- and voltage-dependent, and their coupling via $Ca^{2+}$ influx to plasticity-related intracellular signaling, has led to the notion that they might play a crucial role in synaptic efficacy and plasticity, but their specific features are still unknown.

Neurotrophins such as brain-derived neurotrophic factor or neural growth factor also seem to greatly influence plasticity because their production and release depend on visual activity. In turn, neurotrophins can modulate electrical activity and synaptic transmission at both presynaptic and postsynaptic levels. They can have actions that are both fast, for instance, by increasing transmitter release or by directly depolarizing neurons, and ones that are slow, by modulating gene expression (McAllister, Katz, & Lo, 1999). This reciprocal regulation between neurotrophins and neural activity might provide a means by which active neuronal connections are selectively reinforced, and therefore, play a role in visual cortical synaptic efficacy and plasticity.

Early in development, internally generated spontaneous activity shapes circuits on the basis of genetic estimates of the initial configuration of connections necessary for function and survival (genetic nature). With maturation of the sensory organs, the developing brain relies less on natural activity and gradually more on sensory experience (environmental nurture). The sequential grouping of spontaneously generated and experience-dependent neural activity gives the brain an ongoing capability to adapt to dynamically changing inputs throughout growth and during life.

## References

Bach-y-Rita, P., Kaczmarek, K. A., Tyler, M. E., & Garcia-Lara, J. (1998). Form perception with a 49-point electrotactile stimulus array on the tongue: A technical note. *Journal of Rehabilitation Research and Development, 35,* 427–430.

Bavelier, D., & Neville, H. J. (2002). Cross-modal plasticity: Where and how? *Nature Reviews Neuroscience, 3,* 443–452.

Beaulieu, C., & Cynader, M. (1990). Effect of the richness of the environment on neurons in cat visual cortex: II. Spatial and temporal frequency characteristics. *Developmental Brain Research, 53,* 82–88.

Berardi, N., Pizzorusso, T., & Maffei, L. (2000). Critical periods during sensory development. *Current Opinion in Neurobiology, 10,* 138–145.

Berardi, N., Pizzorusso, T., Ratto, G. M., & Maffei, L. (2003). Molecular basis of plasticity in the visual cortex. *Trends in Neuroscience, 26,* 369–378.

Bittar, R. G., Ptito, M., Faubert, J., Dumoulin, S. O., & Ptito, A. (1999). Activation of the remaining hemisphere following stimulation of the blind hemifield in hemispherectomized subjects. *NeuroImage, 10,* 339–346.

Blakemore, C., & Cooper, G. F. (1971). Modification of the visual cortex by experience. *Brain Research, 31,* 366.

Boire, D., Theoret, H., Herbin, M., Casanova, C., & Ptito, M. (2000). Retinogeniculate projections following early cerebral hemispherectomy in the vervet monkey. *Experimental Brain Research, 135,* 373–381.

Boire, D., Theoret, H., & Ptito, M. (2001). Visual pathways following cerebral hemispherectomy. *Progress in Brain Research, 134,* 379–397.

Bronchti, G., Heil, P., Sadka, R., Hess, A., Scheich, H., & Wollberg, Z. (2002). Auditory activation of "visual" cortical areas in the blind mole rat (*Spalax ehrenbergi*). *European Journal of Neuroscience, 16,* 311–329.

Chino, Y. M. (1999). The role of visual experience in the cortical topographic map reorganization following retinal lesions. *Restorative Neurology and Neuroscience, 15,* 165–176.

Cohen, L. G., Celnik, P., Pascual-Leone, A., Corwell, B., Falz, L., Dambrosia, J., et al. (1997). Functional relevance of cross-modal plasticity in blind humans. *Nature, 389,* 180–183.

Coq, J. O., & Xerri, C. (1998). Environmental enrichment alters organizational features of the forepaw representation in the primary somatosensory cortex of adult rats. *Experimental Brain Research, 121,* 191–204.

Cowey, A. (2004). The 30th Sir Frederick Bartlett lecture: Fact, artefact, and myth about blindsight. *Quarterly Journal of Experimental Psychology Section A, 57,* 577–609.

De Volder, A. G., Bol, A., Blin, J., Arno, P., Grandin, C., Michel, C., & Veraart, C. (1997). Brain energy metabolism in early blind subjects: Neural activity in the visual cortex. *Brain Research, 750,* 235–244.

Di Stefano, M., Ptito, M., Quessy, S., Lepore, F., & Guillemot, J. P. (1995). Receptive field properties of areas 17–18 neurons in strabismic cats with the early section of the optic chiasm. *Journal für Hirnforschung, 36*, 277–281.

Dreher, B., Burke, W., & Calford, M. B. (2001). Cortical plasticity revealed by circumscribed retinal lesions or artificial scotomas. *Progress in Brain Research, 134,* 217–246.

Fendrich, R., Wessinger, C. M., & Gazzaniga, M. S. (2001). Speculations on the neural basis of islands of blindsight. *Progress in Brain Research, 134,* 353–366.

Frost, D. O., Boire, D., Gingras, G., & Ptito, M. (2000). Surgically created neural pathways mediate visual pattern discrimination. *Proceedings of the National Academy of Sciences (USA), 97,* 11068–11073.

Herbin, M., Boire, D., Theoret, H., & Ptito, M. (1999). Transneuronal degeneration of retinal ganglion cells in early hemispherectomized monkeys. *Neuroreport, 10,* 1447–1452.

Izraeli, R., Koay, G., Lamish, M., Heicklen-Klein, A. J., Heffner, H. E., Heffner, R. S., & Wollberg, Z. (2002). Cross-modal neuroplasticity in neonatally enucleated hamsters: Structure, electrophysiology and behaviour. *European Journal of Neuroscience, 15,* 693–712.

Johansson, B. B., & Belichenko, P. V. (2002). Neuronal plasticity and dendritic spines: Effect of environmental enrichment on intact and postischemic rat brain. *Journal of Cerebral Blood Flow and Metabolism, 22,* 89–96.

Kolb, B., & Whishaw, I. Q. (2001). *An introduction to brain and behavior.* New York: Worth Publishers.

Krubitzer, L., & Kahn, D. M. (2003). Nature versus nurture revisited: An old idea with a new twist. *Progress in Neurobiology, 70,* 33–52.

Kujala, T., Alho, K., & Näätänen, R. (2000). Cross-modal reorganization of human cortical functions. *Trends in Neuroscience, 23,* 115–120.

Kupers, R., & Ptito, M. (2004). "Seeing" through the tongue: Cross-modal plasticity in the congenitally blind. *International Congress Series, 1270,* 79–84

Lyckman, A. W., & Sur, M. (2002). Role of afferent activity in the development of cortical specification. *Results and Problems in Cell Differentiation, 39,* 139–156.

McAllister, A. K., Katz, L. C., & Lo, D. C. (1999). Neurotrophins and synaptic plasticity. *Annual Review of Neuroscience, 22,* 295–318.

Melchner, L. von, Pallas, S. L., & Sur, M. (2000). Visual behaviour mediated by retinal projections directed to the auditory pathway. *Nature, 404,* 871–876.

Olausson, H., Ha, B., Duncan, G. H., Morin, C., Ptito, A., Ptito, M., Marchand, S., & Bushnell, M. C. (2001). Cortical activation by tactile and painful stimuli in hemispherectomized patients. *Brain, 124,* 916–927.

Pascual-Leone, A., & Torres, F. (1993). Plasticity of the sensorimotor cortex representation of the reading finger in Braille readers. *Brain, 116,* 39–52.

Payne, B. R., & Lomber, S. G. (2002). Plasticity of the visual cortex after injury: What's different about the young brain? *Neuroscientist, 8,* 174–185.

Ptito, A., Fortin, A., & Ptito, M. (2001). "Seeing" in the blind hemifield following hemispherectomy. *Progress in Brain Research, 134,* 367–378.

Ptito, M., Bouchard, P., Lepore, F., Quessy, S., Di Stefano, M., & Guillemot, J. P. (1995). Binocular interactions and visual acuity loss in esotropic cats. *Canadian Journal of Physiology & Pharmacology, 73,* 1398–1405.

Ptito, M., Dalby, M., & Gjedde, A. (1999). Visual field recovery in a patient with bilateral occipital lobe damage. *Acta Neurologica Scandinavica, 99*, 252–254.

Ptito, M., Giguere, J. F., Boire, D., Frost, D. O., & Casanova, C. (2001). When the auditory cortex turns visual. *Progress in Brain Research, 134*, 447–458.

Ptito, M., Johanssen, P., Faubert, J., & Gjedde, A. (1999). Activation of human extrageniculostriate pathways after damage to area V1. *NeuroImage, 9* (1), 97–107.

Rampon, C., & Tsien, J. Z. (2000). Genetic analysis of learning behavior-induced structural plasticity. *Hippocampus, 10*, 605–609.

Rauschecker, J. P. (1995). Compensatory plasticity and sensory substitution in the cerebral cortex. *Trends in Neuroscience, 18*, 36–43.

Rebillard, G., Carlier, E., Rebillard, M., & Pujol, R. (1977). Enhancement of visual responses on the primary auditory cortex of the cat after an early destruction of cochlear receptors. *Brain Research, 129*, 162–164.

Röder, B., & Rösler, F. (2003). The principle of brain plasticity. In R. H. Kluwe, G. Lüer, & F. Rösler (Eds.), *Principles of learning and memory* (pp. 27–50). Basel, Switzerland: Birkhäuser.

Röder, B., Stock, O., Bien, S., Neville., H. J., & Rösler, F. (2002). Speech processing activates visual cortex in congenitally blind adults. *European Journal of Neuroscience, 16*, 930–936.

Sadato, N., Pascual-Leone, A., Grafman, J., Deiber, M. P., Ibanez, V., & Hallett, M. (1998). Neural networks for Braille reading by the blind. *Brain, 121*, 1213–1229.

Sengpiel, F., & Kind, P. C. (2002). The role of activity in development of the visual system. *Current Biology, 12*, 818–826.

Toldi, J., Farkas, T., & Volgyi, B. (1994). Neonatal enucleation induces cross-modal changes in the barrel cortex of rat: A behavioural and electrophysiological study. *Neuroscience Letters, 167*, 1–4.

Toldi, J., Feher, O., & Wolff, J. R. (1996). Neuronal plasticity induced by neonatal monocular (and binocular) enucleation. *Progress in Neurobiology, 48*, 191–218.

Tomaiuolo, F., Ptito, M., Marzi, C. A., Paus, T., & Ptito, A. (1997). Blindsight in hemispherectomized patients as revealed by spatial summation across the vertical meridian. *Brain, 120*, 795–803.

Wiesel, T. N., & Hubel, D. H. (1965). Comparison of the effects of unilateral and bilateral eye closure on cortical unit responses in kittens. *Journal of Neurophysiology, 28*, 1029–1040.

Weiskrantz, L. (2004). Roots of blindsight. *Progress in Brain Research, 144*, 229–241.

Weiskrantz, L., Warrington, E. K., Sanders, M. D., & Marshall, J. (1974). Visual capacity in the hemianopic field following a restricted occipital ablation. *Brain, 97*, 709–728.

Zeki, S. (1991). Cerebral akinetopsia (visual motion blindness): A review. *Brain, 114*, 811–824.

# 6

# Blindness: A Source and Case of Neuronal Plasticity

Brigitte Röder

ABSTRACT

*The sensory deprivation model provides an opportunity to study the dependence of brain functions on experience in humans. This chapter reports studies on spatial and memory functions in blind humans to demonstrate that the lack of a particular environmental input results in specific behavioral and neural adaptations. It is concluded that neural networks established during development set the limits of adaptive capacities later in life.*

## INTRODUCTION

The capability of the brain to adapt to new requirements is called neuronal plasticity. Research has shown that the ability to change is a lifelong feature characteristic of the central nervous system (CNS) and is indeed the basis for learning and memory. Nevertheless, the extent of possible changes varies across the lifespan, and experience early in life may essentially determine the dynamic range for adaptations later in life. The existence of so-called critical periods in development (i.e., time windows during which adequate experience can cause normal development) is well accepted. The windows vary for different functions and seem to exist for basic sensory processes, as well as for more complex functions such as social behavior (e.g., Chapter 3). Although the time windows of increased plasticity vary for different functions, the principles of how experience shapes brain systems are most likely similar across functional domains (Bavelier & Neville, 2002). Therefore, research on the developmental principles of perceptual-cognitive functions will contribute to the understanding of biocultural co-constructivism in lifespan development.

For example, it has been asked how sensory experience contributes to the development of both perceptual and higher cognitive functions.

Prospective developmental approaches study infants and children at different ages. Retrospective developmental approaches use deprivation models to investigate the consequences of a particular change in experience at a given time during ontogeny on the functionality of neurocognitive systems. Among other models, researchers have used the visual deprivation model to examine the unique contribution of vision to the emergence of particular brain systems (e.g., spatial representations) and to investigate to what extent the spared senses are able to compensate for lost visual input.

In the following, spatial and memory functions in blind humans is discussed to demonstrate the heterogeneous time course of experience dependencies across different perceptual-cognitive domains that may be characteristic for biocultural co-constructivism.

## DEVELOPMENT OF MULTISENSORY PROCESSES

Researchers have wondered whether different sensory systems develop independently or whether there is a mutual dependency in the emergence of sensory functions. Two main views can be distinguished: according to a hierarchical account of development, the different sensory systems develop independently at the beginning and the links between modalities and integration across senses emerge gradually after the single senses have differentiated (Piaget, 1952). An alternative view assumes that initially all sensory systems are linked, a situation called "blooming buzzing confusion" (James, 1890) or "neonatal synaesthesia" (Maurer, 1997).

The first view is supported by the observation that different sensory systems display different developmental time courses. According to Gottlieb (1971, in Turkewitz & Kenny, 1982) the somatosensory system develops first, followed by the vestibular, olfactory, auditory, and finally the visual system. For example, some animals are born with closed eyes that open at a later postnatal stage. Taking into account the heterogeneous developmental time courses of the sensory periphery and the linked central brain areas (Huttenlocher & Dabholkar, 1997), Turkewitz and Kenny (1982) proposed, as an extension of this view, that earlier developing systems not only influence later developing systems, but also that the later emerging systems can change the functional organization of early developing systems. As a consequence, the lack of input to an earlier developing system may disrupt the development of a later developing system. In contrast, the lack of input to a later developing system should interfere less with the functionality of systems developing earlier and may even result in an expansion of the systems emerging earlier. Such an expansion of the auditory and/or somatosensory system into visual subparts of multisensory cortex or predominantly visually responsive areas has been reported for both visually deprived animals and humans (for a review, see Röder & Rösler, 2004). Contrary to this view, the visual system also seems to expand similarly when auditory input is absent from birth (Bavelier & Neville, 2002). However, this might be explained by the fact that multisensory areas reach their functional maturity later than the sensory areas that are dominated by one modality.

The idea of initially highly interwoven sensory systems is supported by the fact that many transient connections and/or less efficient inhibitory influences across modalities exist after birth. Maurer (1997) argued that newborn infants are synesthetic. For example, in contrast to adults, the optimal stimulation level of infants seems to be determined by the sum of input across modalities.

There are two main approaches to studying the emergence of multisensory functions and the mutual dependencies across modalities: (1) prospective developmental studies investigate either the same or different individuals at different ages, and test how and when adult-like behavior or neural organization is achieved; and (2) retrospective developmental studies investigate individuals with specific or deviating experiences. This approach tests whether and how a particular event or condition has changed the organization of the adult system.

Prospective studies in cats and monkeys have provided evidence for the existence of neurons with multisensory responsiveness from birth on. For example, the distribution of unimodal and multisensory neurons in the superior colliculus is by and large similar in newborn and adult monkeys. Receptive fields are generally larger, but they already spatially overlap for the different senses at birth – however, specific multisensory interactions are lacking. Although in the mature system spatially congruent bimodal stimulation results in an increase in neural firing rate that far exceeds the maximal unisensory response rate, such a multisensory facilitation is not observed in newborns and seems to develop slowly within the first postnatal weeks and months (Wallace & Stein, 2001).

Researchers have used behavioral paradigms, including habituation and pair matching paradigms, to study multisensory integration functions in humans of different ages (Lewkowicz, 2002; Lewkowicz & Lickliter, 1994). Lewkowicz (2002) proposed two main principles, heterogeneity and heterochrony, which suggest that multisensory perception consists of many different subfunctions that are acquired at different ages. For example, he showed that cross-modal matching based on temporal synchrony, duration, temporal rate, and rhythm emerges sequentially.

The sensory deprivation approach has been used to study the experience dependence of sensory functions (retrospective approach; see Chapter 5). It is well known that monocular deprivation results in functional blindness of the deprived eye if deprivation exceeds the critical period. This approach has been proven fruitful to investigate which functions depend on experience and whether an environmental influence is limited to a critical period in development. However, the sensory deprivation approach can also be used to study interactions in the development of specific functions and to delineate the unique contribution of a deprived sense for a particular multimodal or cognitive function.

For blind humans, it has been demonstrated that basic (sensory thresholds, sensory discrimination) and more complex tactile and auditory functions (imagery, speech perception, memory) fully develop without visual input. Moreover, in many auditory and tactile perceptual and cognitive tasks, a superiority of the blind has been observed, suggesting that the specific sensory experience of the blind significantly influences the development of auditory and tactile functions (for a review, see Röder & Rösler, 2004; cf. Bavelier & Neville, 2002; Kujala, Alho, & Näätänen, 2000).

The following two sections discuss spatial and memory functions in blind adults, that is, changes due to visual deprivation starting at different ages. The findings show that different functional domains vary in their susceptibility to experience and in the time course of plasticity effects.

SPATIAL FUNCTIONS

The visual sense provides the most accurate spatial information. Therefore, it has been assumed that visual input essentially contributes to the development of spatial functions in the auditory and tactile modalities as well. Given the host of findings that space is used to link input across modalities, cross-modal interdependencies in the emergence of spatial function do not seem to be unlikely. For example, bimodal stimuli are detected faster than unimodal stimuli, and these processing gains suggest that a multimodal integration instance exists along the processing pathway. If two parts of a bimodal stimulus (e.g., the auditory and the visual part) are presented from different locations rather than the same location, an additional activation is seen in the event-related brain potential (ERP) over parietal cortex starting at about 150 ms after the event (Gondan, Niederhausen, Rösler, & Röder, 2005. This also supports the idea of multimodal processing steps because the parietal cortex seems to be essential for the transformation of modality-specific reference frames into a supramodal coordinate system (Cohen & Andersen, 2002; Gondan et al., 2005).

## Spatial Selective Attention

The influence of spatial attention on the processing of stimuli of different modalities has substantiated the assumption that the different senses access common spatial representations at early processing stages. For example, Hötting, Rösler, and Röder (2003) presented tactile stimuli at the left and right index fingers and tones from speakers located near the hands. Auditory and tactile stimuli were presented successively in a random sequence. It was the participants' task to attend to one modality (either touch or audition) and one side (either the left or the right) to detect rare deviant stimuli (with a gap) at that location and in that modality. As is well known from previous work, spatial attention enhances early processing steps associated with the sensory encoding of stimuli. If space is used for cross-modal binding, the processing of task irrelevant stimuli in one modality should be enhanced if they are presented at a location in space that is attended to in the other modality (e.g., if left auditory stimuli are task relevant, processing of left tactile stimuli, although irrelevant, should be boosted compared with right tactile stimuli). This hypothesis can be tested using ERP methodology because the electric brain response to stimuli that do not require any response can be recorded. Indeed, Hötting et al. (2003) and others (Eimer, 2004a) have demonstrated such an enhanced processing of ignored stimuli that fell into the focus of spatial attention. Thus, spatial representations shared by different sensory systems are accessed as early as within the first 150 ms after stimulus presentation (Fig. 6.1).

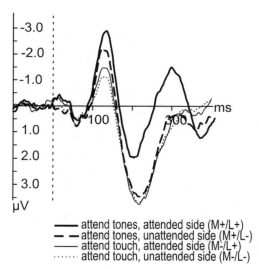

—— attend tones, attended side (M+/L+)
— — attend tones, unattended side (M+/L-)
—— attend touch, attended side (M-/L+)
······ attend touch, unattended side (M-/L-)

FIGURE 6.1. Grand mean ERPs for tones (1) when audition was task relevant and they were presented at the attended side (M+/L+), (2) when audition was task relevant but they were presented from an unattended location (M+/L−), (3) when audition was task irrelevant and they were presented at the attended side (M−/L+), and (4) when audition was task irrelevant but they were presented from an unattended location (M−/L−). Even when sound could be ignored, the processing of tones that were presented at a location at which tactile stimuli had to be monitored were enhanced, compared with tones from a location that was unattended in touch as well. (Adapted from Hötting et al., 2003.)

Given this vivid interaction across modalities in localizing events, one may wonder if similar cross-talk between senses already exists early in development. Studies in owls have indeed demonstrated a massive influence of visual input on the formation of auditory spatial maps (Knudsen, 2002). If an animal grows up wearing prisms that cause a shift of the world to one side, a corresponding shift is observed in the representation of auditory space. It has, furthermore, been suggested that the fine-tuning of auditory spatial representations depends on instructive signals of the visual system because the more ambiguous auditory localization cues have to be disambiguated by more precise visual information (Knudsen, 2002). This would mean that spatial representations of the different senses do not develop independently and, as a consequence, that blind individuals should display impairments in sound localization. In contrast, others have hypothesized that each modality is capable of generating spatial representations by direct sensory-motor feedback loops and, thus, no differences in auditory localization skills between sighted and blind individuals should exist. From a cross-modal compensation point of view, one may even suggest that if an individual has lost one distal sense (vision), the precision of the other (hearing) should improve. Indeed, Rauschecker (1995) reported enhanced auditory localization skills for lateral and rear sound sources in visually deprived cats. Moreover, Rauschecker and co-workers were able to demonstrate that the "visual" parts of a multisensory cortical structure (the anterior ectosylvian cortex) responded to auditory stimuli and that the spatial tuning of the neurons in these areas was more precise.

The human literature on auditory localization skills in the blind is highly inconsistent. Worse, equal, and better auditory localization skills have been reported (see Röder & Rösler, 2004). Röder et al. (1999) conducted an experiment closely modeled after the Rauschecker et al. study of visually deprived cats. They compared auditory localization skills of sighted and blind human adults both for central and peripheral (lateral) sound sources. Congenitally blind adults localized sounds from a speaker array positioned in front of them as precisely as sighted people, but they were superior to the sighted for lateral sound sources. Analogous to the finding in visually deprived cats, concurrent ERP recordings uncovered a sharper spatial tuning of neural networks encoding peripheral sound positions for the blind than for the sighted. Moreover, the scalp distribution of the electric activity associated with spatial attention was shifted posteriorly in the blind compared with the sighted. This was interpreted as evidence for a reorganization of multisensory areas, analogous to that found in visually deprived cats. Interestingly, the same ERP component (in the N1 epoch) has been repeatedly found to be susceptible to cross-modal attention effects (cf. Eimer, 2004a; Hötting et al., 2003). Supporting evidence for a reorganization of multisensory cortex after visual deprivation is now also available from brain imaging studies (Weeks et al., 2000).

In sum, although vision normally seems to modulate the spatial representations of, for example, the auditory sense, the results of Röder et al. (1999) suggest that when vision is absent in human development, the auditory spatial representations are further refined, possibly by recruiting normally visually dominated subparts of multisensory association areas.

## Spatial Imagery

Another possibility to acquire knowledge about where objects are located in the world, at least in peripersonal space, is by means of the haptic sense. The haptic sense comprises touch (i.e., information from the skin receptors) and proprioception (i.e., signals from the joints that inform about the position of a limb). A main difference between the visual and haptic sense is the manner in which each acquires spatial layouts. Although the visual sense is able to gain information from all three dimensions in parallel, the haptic sense acquires information serially and has to integrate these pieces of information successively (e.g., Millar, 1994). To test whether spatial layouts are encoded similarly when acquired by the haptic or the visual sense, Röder and Rösler (1998) used a layout that consisted of five different landmarks. Initially, participants had to learn the location of the objects either visually or haptically. In a second test phase, they were instructed to imagine a small plastic coin flying from a first to a second object location. The time needed for this mental image scanning was measured. From similar studies using visually perceived layouts, it is known that mentally walking along an imaged map seems to be analogous to a real walk, that is, the time needed to reach the destination is a function of the distance between the landmarks. This result was replicated and extended by showing that the mental scanning times, although dependent on the distance between the landmarks on the initial map, were independent of the modality that had been used to encode the spatial layout. Therefore, it was concluded that the underlying spatial representation is independent of the modality used to acquire the layout, although the original motor actions (hand movements vs. eye movements) differed in speed.

To further test this hypothesis, a group of congenitally blind adults was tested with the same paradigm. Because they performed similarly to the sighted, it was concluded that they access similar spatial representations that are acquired independently of the visual input. This conclusion would be substantiated if blind and sighted people were to activate similar brain areas in spatial imagery tasks. In fact, this could be shown by evidence from another spatial imagery study (Röder, Rösler, & Hennighausen, 1997). Participants first had to touch a nonsense form in a two-dimensional tactile display; in the consecutive transformation phase, a tone signaled to them how much they had to mentally rotate the form. Consistent with earlier studies (mainly with visual stimuli), increasing mental rotation times with increasing rotational load were obtained again, both in blind and sighted adults. Concurrently recorded slow ERPs showed the maximal increase in brain activation with increasing rotational load over parietal cortex in sighted people, which is consistent with recent brain imaging studies. Importantly, the blind showed a highly similar effect over the parietal cortex, too, suggesting that spatial representations can not only be accessed through the haptic sense, but can also be acquired without or independently of any visual input.

So far, we have learned that space is an essential feature for the communication between modality systems. We have also seen that spatial representations acquired through the haptic modality have similar properties and are present in similar brain areas to those representations acquired visually. So, isn't there any unique contribution of vision to spatial processes? In the context of auditory localization, it has been argued that in healthy individuals auditory localization may be biased by vision, whereas the emergence of auditory spatial representations is independent from vision.

## Spatio-Temporal Discrimination

In healthy individuals, haptic exploration is usually tightly linked to the visual system. There are neurons in premotor and other cortical areas that have bimodal visuosomatosensory receptive fields (RFs). Interestingly, the visual RF is linked to a body part (e.g., an arm) and follows that body part when it is moved to a new location (Graziano, Cooke, & Taylor, 2000). This system has been proposed to be part of a matching mechanism that links modality-specific coordinate systems. Moreover, it has been shown that the spatial location of inputs of different modalities is important for cross-modal binding. Behavioral and ERP studies on multisensory spatial attention, as well as computational studies, have suggested that all input senses are mapped into an allocentric or an eye-centered frame of reference. This has been attributed to the dominant role of vision and the need to move the eyes toward the relevant event to bring it into one's fovea.

There are many demonstrations on how vision affects auditory and tactile perception in humans. The ventriloquist illusion (i.e., the perception of the ventriloquist's voice at the puppet's lips) is one example of how auditory space perception is modulated by visual input. The rubber arm illusion, in which tactile stimuli are perceived at the position of a visible rubber arm instead of at the location of one's own arm, provides evidence for a visual-tactile ventriloquist-like effect. Interestingly, studies that manipulated the location of limbs, for example, by crossing the arms, suggest that tactual perception may operate in a visual or external frame of reference, even when vision is task irrelevant or not available (e.g., when the task is performed in absolute darkness). If two touches are presented subsequently to the left and the right hand and people are asked to decide which

*Brigitte Röder*

**All participants**                                  **Matched groups**

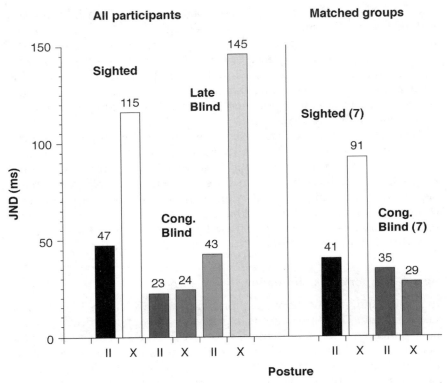

FIGURE 6.2. Just noticeable differences (JNDs) for two tactile stimuli, one presented to the left and one presented to the right hand (II, uncrossed condition; X, crossed condition). Congenitally blind participants not only demonstrated smaller JNDs (i.e., better tactile temporal resolution), they were, in contrast to sighted and late blind participants, also unaffected by crossing their hands. This suggests that a remapping of tactile stimuli into an allocentrically anchored coordinate system is induced by the visual input. The left panel demonstrates that the lack of a hand-crossing effect was not due to the higher temporal resolution of the congenitally blind. Even when matched for JNDs in the uncrossed condition, the sighted displayed impaired spatiotemporal tactile perception in the crossed compared with the uncrossed condition, whereas the congenitally blind subgroup did not. (Adapted from Röder et al., 2004.)

of the two fingers was touched first, the performance depends strongly on whether the hands are in the normal or crossed-over position. In the crossed position, the time for an exact discrimination more than doubles (Fig. 6.2). This is surprising because the position of the hand in external space is totally irrelevant. It has been argued that this performance decline is due to a conflict between an externally based and an anatomically (soma-totopically) organized frame of reference. If stimuli have to be localized first – before their temporal relation can be determined – longer and just noticeable differences are predicted. It seems as if tactile percepts are projected into the "visual" reference frames resulting in impaired performance if the original modality-specific coordinates are misaligned. In this context, it is interesting to note that monkeys produce saccades elicited by touches to one hand initially to the wrong side when their hands are crossed (Groh & Sparks, 1996). Because tactile and auditory orienting emerges earlier in ontogeny than visual orienting, it could be hypothesized that vision gains control over tactile (and auditory) perception at later developmental stages. If no visual input is available during development, as in congenitally blind people, not only modality-specific (e.g., auditory spatial) representations should be refined, but also qualitative changes should occur; for example, the default coordinate systems of their "spatial platform" should change.

In agreement with this hypothesis is the finding that hand crossing does not impair tactile performance (in the temporal order judgment tasks described previously) in congenitally blind adults (Röder, Rösler, & Spence, 2004; Fig. 6.2). Furthermore, this finding supports the view that it is indeed vision that "impairs" tactile performance in the sighted. Interesting and most important for theories on neurofunctional development is the observation that people who became blind after the age of 12 years are, similar to the sighted, confused by crossing their hands (Fig. 6.2), even when sight has been absent for more than 40 years. Because studies in primates have demonstrated that specific multisensory processing capacities are not present immediately after birth but develop later (Wallace & Stein, 2001), it seems that the establishment of specific visual-tactile connections requires adequate stimulation. The finding that late blind individuals' tactile perception was still influenced by a "visual" reference frame may be interpreted as evidence for the involvement of both selective (pruning of connections) and constructive mechanisms (growth of connections) in the development of functions.

A visually defined reference frame has also been observed for auditory localization. In healthy sighted adults, it has been demonstrated that turning the head to one side resulted in a shift of the subjective auditory median plane toward the same direction, that is, a sound that had been perceived in the middle of the head shifted slightly into the opposite direction of the head turn. This phenomenon has been attributed to a mismatch between head-centered coordinates and trunk-centered coordinates, which have to be related to localize sounds. Similar to the studies on the effects of posture change on tactile perception, the auditory localization bias has been argued to originate from a process that remaps auditory input into a world-based coordinate system. Congenitally blind people do not show this effect (Schicke, Demuth, & Röder, 2002), suggesting that this bias in auditory space perception is indeed acquired due to visual input.

In sum, these data impressively demonstrate how experience triggers not only quantitative, but also qualitative changes in brain functions (Eimer, 2004b). When and for what length of time experience is capable of shaping the underlying neural networks is not yet known. However, it is important to note that although vision becomes the dominant modality for space perception during ontogeny, the auditory and the haptic senses fully develop without concurrent visual input. This might reflect a kind of safety buffer that increases the chances of survival in case of an injury and may also guarantee an optimal adaptation of a species in changing environments.

MEMORY

Because the capability to change throughout life is an inherent feature of nervous systems, it can be hypothesized that memory functions as such are particularly mutable and contribute to compensatory performance in the blind.

Developmental studies suggest that different forms of memory have different developmental time courses (Cycowicz, 2000) and are differentially affected by aging (Friedman, 2000). Based on data from neuropsychology, item and source memory have been distinguished within episodic memory. Although item memory refers to the occurrence of a particular stimulus or event, source memory describes the circumstances (time, place etc.) under which a fact has been acquired (e.g., Curran & Schacter, 2000; Cycowicz, 2000). Some patients with frontal lobe damage show intact item memory but deficient source memory (Curran & Schacter, 2000) and produce an elevated number of false memories for lures belonging to the same category as the originally encountered items (Curran & Schacter, 2000). Source memory and retrieval monitoring have, therefore, been closely associated with (prefrontal) lobe functions. Due to the prolonged development of frontal brain areas (Huttenlocher & Dabholkar, 1997; Webb, Monk, & Nelson, 2001), source memory also develops later than item memory or implicit memory (Cycowicz, 2000). Because the normal development of sensory and attentional functions seems to change substantially in blind people, it can be expected that the most flexible and latest-developing memory functions would also develop differently in the blind. We hypothesized that episodic memory functions would show compensatory capacities in blind humans and that the blind would develop special advantages in source memory. Because short- and long-term memory functions dissociate (e.g., Curran & Schacter, 2000), the two were investigated separately.

## Short-Term Memory Functions

Short-term memory skills have most often been investigated with digit-span and word-span tasks. Although some authors found evidence for higher short-term spans in blind children and adolescents (Hull & Mason,

1995), others did not (Wyver & Markham, 1998). These inconsistencies are most likely due to sample differences. Wyver and Markham included blind children with some rudimentary but useful vision, that is, a group for which Hull and Mason (1995) had not found enhanced digit spans. The latter authors found higher digit spans only for blind participants whose visual deficit was congenital and total or nearly total.

To test whether blind adults possess higher short-term memory capacities, a group of congenitally blind adults was given a digit- and word-span task (forward and backward spans). The blind adults reached higher scores than a control group of sighted adults matched for age, gender, handedness, and education (Fig. 6.3). A group of late blind adults was also tested

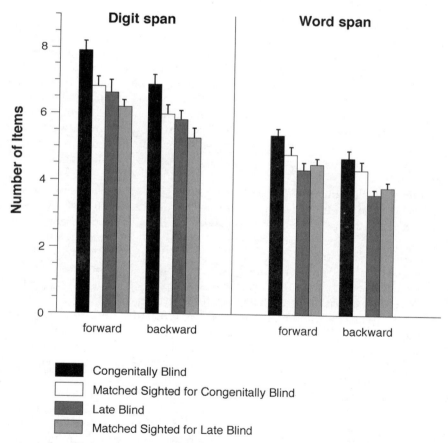

FIGURE 6.3. Digit and word spans for both a group of congenitally blind adults and an age-, gender-, and education-matched sighted control group and a group of late blind adults and a matched sighted control group. The congenitally blind showed enhanced short-term memory compared with their controls, whereas the late blind did not have higher memory spans than their control group.

and compared with another sighted group matched for age, handedness, gender, and education. The performance of the latter two groups differed neither in the digit nor in the word spans (Fig. 6.3). This suggests that acquiring better short-term memory capacities to compensate for the loss of vision is less likely in adulthood. It is notable that Hull and Mason (1995) reported a superiority of the congenitally blind already at the age of 6 years, that is, an age at which the late blind of this study still had some useful vision. Therefore, it might be concluded that short-term memory functions display less compensatory capacity in adulthood than during early childhood.

## Long-Term Memory Functions

### Recognition Memory

Studies on long-term memory functions in the blind have focused on whether blind people can make use of imagery strategies to improve their memory, as sighted people are known to do. It has been shown that blind people remember items with high imagery ratings better than items with low imagery ratings unless these ratings are based on visual features only (De Beni & Cornoldi, 1988; Marchant & Malloy, 1984). Rönnberg and Nilsson (1987) hypothesized that blind people should show lower long-term memory capacity than sighted persons because they lack an access to visual encoding modes and must rely on a presumably shallower auditory code.

Röder, Rösler, and Neville (2001) used ERPs to compare the neural bases of encoding and retrieval in blind and sighted adults. The use of ERPs has proven fruitful in studying memory because they allow different memory functions to be dissociated (e.g., Rugg, 1995). Two memory-related ERP effects were studied. First, the so-called old/new effect (recognition effect), which is a more positively directed potential for successfully recognized old words than for correctly classified new words. This effect is observed in explicit recognition tasks after both an incidental and an intentional study phase. Second, the so-called DM effect (difference according to memory) was analyzed, which is a positive potential shift following items of the study phase that subsequently will be recognized as compared with later not recognized items. Whereas the old/new effect reflects retrieval processes, the DM effect relates to encoding.

In an experiment by Röder et al. (2001), participants first listened to sentences and had to decide whether the last word fit the sentence context (study phase). An unexpected recognition test followed after a short break. All sentence terminal words were presented again but mixed with an identical number of new words. Participants had to decide whether they had encountered the words before. Behavioral measures showed that congenitally blind participants had significantly higher recognition scores than the sighted controls. Whereas ERP old/new effects were not reliable in the sighted, the blind had more positively directed potentials to old than new words over frontocentrotemporal areas of the right hemisphere (Fig. 6.4).

To test if this group difference was due to the higher memory scores of the blind rather than to blindness per se, an attempt was made to recruit a group of sighted participants matched to the blind with respect to memory performance.[1] However, in an enlarged sample of 36 sighted adults, there were only four with d' larger than 1 (whereas the mean of the congenitally blind was 1.33). Therefore, nine sighted participants with a d' higher than 0.75 (mean, 0.95) were used for the comparison. These "high-performing" sighted participants showed an ERP old/new effect similar (although weaker) to the blind, indicating that the lack of an ERP old/new effect in the original matched sighted group was due to lower memory performance rather than sightedness per se (Fig. 6.4).

For the study phase, ERPs were separately averaged for words that were later recognized and for words that were later not recognized. In the sighted, a positivity associated with words that were subsequently recognized was observed over frontocentral brain regions (DM effect; Fig. 6.4). A much stronger and left-lateralized DM effect was detected in the congenitally blind. Again, the high-performing sighted group had a more pronounced DM effect than the sighted group matched to the blind group (Fig. 6.4).

A comparison of the scalp distribution of the old/new and the DM effects did not show any group differences (congenitally blind vs. high-performing sighted participants) in the anterior-posterior distribution of ERPs. This suggests that similar brain areas mediate memory functions in blind and sighted adults, but that these systems may work more efficiently in the blind. In fact, animal studies have shown that use-dependent reorganizations are not always accompanied by a detectable increase in cortical representations (for discussion, see Gilbert, Sigman, & Crist, 2001). However, in our study sighted and blind participants differed in the overall activation pattern. Although the sighted had pronounced frontal negative potentials that decreased toward posterior areas, the blind had potentials of similar amplitude over anterior and posterior brain areas; in other words, they had higher negativities over posterior (visual) brain areas than the sighted. Similar, relatively stronger negative potentials over the posterior scalp had been observed in blind people in earlier studies (e.g., Röder et al., 1997). Because the posterior negative potentials of the blind did not vary with memory performance in this study, a direct contribution to the higher recognition scores has to be questioned. Nevertheless,

---

[1] Hit (correctly recognized old words) and false alarm rates (new words that were judged as old) were calculated and combined to derive the recognition score d'.

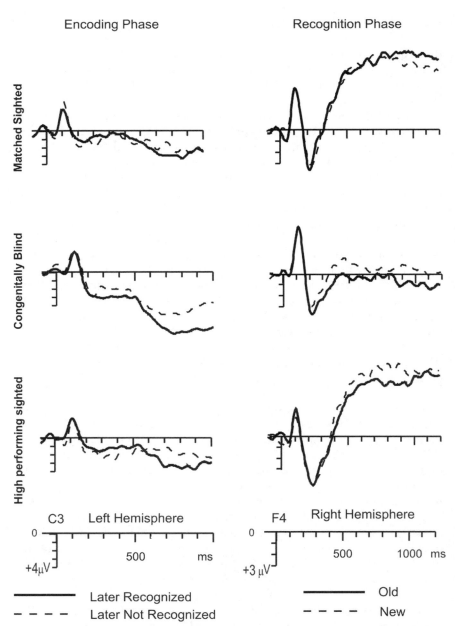

FIGURE 6.4. Grand mean ERPs for a group of congenitally blind adults, a matched sighted control, and a group of high-performing sighted adults during the encoding (left central electrode site) and recognition phase (right frontal site). The ERPs of congenitally blind differed for later recognized and later not recognized items during encoding and for successfully recognized and new items during the recognition phase. Similar effects were seen in a group of high-performing sighted adults, but not in an age-, gender-, and education-matched group of sighted adults. It was suggested that the congenitally blind use superior encoding strategies. (Adapted from Röder et al., 2001.)

a recent brain imaging study substantiates the ERP results that suggest a more pronounced involvement of posterior brain areas. Amedi, Raz, Pianka, Malach, and Zohary (2003) showed a higher occipital cortex activation in blind than in sighted adults in a long-term memory task, which moreover correlated with behavioral measures of memory capacities.

The largest ERP differences between the blind and the sighted were found in the retrieval task for the frontally distributed part of the old/new effect. This subcomponent has been associated with postretrieval processes, such as monitoring or postretrieval evaluation, and source memory processes, and it has been linked to frontal "executive" brain functions. It is known from developmental neuroscience that frontal brain areas are the latest to mature; that is, they do not reach adult level before the second decade (e.g., Webb et al., 2001, for a review). For visual functions, it has been shown that late-developing systems are particularly susceptible to altered input (i.e., visual deprivation; reviewed in Maurer & Lewis, 2001).

The results observed for the congenitally blind match with findings from other brain imaging studies on elaborative processing. For example, a left-lateralized DM effect and corresponding functional magnetic resonance imaging activations have been reported to occur only with semantic, rather than with physical, encoding strategies. In the Röder et al. (2001) experiment, semantic processing was required in the study phase. Therefore, the superior performance of the blind and their more pronounced, left-lateralized DM effect suggest that conceptual encoding strategies were employed. However, this interpretation disagrees with what has been proposed in the literature for memory strategies of blind as compared with sighted people. Pring, Freistone, and Katan (1990) hypothesized that the blind use data-driven rather than concept-driven memory strategies. The authors reported that sighted children recalled auditorily presented words with a higher probability when the words were generated by the participants themselves, rather than when they had only been rehearsed (the so-called generation effect). However, the reverse was found for the blind participants; that is, they remembered the self-generated words less well than the mechanically rehearsed ones.

## Levels of Processing

Because the generation but not the rehearsal of words requires an activation of semantic networks, impairments of the blind in conceptual processing were proposed. In the study conducted by Röder et al. (2001), the test items were exactly the same sound files as the study items. Therefore, although the brain activation pattern implied a "deep" encoding strategy, it cannot be excluded that data-driven encoding strategies contributed to the superiority of the blind. To test this, the next study compared the efficiency of semantic versus physical encoding strategies in blind versus sighted adults (Röder & Rösler, 2003). In addition, this experiment explicitly investigated source memory functions by introducing a false memory manipulation. Röder and Rösler (2003) manipulated the "depth" of encoding and the similarity of lures independently. It is well known from the level-of-processing approach that encoding strategies that involve processing of the items for meaning (semantic, elaborative, or "deep" encoding) result in higher recognition than encoding strategies that focus on physical features of the stimuli (physical or "shallow" encoding).

Participants first heard environmental sounds that they either had to name or rate as harsh or soft. In the recognition phase, all encountered sounds were presented again, intermixed with the same number of new sounds. Although 70% of the new sounds were both physically and semantically distinct, the remaining were physically distinct but represented the same concept as an item in the study phase; that is, they had been named the same in a preexperiment (e.g., the sound of another car). These "pseudo-old" sounds were introduced to study false memory effects as a function of encoding instruction and visual status. Because the false memory literature predicts that false alarm rates are higher when the the semantic relation between old and distractor items is closer, we hypothesized that physical encoding should reduce false memory rates and that this should be particularly true for blind participants. The performance of university students was compared with that of congenitally blind adults of a similar age and with a similar educational background.

Results show that semantic encoding led to higher memory performance than physical encoding, demonstrating a level-of-processing effect for environmental sounds (Fig. 6.5). Importantly, the pattern of results did not differ between sighted and blind groups; that is, blind people gained from semantic encoding strategies as much as the sighted did. However, the overall performance level was higher in the blind, demonstrating a general superiority in long-term retention for environmental sounds (Fig. 6.5). A comparison of false memory rates (the probability of classifying a pseudo-old item as old minus the probability of responding to a physically and semantically distinct new item with "old") revealed fewer false recognitions in the physically encoding, congenitally blind group than in any other group. This result suggests that blind people are able to make extended use of physical features if they focus on them explicitly.

The fact that explicit but not implicit physical encoding reduced false memories in the blind is pertinent to the finding that explicit memory functions show a more extended developmental time course than implicit memory functions do (Cycowicz, 2000). Cobb, Lawrence, and Nelson (1979) did not find any superiority in the performance of their blind participants in a recognition task with environmental sounds, and Rönnberg and Nilsson (1987) reported no advantage of their blind group in a memory task with words but rather "... signs of inferior performance" (p. 279). However, it

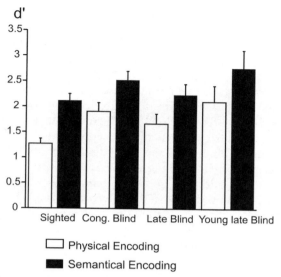

FIGURE 6.5. Recognition scores (d') for environmental sounds for congenitally blind, late blind, and sighted adults who encoded the stimuli either physically or semantically. The congenitally blind had higher memory scores than the sighted, irrespective of encoding mode. When matched for age, the late blind ("young late blind") showed similarly high performance as the congenitally blind. (Adapted from Röder & Rösler, 2003.)

has to be noted that an exact description of the participants of the first study is missing, and that the sample of Rönnberg and Nilsson (1987) comprised late blind adults with different degrees of visual impairments. It has repeatedly been shown that, compared with normal sighted controls, partially sighted individuals show inferior performance in their intact sensory systems. Moreover, if the development of compensatory memory functions is linked to critical periods, late blind adults should not be superior to sighted controls.

To test the age dependence of compensatory memory functions, another study was conducted with a group of late blind participants (Röder & Rösler, 2003). If the compensatory capacity of auditory memory functions is smaller in adulthood than in early childhood, the late blind group should show higher memory performance than the sighted but lower memory performance than the congenitally blind group. In contrast, if compensation through auditory memory is restricted to early childhood, no differences between late blind and sighted individuals should be expected. Rather, both groups should not perform as well as the congenitally blind group (Fig. 6.5).

The memory scores of the late blind lay between those of the sighted and those of the congenitally blind, supporting the first hypothesis. However, the late blind were (1) on average older than the congenitally blind and (2) not blind for a similar amount of time as the congenitally blind. To test whether late blindness as such or one of these two confounding factors could explain the somewhat lower performance of the late blind, the group was first divided into younger and older late blind subgroups. The young late blind participants showed better recognition than the older late blind and sighted participants. Important to note was that the young late blind did not differ from the congenitally blind, whereas the older late blind did (Fig. 6.5). In contrast, memory performance in the late blind group did not correlate with the duration of total blindness. Taken together, these results indicate that the absolute age difference between the congenitally and the late blind groups is responsible for the lower memory scores of the late blind. Therefore, it is justified to conclude that compensatory long-term memory functions can also emerge later in life and are not linked to critical periods in early childhood.

*Memory for Voices*
Another important field in everyday life in which memory plays an essential role is the recognition of members of one's own species. Most sighted people recognize other people mainly on the basis of facial information. It has been argued that due to the high biological importance of recognizing people, specialized brain systems have evolved for face processing. Blind people have hardly any access to face information because it is normally socially inappropriate and too time consuming to haptically explore another person's face. Therefore, blind persons rely mainly on auditory cues such as the sounds people produce while walking, and most important, their voices. To test whether blind people remember voices better than sighted people, different voice probes presented first in a study phase had to be recognized later when presented again intermixed with new voice probes (for details, see Röder & Neville, 2003). As predicted, higher recognition scores were obtained for the congenitally blind than for the sighted controls.

One may wonder if blind people are able to substitute face information by voice cues, that is, recognize people on the basis of their voices as easily as sighted people do on the basis of face or both face and voice information. To answer this question, only a picture or a picture plus the voice of a person were presented to two new groups of sighted participants. Sighted participants who saw the faces of the speakers showed much higher person recognition than the blind based on voice information. These results suggest that the intact sensory systems improve in the blind, but that this compensation is not sufficient to fully substitute for visual information.

CONCLUSION

Neville (1995) suggested that brain systems whose organization is based on associative learning mechanisms display high plasticity throughout life; for example, sensory maps (i.e., temporal coincidence maps) or lexical representations (i.e., the learning of object–word associations) belong to this category. In contrast, systems that are based on the "perception of rule-based invariance" (Neville, 1995, p. 229) require specific input during restricted times in life to establish their full capacities (i.e., they display sensitive periods); therefore, they are less plastic throughout life. Episodic memory belongs to the first category, and the results indicating that congenitally and late blind people show similar compensatory behavioral improvements are in agreement with the suggestion that systems based on associative learning mechanisms demonstrate lifelong adaptive capacities. In contrast, spatial representations and cross-modal transformation rules may at least partially belong to the first category. Correspondence between spatial cues is detected and subsequently consolidated during development; changes are restricted more to childhood.

Black, Jones, Nelson, and Greenough (1998) distinguished (1) *gene-driven*, (2) *experience-expectant*, and (3) *experience-dependent* neural processes. The first are largely insensitive to experience, and research suggests they guide the basic set-up of the CNS common to all members of a species. In contrast, experience-expectant neural processes are built on a readiness of the brain for specific types of information provided by the environment. The susceptibility for this specific input is common to all members of a species and limited to a particular time period of development. The concept of experience-expected development corresponds to that of sensitive periods and has been associated with the overproduction of synaptic connections (Bourgeois, Goldman-Rakic, & Rakic, 2000), but it may involve constructive elements (growth processes) as well (Knudsen, 2002). Experience-dependent processes constitute the ability of the brain to adapt to individual specific variations of an "average environment" present during development. They are proposed to be active throughout life but may build on earlier experience-expectant processes (Knudsen, 1998). It could be speculated that *experience-expectant* functions initially recruit subparts of an exuberance of connections during early development. The remaining connections are either inhibited (Berardi, Pizzorusso, & Maffei, 2000) or eliminated (Bourgeois et al., 2000; Huttenlocher & Dabholkar, 1997). The surviving connections extend further (increase in dendritic branching, etc.) and may be stabilized by the growth of new connections.

Experience-dependent adult plasticity may be due to changing the excitatory/inhibitory balance of existing connections and the local influence of newly generated neurons. It is interesting to note that although the number of newly generated neurons is relatively small, their survival seems to be necessary for some forms of learning (van Praag, Schinder, Christie, Toni, Palmer, & Gage, 2002; cf. Chapter 4). The degree of plasticity in the brain at a given age is possibly determined by the number of existing excitatory and inhibitory connections, as well as the degree and the extent of growth processes (constructive capabilities). Therefore, the functionality of the adult brain and its adaptive capacities depends on the richness of the networks set up during ontogeny, which again depend on the expected and actual range of variation in experience during development.

Evidence for all three processes is also provided by the systematic comparisons of sighted, congenitally blind, and late blind individuals (Röder et al., 2004; see also Schicke et al., 2002). In sum, as shown in animal models and in humans with other selective sensory deficits (e.g., deaf people), these findings with blind people show convincingly that brain systems are highly plastic and can adapt to changed input conditions. Although the genetically determined and environmentally shaped brain systems set limits for learning and adult plasticity, the findings are a clear case for the co-construction hypothesis.

**References**

Amedi, A., Raz, N., Pianka, P., Malach, R., & Zohary, E. (2003). Early "visual" cortex activation correlates with superior verbal memory performance in the blind. *Nature Neuroscience, 6* (7), 758–766.

Bavelier, D., & Neville, H. J. (2002). Cross-modal plasticity: Where and how. *Nature Reviews Neuroscience, 3,* 443–452.

Berardi, N., Pizzorusso, T., & Maffei, L. (2000). Critical periods during sensory development. *Current Opinion in Neurobiology, 10,* 138–145.

Black, J. E., Jones, T. A., Nelson, C. A., & Greenough, W. T. (1998). Neuroplasticity and the developing brain. In N. Alessi, J. T. Coyle, S. I. Harrison, & S. Eth (Eds.), *The handbook of child and adolescent psychiatry* (Vol. 6, pp. 31–53). New York: Wiley.

Bourgeois, J.-P., Goldman-Rakic, P. S., & Rakic, P. (2000). Formation, elimination, and stabilization of synapses in the primate cerebral cortex. In M. S. Gazzaniga (Ed.), *The new cognitive neurosciences* (2nd ed., pp. 45–53). Cambridge, MA: MIT Press.

Cobb, N., Lawrence, D. M., & Nelson, N. D. (1979). Report on blind subjects' tactile and auditory recognition for environmental stimuli. *Perceptual and Motor Skills, 48,* 363–366.

Cohen, Y. E., & Andersen, R. A. (2002). A common reference frame for movement plans in the posterior parietal cortex. *Neuroscience, 3,* 553–562.

Curran, T., & Schacter, D. L. (2000). Amnesia II: Cognitive neuropsychological issues. In M. J. Farah & T. E. Feinberg (Eds.), *Patient-based approaches to cognitive neuroscience* (pp. 291–299). Cambridge, MA: MIT Press.

Cycowicz, Y. M. (2000). Memory development and event-related brain potentials in children. *Biological Psychology, 54,* 145–174.

De Beni, R., & Cornoldi, C. (1988). Imagery limitations in totally congenitally blind subjects. *Journal of Experimental Psychology: Learning, Memory, and Cognition, 14* (4), 650–655.

Eimer, M. (2004a). Electrophysiological studies of multisensory attention. In G. A. Calvert, C. Spence, & B. E. Stein (Eds.), *The handbook of multisensory processes* (pp. 549–562). Cambridge, MA: MIT Press.

Eimer, M. (2004b). Multisensory integration: How visual experience shapes spatial perception. *Current Biology, 14* (3), R115–R117.

Friedman, D. (2000). Event-related brain potential investigations of memory and aging. *Biological Psychology, 54,* 174–206.

Gilbert, C. D., Sigman, M., & Crist, R. E. (2001). The neural basis of perceptual learning. *Neuron, 31,* 681–697.

Gondan, M., Niederhausen, B., Rösler, F., & Röder, B. (2005). Multisensory processing in the redundant target effect: A behavioral and event-related potential study. *Perception and Psychophysics, 67* (4), 713–726.

Graziano, M.S., Cooke, D. F., & Taylor, C. S. (2000). Coding the location of the arm by sight. *Science, 290* (5497), 1782–1786.

Groh, J. M., & Sparks, D. L. (1996). Saccades to somatosensory targets: I. Behavioral characteristics. *Journal of Neurophysiology, 75* (1), 412–427.

Hötting, K., Rösler, F., & Röder, B. (2003). Crossmodal and intermodal attention modulates event-related brain potentials to tactile and auditory stimuli. *Experimental Brain Research, 148,* 26–37.

Hull, T., & Mason, H. (1995). Performance of blind children on digit-span tests. *Journal of Visual Impairment & Blindness, 89,* 166–169.

Huttenlocher, P. R., & Dabholkar, A. S. (1997). Regional differences in synaptogenesis in human cortex. *Journal of Comparative Neurology, 387,* 167–178.

James, W. (1890). *Principles of psychology.* New York: Holt.

Knudsen, E. I. (1998). Capacity for plasticity in the adult owl auditory system expanded by juvenile experience. *Science, 279,* 1531–1533.

Knudsen, E. I. (2002). Instructed learning in the auditory localization pathway of the barn owl. *Nature, 417,* 322–328.

Kujala, T., Alho, K., & Näätänen, R. (2000). Cross-modal reorganization of human cortical functions. *Trends in Neuroscience, 23* (3), 115–120.

Lewkowicz, D. J. (2002). Heterogeneity and heterochrony in the development of intersensory perception. *Cognitive Brain Research, 14,* 41–63.

Lewkowicz, D. J., & Lickliter, R. (Eds.). (1994). *The development of intersensory perception.* Hillsdale, NJ: Erlbaum.

Marchant, B., & Malloy, T. E. (1984). Auditory, tactile and visual imagery in PA learning by congenitally blind, deaf, and normal adults. *Journal of Mental Imagery, 8,* 19–32.

Maurer, D. (1997). Neonatal synaesthesia: Implications for the processing of speech and faces. In S. Baron-Cohen & J. E. Harrison (Eds.), *Synaesthesia: Classical and contemporary readings* (pp. 224–242). Oxford, UK: Blackwell.

Maurer, D., & Lewis, T. L. (2001). Visual acuity and spatial contrast sensitivity: Normal development and underlying mechanisms. In C. A. Nelson & M. Luciana (Eds.), *Handbook of developmental cognitive neuroscience* (pp. 237–251). Cambridge, MA: MIT Press.

Millar, S. (1994). *Understanding and representing space: Theory and evidence from studies with blind and sighted children*. Oxford, UK: Clarendon Press.

Neville, H. J. (1995). Developmental specificity in neurocognitive development in humans. In M. S. Gazzaniga (Ed.), *The cognitive neurosciences* (pp. 219–231). Cambridge, MA: MIT Press.

Piaget, J. (1952). *The origins of intelligence in children*. New York: International University Press.

Pring, L., Freistone, S. E., & Katan, S. A. (1990). Recalling pictures and words: Reversing the generation effect. *Current Psychology: Research & Reviews, 9* (1), 35–45.

Rauschecker, J. P. (1995). Compensatory plasticity and sensory substitution in the cerebral cortex. *Trends in Neuroscience, 18* (1), 36–43.

Röder, B., & Neville, H. (2003). Developmental functional plasticity. In J. Grafman & I. Robertson (Eds.), *Handbook of neuropsychology* (Vol. 9, pp. 231–270). Amsterdam: Elsevier.

Röder, B., & Rösler, F. (1998). Visual input does not facilitate the scanning of spatial images. *Journal of Mental Imagery, 22* (3/4), 165–182.

Röder, B., & Rösler, F. (2003). Memory for environmental sounds in sighted, congenitally blind and late blind adults: Evidence for cross-modal compensation. *International Journal of Psychophysiology, 50*, 27–39.

Röder, B., & Rösler, F. (2004). Compensatory plasticity as a consequence of sensory loss. In G. A. Calvert, C. Spence, & B. E. Stein (Eds.), *The handbook of multisensory processes* (pp. 719–748). Cambridge, MA: MIT Press.

Röder, B., Rösler, F., & Hennighausen, E. (1997). Different cortical activation patterns in blind and sighted humans during encoding and transformation of haptic images. *Psychophysiology, 34*, 292–307.

Röder, B., Rösler, F., & Neville, H. J. (2001). Auditory memory in congenitally blind adults: A behavioral-electrophysiological investigation. *Cognitive Brain Research, 11* (2), 289–303.

Röder, B., Rösler, F., & Spence, C. (2004). Early vision impairs tactual perception in the blind. *Current Biology, 14* (2), 121–124.

Röder, B., Teder-Sälejärvi, W., Sterr, A., Rösler, F., Hillyard, S. A., & Neville, H. J. (1999). Improved auditory spatial tuning in blind humans. *Nature, 400*, 162–166.

Rönnberg, J., & Nilsson, L. (1987). The modality effect, sensory handicap, and compensatory functions. *Acta Psychologica, 65*, 263–283.

Rugg, M. D. (1995). ERP studies of memory. In M. D. Rugg & M. G. H. Coles (Eds.), *Electrophysiology of mind* (pp. 132–170). Oxford, UK: Oxford University Press.

Schicke, T., Demuth, L., & Röder, B. (2002). Influence of visual information on the auditory median plane of the head. *Neuroreport, 13* (13), 1627–1629.

Turkewitz, G., & Kenny, P. A. (1982). Limitations on input as a basis for neural organization and perceptual development: A preliminary theoretical statement. *Developmental Psychobiology, 15*, 357–368.

van Praag, H., Schinder, A. F., Christie, B. R., Toni, N., Palmer, T. D., & Gage, F. H. (2002). Functional neurogenesis in the adult hippocampus. *Nature, 415* (6875), 1030–1034.

Wallace, M. T., & Stein, B. E. (2001). Sensory and multisensory responses in the newborn monkey superior colliculus. *Journal of Neuroscience, 21* (22), 8886–8894.

Webb, S. J., Monk, C. S., & Nelson, C. A. (2001). Mechanisms of postnatal neurobiological development: Implications for human development. *Developmental Neuropsychology, 19* (2), 147–171.

Weeks, R., Horwitz, B., Aziz-Sultan, A., Tian, B., Wessinger, C. M., Cohen, L. G., Hallett, M., & Rauschecker, J. P. (2000). A positron emission tomographic study of auditory localization in the congenitally blind. *Journal of Neuroscience, 20* (7), 2664–2672.

Wyver, S. R., & Markham, R. (1998). Do children with visual impairments demonstrate superior short-term memory, memory strategies, and metamemory? *Journal of Visual Impairment & Blindness, 92* (11), 799–811.

# PART FOUR

# BIOCULTURAL CO-CONSTRUCTION: SPECIFIC FUNCTIONS AND DOMAINS

# 7

# Language Acquisition: Biological Versus Cultural Implications for Brain Structure

## Angela D. Friederici and Shirley-Ann Rüschemeyer

ABSTRACT

*In the discussion on co-constructivism of culture and brain, language is particularly interesting because it is clearly a cultural construction, yet deeply rooted biologically. Cross-linguistic data strongly suggest that the same brain areas, functionally identified to be specific for syntax, semantics, and phonology, are active in participants across languages. However, comparisons between first (native) and second (nonnative) language processing reveal differences with respect to the recruitment of the different subcomponents in a common neuronal network of language processing. Native language processing thus seems to be similar across different languages, but the strategies used to process a nonnative language appear to be different.*

## INTRODUCTION

One of the intriguing issues discussed in the context of the nature–nurture debate (also known as the biology–culture debate) is the question of how different languages influence the brain basis of language processing. This question is particularly interesting in light of the fact that language is clearly a cultural construct and that cultural parameters have been shown to influence development and organization. Thus, a direct assumption following from these observations could be that different languages result in different neural structures.

There is clear evidence that cultural parameters present during development and learning, in general, influence the representation of particular cognitive and motor functions in the brain. A number of brain imaging studies have demonstrated reliable differences in brain activation as a function of training and expertise. For example, musicians, highly trained experts in acoustics and mechanical skills related to their specific instruments, show different brain activations than nonmusicians do when presented with musically related stimuli. Violin players, who depend on the dexterity of the left fingers to produce different notes on the violin, show different activation patterns over somatosensory cortex than nonmusicians do in response to the application of pressure to left digits, but not to right digits (Elbert, Pantev, Wienbruch, Rockstroh, & Taub, 1995). Musicians' neurophysiological response was also found to be different when participants were presented with piano (musically relevant) tones versus pure acoustic tones not found in music. This dissociation between different types of acoustic stimuli was not observed in nonmusicians (Pantev, Oostenveld, Engelien, Ross, Roberts, & Hoke, 1998). Musicians and nonmusicians also showed different electrophysiological responses to deviant complex chords based on the saliency of the deviation. Very obvious harmonic disturbances brought on similar event-related brain potential (ERP) components in both groups, whereas less salient errors elicited a modulated response in musicians only (Koelsch, Gunter, Friederici, & Schröger, 2000; Koelsch, Schröger, & Tervaniemi, 1999). Such findings suggest that basic parameters of a given cognitive function (in this case, acoustic processing) may be represented in the brain independent of the amount of input or training, whereas higher-level processes (i.e., processing of complex musical stimuli) are not (see Chapter 10).

However, the picture with respect to language may be more complicated because it is not immediately clear exactly what parameters within language might influence the cerebral organization of a speaker's language processing system. On the one hand, languages are clearly cultural constructs and differ substantially in their surface form across cultures. On the other hand, there is a strictly formulated linguistic theory claiming that despite differences in the surface structures of natural languages, the underlying "deep" structure of all human languages is universal, and the acquisition of this universal structure is biologically determined (Chomsky, 1981). Thus, predictions with respect to the possible influence of a particular language on brain structure during learning are not obvious. If surface differences between languages are the relevant parameters influencing cerebral organization of language, one would expect different brain activation patterns as a function of different languages. If, however, the underlying universal structure is the relevant parameter of influence, one would expect similar brain activation patterns for different languages.

Predictions regarding the brain–language/language–brain relationship are complicated not only by the fact that it is not known which language parameters affect cerebral organization, but also by the fact that we do not know whether a normal healthy native speaker of a given language should be considered to be an "expert" of language processing in his or her native tongue. Clearly, there is a large degree of variability in the ability of adults to produce free speech or text. But is a novelist an expert user of language in the same manner that a violinist is an expert in music? Or is it rather that each healthy native speaker is an expert in his or her mother tongue – at least with respect to everyday language use?

In the following, we review studies that address this problem. Two approaches are taken to highlight the issue under consideration. First, the neural representation of language processes across different languages is compared. In this section, we demonstrate that although languages differ quite dramatically in how they encode lexical and syntactic information, the functional neuroanatomy is rather similar, as are the electrophysiological markers of lexical-semantic and syntactic processes. In the second section, studies are reviewed that directly compare neural representation of two languages in one person. For these studies comparing the processing of the native first language and a nonnative second language, we discuss in detail at what age the second language was acquired, as well as the individual's proficiency, or expertise, in each language. In this chapter, we do not consider issues concerning different writing systems (i.e., the difference between processing phonetically based alphabetic systems, such as in English, versus character-based orthographies, such as in Chinese). Although this topic is certainly interesting, we focus on different spoken languages as the primary issue under consideration because natural spoken languages constitute the primary language system. We make a brief excursion to describe several findings concerning sign language, which also constitutes a natural language, despite its dependency on visual input. Writing systems are considered to be secondary systems from both an evolutionary perspective because they developed long after the spoken languages and from a functional perspective because they cannot exist (as a language) without the spoken language.

Before turning to the different studies in more detail, the brain imaging techniques used in these studies are presented briefly.

## METHODS OF BRAIN IMAGING

The brain imaging techniques currently employed to study cognitive functions are restricted with respect to either their temporal or their spatial resolution. Functional magnetic resonance imaging (fMRI) and positron emission tomography measure changes in regional blood flow, aspects that correlate with neural activity. The spatial resolution of today's fMRI with 2 mm is excellent, whereas its temporal resolution with 1 to 3 s is less optimal for time-sensitive processes such as online language use.

Temporal parameters are captured in detail by electroencephalography or magnetoencephalography because these methods register the neural activity online, millisecond by millisecond. The ERP or event-related magnetic field reflects the summation of the synchronous postsynaptic activity of large populations of neurons time locked to critical stimuli. To achieve a better signal-to-noise ratio for a given event, the brain's activity is averaged over a number of events of the same type. The time-locked average wave forms in the ERP typically display a number of positive and negative peaks after the onset of a given stimulus. The ERP provides three dimensions as defining variables: the latency, measured in milliseconds; the amplitude, which is modified as a function of the difficulty of the cognitive process under investigation; and the topography, which allows for the differentiation of various cognitive processes based on the activation of a variety of neural structures. Here, we should point out that the spatial information provided by ERPs refers to positions over the scalp, and not to specific neural generators. Thus, these latter methods provide an excellent temporal resolution (on the order of milliseconds) but are less optimal in their spatial parameters.

## NEURAL REPRESENTATIONS ACROSS DIFFERENT LANGUAGES

More recently, quite a few studies have investigated the neural basis of language processing in healthy participants. These studies have been conducted for different languages, using both fMRI and ERP measures. Clearly, a different pattern of results would be expected for participants under various pathological conditions, such as participants who have undergone hemispherectomy, cochlear implants, or suffered various forms of cerebral insult. However, the way in which specific language components are modulated under such conditions is not the primary topic addressed in this chapter; therefore, we restrict further discussion to findings surrounding healthy participant groups. A second important factor to keep in mind is that a fair degree of variability can be observed even between nonpathological participants performing various language tasks. Interindividual differences are diminished by looking at results obtained from large groups of participants. In the following, we also restrict our discussion to findings pertaining to group studies.

### Brain Activation Patterns Across Languages

fMRI language processing studies have been conducted in languages as different as English, Japanese, German, Italian, Hebrew, Dutch, French, and Thai (for recent reviews of fMRI studies and language processing, see Bookheimer, 2002; Cabeza & Nyberg, 2000). Although these studies used different stimulus materials and tasks, common patterns of brain activation have been observed across the different languages. Semantic aspects of processing are supported by the posterior portion of the left superior temporal gyrus (STG) and the middle temporal gyrus, as well as the left inferior frontal gyrus (IFG), in particular, Brodmann's areas (BAs) 45 and 47. Syntactic processes are subserved by the left anterior portion of the STG and BA 44 in the left IFG. The latter brain area has been discussed as the crucial region involved in the processing of syntactic operations necessary to comprehend noncanonical sentence structures (Grodzinsky, 2000) and syntactic operations of natural languages (as compared with unnatural structures) in general (Musso, Weiller, Kiebel, Müller, Bülau, & Rijntjes, 2003).

Of crucial interest in a comparison of the underlying brain systems between different languages are those languages that mark the same function by different cues. For example, English marks grammatical function (subject, object) by word order, whereas German can mark it by case (nominative, accusative). However, speakers of both languages rely on the same underlying neural network consisting of superior temporal and inferior frontal regions to parse language stimuli. A more extreme example comes from Thai, which marks lexical-semantic differences by tone (e.g., high low vs. low high) and not necessarily by phonemes as most languages do (e.g., *mouse* vs. *house*). This comparison is quite relevant because prosodic information is known to be processed predominantly in the right hemisphere, whereas phonemic and lexical-semantic information is processed in the left hemisphere (for a review, see Friederici & Alter, 2004). If the coding (tone vs. phoneme) of the information determines the brain activation, one would expect clear differences between Thai and other languages. If, however, brain activation patterns are determined by the linguistic function (lexical-semantic), then one would expect no differences between the languages. A number of brain imaging studies conducted with Thai native speakers (Gandour, Wong, Hsieh, Weinzapfel, Van Lancker, & Hutchins, 2000) indicate that tonal differences are processed in the left hemisphere when they encode lexical-semantic information. Thus, it appears that the function, rather than the encoding parameters, determines the laterality of the brain activation.

Further evidence for the biological determination of different language function comes from studies looking at sign languages. Sign languages provide valuable insights into human language capacities because they represent a natural linguistic form of communication completely dissociated from auditory input. Sign languages are complex, natural human languages that are acquired by children in the same developmental stages as seen for spoken language acquisition (Corina & McBurney, 2001). Despite the clearly different input modalities and types of information used to encode a communicative act in spoken and sign languages, the same brain areas appear to be responsible for processing both language types (Corina & McBurney, 2001; Hickok, Kirk, & Bellugi, 1998). A comprehensive review of individual case studies describing deaf aphasics shows that right-handed signers, like right-handed hearing individuals, exhibit language disturbances only after insult to critical left hemispherical language sites (Corina, 1998; Corina & McBurney, 2001). Furthermore, language breakdown occurs along linguistically motivated lines – meaning that aphasias in sign languages follow the same linguistic patterns observed in aphasias of spoken languages. Thus, comprehension deficits appear to arise after insult to posterior lesions in left temporal cortex, whereas production deficits tend to be the result of legions in left anterior cortical structures (Corina & McBurney, 2001).

Lateralization of sign language processing has been a matter of debate in recent years. It has been suggested that processing of sign language relies more heavily on right hemispheric structures than does spoken language processing. A recent neuroimaging study comparing activation patterns in deaf and hearing subjects processing both sign and written English language stimuli shows additional involvement of right hemispheric regions when subjects were required to process signs (Neville et al., 1998). The authors suggest that the specific nature and structure of American Sign Language (ASL) lead to this additional recruitment of right hemisphere into the language processing system (but see Hickok, Kirk, & Bellugi, 1998). Specifically, it is proposed that certain linguistic properties (e.g., classifiers) are encoded in ASL in a visuospatial manner not existent in spoken languages (Corina & McBurney, 2001). Such visuospatial information in the language signal could be the cause of additional right hemispheric activation for sign language processing. However, as in the case of Thai, it is assumed that the linguistic information extracted from the incoming signal is further processed by classical language areas (Corina, 1998).

fMRI studies from our own laboratory have directly investigated the processing of comparable linguistic phenomena in German and Russian. In both languages, we investigated lexical-semantic and syntactic processes operationalized in sentences containing a semantic violation or a syntactic phrase structure violation. The semantic violation was realized as a selectional restriction error violating basic semantic features such as animacy (e.g., *The honey was murdered*). The syntactic violation was realized as a word category error within a prepositional phrase; that is, a verb instead of a noun completed the prepositional phrase (e.g., *in the eaten* instead of *in the restaurant*). Sentences with these types of errors were constructed in both German (e.g., semantic violation: *Der Vulkan wurde gegessen [The volcano was eaten]*; syntactic violation: *Das Eis wurde im gegessen [The ice cream was in the eaten]*) and Russian (semantic violation: *Ja dumaju, shto njebo prokisnjet [I think that the sky is sour]*; syntactic violation: *Ja dumaju, shto krjepljenje dlja upadjot [I think that the fastening for falls down]*). The study tested a group of German natives ($N = 7$) and a group of Russian native speakers ($N = 7$). The stimulus material contained semantically incorrect sentences, syntactically incorrect sentences, and correct sentences. Participants were asked to listen to the sentences over headphones, and then to judge whether the sentences were well formed and sensible.

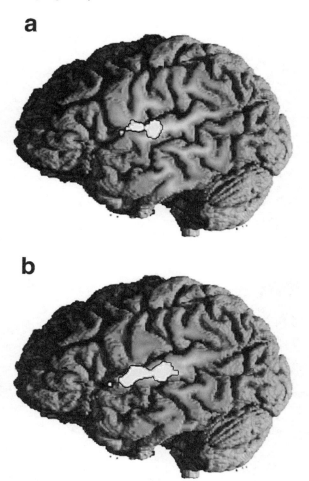

FIGURE 7.1. (a) Increased activation in response to German sentences containing a syntactic violation versus correct sentences in seven German participants (Z > 2.57; $p$ < 0.005, uncorrected). (b) Increased activation in response to Russian sentences containing a syntactic violation verus correct sentences in seven Russian participants (Z > 2.57; $p$ < 0.005, uncorrected).

The performance of the two groups indicates that each group is well in control of their native language. The fMRI results demonstrate a high similarity between the two groups. For the syntactic violation as compared with the correct sentences, both groups show increased activation in the left STG, lateral to the Heschl's gyrus and anterior to this (Fig. 7.1).

For the semantic violation condition, increased levels of activation were found in the IFG, namely, within BA 45/47, in both groups (Fig. 7.2). Note

**a**

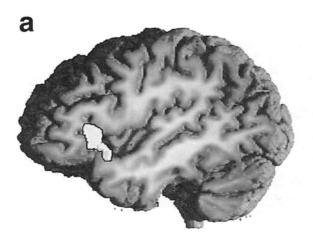

**b**

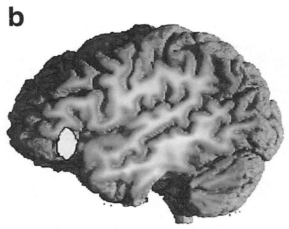

FIGURE 7.2. (a) Increased activation in response to German sentences containing a semantic violation versus correct sentences in seven German participants ($Z >$ 2.57; $p < 0.005$, uncorrected). (b) Increased activation in response to Russian sentences containing a semantic violation versus correct sentences in seven Russian participants ($Z > 2.57$; $p < 0.005$, uncorrected).

that the activation locus is not identical in the two groups, but the peaks of activation lie in anatomically comparable areas within the anterior portion of the left IFG.

Thus, the data from the Russian and German natives suggest that the observed brain activation is determined by the linguistic function (semantic vs. syntax) rather than by the language (German vs. Russian).

Again, it should be noted that only a small sample of participants was investigated here ($N = 7$) and that, although the pattern emerging from these data seems relatively clear, more subtle differences might well become evident with the use of more advanced technology in the future or on investigation of a larger group (see also Rüschemeyer et al., 2005). Furthermore, we make the argument that the observed similarities in brain activation in response to similar linguistic cues is a reflection of identical processes in our two groups of participants. This argumentation is relatively logical and by no means incorrect; however, it is important to keep in mind that the same cerebral areas can be employed for any number of cognitive skills so same brain activation does not always imply same processes. In other words, although it appears that our two participant groups are processing the sentence stimuli in a similar manner, we cannot be absolutely sure on the basis of these data alone that the cognitive processes supported by the observed activations are identical. We feel comfortable, however, in saying that the data are a good indication that two typologically different languages are supported by similar cerebral structures. Although further studies would be necessary to rule out all eventualities, the results from the studies at hand and the current literature seem to support the notion that, in the domain of language, brain activation patterns are not influenced by cultural differences (i.e., by language differences).

## LANGUAGE-RELATED ELECTROPHYSIOLOGICAL COMPONENTS ACROSS LANGUAGES

Having seen evidence that the brain activation registered with fMRI is similar across two typologically different languages, one might wonder whether the same holds true for electrophysiological measures. Particular ERP components have been identified as correlates of specific aspects of language processing, such as, for example, semantic and syntactic processing.

The processing of a *semantic* anomaly, measured using ERPs, was first reported by Kutas and Hillyard (1980). They showed that the impossibility of integrating a semantically inappropriate word into a preceding sentence context leads to a negative ERP deflection with a centroparietal distribution present 300 to 500 ms postonset, termed the *N400 component*. The N400 component was found to correlate in amplitude with the semantic fit between a target word and the restrictions provided by a sentential or word context (Kutas & Hillyard, 1984), and has been supposed to be a marker of semantic integration, in particular (Chwilla, Brown, & Hagoort, 1995).

The N400 component was first identified in reading experiments (Kutas & Hillyard, 1980), but was also later observed during auditory language processing (Holcomb & Neville, 1990). Moreover, it is important to note that this component is found as a correlate for lexical-semantic processes in a number of different languages, such as English (Holcomb & Neville,

1990; Kutas & Hillyard, 1980), German (Friederici, Pfeifer, & Hahne, 1993), Dutch (Chwilla et al., 1995), French (Radeau, Besson, Fonteneau, & Castro, 1998), Italian (Angrilli et al., 2002), Hebrew (Deutsch & Bentin, 2001), and even for ASL (Neville, Mills, & Lawson, 1992).

As for *syntactic* processing, two components have been identified: an (early) left-anterior negativity (which is termed *ELAN* or *LAN*, depending on latency) and a late centroparietal positivity (referred to as the *P600* component).

Left anterior negativities with a maximum latency below 200 ms have been found to occur with phrase structure violations in English (Neville, Nicol, Barss, Forster, & Garrett, 1991) and German (Friederici et al., 1993) and have been termed *early left anterior negativity (ELAN)*. The finding that this component varies with probability (Hahne & Friederici, 1999) indicates that it reflects highly automatic processes. There is some evidence that the ELAN is dependent on input parameters because it did not show up consistently in studies also employing visual word-by-word presentation and because its latency has been shown to depend on visual contrast (Gunter, Friederici, & Hahne, 1999). *Left anterior negativity (LAN)* effects, between 300 and 500 ms, follow violations based on syntactic information other than word category, such as different types of agreement phenomena (in Dutch: Gunter, Stowe, & Mulder, 1997; in German: Münte, Matzke, & Johannes, 1997; in Italian: Angrilli et al., 2002; and in Hebrew: Deutsch & Bentin, 2001).

The *P600 component is* a positive deflection in the ERP that develops from 500 ms onward and has a centroparietal maximum around 600 ms. It has been found for ungrammatical sentences such as phrase structure violations, verb-argument structure and subcategorization violations (in English: Coulson, King & Kutas, 1998; in German: Friederici & Frisch, 2000), subjacency violations (in English: Neville et al., 1991), agreement violations (in Dutch: Gunter et al., 1997), and for nonpreferred disambiguation of ambiguous sentences (in English: Osterhout & Holcomb, 1992; in German: Frisch, Schlesewsky, Saddy, & Alpermann, 2002). In recent studies, it is more generally conceived of as a marker for syntactic integration cost (Kaan, Harris, Gibson, & Holcomb, 2000).

In the syntactic domain, there are, however, some reports that point to a divergence of syntactic ERP effects between different languages. Because most of the ERP studies on syntactic processing have been conducted in English, Dutch, and German, the available data are limited. Moreover, the crucial studies differ with respect to the speed of input because some studies presented the stimulus material auditorily as connected speech and some visually in a word-by-word manner. It has been shown that this aspect affects the ELAN, even within one language, for the same sentence material (Gunter et al., 1999). Moreover, visual word by word also appears to affect the presence of the LAN effect during agreement processes in

English (Osterhout & Mobley, 1995) and in Dutch (Hagoort, Brown, & Groothusen, 1993). Because the LAN is sometimes observed in these languages (in Dutch: Gunter et al., 1997; in English: Coulson et al., 1998) and is sometimes not (in Dutch: Hagoort et al., 1993; in English: Osterhout & Mobley, 1995), the absence of the LAN in these studies cannot be taken to reflect language-specific differences.

Another crucial consideration is to what extent differences between languages are reflected in the ERPs. Take, for example, the obvious difference between languages with relatively strict word order (e.g., English and Dutch) and those with relatively free word order (e.g., German, Russian, Japanese). In the latter languages, grammatical relations between the arguments in a sentence can be marked by means of case. Thus, various processes may be applied in these different languages during sentence processing to build up grammatical relations. Whereas word order-based processes are most relevant during online comprehension of English sentences, case information-based processes are applicable for German, Russian, and Japanese. A recent model of language comprehension has captured this processing difference by assuming two processing streams for the assignment of grammatical relations and thematic roles in the human parsing system (Bornkessel, 2002).

The activation of each of these two processing streams is assumed to be a function of the type of information (word order vs. case information) in a given language. ERP experiments with German sentences containing unambiguous case marking have shown that incorrect case marking can lead to an N400 effect in German (Frisch & Schlesewsky, 2001) and to a LAN effect in English (Coulson et al., 1998). This difference is predicted by the model cited previously in that it assumes that when unambiguous case information is available, the system assigns the thematic/semantic role immediately on the basis of this information. For example, an argument marked in the nominative case is most likely to correspond to the actor in the sentence. A violation of expected case information (e.g., two arguments marked nominative in one sentence) makes the assignment of thematic/semantic roles impossible and therefore leads to an N400 as shown by Frisch and Schlesewsky (2001). In English, no such direct mapping is possible because grammatical relations are indicated by position. Thus, in a sentence such as *The plan took we to paradise,* the parsing system detects that the word "we" signaling subjecthood is in the incorrect position, and the brain elicits an LAN, a syntactic ERP component (Coulson et al., 1998). Thus, it appears that violation of case marking evokes different ERP components, depending on whether the language provides the possibility for direct mapping from case information to thematic roles.

When these data are considered with respect to the issue of biologically constrained universality of the neural basis of language processing versus the notion of a culturally determined brain basis, the data reviewed

Angela D. Friederici and Shirley-Ann Rüschemeyer

can be taken to reflect universality, as case marking in German allows for thematic role assignment in a manner quite similar to animacy (in most languages, animacy is a crucial cue for actorhood). Under the hypothesis of functional universality, one would predict violations of both (case marking and animacy) to elicit an N400 independent of language. This is what the combined data suggest.

## REPRESENTING TWO LANGUAGES IN ONE BRAIN

Another angle from which the issue of biological versus cultural implications for the neural representation of language can be approached is the investigation of language processing in bilinguals.

### Brain Activation Patterns in Bilinguals

In recent years, a number of neuroimaging studies have focused on just this issue. Early findings were not univocal with respect to whether the first language (L1) and second language (L2) have the same neural representation. Whereas some observed different neural patterns for L1 and L2 (Kim, Relkin, Lee, & Hirsch, 1997; Perani et al., 1998), others did not (Klein, Milner, Zatorre, Meyer, & Evans, 1995). However, it should be pointed out that the experimental paradigms, modality of investigation, methods, and participant groups investigated in these studies differed greatly, making direct comparisons of findings impossible. Nevertheless, several very general statements can be made safely. First, different aspects of L1 and L2 can be supported by separate or shared neural networks, and inconsistencies can also be observed within individuals (Kim et al., 1997). For example, it is possible that the networks supporting semantic processing in L1 and L2 are more similar than the networks underlying syntactic processing in L1 and L2. Because of this, results across studies are incredibly difficult to compare. The same participants may show similar neural activation patterns in L1 and L2 in a word comprehension paradigm, but different neural activation patterns in L1 and L2 during sentence production. A study directly comparing various paradigms does not exist to our knowledge; however, in a moment we consider a study of our own in which semantic and syntactic processing in L1 and L2 are directly compared. Second, attained proficiency, language exposure, and age of acquisition are factors that can differentially influence the representation of L2 in the brain (Perani et al., 1998). Last, studies investigating language comprehension provide more uniform results than studies looking at language production in bilinguals (for a review, see Abutalebi, Cappa, & Perani, 2001).

Our own findings suggest that relatively proficient nonnative speakers who have acquired their second language late in life rely on slightly different processing strategies to parse even simple, correct sentences in their L2 (see also Rüschemeyer et al., 2005). To describe the brain activation pattern observable for L2 learners in comparison with L1 processing in natives, we conducted an fMRI experiment identical to that described previously comparing processing of German and Russian, however, with Russian natives who had learned German to a high degree of proficiency (89% correct on a language proficiency test), but who had started to learn German late in life (on average at 18 years of age). The participants ($N = 7$) were between the ages of 26 and 31, had been learning German intensively (usually in Germany) for an average of 7.5 years, and reported speaking German in approximately 50% of their free time (usually participants reported speaking Russian at home and with family 100% of the time, and German with colleagues and at school/university 100% of the time). The stimulus material was German and identical to that used for native German speakers.

Compared with natives (Figs. 7.1 and 7.2), L2 learners displayed less activation in the STG and more activation in the IFG (Fig. 7.3).

This activation pattern was observed not only for the processing of correct sentences, but also for the processing of incorrect sentences. Thus, it appears that the neural network active during L1 and L2 is the same in principle, but additional activation for L2 processing is observed in the IFG. This brain area is known to come into play in L1 processing when semantic tasks get more strategic (Fiez, 1997; Thompson-Schill, D'Esposito, Aguirre, & Farah, 1997) or the stimulus materials get syntactically more complex (Stromswold, Caplan, Alpert, & Rauch, 1996). The fact that this area becomes more active in L2 learners for not very demanding stimulus sentences (simple correct sentences) suggests that processing these sentences is already quite demanding for L2 learners. On the basis of these data alone, increased IFG activation in L2 speakers could be interpreted as either (1) increased difficulty in breaking down syntactic structure in L2, or (2) increased difficulty in selecting a specific word from the mental lexicon in L2. The increased activation observed in native speakers in STG could well reflect a greater role of fast acoustic processing directly in auditory association cortex.

## Language-Related Electrophysiological Components in Bilinguals

ERP studies in bilinguals have systematically investigated lexical-semantic and syntactic processes looking at the three language-related components N400, (E)LAN, and P600 (review see Mueller, 2005).

As discussed previously, the N400 reflects processes of lexical-semantic integration in sentence comprehension. In highly proficient bilingual participants, a delayed (but otherwise characteristic) N400 has been observed when stimulus material is presented in L2 (Ardal, Donald, Meuter, Muldrew, & Luce, 1990). In less proficient participants, the delayed N400 is additionally reduced in its amplitude (Kluender, 1991). Although the

**a**

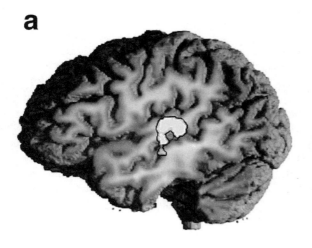

**b**

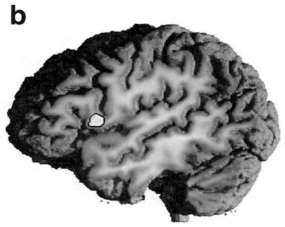

FIGURE 7.3. (a) Increased activation in STG for German native speakers ($N = 7$) compared with nonnative speakers of German ($N = 7$) listening to correct sentences in German ($Z > 2.3$; $p < 0.01$, uncorrected). (b) Increased activation in IFG for nonnative speakers of German ($N = 7$) compared with German native speakers ($N = 7$) listening to correct sentences in German ($Z > 2.3$; $p < 0.01$, uncorrected).

proficiency of participants appears to modify the parameters of the N400 slightly, the effect is nevertheless observable in groups of more and of less proficient L2 speakers. Age of acquisition of L2 similarly has no effect on the presence of the N400. Weber-Fox and Neville (1996) tested five groups of L2 learners, that is, native speakers of Chinese learning English. The groups differed in the age at which participants acquired English: 1 to 3 years, 3 to 6 years, 7 to 10 years, 11 to 13 years, and after 16 years of age. All groups showed an N400 component in response to sentence stimuli in L2. Interestingly, the linguistic relationship of the native language to the second language seems to play little role in the elicitation of the N400 component. L2 learners of German with quite different native languages (Russian vs. Japanese) have been tested using sentence materials in German (Hahne, 2001; Hahne & Friederici, 2001). Both groups show a reliable N400 effect in response to semantic anomalies; however, the N400 is again delayed in the participants who learned German after the age of 11.

The ERP components we have discussed with regard to syntactic processing are the (E)LAN and the P600. In the Weber-Fox and Neville (1996) study mentioned previously, syntactic processing was also investigated in each different group. Sentences that were syntactically anomalous due to the presence of a word category violation elicited an ELAN (N125) followed by a later LAN (N300–500) and a P600 in natives. The P600 was observed in all but one group (>16 years). The ELAN was not found for L2 learners, but the later LAN (N300–500) was, albeit with a more bilateral distribution when L2 was learned late (after 11 years). This finding was taken to support the view that syntactic processing, in particular, is subject to age-of-acquisition effects, thereby providing evidence for the notion of a critical period.

Our own ERP experiments with bilinguals have focused on two issues: (1) whether different types of native languages influence L2 processing, and (2) whether L2 proficiency is reflected in brain activation measurements.

In a series of ERP experiments, semantically and syntactically anomalous sentences were presented over headphones to L2 learners with quite different native languages (Hahne, 2001; Hahne & Friederici, 2001). One group included Russian native speakers and one group included Japanese natives. Although both languages are case marked, their underlying syntactic structures are quite different. Russian, like German (or English), is left branching in its structural tree, whereas Japanese is right branching. Participants listened to German sentences that were either correct or semantically or syntactically incorrect (for examples, see the previous German/Russian study). After each sentence, participants were required to judge the sentence's correctness. Behavioral data revealed that judgment performance for the Russian participants was quite good (approximately 8% errors in all conditions), whereas Japanese participants were not quite as proficient (approximately 20% errors for correct and semantically incorrect sentences; 33% errors for syntactic anomalies).

Both groups of participants (Russian and Japanese natives) showed an ERP pattern in response to semantic violations that was very similar to that seen in native German speakers. In other words, both Russian and Japanese natives showed an N400 component for German sentences that were semantically incorrect. The ERP pattern for the syntactically incorrect sentences, however, was different between natives and nonnative speakers. Natives demonstrated a biphasic pattern consisting of both an

ELAN and a P600 in response to phrase structure anomalies. In L2 learners from both groups, in contrast, no early component (ELAN) could be seen. Regarding the later ERP component, Russian natives demonstrated a P600 effect, with a more positive-going wave for the syntactically incorrect versus the correct sentences, whereas in Japanese natives no P600 effect was detectable. The absence of a P600 effect in Japanese participants is due to the fact that correct sentences already elicited a positive-going wave in this time window, suggesting that processing of correct sentences was already quite demanding for this group. No difference was therefore observable in the comparison of syntactically anomalous versus correct sentences.

This observation is in line with our fMRI finding that the processing of correct sentences in L2 learners can lead to activation patterns that are reported for L1 when processing becomes difficult (see the previous section). Taken together, the ERP data suggest that the highly automatic syntactic processes of initial phrase structure building are not established, even in moderately proficient L2 speakers. The fact that this is the case for both groups, although they come from source languages as different from one another as Russian and Japanese, again seems to support the view that the neural basis of language processing for L2 learning follows a universal pattern. Moreover, the data suggest that not only age of acquisition, but also proficiency plays a crucial role in determining the brain activation pattern, as both the Russian and the Japanese natives learned L2 after puberty.

This clearly raised the question of whether a normal biphasic ELAN-P600 could be elicited in late learners of L2 once they had obtained a high level of proficiency. To control the acquisition style, age of acquisition, amount, and type of input participants received, we conducted an ERP experiment with participants that had learned a novel (nonexisting) language that followed the structural principles of a natural language (Friederici, Steinhauer, & Pfeifer, 2002). It would go beyond the limits of this chapter to describe the study in detail, but the crucial outcome was the following. After participants had learned this novel language to a criterion of 100% correct in an implicit learning setting, they entered the ERP session. Sentences in the novel language were presented to participants via headphones. Following the set-up of the previously discussed studies, the sentences presented were either correct or incorrect with respect to the underlying syntactic structure of the novel language. Syntactically incorrect sentences elicited a biphasic ERP pattern consisting of an early negativity and a late positivity quite similar to the effect observed in natives (Hahne & Friederici, 2002). If this result can be generalized to L2 learning of existing natural languages, one can conclude that proficiency is the crucial factor and that once proficiency of L2 is very high, similar brain responses are observable in L1 and L2.

## IN SEARCH OF LANGUAGE-SPECIFIC BRAIN ACTIVATION PATTERNS

Having seen that the variance of brain activation patterns for a given linguistic domain is larger within language than between languages, one wonders whether there are any brain reactions specific to a particular language.

Behaviorally, there is ample evidence that specific language input affects the perceptual abilities of listeners. It was shown that infants discriminate speech sounds according to a universal set of phonetic categories without prior specific language experience (Werker, Gilbert, Humphrey, & Tees, 1981), but that this ability declines as a function of specific language experience (Eimas, 1975; Werker & Tees, 1983, 2002). This decline is already evident at the end of the first year of life, when infants begin to understand and produce sounds of their native language (Werker & Tees, 2002). These results suggest a clear influence of cultural variables on language behavior.

It is an open question, however, how such behavioral aspects are implemented in the brain. In principle, there are two ways in which these input-related changes could be implemented. One possibility is that the connection strength between neurons or neuronal assemblies changes as a function of specific language input. Another possibility is that different brain areas are recruited as a function of different inputs.

Unfortunately, the neuroimaging methods available do not allow us to evaluate the former possibility empirically. The latter possibility, however, is open to evaluation by today's brain imaging tools.

In a recent developmental study using the ERP methodology, it was shown, for example, that sensitivity to particular phonetic contrasts varies as a function of language input (Cheour et al., 1998). The study used a so-called auditory mismatch negativity paradigm in which a sequence of identical stimuli is interrupted by infrequent deviant stimuli. The deviant stimuli are known to elicit a characteristic negative-going wave form in the ERP signal, which peaks shortly after onset of the deviant stimuli and has been dubbed the mismatch negativity (MMN). The MMN has been used to illustrate adults' categorical perception of phonemes in several languages, including Finnish (Näätänen et al., 1997), Estonian (Cheour et al., 1998; Näätänen et al., 1997), English (Rivera-Gaxiola, Johnson, Csibra, & Karmiloff-Smith, 2000), and French (Dehaene-Lambertz, Dupoux, & Gout, 2000). In the Cheour et al. (1998) study, the authors set out to investigate whether the language-specific categorization of phonemes seen in adult native speakers of a language could also be seen in prelinguistic infants. In other words, previous studies had shown that an MMN is elicited in native-speaking adults confronted with an acoustically presented, deviant phoneme in a string of identical phonemes, only if both phonemes are represented in their native language. Adult listeners show no phonetic, left-lateralized MMN if the deviant phoneme is not represented in their native tongue (Näätänen et al., 1997). Applying the same stimuli previously used in studies looking at adults, Cheour and colleagues conducted a longitudinal study of prelinguistic children. The findings show that 6-month-old infants perceive differences in phonemes not represented in their (to-be) native language. This is an ability that adult speakers no longer have. At the age of approximately 1 year, infants begin to show a pattern more similar to that seen in adults. In other words, after receiving enough linguistic input, the categorical perception of phonemes is determined by the native language. This is reflected in brain activation measured in infants at 1 year of age, but not in younger infants.

These data indicate that the brain loses its sensitivity to those phonetic contrasts that are not phonemically relevant for the target language; however, the brain system that processes phonemically relevant aspects and supports the differentiation between different phonemes in a language appears to be the same. This again supports the notion that it is the function a particular linguistic cue plays in a given language that determines the brain activation pattern.

To conclude, the data at hand indicate that the brain basis for different languages is surprisingly similar, at least at a macroscopic level as accessible by ERP and fMRI. This does not exclude that differences in the connectivity are present at the level of neurons and neural assemblies, but these are not currently accessible. Those differences that are observed in the ERP patterns and in the fMRI activations are clearly due to the form in which linguistic information is encoded and not due to the linguistic function. Rather, the brain basis of language processing is determined by the linguistic function independent of the form in which it is encoded. In this respect, the brain basis of language is universal.

**References**

Abutalebi, J., Cappa, S., & Perani, D. (2001). The bilingual brain as revealed by functional neuroimaging. *Bilingualism: Language and Cognition, 4*, 179–190.
Angrilli, A., Penolazzi, B., Vespignani, F., De Vincenzi, M., Job, R., Ciccarelli, L., et al. (2002). Cortical brain responses to semantic incongruity and syntactic violation in Italian language: An event-related potential study. *Neuroscience Letters, 322*, 5–8.
Ardal, S., Donald, M.W., Meuter, R., Muldrew, S., & Luce, M. (1990). Brain responses to semantic incongruity in bilinguals. *Brain and Language, 39*, 187–205.
Bookheimer, S. (2002). Functional MRI of language: New approaches to understanding the cortical organization of semantic processing. *Annual Review of Neuroscience, 25*, 151–188.
Bornkessel, I. (2002). *The argument dependency model: A neurocognitive approach to incremental interpretation* (MPI Series in Cognitive Neuroscience, 28). Leipzig, Germany: Max Planck Institute of Cognitive Neuroscience.

Cabeza, R., & Nyberg, L. (2000). Imaging cognition II: An empirical review of 275 PET and fMRI studies. *Journal of Cognitive Neuroscience, 12* (1), 1–47.

Cheour, M., Ceponiene, R., Lehtokoski, A., Luuk, A., Allik, J., Alho, K., & Näätänen, R. (1998). Development of language-specific phoneme representations in the infant brain. *Nature Neuroscience, 1,* 351–353.

Chomsky, N. (1981). Knowledge of language: Its elements and origins. *Philosophical Transactions of the Royal Society of London (Series B), 295,* 223–234.

Chwilla, D. J., Brown, C. M., & Hagoort, P. (1995). The N400 as a function of the level of processing. *Psychophysiology, 32,* 274–285.

Corina, D. (1998). Aphasia in users of signed languages. In P. Coppens, Y. Lebrun, & A. Basso (Eds.), *Aphasia in atypical populations* (pp. 261–309). Hillsdale, NJ: Erlbaum.

Corina, D. P., & McBurney, S. L. (2001). The neural representation of language in users of American Sign Language. *Journal of Communication Disorders, 34,* 455–471.

Coulson, S., King, J., & Kutas, M. (1998). Expect the unexpected: Event-related brain responses of morpho-syntactic violations. *Language and Cognitive Processes, 13,* 21–58.

Dehaene-Lambertz, G., Dupoux, E., & Gout, A. (2000). Electrophysiological correlates of phonological processing: A cross-linguistic study. *Journal of Cognitive Neuroscience, 12,* 635–647.

Deutsch, A., & Bentin, S. (2001). Syntactic and semantic factors in processing gender agreement in Hebrew: Evidence from ERPs and eye movements. *Journal of Memory and Language, 45,* 200–224.

Eimas, P. D. (1975). Auditory and phonetic coding of the cues for speech: Discrimination of [r − l] distinction by young infants. *Perception and Psychophysics, 18,* 341–347.

Elbert, T., Pantev, C., Wienbruch, C., Rockstroh, B., & Taub, E. (1995). Increased cortical representation of the fingers of the left hand in string players. *Science, 270,* 305–307.

Fiez, J. A. (1997). Phonology, semantics, and the role of the left inferior prefrontal cortex. *Human Brain Mapping, 5,* 79–83.

Friederici, A. D., & Alter, K. (2004). Lateralization of auditory language functions: A dynamic dual pathway view. *Brain and Language, 89,* 267–276.

Friederici, A. D., & Frisch, S. (2000). Verb–argument structure processing: The role of verb-specific and argument-specific information. *Journal of Memory and Language, 43,* 476–507.

Friederici, A. D., Pfeifer, E., & Hahne, A. (1993). Event-related brain potentials during natural speech processing: Effects of semantic, morphological and syntactic violations. *Cognitive Brain Research, 1,* 183–192.

Friederici, A. D., Steinhauer, K., & Pfeifer, E. (2002). Brain signatures of artificial language processing: Evidence challenging the "critical period" hypothesis. *Proceedings of the National Academy of Sciences (USA), 99,* 529–534.

Frisch, S., & Schlesewsky, M. (2001). The N400 reflects problems of thematic hierarchizing. *Neuroreport, 12,* 3391–3394.

Frisch, S., Schlesewsky, M., Saddy, D., & Alpermann, A. (2002). The P600 as an indicator of syntactic ambiguity. *Cognition, 85,* B83–B92.

Gandour, J., Wong, D., Hsieh, L., Weinzapfel, B., Van Lancker, D., & Hutchins, G. D. (2000). A crosslinguistic PET study of tone perception. *Journal of Cognitive Neuroscience, 12,* 207–222.

Grodzinsky, Y. (2000). The neural substrate of the language faculty: Suggestions for the future. *Brain and Language, 71,* 82–84.

Gunter, T. C., Friederici, A. D., & Hahne, A. (1999). Brain responses during sentence reading: Visual input affects central processes. *Neuroreport, 10,* 3175–3178.

Gunter, T. C., Stowe, L. A., & Mulder, G. (1997). When syntax meets semantics. *Psychophysiology, 34,* 660–676.

Hagoort, P., Brown, C., & Groothusen, J. (1993). The syntactic positive shift (SPS) as an ERP measure of syntactic processing. *Language and Cognitive Processes, 8,* 439–483.

Hahne, A. (2001). What's different in second-language processing? Evidence from event-related brain potentials. *Journal of Psycholinguistic Research, 30,* 251–266.

Hahne, A., & Friederici, A. D. (1999). Electrophysiological evidence for two steps in syntactic analysis: Early automatic and late controlled processes. *Journal of Cognitive Neuroscience, 11,* 194–205.

Hahne, A., & Friederici, A. D. (2001). Processing a second language: Late learners' comprehension strategies as revealed by event-related brain potentials. *Bilingualism: Language and Cognition, 4,* 123–141.

Hahne, A., & Friederici, A. D. (2002). Differential task effects on semantic and syntactic processes as revealed by ERPs. *Cognitive Brain Research, 13,* 339–356.

Hickok, G., Kirk, K., & Bellugi, U. (1998). Hemispheric organization of local- and global-level visuospatial processes in deaf signers and its relation to sign language aphasia. *Brain and Language, 65,* 276–286.

Holcomb, P. J., & Neville, H. J. (1990). Auditory and visual semantic priming in lexical decision: A comparison using event-related brain potentials. *Language and Cognitive Processes, 5,* 281–312.

Kaan, E., Harris, A., Gibson, E., & Holcomb, P. (2000). The P600 as an index of syntactic integration difficulty. *Language and Cognitive Processes, 15,* 159–201.

Kim, K. H. S., Relkin, N. R., Lee, K. M., & Hirsch, J. (1997). Distinct cortical areas associated with native and second languages. *Nature, 388,* 171–174.

Klein, D., Milner, B., Zatorre, R. J., Meyer, E., & Evans, A. C. (1995). The neural substrates underlying word generation: A bilingual functional-imaging study. *Proceedings of the National Academy of Sciences (USA), 92,* 2899–2903.

Kluender, K. R. (1991). Effects of first formant onset properties on voicing judgments result from processes not specific to humans. *Journal of the Acoustical Society of America, 90,* 83–96.

Koelsch, S., Gunter, T. C., Friederici, A. D., & Schröger, E. (2000). Brain indices of music processing: Non-musicians are musical. *Journal of Cognitive Neuroscience, 12,* 520–541.

Koelsch, S., Schröger, E., & Tervaniemi, M. (1999). Superior pre-attentive auditory processing in musicians. *Neuroreport, 10,* 1309–1313.

Kutas, M., & Hillyard, S. A. (1980). Reading senseless sentences: Brain potentials reflect semantic incongruity. *Science, 207,* 203–205.

Kutas, M., & Hillyard, S. A. (1984). Brain potentials during reading reflect word expectancy and semantic association. *Nature, 307,* 161–163.

Mueller, J. (2005). Electrophysiological correlates of second language processing. Second Language Research, 21(2), 152–174.

Münte, T. F., Matzke, M., & Johannes, S. (1997). Brain activity associated with syntactic incongruencies in words and pseudo-words. *Journal of Cognitive Neuroscience*, 9, 318–329.

Musso, M., Weiller, C., Kiebel, S., Müller, S. P., Bülau, P., & Rijntjes, M. (2003). Training-induced brain plasticity in aphasia. *Brain*, 122, 1781–1790.

Näätänen, R., Lehtokoski, A., Lennes, M., Cheour, M., Huotilainen, M., Iivonen, A., et al. (1997). Language-specific phoneme representations revealed by electric and magnetic brain responses. *Nature*, 385, 432–434.

Neville, H. J., Bavelier, D., Corina, D., Rauschecker, J., Karni, A., Lalwani, A., et al. (1998). Cerebral organization for language in deaf and hearing subjects: Biological constraints and effects of experience. *Proceedings of the National Academy of Sciences (USA)*, 95, 922–929.

Neville, H. J., Mills, D., & Lawson, D. (1992). Fractionating language: Different neural subsystems with different sensitive periods. *Cerebral Cortex*, 2, 244–258.

Neville, H. J., Nicol, J. L., Barss, A., Forster, K., & Garrett, M. (1991). Syntactically based sentence processing classes: Evidence from event-related brain potentials. *Journal of Cognitive Neuroscience*, 3, 151–165.

Osterhout, L., & Holcomb, P. J. (1992). Event-related brain potentials elicited by syntactic anomaly. *Journal of Memory and Language*, 31, 785–806.

Osterhout, L., & Mobley, L. A. (1995). Event-related brain potentials elicited by failure to agree. *Journal of Memory and Language*, 34, 739–773.

Pantev, C., Oostenveld, R., Engelien, A., Ross, B., Roberts, L. E., & Hoke, M. (1998). Increased auditory cortical representation in musicians. *Nature*, 392, 811–814.

Perani, D., Paulesu, E., Galles, N. S., Dupoux, E., Dehaene, S., Bettinardi, V., et al. (1998). The bilingual brain: Proficiency and age of acquisition of the second language. *Brain*, 121, 1841–1852.

Radeau, M., Besson, M., Fonteneau, E., & Castro, S. (1998). Semantic repetition and rime priming between spoken words: Behavioral and electrophysiological evidence. *Biological Psychology*, 48, 183–204.

Rivera-Gaxiola, M., Johnson, M., Csibra, G., & Karmiloff-Smith, A. (2000). Electrophysiological correlates of category goodness. *Behavioural Brain Research*, 112, 1–11.

Rüschemeyer, S.-A., Fiebach, C.J., Kempe, V. & Friederici, A.D. (2005). Processing lexical semantic and syntactic information in first and second language: fMRI evidence from Russian and German. *Human Brain Mapping*, 25, 266–286.

Stromswold, K., Caplan, D., Alpert, N., & Rauch, S. (1996). Localization of syntactic comprehension by positron emission tomography. *Brain and Language*, 52, 452–473.

Thompson-Schill, S. L., D'Esposito, M., Aguirre, G. K., & Farah, M. J. (1997). Role of left inferior prefrontal cortex in retrieval of semantic knowledge: A reevaluation. *Proceedings of the National Academy of Sciences (USA)*, 94, 14792–14797.

Weber-Fox, C., & Neville, H. J. (1996). Maturational constraints on functional specializations for language processing: ERP and behavioral evidence in bilingual speakers. *Journal of Cognitive Neuroscience*, 8, 231–256.

Werker, J. F., Gilbert, J. H., Humphrey, K., & Tees, R. C. (1981). Developmental aspects of cross-language speech perception. *Child Development, 52,* 349–355.

Werker, J. F., & Tees, R. C. (1983). Developmental changes across childhood in the perception of non-native speech sounds. *Canadian Journal of Psychology, 37,* 278–286.

Werker, J. F., & Tees, R. C. (2002). Cross-language speech perception: Evidence for perceptual reorganization during the first year of life. *Infant Behavior & Development, 25,* 121–133.

# 8

# Reading, Writing, and Arithmetic in the Brain: Neural Specialization for Acquired Functions

## Thad A. Polk and J. Paul Hamilton

ABSTRACT

*Different parts of the brain perform different, relatively self-contained functions. In many cases, this functional modularity is undoubtedly innately predetermined, but in other cases it seems likely that experience plays a significant role. We review evidence for experience-dependent neural modularity in three domains: reading, writing, and arithmetic. These skills are recent developments on an evolutionary time scale, they are not shared with nonhuman species, and they do not develop in humans without explicit, systematic instruction. It is therefore unlikely that their neural organization is innate. Nevertheless, findings from case studies of neurological patients and, more recently, from neuroimaging experiments suggest that the brains of educated adults do include neural modules dedicated to these functions.*

### READING, WRITING, AND ARITHMETIC IN THE BRAIN: NEURAL SPECIALIZATION FOR ACQUIRED FUNCTIONS

One of the central tenets of modern cognitive neuroscience is that the cortical architecture underlying cognition is organized into anatomically segregated subsystems (modules) that perform different functions. Most of the evidence for a modular organization comes from work with patients who are brain damaged. Focal brain lesions occasionally produce impairments that seem to affect a single behavioral function (e.g., color processing, visual object recognition, motor control on one side of the body) without significantly affecting others. A natural (although not always valid) interpretation of such dissociations is that the impaired function depends on a neural subsystem or module that is anatomically segregated from other functions and that is therefore vulnerable to selective damage. What might lead certain functions to become anatomically segregated from others?

In most cases, it is plausible to assume that the underlying neural seg-regation was genetically predetermined. Color processing, object recogni-tion, motor control, and many other behavioral functions that are vulner-able to selective impairment share characteristics that suggest a genetic account: they are old on an evolutionary scale, they are shared by non-human species, they provide a clear adaptive advantage, and they develop without systematic instruction. It is therefore natural to assume that genet-ics played a significant role in the localization and segregation of many of these functions.

However, a growing body of evidence from neuroscience has demon-strated conclusively that experience can and does lead to changes in neural organization (e.g., see Chapters 5 and 6). Receptive field sizes can be rapidly modified by the presentation of stimuli outside the previous receptive field, and somatosensory, auditory, visual, and motor maps (both cortical and subcortical) reorganize as a result of experience in a variety of species (e.g., Merzenich & Kaas, 1982). Changes in cortical maps can occur in days to weeks, and changes in sensory representations can occur even faster (min-utes to hours). Recent human studies have demonstrated similar effects. For example, the size of the posterior hippocampi correlates with amount of experience as a taxi driver (Maguire et al., 2000), consistent with the hypothesis that this brain area is important in spatial navigation and grows as a result of relevant experience. Similarly, the cortical representation of the fingers on the left hand is larger in right-handed string players than in control subjects, and the amount of reorganization correlates with the age at which the musician started playing (Elbert, Pantev, Wienbruch, Rockstroh, & Taub, 1995).

These studies have demonstrated what one might call *quantitative* effects on neural organization. The effects typically involve changes in the size or shape of a brain area devoted to a specific function, rather than the anatomic segregation of a function that was not previously localized (what one might call a *qualitative* change). For example, a somatosensory area that responds to sensation in the right index finger might grow larger with increasing stimulation of that finger, or it might invade and take over a neighboring area that was previously devoted to a finger whose sensory input was removed.

But given this quite compelling evidence for quantitative effects on neural organization, it is natural to ask whether experience can also lead to *qualitative* changes in brain organization, such as experience-dependent neural segregation of functions. The issue therefore is not simply whether the environment can influence the brain (it obviously can and does), nor is it whether some functions are anatomically localized in the brain (they obviously are). Rather, the issue is whether *experience* can lead to *quali-tative* changes in the brain's modular organization, specifically, whether behavioral functions that were not previously localized can become anatomically segregated as a result of experience. In this chapter, we review evidence regarding the neural substrates of reading, writing, and arithmetic that suggests that experience (in this case, schooling) can and does lead to qualitative changes in the brain's modular organization. Before doing so, however, it is worth being clear on what we mean by a neural "module."

## MODULARITY

In standard usage, the word module refers to a part or component of a larger system that performs a specific function and whose operation is relatively self-contained. For example, a typical computer system includes a keyboard, mouse, and monitor, in addition to the computer itself. Each component performs a specific function, and its operation is relatively self-contained (e.g., their operation does not depend critically on the operation of the rest of the system, aside from inputs, and the operation of the rest of the system does not depend critically on the operation of the module, aside from the module's outputs). Accordingly, these components could be described as modules in the overall computer system.

A widespread, if sometimes controversial, assumption in cognitive science is that the human mind and brain is also composed of modules. Fodor (1983) is best known for this claim. He provided an explicit set of criteria that, he argued, modules tend to satisfy, and then made the case that certain human input systems, but not more central cognitive systems, are modules. Like the common-sense definition just discussed, Fodor assumes that modules perform specific functions (i.e., they are domain specific) and that they are self-contained, both in terms of the computational resources they use and in terms of the information to which they have access (in Fodor's terms, they are computationally autonomous and informationally encapsulated). Fodor further assumes that modules are often self-contained anatomically; that is, they are anatomically localized in the brain.

To illustrate some of the issues that arise in discussing modularity, consider the case of face processing in ventral visual cortex. It is well known that damage to parts of extrastriate cortex can, in rare cases, lead to a deficit in recognizing faces without a corresponding deficit in the ability to recognize other categories of visual stimuli (Damasio, Damasio, & Van Hoesen, 1982). Neuroimaging results confirm that parts of ventral visual cortex (particularly, the fusiform gyrus) are activated significantly more by face stimuli than by other control stimuli (Kanwisher, McDermott, & Chun, 1997). Figure 8.1 illustrates the location of the fusiform gyrus, as well as many other neural structures that are mentioned in this chapter. Thus, there would seem to be evidence for domain specificity (for faces, but not other stimulus categories) and for self-containment (anatomical localization), as one would expect of a face processing module.

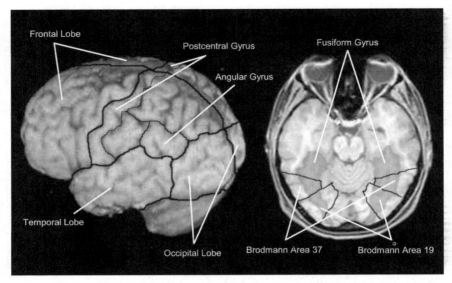

FIGURE 8.1. Location of a number of brain structures discussed in this chapter. (Left) Structures on the external surface of the left hemisphere. (Right) Structures on the ventral (bottom) surface of the brain.

This interpretation is controversial, however. Gauthier and colleagues argued that the so-called fusiform face area actually responds whenever people view stimuli that they are experts at recognizing. For example, car and bird experts activate this area when recognizing cars and birds (Gauthier, Skudlarski, Gore, & Anderson, 2000), and practice in recognizing unfamiliar nonface objects (so-called "greebles") also leads to activation in this area (Gauthier, Tarr, Anderson, Skudlarski, & Gore, 1999). These results undermine the claim that this area is devoted specifically to face recognition (i.e., that it is domain specific). Furthermore, Haxby and colleagues presented evidence suggesting that the cortical representation of faces is not, in fact, localized to the fusiform gyrus, potentially undermining the claim that it is self-contained (Haxby et al., 2001). These examples illustrate the importance of analyzing with great care the evidence for both domain specificity and self-containment. For present purposes, it is most important that, even if a neural face module could be firmly established, it would not demonstrate that *experience* can lead to the creation of new modules. The problem is that face recognition could well be innate: it is shared with other species, it develops without systematic instruction, it provides a clear adaptive advantage, and it is old on an evolutionary time scale.

In this chapter, we present evidence consistent with the claim that some of the neural systems involved in reading, writing, and arithmetic satisfy the two basic criteria of modularity, namely, domain specificity and self-containment. This claim is based primarily on evidence that brain damage can lead to behavioral deficits that are specific to these domains (although we also review other types of evidence as appropriate). We argue that the most natural explanation in each case is that the damaged tissue is dedicated to the acquired function, that it is self-contained both functionally and anatomically, and that it therefore constitutes a neural module. Furthermore, because these functions are acquired, are unique to humans, and are recent developments on an evolutionary time scale, it is unlikely that they could be innate. We thereby hope to provide support for the claim that experience can lead to the creation of new functional and anatomic modules in the human brain.

## READING

It is now well established that the ability to recognize visual words can be selectively impaired by brain damage, even while the ability to write, recognize other visual objects, and comprehend spoken language is relatively preserved. This pattern of impairments is known as *pure alexia* (Dejerine, 1892; Patterson & Kay, 1982; Warrington & Shallice, 1980). In most cases of pure alexia, the identification of individual letters is better than that of words and, indeed, pure alexic patients typically partially compensate for their impairment by naming the individual letters in a word to try to identify it. This letter-by-letter strategy leads to a number of characteristic effects: longer words take significantly longer to read than shorter words (typically, at least a 1-s increase with each additional letter), errors in letter identification lead to corresponding word identification errors (e.g., a patient who incorrectly names the letters in "hall" as "b-a-l-l" may incorrectly identify the word as "ball"), and linguistic factors (e.g., part of speech, orthographic regularity, concreteness) do not influence word recognition accuracy like they do in normal readers. There is also evidence that some pure alexics can extract partial information from words that they cannot explicitly recognize (e.g., performing above chance on lexical decision and semantic categorization tasks with briefly presented words that they fail to identify; Coslett & Saffran, 1989). The syndrome is typically associated with damage to the posterior portion of the left hemisphere (Binder & Mohr, 1992).

Given that pure alexia dissociates from other visual recognition deficits and from other language deficits, it is natural to assume it reflects damage to a neural system that includes modules specialized for orthography. Many theories of pure alexia do indeed make that assumption. For example, the traditional account of pure alexia is that it is due to a *disconnection* between visual information in the right hemisphere and an orthography-specific module in the left angular gyrus that represents the "optical image for words" (Dejerine, 1892; Geschwind, 1965; see Fig. 8.1 for localization of the angular gyrus). Warrington and Shallice (1980) proposed that pure alexia reflects damage to a word form system that is used to represent all word-like stimuli (but not other visual stimuli). Patterson and Kay (1982) also assumed a reading-specific module such as the word form system, although they attributed pure alexia to an impairment in the transmission of letter information to that module. Arguin and Bub (1993) suggested that the processing of letters themselves (specifically, the computation of abstract orthographic codes) was impaired, but again this theory assumes a neural module that is specialized for reading.

In a positron emission tomography study, Petersen, Fox, Snyder, and Raichle (1990) found areas in left medial extrastriate cortex that behaved like one might expect cortical areas devoted to reading to behave. They responded significantly more to word-like stimuli (words and pseudowords) than to letter strings that were not word-like (consonant string nonwords). A number of subsequent imaging studies have also found that words and word-like visual stimuli lead to activation in left ventral visual cortex and have localized this activity to be on or near the posterior part of the left fusiform gyrus in Brodmann's area 37 or 19 (Fig. 8.1; Cohen et al., 2000; Polk & Farah, 1998, 2002; Polk et al., 2002) or in a more superior temporal site (Howard et al., 1992).

Although these results are consistent with neural specialization for reading, other theories have explained pure alexia in terms of a more general perceptual problem, without appealing to a neural module that is specialized for orthography. For example, Kinsbourne and Warrington (1962) presented evidence consistent with the hypothesis that pure alexia arises from a difficulty in encoding many separate visual forms simultaneously or in very rapid succession. According to this view, the fact that the impairment manifests itself most clearly in reading simply reflects the fact that reading, perhaps more than any other visual recognition task, requires the simultaneous recognition of multiple forms (i.e., the letters in words). In particular, such theories need not assume the existence of a neural module that is specialized for reading. Similarly, Rapp and Caramazza (1991) proposed that pure alexic patients may have impaired feature representations toward the right side of stimuli (in both retinocentric and stimulus-centered frames of reference) and that this perceptual impairment could give rise to the reading deficits observed in pure alexia. Again, according to this hypothesis, one need not posit a reading-specific neural module.

In short, the issue of whether pure alexia implies reading-specific neural modules (and therefore experience-dependent neural segregation) is unresolved. The evidence certainly suggests the existence of such modules, but it is not yet possible to rule out alternative interpretations. Part of the problem is that words differ from other visual stimuli along a variety of dimensions, and thus perceptual impairments that selectively affect such a dimension could manifest themselves as visual word recognition deficits.

There is, however, some evidence for a much cleaner dissociation, namely, a selective deficit in recognizing letters but not digits. In rare cases, patients who have a profound deficit in recognizing letters nevertheless do not have difficulty (or significantly less difficulty) in recognizing digits and numbers (Anderson, Damasio, & Damasio, 1990). This suggests that even letter and digit recognition may depend on independent neural substrates. Consistent with this hypothesis, Allison, McCarthy, Nobre, Puce, and Belger (1994) studied patients with electrodes chronically implanted in ventral visual cortex and found that letter strings and numbers evoked negative potentials at different locations.

Previous neuroimaging experiments have found a similar dissociation: an area in left inferior occipitotemporal cortex that responds significantly more to consonant strings than number strings (Polk & Farah, 1998; Polk et al., 2002). These results are more compelling than are selective impairments in visual word recognition because letters and digits are very closely matched along most stimulus dimensions. Indeed, Polk et al. (2002) found evidence of specialization for letter recognition in Brodmann's area 37 in the left hemisphere (Fig. 8.1), even after controlling for differences in the physical features that make up letters and digits, in the number of characters presented from each category, and in the frequency with which each individual character was presented. These results provide some of the strongest evidence in support of the hypothesis that experience can lead to neural specialization and against the idea that neural organization is genetically predetermined.

## WRITING

Like reading, writing can also be selectively impaired by brain damage, even while spoken language and motor control are relatively preserved. A number of case studies exhibiting such a *pure dysgraphia* have been reported (Alexander, Fischer, & Friedman, 1992). Only a few neuroimaging studies have investigated writing, but they also support the claim that writing elicits activation in brain areas that are not used in other language production and motor control tasks (e.g., Katanoda, Yoshikawa, & Sugishita, 2001). Writing is a particularly demanding fine-motor control task, so impairments in motor control could certainly disproportionately affect writing compared with other motor tasks. Nevertheless, many cases of dysgraphia are best characterized as central spelling deficits rather than more peripheral writing deficits because they affect oral spelling and handwriting (Beauvois & Derouesne, 1981; Shallice, 1981). Indeed, in most cases of pure dysgraphia, the patients are able to make well-formed letters, hence demonstrating relatively preserved motor control. Their spelling is what is most impaired. Spelling is an acquired skill that presumably has no genetic basis, so these findings provide further evidence that experience (in this case, learning to write) can lead to neural specialization for an acquired function.

Furthermore, evidence suggests that a number of component processes in writing are themselves localized and are therefore vulnerable to selective impairment. For example, within the more central spelling system, there appear to be at least two (and potentially more) different routes to spelling: a phonological route in which words are spelled by sounding them out and a lexical route in which the spelling of familiar words is simply retrieved from memory. The main evidence for this division comes from patients in whom one or the other route is selectively impaired. Lexical dysgraphics (also called surface dysgraphics) are disproportionately impaired at spelling irregular words (e.g., *yacht*) whose pronunciation does not correspond to its spelling, compared with words (or nonwords) whose spelling is more regular (Beauvois & Derouesne, 1981). Such patients are typically assumed to have a selective impairment in the lexical (whole word) route to spelling. The assumption is that they are unable to look up a word's spelling directly in the lexicon (because of damage to the lexical spelling route), so they must therefore sound words out and guess their spelling based on how they sound (i.e., by using their alternative phonological route to spelling). A lexical dysgraphic might therefore produce *yot* as a potential spelling for *yacht* because *yot* is what the word sounds like.

Conversely, phonological dysgraphics can spell most real words, regardless of whether they are irregular, but are severely impaired when it comes to spelling nonwords such as *plid* or *sart* (Shallice, 1981). These patients are assumed to have a selective impairment in the phonological (sound-it-out) route to spelling, which leads them to rely on the lexical (look-it-up) route. Of course, the lexical route only works for real words because nonwords would not have an entry in the lexicon. This assumption explains why phonological dysgraphics are able to spell both regular and irregular real words (they can look them up), but are unable to spell nonwords (which must be sounded out because they cannot be looked up).

The output of the spelling system is typically assumed to be a graphemic code that represents the identities of the letters to be produced, but not the details of their case, style, size, and so on. The more peripheral motor side of writing involves converting this abstract graphemic representation into a sequence of motor movements, and evidence suggests that there is modularity at this level of processing as well. Most models of writing specify at least two additional stages of processing after the graphemic representation has been computed: an allographic stage and a graphomotor stage. In the allographic stage, a visuospatial representation of the letters is computed that includes their specific physical characteristics (e.g., case, style). In the graphomotor stage, allographic representations are converted into the motor programs necessary to execute the set of strokes involved in writing the letters. Evidence suggests that these two stages of writing can be selectively impaired by brain damage.

For example, numerous patients have been reported who have writing deficits despite being able to write individual letters and being able to spell orally (De Bastiani & Barry, 1989; Goodman & Caramazza, 1986). At least two patients have been described who mistakenly mixed upper- and lowercase letters (e.g., "forza" written as F-o-r-Z-A) when writing aurally presented and internally generated words (despite relatively correct spelling and well-formed letters; De Bastiani & Barry, 1989). The fact that oral spelling is relatively preserved in these patients suggests that their impairment affects a processing stage that is downstream from the abstract graphemic representation that spelling computes. The fact that they can write well-formed letters suggests that the final graphomotor stage is also relatively preserved. The deficit is therefore typically attributed to the allographic stage of processing (or to a process that transforms the graphemic representation into an allographic representation).

There is also evidence that the graphomotor stage of writing can be selectively impaired by brain damage, even without a more general motor programming deficit (an apraxia). For example, Otsuki, Soma, Arai, Otsuka, and Tsuji (1999) reported a Japanese patient who could execute meaningful motor gestures and copy complex figures. His oral spelling of words was also intact, and he could even give correct verbal descriptions of how to write characters in both Kanji and Kana alphabets. Nevertheless, the patient made frequent errors in writing the characters. Twenty-five percent of the time, the patient either demonstrated unusual stroke sequences, rendered malformed strokes, or did not use the proper set of strokes for a letter. This deficit points to a decrement at the graphomotor level of word and letter writing.

Perhaps most surprising, a number of cases have been reported in which writing was selectively impaired for a particular style of writing (e.g., cursive vs. print), for lower- versus uppercase, and for letters but not digits. Venneri and Pestell (2002) described two mild Alzheimer's patients who exhibited a double dissociation between writing in cursive and in print, despite intact reading, oral spelling, and copying of letters. Hanley and Peters (1996) reported a patient with a selective deficit in writing lowercase but not uppercase letters. Furthermore, this impairment was restricted to print (the patient could still write lowercase letters in cursive). Anderson et al. (1990) described a patient who exhibited writing deficits that were much more severe for letters than numbers. The distinctions between cursive and print, between uppercase and lowercase, and between letters and digits are obviously all culturally defined and are learned by experience. These cases therefore support the hypothesis that cortical areas can become specialized for acquired functions that have no genetic basis.

ARITHMETIC

In the early twentieth century, a number of neurologists described patients with brain damage suffering from what has come to be called *acalculia*, that is, an impairment in mathematical calculation (Lewandowsky & Stadelmann, 1908; Peritz, 1918). There has been some debate over whether calculation is dependent on language processing, but some recent cases have demonstrated a clear double dissociation (Rossor, Warrington, & Cipolotti, 1995). Even before this dissociation was established, however, many theorists had proposed a neurally segregated calculation center in the brain. Lewandowsky and Stadelmann (1908) located this center in the left occipital lobe, whereas Peritz (1918) located it in the left angular gyrus. Goldstein (1948) argued that the left parietal-occipital region and/or frontal lobes were impaired in most cases of acalculia (Fig. 8.1 illustrates the location of some of these areas). Hecaen, Angelergues, and Houillier (1961) argued that calculation should be localized to the parietal lobes bilaterally. More recently, Ojemann (1974) demonstrated that backward counting and simple calculations could be disrupted by bilateral stimulation of the ventrolateral thalamus.

Obviously, a variety of different brain areas have been implicated in calculation, so it is natural to wonder whether calculation is a unitary process that is anatomically localized or whether instead it should be broken down into subprocesses. Collignon, Leclercq, and Mahy (1977) studied the calculation abilities of 26 neurological patients with a variety of different lesion sites and concluded that acalculia could arise from damage to many different brain areas. Similarly, Kahn and Whitaker (1991) performed an extensive review of reported cases of acalculia and concluded that acalculia could be associated with lesions in anterior or posterior areas, in left or right hemisphere, and in both cortical and subcortical structures. These authors argued that the evidence undermined the idea of a localized neural calculation center.

Recent work on acalculia has focused on breaking down number processing into subprocesses, some of which have been hypothesized to be anatomically localized. For example, Dehaene and Cohen (1991) described a patient whose *precise* knowledge of numbers and arithmetical operations was dramatically impaired, but whose ability to *approximate* quantities and to make use of approximations was intact. For example, this patient could quickly and accurately reject arithmetic problems in which the answer was not even approximately correct (e.g., 2 + 2 = 9); however, the patient could not reject problems in which the answer was close but still incorrect (e.g., 2 + 2 = 5). This distinction between exact and approximate calculation is also supported by both neuroimaging evidence and behavioral results (Dehaene, Spelke, Pinel, Stanescu, & Tsivkin, 1999). Dehaene and Cohen (1995) proposed that the brain includes a module for processing analogue quantities and localized the module to the inferior parietal cortex (which includes the angular gyrus; Fig. 8.1).

We would argue that these findings provide less compelling evidence for experience-dependent neural specialization than the data from reading and writing, however. There is evidence to suggest that nonhuman animals and preverbal infants can represent and manipulate quantity information (Gallistel & Gelman, 1992), so it is natural to assume that this ability has a genetic basis. Thus, even if certain cortical areas are specialized for processing quantity information, this would not provide strong evidence in favor of *experience-dependent* neural specialization; the specialization may be genetic.

Perhaps the most promising evidence for experience-dependent specialization in number processing is based on selective impairments in semantic knowledge about numbers. A number of patients have now been described whose number knowledge seems to be disrupted. For example, Warrington (1982) described a patient, DRC, whose knowledge of arithmetic facts was selectively impaired. DRC understood the concept of quantity and what individual numbers referred to, yet he was unable to perform basic arithmetical operations (addition, subtraction, multiplication) normally. He did appear to understand how these operations worked (e.g., that multiplication corresponds to repeated addition), but he had lost his knowledge of memorized math facts (e.g., that $3 + 5 = 8$ and $9 - 6 = 3$). Warrington concluded that semantic memory is organized categorically at an anatomical level (in distinct modules), and that arithmetic facts constitute one subcategory that can be selectively impaired. Because this category of information is not innate, it supports the hypothesis that experience (in this case, learning and using the facts of arithmetic) can lead to neural segregation of function. Cipolotti, Butterworth, and Denes (1991) described a similar patient, CG, who exhibited a relatively preserved ability to deal with numbers less than 4, but not with numbers higher than 4. This dissociation was apparent across modalities and across a wide range of tasks. CG did not have a more general semantic impairment or reasoning deficit, so the authors concluded that she had a selective deficit in number knowledge.

Polk, Reed, Keenan, Hogarth, and Anderson (2001) presented a similar patient, MC, who exhibited a domain-specific impairment in number knowledge following a left middle cerebral artery stroke. She was dramatically impaired on all tasks involving number symbols: identifying and comparing the magnitude of Arabic numbers, counting, performing simple calculations, and writing numbers to dictation. Her impairment was apparent in auditory and tactile tasks, suggesting that her impairment was modality independent. Her deficit also extended to concepts related to numbers. For example, she had lost her knowledge of Roman numerals, of cardinal facts (e.g., how many days in a week? hours in a day?), and of what arithmetical symbols meant (e.g., $+, -, =, \%, \div$, decimal point). Even

TABLE 8.1. *Definitions of Number-Related Words Given by Patient MC After a Left Middle Cerebral Artery Stroke*

| Word | Response |
|------|----------|
| Dozen | No idea, no guess |
| Half | Half a gallon |
| Score | Keep score when bowling |
| Pair | Pair of nylons |
| Single | I'm single and available |
| Gross | Yucky |
| Trio | No guess |
| Quartet | Music guys |
| Twin | Had twins, two kids |
| Unit | Stereo unit |
| Quarter | Coin |
| Sextet | No guess |

her definitions of number-related words were impaired and often failed to convey the aspect of the definition related to numbers (Table 8.1).

In contrast to her dramatic impairment in number knowledge, her knowledge of other semantic categories was well preserved. She could identify and name pictures of living and nonliving things quickly and easily. She could provide reasonable definitions for nonnumber words and identify synonyms. She could fluently generate lists of fruits, animals, and vegetables. Even her knowledge of nonnumeric sequences (e.g., days of the week, alphabet) was preserved.

Furthermore, MC was quite capable of dealing with analogue magnitudes. She could order objects by size or pick out the largest or smallest of a set. When shown two piles of pennies or two glasses of water, she could choose the one with "more." She could also correctly answer questions about imagined quantities, such as "Would there be more coffee beans or sugar grains in a cup?" She could also accurately determine which of two words occurred more often in a list (although she would not be able to report the actual number of times a word occurred).

We would characterize MC's deficit as impaired access to symbolic knowledge about numbers. A natural interpretation of MC's case is that symbolic knowledge about numbers is anatomically segregated from knowledge of other domains. Because symbolic number knowledge is acquired (typically, in school), this case is consistent with the hypothesis that cortical areas can become specialized for behavioral functions that are acquired and have no genetic basis. Furthermore, MC's deficits cannot be attributed to an impaired quantity representation module (whose anatomical localization might plausibly be assumed to have a genetic basis as previously discussed). Indeed, her processing of analogue quantity information was intact. The number knowledge that MC lost was the very knowledge that is acquired. Her case therefore provides some of the strongest evidence for experience-dependent neural specialization within the general domain of arithmetic and number processing.

GENERAL DISCUSSION

In this chapter, we review evidence for neural specialization in the domains of reading, writing, and arithmetic. These results provide some of the most compelling evidence in support of the hypothesis that experience can lead to neural specialization and against the idea that the modular organization of cortex is determined exclusively by genetics. The paradox is that reading, writing, and arithmetic are very recent developments on an evolutionary scale; there simply has not been time for evolution to develop specialized mechanisms to deal with them. They are also obviously unique to the human species so there is no obvious phylogenetic source on which evolution can draw. These skills may provide some adaptive advantage, but it is clearly less significant than the advantages provided by sensorimotor functions and other examples of localized functions, especially considering that a large portion of the world's population is not literate or trained in math. Finally, these skills obviously do not develop automatically; they require years of systematic training.

The most natural explanation is an important one: somehow, the cultural experiences of learning to read, write, and do arithmetic are producing significant, qualitative changes in brain organization. These are not simply cases in which experience is modulating the size of a brain area. Rather, they suggest that experience can lead to the development of new functional brain areas that perform functions acquired through experience.

It is important to note that reading, writing, and arithmetic all depend on a variety of cognitive and neural mechanisms that presumably *are* innate. For example, reading depends on the rapid recognition of multiple shapes (not to mention more basic visual processes), writing depends on fine manual motor control, and mathematics depends on the ability to represent analogue quantity. Heredity could play a significant role in the development and neural organization of any or all these functions, so it would not be surprising to find that developmental dyslexia or some other disorder of reading, writing, or arithmetic has a hereditary component (see Fischer & DeFries, 2002, for evidence of such a hereditary component in developmental dyslexia). We would suggest, however, that such genetic links reflect aspects of these skills that are not domain specific. Otherwise, one would have to explain how evolution managed to produce an innate neural organization for a function that is recent in evolutionary time, is not shared with other species, and does not develop without instruction. That said, we have tried to make clear that the evidence does suggest that neural specialization can occur for functions that *are* specific to these skills. In our view, the most natural explanation is that experience has led to the development of specialized tissue to deal with these functions.

Why would the brain develop specialized tissue for these skills rather than for some others? One obvious explanation is that reading, writing, and arithmetic are perhaps the most important intellectual skills that are acquired by instruction. They are explicitly taught to children and are practiced extensively throughout life by those who have acquired them. Apparently, the brain can reshape its modular architecture in response to the most important demands of its culture. These domains therefore provide a particularly clear example of biocultural co-construction: biology and culture are interacting to construct the mind's neural architecture.

## References

Alexander, M. P., Fischer, R. S., & Friedman, R. (1992). Lesion localization in apractic agraphia. *Archives of Neurology, 49* (3), 246–251.
Allison, T., McCarthy, G., Nobre, A., Puce, A., & Belger, A. (1994). Human extrastriate visual cortex and the perception of faces, words, numbers, and colors. *Cerebral Cortex, 4,* 544–554.
Anderson, S. W., Damasio, A. R., & Damasio, H. (1990). Troubled letters but not numbers. *Brain, 113,* 749–766.
Arguin, M., & Bub, D. N. (1993). Single-character processing in a case of pure alexia. *Neuropsychologia, 31,* 435–458.
Beauvois, M. F., & Derouesne, J. (1981). Lexical or orthographic agraphia. *Brain, 104,* 21–49.
Binder, J. R., & Mohr, J. P. (1992). The topography of callosal reading pathways: A case-control analysis. *Brain, 115,* 1807–1826.
Cipolotti, L., Butterworth, B., & Denes, G. (1991). A specific deficit for numbers in a case of dense acalculia. *Brain, 114,* 2619–2637.
Cohen, L., Dehaene, S., Naccache, L., Lehericy, S., Dehaene-Lambertz, G., Henaff, M. A., & Michel, F. (2000). The visual word form area: Spatial and temporal characterization of an initial stage of reading in normal subjects and posterior split-brain patients. *Brain, 123,* 291–307.
Collignon, R., Leclercq, C., & Mahy, J. (1977). Symptomatology of dyscalculia in the presence of cortical lesions. *Acta Neurologica Belgica, 77* (5), 257–275.
Coslett, H. B., & Saffran, E. M. (1989). Evidence for preserved reading in pure alexia. *Brain, 112,* 327–359.
Damasio, A. R., Damasio, H., & Van Hoesen, G. W. (1982). Prosopagnosia: Anatomic basis and behavioral mechanisms. *Neurology, 32,* 331–341.
De Bastiani, P., & Barry, C. (1989). A cognitive analysis of an acquired dysgraphic patient with an allographic writing disorder. *Cognitive Neuropsychology, 6* (1), 25–41.

Dehaene, S., & Cohen, L. (1991). Two mental calculation systems: A case study of severe acalculia with preserved approximation. *Neuropsychologia, 29* (11), 1045–1074.

Dehaene, S., & Cohen, L. (1995). Towards an anatomical and functional model of number processing. *Mathematical Cognition, 1,* 83–120.

Dehaene, S., Spelke, E., Pinel, P., Stanescu, R., & Tsivkin, S. (1999). Sources of mathematical thinking: Behavioral and brain-imaging evidence. *Science, 284,* 970–974.

Dejerine, J. (1892). Contribution à l'étude anatomo-pathologique et clinique des différentes variétés de cécité verbale [Contribution to the anatomo-pathologic and clinical study of the different varieties of verbal blindness]. *Mémoires de la Société de Biologie, 4,* 61–90.

Elbert, T., Pantev, C., Wienbruch, C., Rockstroh, B., & Taub, E. (1995). Increased cortical representation of the fingers of the left hand in string players. *Science, 270,* 305–307.

Fisher, S. E., & DeFries, J. C. (2002). Developmental dyslexia: Genetic dissection of a complex cognitive trait. *Nature Reviews Neuroscience, 3,* 767–780.

Fodor, J. (1983). *Modularity of mind.* Cambridge, MA: MIT Press.

Gallistel, C. R., & Gelman, R. (1992). Preverbal and verbal counting and computation. *Cognition, 44* (1–2), 43–74.

Gauthier, I., Skudlarski, P., Gore, J. C., & Anderson, A. W. (2000). Expertise for cars and birds recruits brain areas involved in face recognition. *Nature Neuroscience, 3,* 191–197.

Gauthier, I., Tarr, M. J., Anderson, A. W., Skudlarski, P., & Gore, J. C. (1999). Activation of the middle fusiform "face area" increases with expertise in recognizing novel objects. *Nature Neuroscience, 2,* 568–573.

Geschwind, N. (1965). Disconnection syndromes in animals and man. *Brain, 88,* 237– 294, 585–644.

Goldstein, K. (1948). *Language and language disturbances.* New York: Grune & Stratton.

Goodman, R. A., & Caramazza, A. (1986). Dissociation of spelling errors in written and oral spelling: The role of allographic conversion in writing. *Cognitive Neuropsychology, 3* (2), 179–206.

Hanley, J. R., & Peters, S. (1996). A dissociation between the ability to print and write cursively in lower-case letters. *Cortex, 32* (4), 737–745.

Haxby, J. V., Gobbini, M. I., Furey, M. L., Ishai, A., Schouten, J. L., & Pietrini, P. (2001). Distributed and overlapping representations of faces and objects in ventral temporal cortex. *Science, 293,* 2425–2430.

Hecaen, H., Angelergues, R., & Houillier, S. (1961). Les variétés cliniques des acalculies au cours lésions retrorolandiques: Aproche statistique du problème [The clinical varieties of acalculias during retrorolandic lesions: Statistical approach to the problem]. *Revue Neurologique, 105,* 85–103.

Howard, D., Patterson, K., Wise, R., Brown, W. D., Friston, K., Weiller, C., & Frackowiak, R. (1992). The cortical localization of the lexicons: Positron emission tomography evidence. *Brain, 115,* 1769–1782.

Kahn, H. J., & Whitaker, H. A. (1991). Acalculia: An historical review of localization. *Brain and Cognition, 17* (2), 102–115.

Kanwisher, N., McDermott, J., & Chun, M. M. (1997). The fusiform face area: A module in human extrastriate cortex specialized for face perception. *Journal of Neuroscience, 17,* 4302–4311.

Katanoda, K., Yoshikawa, K., & Sugishita, M. (2001). A functional MRI study of the neural substrates for writing. *Human Brain Mapping, 13,* 34–42.

Kinsbourne, M., & Warrington, E. K. (1962). A disorder of simultaneous form perception. *Brain, 85,* 461–486.

Lewandowsky, M., & Stadelmann, E. (1908). Über einen bemerkenswerten Fall von Hirnblutung und über Rechenstörungen bei Herderkrankung des Gehirns [On a remarkable case of brain bleeding and on calculation disturbances in focal disease of the brain]. *Journal fur Psychologie und Neurologie, 11,* 249–265.

Maguire, E. A., Gadian, D. G., Johnsrude, I. S., Good, C. D., Ashburner, J., Frackowiak, R. S. J., & Frith, C. D. (2000). Navigation-related structural change in the hippocampi of taxi drivers. *Proceedings of the National Academy of Sciences (USA), 97,* 4398–4403.

Merzenich, M. M., & Kaas, J. H. (1982). Reorganization of mammalian somatosensory cortex following peripheral nerve injury. *Trends in Neuroscience, 5,* 434–436.

Ojemann, G. A. (1974). Mental arithmetic during human thalamic stimulation. *Neuropsychologia, 12,* 1–10.

Otsuki, M., Soma, Y., Arai, T., Otsuka, A., & Tsuji, S. (1999). Pure apraxic agraphia with abnormal writing stroke sequences: Report of a Japanese patient with a left superior parietal haemorrhage. *Journal of Neurology, Neurosurgery and Psychiatry, 66* (2), 233–237.

Patterson, K. E., & Kay, J. (1982). Letter-by-letter reading: Psychological descriptions of a neurological syndrome. *Quarterly Journal of Experimental Psychology, 34A,* 411–441.

Peritz, G. (1918). Zur Pathopsychologie des Rechnens. *Deutsche Zeitschrift fur Nervenheilkunde, 61,* 234–340.

Petersen, S. E., Fox, P. T., Snyder, A. Z., & Raichle, M. E. (1990). Activation of extrastriate and frontal cortical areas by visual words and word-like stimuli. *Science, 249,* 1041–1044.

Polk, T. A., & Farah, M. J. (1998). The neural localization of letter recognition: Behavioral, computational, and neuroimaging studies. *Proceedings of the National Academy of Sciences (USA), 95,* 847–852.

Polk, T. A., & Farah, M. J. (2002). Functional MRI evidence for an abstract, not visual, word-form area. *Journal of Experimental Psychology: General, 131* (1), 65–72.

Polk, T. A., Reed, C. L., Keenan, J. M., Hogarth, P., & Anderson, C. A. (2001). A dissociation between symbolic number knowledge and analogue magnitude information. *Brain and Cognition, 47* (3), 545–563.

Polk, T. A., Stallcup, M., Aguirre, G. K., Alsop, D. C., D'Esposito, M., Detre, J. A., & Farah, M. J. (2002). Neural specialization for letter recognition. *Journal of Cognitive Neuroscience, 14* (2), 145–159.

Rapp, B. C., & Caramazza, A. (1991). Spatially determined deficits in letter and word processing. *Cognitive Neuropsychology, 8* (3–4), 275–311.

Rossor, M. N., Warrington, E. K., & Cipolotti, L. (1995). The isolation of calculation skills. *Journal of Neurology, 242* (2), 78–81.

Shallice, T. (1981). Phonological agraphia and the lexical route in writing. *Brain*, *104*, 413–429.

Venneri, A., & Pestell, S. J. (2002). Independent representations for cursive and print style: Evidence from dysgraphia in Alzheimer's disease. *Cognitive Neuropsychology*, *19* (5), 387–400.

Warrington, E. K. (1982). The fractionation of arithmetical skills: A single case study. *Quarterly Journal of Experimental Psychology*, *34A*, 31–51.

Warrington, E. K., & Shallice, T. (1980). Word-form dyslexia. *Brain*, *103*, 99–112.

# 9

## Emotion, Learning, and the Brain: From Classical Conditioning to Cultural Bias

Elizabeth A. Phelps

ABSTRACT

*Classical conditioning, described by Pavlov, has emerged as an important tool in our efforts to understand the mechanisms of emotional learning. Using a classical fear conditioning paradigm, research with nonhuman animals has identified the amygdala as a critical structure for emotional learning. This chapter reviews how studies in humans have extended the role of the amygdala to social means of emotional learning and culturally acquired race bias. Although cultural knowledge and some forms of social communication may be uniquely human characteristics, how emotional value is expressed in these domains seems to rely on basic mechanisms that are shared across species.*

OVERVIEW

The basic principles of classical conditioning were identified by Ivan Pavlov more than a century ago when he showed that dogs would salivate to the ringing of a bell that had previously been paired with the delivery of food. More recently, investigators have used classical conditioning paradigms to help understand the neural mechanisms of emotional learning. These studies have focused on classical fear conditioning. In a typical fear conditioning paradigm, a neutral stimulus, called the conditioned stimulus (CS), is paired with an aversive event, the unconditioned stimulus (UCS). After a few pairings, the animal learns that CS predicts the UCS, and this previously neutral stimulus begins to elicit a fear response, called the conditioned response (CR). Using this paradigm, scientists studying nonhuman animals have been able to map the neural pathways of emotional learning from stimulus input to response output (see LeDoux, 2002, for a review).

Simple learning paradigms, such as classical conditioning, are powerful tools in our efforts to understand the neural mechanisms of emotion for a number of reasons – the basic parameters are precisely defined, the principles are consistent across species, and they are relatively easy to study in the laboratory. However, a potential disadvantage of using classical fear conditioning as a general model for emotional learning is that it may be too simple to capture the complex social and cultural interactions that comprise most everyday human emotional learning situations. Although pairing a tone (CS), for instance, with a shock (UCS) may be an adequate analogy for a child learning to avoid putting his or her hand near a stove after accidentally being burned, it may not be an adequate model for learning the subtleties of social dynamics or cultural biases.

In this chapter, I present evidence suggesting that even though classical fear conditioning is a relatively simple, nonsocial form of associative learning, the basic neural mechanisms of emotional learning identified with this model paradigm may also underlie a range of social and cultural learning circumstances. The similarity in the neural mechanisms of classical conditioning and social learning implies that the basic principles of emotional learning may be the same, even though the content and complexity of stimuli may vary widely. By examining the similarities and differences in neural circuits of fear learning across social and nonsocial domains, we can draw on detailed animal models to help inform our understanding of complex human behaviors. We can also begin to understand how social communication results in changes in the neural systems of emotion, and how these changes in brain function may underlie both individual and cultural differences.

Our understanding of the neural systems of emotion in humans is just beginning to emerge, and this initial work is somewhat limited in that it focuses on a few brain structures and is largely confined to adult populations. In an effort to provide a comprehensive review of how a simple associative learning model may help inform complex cultural learning, this chapter focuses on the role of a phylogenetically old, subcortical brain structure, the amygdala, and research conducted in healthy adults.

## NEURAL MECHANISMS OF FEAR CONDITIONING: FROM RATS TO HUMANS

Recent investigations of fear conditioning in nonhuman animals have identified the neural circuits of emotional learning and determined that the amygdala plays a key role. The amygdala is a small almond-shaped structure in the medial temporal lobe that sits anterior and adjacent to the hippocampus (Fig. 9.1). It was first identified as a potentially important region in emotion processing when Kluver and Bucy (1937) damaged the medial temporal lobes in monkeys and observed a range of odd emotional responses, including the tendency to approach feared objects. Weiskrantz (1956) later isolated the amygdala as the primary structure

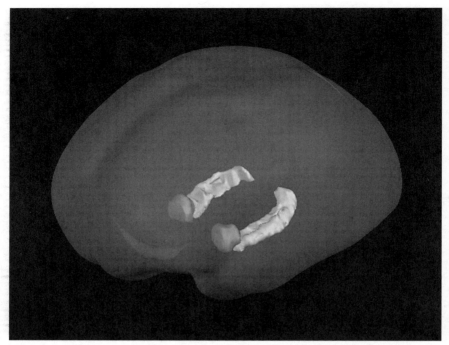

FIGURE 9.1. Human amygdala (dark) and hippocampus (light). (Adapted from Phelps, 2004.)

whose damage resulted in what came to be known as Klüver-Bucy syndrome. It has been proposed that the amygdala is a key structure in a network of brain regions believed to be important for normal emotion processing (Papez, 1937). A modified version of this network identified by Papez has been referred to as the "limbic system," although there is now considerable debate as to whether this is an appropriate term given that there are no clear inclusion or exclusion criteria for "limbic" structures (LeDoux, 1996).

One of the amygdala's primary roles in emotion processing is emotional learning, and it has been shown to be critical for the acquisition and expression of fear conditioning (Davis, 1997; Kapp, Frysinger, Gallagher, & Haselton, 1979; LeDoux, 1996). For instance, in a typical fear conditioning paradigm in rats, a tone (CS) is paired with a footshock (UCS). Although the tone by itself does not normally elicit a strong response, after a few pairings with the shock, the rat will show classic fear reactions, such as freezing and increased heart rate, to the presentation of the tone alone. However, if the amygdala is lesioned, the rat will fail to demonstrate any conditioned fear response to the tone, although it will continue to respond to the shock. By using a combination of neuroscience techniques in rats, researchers have determined that the amygdala plays a role in all stages of fear conditioning – acquisition, storage, and expression (see LeDoux, 2002, for a review). Recent evidence suggests that the amygdala may also be important for extinction learning, in which a CS that was previously paired with a UCS is then presented without the UCS for a number of trials, and the animal learns that the CS no longer predicts an aversive consequence (Falls, Miserendino, & Davis, 1992).

It is not possible to study the neural systems in humans with the same level of specificity as in nonhuman animals; however, studies examining human brain function are largely consistent with the mechanisms of fear learning identified in rats. In humans, a typical fear conditioning paradigm might consist of a neutral stimulus, such as a blue square (CS), being paired with mild shock to the wrist (UCS). After a few pairings, the blue square by itself will begin to elicit a range of physiological responses indicative of fear or arousal, such as increased sweating (as assessed by the skin conductance response), changes in heart rate, or increased startle. However, much like in rats, if the human amygdala is damaged, these conditioned fear responses are not expressed, even though the response to shock is normal (Bechara et al., 1995; LaBar, LeDoux, Spencer, & Phelps, 1995). Studies using functional magnetic resonance imaging (fMRI) have observed activation of the amygdala to a CS during fear conditioning (Buchel, Morris, Dolan, & Friston, 1998; LaBar, Gatenby, Gore, LeDoux, & Phelps, 1998). The strength of this activation is correlated with the magnitude of the CR, as assessed physiologically by the skin conductance response. In addition, a recent fMRI study on extinction reported amygdala activation during the initial stages of extinction learning (Phelps, Delgado, Nearing, & LeDoux, 2004). These studies suggest that neural mechanisms of fear conditioning are preserved across species.

Although the results from studies of fear conditioning in humans are similar to those reported in rats, there are some fundamental differences. Unlike other animals, humans can express learning through verbal communication, as well as physical or physiological measures. When patients with amygdala damage participate in a fear conditioning paradigm, they are able to verbally report the parameters of fear conditioning, indicating an explicit representation and awareness of the events of fear conditioning (LaBar et al., 1995). For instance, patient SP, who suffers from bilateral amygdala damage, and normal control subjects were shown a blue square that was paired with a mild shock to the wrist. In both SP and the control subjects, the shock elicited a change in the skin conductance response, a physiological measure of fear or arousal. After a few pairings, the blue square also elicited a skin conductance response in control subjects, indicating conditioned fear. However, SP failed to demonstrate this conditioned fear response. After the study, SP was shown her data indicating a lack of a CR to the blue square and commented:

> I knew that there was an anticipation that the blue square, at some particular point in time, would bring in one of the volt shocks. But even though I knew that, and I knew that from the very beginning, except for the very first one when I was surprised. That was my reaction – I knew it was going to happen. So I learned from the very beginning that it was going to happen: blue–shock. And it happened. I turned out to be right! (Phelps, 2002, p. 559)

As SP's remarks indicate, even though she does not demonstrate fear conditioning as indicated by a physiological response, she has a good understanding and explicit knowledge of the events of fear conditioning. The acquisition of this explicit knowledge depends on a neighboring medial temporal lobe structure, the hippocampus. Patients with damage to the hippocampus, but with intact amygdala, show the opposite pattern, that is, they demonstrate a normal CR as measured by skin conductance, but are unable to explicitly report the events of fear conditioning (Bechara et al., 1995).

This dissociation between an implicit physiological response and an explicit awareness and understanding suggests that emotional learning is represented by multiple, independent learning or memory systems. The physical manifestation of fear conditioning, which is common across species, depends on the amygdala; however, a cognitive awareness and understanding of the events of fear conditioning are independent. This intact awareness and understanding of the fear conditioning paradigm with amygdala damage suggest that the applicability of the fear conditioning models of emotion to complex human social learning may be limited. However, in the next section, I argue that even though the mechanisms of social learning may differ, the amygdala still plays a critical role.

EXTENDING THE MECHANISMS OF FEAR CONDITIONING
TO SOCIAL LEARNING

Cultural knowledge is conveyed through social interaction and social learning. One form of social learning is symbolic, such as language. When patient SP was asked about fear conditioning, she was able to verbally report the events that occurred and the relation between them. Her explicit memory, which relies on the hippocampus, is intact. If she was simply told that a blue square predicted a shock, she would be able to remember this information, verbally report it when asked, and even use this information to avoid the blue square, if possible. Through language and instruction, individuals can acquire an understanding and awareness of the emotional significance of an event or circumstance. This social, symbolic means of human emotional learning appears, at first, to be independent of the amygdala.

However, even though the acquisition of emotional knowledge learned through verbal communication does not depend on the amygdala, recent studies suggest the amygdala does play some role in the expression of this learning. This was investigated using a paradigm called instructed fear. In instructed fear, subjects are told that a presentation of a blue square predicts the possibility of a mild shock to the wrist. They are told that they will not receive a shock every time the blue square is presented, but on some proportion of the trials a shock will be presented. However, in this paradigm, a shock is never actually delivered. It has been reported previously that fear learning through instruction results in robust fear responses, as assessed with physiological measures (Hugdahl & Ohman, 1977). Two recent studies examined whether the amygdala mediates this physiological expression of instructed fear.

The first study used fMRI to compare brain responses to a blue square, "threat" stimulus, which was verbally linked to the possibility of a mild shock, with responses to a yellow square, "safe" stimulus, which was not linked to the possibility of shock. Although none of the subjects actually received a shock in the study, they showed a greater skin conductance response to the blue square, indicating arousal or fear. When the study was complete, the subjects reported they believed a shock would be presented with the blue square. Activation of the left amygdala was observed to the threat (vs. safe) stimulus (Fig. 9.2). As in fear conditioning, the strength of

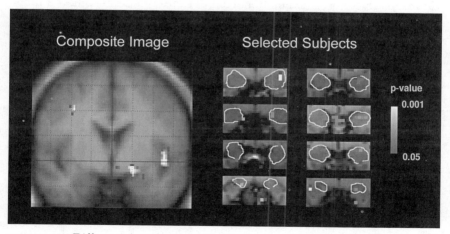

FIGURE 9.2. Differential activation of the left human amygdala to a stimulus verbally paired with shock (threat) versus a stimulus not paired with shock (safe): left, a group composite activation map; right, examples of activation for individual subjects. (Adapted from Phelps et al., 2001.)

this amygdala response correlated with the skin conductance response to the threat stimulus (Phelps et al., 2001).

This study suggests that a symbolic representation of the emotional significance of an event can alter the amygdala's response. However, brain imaging techniques show correlations between brain responses and stimuli or behaviors, but they cannot indicate if a brain region plays a critical role in the expression of behavior. A follow-up study examining patients with amygdala damage found that the physiological expression of fear to a threat stimulus was impaired by damage to the left amygdala, a finding consistent with the conclusion that the amygdala is critical for the expression of instructed fears (Funayama, Grillon, Davis, & Phelps, 2001).

Although only the left amygdala appears to play a role in instructed fear, perhaps because of the verbal nature of the learning, these results suggest that the expression of fears acquired through direct aversive experience (fear conditioning) and symbolic, social means (instructed fear) rely on overlapping neural circuits. This is important because it extends the mechanisms of fear conditioning to situations typical of human experience. In humans, many of our fears are imagined and anticipated but never actually experienced. The studies with instructed fear suggest that these imagined, socially conveyed fears can modulate the amygdala, which in turn is critical for the indirect, physiological expression of these fears.

Another means of social learning is observation. A number of studies have shown that information learned vicariously, through observing others, can have a significant impact on behavior (e.g., Bandura, Ross, & Ross, 1961). Observational learning has been demonstrated as a powerful means to convey the emotional significance of stimuli across a range of populations – from toddlers observing fear reactions in their mothers (Gerull & Rapee, 2002) to monkeys learning to fear a toy snake by watching another monkey's response (Mineka, Davidson, Cook, & Keir, 1984).

A recent study examined the expression of fears learned vicariously through observation and found that they were similar to conditioned fears. This study compared fear learning through classical conditioning, instruction, and observation (Olsson & Phelps, 2004). In classical fear conditioning, the expression of learned fears can be independent of awareness of the presence of the CS. If a CS is presented subliminally – so quickly that subjects are unaware it was presented – the fear will still be expressed, although this can depend on the nature of the CS (see Ohman & Mineka, 2001, for a review). Olsson and Phelps (2004) examined whether awareness of the CS was necessary for the expression of fears learned through social (observation and instruction) and nonsocial (classical conditioning) means. In this study, the CS+ and CS– were pictures of angry faces of different individuals. Awareness was manipulated by presenting some presentations of each CS for 6 s (the supraliminal condition) and others for 30 ms, followed by a 5,970-ms mask, which was the face of another individual with a neutral expression (subliminal condition). All subjects indicated they were unaware of the presentation of the CS+ and CS− angry faces in the subliminal condition.

In the observational fear conditioning group, subjects were told they were going to watch a video of another subject undergoing the same procedure they would subsequently participate in themselves. In the video, a confederate received a mild shock to the wrist paired with some presentations of the observational CS+. The two other faces (the observational CS− and mask) were also presented but were never paired with shock. Watching the video was the *acquisition phase*. In the *test phase*, subjects were told they were now going to undergo the same procedure. They were presented with both supraliminal and subliminal versions of the CS+ (linked to shock) and CS− (not linked to shock). None of these subjects actually received a shock during the test phase. The instructed and classical conditioning groups used the same stimuli and basic procedure, except for the means of acquisition. The instructed fear group was simply told that one of the faces was going to be paired with shock and the others would not. The test phase for the instructed group was identical to the observation group. The classical conditioning group actually received a shock paired with supraliminal presentations of the CS+.

The results for the classical conditioning group replicated results from previous studies (Hygge & Ohman, 1978); conditioned fears were expressed regardless of whether subjects were aware of the presentation of the CS+. Subjects in the instructed group (which had an awareness of the emotional significance of the CS+ acquired symbolically through language) did not show any indication of a fear response when the CS+ was presented subliminally, although consistent with studies mentioned earlier, instruction resulted in a robust physiological expression of the fear with awareness. Interestingly, the results from the observational group were similar to fear conditioning. A fear response was expressed when the CS+ was presented with or without awareness. In other words, the behavioral expression of vicarious, observational learning resembles learning through classical conditioning and can be expressed without awareness, whereas fear learning through language and instruction requires awareness for expression.

The primary difference between social learning through instruction and observation is, of course, the means of acquisition. With verbal instruction, individuals could learn about the emotional significance of a stimulus or event long before encountering the stimulus, when they are far removed from any emotional situation or threat. Observational fear learning, however, could result in a vicarious experience of emotion. Watching another experience a nervous reaction can evoke an emotional reaction in the observer, as well as corresponding activation of a subset of a network of brain regions that are involved in experienced pain (Singer et al., 2004). In this way, observational fear learning is similar to classical conditioning – a stimulus is paired with an aversive event – although in observational fear the aversive event is watching someone else's discomfort. The ability of patients with amygdala damage to remember and verbally report instructions given suggests the amygdala is not important for the acquisition of instructed fear, although it does play a role in its expression (Funayama et al., 2001). However, the similarity in the expression of fears acquired through observation and classical conditioning indicate that the amygdala might play a role in the acquisition, as well as expression, of observational fear.

To test this hypothesis, Olsson, Nearing, Zeng, and Phelps (2004) used fMRI to examine amygdala activation during both the acquisition and test phases of observational fear learning. In acquisition, subjects watched a confederate receive mild shocks to the wrist paired with some presentations of a blue square (the observational CS+), whereas presentations of a yellow square (the observational CS−) were never paired with shock. In the test phase, the subjects were told they would participate in a similar paradigm, although none of the subjects actually received a shock. Amygdala activation, as well as enhanced skin conductance response to the CS and UCS, was observed in both the acquisition and test phases of the study. These results demonstrate that, similar to fear conditioning, the amygdala is involved in both the acquisition and expression of observational fear learning.

The studies on social learning of fear indicate that the neural systems of emotion identified in animal models of classical conditioning may also be applicable to social learning situations. The amygdala is a critical structure in fear acquisition and expression acquired through both social and nonsocial means. This research suggests the possibility that the neural systems in fear conditioning could be important for more complex social interactions and cultural learning. In the next section, we explore whether the mechanisms of fear conditioning can help identify systems of culturally acquired bias.

## EXTENDING THE MECHANISMS OF FEAR CONDITIONING TO CULTURAL BIAS

Thus far, I have described studies with blue squares, mild shocks, and indirect, physiological expressions of emotional learning. These types of simple paradigms have demonstrated that the elegant models outlining the neural circuits of emotional learning in nonhuman animals can also help explain social learning in humans. The similarities in neural systems underlying these different types of learning suggest that it is not necessary to invoke special neural mechanisms for learning through social versus nonsocial means. However, the social learning paradigms described previously are constrained. The stimuli are simple geometric shapes, and the learning is expressed through skin conductance. If the basic mechanisms of fear conditioning are relevant to complicated social interactions and the acquisition of cultural knowledge, we should be able to use this model to help us understand and predict the expression of cultural learning.

In a series of studies we used the classical fear conditioning model as a basis for exploring the neural systems and behavioral expression of culturally acquired race bias. In the United States, the last several decades have seen a decline in attitudes expressing race bias (Biernat & Crandall, 1999; Schuman, Steeh, & BoBo, 1997). On question and answer surveys conducted today, White Americans generally express relatively unbiased attitudes toward Black and White race groups. However, this lack of bias as expressed through explicit attitudes is not consistent with the prevalence of racially biased acts. The expression of race bias may be minimal on explicit questionnaires, but actions and indirect assessments of race attitudes suggest that race bias is a persistent cultural issue (Nosek, Cunningham, Banaji, & Greenwald, 2000).

Social psychologists investigating attitudes toward social groups have differentiated explicit attitudes, which are consciously and directly expressed through verbal communication, from implicit attitudes, which are expressed through actions without conscious effort or control (Greenwald & Banaji, 1995). Although in some cases attitudes expressed explicitly and implicitly are similar, for many social groups they are not (Fazio, Jackson, Dunton, & Williams, 1995; Greenwald, McGhee, & Schwartz, 1998). A classic test to assess implicit attitudes is the Implicit Association Test (IAT). This is a reaction time task used to measure cognitive conflict by pairing stimuli whose evaluative characteristics may differ. In a typical IAT, a subject will be given a series of trials. On some trials, the subject will see either a word that represents something "good" (e.g., lucky, fun, trust) or "bad" (e.g., funeral, fail, harm). On other trials, subjects see a stimulus that represents one race group or another, such as a picture of the face of a White or Black individual. For half the trials, subjects will be asked to press one button as quickly as possible whenever a "good" word or White face is presented, and another button whenever a "bad" word or Black face is presented. For the remaining half of these trials, the pairings are reversed. The difference in the reaction time between the Black + good/White + bad and White + good/Black + bad conditions is the measure of implicit attitude or race bias.

Using the IAT as measure of implicit attitudes has shown that even though White Americans, in general, explicitly express relatively unbiased race attitudes, there are persistent negative attitudes toward Black Americans expressed implicitly. Black Americans generally express a relatively positive attitude toward their own race group when their attitudes are explicitly assessed by question-and-answer survey. However, when attitudes are assessed implicitly using the IAT, they tend to be less positive and sometimes even negative toward their own race group. On all these measures, there is substantial variability among individuals (especially among Black Americans), but the general trends suggest that the explicit and implicit assessment of race attitudes reveal different patterns of race bias (Phelps & Banaji, 2005).

This dissociation between evaluative attitudes that are expressed explicitly through verbal report and implicitly through physical reaction time responses is reminiscent of the dissociation observed with fear conditioning following damage to the amygdala or hippocampus. With amygdala damage, it is possible to explicitly report the emotional significance of a stimulus, even if the implicit, physiological assessment of this learning is impaired. The opposite pattern emerges following damage to the hippocampus. This dissociation suggests that different neural mechanisms underlie the implicit and explicit expression of emotional evaluation. Given this, we asked if the amygdala might be related to the implicit expression of race bias.

Amygdala responses were assessed in White American subjects using fMRI. During brain imaging, subjects were shown pictures of unfamiliar Black and White males' faces. Subjects were simply asked to press a button indicating whether a face was repeated. After imaging, subjects were given three assessments of race attitudes. One was an explicit question and answer survey (the Modern Racism Scale [MRS]; McConahay, 1986). The other two were implicit. The first was an IAT, described previously, in which the same male faces shown during imaging were used as the Black or White stimuli. The second was a physiological assessment, the startle eyeblink. The startle reflex is a natural response to a loud noise and an early component of this reflex response is an eyeblink. The startle eyeblink is potentiated by the emotional state of the subject – if a loud noise is presented when someone is slightly anxious, he or she will startle more than when relaxed or calm (Lang, Bradley, & Cuthbert, 1990). Studies on fear conditioning have shown potentiated startle responses in the presence of a CS, which are impaired following amygdala damage (Davis, 1997). In the race bias study, we presented the pictures of the Black and White male faces and startled subjects by presenting a loud white noise. The difference in the magnitude of the startle eyeblink response while viewing the Black versus the White faces was our physiological measure of race bias.

Although the majority of White American subjects showed greater amygdala activation to the Black as compared with the White faces, there was some variability. When exploring how this variability in amygdala response was related to the variability in our assessment of race bias, an interesting pattern emerged. There was no correlation between the amygdala response and the MRS score, the explicit measure of race bias. However, both implicit measures were significantly correlated with the magnitude of amygdala activation – the more negative the bias toward Black,

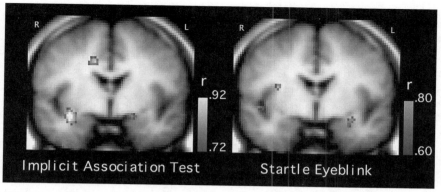

FIGURE 9.3. Regions that show a correlation between differential activation to Black versus White unfamiliar faces, and the magnitude of implicit race bias as measured by the IAT (left) and startle eyeblink (right). For both measures, a region of the right amygdala predicts race bias scores across subjects. (Adapted from Phelps et al., 2000.)

the stronger the amygdala activation to the Black versus the White faces. It did not matter if the assessment of implicit race attitudes was a reaction time measure (IAT) or a physiological assessment (startle eyeblink); the strength of the correlation with amygdala activation was similar (Phelps et al., 2000; Fig. 9.3).

These results were the first to show that culturally acquired information may rely on the same neural systems for expression as basic fear conditioning. Although the Phelps et al. (2000) study did not include Black American subjects, a study by Hart and colleagues (2000) reported greater amygdala activation to White versus Black faces in Black American subjects, suggesting the neural mechanisms of race evaluation extend to out-group faces across race groups.

The amygdala is a region believed to be important for emotional learning. The Phelps et al. (2000) study suggests that the amygdala's role in emotional learning may extend to culturally acquired race bias. As the variability in both amygdala activation and measures of race bias in the White American subjects indicates, the strength of a culturally acquired bias, along with its neural signature, can vary across individuals, even though there are general patterns for the social group as a whole. It is also possible that the expression of race bias can vary, depending on the identity of the individuals of the other race. Although a person may express a social group bias toward someone with whom they are unfamiliar, this may be diminished (or extinguished) to someone from the same race group who is familiar and well liked.

Familiarity is an important component of extinction learning. Extinction learning occurs when a CS that previously predicted the presentation of the

UCS is no longer paired with a UCS and, eventually, the learned emotional response (CR) is diminished. In other words, familiarity with a CS, without negative consequences, reduces the negative evaluation. The amygdala has been shown to play a role in initial extinction learning across species (Falls et al., 1992; Phelps et al., 2004); however, when a response to a CS has been previously extinguished, the amygdala response is diminished (Phelps et al., 2004). Given this, we might expect a different pattern of amygdala activation when viewing familiar Black and White individuals with generally positive images.

We tested this hypothesis by repeating the race bias study described previously, with one exception: the pictures were of faces belonging to culturally familiar Black and White individuals with relatively positive public images (e.g., John F. Kennedy, Martin Luther King, Harrison Ford, Denzel Washington). In this variation of the task, there was no consistent pattern of amygdala activation to the Black versus White faces and no correlation between any measure of race bias and the amgydala response. This lack of an amygdala response is similar to the diminished amygdala response observed to previously extinguished CS (Phelps et al., 2004). Although the interpretation of a null finding is always problematic, these results suggest that the neural mechanisms of culturally acquired race bias can be altered by exposure and familiarity. In this study, we examined changes in brain function as a result of familiarity induced by culturally popular images in the United States. However, the mechanisms identified here are general learning mechanisms that should respond broadly to social and emotional stimuli in any environment. Therefore, we would expect cross-cultural differences to also change the neural systems of learned emotional responses and social bias.

The studies on the neural systems of culturally acquired race bias indicate that models derived from simple conditioning paradigms are useful in understanding complex social behaviors. In this case, being able to show different neural circuits underlying the expression of implicit and explicit race biases supports the psychological research, suggesting that distinct mechanisms may underlie the expression of different types of attitudes. As we move forward, we should be able to use these models to provide clues as to how these culturally acquired biases may be expressed, modified, and diminished.

CONCLUSION

Once an object or event acquires an emotional significance, the way it is processed from that point on is altered. Previous studies have shown that the emotional quality of a stimulus can influence a range of cognitive processes, including working memory (Kensinger & Corkin, 2003), long-term memory (Hamann, 2002), attention (Ohman, Flykt, & Esteves, 2001), and even the earliest stages of perception (Ling, Phelps, Holmes, & Carrasco, 2004). Given this, understanding how items, situations, and even people acquire their emotional properties in social and cultural frameworks is important in understanding many other aspects of behavior as well.

In this review, I focus on research in normal healthy adults, primarily because the literature on changes in amygdala function over the lifetime is limited. However, some evidence is starting to emerge indicating that normal aging may alter the pattern of amygdala response. Although in young adults, the amygdala responds to both positive and negative arousing stimuli (e.g., Hamann, 2002), there tends to be a bias for the amygdala to code negative or threatening stimuli (e.g., Adolphs et al., 1999; Whalen, 1998). However, a recent study by Mather and colleagues (2004) found that this pattern of amygdala response changes with normal aging, such that the amygdala in older adults shows a more dominant response to positive arousing stimuli. These results are intriguing, but it is difficult to know how they might translate to emotional and social learning. However, they suggest the possibility that the patterns of social and cultural emotional learning may also alter with aging.

The basic principles of classical conditioning described by Pavlov have emerged as an important tool in our efforts to understand the neural and behavioral mechanisms of emotional learning. Using this classical fear conditioning paradigm, detailed neural circuits can be identified in nonhuman animals, which may help us understand even complex human behaviors. The studies from fear conditioning to cultural race bias suggest a similarity in the mechanisms of learning. Although cultural knowledge and some forms of social interaction and communication may be uniquely human characteristics, how emotional value is acquired and expressed in these domains seems to rely on basic mechanisms that are shared across species.

## References

Adolphs, R., Tranel, D., Hamann, S., Young, A. W., Calder, A. J., Phelps, E. A., et al. (1999). Recognition of facial emotion in nine individuals with bilateral amygdala damage. *Neuropsychologia, 37*, 1111–1117.

Bandura, A., Ross, D., & Ross, S. A. (1961). Transmission of aggression through imitation of aggressive models. *Journal of Abnormal Social Psychology, 63*, 575–582.

Bechara, A., Tranel, D., Damasio, H., Adolphs, R., Rockland, C., & Damasio, A. R. (1995). Double dissociation of conditioning and declarative knowledge relative to the amygdala and hippocampus in humans. *Science, 269* (5227), 1115–1118.

Biernat, M., & Crandall, C. S. (1999). Racial attitudes. In J. P. Robinson, P. H. Shaver, & L. S. Wrightsman (Eds.), *Measures of political attitudes* (pp. 291–412). San Diego: Academic Press.

Buchel, C., Morris, J., Dolan, R. J., & Friston, K. J. (1998). Brain systems mediating aversive conditioning: An event-related fMRI study. *Neuron, 20* (5), 947–957.

Davis, M. (1997). Neurobiology of fear responses: The role of the amygdala. *Journal of Neuropsychiatry: Clinical Neuroscience, 9*, 382–402.

Falls, W. A., Miserendino, M. J., & Davis, M. (1992). Extinction of fear-potentiated startle: Blockade by infusion of an NMDA antagonist into the amygdala. *Journal of Neuroscience, 12*, 854–863.

Fazio, R. H., Jackson, J. R., Dunton, B. C., & Williams, C. J. (1995). Variability in automatic activation as an unobtrusive measure of racial attitudes: A bona fide pipeline? *Journal of Personality and Social Psychology, 69*, 1013–1027.

Funayama, E. S., Grillon, C., Davis, M., & Phelps, E. A. (2001). A double dissociation in the affective modulation of startle in humans: Effects of unilateral temporal lobectomy. *Journal of Cognitive Neuroscience, 13*, 721–729.

Gerull, F. C., & Rapee, R. M. (2002). Mother knows best: Effects of maternal modelling on the acquisition of fear and avoidance behaviour in toddlers. *Behaviour Research Therapy, 40*, 279–287.

Greenwald, A. G., & Banaji, M. R. (1995). Implicit social cognition: Attitudes, self-esteem, and stereotypes. *Psychological Review, 102*, 4–27.

Greenwald, A. G., McGhee, J. L., & Schwartz, J. L. (1998). Measuring individual differences in social cognition: The Implicit Association Test. *Journal of Personality and Social Psychology, 74*, 1464–1480.

Hamann, S. (2002). Cognitive and neural mechanisms of emotional memory. *Trends in Cognitive Science, 5*, 394–400.

Hart, A. J., Whalen, P. J., Shin, L. M., McInerney, S. C., Fischer, H., & Rauch, S. L. (2000). Differential response in the human amygdala to racial outgroup vs. ingroup face stimuli. *Neuroreport, 11*, 2351–2355.

Hugdahl, K., & Ohman, A. (1977). Effects of instruction on acquisition and extinction of electrodermal responses to fear-relevant stimuli. *Journal of Experimental Psychology: Human Learning and Memory, 3*, 608–618.

Hygge, S., & Ohman, A. (1978). Modeling processes in the acquisition of fears: Vicarious electrodermal conditioning to fear-relevant stimuli. *Journal of Personality and Social Psychology, 36*, 271–279.

Kapp, B. S., Frysinger, R. C., Gallagher, M., & Haselton, J. R. (1979). Amygdala central nucleus lesions: Effect on heart rate conditioning in the rabbit. *Physiological Behavior, 23*, 1109–1117.

Kensinger, E. A., & Corkin, S. (2003). Effect of negative emotional content on working memory and long-term memory. *Emotion, 3*, 378–393.

Kluver, H., & Bucy, P. C. (1937). "Psychic blindness" and other symptoms following bilateral temporal lobectomy in rhesus monkeys. *American Journal of Physiology, 119*, 352–353.

LaBar, K. S., Gatenby, J. C., Gore, J. C., LeDoux, J. E., & Phelps, E. A. (1998). Human amygdala activation during conditioned fear acquisition and extinction: A mixed-trial fMRI study. *Neuron, 20*, 937–945.

LaBar, K. S., LeDoux, J. E., Spencer, D. D., & Phelps, E. A. (1995). Impaired fear conditioning following unilateral temporal lobectomy in humans. *Journal of Neuroscience, 15*, 6846–6855.

Lang, P. J., Bradley, M. M., & Cuthbert, B. N. (1990). Emotion, attention, and the startle reflex. *Psychological Review, 97*, 377–395.

LeDoux, J. E. (1996). *The emotional brain.* New York: Simon and Schuster.

LeDoux, J. E. (2002). *Synaptic self: How our brains become who we are.* New York: Viking.

Ling, S., Phelps, E. A., Holmes, B. D., & Carrasco, M. (2004). Emotion potentiates attentional effects in early vision [Abstract]. *Journal of Vision, 4* (8), 623a. Available: http://journalofvision.org/4/8/623/, doi:10.1167/4.8.623.

Mather, M., Canli, T., English, T., Whitfield, S., Wais, P., Ochsner, K., et al. (2004). Amygdala responses to emotionally valenced stimuli in older and younger adults. *Psychological Science, 15,* 259–263.

McConahay, J. P. (1986). Modern racism, ambivalence, and the modern racism scale. In J. F. Dovidio & S. L. Gaertner (Eds.), *Prejudice, discrimination and racism* (pp. 91–125). Orlando, FL: Academic Press.

Mineka, S., Davidson, M., Cook, M., & Keir, R. (1984). Observational conditioning of snake fear in rhesus monkeys. *Journal of Abnormal Psychology, 93,* 355–372.

Nosek, B. A., Cunningham, W. A., Banaji, M. R., & Greenwald, A. G. (2000, February). *Measuring implicit attitudes on the internet.* Poster presented at the annual meeting of the Society for Personality and Social Psychology, Nashville, TN.

Ohman, A., Flykt, A., & Esteves, F. (2001). Emotion drives attention: Detecting the snake in the grass. *Journal of Experimental Psychology: General, 130,* 466–478.

Ohman, A., & Mineka, S. (2001). Fears, phobias, and preparedness: Toward an evolved module of fear and fear learning. *Psychological Review, 108,* 483–522.

Olsson, A., Nearing, K., Zeng, J., & Phelps, E. A. (2004, October). *Learning by observing: Neural correlates of fear learning through social observation.* Paper presented at the 34th annual meeting of the Society for Neuroscience, San Diego, CA.

Olsson, A., & Phelps, E. A. (2004). Learned fear of "unseen" faces. *Psychological Science, 15,* 822–828.

Papez, J. W. (1937). A proposed mechanism of emotion. *Archives of Neurology and Psychiatry, 79,* 217–224.

Phelps, E. A. (2002). The cognitive neuroscience of emotion. In M. S. Gazzaniga, R. B. Ivry, & G. R. Magnum (Eds.), *Cognitive neuroscience: The biology of mind* (2nd ed., pp. 537–576). New York: Norton.

Phelps, E. A. (2004). Human emotion and memory: Interactions of the amygdala and hippocampal complex. *Current Opinion in Neurobiology, 14,* 198–202.

Phelps, E. A., & Banaji, M. R. (2005). Animal models of human attitudes: Integrations across behavioral, cognitive, social neuroscience. In J. T. Cacioppo, P. S. Visser, & C. L. Pickett (Eds.), *Social neuroscience: People thinking about thinking people (pp. 229-244).* Cambridge, MA: MIT Press.

Phelps, E. A., Delgado, M. R., Nearing, K. I., & LeDoux, J. E. (2004). Extinction learning in humans: Role of the amygdala and vmPFC. *Neuron, 43,* 897–905.

Phelps, E. A., O'Connor, K. J., Cunningham, W. A., Funayama, E. S., Gatenby, J. C., Gore, J. C., & Banaji, M. R. (2000). Performance on indirect measures of race evaluation predicts amygdala activation. *Journal of Cognitive Neuroscience, 12,* 729–738.

Phelps, E. A., O'Connor, K. J., Gatenby, J. C., Gore, J. C., Grillon, C., & Davis, M. (2001). Activation of the left amygdala to a cognitive representation of fear. *Nature Neuroscience, 4,* 437–441.

Schuman, H., Steeh, C., & BoBo, L. (1997). *Racial attitudes in America: Trends and interpretations.* Cambridge, MA: Harvard University Press.

Singer, Y., Seymour, B., O'Doherty, J., Kaube, H., Dolan, R. J., & Frith, C. D. (2004). Empathy for pain involves the affective but not sensory components of pain. *Science, 303,* 1157–1162.

Weiskrantz, L. (1956). Behavioral changes associated with ablation of the amygdaloid complex in monkeys. *Journal of Comparative Physiology and Psychology, 49,* 381–391.

Whalen, P. J. (1998). Fear, vigilance, and ambiguity: Initial neuroimaging studies of the human amygdala. *Current Directions in Psychological Science, 7,* 177–188.

# 10

## The Musical Mind: Neural Tuning and the Aesthetic Experience

Oliver Vitouch

ABSTRACT

*Music is a human universal. Still, a persuasive evolutionary explanation of its adaptive value is missing. In its refined forms, music can be paradigmatically seen as an exaptation or spandrel, serving no immediate survival or reproductive purpose in a "l'art pour l'art" fashion. Simultaneously, musical training is a model case for neural plasticity, with extended perceptual and motor skills having their morphological and functional imprints on the neocortex. This chapter exemplifies how music shapes the brain – from the early development of absolute pitch, to macroscopic changes in cortical specialization, to "strong experiences with music" and their supposed substrates. These phenomena can only be properly understood from the interplay of evolution, culture, and ontogenesis.*

## A HUMAN UNIVERSAL

In 1977, humans sent two spacecrafts, the *Voyagers*, into different angles of deep space. Aboard each vessel was, apart from technical gear, a small collection of human artifacts. Part of the collection was graphical, including a drawing of a woman and a man (greeting with his open palm) and a drawing representing the position of the Earth within our solar system. The other part was tonal, including a golden disk containing human speech and 27 tracks of music, such as a Glenn Gould recording of the C major Prelude and Fugue from Johann Sebastian Bach's *Well-Tempered Clavier*, Book 2. Obviously, the team of scientists in charge found music to be an achievement sufficiently characteristic of our species to be put into an "information basket" about *Homo sapiens*: "Hi, we are humans living on earth, we have sexual dimorphism, we greet, speak, draw, construct, research, and we play Bach."

There were good reasons for sending music. Music is, just like speech, a human universal. There is no known human culture that does not have any kind of musical activity. Recent archeological evidence even suggests that music is not a specialty of *Homo sapiens* alone, but a characteristic achievement of the entire genus *Homo* (Kunej & Turk, 2000): a more than 40,000-year-old cave bear femur with flute-like holes was found at a Neanderthal burial site in Slovenia, speaking for an even earlier than usually assumed and pan-hominid origin of instrumental music. Other prehistoric flutes are of a somewhat more recent origin but corroborate that instrumental music dates to before Orpheus.

This chapter shows, via different strands of evidence, how human musicality can reveal insights into the biocultural co-construction of minds and brains. Our brains perceive and produce music, and music shapes the brain. "Musical biographies" leave their imprints even in the macromorphology of our cortex. Hence, as far as the musical mind is concerned, the brain is clearly both an independent and a dependent variable.

## PRELUDE: ON EVOLUTION

Since the 1990s, evolutionary psychology (EP) has come very much *en vogue* in explaining human mental faculties. My basic scientific credo is that the inclusion of an evolutionary perspective is both necessary and useful for the mind and brain sciences. Still, the evolutionary paradigm does not restrict the problem space as strongly as typically claimed: the specificity of predictions, arguing from an increased fitness perspective alone, is almost never sufficient to concretely "predict" or "explain" anything – for instance, to explain why we have music. It is, at best, sufficient to *exclude* some things that seem impossible from an evolutionary perspective, such as an extreme waste of resources or accepting high risks without adequate compensation. Even *universality* of a phenomenon does not automatically mean that we have identified a natural principle. Dennett (1995) pointed out that all known human hunters who use spears let them fly tip first. However, this obviously does not suggest the existence of a "human spear tip" gene – rather, we observe a structurally immanent principle resulting from the anatomy, or logic, of a spear. Universality (or transculturality) of a phenomenon can be a very strong cue in looking for its phylogenetic origins, but it does not necessarily imply direct "genetic coding." If we turn back to music, where we have complex sound and a nervous system proficiently able to perceive it, it is probably near at hand to "make something of it," without necessarily assuming an immediate evolutionary function. The salience and survival relevance of auditory cues alone, especially at night, in the ancient environment of evolutionary adaptedness should partly account for the modern "teasing" of the auditory system by rich and quickly modulating sound sceneries.

Are all human mental faculties sufficiently explicable as biological adaptations? This position would amount to a "selection pressure rules" view (cf. Andrews, Gangestad, & Matthews, 2002). Beyond this orthodox view of EP, there are other evolution-informed views with a stronger focus on (1) neural and behavioral plasticity and (2) exaptations or spandrels (Gould & Lewontin, 1979), novel mental abilities capitalizing on resources that had initially been selected for other purposes. A good example is the recent movement of "evo-devo," a courageous attempt to integrate findings from evolutionary and developmental biology. Generally, it is important to keep in mind that increased plasticity and behavioral flexibility are specific products of hominid evolution, and that *Homo plasticus* is a successful phylogenetic product (Hoffrage & Vitouch, 2002). Unfortunately, EP and its axioms do not help much in explaining the "cognitive big bang" (or the series of bangs) that made *Homo* sapiens.

On the conceptual level, EP has a problem that I call "the tricky shortcut of behavioral genetics." The problem is that the angle of observation implies a direct shortcut from (A) "gene" to (B) "behavior/mind." On the route from (A) to (B), a miracle occurs: there is no explicit model on how this direct link is established. This view is strongly influenced by a variant of Francis H. Crick's *central dogma* of molecular genetics, the concept that information flows on a one-way route from genotype to phenotype, but never the other way round. The dogma has strong merits because it helped vaccinate genetic thinking against Lamarckian ideas of "individual experience writing back into the genome." It can, however, be conceptually misleading in a somewhat different context because its "production" focus is too much on the genotype side, and aspects such as interactive epigenesis are downplayed (see Gottesman & Hanson, 2005; Gottlieb, 1998; Chapter 2). Future anthropologists will be smiling at the gene concept of the twentieth century and may even call out "phlogiston!" Genes were used as a catchall category, the magic entity that conceals the answer for all riddles about life.

A more recent road map from (A) to (B) would include the following stations: information is expressed from the *genome* into the *proteome*, which provides the material for building our brain tissues. After all, it is the *brain* that comprises the mind and produces behavior. But here is an important loop in the system: at least in *Homo sapiens*, the mind/behavior level includes the production of *culture* (still a four-letter word for some reductionists), which via countless channels works back on the brain. This is not the only loop in the system – for instance, environmental factors can also influence which parts of the genome are ontogenetically expressed into the proteome and which stay mute. (The looping depends on what your concrete definition of "culture" subsumes [e.g., rearing and nutrition].) It is, however, the most obvious loop: human brains generate culture, and culture generates brain changes. As individual brains become more individualized through individual experience, the brain must be conceptualized not only as an independent, but also as a dependent variable.

Evolution is an important chapter in the storybook of life, and in many respects, it is *the* most important chapter. The misunderstanding is rather to believe that from an understanding of the basic principles of evolution alone, we would be able to consistently retell the whole story. This is what the adaptationist or "neo-Darwinian" school of EP (Darwin's own convictions notwithstanding) seems to assume. For the species of *Homo sapiens*, however, the exaptations are at least as specific as the adaptations. It is therefore high time to borrow from Immanuel Kant, one of the implicit forefathers of EP and the idea of innate concepts, and from his *Critique of Pure Reason.* Contemporary psychology is in need of a *Critique of Pure Evolution* (e.g., Sternberg & Kaufman, 2002; Tomasello, 1999), as well as of integrative concepts suited to properly unify evolutionary accounts and cultural/learning accounts of "human architecture."

## EVOLUTIONARY THEORIES OF HUMAN MUSICALITY

As neither the enjoyment nor the capacity of producing musical notes are faculties of the least use to man in reference to his daily habits of life, they must be ranked among the most mysterious with which he is endowed. (Darwin, 1871, p. 878)

Similar to our not having an accurate model of the concrete combination or sequence of factors that made *Homo* sapiens, we have no sound theoretical basis until now for what made them musical and why we differ so clearly in this respect from our close relatives. Although the macaque's auditory cortex shows strong resemblance to the matching structures of the human cortex, neither monkeys nor apes sing, nor have they made it into the charts thus far.

As to tentative evolutionary accounts of why we have music, there is not just *one* single theory. Rather, we can choose from about a dozen rivaling theory families. Worse still, it is even unsettled whether we should prefer a *natural selection* or a *sexual selection* explanation (or both). Although Charles Darwin himself strongly favored a sexual selection account (as expressed in his "Descent" of 1871, published 12 years after the "Origin of Species"), the current conceptual situation is less clear. An exemplary range of candidate factors is shown in Table 10.1. Of course, it is also feasible to speculate about multiple origins of music, which mutually amplified each other.

For example, authors favoring social cohesion explanations argue that more than one person *speaking* at the same time does not work properly (although couples, politicians, and conference participants sometimes try), whereas singing at the same time works well, even in large groups. Aficionados of group effort theories, for the sake of another example, hold that (rhythmic) music is well suited to facilitate the coordination of movements of several people. This is why the Royal Navy invented the *shanties*: just imagine a group of men, singing "*What* shall we do with the / *drunken* sailor" while setting the sails. Here, we have a clear selection advantage – or didn't Britannia rule the waves for the longest time?

TABLE 10.1. *Candidate Factors for an Evolutionary "Explanation" of Human Musicality*

| | |
|---|---|
| Mate choice (sexual selection) | Conflict reduction |
| Social cohesion | Safe time passing |
| Group effort | Transgenerational communication |
| Perceptual development | Mother–child bonding |
| Motor skill development | Communication at a distance |

*Note:* Adapted from Huron (2001; cf. Hauser & McDermott, 2003; Panksepp & Bernatzky, 2002; Wallin, Merker, & Brown, 2000).

Perhaps the most interesting and, at the same time, most debatable case is sexual selection. Huron (2001) argued that for a trait operated on by sexual selection, you would, by comparison with other traits and species, clearly expect sexual dimorphism (e.g., singing males and silent females) – an untenable view after even the Vienna Philharmonic recently dropped this assumption. Others disagree and make a point for a sexually selected trait with both sexes being musical (e.g., Merker, 2003; Miller, 2000). However, it is certainly evident that most approaches really have a problem explaining how music adaptively evolved from vocal to instrumental, and from an early choir to a Beethoven sonata. The sexual selection view is apparently better suited to argue for a continuous aesthetic refinement on adaptive grounds because the best musicians may be the most attractive mates. This seems to hold at least anecdotally, from early pop stars such as Franz Liszt or Johann Strauss, Jr. (who regularly found his dressing room full of bouquets sent by female admirers) to Mick Jagger or Robbie Williams. However, it is an open question who the best musician of a certain epoch is (and why), and to what degree the music (and its quality . . . ) makes that person attractive.

To conclude, the immediate survival or reproductive purpose of music is still unclear, or at least very debatable. Still, it is a remarkable fact that the foremost export sector in the U.S. economy is not high technology, but *entertainment*, and that the music industry is larger than the pharmaceutical industry (Huron, 2001). The latest Austrian "Youth Radar" Survey[1] found that "listening to music" is the foremost leisure activity for adolescents and young adults (both genders), followed by "listening to the radio," clearly topping TV, cell phones, and the Internet. As recently demonstrated by Zdrahal-Urbanek and Vitouch (2003), famous pieces of music are often instantaneously recognized, sometimes with only split-second latencies. All this points to a very special role that music is playing for humans – a specialty with as yet unsettled biocultural origins.

[1] Jugendradar 2003 ($N = 1549$), initiated by the Austrian Federal Ministry of Social Security, Generations, and Consumer Protection (http://www.bmsg.gv.at).

MUSIC SHAPES THE BRAIN

Music is a very suitable domain for the investigation of ontogenetic neuroadaptive processes (cf. Münte, Altenmüller, & Jäncke, 2002). An influential stream of expertise theory, the *deliberate practice* approach (Ericsson, Krampe, & Tesch-Römer, 1993; for a music-centered overview, see Vitouch, 2005a), is essentially based on the "10-years rule of deliberate practice." It assumes an extended period of constant, systematic training as a necessary condition for high-level skill acquisition, for example, for becoming an eminent musician. This long-term training regimen leaves its imprints in the human neocortex. We therefore expect not only the minds, but also the brains of expert musicians to differ from their amateur counterparts, a supposition that has been confirmed in a number of brain imaging studies since the mid-1990s.

## Music Performance

(. . .) the work of a pianist (. . .) is inaccessible for the untrained human, as the acquisition of new abilities requires many years of mental and physical practice. In order to fully understand this complicated phenomenon it is necessary to admit, in addition to the strengthening of pre-established organic pathways, the establishment of new ones, through ramification and progressive growth of dendritic arborizations and nervous terminals. (. . .) Such a development takes place in response to exercise, while it stops and may be reversed in brain spheres that are not cultivated. (Ramón y Cajal, 1899, cited in Pascual-Leone, 2001, p. 316)

In what soon became a citation classic, Elbert, Pantev, Wienbruch, Rockstroh, and Taub (1995) used high-resolution magnetoencephalography (MEG) and source localization models to investigate the plasticity of finger representations in the primary somatosensory cortex. They assumed that the strong fine-sensorimotoric requirements for string players and the specifically intensified afferent input should lead to a long-term plastic reorganization of the sensory homunculus, best visible from the representations of the second to fifth digit (D2 to D5) of the left hand (which projects contralaterally to the right cortical hemisphere). Elbert and his colleagues compared nine musicians (violinists, cellists, and guitar players with 7 to 17 years of musical training) with six age-matched controls in their cortical responses to pneumatic stimulation of the tips of D1 (thumb) and D5 of both hands. They found positive evidence for expertise-related morphological changes: as compared with the controls, the mean dipoles for the left hand of musicians were medially shifted, with a stronger shift for D5 than for D1, meaning that their left-hand finger representations spanned a somewhat larger area. Moreover, the dipole moments (resulting from the amplitudes of the cortical responses) were significantly larger for the musicians, again, more so for D5 than for the passive thumb. No such

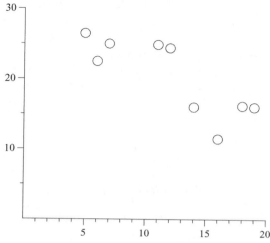

FIGURE 10.1. Correlation between age at inception of musical practice (x-axis) and D5 dipole strength (in nA × m; y-axis) in string players. Dipole strengths of controls ranged from 5 to 11 nAm. (Adapted from Elbert et al., 1995.)

between-group differences were found in the left hemisphere for the representations of the right (bow) hand.

Perhaps the most important result of this study, however, was a difference within the musicians' group. Elbert et al. (1995) found a strong effect for the time of inception of musical practice. Those string players who had started early (at ages 5 to 12 years) with their regular training showed a substantially larger D5 dipole moment than the late beginners. This indicates, in concordance with cell-biological evidence, that only the early beginners strongly morphed their cortices, whereas the adolescent brains had already lost much of their former (macro)elasticity (Fig. 10.1). Early training of string players seems to induce the recruitment of a more extended cortical network for the single-finger representations of the left hand, with the active fingers competitively occupying a larger territory. Similar effects were found earlier for the D2 representations of blind Braille readers, which strongly speaks for a causal interpretation of these findings and for training-induced reorganization, instead of the notion of innate person factors constituting a priori group differences (cf. Vitouch, 2005a). (Early) experience shapes brains – *q.e.d.*

Amunts et al. (1997) conducted a similar study, using in vivo morphometry of the human cortex by means of structural magnetic resonance imaging (MRI). They measured an anatomical marker for the extension of the primary motor cortex, the intrasulcal length of the precentral gyrus (ILPG), in 21 right-handed pianists. As compared with controls, who had shown a strong ILPG asymmetry in favor of the dominant hand, the pianists' left and right ILPG were nearly symmetric. Hence, the pianists' right ILPGs (controlling the left hand) spanned a larger area than those of the controls. This finding matched the results of a unimanual D2 tapping task on the behavioral level. Just like Elbert et al. (1995), Amunts et al. (1997) found a clear connection between age at inception of piano practice and ILPG, with correlations of $r = -.63$ for the right and $r = -.60$ for the left hemisphere.

## Music Perception

As convincing as these practice-induced testimonies of cortical plasticity in the motoric realm may be, are they particularly specific for *music*? Although musical training is a model case for neural plasticity, as well as a perfect ecological domain for the study of early-onset and long-term effects in humans, one could well argue that the nature of such changes does not structurally differ from those in people who become expert typists. To dig deeper into the hard wiring of the musical mind, we have to look out for the brain substrates (or at least correlates) of differences in music *perception*. Irrespective of some fictitious "Mozart effect," the empty promise to improve your children's brains with the "just add water" ease of instant soup,[2] there are some well-controlled studies that demonstrate music-induced brain plasticity in the perceptual realm. They show that the way we hear music – the frequency and the framework of doing it – works back on the underlying cortical architecture.

Pantev et al. (1998) transferred the basic design of the Elbert et al. (1995) study from the haptic into the tonal world. By means of MEG, they gauged the cortical tonotopy of passive responses to sine tones and piano tones of different frequencies in the primary auditory cortices of 20 musicians. Although Pantev and colleagues found no "geographical" differences between the tonotopical organization of musicians' brains and those of controls, they found that musicians' dipole moments in response to piano tones, as compared with those of the controls, were increased by 25%. In addition, they found the already well-known contingency between onset of training and size of the effect, although in a somewhat weaker form ($r = -.43$). Their results speak for a use-dependent functional reorganization of the auditory cortex during the development of musical skill. More recently, Schneider et al. (2002) presented even clearer findings in this direction. They found both physiological (strength of early magnetic field components in response to sinusoidal tones) and morphological differences (gray matter surface volume reconstructions) between musicians and nonmusicians in Heschl's gyrus, the site of the primary auditory cortex.

[2] For a requiem, see the series of papers in *Nature*, 1999 (Vol. 400, pp. 826ff), and most recently and comprehensively, Steele (2003).

In the same year as Elbert et al. (1995), Schlaug, Jäncke, Huang, and Steinmetz (1995) published a paper that methodologically preceded the Amunts et al. (1997) study. By means of in vivo structural MRI morphometry, they found that the surface of the left planum temporale, as defined by anatomical markers, was larger in musicians than in nonmusicians in their sample, with the musicians therefore showing an even stronger left-sided asymmetry of this structure. Remarkably, these differences were even more pronounced for those musicians possessing absolute pitch, a finding that can be attributed to either early training or innate differences (or to an interaction of both; for the debate on the genesis of absolute pitch, refer to the next section). The data of Schlaug et al. (1995) also opened a discussion about the planum temporale, formerly an area associated mainly with speech perception, being a potential "substrate area" for absolute pitch (see Vitouch, 2005b). Gaser and Schlaug (2003) presented new morphological data on the pronounced hemispheric asymmetry of this structure in musicians.

Koelsch, Schröger, and Tervaniemi (1999) used an early component difference in the event-related electroencephalogram, the mismatch negativity (MMN), to investigate expertise effects in responses to mistuned chords. The MMN is generated in the primary auditory cortex and is a correlate of preattentive stimulus processing (independent of the direction of attention). On this basic level of processing, they found that violinists' MMN was sensitive to even small frequency deviations ($<1\%$) of the middle tone of a chord.

Münte, Kohlmetz, Nager, and Altenmüller (2001) used an attention-dependent event-related component, the N100, to demonstrate improved auditory spatial tuning in conductors. The participants' task was to locate the sources of sounds in the auditory periphery exactly. The N100 of conductors, as compared with both pianists and nonmusicians, was more selectively tuned to the correct source, and matched their performance advantage on the behavioral level. This points to a domain-specific narrowing of professional conductors' "attentional fan." Similar results have previously been found for blind people (see Chapter 6), which again speaks strongly for a plasticity rather than an innateness account for these findings.

Of course, it is often possible to argue that expertise-correlated differences are merely reflections of innate person factors and that the brains under investigation already differed a priori, or had different potentials for becoming shaped or "tuned." It therefore is important to rule out such alternative explanations by means of converging evidence, and by evidence that logically supports the "tuning by training" causal relationship, as in the previous case of conductors and blind people. The most elegant and direct approach, namely, conducting experimentally controlled longitudinal training studies, has rarely been accomplished in the brain imaging domain so far. Some recent studies, however, aimed to functionally track training-induced changes, at least over brief periods of time (Bangert & Altenmüller, 2003; Gaab & Schlaug, 2003).

### Early Plasticity: The Case of Absolute Pitch

Absolute pitch (AP) – the ability to name the pitch class of a tone (e.g., "F sharp") independently of a tonal reference or anchor – has long been treated as the apex of musical genius (Vitouch, 2005b). Owing to its increased prevalence among composers, conductors, and child prodigies, AP (or, colloquially, "perfect pitch") was thought of as a rare innate gift and a clear sign of musical excellence. Today, in the light of new evidence, many authors subscribe to an *early learning* view of this ability (Takeuchi & Hulse, 1993), connecting it rather to perceptual styles than to prodigious memory feats. Evidence for the early learning model is summarized in Table 10.2 (for current contributions to the debate, see Levitin & Zatorre, 2003; Russo, Windell, & Cuddy, 2003; Vitouch, 2003).

"Early learning" means that the ability can be acquired within a certain ontogenetic time window (a sensitive period or critical age; see Neville & Bavelier, 2000), which in the case of AP seems to last up to an age of 5 to 6 years, but is practically impossible at later ages. The acquisition of AP may therefore be a special case of *perceptual learning*, although with a hard age limit. It shows remarkable parallels to the phonetic characteristics of first-language (L1) acquisition (see Vitouch, 2003, 2005b; cf. Deutsch, Henthorn, & Dolson, 2004; Chapter 7). Within this "plasticity window" view, however, it is still a matter of debate as to whether early learning is a *necessary* or *sufficient* condition for the development of AP, that is, if a special genetic endowment is needed as a basis (or at least as a facilitator) for AP acquisition. This makes AP an intriguing model case for the interplay of genetic and developmental factors (Zatorre, 2003). To those who do not

TABLE 10.2. *Lines of Evidence in Favor of an "Early Learning" Model of Absolute Pitch*

1. Increased incidence in the congenitally and early blind
2. Increased incidence among musicians in Japan, a country with a special tradition of early music training
3. Increased incidence in *different* types of genetically based cognitive deficit syndromes
4. High frequency of absolute pitch in latent forms
5. Strong parallels to first language (L1) acquisition
6. Consistently strong correlations between early music training and the manifestation of AP in adolescence

*Note:* See Vitouch (2003) for details.

possess it, AP typically seems completely mysterious, like a magic trick. It is not a "fixed" ability, something that pops out of the genotype by mere individual preparedness, but is subject to developmental processes at an early age. From what we know today, the brains of persons possessing AP are shaped by early experience to become what they are.

## Scale Systems: Likings in Major and Minor

It is almost trivial to note that we find a broad diversity of musical likings in the real world: there is strong heterogeneity of stylistic preferences between generations, between cultures with different music traditions, between subcultures within a society, and so on. This is field evidence for the culture-driven and moldable aspects of musical likings, as well as for the role of musical socialization.

For the sake of further demonstration, let us briefly touch the more specific issue of musical scale systems. It has been a traditional discussion in the history of both musicology and psychology whether the perception of consonance versus dissonance, and the emergence of musical scales, is a product of physical and physiological givens (founded on the resonance of partials and the anatomy of our inner ear) or a sociocultural construct. The most convincing answer is that it is both. Although there are natural constants in our (and other mammals') perception of tones, such as the phenomenon of octave similarity, the Western music system with its division of the octave into 12 chromatic tones is certainly the most dominant (if not imperialist), but of course not the only existing system. Carterette and Kendall (1999) gave a comparative overview of scale systems that fundamentally differ from the occidental pattern, such as the traditional Balinese *slendro* and *pelog* modes, which show very little overlap with the major/minor key tones. It has been argued that these scales partly reflect the particular nonharmonic structure of partials of the metallophonic instruments that are prominent in this culture (*gamelan* ensemble music). This would mean that scale systems arise from the flexible adaptation to specific resonance structures. However, we are obviously not "determined" from birth to like a certain music system – there are no innate scales. Music is universal; scale systems and musical likings are not. As a general note, although comparative musicology and ethnomusicology have a very long tradition in Europe, experimental psychology of music about other musical ethnicities is rare (see Ayari & McAdams, 2003).

Moving from the macro- to the microlevel, we find similarly interesting effects of how cognitive anatomy interacts with cultural shaping when we look at *tuning systems*. In the history of Western music, different tunings have been in use, reflecting a physical dilemma (known since Pythagoras) between purity of intonation and the usage of different keys. The modern tuning standard, equal temperament, is a compromise between purity and flexibility. In equal temperament, all semitones have exactly the same size (100 cents), which means that all musical keys are in the same condition on a keyboard instrument with fixed intonation. Chromatic modulations are perfectly possible, and all chromatic keys are available, an essential requirement since the advent of the romantic period with its complex chromatic harmonics. The price for this flexibility is a small loss in tuning accuracy for all intervals but the octave. For instance, as compared with just intonation, the major third from the tonic (C–E in C major) is somewhat "too large" in equal temperament, whereas the minor third (C–Eb in C minor) is somewhat "too narrow." These deviations from the perfect frequency ratios remain below the threshold of audible misintonations, but they affect the brilliance of sound and result in a phenomenon known as "beating" – amplitude oscillations that you can hear with the thirds or fifths on every concert grand.

How do musicians live with this compromise? We hypothesized that string players, who have the possibility of just intonation in ensembles without keyboards, should show a clear preference for just intervals, whereas pianists, who grew up in an equal-tempered environment, may have grown accustomed to the characteristics of this intonation. For instance, a just third may actually sound "too large" for a pianist. Effects in this direction were found by Loosen (1995), using melodic (sequential) musical scales. Hahn and Vitouch (2002) used more complex and harmonic musical material in a study with string players, pianists, and nonmusicians. In a number of paired-choice trials, participants had to judge which of two versions of a musical sequence they preferred. The pairs were "digital twins" of the same sequence, identical except for the difference in tuning. Some of the results are given in Figure 10.2. What we found was a specific effect of experience, namely, of the kind of instrument played on

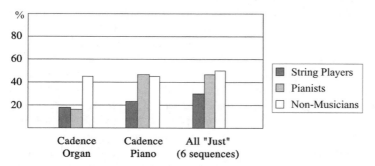

FIGURE 10.2. Preference for the equal-tempered (vs. just) version, in percent of trials. Cadence Organ, major-mode cadence in pipe organ timbre; Cadence Piano, major-mode cadence in piano timbre; All "Just" (six sequences): all six music sequences (pooled) with pairs of equal temperament versus just intonation. (Adapted from Hahn & Vitouch, 2002.)

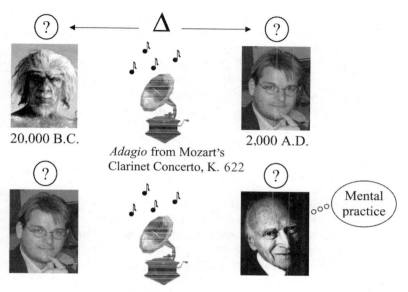

FIGURE 10.3. Issues in biocultural co-constructivism. See text for explanation.

tuning preferences (in interaction with characteristics of the sequence): string players showed a clear preference for the "just intonation" trials for most of the sequences, whereas pianists and nonmusicians mostly had no clear preference for either version. Musical likings are not just the manifestation of some homogeneous cognitive anatomy, but are modulated by cultural background (musical scale systems) and individual experience (tuning systems within the Western scale system).

## THE AESTHETIC EXPERIENCE

Be prepared for a little *Gedankenexperiment*. Figure 10.3 is at the core of biocultural co-constructivism, touching questions about the interplay of evolution, culture, and individual ontogenetic experience. First, have a look at the two persons in the upper row. One is living in 20,000 B.C., and we can safely assume that he had no formal music education, nor has he – compared with modern standards – grown up in an especially enriched musical environment. The other is living at the beginning of the twenty-first century. Evolutionary psychology holds that these two have a very similar genetic endowment – the genome of the person to the right is the heritage of his hunter-gatherer ancestor to the left, and some 20 millennia are too short for major genetic breakthroughs. Now they are both presented with the second movement from W. A. Mozart's *Concerto for Clarinet and Orchestra*, K. 622 (Mozart's last concerto). What is the phenomenological difference between Mr. 20,000's and Mr. 2,000's subjective music experience? As a result of the listening process, do they live through similar perceptual qualities (*qualia*), or are there elementary differences between what they hear and what they feel? Of course, the two differ with respect to their prior experience with music, and they have "different brains." However, they still share the same basic hardware for processing sound and music (as compared with, say, a Martian with a different genome and cognitive anatomy).

Now, look at the lower row. Here, we have Mr. 2,000 again, plus a contemporary, Sir Yehudi Menuhin (who died in 1999). It seems as if the roles had switched: our modern person becomes the aborigine, and Sir Yehudi takes over the learned part. Consider that Sir Yehudi could probably influence the microstructure of his auditory cortices even by means of mental practice (Rauschecker, 2001). Imagine that under the right conditions he just had to *think* about music to shape his musical brain. Is the difference between the music perceptions of Sir Yehudi and yours truly the same as in the previous row? Or is there a more fundamental difference between rows because Yehudi and I both had much better early environmental conditions (already in utero), such as rich nutrition and a rich culture, for developing extended plasticity? Is the aesthetic experience of these three persons essentially the same or different?

In the previous section, we saw that cortical correlates of *music perception* change with musical training as a result of brain plasticity, but from this basic level of observation, it is still a long way to the realm of *aesthetic experience*. Can we assume that the architectural changes in the musician's brain come along with structural changes in subjective experience, with altered states of musical consciousness?

Subjective experience has never been an easy topic for psychology and the neurosciences; and the experience of music is no exception. Recently, the *Spiegel* (No. 31/2003), Germany's major weekly, featured a cover story entitled "Music: The Mathematics of Feelings." Strange as it may seem to the layperson, the learned psychologist will not be surprised that "music and emotion" is not a well-researched topic in music psychology. In the name of my fellow music psychologists, let me make a confession: we still have more "tone psychology" (sometimes "chord psychology") than music psychology in the major journals. This is a chronified symptom of psychology's bottom-up orientation, and explains why aesthetic experience is a topic in philosophy, phenomenology, and aesthetics, but not so much in the cognitive psychology and the cognitive neurosciences of music.

Even psychologists, however, agree that music *does* evoke feelings and strong experiences. After all, this is precisely the reason why we listen to it. Among the abstract arts, music is probably the most intense trigger of emotional reactions. You can see people crying in a concert, whereas this rarely ever happens in a picture gallery. The effect is even stronger in combination with the performing arts: music in the movies (and, centuries earlier, opera) is an efficient source of emotional roller-coasting.

As a concomitant of the recent boom of "emotional science" (including emotional neuroscience), the topic of music and emotion had a renaissance that was overdue (see Juslin & Sloboda, 2001). How are we affected by music? One of the most inspired approaches to this is the concept of "chills & thrills" (Sloboda, 1991), which takes subjective bodily reactions to music as indicators of musical climaxes (the moments that producers try to maximize on "best of" samplers). Frequently reported correlates of such musical peak experiences are shivers down the spine ("chills"), gooseflesh, beating of the heart, lump in one's throat, tears, smiling, and so forth. Overlap of people's judgments is then used to identify common structural features of eminent musical moments or sequences. A similar but more qualitative, verbal approach has been taken by Gabrielsson (2001) with his autobiographical concept of "strong experiences with music."

If you want to see someone experiencing musical thrills, see the scene in Milos Forman's *Amadeus* (1984) in which the aged composer Antonio Salieri (F. Murray Abraham) is remembering the first time he heard a tune by Mozart, the *Adagio* from the *Gran Partita* (Serenade for 13 Winds, K. 361). Salieri, living in an insane asylum, describes the beginning of the third movement to his interviewer, a young reverend, while in the film you can hear the music. The subtlety of the scene is its suggestion that with sufficient musical expertise, you can experience musical thrills from imagery alone.[3]

These thrills are, of course, not restricted to classics. In an Internet study, Schönberger (2003) collected reports about chills and thrills with popular music. One of the tunes with the most significant interindividual overlap of thrill nominations was Whitney Houston's "I Will Always Love You" (written by Dolly Parton and featured in *The Bodyguard*, 1992). The song is structurally interesting in several respects, also because its refrain consists basically of a single note (with some appoggiaturas and grace notes). Although this is not the place for a comprehensive analysis, just consider the oddity that Salieri also emphasizes the single, high note at the beginning of the theme from the *Adagio*. In a ranking of the "top 100 million-selling songs" compiled by the U.S. radio station 90–92 FM, Houston's song came

---

[3] I am indebted to John Sloboda for guiding my attention to this scene. A similar instance of music commented online can be found in Jonathan Demme's *Philadelphia* (1993), where Tom Hanks "explains" the Aria *La mamma morta* from Umberto Giordano's *Andrea Chénier* (sung by Maria Callas) to Denzel Washington. If you want to feel pure chills for yourself, I recommend the airport showdown of Terry Gilliam's *Twelve Monkeys* (1995) with the solo violin theme (music by Paul Buckmaster).

out sixth, which was the best rank of a female voice – the next female voice was No. 24, Gloria Gaynor's "I Will Survive."[4]

The thrills framework has found resonance and support in the neurosciences. As far as the specific "chills" experience is concerned, Panksepp (1995; Panksepp & Bernatzky, 2002) has promoted the hypothesis of a substrate function of the opioid axis. According to Panksepp, the actual experience of chills does not result from the docking of endorphines on the receptors, but from their subsequent withdrawal – a music-induced "cold turkey." Following an earlier study on the perception of consonance-dissonance, Blood and Zatorre (2001) conducted an intriguing functional MRI study on intensely pleasurable responses to music. The main point of their study was that they used music self-selected by their participants, which as experimental stimuli should reliably trigger strong experiences. They found that the experience of thrills was correlated with activity changes in the reward–motivation and emotion centers of the brain, including the ventral striatum, midbrain (especially the periaqueductal gray), amygdala, orbitofrontal cortex, and ventral medial prefrontal cortex. A similar network of regions has been shown to be active in response to pleasurable stimuli such as sexual activity, food intake, cocaine rush in cocaine-dependent subjects, and chocolate consumption. It therefore is legitimate to conclude from the Blood and Zatorre (2001) study that sex, drugs, and "rock'n'roll" involve similar brain regions, and that music can have effects similar to those of biologically salient stimuli.

For the topic of biocultural co-constructivism, an essential aspect of this study is the central role of *individuality*: The self-selected experimental stimuli of one person were used as the control stimuli for another person, and all results were obtained in a (treatment–control) subtraction paradigm. Reactions to music crucially depend on *who* listens to it: on the likings and preferences of individuals, and on familiarity. What we see are individualized, biological responses, resulting from interactions of preparedness (for musical sound per se) with acquisition and learning (likings and styles). Individual musical minds are the resonant vibrations of individualized musical brains.

POSTLUDE: A BEAUTIFUL MIND

Finally, let us loop back to evolutionary theories about music. We have not been straightforwardly programmed to produce, and to like, three-part inventions. It is plausible to assume that music has *multiple origins* and that its contemporary sophistication in many, if not most, cultures has

[4] The top five songs were (1) Elton John's "Candle in the Wind," (2) Bill Haley's "Rock Around the Clock," (3) The Beatles' "I Want To Hold Your Hand" and (4) "Hey Jude," and (5) Elvis Presley's "It's Now or Never."

long been unleashed from selection pressures. Bach's fugues, Beethoven's string quartets, or Radiohead's sound weavings are nothing other than exaptations: highly refined, artful, cognitive mosaics that may capitalize on some ancient, evolutionarily useful capabilities but serve no immediate evolutionary purpose. Making music, from this perspective, is a bit like playing chess: it is something that humans *can* do based on a repertoire of underlying cognitive resources, it shapes your brain, and it is a reward by itself. Music, however, has a notable advantage: it sounds much better than chess. So, perhaps we should again borrow from philosophy, this time from Ludwig Wittgenstein, and say "Music happens when the mind goes party."

ACKNOWLEDGMENTS

I am indebted to my family, especially to Judith, Jonas, and Claudia, for granting me the extra time and support to work on this chapter, and to three anonymous reviewers for their helpful comments.

**References**

Amunts, K., Schlaug, G., Jäncke, L., Steinmetz, H., Schleicher, A., Dabringhaus, A., & Zilles, K. (1997). Motor cortex and hand motor skills: Structural compliance in the human brain. *Human Brain Mapping, 5,* 206–216.

Andrews, P. W., Gangestad, S. W., & Matthews, D. (2002). Adaptationism: How to carry out an exaptationist program. *Behavioral and Brain Sciences, 25,* 489–553.

Ayari, M., & McAdams, S. (2003). Aural analysis of Arabic improvised instrumental music (Taqsīm). *Music Perception, 21,* 159–216.

Bangert, M. W., & Altenmüller, E. O. (2003). Mapping perception to action in piano practice: A longitudinal EEG study. *BMC Neuroscience, 4* (26). Available: http://www.biomedcentral.com/1471-2202/4/26.

Blood, A. J., & Zatorre, R. J. (2001). Intensely pleasurable responses to music correlate with activity in brain regions implicated in reward and emotion. *Proceedings of the National Academy of Sciences (USA), 98,* 11818–11823.

Carterette, E. C., & Kendall, R. A. (1999). Comparative music perception and cognition. In D. Deutsch (Ed.), *The psychology of music* (2nd ed., pp. 725–791). San Diego: Academic Press.

Darwin, C. R. (1871). *The descent of man, and selection in relation to sex* (2 vols.). London: Murray.

Dennett, D. C. (1995). *Darwin's dangerous idea.* New York: Simon & Schuster.

Deutsch, D., Henthorn, T., & Dolson, M. (2004). Absolute pitch, speech, and tone language: Some experiments and a proposed framework. *Music Perception, 21,* 339–356.

Elbert, T., Pantev, C., Wienbruch, C., Rockstroh, B., & Taub, E. (1995). Increased cortical representation of the fingers of the left hand in string players. *Science, 270,* 305–307.

Ericsson, K. A., Krampe, R. T., & Tesch-Römer, C. (1993). The role of deliberate practice in the acquisition of expert performance. *Psychological Review, 100,* 363–406.

Gaab, N., & Schlaug, G. (2003). Training non-musicians on a musical task: An fMRI study. In R. Kopiez, A. C. Lehmann, I. Wolther, & C. Wolf (Eds.), *Proceedings of the 5th triennial conference of the European Society for the Cognitive Sciences of Music* (CD-ROM, pp. 539–541). Hanover, Germany: Hanover University of Music and Drama.

Gabrielsson, A. (2001). Emotions in strong experiences with music. In P. N. Juslin & J. A. Sloboda (Eds.), *Music and emotion: Theory and research* (pp. 431–449). Oxford, UK: Oxford University Press.

Gaser, C., & Schlaug, G. (2003). Brain structures differ between musicians and non-musicians. *Journal of Neuroscience, 23,* 9240–9245.

Gottesman, I. I., & Hanson, D. R. (2005). Human development: Biological and genetic processes. *Annual Review of Psychology, 56,* 263–286.

Gottlieb, G. (1998). Normally occurring environmental and behavioral influences on gene activity: From central dogma to probabilistic epigenesis. *Psychological Review, 105,* 792–802.

Gould, S. J., & Lewontin, R. C. (1979). The spandrels of San Marco and the Pan-glossian paradigm: A critique of the adaptationist programme. *Proceedings of the Royal Society of London (Series B), 205,* 581–598.

Hahn, K., & Vitouch, O. (2002). Preference for musical tuning systems: How cognitive anatomy interacts with cultural shaping. In C. Stevens, D. Burnham, G. McPherson, E. Schubert, & J. Renwick (Eds.), *Proceedings of the 7th international conference on Music Perception & Cognition* (CD-ROM, pp. 757–760). Adelaide, Australia: Causal Productions.

Hauser, M. D., & McDermott, J. (2003). The evolution of the music faculty: A comparative perspective. *Nature Neuroscience, 6,* 663–668.

Hoffrage, U., & Vitouch, O. (2002). Evolutionspsychologie des Denkens und Problemlösens [Evolutionary psychology of thinking and problem solving]. In J. Müsseler & W. Prinz (Eds.), *Allgemeine Psychologie* (pp. 734–794). Heidelberg, Germany: Spektrum.

Huron, D. (2001). Is music an evolutionary adaptation? In R. J. Zatorre & I. Peretz (Eds.), *The biological foundations of music* (Annals of the New York Academy of Sciences, Vol. 930, pp. 43–61). New York: The New York Academy of Sciences.

Juslin, P. N., & Sloboda, J. A. (Eds.). (2001). *Music and emotion: Theory and research.* Oxford, UK: Oxford University Press.

Koelsch, S., Schröger, E., & Tervaniemi, M. (1999). Superior attentive and pre-attentive auditory processing in musicians. *Neuroreport, 10,* 1309–1313.

Kunej, D., & Turk, I. (2000). New perspectives on the beginnings of music: Archeological and musicological analysis of a middle Paleolithic bone 'flute.' In N. L. Wallin, B. Merker, & S. Brown (Eds.), *The origins of music* (pp. 235–268). Cambridge, MA: MIT Press.

Levitin, D. J., & Zatorre, R. J. (2003). On the nature of early music training and absolute pitch: A reply to Brown, Sachs, Cammuso, and Folstein. *Music Perception, 21,* 105–110.

Loosen, F. (1995). The effect of musical experience on the conception of accurate tuning. *Music Perception, 12,* 291–306.

Merker, B. (2003). Is there a biology of music, and why does it matter? In R. Kopiez, A. C. Lehmann, I. Wolther, & C. Wolf (Eds.), *Proceedings of the 5th triennial conference of the European Society for the Cognitive Sciences of Music* (CD-ROM, pp. 257–260). Hanover, Germany: Hanover University of Music and Drama.

Miller, G. (2000). Evolution of human music through sexual selection. In N. L. Wallin, B. Merker, & S. Brown (Eds.), *The origins of music* (pp. 329–360). Cambridge, MA: MIT Press.

Münte, T. F., Altenmüller, E., & Jäncke, L. (2002). The musician's brain as a model of neuroplasticity. *Nature Reviews Neuroscience, 3,* 473–478.

Münte, T. F., Kohlmetz, C., Nager, W., & Altenmüller, E. (2001). Superior auditory spatial tuning in conductors. *Nature, 409,* 580.

Neville, H. J., & Bavelier, D. (2000). Specificity and plasticity in neurocognitive development in humans. In M. S. Gazzaniga (Ed.), *The new cognitive neurosciences* (2nd ed., pp. 83–98). Cambridge, MA: MIT Press.

Panksepp, J. (1995). The emotional sources of 'chills' induced by music. *Music Perception, 13,* 171–207.

Panksepp, J., & Bernatzky, G. (2002). Emotional sounds and the brain: The neuro-affective foundations of musical appreciation. *Behavioural Processes, 60,* 133–155.

Pantev, C., Oostenveld, R., Engelien, A., Ross, B., Roberts, L. E., & Hoke, M. (1998). Increased auditory cortical representation in musicians. *Nature, 392,* 811–814.

Pascual-Leone, A. (2001). The brain that plays music and is changed by it. In R. J. Zatorre & I. Peretz (Eds.), *The biological foundations of music* (Annals of the New York Academy of Sciences, Vol. 930, pp. 315–329). New York: The New York Academy of Sciences.

Rauschecker, J. P. (2001). Cortical plasticity and music. In R. J. Zatorre & I. Peretz (Eds.), *The biological foundations of music* (Annals of the New York Academy of Sciences, Vol. 930, pp. 330–336). New York: The New York Academy of Sciences.

Russo, F. A., Windell, D. L., & Cuddy, L. L. (2003). Learning the "special note": Evidence for a critical period for absolute pitch acquisition. *Music Perception, 21,* 119–127.

Schlaug, G., Jäncke, L., Huang, Y., & Steinmetz, H. (1995). In-vivo evidence of structural brain asymmetry in musicians. *Science, 267,* 699–701.

Schneider, P., Scherg, M., Dosch, H. G., Specht, H. J., Gutschalk, A., & Rupp, A. (2002). Morphology of Heschl's gyrus reflects enhanced activation in the auditory cortex of musicians. *Nature Neuroscience, 5,* 688–694.

Schönberger, J. (2003). *Zum Erleben von Thrills und anderen starken emotionalen Reaktionen beim Musikhören* [The experience of thrills and other strong emotional reactions to music]. Unpublished Master's thesis, University of Vienna, Vienna, Austria.

Sloboda, J. A. (1991). Music structure and emotional response: Some empirical findings. *Psychology of Music, 19,* 110–120.

Steele, K. M. (2003). Do rats show a Mozart effect? *Music Perception, 21,* 251–265.

Sternberg, R. J., & Kaufman, J. C. (Eds.). (2002). *The evolution of intelligence.* Mahwah, NJ: Erlbaum.

Takeuchi, A. H., & Hulse, S. H. (1993). Absolute pitch. *Psychological Bulletin, 113,* 345–361.

Tomasello, M. (1999). *The cultural origins of human cognition.* Cambridge, MA: Harvard University Press.

Vitouch, O. (2003). Absolutist models of absolute pitch are absolutely misleading. *Music Perception, 21,* 111–117.

Vitouch, O. (2005a). Erwerb musikalischer Expertise [Acquisition of musical expertise]. In T. H. Stoffer & R. Oerter (Eds.), *Enzyklopädie der Psychologie: Vol. D/VII/1. Allgemeine Musikpsychologie* (pp. 657–715). Göttingen, Germany: Hogrefe.

Vitouch, O. (2005b). Absolutes Gehör [Absolute pitch]. In T. H. Stoffer & R. Oerter (Eds.), *Enzyklopädie der Psychologie: Vol. D/VII/1. Allgemeine Musikpsychologie* (pp. 717–766). Göttingen, Germany: Hogrefe.

Wallin, N. L., Merker, B., & Brown, S. (Eds.). (2000). *The origins of music.* Cambridge, MA: MIT Press.

Zatorre, R. J. (2003). Absolute pitch: A model for understanding the influence of genes and development on neural and cognitive function. *Nature Neuroscience, 6,* 692–695.

Zdrahal-Urbanek, J., & Vitouch, O. (2003). Recognize the tune? A study on rapid recognition of classical music. In R. Kopiez, A. C. Lehmann, I. Wolther, & C. Wolf (Eds.), *Proceedings of the 5th triennial conference of the European Society for the Cognitive Sciences of Music* (CD-ROM, pp. 257–260). Hanover, Germany: Hanover University of Music and Drama.

# PART FIVE

# PLASTICITY AND BIOCULTURAL
# CO-CONSTRUCTION IN LATER LIFE

# Influences of Biological and Self-Initiated Factors on Brain and Cognition in Adulthood and Aging

Lars Nyberg and Lars Bäckman

ABSTRACT

*Age-related memory deficits are most pronounced on demanding tests of working memory and episodic memory, and are more pronounced in some older individuals than in others. In this chapter, we review individual-difference factors that influence memory functioning in adulthood and aging. A distinction is drawn between two categories of factors. The first includes biological factors that impose constraints by predisposing the aging brain toward cognitive decline. The second category includes a more heterogeneous collection of factors that are self-initiated and may be seen as offering possibilities rather than imposing constraints. We conclude by presenting some intriguing avenues for future research.*

INTRODUCTION

*Increasing age leads to impaired memory function.* Although this bold and perhaps depressing opening statement has been supported by numerous empirical observations, it has to be qualified in several ways. First, all memory functions are not uniformly affected by aging. In the domain of short-term working memory, age differences are modest on tasks that involve the passive holding of information over some restricted time period, whereas tasks that more heavily tax executive processes by requiring both holding and manipulation of memory information are associated with much more pronounced age differences. Within the domain of long-term memory, declarative (i.e., episodic and semantic) memory is more age sensitive than nondeclarative (i.e., procedural) memory. Also, within declarative memory, aging seems to have quite differential effects (e.g., Nyberg, Maitland et al., 2003; Fig. 11.1). At least up to young-old age (younger than age 70), performance on semantic memory tests such as vocabulary and general knowledge tends to *improve* with advancing age. Improved

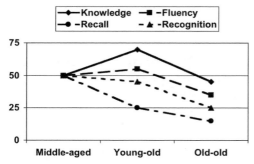

FIGURE 11.1. Age-related changes in declarative memory. Middle-age = 35–50 y; Young-old = 55–65 y; Old-old = 70–80 y. Performance on the y-axis is expressed in arbitrary units to illustrate relative age-related changes for different memory functions. (Adapted from Nyberg, Maitland et al., 2003.)

episodic memory performance with advancing age is atypical, but the negative effects of aging on episodic memory performance are moderated by the amount of retrieval support: age differences are less pronounced on supported tests (e.g., recognition tests) and more pronounced on demanding tests such as free recall (e.g., Nyberg, Maitland et al., 2003). Second, the statement that aging leads to impaired memory refers to the population level. At the individual level, it is certainly the case that many older individuals will show a level of memory functioning that exceeds that of many younger individuals (Rowe & Kahn, 1987). Thus, to better characterize the relation between aging and memory, the opening statement should be modified to be similar to the following: *Increasing age leads to impaired memory function that is most apparent on demanding tests of working memory and episodic memory and that is much more pronounced for some older individuals than for others.*

In this chapter, we elaborate on this characterization of the aging–memory relationship. Specifically, we discuss selected examples of individual difference factors that influence episodic and working memory functioning in adulthood and aging. In the spirit of this volume, we make a distinction between two categories of factors. The first category includes various biological factors that may be seen as imposing constraints by predisposing the aging brain toward cognitive decline. The second category includes a more heterogeneous set of factors that have in common that they are self-initiated rather than biologically determined. These factors may be seen as offering possibilities rather than imposing constraints. Note that the term "self-initiated" is used loosely to include self-initiated activities and more passive factors related to the environment (e.g., living conditions). Whereas these self-initiated factors are different than participating in courses and social events, they are similar in that they *in principle* can be changed by an individual's action. Finally, in the concluding section, we outline some outstanding issues on the research agenda in this field as we see them.

## CONSTRAINTS: INFLUENCES OF BIOLOGICAL FACTORS ON MEMORY PERFORMANCE

### Genetics

We begin our discussion of biological factors by considering genetic influences. Today, genetic influences are not conceived of as truly deterministic factors. Instead, the critical importance of gene–environment interactions has been emphasized in recent accounts of the genetics of behavioral aging (McClearn & Vogler, 2001). Studies that have examined the relative influence of genetic and environmental factors on memory in adulthood and aging indicate that as much as 50% of the variability in episodic memory performance can be accounted for by genetic factors (e.g., Johansson et al., 1999). With regard to the influence of specific genes, much attention has been directed at the gene that codes for apolipoprotein E (APOE). One of the APOE alleles, APOE $\varepsilon$4, has been shown to be a risk factor for Alzheimer's disease (Strittmatter et al., 1993). There is also some evidence that APOE $\varepsilon$4-positive nondemented individuals show memory deficits (e.g., O'Hara et al., 1998), although preclinical dementia may account for this association in part (e.g., Small, Basun, & Bäckman, 1998).

Recent functional brain imaging studies have examined whether differences in brain activity patterns are seen when comparing APOE $\varepsilon$4-positive and APOE $\varepsilon$4-negative individuals. The pattern of results is still somewhat mixed, but there is evidence for reduced brain activity in task-relevant regions for APOE $\varepsilon$4-positive individuals (e.g., Smith et al., 1999). We recently used functional magnetic resonance imaging (fMRI) to contrast 30 APOE $\varepsilon$4-positive individuals with 30 APOE $\varepsilon$4-negative individuals when they were engaged in a semantic classification task (Lind et al., 2005). Great care was taken both to exclude persons that might be in a preclinical stage of dementia and to match the groups on relevant demographic variables. Preliminary results suggest that the APOE $\varepsilon$4-positive individuals had reduced parietal cortex activity. This observation strongly agrees with the results of a recent study in which metabolic brain activity in APOE $\varepsilon$4-positive and APOE $\varepsilon$4-negative younger individuals was examined ($M_{age} = 31$ years; Reiman et al., 2004). Because of their young age, the individuals studied were unlikely to have been in a preclinical stage of dementia. Genetic variation therefore seems to relate to brain activity in a systematic way and may, sooner or later, translate into impaired cognitive performance. Importantly, there is also some evidence that a genetic predisposition will influence how one is affected by various incidents, for example, a synergistic interaction between APOE ε4 and head injury for the risk of dementia (Mayeux et al., 1995).

## Neurotransmission

A second biological factor relevant for our understanding of impaired memory functioning in old age is neurotransmission. There are many neurotransmitters in the central nervous system, and several may be of relevance for understanding age-related cognitive deficits. Here, we focus on the nigrostriatal dopamine system, although the mesolimbic and tegmental-neocortical dopamine systems are also relevant. It is well established that the nigrostriatal system is critical for efficient motor functioning. In addition, converging evidence from studies of Huntington and Parkinson patients, animal lesion studies, animal and human pharmacological studies, developmental studies, and computational studies show that dopamine is also critical for higher-order cognitive functions (for a review, see Bäckman & Farde, 2004). The cognitive function most studied in relation to dopamine is working memory, but associations with episodic memory have also been demonstrated repeatedly (see Braver et al., 2001).

Positron emission tomography (PET) and single photon emission tomography can be used for in vivo imaging of neurotransmission systems. Such studies have provided strong evidence that with increasing age various dopaminergic markers are reduced (e.g., Rinne, Lönnberg, & Marjamäki, 1990). The exact nature of the age–dopamine relation remains to be determined, but several studies suggest that decreases are apparent in early adulthood and subsequently magnified in an approximately linear fashion (see Reeves, Bench, & Howard, 2002). There is some evidence that the decline becomes more pronounced after 55 years of age (e.g., Bannon & Whitty, 1997), which, speculatively, may relate to recent observations in longitudinal studies that a reduction in episodic memory appears around the age of 60 (Rönnlund, Nyberg, Bäckman, & Nilsson, 2005). More direct evidence for a relation between age, dopamine functions, and memory performance comes from PET dopamine imaging studies that included age heterogeneous samples and assessed cognitive functioning before or after PET scanning (e.g., Volkow et al., 1998; Wang et al., 1998). The results of one such study provided especially strong support for age-related reductions in dopaminergic functioning as a salient biological factor for explaining age-related reductions in cognitive functioning (Bäckman et al., 2000; Table 11.1). Specifically, Bäckman and colleagues used hierarchical regression analyses to tease apart the relative influence of age and dopamine on cognitive test performance. In one such analysis, it was found that dopamine could account for a substantial portion of the variability in cognitive performance, and chronological age did not explain any additional variance when it was entered after the PET-derived measure of dopamine.

TABLE 11.1. *Amount of Variance ($R^2$) in Cognitive Performance Accounted for by Age and Dopamine $D_2$ Receptor Binding as a Function of Order of Entry*

|  | Perceptual Speed | | Episodic Memory | |
|---|---|---|---|---|
|  | Dots | Trail Making | Word Recognition | Face Recognition |
| Age | .52 | .34 | .13 | .27 |
| $D_2$ | .11 | .22 | .27 | .24 |
| Total | .63 | 56 | .40 | .51 |
| $D_2$ | .61 | .55 | .38 | .48 |
| Age | .02 | .01 | .02 | .03 |
| Total | .63 | .56 | .40 | .51 |

*Note:* Adapted from Bäckman et al. (2000).

In the reverse analysis, when age was entered into the equation before the dopamine measure, it was found that the amount of explained variance increased significantly when the dopamine measure was entered.

## Structural Brain Changes

A third critical biological factor to consider is age-related structural change in the brain. Much attention has been devoted to gray matter changes with increasing age. The most studied regions in this regard are the hippocampus and regions within the frontal cortex. The hippocampus has long been implicated in declarative memory functioning, and there is evidence that this brain region is also involved in certain working memory functions (see Ranganath & D'Esposito, 2001). Frontal brain regions are strongly associated with working memory and executive functions (see Cabeza & Nyberg, 2000), but imaging (e.g., Habib, Nyberg, & Tulving, 2003) and lesion (e.g., Wheeler, Stuss, & Tulving, 1995) data show that frontal regions are also important for declarative memory.

Hippocampal volume estimations with structural MRI studies provide evidence for volume decreases with advancing age, although some studies have found no age–volume relationship (see Albert & Killiany, 2001). Several factors, including APOE status (Kaye et al., 1997), may account for the mixed findings. When observed, the magnitude of the decrease has been quantified as mild to moderate on the basis of cross-sectional data. In a recent longitudinal study (Raz, Rodrigue, Head, Kennedy, & Acker, 2004), hippocampal volume was found to decrease with about one standard deviation over a 5-year period, and the rate of hippocampal shrinkage appeared to be higher for older than for younger adults. When measures of hippocampal volume have been related to level of memory performance, positive correlations have been observed in some studies, although in several studies no or only weak correlations were found (Albert & Killiany, 2001).

Measures of volumetric reductions of frontal regions are quite consistent in showing reduced frontal lobe volume in older age (see Albert & Killiany, 2001). Perseverative errors on the Wisconsin Card Sorting Test have been found to correlate (negatively) with frontal volume (Gunning-Dixon & Raz, 2003), providing evidence for a link between the integrity of the frontal lobes and executive functions.

In the study by Gunning-Dixon and Raz (2003), the volume of white matter hyperintensities was also related to the number of perseverative errors on the Wisconsin Card Sorting Test. This finding is in accordance with the results of other studies in which the magnitude of age-related white-matter hyperintensities was found to be pronounced in older samples and to correlate with cognitive performance (e.g., Söderlund, Nyberg, Nilsson, & Launer, 2003). White-matter hyperintensities signal impaired integrity of white matter tracts. A fairly recent MRI development consists of using diffusion tensor imaging (DTI) to examine the integrity of white matter tracts. O'Sullivan et al. (2001) used DTI to study white matter tract disruption with normal aging and correlated white matter changes with cognitive performance. In a comparison of a group of older adults with younger adults, they found evidence for reduced white matter integrity in the older group, and within the older group, white matter integrity correlated with age. The effects were most pronounced in the anterior white matter. Furthermore, in keeping with the findings by Gunning-Dixon and Raz (2003), measures of anterior white matter integrity correlated with performance on a test of executive function (the Trail Making Test).

This discussion of age-related structural brain changes concludes our brief review of biological factors that contribute to declining cognitive functioning in older age. We now examine how various self-initiated factors may help compensate for these and other biological constraints.

## POSSIBILITIES: INFLUENCES OF SELF-INITIATED FACTORS ON MEMORY PERFORMANCE

### Cognitive Compensation

One approach toward helping older adults to overcome cognitive decline is guided training in select cognitive abilities. There is much evidence that older adults can benefit from training and substantially increase their cognitive performance. One recent large-scale study included 2,832 individuals between ages 65 and 94 who had been randomly divided into a control group and three intervention groups (Ball et al., 2002). One intervention consisted of memory training, another of reasoning training, and a third of speed-of-processing training. It was found that all forms of intervention led to improved performance in the specific domain that had been trained. However, although these positive intervention effects remained over time (up to 2 years), transfer effects to nontrained tasks were minimal. In addition, although older adults benefit from cognitive training, age-comparative studies have shown that the size of memory training gains is greater for younger than older adults (e.g., Verhaeghen & Marcoen, 1996). Verhaeghen and Marcoen found that one reason for the negative age difference in training-related gains was an age-related decrease in basic processing capacity and a second reason was *noncompliance* (i.e., not using the trained strategy/technique). The negative age effect thus seemed to partly reflect a processing deficit and partly a utilization deficit. The results of a recent functional brain imaging study support this interpretation (Nyberg, Sandblom et al., 2003). Specifically, relative to pretest, memory encoding after training on the loci mnemonic was associated with increased activity in prefrontal and occipitoparietal cortex for younger adults. The older adults split into two groups: one comprising individuals whose performance was facilitated by training, and one with individuals who did not improve their performance after training. Both older groups had reduced frontal activity relative to the younger group, which may reflect a processing deficit. Moreover, it was found that the young and the facilitated older adults showed increased posterior activity (Fig. 11.2). The nonfacilitated and facilitated older adults did not differ on measures of processing capacity; therefore, the posterior effect was suggested to reflect a utilization deficit on the part of the nonfacilitated older adults.

More generally, based on imaging studies of brain activity related to exceptional performance (e.g., Maguire, Valentine, Wilding, & Kapur, 2003), it has been argued that superior memory is acquired rather than given by nature (Ericsson, 2003). Maguire and colleagues found that in a sample of ten "superior memorizers," all reported using mnemonics to support their memory. Thus, these individuals acquired a superior memory through self-initiated practice. As noted by Ericsson, however, only some people persist with training and reach high performance levels. It is unclear why some, but not others, are willing to put in the required effort. Similarly, it is unclear why some older adults seem to suffer from a utilization deficiency and appear unable or unwilling to adhere to training programs. This question is also of significance when it comes to nonguided or spontaneous compensatory activities. Recently, much attention has been devoted to findings of relatively increased brain activity in older as compared with younger adults. A salient example is that younger adults recruit right prefrontal brain regions during episodic memory retrieval, and older adults recruit bilateral prefrontal regions (e.g., Bäckman et al., 1997). It has been argued that such age-related increases in functional brain activity serve a compensatory function (Cabeza, 2002; Reuter-Lorenz, 2002).

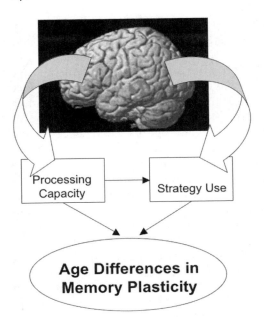

FIGURE 11.2. Schematic illustration of the relation of frontal and posterior brain regions to age-related processing and utilization deficiencies during use of the loci mnemonic. (Adapted from Nyberg, Sandblom et al., 2003.)

Findings of bilateral prefrontal activity in cognitively high- but not low-performing older adults support this view (Cabeza, Anderson, Locantore, & McIntosh, 2002). More pronounced bilaterality in the activation patterns of demented older adults (Bäckman et al., 1999), as well as in those of healthy older adults showing declining rather than stable levels of memory performance over time (Persson et al., 2005), suggests that such activity does not always accompany good cognitive performance, but may nevertheless reflect some kind of compensatory processes. As noted previously, a critical question is why some but not other older adults, as in the study by Cabeza et al. (2002), seem able to recruit additional brain regions for compensatory purposes. This interindividual difference possibly relates to the factors discussed in the next section on lifestyle.

### Lifestyle Factors

One class of lifestyle factors that has been considered to be of potential importance is substance use. In a recent study, we found evidence that, across the adult age span, current smokers outperformed people who never smoked on cognitively demanding tasks such as free recall and block design (Hill, Nilsson, Nyberg, & Bäckman, 2003). Although this observation is consistent with some prior observations, the collective pattern of results is quite variable, and it has been concluded that use of substances such as tobacco and alcohol has a rather limited effect on memory performance in adulthood and aging (Bäckman, Small, & Wahlin, 2001). A class of lifestyle factors that seems to account for more of the age-related variability in cognitive performance is engagement in social, cognitive, and physical activities (Bäckman et al., 2001; Scarmeas & Stern, 2003). In healthy aging, social disengagement seems to contribute to cognitive decline (Bassuk, Glass, & Berkman, 1999), and a rich social network has been found to exert a protective effect against dementia (Fratiglioni, Wang, Ericsson, Maytan, & Winblad, 2000). Similar effects have been observed for cognitive activities (e.g., Wilson et al., 2002) and aerobic fitness (Colcombe & Kramer, 2003).

Brain imaging studies have provided some clues on how the latter class of lifestyle factors can affect brain and cognition. Colcombe et al. (2003) showed that measures of aerobic fitness in a sample of 55 community-dwelling older adults moderated age-related decline in gray and white matter tissue density. Interestingly, the sparing effects of fitness on gray and white matter were pronounced in frontal regions (cf. see "Structural Brain Changes" section). For leisure and social activities, Scarmeas et al. (2003) demonstrated an inverse correlation between activity status and brain blood flow measured with PET. Similar observations have been reported for educational and occupational attainments (see Scarmeas et al., 2003). These findings have been related to the *cognitive reserve hypothesis*, which states that individual differences in the ability to cope with dementia-related pathological processes can in part be accounted for by aspects of life experience. Thus, on this view, engagement in activities may supply a reserve that allows individuals to cope for a longer time before the dementia becomes clinically manifest. This may also explain why apparently nondemented individuals at autopsy can show neuropathological changes typical for dementia (Goldman et al., 2001). In the context of lifestyle, it should finally be noted that stressful life situations may also serve to magnify age-related changes in cognitive functioning. Lupien et al. (1998) registered cortisol levels in older adults during a 30-day period. They found that persons with increasing or high cortisol reported higher feelings of stress than a decreasing or moderate cortisol group. In addition, the high cortisol/stress group had impaired performance on tests of delayed recall and path finding, as well as reduced hippocampal volume. On the basis of their findings, Lupien et al. concluded that increases in cortisol secretion in later life may result in cognitive deficits, suggesting that avoiding prolonged stress may be yet another self-initiated factor of importance.

In sum, studies of various kinds of self-initiated factors provide suggestive evidence that it is possible to compensate for various biological factors that predispose the aging brain toward cognitive decline. In some cases, as in the effect of aerobic fitness on gray and white matter degeneration, the expression of biological factors may actually be moderated by self-initiated activity. In other cases, such as engaging in social activities, the positive result may not affect the biological process itself (e.g., neuropathological changes associated with dementia), but rather make the individual better able to cope with these processes. Effectively, this would mean that if a pathological process has reached exactly the same point in two different individuals (e.g., affected the same number of gray/white matter neurons/pathways), the manifestation of these effects at the behavioral level would differ such that the more active individual is less severely affected as assessed by observations, neuropsychological tests, and reports by relatives.

OUTSTANDING ISSUES

We begin this chapter by characterizing cognitive aging as an impairment of memory function that is most apparent on demanding tests of working memory and episodic memory, and that is much more pronounced in some older individuals than in others. The review of biological and self-initiated factors shed some light on this characterization. The increased sensitivity of these particular memory functions can at least in part be accounted for in terms of their brain correlates, that is, age-related changes of the nigrostriatal system, as well as gray and white matter structural changes in frontal and medial-temporal brain regions, seem to explain significant portions of the age-related change in cognitive performance. Furthermore, between-individual variation in the magnitude of age-related decline seems to relate to both genetic and lifestyle-related factors. Although these and related results provide support for reciprocal influences between biological and nonbiological factors, the evidence is still largely indirect. In this final section, we discuss some avenues of research that could potentially further substantiate the link.

One significant issue concerns a more direct mapping of how structural brain changes in neurotransmission and gray/white matter volume relate to age-related differences in functional brain activity. Numerous fMRI studies have found relative regional underactivation during memory processing when older persons' brain activity was compared with that of younger persons. This pattern may reflect age-related structural brain changes that translate into lowered functional brain activity. However, as was discussed previously, there are many examples of relatively higher brain activity in older compared with younger adults, and it has been shown that age-related underrecruitment of frontal regions during intentional memory encoding can be reversed by guided task instructions (i.e., incidental encoding; Logan, Sanders, Snyder, Morris, & Buckner, 2002). Clearly, the latter set of findings suggests that the structural changes that accompany normal aging are not of sufficient magnitude to make normal functional responses impossible. One possibility that has been proposed instead is that what may be affected by aging is modulation of cortical signal-to-noise relations by relevant neurotransmitters (Esposito, Kirby, Van Horn, Ellmore, & Faith Berman, 1999). In brief, this account rests on the assumption that an optimal function of cortical brain areas, notably in prefrontal cortex, requires an optimal range of dopaminergic tone (cf. Li, Lindenberger, & Sikström, 2001). At younger ages, tonic regulation dependent on task conditions (e.g., intentional vs. incidental encoding) ensures that optimal levels and corresponding increases and decreases in activity are instantiated. In contrast, at older ages, the regulation is impaired, which may result in suboptimal levels under certain task conditions (e.g., intentional encoding) but not others (e.g., incidental encoding). Empirical approaches that may shed light on this account include "pharmacological brain imaging" (e.g., Bullmore et al., 2003), as well as multimodal imaging (e.g. combined molecular and functional imaging).

Another significant issue has to do with more direct assessment of the effects of self-initiated factors on cognitive and brain function in older age. We noted previously that older adults benefit from skills that are learned in directed training programs, but there seem to be severe limitations on how these skills transfer to facilitate untrained functions and everyday activities (e.g., Ball et al., 2002). It is possible that other forms of training that tap basic cognitive (e.g., working memory) and neural (e.g., frontal cortex) systems may foster greater generalization (Olesen, Westerberg, & Klingberg, 2004). However, at the population level, stimulating activities in the form of leisure and social activities probably have greater potential than guided training programs. We reviewed evidence that such activities have positive effects on cognition and also on brain function, and we have preliminary data to suggest that those older adults who display "successful" aging by showing minimal cognitive impairment have more close friends and are less often alone than the majority of older adults who display "normal" cognitive aging (Habib, Nyberg, & Nilsson, 2005). To date, however, most studies that have examined the influence of lifestyle factors on brain and cognition in adulthood and aging have used a cross-sectional design, so conclusions about cause or effect remain tentative. A longitudinal design was used in a study of time-related structural brain changes in high-performing older adults, but that study did not include any control group of "normal" older adults or any measures of lifestyle factors (Wahlund, Almkvist, Basun, & Julin, 1996). Longitudinal studies, perhaps of a quasiexperimental nature, will be needed to more conclusively determine whether lifestyle activities have causal influences on brain and cognition.

In conclusion, the complexity of interactions between biological and cultural factors in developmental processes has currently received considerable attention. In this chapter, we focus on the interaction between biology and behavior, whereas in Chapter 12, environmental and cultural factors are discussed in depth. In a recent contribution, Buckner (2005) concluded:

> The fundamental assumption is that the varied cognitive states of older individuals are caused by the many age-associated brain changes that are taking place, their responses to these changes, how they sum and interact, and how the experiences and external interactions in a person's life influence these changes. Full description of why some individuals present in one manner and others quite differently will require that theories and measurement span multiple levels of organization – from the genetic to the behavioral. (p. 282)

We believe that the efforts summarized in this volume represent a significant step in this direction.

ACKNOWLEDGMENTS

Preparation of this chapter was supported by grants from the Swedish Research Council to Lars Nyberg, and from the Swedish Research Council and the Bank of Sweden Tercentenary Foundation to Lars Bäckman.

**References**

Albert, M. S., & Killiany, R. J. (2001). Age-related cognitive change and brain–behavior relationships. In J. E. Birren & K. W. Schaie (Eds.), *Handbook of the psychology of aging* (5th ed., pp. 161–185). San Diego: Academic Press.

Bäckman, L., Almkvist, O., Andersson, J., Nordberg, A., Reineck, R., Winblad, B., & Långström, B. (1997). Brain activation in young and older adults during implicit and explicit retrieval. *Journal of Cognitive Neuroscience, 9*, 378–391.

Bäckman, L., Andersson, J. L. R., Nyberg, L., Winblad, B., Nordberg, A., & Almkvist, O. (1999). Brain regions associated with episodic retrieval of verbal information in normal aging and Alzheimer's disease. *Neurology, 52*, 1861–1870.

Bäckman, L., & Farde, L. (2004). The role of dopamine systems in cognitive aging. In R. Cabeza, L. Nyberg, & D. C. Park (Eds.), *Cognitive neuroscience of aging: Linking cognitive and cerebral aging* (pp. 58–84). Oxford, UK: Oxford University Press.

Bäckman, L., Ginovart, N., Dixon, R. A., Robins Wahlin, T.-B., Wahlin, Å., Halldin, C., & Farde, L. (2000). Age-related cognitive deficits mediated by changes in the striatal dopamine system. *American Journal of Psychiatry, 157*, 635–637.

Bäckman, L., Small, B. J., & Wahlin, Å. (2001). Aging and memory: Cognitive and biological perspectives. In J. E. Birren & K. W. Schaie (Eds.), *Handbook of the psychology of aging* (5th ed., pp. 349–377). San Diego: Academic Press.

Ball, K., Berch, D. B., Helmers, K. F., Jobe, J. B., Leveck, M. D., Marsiske, M., et al. (2002). Effects of cognitive training interventions with older adults: A randomized controlled trial. *JAMA, 13*, 2271–2281.

Bannon, M. J., & Whitty, C. J. (1997). Age-related and regional differences in dopamine mRNA expression in human midbrain. *Neurology, 48*, 969–977.

Bassuk, S. S., Glass, T. A., & Berkman, L. F. (1999). Social disengagement and incident cognitive decline in community-dwelling elderly persons. *Annals of Internal
Medicine, 131,* 165–173.

Braver, T. S., Barch, D. M., Keys, B. A., Carter, C. S., Cohen, J. D., Kaye, J. A., et al.
(2001). Context processing in older adults: Evidence for a theory relating cognitive control to neurobiology in healthy aging. *Journal of Experimental Psychology:
General, 130,* 746–763.

Buckner, R. L. (2005). Three principles for cognitive aging research: Multiple causes
and sequelae, variance in expression and response, and the need for integrative
theory. In R. Cabeza, L. Nyberg, & D. C. Park (Eds.), *Cognitive neuroscience of aging:
Linking cognitive and cerebral aging* (pp. 267–285). Oxford, UK: Oxford University
Press.

Bullmore, E., Suckling, J., Zelaya, F., Long, C., Honey, G., Reed, L., et al. (2003).
Practice and difficulty evoke anatomically and pharmacologically dissociable
brain activation dynamics. *Cerebral Cortex, 13,* 144–154.

Cabeza, R. (2002). Hemispheric asymmetry reduction in older adults: The HAROLD
model. *Psychology and Aging, 17,* 85–100.

Cabeza, R., Anderson, N. D., Locantore, J. K., & McIntosh, A. R. (2002). Aging grace-
fully: Compensatory brain activity in high-performing older adults. *NeuroImage,
17,* 1394–1402.

Cabeza, R., & Nyberg, L. (2000). Imaging cognition II: An empirical review of 275
PET and fMRI studies. *Journal of Cognitive Neuroscience, 12,* 1–47.

Colcombe, S. J., Erickson, K. I., Raz, N., Webb, A. G., Cohen, N. J., McAuley, E., &
Kramer, A. F. (2003). Aerobic fitness reduces brain tissue loss in aging humans.
*Journal of Gerontology: Medical Sciences, 58A,* M176–M180.

Colcombe, S., & Kramer, A. F. (2003). Fitness effects on the cognitive function of
older adults: A meta-analytic study. *Psychological Science, 14,* 125–130.

Ericsson, K. A. (2003). Exceptional memorizers: Made, not born. *Trends in Cognitive
Sciences, 7,* 233–235.

Esposito, G., Kirby, G. S., Van Horn, J. D., Ellmore, T. M., & Faith Berman, K. (1999).
Context-dependent, neural system-specific neurophysiological concomitants of
ageing: Mapping PET correlates during cognitive activation. *Brain, 122,* 963–
979.

Fratiglioni, L., Wang, H. X., Ericsson, K., Maytan, M., & Winblad, B. (2000). Influence
of social network on the occurrence of dementia: A community-based longitudinal study. *Lancet, 355,* 1315–1319.

Goldman, W. P., Price, J. L., Storandt, M., Grant, E. A., McKeel, D. W., Rubin, E. H.,
& Morris, J. C. (2001). Absence of cognitive impairment or decline in preclinical
Alzheimer's disease. *Neurology, 56,* 361–367.

Gunning-Dixon, F. M., & Raz, N. (2003). Neuroanatomical correlates of selected
executive functions in middle-aged and older adults: A prospective MRI study.
*Neuropsychologia, 41,* 1929–1941.

Habib, R., Nyberg, L., & Nilsson, L.-G. (in press). Cognitive and Non-Cognitive Factors Contributing to the Longitudinal Identification of Successful Older Adults
in the *Betula* Study. *Aging, Neuropsychology, and Cognition.* Manuscript accepted
for publication.

Habib, R., Nyberg, L., & Tulving, E. (2003). Hemispheric asymmetries of memory:
The HERA model revisited. *Trends in Cognitive Science, 7,* 241–245.

Hill, R. D., Nilsson, L.-G., Nyberg, L., & Bäckman, L. (2003). Cigarette smoking and cognitive performance in healthy Swedish adults. *Age and Ageing, 32,* 548–550.

Johansson, B., Whitfield, K., Pedersen, N. L., Hofer, S. M., Ahern, F., & McClearn, G. E. (1999). Origins of individual differences in episodic memory in the oldest-old: A population-based study of identical and same-sex fraternal twins aged 80 or older. *Journal of Gerontology: Psychological Sciences, 54,* P173–P179.

Kaye, J. A., Swihart, T., Howieson, D., Dame, A., Moore, M. M., Karnos, T., et al. (1997). Volume loss of the hippocampus and temporal lobe in healthy elderly persons destined to develop dementia. *Neurology, 48,* 1297–1304.

Li, S.-C., Lindenberger, U., & Sikström, S. (2001). Aging cognition: From neuromodulation to representation to cognition. *Trends in Cognitive Science, 5,* 479–486.

Lind, J., Persson, J., Ingvar, M., Larsson, A., Cruts, M., van Broeckhoven, C., Adolfsson, R., Bäckman, L., Nilsson, L-G., Petersson, K.-M., & Nyberg, L. (in press). *Reduced functional brain activity in cognitively intact apolipoprotein e4 carriers.* Manuscript submitted for publication.

Logan, J. M., Sanders, A. L., Snyder, A. Z., Morris, J. C., & Buckner, R. L. (2002). Under-recruitment and nonselective recruitment: Dissociable neural mechanisms with aging. *Neuron, 33,* 827–840.

Lupien, S. J., de Leon, M., Desanti, S., Convit, A., Tarshish, C., Nair, N. P. V., et al. (1998). Cortisol levels during human aging predict hippocampal atrophy and memory deficits. *Nature Neuroscience, 1,* 69–73.

Maguire, E. A., Valentine, E. R., Wilding, J. M., & Kapur, N. (2003). Routes to remembering: The brains behind superior memory. *Nature Neuroscience, 6,* 90–95.

Mayeux, R., Ottman, R., Maestre, G., Ngai, C., Tang, M.-X., Ginsberg, H., et al. (1995). Synergistic effects of traumatic head injury and apolipoprotein-ε4 in patients with Alzheimer's disease. *Neurology, 45,* 555–557.

McClearn, G. E., & Vogler, G. P. (2001). The genetics of behavioral aging. In J. E. Birren & K. W. Schaie (Eds.), *Handbook of the psychology of aging* (5th ed., pp. 109–131). San Diego: Academic Press.

Nyberg, L., Maitland, S. B., Rönnlund, M., Bäckman, L., Dixon, R. A., Wahlin, Å., & Nilsson, L.-G. (2003). Selective adult age differences in an age-invariant multi-factor model of declarative memory. *Psychology and Aging, 18,* 149–160.

Nyberg, L., Sandblom, J., Jones, S., Stigsdotter Neely, A., Petersson, K. M., Ingvar, M., & Bäckman, L. (2003). Neural correlates of training-related memory improvement in adulthood and aging. *Proceedings of the National Academy of Sciences (USA), 100,* 13728–13733.

O'Hara, R., Yesavage, J. A., Kraemer, H. C., Mauricio, M., Friedman, L. F., & Murphy G. M., Jr. (1998). The APOE epsilon 4 allele is associated with decline on delayed recall performance in community-dwelling older adults. *Journal of the American Geriatrics Society, 46,* 1493–1498.

Olesen, P. J., Westerberg, H., & Klingberg, T. (2004). Increased prefrontal and parietal activity after training of working memory. *Nature Neuroscience, 7,* 75–79.

O'Sullivan, M., Jones, D. K., Summers, P. E., Morris, R. G., Williams, S. C. R., & Markus, H. S. (2001). Evidence for cortical "disconnection" as a mechanism of age-related cognitive decline. *Neurology, 57,* 632–638.

Persson, J., Nyberg, L., Lind, J., Larsson, A., Nilsson, L.-G., Ingvar, M., & Buckner, R. L. (2005). Structure–function correlates of cognitive decline in aging. *Cerebral Cortex,*

Ranganath, C., & D'Esposito, M. (2001). Medial temporal lobe activity associated with active maintenance of novel information. *Neuron, 31,* 865–873.

Raz, N., Rodrigue, K. M., Head, D., Kennedy, K. M., & Acker, J. D. (2004). Differential aging of the medial temporal lobe: A study of five-year change. *Neurology, 62,* 433–438.

Reeves, S., Bench, C., & Howard, R. (2002). Aging and the nigrostriatal dopamine system. *International Journal of Geriatric Psychiatry, 17,* 359–370.

Reiman, E. M., Chen, K. W., Alexander, G. E., Caselli, R. J., Bandy, D., Osborne, D., et al. (2004). Functional brain abnormalities in young adults at genetic risk for late-onset Alzheimer's dementia. *Proceedings of the National Academy of Sciences (USA), 101,* 284–289.

Reuter-Lorenz, P. A. (2002). New visions of the aging mind and brain. *Trends in Cognitive Sciences, 6,* 394–400.

Rinne, J. O., Lönnberg, P., & Marjamäki, P. (1990). Age-dependent decline of dopamine-D$_1$ and dopamine-D$_2$ receptor. *Brain Research, 508,* 349–352.

Rönnlund, M., Nyberg, L., Bäckman, L., & Nilsson, L.-G. (2005). Stability, improvement, and decline in adult-life span development of declarative memory: Cross-sectional and longitudinal data from a population-based sample. *Psychology and Aging.*

Rowe, J. W., & Kahn, R. L. (1987). Human aging: Usual and successful. *Science, 237,* 143–149.

Scarmeas, N., & Stern, Y. (2003). Cognitive reserve and lifestyle. *Journal of Clinical and Experimental Neuropsychology, 25,* 625–633.

Scarmeas, N., Zarahn, E., Anderson, K. E., Habeck, C. G., Hilton, J., & Flynn, J. (2003). Association of life activities with cerebral blood flow in Alzheimer's disease. *Archives of Neurology, 60,* 359–365.

Small, B. J., Basun, H., & Bäckman, L. (1998). Three-year changes in cognitive performance as a function of apolipoprotein E genotype: Evidence from very old adults without dementia. *Psychology and Aging, 13,* 80–87.

Smith, C. D., Andersen A. H., Kryscio, R. J., Schmitt, F. A., Kindy, M. S., Blonder, L. X., & Avison, M. J. (1999). Altered brain activation in cognitively intact individuals at high risk for Alzheimer's disease. *Neurology, 53,* 1391–1396.

Söderlund, H., Nyberg, L., Nilsson, L.-G., & Launer, L. J. (2003). High prevalence of white matter lesions in normal aging: Relation to blood pressure and cognition. *Cortex, 39,* 1093–1105.

Strittmatter, W. J., Saunders, A. M., Schmechel, D., Pericak-Vance, M., Enghild, J., Salvesen, G. S., & Roses, A. D. (1993). Apolipoprotein E: High-avidity binding to beta-amyloid and increased frequency of type 4 allele in late-onset familial Alzheimer's disease. *Proceedings of the National Academy of Sciences (USA), 90,* 1977–1981.

Verhaeghen, P., & Marcoen, A. (1996). On the mechanisms of plasticity in young and older adults after instruction in the method of loci: Evidence for an amplification model. *Psychology and Aging, 11,* 164–178.

Volkow, N. D., Gur, R. C., Wang, G.-J., Fowler, J. S., Moberg, P. J., Ding, Y. S., et al. (1998). Association between decline in brain dopamine activity with age and cognitive and motor impairment in healthy individuals. *American Journal of Psychiatry, 155,* 344–349.

Wahlund, L.-O., Almkvist, O., Basun, H., & Julin, P. (1996). MRI in successful aging: A 5-year follow-up study from the eighth to ninth decade of life. *Magnetic Resonance Imaging, 14,* 601–608.

Wang, Y., Chan, G. L. Y., Holden, J. E., Dobko, T., Mak, E., Schulzer, M., et al. (1998). Age-dependent decline of dopamine $D_1$ receptors in human brain: A PET study. *Synapse, 30,* 56–61.

Wheeler, M. A., Stuss, D. T., & Tulving, E. (1995). Frontal lobe damage produces memory impairment. *Journal of the International Neuropsychological Society, 1,* 525–536.

Wilson, R. S., Mendes de Leon, C. F., Barnes, L. L., Schneider, J. A., Bienias, J. L., Evans, D. A., & Bennett, D. A. (2002). Participation in cognitively stimulating activities and risk of incident Alzheimer disease. *JAMA, 287,* 742–748.

# 12

# The Aging Mind and Brain: Implications of Enduring Plasticity for Behavioral and Cultural Change

Patricia A. Reuter-Lorenz and Joseph A. Mikels

ABSTRACT

*Although aging is broadly characterized by decline, the potential for new learning and plasticity persists well into the later decades of life. Scientific advances are yielding a deeper understanding of the limitations that biological aging imposes on cognitive function, as well as new insights into how the human mind and brain respond adaptively to the aging process. Neurocognitive investigations of the reciprocity between mind and brain reveal new avenues to influence and shape neural processes that underlie mental fitness, especially in the golden years. We explore these ideas to illustrate the co-constructivist framework in operation across neural, cognitive, behavioral, and cultural dimensions as they influence late-life development.*

OVERVIEW

The persistence of behavioral adaptation and plasticity (i.e., modifiability) in later life has been recognized by the field of cognitive aging for several decades (e.g., Baltes, 1997). Training procedures of various sorts have been shown to enhance cognitive performance and produce long-term gains, even for older adults well into their seventies (e.g., Willis & Nesselroade, 1990). With the recent advances in genetics, in the basic neurosciences, and in brain imaging technologies, the scope and potential of age-related reorganizational processes have attained a new level of analysis and persuasion, especially for researchers whose theoretical orientation is closely linked to brain correlates of plasticity (Park, Polk, Mikels, Taylor, & Marshuetz, 2001; Reuter-Lorenz, 2002). As documented in other contributions to this volume, and in this chapter, adult neurogenesis, cognitive improvement with physical exercise, and compensatory brain activity patterns are but a few of the more recent additional indications that behavioral and biological plasticity, even in the golden years, is a fact of life. Indeed, identifying the sources, mechanisms, and limitations of later-life plasticity, whether they are due to nature (i.e., genetics), nurture, or both, is an endeavor of great practical and intellectual interest and, in many respects, forms the bedrock of a biocultural co-constructivist agenda for aging research.

Biocultural co-constructivism recognizes that individual lifespan development is the result of the co-constructive influences of biology and culture (i.e., experience and environment). However, co-constructivism takes the nature–nurture inquiry several steps further by examining the recursive influences of the individual on his or her own biology, of biology on the environment, and vice versa. For example, in the context of developmental changes over the lifespan, we can inquire about how the individual system adapts, both behaviorally and neurophysiologically, to its own reorganization. Moreover, one can investigate whether and how the reorganized system alters its environment and, in turn, brings new influences on itself. Understanding this kind of recursion at different levels of analysis is at the heart of the co-constructive endeavor and is one of the greatest and most novel challenges it poses.

No forum could be more appropriate than the present one to attempt to take on this challenge as it pertains to aging. We do so from a perspective framed by a novel theory that has grown out of our own research on age-related alterations in working memory and their neural underpinnings. We refer to this view as the *compensation-related utilization of neural circuits hypothesis* (or CRUNCH). This hypothesis recognizes that the aging brain adapts to its own decline by recruiting additional neural circuits not typically engaged by younger brains to optimize information processing. Such forms of compensation may have a cost in that more neural resources must be expended by an older brain to accomplish computational goals that can be completed more efficiently (i.e., with fewer circuits) by younger brains. Nevertheless, we are beginning to understand the processes of compensation and adaptation from a biological perspective, and this understanding can permit a more complete analysis of the co-constructive influences on the later stages of life.

Although this chapter focuses on an individual brain-oriented approach, we draw attention to the fact that the notion of compensation is also a cultural construct. For some cultural anthropologists (Gehlen, 1988), culture is inherently a system of compensations, usually inventions and resources that "compensate" for the shortcomings of the biological make-up of humans. Thus, although it is not the primary focus of this chapter, we want to acknowledge the view that compensatory forces are also part of the environment and through experience can shape the brain in directions similar to the brain-based account of CRUNCH (see, e.g., Baltes, 1997; Chapter 14).

As background, we begin with a basic but broad-stroke review of what is known about the declines that normally accompany neural and cognitive aging, followed by an overview of evidence indicating the extent to which plasticity endures in older age (see Chapters 2 and 11). By way of introduction to our own neurocognitive hypothesis, we discuss two related macro-level theories that were derived on purely behavioral grounds: the theory of selection, optimization, and compensation (SOC; see Baltes, 1997) and socioemotional selectivity theory (SST; see Carstensen, Isaacowitz, & Charles, 1999). After discussing CRUNCH and its empirical foundations, we close with some speculations that it is hoped will point to future research that considers the dynamic reciprocity inherent in the co-constructive approach.

## REALITY OF NEURAL AND COGNITIVE DECLINES

In various places throughout this chapter, we distinguish between the aging mind and the aging brain, recognizing the separable disciplines that have generated largely independent descriptions and accounts of the aging process. Neurobiological descriptions of the aging process emphasize structural changes, along with functional alterations, that are measured physiologically. This approach, largely devoid of reference to psychological function, is what we refer to as the aging brain. Conversely, the psychological accounts of the aging process emphasize functional changes in the performance of the "system." Psychological theories explain performance changes by appealing to psychological constructs, mental operations, and the environmental/experiential dynamics that shape them, with minimal reference to neurobiological substance that embodies and implements these processes. This approach is captured by our phrase "the aging mind."

In truth, as cognitive neuroscientists, we believe this to be a false dichotomy in that mental events have an underlying neurobiology that can influence other neurobiological processes, neurobiological processes give rise to mental events, and our methods enable us to investigate both levels of analysis in tandem. Nevertheless, the dichotomy recognizes the disciplinary boundaries that have largely characterized the study of aging, with emphasis on behavioral/performance measures and psychologically based theories on the one side, versus neural and biologically based explanations on the other.

Aging is accompanied by global declines in brain structure as well as specific and localized alterations (for a review, see Raz, 2000). On the macro level, brain weight and volume decline approximately 2% per decade in a relatively linear fashion. This decrease is related to the expansion of the cerebral ventricles and the enlargement of the cerebral sulci. On a micro level, these declines in brain weight and volume are manifest in neuron shrinkage; debranching of the dendrites; declines in synaptogenesis; declines in dopamine receptors, transporters, and storage vesicles; and generalized white and gray matter loss.

It is also recognized that atrophy of the aging brain is not fully global and that some areas are more affected than others. In the neocortex, the prefrontal association cortex is especially vulnerable to age-related atrophy relative to more moderate declines in the temporal, parietal, and occipital cortices and minimal age-related decline in the anterior cingulate gyri. Moreover, lateral prefrontal areas may be more affected than orbital frontal cortex, an effect that has interesting implications given the divergent trajectories of cognitive decline and emotional preservation and improvement.

Differential age-related atrophy is also evident subcortically. Moderate shrinkage of the amygdala, hippocampus, mammillary bodies, caudate, putamen, and globus pallidus have all been documented, whereas the pons appears less sensitive to the effects of age, at least with respect to volume. The extent to which these patterns of spared versus moderate to extensive neural atrophy align with patterns of preservation versus decline in the aging mind is the subject of vigorous and ongoing research.

The characterization of the aging mind has been strongly influenced by the psychometric tradition of intelligence testing. Accordingly, developmental psychologists conceive of the mind as a multidimensional system that is comprised of different intellectual abilities that have different life course trajectories (Schaie, 2005). In particular, decades of research on cognitive aging have documented a steady decline over the lifespan on tests that are believed to measure fluid intelligence, such as reasoning, problem solving, and tests of associative and recollective memory. In contrast, measures of knowledge-rich, crystallized intelligence, such as tests of vocabulary, numerical abilities, and world knowledge are relatively well preserved in older adults (for reviews, see Craik & Salthouse, 2000).

Several theories have been proposed to account for the differential effects of aging on these two broad classes of mental abilities. One sort of model appeals to the underlying construct of cognitive resources, such as processing capacity (i.e., mental workspace) or processing speed. Tasks that tap fluid intelligence are posited to be more resource demanding and more dependent on mental effort than measures of crystallized intelligence (Hasher & Zacks, 1979; Salthouse, 1996). Consequently, performance changes due to aging will be more evident on tasks that are resource dependent. A different but related view is that, relative to knowledge-based intellectual abilities, fluid facets of intelligence, also referred to as cognitive mechanics, are more constrained by the integrity of biological mechanisms (Baltes, 1997). Knowledge-based abilities are more exogenously influenced, contextualized, and closely linked to the cultural and experiential history of an individual. The biological declines that accompany aging are therefore more evident in measures of fluid intelligence.

The information processing tradition of cognitive psychology has fostered a characterization of the aging mind in terms of constituent mental operations or processes. This tradition emphasizes the use of "model" experimental paradigms to analyze elementary perceptual and cognitive processes that are viewed as the building blocks or constituents of complex mental abilities. The goal here is to identify the basic operations that are most affected by the aging process. One of the most influential accounts of this type proposed by Hasher and Zacks (1988) posits that a fundamental source of age-related changes in cognition is a decline in inhibitory processes. According to this view, aging reduces the ability to filter out irrelevant information, to delete no longer relevant information, and to resolve conflict between competing inputs and competing response tendencies. By considering such elementary mental operations as cognitive mechanics, it becomes possible to integrate the information processing view of cognitive aging with accounts arising from the psychometric tradition (see Li et al., 2004). There is a need for future research in aging and lifespan development to achieve a more thorough integration of the intellectual abilities framework and the information processing approach, especially in an effort to understand the neuropsychological basis of aging.

Nevertheless, the information processing approach to cognitive aging has lent itself to a more brain-based, neuropsychological framework in which to understand the aging mind. Although the psychometric tradition clearly recognizes that age-related changes in intelligence must have biological correlates, a focus on basic cognitive operations permits a more direct mapping to neurological mechanisms. Thus, the information processing approach has enabled a fertile integration of biological and behavioral approaches. From this perspective, researchers have tried to understand age declines by identifying similarities between the cognitive and task performance profiles of older adults and those obtained from patient populations who have well-described, circumscribed neurological deficits. One merit of this approach is that it has generated hypotheses that link cognitive declines in aging to alterations in specific neural subsystems. For example, aging of the hippocampus is viewed as a critical source of age declines in associative and recollective memory. Neural declines in prefrontal cortex are the hypothesized cause of declines in reasoning, problem solving, and the class of processes referred to as executive functions.[1] At the same time, analogies with the effects of brain damage have tended to promote a pessimistic view of the aging process that emphasizes loss rather than reorganization and the possibility of continued modifiability.

---

[1] Although a consensual definition of executive functions is lacking, most taxonomies include such processes as inhibition, planning, goal shifting, and rule formation and implementation (see Smith & Jonides, 1999, for a review).

More generally, behavioral analyses are associated with the temptation to assume that preserved performance indicates that the mechanisms underlying task performance are also preserved. Although the use of compensatory strategies has figured prominently in some accounts of cognitive aging (Bäckman & Dixon, 1992; Baltes, 1997), the equation of spared and impaired performance with spared and impaired underlying processes, respectively, has been the predominant neuropsychological approach to aging until recently. The interpretation of spared performance is especially important to consider because it could signal preservation of underlying circuitry, compensatory processes, or some combination thereof. By using brain imaging technology to assess neural activity while older adults are engaged in different cognitive tasks, it has become possible to identify the substrates of spared versus impaired performance, and to characterize the corresponding utilization of neural resources. The additional leverage, thus provided, has proven essential in the view we develop here about the role of compensation and functional reorganization in the circuitry that supports cognitive performance in older age (see also, e.g., Park et al., 2001).

PLASTICITY IN AGING

Against a backdrop of neural and cognitive declines, resilience, plasticity, and the capacity for reorganization endure through the latter decades of life according to multiple sources of evidence. One of the most direct ways to identify an enduring capacity for plasticity is to examine the effects of training interventions on the performance of older adults. Indeed, the ability of older adults to benefit from training and to acquire new skills well into the ninth decade of life were extensively studied and well established nearly two decades ago (Baltes & Lindenberger, 1988). For example, the method of loci, widely used to improve long-term memory, involves associating new materials with a series of well-known landmarks. Like most abilities, the ability to acquire new skills and the benefits of training interventions, such as the method of loci, decrease with age. Consequently, in training studies, age differences are most pronounced when skills have been learned and acquired to asymptotic levels (i.e., the method of testing the limits; Kliegl, Smith, & Baltes, 1990). Nevertheless, the capacity for improvement remains across the lifespan, and one goal of aging successfully is to achieve a full realization of one's potential for plasticity.

Of course, the seeds for successful aging are sown throughout the life cycle by experiential contexts that shape neural and cognitive functioning. There is accumulating evidence to indicate that the quality of cognitive functioning in older age is influenced by work experience (see Chapter 14), socioeconomic status, ethnicity, race, and culture (see Stern & Carstensen, 2000, for a review). The "training" benefits accrued and the "healthfulness" promoted by particular life experiences and cultural contexts have been proposed as causal mechanisms underlying these effects. Yet, we are only beginning to understand the principles by which life experiences and the inputs and feedback from the environment shape the brain's structure and function. Here, we summarize recent cognitive neuroscience evidence demonstrating that even in older age there is sufficient plasticity to permit beneficial effects of experiential and environmental interventions that can promote successful aging.

The evidence for positively transformative effects of diet and exercise in older age is particularly exciting. Aging decreases the ability to combat chemical imbalances, such as increases in free radicals that damage cellular structure and have been compellingly linked to the deleterious effects of aging on the brain (Finch & Cohen, 1997). Antioxidants can correct such imbalances by deactivating these free radicals, thus preventing and potentially reversing the detrimental effects of aging. Specifically, dietary consumption of foods high in antioxidants – such as blueberries, strawberries, and spinach – have been shown not only to prevent the onset of neural and cognitive degradation, but also to reverse these decrements once already in motion (Joseph et al., 1999).

Apart from the benefits of weight control and an improved sense of well-being, a decade of research has established that higher levels of physical fitness can maintain and even enhance aspects of cognitive functioning (Churchill et al., 2002). Compared with older people who are low in cardiovascular fitness, highly fit seniors not only perform better on cognitive measures of attention and conflict resolution, but they also demonstrate more efficient recruitment of the neural circuitry critical for implementing cognitive control (Colcombe et al., 2004). There is some evidence to indicate that even a short-term program of aerobic exercise can actually reverse the downward trajectory that characterizes measures of fluid intelligence and effortful processing tasks (Churchill et al., 2002). Animal models have demonstrated that brain function is a direct recipient of the benefits of aerobic training through increased neurogenesis, and other neurophysiological changes that foster neuronal survival and plasticity (van Praag, Christie, Sejnowski, & Gage, 1999). Moreover, increased vascularity in physically fit individuals could also improve neurophysiological function (Churchill et al., 2002). The benefits of diet and exercise could also operate indirectly; that is, fit bodies may function self-sufficiently in that they require less monitoring and fewer cognitive resources, thereby making a larger share of cognitive resource available for cognitive activity (see, e.g., Li, Lindenberger, Freund, & Baltes, 2001).

Animal models have clearly established the importance of enriched environments on neural and behavioral development. Not only is such exposure vital in the early stages of the life cycle, but also its influence can persist in later life as well. The exposure of old mice and rats to complex environments, for instance, with more opportunities to explore novel situations, objects, and social interactions, improves performance on cognitive and behavioral tasks (Winocur, 1998). Such behavioral improvements occur when the animals are moved from impoverished to enriched environments. Moreover, when the animals are moved from enriched to impoverished environments, opposite results emerge as declines in performance (Winocur, 1998). Thus, behaviorally it appears that the effects of the environment on behavior and cognition are somewhat reversible and plastic even in older age. There has been considerable progress in identifying the neural correlates associated with environmental influences in the mature adult brain. Enriched environments have been associated with synaptogenesis, dendritic branching, neurogenesis, and plasticity of supportive elements such as glial cells (see Churchill et al., 2002; Chapter 4). Plasticity of this sort is likely to underlie the behavioral and cognitive improvements observed in enriched environments into older age.

The factor of social engagement, which can be viewed as the mutual and interactive influence of experiential and environmental factors, has also been shown to influence the aging process. For instance, high levels of social engagement, such as living with a spouse and/or having monthly contact with close family members or friends, improve performance on measures of cognitive ability (Arbuckle, Gold, & Andres, 1986). It may not be the actual social contact that prevents cognitive decline, but rather the social and emotional support received (Seeman, Lusignolo, Albert, & Berkman, 2001).

It is part of the co-constructivist argument that neural and cognitive aging are contingent on extant cultural conditions. Although the mechanisms have yet to be elucidated, neural aging must also reflect the cultural and technological context in which the biology of aging takes place. The fact that vitality and longevity have been extended and continue to be extended must entail fundamental changes in the characteristics of the aging brain. In turn, the presence of an older citizenry within a culture will shape the characteristics of that culture. Although an extensive review of cultural influences on aging is outside the scope of this chapter (see Chapter 2), it is helpful to consider how a "cultural neuroscience" approach to aging can test various hypotheses about the structure of aging cognition and the influence of environmental context. For example, the proposal that cognitive mechanics are more dependent on the integrity of biological mechanisms than knowledge-based intelligence (pragmatics) predicts marked age differences in the neural substrates of fluid intelligence measures along with relative cultural invariance. However, pragmatic aspects of intelligence should be associated with differences that are more pronounced between groups of older adults from different cultural backgrounds than between groups of younger adults (see Park & Gutchess, 2002; Park, Nisbett, & Hedden, 1999, for informative discussions of this research agenda).

In sum, the aging mind and brain exhibit persisting plasticity in response to experiential, environmental, and cultural factors. Although we are just beginning to understand the genetic characteristics that promote successful aging (see Chapter 11), a host of experiential and environmental factors have clear beneficial effects on neurocognitive functioning. However, such adaptive capacities must be understood against the backdrop of neural and cognitive aging processes that impose inevitable limitations on the changing organism. How do the realities of decline and plasticity interact to create a new stage of the life cycle that we identify as old age?

## INTERACTIONIST AND CO-CONSTRUCTIVIST VIEWS OF SOC AND SST

The theory of lifespan development advanced by Paul Baltes and his collaborators (Baltes, 1997) incorporates several concepts that are echoed in the neural account of aging that we present in this section. These concepts are selection, optimization, and compensation. Within the Baltes framework, which is referred to as SOC, the impetus behind adaptive behavioral change is the changing dynamics in the biology–culture interactions mediated by brain and behavior development. One prominent driving force is the increase in "biological vulnerability" due to the aging process. Another is the impact of cultural learning. With the increase in biological vulnerability, regardless of whether wittingly, the individual responds with a strategy of becoming increasingly selective about the repertoire of behaviors and cognitive acts in which he or she will engage. By narrowing one's options, and by allocating resources to the set of behaviors that reflect past developmental acquisitions (i.e., cultural learning) and are most adequate and suitable to one's current life circumstances, one can optimize those behaviors – that is, they can be performed with the fullest force of effort, greatest allocation of resources, and highest quality possible. Overall, this strategy is a form of compensation in which one's resources are not divided across multiple and less essential domains at their expense, but rather, in which the most essential acts are preserved through selective resource allocation. According to the SOC theory, in addition, selective optimization (e.g., practice) strengthens those means that are critical for achieving the selected actions.

One excellent example of SOC in action comes from a recent study by Li, Lindenberger, Freund, and Baltes (2001). This group investigated differences in the selective optimization of concurrent tasks in younger and older adults. Participants were asked to engage in simultaneous memorization and walking tasks, and were also trained in the usage of external aids. Overall, older adults prioritized the walking task over the memorization task. Furthermore, consistent with SOC, the researchers found that when difficulty was elevated for both tasks, only the younger adults successfully implemented aids for the memorization task; conversely, only the older adults benefited from aids for the walking task. Thus, when the level of demand forces selectivity, older adults adopt a sensorimotor focus, thereby optimizing their performance on the task most vital to their safety.

The adaptive allocation of resources has also been demonstrated in the domains of emotional functioning and social interactions through the research program of Laura Carstensen and her colleagues (1999). Their group has shown that as people age, they place higher priority on goals related to emotional meaning, whereas younger adults emphasize intellectual, knowledge-related goals. For instance, with respect to social encounters, older adults prefer to interact with familiar social partners, as compared with unfamiliar ones, due to the emotional significance of closer relationships. According to Carstensen et al.'s (1999) socioemotional selectivity theory (SST), the shift from intellectual, knowledge-related goals to emotion-related goals results from a change in time perspective that comes with aging. Younger adults see time as expansive, whereas for older adults time is more limited, and their goals change accordingly. With an open-ended time perspective, such as that of younger adults, people seek new information and new social partners. In contrast, when time is perceived as limited, as is the case of older adults, goals related to emotional meaning are prioritized such that people seek regulated emotional states and emotionally meaningful social interactions. Because older adults perceive the end of life as much closer in time than do healthy younger adults, their limited time perspective fosters an increased focus on emotion-related goals.

Thus, a change in future time perspective is a causal factor according to SST. However, the increased focus on emotionally meaningful goals is associated with age-related alterations in basic information processing mechanisms (for a review, see Carstensen & Mikels, 2005). Older adults appear to direct their attention away from negatively valenced stimuli and toward positively valenced stimuli, a pattern not observed in younger adults. Furthermore, in both working (short-term) memory and long-term memory, older adults also show a bias for remembering positively valenced stimuli. Thus, social and emotional changes across the lifespan are postulated to be linked to basic changes in information processing. The causal links between emotional, motivational, and cognitive age-related changes remain unclear; however, the current body of empirical support for SST makes evident the reciprocal relationship between these factors.

SOC and SST share the central idea that the cognitive, emotional, and behavioral repertoire that distinguishes the older adult from the younger adult is not simply caused by an aging biological substrate. Instead the aging mind represents the outcome of co-construction by biological and cultural forces. In addition, the aging mind responds adaptively to the reality of its own aging; by so doing, it alters its own psychological architecture, and ultimately, the social and cultural milieu in which it thrives. Although to date, neither of these theories has been explicitly examined from a brain science point of view, cognitive neuroscience research on aging cognition, from our lab and others, has discovered principles of adaptation, compensation, and compromise that we believe stem from the brain's response to its own aging process, rather than reflecting a passive consequence of biological aging. In this sense, our brain-based approach offers an additional perspective on the co-construction of the aging mind and brain. In our view, the results display consistency with some of the principles that have derived from research conducted within a more behavioral, cultural learning framework.

CRUNCH

Reuter-Lorenz, Stanczak, and Miller (1999) published a report, entitled "Neural recruitment and cognitive aging: Two hemispheres are better than one, especially as you age," which supports the basic idea that as we age, declining neural efficiency requires that more neural circuitry get recruited at lower levels of task demand compared with younger adults. This hypothesis, CRUNCH, has its roots in these earlier observations and proposes that older adults in general tend to recruit more neural resources for any given task than their younger counterparts. Therefore, older adults are more likely to reach their resource ceiling at lower levels of task demand than young adults.

This view is similar to arguments by behaviorally oriented, cognitive aging researchers discussed earlier in the chapter, who claim that diminishing resources increase the level of difficulty or effort required for older adults, relative to their younger counterparts. Now, through the combined use of cognitive tasks that are analytical with respect to the underlying processes and functional neuroimaging, we are in a position to delineate which neural processes decline and which processes compensate in older age, and to identify the costs of compensation. We believe this compensation can take at least two forms. We refer to one as compensation by recruiting "more of the same" neural process, whereby more time is devoted to a particular process, or whereby more neural nodes are used from a pool of nodes specialized for this process. The other form we refer to as compensation by "supplementary processes," whereby additional operations or strategies are recruited to compensate for deficiencies that render the usual circuitry insufficient to perform the task alone.

Indeed, there is evidence from neuroimaging studies of younger adults that principles like "more of the same" and "supplementary processes" seem to be implemented by the brain to meet increasing task demand. For example, when task difficulty is varied parametrically by increasing the number of items that have to be held in working memory (i.e., over a retention interval of 3–10 s), several studies have reported that activity in task-relevant areas increases linearly as a function of set size (e.g., Jonides et al., 1998). This would be an example of recruiting "more of the same" neural circuits to meet increased task demand. Task difficulty can also be increased by requiring that the individual perform one or more additional operations at some stage during task processing. Explicit changes in task demands have been shown to recruit additional brain areas that map onto the kind of processing introduced into the task. For example, the introduction of response conflict can lead to activation of the anterior cingulate (Nelson, Reuter-Lorenz, Sylvester, Jonides, & Smith, 2003), whereas requiring subjects to reorder items in a list rather than recall them verbatim recruits lateral prefrontal regions (Postle, Berger, & D'Esposito, 1999).

In the older brain, where neural efficiency declines from the host of biological factors reviewed earlier in the chapter, it follows that optimal processing would require additional neural recruitment at lower levels of task demand compared with the younger brain. Thus, older brains should activate like younger brains performing a more demanding task. This age difference in activation is what we hypothesize to be the compensatory utilization of neural circuits. However, the net effect of this neural strategy in combination with age-related loss of neural resources is that fewer resources are available to meet the processing requirements of more complex tasks – this is the "crunch." In general terms, the resource ceiling is reached to complete the cognitive operations required of more rudimentary tasks; as a result, performance on more complex tasks suffers from the lack of additional resources and from the more global adverse consequences of declining neural efficiency.

## EMPIRICAL BASES OF CRUNCH

One of the most exciting discoveries that has emerged from the use of neuroimaging to study aging cognition is finding that neurologically intact, healthy older adults show signs of overactivation – greater levels of activity – compared with younger adults performing the same task. Overactivity was an unexpected outcome because, given the shrinkage of neural tissue and the lesion model framework of cognitive aging, it was assumed that older brains would be less able than younger brains to engage the relevant circuitry, leading to underactivation as the dominant age-specific pattern. Indeed, overactivation in some brain regions is sometimes found to be accompanied by underactivation in others. Of paramount importance is that in many studies these age-unique activity patterns are the neural correlates of preserved performance, and several studies have now linked overactivation to high-performing subgroups of older adults (see Reuter-Lorenz & Lustig, 2005, for a review).

Not surprisingly, the majority of neuroimaging studies on cognitive aging have focused on memory; therefore, this is the domain in which age-related overactivation is most widely reported (see Cabeza, Nyberg, & Park, 2005, for reviews). Initial studies using positron emission tomography (PET; see, e.g., Chapter 11) reported overactivation in the left frontal regions of older adults during retrieval from long-term memory, which typically activates right frontal sites in younger adults. With PET, it is not possible to eliminate the activation associated with erroneous trials. Because older adults make more errors than younger adults, the contributions of age versus differing performance level can be confounded. One study on spatial working memory from our lab (Reuter-Lorenz et al., 2000) got around this problem by selecting older adults who performed as well as or better than younger adults. We found that older adults showed more left hemisphere activation on this spatial task, which activated primarily right hemisphere sites in younger adults. That is, older adults showed activity that was more bilateral than younger adults, and the sites of overactivation were localized to regions of prefrontal cortex – brain regions that are activated by younger adults in response to higher task demands.

To date, regions of overactivation have characterized the activity patterns of older relative to younger adults across a wide range of tasks, including perceptual and attentional tasks, tests of language processing, tests of motor control, verbal working memory, episodic memory encoding, and autobiographical memory (see Reuter-Lorenz & Lustig, 2005). The sites of additional activity in older adults are frequently found in approximately mirror symmetric regions in the hemisphere opposite to the most active sites in younger adults, which yields a pattern of reduced asymmetry in older adults (Fig. 12.1). However, bilaterality is not always the dominant pattern, and in many cases, older adults tend to overactivate regions of prefrontal cortex. Of course, the pressing question is "What functions are served by regions of overactivation?" We briefly consider several interpretations, including the one that we favor, which is the possibility that these regions function in a compensatory manner (see also Grady & Kapur, 1999).

One obvious possibility is that older adults are engaging different and possibly more numerous cognitive strategies than younger adults. In its simplest form, we find this explanation to be inadequate. In our neuroimaging studies of working memory, using both self-report and performance measures of strategy use, we found no differences between the two age groups. In some reports, the stimulus materials used are so basic (e.g., Gabor patches of selected spatial frequencies) that they do not readily lend themselves to multiple strategies (see Reuter-Lorenz, 2002, for a review). Moreover, at least one report examining episodic memory has shown underactivation in older adults relative to younger adults when no strategy was provided, as well as bilateral activation in older relative to younger adults when both groups were given a specific encoding strategy (Logan, Sanders, Snyder, Morris, & Buckner, 2002). Another possibility is that older adults are simply trying harder than younger adults,

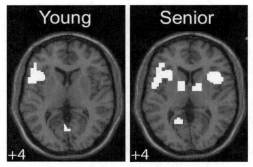

FIGURE 12.1. Horizontal sections showing BOLD activity obtained in younger (left-hand panel) and older (right-hand panel) adults. These images indicate the regions that are uniquely activated by a verb generation task condition that has high selection/interference resolution demands compared with a less demanding verb generation condition. In younger adults, activation is evident in the left inferior frontal gyrus. A pattern of age-specific overactivation is evident in the older adults who show bilateral activity in the left and right inferior frontal gyrus, and bilateral activation of the basal ganglia. Older adults are slower at verb generation overall compared with younger adults; however, the effect on performance of increasing the selection demand does not differ between the two age groups. We interpret the pattern of overactivation that occurs in the context of comparable performance effects to be consistent with compensatory processes in older adults. For more details, see Persson et al. (2004).

and this greater effort is manifest neurally as more active sites. One recent study addressed this possibility in the motor domain, using grip strength as the performance measure of interest. Both older and younger adults were asked to grip a dynamometer using their maximum grip strength, and then were scanned while gripping with different percentages of that maximum. The fact that the output was tailored to the ability level of each individual makes it difficult to account for the age-unique activation patterns by claiming that older adults expended more effort than younger adults (Ward, Brown, Thompson, & Frackowiak, 2003).

So, on what basis can we claim that these additional sites of overactivation in older adults are functioning in a compensatory manner? We offer four types of evidence that support this interpretation. First, there have been reports from studies of patients with focal lesions that indicate that certain language abilities lost after left hemisphere damage may be subsequently regained because the function has been taken over by the right hemisphere (see Reuter-Lorenz, 2002, for a review). Indeed, neuroimaging of patients with preserved language abilities after focal damage has revealed increased activity in right hemisphere regions homologous to the damaged sites but not typically associated with these abilities. Data such as these establish compensatory potential at the neurocognitive level.

A second piece of evidence comes from our own behavioral studies of older adults that used the divided visual field methodology to evaluate age-related changes in interhemispheric cooperation. Because of the way the left and right visual fields are mapped onto the retinas, it is possible to project initially to one side of the brain or the other. Consider a task in which a subject has to decide whether two items match, based on their physical appearance. Presenting the two items of such physical matches to the same visual field, thereby projecting to the same hemisphere, elicits better performance than when the items are presented to different visual fields. If the match is made more difficult by increasing the number of items or by requiring an abstract property such as the name of an item, it becomes advantageous for the items to appear in opposite visual fields, thereby engaging both hemispheres in the matching process. This is known as the bilateral field advantage. We have shown that, relative to younger adults, older adults show a stronger bilateral field advantage at lower levels of task demand (Reuter-Lorenz et al., 1999). We interpret this result to indicate that older adults benefit from engaging more neural circuitry and that this increased recruitment serves to compensate for declining neural efficiency.

The third piece of evidence supporting the compensation interpretation is the link between overactivation found in brain imaging studies of episodic and working memory and higher performance levels in senior subjects. In at least three studies of working memory, increased prefrontal activation has been correlated with higher levels of performance in older adults (see Reuter-Lorenz & Sylvester, 2005, for a review). Likewise, in studies of episodic memory that have examined high- and low-performing subgroups of seniors, the higher-performing subgroup has been the one showing greater overactivation (see Reuter-Lorenz & Lustig, 2005, for a review). Results such as these challenge the proposal that overactivation is a sign of neural dysfunction (due possibly to a breakdown in inhibition) and that it plays a causal role in impaired performance in older age (see Reuter-Lorenz, 2002; Reuter-Lorenz & Lustig, 2005). Finally, the neural correlates of cognitive processing can now be examined on a trial-by-trial analysis using event-related functional magnetic resonance imaging. Using this approach, researchers have been able to separately analyze the activation patterns associated with mnemonic encoding that ultimately lead to successful versus unsuccessful memory retrieval. To date, *successful* memory encoding has been associated with greater activation in prefrontal cortex in older adults than in younger adults. The activation is either bilaterally distributed or right localized, and it co-occurs with diminished activity in medial temporal lobe regions, suggesting that the prefrontal activity serves to compensate for age-related diminution of hippocampal efficiency (see Reuter-Lorenz & Lustig, 2005, for a review).

Ongoing research is now attempting to link sites of overactivation to specific neurocognitive processes to determine how compensation occurs, and whether a particular patterns falls into the "more of the same," the "supplementary processes," or some other category. In cases where there is additional activation in homologous regions of the cortex, as we have found in both dorsolateral and inferior frontal gyri, compensatory recruitment of the "more of the same" cognitive process is arguably the most plausible interpretation. However, in cases where frontal overactivation accompanies hippocampal underactivation, for example, the "additional process" interpretation would seem more compelling. Indeed, the fact that overactivation in seniors is frequently found in prefrontal sites has been taken as evidence that older adults rely on executive processes to a greater extent than do younger adults (see Reuter-Lorenz & Lustig, 2005). Likewise, on the basis of behavioral results, Baltes, Lindenberger, and their colleagues have proposed that pragmatic aspects of intelligence, including knowledge-based and strategic processes, are relied on extensively to compensate for declines in cognitive mechanics that are more vulnerable to age-related biological loss (e.g., Li et al., 2004). More work is needed to map the pragmatic/mechanic distinction onto such taxonomies as those applied to the central executive, where inhibition, selection, and goal shifting are defined as executive functions. In any case, a neuroimaging approach to cognitive aging should be able to evaluate this and other proposals in the future when a more thorough linkage of cognitive operations to specific activations patterns has been achieved.

So, what evidence exists to indicate that overactivation in older adults comes at an eventual cost? To date, there is little in the way of neuroimaging data to support this idea. According to CRUNCH, the lower the level of task demand for which additional recruitment must occur, the lower the level of task demand for which the resource ceiling will be reached. At higher levels of task demand, recruitment could reach asymptotic levels and, having reached this capacity limit, there is no further benefit to performance. There is at least one study of dual task performance that has related extensive recruitment in older adults on the single task conditions to underactivation and poorer performance in the dual task condition (DiGirolamo et al., 2001). More data along these lines are needed to test the resource limitation ideas of CRUNCH. In addition, neural efficiency is likely to depend on the effectiveness of connectivity or communication between task-relevant regions, as well as levels of regional activity. A full evaluation of CRUNCH will also require an extensive examination of the relationship between connectivity, activation levels, and performance.

## IMPLICATIONS FOR ENVIRONMENTAL–CULTURAL CHANGE

The dramatic increase in human life expectancy since the early 1900s holds the promise of richer, fuller, and longer lives. What new insights have emerged from studying the aging mind and its neural underpinnings that can improve the way we age? How can we reframe our understanding of the lifelong developmental process to foster more successful aging? We believe that appreciating the recursive nature of the aging process offers a pivotal insight: when we study the aging mind and brain, we are investigating a system that reflects in its outcome the result of past experiential and cultural learning and, in the context of the present, responds to its own aging. The measurements we take, whether they are behavioral or neural, are not mere indices of the consequences of biological aging in the narrow sense. They include the enduring plastic effects of the mind and brain as these systems adapt, reorganize, select, prioritize, and compensate in response to biological aging and environmental pressures. Behavioral measures constitute the end product of these dynamics and thus defy a one-to-one mapping with underlying mechanisms.

Consider a key lesson from neuroimaging: some tasks that are spared in subgroups of older adults, such as the short-term retention of spatial locations, are accomplished by a different neurocognitive route than when the task is performed by the younger brain. Spared performance does not imply that the underlying circuitry is unaltered due to aging. Rather, sparing of performance, the output of the system if you will, may well result from the brain's ability to allocate the necessary neural resources to the storage operations required by this task. Although the precise resources that are used are currently unknown, executive operations and increased cognitive control are likely candidates to be recruited to assist with and supplement rudimentary subtasks, such as storage, that in younger years did not require this additional support. This hypothesis implies that processes that are relatively resource free in the younger brain become more resource intensive in the older brain. Processes can appear spared in older adults because the compensatory contributions of executive functions, for example, maintain the behavioral performance of older adults. However, the increased reliance on executive processes that characterizes aging cognition makes executive functions themselves increasingly vulnerable to overload. The idea derived from behaviorally oriented research that in later life there is a compensatory shift away from some cognitive functions, with increasing reliance on others, is clearly echoed in the brain imaging results of older adults.

So, if this is the state of affairs in the aging mind and brain, then what can we do to promote successful aging? First, we recommend engaging in conditions that produce automaticity in younger years and the persistence of this training into older age. Skill development and knowledge acquisition occur in stages that initially require deliberative and declarative processing but ultimately can become proceduralized and automatic. The larger the repertoire of automatic behaviors one develops over one's life course, the longer such behaviors can operate free of executive control (see Rogers, 2000). Importantly, the protective effects of training and proceduralization, as in the development of expertise, are highly domain specific (Kramer & Willis, 2002). Thus, the acquisition of a large and diverse repertoire of automatic behaviors would be necessary. By the same token, it will be important to rethink intervention strategies and methods for improving quality of life for the older generation. According to our hypothesis, one source of the "crunch" in aging comes from the increased need to allocate executive resources for low-level tasks. Thus, if interventions are targeted at these tasks, it will relieve some of the burden on executive processes. This approach is similar to providing environmental support to older adults to overcome their failure to self-initiate strategy use. (See Chapter 16 for an extensive treatment of the importance of co-constructive considerations for the development of assistive technologies.)

Second, we recommend lifelong training in executive skills. To the extent that these processes become the backbone of cognition in later years, their optimization in early years can increase their endurance and youthfulness. Recent support for this speculation comes from a study of bilingualism and aging (Bialystok, Craik, Klein, & Viswanathan, 2004). Older adults who were bilingual showed better performance on measures of executive control than age-matched monolingual individuals. These performance differences emerged despite the fact that groups were otherwise indistinguishable on other critical measures, including education, vocabulary, intelligence, and basic measures of working memory. Bialystok and her colleagues argued that the increased cognitive demands presented by the requirement to adjudicate between two languages fosters the development of executive control processes, which in turn protect against some cognitive effects of aging. One potential future use of neuroimaging methods can be to identify the operations that function in a supplemental, compensatory fashion and to train or exercise these operations throughout life to ensure their viability in older age.

The multiple arguments in favor of lifelong physical fitness need not be reiterated here, except to say that the benefits of cardiovascular fitness and good diet on mental fitness in older age are striking. New evidence suggests that fit seniors are more apt to engage task-relevant brain regions, and thus may be less reliant on compensatory neural strategies than their less fit peers (Colcombe et al., 2004). Furthermore, given the evidence that physical challenge exacts a larger cognitive toll in older than younger adults (Li et al., 2001), the sense of physical well-being that comes with physical fitness means a greater availability of neurocognitive resources for cognitive rather than physical effort.

In summary, we argue for the optimization of biocultural and co-constructive processes across the lifespan so as to render brain status high. Plasticity of the brain and plasticity of the environment-driven input–output conditions create brain resources that endure across the lifespan. As we supplant the myths of aging with a deeper understanding of the cognitive, affective, and neurobiological processes at work, we can develop educational goals that include a proactive approach to aging and the shaping of the brain. We can begin to shift the focus of our youth-oriented culture to one that is oriented toward the lifespan. Our understanding of living well can expand beyond eating well and exercising to include thinking well and establishing the cognitive foundations that optimize our mental machinery for the later years. Such cultural change can promote the benefits of mind–brain reciprocity so the brain's response to its own aging and the demands posed by environmental conditions are influenced by the mind's understanding of itself as a changing body in a changing environment.

ACKNOWLEDGMENTS

We thank Sam Maglio and Laura Zahodne for their valuable assistance with the preparation of this chapter and Jonas Persson for his comments on an earlier version of this manuscript. We acknowledge the support of the National Institute on Aging with research grant AG18286 to PARL and Ruth L. Kirschstein National Research Service Award AG022264 to JAM.

References

Arbuckle, T. Y., Gold, D., & Andres, D. (1986). Cognitive functioning of older people in relation to social and personality variables. *Psychology and Aging, 1* (1), 55–62.
Bäckman, L., & Dixon, R. A. (1992). Psychological compensation: A theoretical framework. *Psychological Bulletin, 112* (2), 259–283.
Baltes, P. B. (1997). On the incomplete architecture of human ontogeny: Selection, optimization, and compensation as foundation of developmental theory. *American Psychologist, 52* (4), 366–380.
Baltes, P. B., & Lindenberger, U. (1988). On the range of cognitive plasticity in old age as a function of experience: 15 years of intervention research. *Behavior Therapy, 19* (3), 283–300.
Bialystok, E., Craik, F. I. M., Klein, R., & Viswanathan, M. (2004). Bilingualism, aging, and cognitive control: Evidence from the Simon task. *Psychology and Aging, 19* (2), 290–303.
Cabeza, R., Nyberg, L., & Park, D. (Eds.). (2005). *Cognitive neuroscience of aging: Linking cognitive and cerebral aging*. London: Oxford University Press.
Carstensen, L. L., Isaacowitz, D. M., & Charles, S. T. (1999). Taking time seriously: A theory of socioemotional selectivity. *American Psychologist, 54* (3), 165–181.
Carstensen, L. L., & Mikels, J. A. (2005). At the intersection of emotion and cognition: Aging and the positivity effect. *Current Directions in Psychological Science. 14* (3), 117–121.
Churchill, J. D., Galvez, R., Colcombe, S., Swain, R. A., Kramer, A. F., & Greenough, W. T. (2002). Exercise, experience and the aging brain. *Neurobiology of Aging, 23* (5), 941–955.

Colcombe, S. J., Kramer, A. F., Erickson, K. I., Scalf, P., McAuley, E., Cohen, N. J., et al. (2004). Cardiovascular fitness, cortical plasticity, and aging. *Proceedings of the National Academy of Sciences (USA), 101* (9), 3316–3321.

Craik, F. I. M., & Salthouse, T. A. (Eds.). (2000). *The handbook of aging and cognition* (2nd ed.). Mahwah, NJ: Erlbaum.

DiGirolamo, G. J., Kramer, A. F., Barad, V., Cepeda, N. J., Weissman, D. H., Milham, M. P., et al. (2001). General and task-specific frontal lobe recruitment in older adults during executive processes: A fMRI investigation of task-switching. *Neuroreport, 12* (9), 2065–2071.

Finch, C. E., & Cohen, D. M. (1997). Aging, metabolism, and Alzheimer's disease: Review and hypotheses. *Experimental Neurology, 143*, 82–102.

Gehlen, A. (1988). *Man, his nature and place in the world.* New York: Columbia University Press.

Grady, C. L., & Kapur, S. (1999). The use of neuroimaging in neurorehabilitative research. In D. T. Stuss, G. Winocur, & I. H. Robertson (Eds.), *Cognitive neurorehabilitation* (pp. 47–58). New York: Cambridge University Press.

Hasher, L., & Zacks, R. T. (1979). Automatic and effortful processes in memory. *Journal of Experimental Psychology: General, 108* (3), 356–388.

Hasher, L., & Zacks, R. T. (1988). Working memory, comprehension, and aging: A review and a new view. In G. Bower (Ed.), *The psychology of learning and motivation: Advances in research and theory* (Vol. 22, pp. 193–225). San Diego: Academic Press.

Jonides, J., Schumacher, E. H., Smith, E. E., Koeppe, R. A., Awh, E., Reuter-Lorenz, P. A., et al. (1998). The role of parietal cortex in verbal working memory. *Journal of Neuroscience, 18* (13), 5026–5034.

Joseph, J. A., Shukitt-Hale, B., Denisova, N. A., Bielinski, D., Martin, A., McEwen, J. J., & Bickford, P. C. (1999). Reversals of age-related declines in neuronal signal transduction, cognitive, and motor behavioral deficits with blueberry, spinach, or strawberry dietary supplementation. *Journal of Neuroscience, 19* (18), 8114–8121.

Kliegl, R., Smith, J., & Baltes, P. B. (1990). On the locus and process of magnification of age differences during mnemonic training. *Developmental Psychology, 26* (6), 894–904.

Kramer, A. F., & Willis, S. L. (2002). Enhancing the cognitive vitality of older adults. *Current Directions in Psychological Science, 11* (5), 173–177.

Li, K. Z. H., Lindenberger, U., Freund, A. M., & Baltes, P. B. (2001). Walking while memorizing: Age-related differences in compensatory behavior. *Psychological Science, 12* (3), 230–237.

Li, S.-C., Lindenberger, U., Hommel, B., Aschersleben, G., Prinz, W., & Baltes, P. B. (2004). Transformations in the couplings among intellectual abilities and constituent cognitive processes across the life span. *Psychological Science, 15* (3), 155–163.

Logan, J. M., Sanders, A. L., Snyder, A. Z., Morris, J. C., & Buckner, R. L. (2002). Under-recruitment and nonselective recruitment: Dissociable neural mechanisms associated with aging. *Neuron, 33* (5), 827–840.

Nelson, J. K., Reuter-Lorenz, P. A., Sylvester, C. Y., Jonides, J., & Smith, E. E. (2003). Dissociable neural mechanisms underlying response-based and familiarity-based conflict in working memory. *Proceedings of the National Academy of Sciences (USA), 100* (19), 11171–11175.

Park, D. C., & Gutchess, A. H. (2002). Aging, cognition, and culture: A neuroscientific perspective. *Neuroscience & Biobehavioral Reviews, 26* (7), 859–867.

Park, D. C., Nisbett, R., & Hedden, T. (1999). Aging, culture, and cognition. *Journals of Gerontology: Psychological Sciences & Social Sciences, 54B* (2), P75–P84.

Park, D. C., Polk, T. A., Mikels, J. A., Taylor, S. F., & Marshuetz, C. (2001). Cerebral aging: Integration of brain and behavioral models of cognitive function. *Dialogues in Clinical Neuroscience, 3* (3), 151–165.

Persson, J., Sylvester, C. Y., Nelson, J. K., Welsh, K. M., Jonides, J., & Reuter-Lorenz, P. A. (2004). Selection requirements during verb generation: Differential recruitment in older and younger adults. *NeuroImage, 23*, 1382–1390.

Postle, B. R., Berger, J. S., & D'Esposito, M. (1999). Functional neuroanatomical double dissociation of mnemonic and executive control processes contributing to working memory performance. *Proceedings of the National Academy (USA), 96* (22), 12959–12964.

Raz, N. (2000). Aging of the brain and its impact on cognitive performance: Integration of structural and functional findings. In F. I. M. Craik & T. A. Salthouse (Eds.), *The handbook of aging and cognition* (2nd ed., pp. 1–90). Mahwah, NJ: Erlbaum.

Reuter-Lorenz, P. A. (2002). New visions of the aging mind and brain. *Trends in Cognitive Sciences, 6* (9), 394–400.

Reuter-Lorenz, P. A., Jonides, J., Smith, E. E., Hartley, A., Miller, A., Marshuetz, C., & Koeppe, R. A. (2000). Age differences in the frontal lateralization of verbal and spatial working memory revealed by PET. *Journal of Cognitive Neuroscience, 12* (1), 174–187.

Reuter-Lorenz, P. A., & Lustig, C. (2005). Brain aging: Reorganizing discoveries about the aging mind. *Current Opinion in Neurobiology, 15* (4), 245–251.

Reuter-Lorenz, P. A., Stanczak, L., & Miller, A. C. (1999). Neural recruitment and cognitive aging: Two hemispheres are better than one, especially as you age. *Psychological Science, 10* (6), 494–500.

Reuter-Lorenz, P. A., & Sylvester, C.-Y. C. (2005). The cognitive neuroscience of working memory and aging. In R. Cabeza, L. Nyberg, & D. C. Park (Eds.), *Cognitive neuroscience of aging: Linking cognitive and cerebral aging* (pp. 186–217). London: Oxford University Press.

Rogers, W. A. (2000). Attention and aging. In D. C. Park & N. Schwarz (Eds.), *Cognitive aging: A primer* (pp. 57–73). Philadelphia: Psychology Press.

Salthouse, T. A. (1996). The processing-speed theory of adult age differences in cognition. *Psychological Review, 103* (3), 403–428.

Schaie, K. W. (2005). *Developmental influences on adult intelligence: The Seattle Longitudinal Study.* London: Oxford University Press.

Seeman, T. E., Lusignolo, T. M., Albert, M., & Berkman, L. (2001). Social relationships, social support, and patterns of cognitive aging in healthy, high-functioning older adults: MacArthur Studies of Successful Aging. *Health Psychology, 20* (4), 243–255.

Smith, E. E., & Jonides, J. (1999). Storage and executive processes in the frontal lobes. *Science, 283* (5408), 1657–1661.

Stern, P., & Carstensen, L. L. (Eds.). (2000). *The aging mind: Opportunities in cognitive aging.* Washington, DC: The National Academies Press.

van Praag, H., Christie, B. R., Sejnowski, T. J., & Gage, F. H. (1999). Running enhances neurogenesis, learning, and long-term potentiation in mice. *Proceedings of the National Academy of Sciences (USA), 96* (23), 13427–13431.

Ward, N. S., Brown, M. M., Thompson, A. J., & Frackowiak, R. S. J. (2003). Neural correlates of motor recovery after stroke: A longitudinal fMRI study. *Brain, 126* (11), 2476–2496.

Willis, S. L., & Nesselroade, C. S. (1990). Long-term effects of fluid ability training in old-old age. *Developmental Psychology, 26* (6), 905–910.

Winocur, G. (1998). Environmental influences on cognitive decline in aged rats. *Neurobiology of Aging, 19* (6), 589–597.

# BIOCULTURAL CO-CONSTRUCTION: FROM MICRO- TO MACROENVIRONMENTS IN LARGER CULTURAL CONTEXTS

# 13

# Characteristics of Illiterate and Literate Cognitive Processing: Implications of Brain–Behavior Co-Constructivism

Karl Magnus Petersson and Alexandra Reis

ABSTRACT

*Literacy and education represent essential aspects of contemporary society, and subserve important aspects of socialization and cultural transmission. The study of illiterate subjects represents one approach to investigating the interactions between neurobiological and cultural factors in cognitive development, individual learning, and their influence on the functional organization of the brain. In this chapter, we review some recent cognitive, neuroanatomic, and functional neuroimaging results indicating that formal education influences important aspects of the human brain. Taken together, this provides strong support for the idea that the brain is modulated by literacy and formal education, which in turn change the brain's capacity to interact with its environment, including the individual's contemporary culture. In other words, the individual is able to participate in, interact with, and actively contribute to the process of cultural transmission in new ways through acquired cognitive skills.*

## INTRODUCTION

Education plays an essential role in contemporary society. Acquiring reading and writing skills, as well as other cognitive skills, during formal education can be viewed as a structured process of cultural transmission. Formal education and the educational system represent essential aspects of modern society and are cardinal structures of the intelligent information environment. These institutionalized structures subserve important aspects of socialization and cultural transmission. The study of illiterate subjects and matched literate controls provides an opportunity to investigate the interaction between neurobiological and cultural factors in cognitive development and learning. Alternative approaches have also been explored with respect to cross-cultural variation, including the implications of transparent and nontransparent orthographies on brain function (Paulesu et al., 2000), as well as their consequences for the expression of dyslexia (Paulesu et al., 2001).

Reading and writing represent cognitive abilities that depend on human cultural evolution (Vygotsky, 1962). Writing was a relatively late invention in human history, invented some 6,000 years ago. It seems unlikely that specific brain structures have developed for the purpose of mediating reading and writing skills (Ardila, 2004). Instead, it is likely that reading and writing are supported by preadapted brain structures. A preadaptation is a structure that has evolved to serve a specific function but has come to serve as a means for a different end. Several cognitive skills acquired through formal education, including reading, do not represent a specieswide adaptation of the kind that natural language is a paradigmatic example of. Varney (2002) emphasized that reading and writing "evolved through cultural developments that were only acquired as 'typical' human abilities within the last 200 years in Europe and America, and only after World War II in the rest of the world" (Varney, 2002, p. 3). In fact, reading and writing skills are still far from universal at the beginning of the twenty-first century. At present, it is estimated that there are close to 1 billion illiterate humans in the world (about two-thirds are women; EFA Global Monitoring Report Team, 2003/04), whereas the mean educational level is only about 3 to 4 years of schooling (Abadzi, 2003).

Natural language is a system of knowledge, a system of representation and processing of these representations, and a system for communicative use (Chomsky, 1986). However, aspects of language can also be an object of cognition, and metalinguistic awareness involves explicit processing and intentional control over aspects of phonology, syntax, semantics, discourse, and pragmatics. These processes are different from the implicit language processing used in comprehension and production. During the acquisition of reading and writing skills, the child creates the ability to represent aspects of the phonological component of language by an orthographic representation and relate this to a visuographic input–output code. This is commonly achieved by means of a supervised learning process (i.e., teaching). This is in contrast to natural language acquisition, which is largely a spontaneous, nonsupervised, and self-organized acquisition process. A similar perspective can be taken on formal education in general.

In addition to the acquisition of language, children gradually create explicit representations and acquire processing mechanisms that allow for reflecting and analyzing different aspects of language function and language use (Karmiloff-Smith, Grant, Sims, Jones, & Cuckle, 1996). Several researchers have investigated the relationship between reading and metalinguistic awareness (Morais, 1993). Children do not learn language passively but actively construct representations on the basis of linguistically relevant constraints and abstractions of the linguistic input

(Karmiloff-Smith et al., 1996). Metacognitive and metalinguistic awareness develops progressively over the early years of life (Karmiloff-Smith, 1992). When children subsequently learn to read, this has repercussions on the phonological representations of spoken language (Morais, 1993; Petersson, Reis, Askelöf, Castro-Caldas, & Ingvar, 2000). For example, there seems to be an intricate interplay between metalinguistic awareness and reading, rather than simply a one-way influence. Furthermore, it appears that various types of metalinguistic skills (including phonological awareness) correlate with literacy skills and levels of formal education (Ravid & Tolchinsky, 2002).

Literacy, reading and writing, and printed media represent extensive cultural complexes and, like all cultural expressions, they originate in human cognition and social interaction. Goody's work on literacy emphasizes the role that written communication has played in the emergence, development, and organization of social and cultural institutions in contemporary societies (e.g., Goody, 2000). The emergence of writing transformed human culture, including the ability to preserve speech and knowledge in printed media. This allowed societies with a literate tradition to develop and accumulate knowledge and control over their environment and living conditions in a general sense. In addition, the nature of oral communication has a considerable effect on both the content and transmission of the cultural repertoire of a society. For example, the content of the cultural traditions and knowledge has to be held in memory when a written record is not an option. Instead, individual memory will mediate the cultural heritage between generations, and new experience will be integrated with the old by a process of interpretation. The invention of new communication media have a significant impact on the way information is created, stored, retrieved, transmitted, and used, and on cultural evolution as a whole. Furthermore, reading and writing makes possible an increasingly articulate feedback, as well as independent self-reflection, and promotes the development of metacognitive skills. Although auditory-verbal language use is oriented toward content, aspects of this knowledge can become explicitly available to the language user in terms of cognitive control and analytical awareness. It has thus been suggested that the acquisition of reading and writing skills, as well as formal education more generally, facilitates this through a process of representational construction and reorganization (Karmiloff-Smith, 1992). Ravid and Tolchinsky (2002) suggested that metalinguistic development is related to the acquisition of literacy and school-based knowledge. In other words, the acquisition of written language skills promotes flexible and manipulable representations for metalinguistic use (Karmiloff-Smith, 1992).

In this chapter, we review some recent cognitive, neuroanatomical, and functional neuroimaging data indicating that formal education and its use influence aspects of the human brain and, taken together, provide strong support for the hypothesis that the functional architecture of the brain is modulated by literacy. In particular, we focus on results from a series of experiments with an illiterate population and their matched literate controls living in the south of Portugal. We conclude that literacy and formal education exert an interesting influence on the development of the human brain and its capacity to interact with its environment.

## Study Population of Southern Portugal

The fishermen village Olhão of Algarve in southern Portugal, where all our studies have been conducted, is socioculturally homogeneous, and the majority of the population has lived most of their lives within the community. Mobility within the region has been limited, and the main source of income is related to agriculture or fishing. Illiteracy occurs in Portugal due to the fact that 40 or 50 years ago it was common for older daughters of a family to be engaged in daily household activities; therefore, they did not enter school. Later in life, they may have started to work outside the family. In larger families, the younger children were generally sent to school when they reached the age of 6 or 7, whereas the older daughters typically helped out with the younger siblings at home.

Literate and illiterate subjects live intermixed in this region of Portugal and participate actively in this community. Illiteracy is not perceived as a functional handicap, and the same sociocultural environment influences both literate and illiterate subjects on similar terms. Some of the literate and illiterate subjects in our studies are from the same family, increasing the homogeneity in background variables. In addition, most literate subjects participating in our studies are not highly educated, and most often they have had approximately 4 years of schooling. In this context, it is important to ensure that the subjects investigated are not cognitively impaired and also that the illiterate are matched to the literate subjects in as many relevant respects as possible, except for the consequences of not having had the opportunity to receive formal education. In our studies, we have attempted to match the different literacy groups as far as possible in terms of several relevant variables, including, for example, age, sex, general health, sociocultural background, and level of everyday functionality. (For a more detailed characterization of our study population and our selection procedures, see Reis, Guerreiro, & Petersson, 2003.) These protocols and procedures ensure with reasonable confidence that the illiterate subjects are cognitively normal; that their lack of formal education has specific sociocultural reasons, as already described; and that their illiteracy is not due to low intelligence, learning disability, or any other pathology potentially affecting the brain. The illiterate subjects and their literate controls included in our studies are also comparable along socioeconomic dimensions.

## RECENT COGNITIVE FINDINGS

Behavioral studies have demonstrated that literacy/illiteracy and the extent of formal education influence the performance of several behavioral tasks commonly used in neuropsychological assessment (for a recent review, see, e.g., Petersson, Reis, & Ingvar, 2001). For example, it appears that the acquisition of written language skills modulates aspects of spoken language processing (e.g., Mendonça et al., 2002; Morais, 1993; Silva et al., 2002). Additional data indicate that formal education influences some visuospatial skills (e.g., Reis, Petersson, Castro-Caldas, & Ingvar, 2001). However, it is still unclear which cognitive processes and brain mechanisms mediate these effects of literacy. A detailed understanding of which parts of the cognitive system and which processing levels are affected is still lacking. In this section, we focus on some aspects of object naming, short-term memory, phonological processing, and word awareness in spoken sentence context, as well as semantic memory. The basic idea is that literacy influences some aspects of spoken language processing related to phonological processing and verbal short-term working memory, as well as visuomotor skills related to reading and writing.

## Object Naming – Color Makes a Difference to Illiterates

Several studies have indicated that the level of formal education and/or literacy influence performance when subjects name two-dimensional (2D) pictorial representations of objects (e.g., Reis, Guerreiro, & Castro-Caldas, 1994). Naming objects or their 2D pictorial representations are common everyday tasks, and the performance on simple object naming tasks depends on the systems for visual recognition, lexical retrieval, and the organization of articulatory speech output, as well as the interaction between these systems (Levelt, 1989). In our study population, practice in interpreting schematic 2D representations commonly took place simultaneously with the acquisition of written Portuguese and other symbolic representations during school attendance. Moreover, reading and writing depend on advanced visual and visuomotor skills in coding, decoding, and generating 2D representations. It is thus likely that the interpretation and production of 2D representations of real objects, as well as the coding and decoding of 2D material in terms of figurative/symbolic semantic content, is more practiced in literate subjects than in illiterate individuals, who generally have received little systematic practice in interpreting conventional visuosymbolic representations. We thus speculated that there may be differences in 3D and 2D object naming skills between literate and illiterate individuals. In a simple visual naming experiment in which the participants named common everyday objects, Reis, Petersson, et al. (2001) reported differences between literate and illiterate subjects related to 2D object naming but found no difference when subjects named real 3D objects, both with respect to naming performance and in terms of response times. In addition, the two groups dissociated in terms of their error patterns, with the illiterate group more prone to make visually related errors (recognition failure or visual recognition error [e.g., pen instead of needle]), whereas the literate group tended to make semantically related errors (no lexical access or lexical semantic errors [e.g., necklace instead of bracelet]).

Although the results with 2D line drawings and real objects were clear in the study of Reis, Petersson, et al. (2001), the results with colored photos did not clearly dissociate between the literacy groups in terms of 2D versus 3D naming skills. We therefore speculated that the semantic significance of object color might play a role, in particular for the illiterate subjects because they are prone to be driven by semantic rather than formal aspects of stimuli or information, a theme we return to in subsequent sections.

In a recent follow-up study (Reis, Faisca, Ingvar, & Petersson, 2005), using a similar experimental set-up as Reis, Petersson, et al. (2001), we presented common everyday objects as black and white (i.e., grayscaled), as well as colored drawings and photos, in an immediate 2D object naming task. Consistent with the results outlined previously, the literate group performed significantly better than the illiterate group on black and white items (i.e., both line drawings and photos). In contrast, there was no significant difference between literacy groups on the colored items (Fig. 13.1). Interestingly, the illiterate participants performed significantly better on colored line drawings compared with black-and-white photos. Preliminary investigations also indicate that the color effect is related to the semantic value of the color in the sense that the effect seems more pronounced for objects with no or little consistency in the color–object relation compared with objects with a consistent relation to its color (e.g., lemons are yellow).

In summary, the absence of group differences when real 3D objects are named, and in particular the absence of response time (RT) differences on correctly named real objects, indicates that the RT differences on drawings and photos are not simply related to slower visual or language processing in general. Instead, the longer processing time in the illiterate group appears to be related to the processing of 2D visual information or the interaction between lexical retrieval and the processing of 2D visual information. The latter possibility would suggest that the interface between the two systems is configured differently in the two literacy groups, leading to differences in the effectiveness of the necessary information transfer. The result of the error analysis is consistent with this interpretation because the illiterate subjects made relatively more visually related than language-related errors, whereas the pattern was the opposite for the literate group. In fact, the qualitative distribution of errors was not significantly different for real object naming between groups. Taken together, this interpretation is consistent with a recent suggestion that orthographic knowledge is an

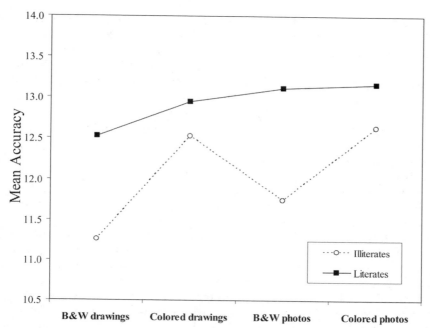

FIGURE 13.1. The 2D stimuli included black and white (B&W) and colored line drawings and photos of common everyday objects. The literate subjects performed significantly better than the illiterate group on B&W items (B&W line drawings: $p = .009$; B&W photos: $p < .001$). In contrast, there was no significant difference between literacy groups on the colored items (colored photos: $p = .21$). Interestingly, the illiterate participants performed significantly better ($p = .02$) on colored line drawings compared with B&W photos.

integral component of the general visual processing system (Patterson & Lambon Ralph, 1999), indicating that the acquisition of alphabetic orthographic knowledge may affect specific components of visual processing. Interestingly, a positive correlation between reading abilities and the capacity to name line drawings has also been reported (Goldblum & Matute de Duran, 2000). Recent findings also indicate that color can play an important role for the illiterate group when naming 2D pictorial representations of common everyday objects. This seems to be true when the semantic value of the color of an object is prominent (Reis, Faísca et al., 2005).

## Phonological Processing, Short-Term Working Memory, and Literacy

As a general background to the following subsections, we note that repetition of pseudowords and digit span tasks are considered as measures of verbal working memory capacities. These measures have been shown to be correlated with reading achievements in children (Baddeley, Gathercole, & Papagno, 1998; Gathercole & Baddeley, 1995). Additional research also points toward a role of verbal working memory and the efficiency of phonological processing in relation to reading skills (Brady, 1991). Verbal short-term working memory is a system subserving the representation and online processing of verbal information. In the Baddeley and Hitch model, one role of the phonological loop, a subsystem for short-term storage of phonologically represented information, is to store unfamiliar sound patterns while more permanent learning changes are formed. This suggests that the phonological loop may serve as a language learning device, and that it may play an integral part in the systems for spoken and written language acquisition (Baddeley et al., 1998).

Several researchers have investigated the relationship between reading and metalinguistic awareness, including so-called phonological awareness (e.g., Morais, 1993). With respect to phonological awareness, this research has indicated that illiterate subjects have some difficulty in dealing with tasks requiring explicit phonological processing. For example, the results of Morais, Cary, Alegria, and Bertelson (1979) showed that illiterate subjects found it more difficult to add and remove phonemes at the beginning of words and pseudowords. One may ask to what extent these tasks are equally natural (i.e., of similar ecological relevance) to literate and illiterate individuals, thus complicating the interpretation of these findings. This issue has recently been emphasized by Reis and colleagues (Reis & Petersson, 2003; Silva, Petersson, Faísca, Ingvar, & Reis, 2004).

Generally speaking, it is still unclear what type of relation exists between phonological processing, verbal working memory, and the acquisition of orthographic knowledge. Moreover, it appears that the phonological processing difficulties in illiterate subjects are not limited to phonological awareness per se but involve other aspects of sublexical phonological processing, as well as skills related to verbal working memory (e.g., phonological recoding in working memory). There is some evidence indicating that these effects may be specific to alphabetic orthographies, and it is unclear whether these generalize to nonalphabetic orthographies. In the following subsections, we review some recent results on short-term memory span, pseudoword processing, and word awareness in sentence context.

### Short-Term Memory – Digit and Spatial Span
Several studies have indicated that there is a difference in digit span between literate and illiterate subjects (e.g., Ardila, Rosselli, & Rosas, 1989; Reis, Guerreiro, Garcia, & Castro-Caldas, 1995). In a recent study, Reis, Guerreiro, and Petersson (2003) showed that the difference in digit span is not a simple effect of literacy as such but that digit span performance appears to depend on the extent of formal education. In particular, illiterate participants had a mean digit span of 4.1 (± 0.9), performing significantly

more poorly than literate participants. However, literate subjects with 4 years of education performed significantly lower ($5.2 \pm 1.4$) than literate subjects with 9 years of education ($7.0 \pm 1.8$). Thus, it appears that not only literacy, but also education more generally, contributes to the observed difference (overall effect $p < .001$).

In a recent follow-up study, we compared literate and illiterate participants directly on the digit span and spatial span subtasks of the Wechsler Memory Scale, 3rd edition. Consistent with the results just described, there was a significant difference between literacy groups on the digit span ($p = .004$), whereas there was no significant difference on the spatial span task ($p = .3$). These results indicate that the illiterate subjects have a lower verbal span compared with literate subjects, whereas this is not the case for spatial span. These results represent a first hint that verbal short-term memory might be influenced by literacy and formal education, and this is possibly related to more effective verbal working memory representations in literate individuals (e.g., chunking; cf., e.g., Olesen, Westerberg, & Klingberg, 2004).

### Word and Pseudoword Processing

Pseudoword repetition is a commonly used task to investigate verbal working memory capacity. Reis and Castro-Caldas (1997) concluded that illiterate subjects performed similarly to literate subjects on word repetition, whereas there was a significant difference on pseudoword repetition. We have suggested that this is related to an inability to handle certain aspects of sublexical phonological structure (Petersson et al., 2000) and indicates that the phonological representations, or the processing of these representations, are differently developed in literate and illiterate individuals (Petersson et al., 2000, 2001). Alternatively, the system for orthographic representations may support phonological processing as an auxiliary interactive processing network (Petersson et al., 2001).

Because several aspects of auditory-verbal language may differ between literate and illiterate subjects, it is of interest to isolate the different sources contributing to these differences in phonological processing. In particular, it is important to study the differences in phonological processing relatively independent of lexicality effects (e.g., vocabulary size and frequency effects), as well as articulatory mechanisms. To do so, we used an immediate auditory-verbal serial recognition paradigm (Gathercole, Pickering, Hall, & Peacker, 2001) in a recent follow-up study (Petersson et al., 2004). In general, immediate serial recognition is independent of speech output. In addition, serial recognition of pseudowords is (relatively) independent of lexicality effects. In this experiment, we compared illiterate and literate subjects on immediate recognition of lists of 3 CVCV-syllable items (C, consonant; V, vowel). The lists varied in lexicality (words/pseudowords) and phonological similarity (dissimilar/similar). The participants were asked to judge whether two lists (presented one after the other) contained items presented in the same or different order. Group comparisons showed significant differences, the literate group performing better than the illiterate, in all conditions (pseudoword/dissimilar, $p < .001$; pseudoword/similar, $p = .03$; word/similar $p = .003$), except for phonologically different words ($p = .2$). Of the four different conditions, the phonologically different word condition is of course the easiest to handle from a phonological point of view. Words are more familiar than pseudowords, and the phonological contrast is greater in the different compared with the similar condition. These results are thus consistent with the differences in pseudoword repetition (literate > illiterate) and digit span performance, and further support the idea that there are differences in verbal working memory capacity between literacy groups. In addition, the results on immediate serial recognition indicate that these differences are (relatively) independent of lexicality effects, articulatory organization (e.g., output phonology), or other speech output mechanisms.

## Awareness of Phonological Form and the Intrusion of Lexical Semantics in Illiterates

A characteristic of problem-solving capabilities in illiterate individuals is their tendency to prefer semantic-pragmatic strategies, if such are possible, over more formally oriented strategies. In other words, when an illiterate individual is confronted with a problem that can be solved by using strategies based on formal/abstract or semantic/pragmatic aspects of the problem, the illiterate individual is generally more likely to base the strategy on the latter type of information. For example, Kolinsky, Cary, and Morais (1987) investigated the notion of phonological word length in literate and illiterate subjects. Even when explicitly asked to attend to the abstract phonological properties of words, the illiterate group still found it difficult to ignore their semantic content; thus, the illiterate group found it difficult to inhibit the intrusion of semantic information when attempting to solve the task based on a form criterion. This suggests that explicit awareness of words as a phonological form may depend on orthographic knowledge or more generally on formal education.

In a recent experiment (Silva et al., 2002; Reis, Faísca, Mendonça, et al., 2005), literate and illiterate participants listened to words and pseudowords during a phonological ("sound") length decision task, in which the participants were asked to decide which item in a pair was the longest in phonological terms. In the word condition, we manipulated the relationship between word length and size of the denoted object, yielding three subconditions: (1) *congruent* – the longer word denoted the larger object; (2) *incongruent* – the longer word denoted the smaller object; and (3) *neutral* – only the phonological length of the words varied, denoting

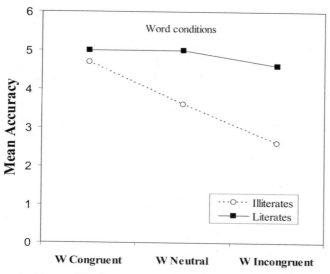

FIGURE 13.2. The literate group performed significantly better than the illiterate group on both words ($p < .001$) and pseudowords ($p = .001$). The results between the different word conditions (i.e., congruent, neutral, incongruent) showed a significant effect in the illiterate group ($p < .001$). There was no significant difference between word (collapsed over conditions) and pseudoword performance in the literate group ($p = .3$). In contrast, the illiterate group showed significantly better performance on pseudowords compared with words ($p = .01$).

objects of similar size. Pseudoword pairs were constructed based on the real word pairs by changing the consonants and maintaining the vowels and word length. All subjects practiced each condition until they fully understood the task.

Two effects were of interest in the results. First, the literate subjects showed no effect of semantic interference, whereas this was clearly the case in the illiterate group (Fig. 13.2). Second, although the literates performed at similar levels on words and pseudowords, the illiterate group performed significantly better on pseudowords compared with words. In fact, the mean performance in the pseudoword condition was slightly better than in the neutral word condition. These results indicate that the illiterate subjects show a greater difficulty in inhibiting the influence of semantic interference, the intrusion of lexical semantics in the decision process (Reis, Faísca, Mendonça, et al., 2005).

## Awareness of Words in Sentence Context

Little is known about how adult illiterate subjects perceive words in sentence context. Awareness of words as independent lexical units has been investigated in children, both before and after acquiring reading skills (e.g., Barton, 1985; Hamilton & Barton, 1983; Karmiloff-Smith et al., 1996), and also in illiterate adults (Cary & Verhaeghe, 1991). The results show that explicit knowledge of words as independent lexical units to some degree depends on literacy. Cary and Verhaegh (1991) suggested that the difficulty for illiterate subjects is to efficiently identify closed-class words because of their relative lack of semantic content. However, given the prominent syntactic role of closed-class words in sentence processing, including sentence comprehension, and the fact that illiterate and literate individuals acquire spoken language on similar terms, we were interested in whether the effects related to closed-class words could be given a phonological explanation. In two recent studies, we revisited these issues (Mendonça et al., 2002). In the first study, we investigated the awareness of words in sentence context, with the aim of clarifying the role of literacy in the recognition of words as independent lexical units and the possible relation to the known phonological processing characteristics of illiterate subjects. We presented short sentences that varied in their constituent structure in random order to the participants. All articles, prepositions, pronouns, and adverbs were included in the closed-class category. We divided this class into phonologically stressed and nonstressed words, where the latter are characterized by the absence of a stressed vowel. Each sentence was orally presented, and subjects were instructed to listen to the sentence, to immediately repeat it, and to identify its constituent words by enumerating them. All spontaneous corrections were considered, and after the experimental session, subjects were asked to correct three of the incorrect segmentations. The behavioral data were scored according to the following aspects: (A) global quantitative: (1) total of correct sentence segmentations (maximum score: 18), (2) spontaneous corrections, and (3) corrections made when probed; (B) segmentation errors: (1) blending (a so-called "clitization" phenomenon) words at the boundaries of sentence's main constituents, and (2) blending words within phrases; (C) omissions of stressed and nonstressed closed-class words.

It is clear from Table 13.1 that the literate group performed significantly better than the illiterate group on the sentence segmentation task. The results also show that illiterate subjects did not spontaneously correct themselves, not even when probed. For all error types investigated, group comparison showed significant differences. Therefore, and to further understand the behavioral pattern of illiterate group, the subsequent error analysis focused on this group only. To compare the incidence of the different error types, percentage of errors was computed based on the total number of possible occurrences for each type. The illiterate group showed a specific pattern of merging or "clitization" of words (Table 13.2 and Fig. 13.3b). There are very few mergers between the major syntactic constituents (1.4% error rate), meaning that illiterates are sensitive to

TABLE 13.1. *Means and Standard Deviations for Sentence Segmentation Scores (Maximum = 18; Between-Group Mann-Whitney U Test)*

| Behavioral Measure | Illiterate | Literate | $p$ Value |
|---|---|---|---|
| Correct sentence segmentation | $3 \pm 2.9$ | $17 \pm 2.0$ | <.001 |
| Spontaneous corrections | $0.1 \pm 0.2$ | $1 \pm 1.3$ | .001 |
| Percentage of questions corrected | $19 \pm 33$ | $80 \pm 45$ | .01 |

the major syntactic structure of the sentence. This was also the case for syntactic boundaries within verb phrases (VPs; 4.3%). Increasing rates of mergers were observed within phrase internal constituents related to noun phrases (NPs) and prepositional phrases (PPs), but this seemed to depend on the particular syntactic context, or alternatively, on the linear sentence position. The words of NPs in subject position were more frequently merged (60%) compared with NPs within VPs or PPs in complement position (47% and 37%, respectively). Within the PPs composed of a preposition or contraction and a noun, the illiterates committed the highest rate of mergers; in differently composed PPs, mergers were less frequent.

The closed-class word analysis revealed that illiterate subjects were unable to correctly segment 50% of the instances. Comparing the stressed and the nonstressed closed-class words showed that the merging tendency was significantly more prominent for the nonstressed closed-class words (Fig. 13.3a).

In a recent follow-up study using a similar experimental design (Mendonça et al., 2003), these effects were replicated. In brief, although there was no significant difference in sentence repetition ($p = .7$), the literate sentence segmentation performance was significantly better than the illiterate performance ($p < .001$), and the mergers related to closed-class words were observed significantly more often with nonstressed as compared with stressed closed-class words in the illiterate group ($p < .001$). More detailed preliminary analysis indicates that the merging effect depends on the type

TABLE 13.2. *Mean and Standard Deviations of Proportions of Segmentation Errors Committed Internal to Phrase Type by Illiterate Group*

| Blending Internal Constituents of Phrases | Percentage |
|---|---|
| Determiner + noun | $51 \pm 22$ |
| Preposition + determiner + noun | $18 \pm 19$ |
| Preposition + determiner | $14 \pm 13$ |
| Preposition + noun | $77 \pm 28$ |
| Contraction + noun | $62 \pm 28$ |

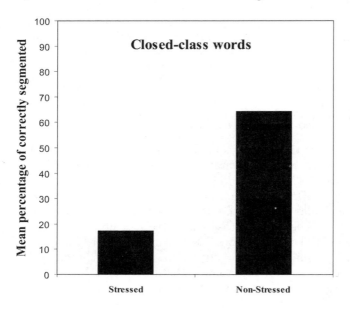

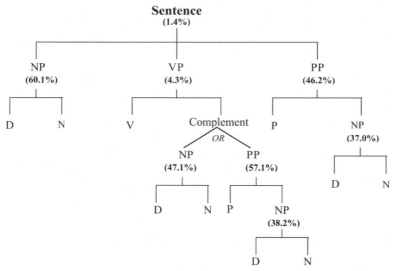

FIGURE 13.3. (a) The proportion of errors related to closed-class words. The closed-class words were either phonologically stressed or nonstressed. The illiterate subjects committed significantly more segmentation errors related to the nonstressed (64 ± 24%) compared with the stressed closed-class words (17 ± 14%; Wilcoxon $p < .001$). (b) The proportion of segmentation errors related to the phrase structure of the sentence (see text for explanation).

of closed class; that is, the stressed versus nonstressed effect was most common for determiners and least common for prepositions. Overall then, the present results corroborate previous suggestions that recognition of words as independent phonological units in sentence context depends on literacy. Cary and Verhaegh (1991) suggested that the difficulty observed in illiterate subjects is related to a difficulty in efficient identification of closed-class words due to their relative lack of semantic content. However, these results show that this cannot serve as a unitary explanation because the segmentation failures did not distribute evenly over closed-class words (not even within subtypes), but occurred more often with phonologically nonstressed than phonologically stressed closed-class words. The illiterate subjects are thus more sensitive to phonologically stressed closed-class words, which they are able to segment quite efficiently. We suggest that illiterate segmentation performance is closely related to sentence internal prosody and phonological stress. Thus, the difficulty seems to be a phonological phenomenon rather than related to lexical semantics. In addition, the "clitization" phenomenon does not seem to be related to phrase structure per se because the illiterate group respected phrasal boundaries; blending mainly occurred within phrases and rarely across phrasal boundaries or boundaries between major sentence constituents. Another contributing factor to segmentation difficulties may be verbal working memory capacity because the performance of the illiterate group increased from the start to the end of sentences. In other words, the linear sentence position may also play a role. In summary, illiterate word segmentation of sentences appears to depend on factors related to phonology, syntactic structure, and linear position, and it does not seem to be related to lexical semantic factors.

## Semantic Fluency – An Example of the Importance of Ecological Relevance

Literacy and formal education are also associated with the acquisition of a broader knowledge base of general information, as well as to process this information in a more systematic abstract and elaborate manner. Hence, literacy and formal education catalyze the development of several cognitive skills in addition to reading and writing skills. Task selection can thus be of importance when investigating populations of different cultural backgrounds. In particular, when the objective is to interpret differences in performance between populations in cognitive terms, it is sometimes important that the task is of comparable ecological relevance to the populations involved. This goes beyond matching populations for background variables related to socioeconomic status and so on (e.g., Coppens, Parente, & Lecours, 1998; Reis & Petersson, 2003). This is illustrated by the results from a recent study of semantic fluency by Silva et al. (2004).

Verbal fluency tasks (i.e., production tasks in which subjects generate as many words as possible during a limited time according to some given criteria) are commonly used in neuropsychological assessment because they are easy to administer, sensitive to brain damage and cognitive deterioration, and have been applied to groups of different cultural background. Clear and consistent differences between literacy groups have been reported when a phonological fluency criterion is used (for a recent review, see Silva et al., 2004). In contrast, several studies comparing literate and illiterate subjects have yielded different results when using semantic criteria. At present, the reasons for this are unclear but might be related to the specific semantic criteria and/or the particular study populations investigated. Reis, Guerreiro, and Petersson (2003) suggested that the non-convergence of results could be related to the ecological or cultural relevance of the chosen semantic criterion. To investigate this issue in greater detail, they decided to use a semantic criterion of equal natural relevance to female literate and illiterate subjects, and asked the participants to name things a person can buy at the supermarket (Reis, Guerreiro, & Petersson, 2001, 2003). The relevance of this criterion springs from the fact that almost all these individuals do the major part of their regular shopping at supermarkets and at comparable levels over time. As expected, Reis et al. found no significant differences between illiterates, subjects with 4 years of education, and subjects with more than 4 years of education.

Silva et al. (2004) attempted to relate the concept of ecological relevance to the level of shared cultural background, except for differences in literacy or formal education. More specifically, Silva et al. compared the performance of the same illiterate and literate subjects on two time-constrained semantic fluency tasks, the first using the semantic category of food items that can be bought at the supermarket (supermarket fluency task), and the second using animal names (animal fluency task). Note that the equal performance on the supermarket task excludes a simple explanation for the performance differences on the animal fluency task (literate > illiterate) in terms of general factors such as cognitive speed or fluency. Instead, the interaction between literacy and semantic criterion might be explained in terms of similarities and differences in shared cultural background, that is, greater for supermarket items and lesser for animals.

This possibly reflects a type of frequency of exposure effect, making lexical access less readily available in illiterate subjects in the animal fluency task. In other words, this difference may be a consequence of education or a secondary effect of literacy. For example, reading skills should facilitate access to information through printed media, thus providing an opportunity to broaden different semantic categories that transcend the shared sociocultural background of the two literacy groups. However, it appears that it is not just that the two semantic categories used in this study are associated with differences in sociocultural background specifically related to literacy/education; they also differ in the level of reference to a concrete knowledge and to specific situations. The observed differences between the literacy groups may not only relate to the semantic category used, but potentially also to the extension (the semantic field; the potential number of available elements) of the semantic category. In this view, written language provides the opportunity to broaden different semantic categories, and by using written language, we can access information that we cannot access through our direct experience. Thus, an important determinant for verbal fluency performance might relate to the type of experience we have with the elements of a semantic category.

We further investigated the effects of formal schooling on the semantic organization of the responses from the animal fluency task (Faísca, Reis, & Petersson, 2003) using a nonmetric multidimensional scaling approach. This approach assumes that the item sequence in a fluency task reflects the semantic organization of a given semantic domain. The most frequent responses in both groups were selected for further analysis, and the serial position was used to build a distance matrix. The matrix for each group was analyzed using multidimensional scaling to represent the results in a 2D semantic space. As can be seen from Figure 13.4, the semantic organization for the common responses is similar in the two literacy groups. Both groups allocated the different exemplars according to the same subcategories (farm birds, farm animals, and wild animals).

In summary, the semantic fluency study illustrates two things. First, significant literacy effects may or may not be observed, depending on the choice of semantic criterion, and this emphasizes the importance of developing instruments that are free of educational and cultural biases. Second, the multidimensional scaling results on the animal category suggest that on the high-frequency responses there is no difference between groups in terms of semantic organization, indicating that differences between groups emerged after the first items of a category had been generated. Thus, it seems that the initial production reflects the shared cultural background, whereas group differences only emerge in the later phase of the animal fluency production.

## FUNCTIONAL AND NEUROANATOMICAL DIFFERENCES BETWEEN LITERACY GROUPS

In a positron emission tomography (PET) study of literate and illiterate subjects, we compared the two literacy groups on immediate verbal repetition. The subjects were instructed to repeat words or pseudowords, and although there were performance differences between groups, these did not correlate with the pattern of brain activations in either group (Petersson et al., 2000). Within-group comparisons indicated that there was a more prominent left-sided inferior parietal (Brodmann's area [BA] 40) activation

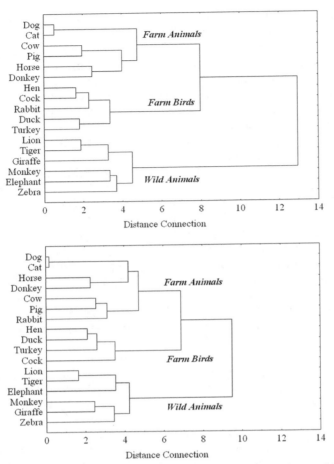

FIGURE 13.4. (a) Hierarchical cluster analysis (Ward's method) of the semantic fluency responses. (b) Multidimensional scaling including the 17 most frequent responses. Note that the results are rotationally invariant so they indicate that the aspects of semantic memory reflected in the data are similarly organized in both literacy groups.

in words versus pseudowords in the literate group, whereas in the reverse comparison, pseudowords versus words, the literate group displayed a significant activation in the anterior insular cortex (BA 14/15) bilaterally and in the right inferior frontal/frontal opercular cortices (BA 44/45/47/49), left perigenual anterior cingulate cortex (BA 24/32), left basal ganglia, midline anterior thalamus/hypothalamus, and midline cerebellum. In the illiterate group, significant activation was only observed in the right middle frontal/frontopolar region (BA 10). These results were generally reflected in the between-group comparisons, including a greater activation of the left

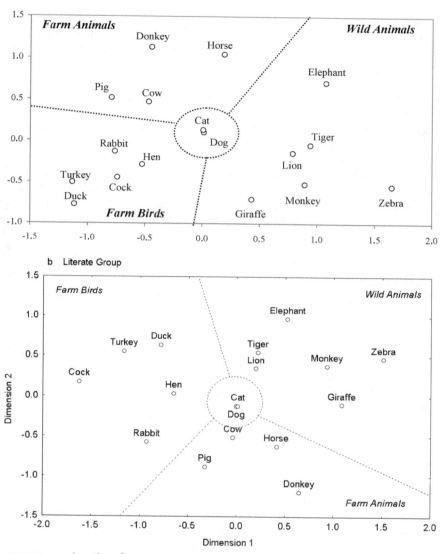

FIGURE 13.4 (*continued*)

inferior parietal region (BA 40) in the literate compared with the illiterate group related to the word versus pseudoword comparison. Taken together with the behavioral findings outlined previously, these results indicate that the functional architecture of auditory–spoken language processing is influenced by literacy, suggesting that a relation between the acquisition of reading and writing skills and aspects of phonological processing also exists in terms of the functional brain organization (see Chapter 7).

A complementary approach to the results outlined in this section takes a network perspective on cognitive brain function. In general, information is believed to be represented as distributed activity in the brain, whereas information processing subserving cognitive functions is believed to emerge from the interactions between different functionally specialized regions. When trying to understand cognitive processing as instantiated in the brain, it is therefore natural to take a network perspective on information processing (Ingvar & Petersson, 2000). Structural equation modeling (SEM) provides one approach to characterize network interactions and to test network hypotheses explicitly. Petersson et al. (2000) employed an SEM analysis of the PET data outlined previously to characterize the functional organization of immediate verbal repetition in literate and illiterate subjects. This approach aimed at characterizing the functional organization in terms of effective connections between regions in a functional-anatomical model. Our objective was to construct a simple network that could explain a sufficient part of the observed covariance in both groups during both word and pseudoword repetition. At the same time, we required that the network model should be both theoretically and empirically plausible based on the literature on the functional organization of language.

In terms of network interactions, the results showed no significant difference in the literate group when comparing the word and pseudoword condition. Neither was there any significant difference between the literate and illiterate group in the word repetition condition. In contrast, there were significant differences between word and pseudoword repetition in the illiterate group and between the illiterate and literate group in the pseudoword condition. The differences between groups were mainly related to the phonological loop, in particular, the interaction between Broca's region and the inferior parietal region.

The absence of significant differences between word and pseudoword repetition in the literate group relates to the fact that the network interactions were similar during word and pseudoword repetition. This indicates that the literate subjects automatically recruit the same processing network during immediate verbal repetition for both word and pseudoword repetition. In contrast, this was not the case for the illiterate group, consistent with the suggestion that phonological processing is differently organized in illiterate individuals due to a different developmental background related to the acquisition of reading and writing skills. Based on this, and in conjunction with the behavioral results outlined previously, we suggest that these differences in the phonological loop interactions might represent a primary difference between the two literacy groups. This is in line with the suggestion that the parallel interactive processing characteristics of the language system differ between literate and illiterate subjects (Petersson et al., 2000).

## The Corpus Callosum and Hemispheric Differences
## Between Literacy Groups

One may wonder whether there are neuroanatomic correlates corresponding to the literacy status. It is well-known that the corpus callosum, the large fiber bundle that interconnects the two brain hemispheres, develops during childhood and into young adulthood. In particular, there is an active myelination process of the neuronal axons running through this structure to establish efficient communication between the brain's two hemispheres (Giedd et al., 1996). Recent evidence suggests that the posterior midbody part of the corpus callosum undergoes extensive myelination during the years of reading acquisition, that is, from 6 to 10 years of age (Thompson et al., 2000). The fibers that cross over in this region of the corpus callosum interconnect the left and right parietotemporal regions (for a general review see, e.g., Zaidel & Iacoboni, 2003). The parietotemporal regions of the brain, in particular in the left hemisphere, are related to language processing, verbal working memory, and reading, and it has been suggested that the corpus callosum plays an important role in the interhemispheric exchange of orthographic and phonological information during reading.

A recent study of the morphology of the corpus callosum in literate and illiterate subjects suggested that the posterior midbody region (Fig. 13.5a) is thinner in the illiterate compared with the literate subjects (Castro-Caldas et al., 1999). Petersson, Reis, Askelöf, Castro-Caldas, and Ingvar (1998) hypothesized that this may be related to a difference in the interhemispheric interactions between literacy groups with respect to the parietotemporal cortices. Behavioral and lesion data have suggested, although not unambiguously so, that certain aspects of language processing in illiterate individuals recruit bilateral brain regions to a greater extent than literate subjects (for a review, see, e.g., Coppens et al., 1998). For example, an early study suggested that the risk of aphasia as a consequence of left hemisphere lesions was lower in illiterate than literate subjects (Cameron, Currier, & Haerer, 1971). More recently, Lecours et al. (1988) suggested that illiterate subjects are more likely to use processing networks that include right hemisphere regions when performing certain language tasks. In a recent study (Petersson, Reis, Castro-Caldas, & Ingvar, 2005), we attempted to characterize the hemispheric left–right differences in two independent data sets acquired with PET from two different samples of illiterate subjects and their matched literate controls. In the first data set, in which the subjects repeated words and pseudowords, we explored the possibility of a left–right difference between literacy groups, predicting a greater left–right difference in the literate compared with the illiterate subjects in the inferior parietal region. To test this prediction, we investigated regions of interest in the angular-supramarginal region (BA 39/40). In a random effect analysis, the left–right difference was greater in

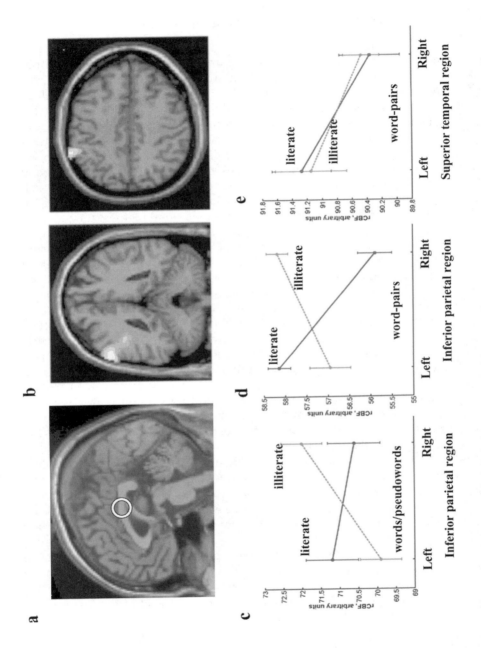

300

the literate group compared with the illiterate for word and pseudoword repetition (Fig. 13.5c). In the second sample, in which subjects listened to and encoded word pairs, we attempted to replicate this finding. Again, the literate group showed greater left–right difference in the angular-supramarginal region (BA39/40) compared with the illiterate subjects, thus replicating the finding from the first study (Figs. 13.5b and 13.5d).

It has recently been indicated that infants are left lateralized in the superior temporal gyrus when listening to speech or speech-like sounds (Dehaene-Lambertz, Dehaene, & Hertz-Pannier, 2002), and to test the specificity of our results with respect to the inferior parietal cortex, we also investigated the superior temporal region (BA 22/41/42). The results showed that both literacy groups were similarly left lateralized in this region (Fig. 13.5e), indicating that the functional lateralization of early speech-related brain regions does not depend on literacy.

It is well accepted that both cerebral hemispheres play a role in language processing. However, the results outlined here lend support to the suggestion that there is a relatively greater involvement of the right hemisphere in illiterate compared with literate subjects in the language tasks investigated. These results provide evidence that literacy, a cultural factor, influences the hemispheric balance in inferior parietal language-related regions. One may speculate that acquiring reading and writing skills at the appropriate age shape not only the local morphology of the corpus callosum, but also the degree of functional specialization and the pattern of interaction between the interconnected inferior parietal regions. Thus, there might be a causal connection between reading and writing acquisition, the development of the corpus callosum, and the hemispheric differences reported here.

---

←

FIGURE 13.5. (a) Differences between literacy groups in the local thickness of the corpus callosum (circle) indicate that this is thinner in illiterate than in literate subjects ($p < .01$). (b) Hemispheric differences (left–right) in activation levels between literacy groups in the inferior parietal region (BA 39/40). (c) In experiment 1, the participants listened to and repeated words and pseudowords. The diagrams show the level of left and right activation levels (regional cerebral blood flow [rCBF], arbitrary units) as a function of literacy group (illiterate: dashed). Differences averaged over conditions $p = .009$ (words: $p = .017$; pseudowords: $p = .006$). (d) In experiment 2, the participants were listening to and encoding word pairs. Again, we observed left–right activation differences (nearest suprathreshold cluster test, $p = .029$, corrected) between literacy groups in the inferior parietal region (BA 39/40). (e) To test the specificity of these left–right results with respect to the inferior parietal cortex, we also investigated the superior temporal region (BA 22/41/42) in the second experiment. The results showed that both literacy groups were similarly left lateralized in this region, indicating that the functional lateralization of early speech-related brain regions does not depend on literacy.

CONCLUSION

Formal education and the educational system can be viewed as an institutionalized process of structured cultural transmission. The study of illiterate subjects and their literate controls represents one approach to investigate the interactions between neurobiological and cultural factors in cognitive development. The results reviewed here indicate that formal education influences important aspects of cognition, as well as structural and functional properties of the brain. Taken together, the evidence provides strong support for the hypothesis that certain functional properties of the brain are modulated by literacy and formal education. In other words, literacy and formal education influence the development of the human brain and its capacity to interact with the environment. This includes the culture of the individual who, through acquired cognitive skills, can actively participate in, interact with, and contribute to, the process of cultural transmission.

ACKNOWLEDGMENTS

This work was supported in part by Fundação para a Ciência e a Tecnologia (FCT/POCTI/41669/PSI/2001), EU grant QLK6-CT-99-02140, the Swedish Medical Research Council (8276,127169), the Knut and Alice Wallenberg Foundation, and the Swedish Dyslexia Foundation. The authors also want to thank Dr. Martin Ingvar, Dr. Alexandre Castro-Caldas, Dr. Francisco Reis, Dr. Francisco Lacerda, Dr. Luis Faísca, Catarina Silva, Susana Mendonça, Alexandra Mendonça, and Simon Askelöf for their contributions to this work.

References

Abadzi, H. (2003). *Improving adult literacy outcomes: Lessons from cognitive research for developing countries*. Washington, DC: The World Bank, Operation Evaluation Department.
Ardila, A. (2004). There is not any specific brain area for writing: From cave-painting to computers. *International Journal of Psychology, 39*, 61–67.
Ardila, A., Rosselli, M., & Rosas, P. (1989). Neuropsychological assessment in illiterates: Visuospatial and memory abilities. *Brain & Cognition, 11*, 147–166.
Baddeley, A., Gathercole, S., & Papagno, C. (1998). The phonological loop as a language learning device. *Psychological Review, 105*, 158–173.
Barton, D. (1985). Awareness of language units in adults and children. In A. W. Ellis (Ed.), *Progress in the psychology of language* (Vol. 1, pp. 187–205). Hillsdale, NJ: Erlbaum.
Brady, S. A. (1991). The role of working memory in reading disability. In S. A. Brady & D. P. Shankweiler (Eds.), *Phonological processes in literacy* (pp. 129–151). Hillsdale, NJ: Erlbaum.
Cameron, R. F., Currier, R. D., & Haerer, A. F. (1971). Aphasia and literacy. *British Journal of Disorders of Communication, 6*, 161–163.

Cary, L., & Verhaeghe, A. (1991). Efeito da prática da linguagem ou da alfabetização no conhecimento das fronteiras formais das unidades lexicais: Comparação de dois tipos de tarefas [Effect of language practice and literacy on the knowledge of formal lexical unit boundaries]. *Actas das Jornadas de Estudos dos Processos Cognitivos*, 33–49.

Castro-Caldas, A., Cavaleiro, M., Carmo, I., Reis, A., Leote, F., Ribeiro, C., et al. (1999). Influence of learning to read and write on the morphology of the corpus callosum. *European Journal of Neurology, 6*, 23–28.

Chomsky, N. (1986). *Knowledge of language*. New York: Praeger.

Coppens, P., Parente, M. A. M. P., & Lecours, A. R. (1998). Aphasia in illiterate individuals. In P. Coppens, Y. Lebrun, & A. Basso (Eds.), *Aphasia in atypical populations* (pp. 175–202). Hillsdale, NJ: Erlbaum.

Dehaene-Lambertz, G., Dehaene, S., & Hertz-Pannier, L. (2002). Functional neuroimaging of speech perception in infants. *Science, 298*, 2013–2015.

EFA Global Monitoring Report Team. (2003/04). *Gender and education for all: The leap to equality*. Paris: UNESCO. Available: http://www.efareport.unesco.org.

Faísca, L., Reis, A., & Petersson, K. M. (2003, October). *O efeito da escolaridade na organização das redes semânticas: Utilização de técnicas de escalonamento no estudo da categoria semântica "animais"* [Semantic networks and literacy: The application of the multidimensional scaling technique to study the "animal" semantic category]. Paper presented at V Simpósio Nacional de Investigação em Psicologia, Lisbon, Portugal.

Gathercole, S. E., & Baddeley, A. D. (1995). *Working memory and language* (Vol. 2). Hillsdale, NJ: Erlbaum.

Gathercole, S. E., Pickering, S. J., Hall, M., & Peacker, S. M. (2001). Dissociable lexical and phonological influences on serial recognition and serial recall. *Quarterly Journal of Experimental Psychology, 54A* (1), 1–30.

Giedd, J. N., Rumsey, J. M., Castellanos, F. X., Rajapakse, J. C., Kaysen, D., Vaituzis, A. C., et al. (1996). A quantitative MRI study of the corpus callosum in children and adolescents. *Developmental Brain Research, 91*, 274–280.

Goldblum, M.-C., & Matute de Duran, E. (2000). Are illiterate people deep dyslexics? *Journal of Neurolinguistics, 2*, 103–111.

Goody, J. (2000). *The power of the written tradition*. Washington, DC: Smithsonian Institution Press.

Hamilton, M. E., & Barton, D. (1983). Adults' definition of "word": The effects of literacy and development. *Journal of Pragmatics, 7*, 581–594.

Ingvar, M., & Petersson, K. M. (2000). Functional maps – cortical networks. In A. W. Toga & J. C. Mazziotta (Eds.), *Brain mapping: The systems* (pp. 111–140). San Diego: Academic Press.

Karmiloff-Smith, A. (1992). *Beyond modularity: A developmental perspective on cognitive science*. Cambridge, MA: MIT Press.

Karmiloff-Smith, A., Grant, J., Sims, K., Jones, M. C., & Cuckle, P. (1996). Rethinking metalinguistic awareness: Representing and accessing knowledge about what counts as a word. *Cognition, 58*, 197–219.

Kolinsky, R., Cary, L., & Morais, J. (1987). Awareness of words as phonological entities: The role of literacy. *Applied Psycholinguistics, 8*, 223–237.

Lecours, A. R., Mehler, J., Parente, M. A., Beltrami, M. Canossa de Tolipan, L., Castro, M. J., et al. (1988). Illiteracy and brain damage: III. A contribution to the study of speech and language disorders in illiterates with unilateral brain damage (initial testing). *Neuropsychologia, 26,* 575–589.

Levelt, W. J. M. (1989). *Speaking: From intention to articulation.* Cambridge, MA: MIT Press.

Mendonça, A., Mendonça, S., Reis, A., Faísca, L., Ingvar, M., & Petersson, K. M. (2003, November). *Reconhecimento de unidades lexicais em contexto frásico: O efeito da literacia* [Recognition of lexical units in sentence context: The effect of literacy]. Paper presented at the Congresso em Neurociências Cognitivas, Évora, Portugal.

Mendonça, S., Faísca, L., Silva, C., Ingvar, M., Reis, A., & Petersson, K. M. (2002). The role of literacy in the awareness of words as independent lexical units. *Journal of the International Neuropsychological Society, 8,* 483.

Morais, J. (1993). Phonemic awareness, language and literacy. In R. M. Joshi & C. K. Leong (Eds.), *Reading disabilities: Diagnosis and component processes* (pp. 175–184). Dordrecht, The Netherlands: Kluwer Academic.

Morais, J., Cary, L., Alegria, J., & Bertelson, P. (1979). Does awareness of speech as a sequence of phones arise spontaneously? *Cognition, 7,* 323–331.

Olesen, P. J., Westerberg, H., & Klingberg, T. (2004). Increased prefrontal and parietal activity after training of working memory. *Nature Neuroscience, 7,* 75–79.

Patterson, K., & Lambon Ralph, M. A. (1999). Selective disorders of reading? *Current Opinion in Neurobiology, 9,* 235–239.

Paulesu, E., Démonet, J.- F., Fazio, F., McCrory, E., Chanoine, V., Brunswick, N., et al. (2001). Dyslexia: Cultural diversity and biological unity. *Science, 291,* 2165–2167.

Paulesu, E., McCrory, E., Fazio, F., Menoncello, L., Brunswick, N., Cappa, S. F., et al. (2000). A cultural effect on brain function. *Nature Neuroscience, 3* (1), 91–96.

Petersson, K. M., Reis, A., Askelöf, S., Castro-Caldas, A., & Ingvar, M. (1998). Differences in inter-hemispheric interactions between literate and illiterate subjects during verbal repetition [Abstract]. *NeuroImage, 7,* S217.

Petersson, K. M., Reis, A., Askelöf, S., Castro-Caldas, A., & Ingvar, M. (2000). Language processing modulated by literacy: A network-analysis of verbal repetition in literate and illiterate subjects. *Journal of Cognitive Neuroscience, 12,* 364–382.

Petersson, K. M., Reis, A., Castro-Caldas, A., & Ingvar, M. (2005). *Literacy: A cultural influence on the hemispheric balance in the inferior parietal cortex.* Manuscript submitted for publication.

Petersson, K. M., Reis, A., & Ingvar, M. (2001). Cognitive processing in literate and illiterate subjects: A review of some recent behavioral and functional data. *Scandinavian Journal of Psychology, 42,* 251–167.

Ravid, D., & Tolchinsky, L. (2002). Developing linguistic literacy: A comprehensive model. *Journal of Child Language, 29,* 417–447.

Reis, A., & Castro-Caldas, A. (1997). Illiteracy: A bias for cognitive development. *Journal of the International Neuropsychological Society, 3,* 444450.

Reis, A., Faísca, L., Silva, C., Fernandes, L., Ingvar, M. & Petersson, K. M. (2003, October). *A influência da escolaridade na nomeação visual de objectos: O estudo do efeito da cor versus o efeito da forma* [The influence of formal schooling on object visual naming: The color effect versus the shape effect]. Paper presented at V Simpósio Nacional de Investigação em Psicologia, Lisbon, Portugal.

Reis, A., Faísca, L., Ingvar, M. & Petersson, K. M. (2005). Color makes a difference: Two-dimensional object naming skills in literate and illiterate subjects. Accepted for publication in *Brain and Cognition*.

Reis, A., Faísca, L., Mendonça, A., Ingvar, M. & Petersson, K. M. (2005). Semantic interference on a phonological task in illiterate subjects. Accepted for publication in *Scandinavian Journal of Psychology*.

Reis, A., Guerreiro, M., & Castro-Caldas, A. (1994). Influence of educational level of non brain-damaged subjects on visual naming capacities. *Journal of Clinical & Experimental Neuropsychology, 16* (6), 939–942.

Reis, A., Guerreiro, M., Garcia, C., & Castro-Caldas, A. (1995). How does an illiterate subject process the lexical component of arithmetics? [Abstract]. *Journal of the International Neuropsychological Society, 1,* 206.

Reis, A., Guerreiro, M., & Petersson, K. M. (2001). Educational level on a neuropsychological battery [Abstract]. *Journal of the International Neuropsychological Society, 7* (4), 422–423.

Reis, A., Guerreiro, M., & Petersson, K. M. (2003). A socio-demographic and neuropsychological characterization of an illiterate population. *Applied Neuropsychology, 10,* 191–204.

Reis, A., & Petersson, K. M. (2003). Educational level, socioeconomic status and aphasia research: A comment on Connor et al. (2001). Effect of socioeconomic status on aphasia severity and recovery. *Brain and Language, 87,* 1795–1810.

Reis, A., Petersson, K. M., Castro-Caldas, A., & Ingvar, M. (2001). Formal schooling influences two- but not three-dimensional naming skills. *Brain and Cognition, 47,* 397–411.

Silva, C., Faísca, L., Mendonça, S., Ingvar, M., Petersson, K. M., & Reis, A. (2002). Awareness of words as phonological entities in an illiterate population [Abstract]. *Journal of the International Neuropsychological Society, 8,* 483.

Silva, C. G., Petersson, K. M., Faísca, L., Ingvar, M., & Reis, A. (2004). The effects of formal education on the quantitative and qualitative aspects of verbal semantic fluency. *Journal of Clinical & Experimental Neuropsychology, 26,* 266–277.

Thompson, P. M., Giedd, J. N., Woods, R. P., MacDonald, D., Evans, A. C., & Toga, A. W. (2000). Growth patterns in the developing brain detected by using continuum mechanical tensor maps. *Nature, 404,* 190–193.

Varney, N. R. (2002). How reading works: Considerations from prehistory to present. *Applied Neuropsychology, 9,* 3–12.

Vygotsky, L. S. (1962). *Thought and language*. Cambridge, MA: MIT Press.

Zaidel, E., & Iacoboni, M. (Eds.) . (2003). *The parallel brain: The cognitive neuroscience of the corpus callosum*. Cambridge, MA: MIT Press.

# 14

## The Influence of Work and Occupation on Brain Development

Neil Charness

ABSTRACT

*Despite its importance, there has been relatively little research on the role of occupational and work environment influences on brain development. I assess some of the existing literature, drawing inferences based on the probable relationship between cognition, and both brain structure and function, and centering particularly on the issue of adult aging. I review research focusing on occupational complexity and intellectual functioning, specific effects of particular occupations on certain brain regions, and protective effects of occupations on the brain during aging and the development of dementia.*

INTRODUCTION

In a popular joke, Sherlock Holmes, the famous detective and Dr. Watson, his constant companion, go camping, and they pitch their tent under the stars. During the night, Holmes wakes his companion and says: "Watson, look up and tell me what you see." Watson says: "I see millions of stars." Holmes says: "What do you deduce from that?" Watson says: "If a few of those have planets, it's quite likely there are some planets like Earth, and if there are a few planets like Earth out there, there might also be life elsewhere in the universe. What do you deduce, Holmes?" Holmes replies: "Watson, you idiot, someone stole our tent!"

Sometimes it is difficult to see what is before our noses. Many of the people reading these words spend 43+ hours per week (if living in the United States) working in a highly structured occupation that provides them with the resources to live in a modern society. Most newborns in developed countries such as the United States will encounter a set of cognitively challenging niches that make striking demands on their brains starting at prekindergarten and continuing at least until age 67 (for those in the U.S. workforce who plan to retire at the current full pension entitlement age in the United States), a span in excess of 60 years. To put that time duration in perspective, it is worth recalling that the life expectancy for Americans in 1900 was about 47 years.

Perhaps surprisingly, we know remarkably little about how occupations affect human development, and particularly, brain function. As an example, a search of the popular database PsycINFO (1840–2004, April) using the terms "brain" and "occupation" yielded just 79 hits, most of them irrelevant, with many referring to recovery from occupationally induced traumatic brain injuries. The same search terms yielded 681 studies on PUBMED. However, here, too, the vast majority of studies are more concerned with occupation as a risk factor for various medical conditions.

I provide an overview of some literatures that speak to the issues of how societies and cultures influence human development, and more specifically, brain development, particularly through the process of creating work/occupations and providing training opportunities for those who occupy such niches. I will also emphasize issues of development in the latter part of the lifespan. In the process, I am going to have to stretch inference a bit, like Dr. Watson, for want of the critical data that were obvious to Holmes in the earlier joke. Hopefully, I can stimulate a few Holmes-like readers to consider turning their attention to these issues.

## Assumptions

There is a paucity of reliable, replicated work on the direct effects of occupation on the brain. The brain imaging work I examine is often based on very small samples that may not generalize well to the general population. Nonetheless, here are some assumptions or guiding principles that I espouse about brain, mind, and culture. They are ordered from less to more speculative.

### Mind–Brain Relationship

My working assumption is that individual differences in cognition are ultimately reflected in brain function differences that are potentially observable with brain imaging techniques such as functional magnetic resonance imaging (fMRI), positron emission tomography (PET), electroencephalography, and magnetencephalography, and possibly also reflected in brain structure differences observable with a tool such as structural MRI. That is, the mind, as viewed with the experimental and observational tools of cognitive science, is instantiated in brain structures and functioning.

### Development and the Brain

The primary benefit to providing plasticity to a brain during an organism's lifespan is to allow that organism to become better attuned to specific

environments. An organism that can be shaped by (and shape) its environment will have a significant advantage (survival, reproduction) as environmental demands change. Cultural/occupational shaping is a very significant force for molding human brains.

### Occupation and the Brain
Different occupations make different demands on the brain and the brain
develops specialized neural networks in response to those demands. For
instance, if skillful occupational performance requires that people rapidly
perceive and respond to re-occurring patterns, the brain will develop networks to support perceiving and responding to those patterns.

### Efficiency and the Brain
Brains develop in a direction that promotes efficient use of metabolic
resources (e.g., glucose, oxygen). Well-developed/trained brains become
highly efficient. A good index of that efficiency is the time that it takes to
accomplish a mental task. Another index is the extent of tissue activated
at any point in time during task performance, where less activation is
better.

### LIFESPAN DEVELOPMENT FRAMEWORK FOR OCCUPATIONS

Borrowing from the framework espoused by Baltes (1979), we can concep-
tualize working life as being influenced by basic determinants – biological/
genetic, environmental, and their joint effects – that can be described in
terms of normative and nonnormative features: that is, normative age
graded, normative history graded, and nonnormative influences. An example of a normative age-graded social influence would be attaining the age
when you can drive, typically age 16 in the United States. There, reaching
age 16 allows you to earn a driver's license that permits you easy access to
many potential part-time work locations or perhaps to a job related directly
to driving, such as driving a delivery vehicle or a taxi. Another example
would be attaining the age of 65 and becoming eligible to receive a full
pension, and then leaving the paid labor force. An example of a (cyclically)
normative history-graded influence would be the presence of an economic
recession that would confront many labor force participants with the loss
of a job or a feeling of job insecurity, or an economic boom that would lure
someone who is retired back into the labor force. A nonnormative influence is one that is not typically experienced by a large proportion of the
population, such as becoming disabled by a workplace injury and leaving
the labor force, or winning the lottery at a young age and leaving the labor
force. These determinants may mold the brains and bodies of workplace
inhabitants in unique ways.

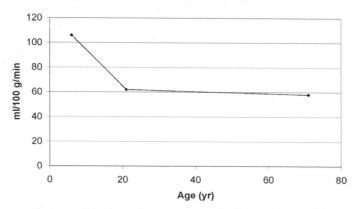

FIGURE 14.1. Lifespan changes in cerebral blood flow. (Data are from Sokoloff, 1989.)

## Principles for Successful Development

Development usually results in more efficient interaction with the environment. Humans progress in just a few decades from reflex-driven behavior as newborns, to adaptive and efficient problem solvers in the workplace environment. One of the hallmarks of such efficiency is speeded performance. In aging, one of the hallmark changes observed is slowing in processing (Salthouse, 1996). One interesting possibility for speed as a marker of efficient processing is that it is a proxy for energy expenditure. Brain tissue, representing 2% of body weight, uses approximately 20% of resting total body oxygen consumption (Sokoloff, 1989). So, the longer a computational process lasts, the more energy it probably consumes, although this may be difficult to detect against the background of normal energy expenditure (homeostatic expenditure). That homeostatic balance seems to be remarkably consistent past maturity across the lifespan, except in the case of disease. Figure 14.1 shows a graph produced from data provided by Sokoloff (1989).

It should be noted that blood flow is at its peak during childhood years (when the cortex is still undergoing significant development), and then declines to a constant from the end of the teen years into old age. It may be profitable to consider energy trade-off in the brain in a fashion similar to the cognitive concept of attentional resources. If some processes demand higher than normal energy expenditure, others may be less able to draw on such resources. Organisms that are efficient from an energy expenditure point of view can make fewer demands on the environment and hence are more likely to survive when local resources shrink. Of course, expending more energy to produce more profitable interactions with the environment is an important trade-off. Adding energy-intensive neocortex to produce a smarter organism paid off for *Homo sapiens*. However, my working assumption is that most people find it difficult to expend energy doing intensive (computationally demanding) thinking for extended periods of time. Diary and questionnaire studies of deliberate practice by musicians, the attention-demanding form of practice aimed at improving performance, shows it to be a not very enjoyable experience (Ericsson, Krampe, & Tesch-Römer, 1993).

## Brain Development

Although the blueprint for the shape of the human brain is undoubtedly framed by the genetic code, its scaffolding is provided by specific environmental influences. It is well known that exposure of a developing fetus to certain chemicals, bacteria, and viruses can have striking negative effects on its developing body and brain. There are also salient examples of how the normal intrauterine environment, by way of the timing of release of estrogens and androgens, determines the morphological and behavioral sexual characteristics of the developing fetus (Vandenbergh, 2003).

One possibility to keep in mind is that the brain structures that people often assume are set solely by DNA instructions function initially as rather general information processing mechanisms that are molded and specialized by interactions with the environment.

As an example, there is enormous proliferation of cells in embryonic development, with programmed cell death (apoptosis) an integral part of development, the so-called "selectionism" view of development. As one example, retinal ganglion cells, a critical component of the mammalian visual system seem to be generated in excessive quantities during the embryonic period with about half dying off before birth (Isenmann, Kretz, & Cellerino, 2003). Subsequently, normal visual stimulation is necessary for the development of adequate levels of visual acuity and binocular vision. Early deprivation usually, although not always, leads to poorer development of visual function, demonstrating a true "use it or lose it" principle for the developing brain.

However, Quartz and Sejnowski (1997) also argued that development is *constructivist*, such that environmental experiences enable greater representational ability and in the process result in brain specialization. There is some compelling evidence that experience-driven development of brain function occurs in humans. For instance, Gauthier and Tarr (2002; see also Tarr & Gauthier, 2000) argued that the region of the visual cortex that has come to be called the fusiform face area is really a flexible fusiform area that responds to experience and expertise training to map many different forms: cars, birds, faces, and even artificial "greebles." Certain behavioral tendencies are probably encoded into developing brain tissue, although undoubtedly in subtle fashion. In summary, the human brain may be a relatively plastic system and both its shape and its function may be molded in diverse ways by environmental influences.

## The Role of Environments on Development

Environments can have powerful effects on behavior and can interact in complex ways with genetic predispositions. A case has been made that human cultural practices can literally affect evolutionary processes by creating niches that select for certain alleles (Laland, Odling-Smee, & Feldman, 2000). One example is the practice of pastoralism and domestication of cattle that has resulted in positive selection in some members of our species for lactose tolerance.

Given that our daily waking environments are mostly a function of where we studied (school) and where we as adults work (occupational building), it is inevitable that our minds and our bodies reflect the impact of such exposure. To give an unpleasant example of a nonnormative influence, there were 5.2 million workplace injuries and illnesses reported in the United States in 2001. Rates varied enormously by sector. The construction industry had a ten times greater rate of injuries from falls than the finance, insurance, and real estate sectors.

## Occupational Environments and the Brain

Simon (1981) hypothesized that the apparent complexity in an ant's path across a beach was more a function of the complexity of its external environment than its internal environment. The ant, seen as a basic information processing mechanism, was relatively simple. Its complex behavior could be seen as the result of adapting to a variegated environment.

The brain may also develop and function in a fairly "simple" way, allocating energy, through blood flow that controls oxygen and glucose metabolism, to brain tissue that is most efficient and effective in information processing. If a problem is difficult to solve, more cortical tissue may have to be recruited. The hemispheric asymmetry reduction in older adults (HAROLD) model expounded by Cabeza (2002) argues that when older adults, who are known to have diminished processing resources, must perform a difficult cognitive task that is typically lateralized to one side of the brain, they are more likely than younger adults to also recruit the homologous area on the other side of the brain to accomplish the task. As task difficulty increases, so does metabolic activity. Aging, which can be viewed as a process that reduces the efficiency and the effectiveness of brain processes, apparently renders many tasks more difficult as judged by studies showing that for a set of tasks performed by young adults, old

TABLE 14.1. *O\*NET Occupational Information*

| Application Specificity | Job-Oriented Descriptors | Worker-Oriented Descriptors |
|---|---|---|
| Cross-occupation descriptors | Generalized work activities<br>Work context<br>Organizational context<br>Labor market information<br>Occupational outlook<br>Wages | Skills<br>Knowledge<br>Education<br>Abilities<br>Interests<br>Work styles<br>Training<br>Experience<br>Licensing |
| Occupation-specific descriptors | Tasks<br>Machines, tools, and equipment<br>Labor market information<br>Occupational outlook<br>Wages | Occupational skills<br>Occupational knowledge<br>Training<br>Experience<br>Licensing |

*Note:* Derived from http://www.onetcenter.org/online.html.

adults take 1.5 to 2.0 times as long to accomplish those same tasks (Hale & Myerson, 1995).

### OCCUPATIONAL DEMANDS

Modern methods for assessing occupational demands and requirements typically involve categorizing work tasks in terms of their characteristics. Jobs and their requisite skills have been described in large tomes such as the U.S. Department of Labor's *Dictionary of Occupational Titles* (1991), which has now been superseded by the Occupational Information Network O\*NET (www.onetcenter.org/online.html). The *Dictionary of Occupational Titles* classifies jobs in terms of a hierarchy, with the highest levels referring to broad categories, such as those jobs dealing primarily with data, with people, or with things (see the following discussion on effect of occupations).

O\*NET classifies jobs on the basis of job requirements, worker attributes, job context, and job content by using several hundred descriptive terms. Table 14.1 shows the classification process.

Jobs are classified based on questionnaires administered both to workers and to job analysts. At the lowest level, person characteristics are determined by ratings of the importance of a diverse set of *abilities* ranging from arm–hand steadiness, to oral and written comprehension, to deductive and inductive reasoning, and to speech recognition and speech clarity. *Knowledge* characteristics can include specific subject areas such as economics and accounting or psychology. Measured *skills* would be social perceptiveness or complex problem solving.

Such classification systems implicitly accept a person–environment fit model, wherein jobs vary in their physical and mental demands, and workers who occupy them bring varying capabilities to those jobs. Presumably, it may take a long time to develop the knowledge, skills, and abilities that qualify someone for a particular occupation. However, it may also be possible to use job demands, and particularly the new information in O*NET on the rated frequency with which abilities are exercised, to evaluate the short- and long-term impact of occupations on workers.

Such attempts will always be problematic because of the changing nature of work and the likelihood that jobs are becoming somewhat more complex over time in terms of prerequisite skills (or at least, the required educational qualifications). As an example, 50 years ago it was not normative to acquire keyboard skills for most occupations. A select few people were interacting with computer systems via keyboards, and only those people headed to commercial sector jobs, such as secretaries, learned how to type in North American (high school) education systems. Today, typing skills are normative for many North American jobs, and few people leave high school without having acquired keyboarding (and mouse) skills. Fifty years from now, interaction with computer systems may be predominantly voice controlled (or perhaps even thought controlled).

## EVIDENCE FOR OCCUPATIONAL INFLUENCE ON THE BRAIN

I now review three lines of research that indicate how occupations can affect the brain. The first concerns how general occupational level influences changes in general intellectual performance across time (and with aging). The second concerns how specific brain areas are affected by specific occupational demands. The third describes how specific occupational demands affect the reserve capacity of the brain as seen in its ability to resist malignant processes such as Alzheimer's disease.

## Occupational Complexity and General Intellectual Performance

An important line of research on the role of intellectually challenging work (Schooler, Mulatu, & Oates, 1999) shows that work can positively influence intellectual functioning, and more so for older than younger workers. In their studies, Schooler et al. (1999) made use of classification schemes at a crude level: whether one works with people or with data or with things. They also developed rating schemes to judge overall intellectual complexity of a job. Their measure of overall substantive complexity for a job also included rated estimates of the amount of time spent on different types of activities at work.

Their study is unique because it made use of a longitudinal sample that was representative of American workers. Although the study started with an all-male sample, it added women on later test occasions. It also evolved in terms of intellectual flexibility measures. It started with a composite derived from relatively crude measures, such as the Embedded Figures Test and interviewer ratings of the intelligence of the interviewee, together with degree of agreement with questions that were phrased positively and negatively during the interview, and answers to hypothetical questions about the merits of cigarette advertising and where best to place a hamburger stand. Later measurement waves also made use of a more sophisticated battery of cognitive measures, such as the primary mental abilities and memory tasks.

The authors tested a reciprocal influence model using structural equation modeling. Their model provided strong support for the hypothesis that substantive complexity in the work environment relates strongly to the degree of intellectual flexibility of the worker. The best-fitting models suggested that the causal arrow runs in both directions simultaneously. Perhaps more surprising was the finding that these paths become even stronger for older workers.

If we assume that aging degrades brain function, then a likely interpretation is that challenging occupational environments are particularly critical for maintaining intellectual functioning across the lifespan. Unfortunately, given the biases of managers in work environments that older workers are less able to benefit from training opportunities, older workers are less likely to be given the opportunity to engage in lifelong learning, or when given it, to take it on (Noe & Wilk, 1993).

Nonetheless, the bottom line from this research program is that being in an intellectually challenging environment can stimulate cognitive functioning and conversely, being in an intellectually sterile environment can dull it. Occupations may have rather direct influences on brain functioning.

Pension schemes and social security systems are features of industrialized nations that permit individuals to cease paid employment long before their lives end. However, it can be argued from the previous example that retirement might be a significant risk factor for negative brain changes. Fortunately, the retirement environment may offer opportunities for stimulation that can replace those available through paid work. The same reciprocal relations seem to hold true between leisure activity complexity and intellectual flexibility (Schooler & Mulatu, 2001). The authors used similar techniques as in their work studies to rate the complexity of leisure activities (ratings of complexity, estimates of time engaged) and used the same measures of intellectual flexibility as in the study of work influences. They again showed that doing more complex leisure activities increased intellectual functioning and doing less complex leisure activities decreased intellectual functioning.

Together, these studies provide strong support for the idea that the type of demands that environments make on intellectual functioning affects the functioning of the brain, and these effects can still occur (and perhaps intensify) late in life.

## Intellectual Capability Increases: Evolution or Revolution?

Evolutionary pressures influence the brain (and brain developmental processes) over the course of millennia. Social and occupational environments can have striking effects on intellectual performance over mere centuries. The theory of reciprocal relationships of intellectual ability and environments has been offered as a potential explanation for the large IQ gains observed over generations, known as the Flynn effect (Flynn, 1987), in conjunction with the finding of the very high heritability for IQ (Dickens & Flynn, 2001). Dickens and Flynn argued that environments and genetic endowments are not independent factors in determining IQ but act in multiplicative (interactive) fashion. Momentary environmental factors can have multiplier effects on the development of intellectual abilities. Hence, standard deviation increases in IQ measured across generations can occur even when there is high heritability of IQ and little apparent variation attributed to environment within a generation.

As Dickens and Flynn (2001) put it,

Thanks to industrialization, it is likely that the cognitive complexity of the average person's job has increased over the last century. There is no doubt that more-demanding educational credentials control access to a wide range of jobs. There are far more people in scientific, managerial, and technical positions than ever before. Increased leisure time is another possible trigger for IQ gains, as some activities undertaken during extended leisure (reading, puzzles, games such as chess) may be honing people's facilities (p. 352).

The biological mechanisms that might support these effects are not yet well understood, but animal models have shown that stimulating environments, including social stimulation, promote neuron growth (Martin, Grimwood, & Morris, 2000).

## Effects of Specific Occupations on Specific Brain Regions

It is reasonably well established (cross-sectionally) that older adult age is associated with reductions in the volume of gray matter in the brain and that the areas of greater loss (e.g., prefrontal cortex) are linked to specific types of cognitive deficits (Raz, Gunning-Dixon, Head, Dupuis, & Acker, 1998). However, it is not yet clear how specific life experiences influence the type and locus of change in the brain across the lifespan. There are intriguing examples, though, of how exercising some physical and mental functions influence cortical development and change.

As first seen in the elegant work of Elbert, Pantev, Wienbruch, Rockstroh, and Taub (1995), extended practice in string instrument players (e.g., violinists) changes the proportion of the sensory homunculus dedicated to the fingers. The change is selective to the left hand (used for fingering movements) compared with the right hand (used for less complex bowing movements). Practice changes the brain structures that support sensori-motor encoding and action. The within-individual control of left versus right hands makes it very difficult to argue for innate brain differences controlling the propensity to engage in stringed instrument playing.

Later work by Pantev et al. (1998) suggests that extensive early music practice by pianists changes the functional organization of auditory cortex, with an associated stronger neural response to piano notes than to pure tones matched for loudness (see Chapter 10).

Similarly, PET studies on taxicab drivers (Maguire, Frackowiak, & Frith, 1997) have shown that areas of the cortex that are most likely to be active during spatial processing, such as the right hippocampus, are differentially active in skilled London taxicab drivers, although this does not occur for simple landmark recall or other unrelated mental activities. More important, when Maguire et al. (2000) conducted a comparison of taxi drivers and a control group using functional MRI scans, they found that the posterior region of the hippocampi of taxi drivers was expanded relative to the control group. In the controls, the anterior region was expanded relative to the taxi drivers. Furthermore, time spent taxi driving was correlated with the extent of the volumetric expansion. They interpreted the data in a fashion similar to Elbert, namely, that specific job experience for taxi drivers had led to the expansion of area for the right posterior hippocampus.

So, here, too, we see that brain architecture responds to the functional demands of an occupation. Although most string players have probably started young enough that one could argue that brain plasticity might be restricted to the first part of the lifespan, the average age of taxi drivers in Maguire et al.'s (2000) study was 44. Few had become professionals until their early 20s, and none would likely have driving experience at all until their late teen years. Still, one could always argue that people with strong spatial memory are more likely both to seek employment that relies on that ability and to have more developed brain regions serving spatial memory.

It is not always the case that structural changes are observed for those who excel in a particular ability. In their study of outstanding mnemonists (who had scored at top levels in a memory competition), Maguire, Valentine, Wilding, and Kapur (2003) did not observe structural brain differences compared with controls. Rather, when mnemonists and controls performed memory tasks that were familiar (digit memory) or unfamiliar (snowflake memory), the investigators observed functional changes specific to regions such as the hippocampus that mnemonists were likely to activate when using a spatial mnemonic such as the Method of Loci. So, strategy was an important intervening variable in determining differences in brain activation between the two groups. Such work argues for some flexibility in activation as opposed to obligatory coding and activation of brain regions.

Another interesting area in which imaging information is becoming available is for chess playing, a task that might be expected to severely stress mental capacities. One important feature of chess playing is the need to generate sequences of chess moves when evaluating which initial move to make. That is, players would need to explore the tree of possible moves from a given position to evaluate a move candidate. A priori, one might expect that such controlled search would strongly activate frontal and prefrontal areas of the brain responsible for executive functioning. However, it is occipital/parietal rather than frontal areas that are most highly activated in brain scans of novice chess players (Atherton, Zhuang, Bart, Hu, & He, 2003). More important, a recent thesis on chess expertise using fMRI recording (Campitelli, 2003) showed that much less brain tissue is needed to compute solutions to domain problems in experts compared with less skilled players. Experts do more with far less brain activation. Here, we see an example of efficiency in activation area. Examining the HAROLD compensation model using older chess players would seem to be an ideal next step.

At the molar behavioral level, the same result is seen within the famous de Groot/Chase and Simon chess experiments, where memory in experts was far superior to memory in novices when each was given a few seconds to glance at a structured chess position (de Groot, 1978), although little advantage was seen for experts with the same brief glance at a randomly arranged set of chess pieces (Chase & Simon, 1973).

A speculative hypothesis is that as people acquire skill, activities that initially occupy metabolically expensive frontal and prefrontal tissue are shifted to less expensive occipital and cerebellar tissue.

An example in the area of cognition is that instead of using so-called general or "weak methods" (Newell, 1990) that involve energy-intensive processes such as planning and search, the brain develops specialized circuits for storing and retrieving solutions. This principle can be seen in the way in which children move from counting strategies to solve simple arithmetic problems, such as $3 + 2 = 5$, to memory retrieval strategies based on pattern recognition (Lemaire & Siegler, 1995).

This principle of specialization can be seen most elegantly in the experimental work on memory experts, where after training for a year or so, ordinary college undergraduates can exceed by an order of magnitude Miller's famous $7 \pm 2$ limit for the span of apprehension. They do so by developing hierarchical long-term working memory structures (Ericsson & Kintsch, 1995) devoted to encoding and retrieving random digits (Ericsson, Chase, & Faloon, 1980). Such structures are very specific to memorizing digits and are useless for memorizing letters. This and much other work investigating expert performance (e.g., see Chapter 8) indicates the narrowness of transfer and hints at the need for domain-specific intensive training to produce durable changes in the brain.

## Lifespan Development: Age and Acquired Knowledge

Aging is a promising area within which to examine ideas about biocultural co-construction. The well-known phenomena of greater interindividual differences for older than younger adult groups is compelling evidence for the nature of the brain changes that can be sculpted by an individual's unique pattern of cultural exposure.

As mentioned previously, the work by Schooler and colleagues provides the most direct evidence of a link between type of work and cognition, with reciprocal influences of intellect and work. The mechanism linking brain and behavior, however, can perhaps best be understood from cognitive experiments and simulations. I draw on one of the model organisms for cognitive psychology (sometimes termed its drosophila) – chess playing.

We can be fairly confident that the ability to move carved pieces of wood skillfully over a chessboard in accord with the rules of chess is unlikely to be selected by evolutionary pressures, although the general-purpose cognitive mechanisms supporting this activity most probably are. A byproduct of the need to rank players objectively to issue invitations to tournaments was the chess rating scale, with a modern, valid one invented by Arpad Elo (1986). This also led, fortuitously, to his study of lifespan development of chess skill (Elo, 1965).

We now know a fair amount about the requirements for reaching world championship levels in terms of time commitment. Charness, Tuffiash, Krampe, Reingold, and Vasyukova (2005) and Charness, Krampe, and Mayr (1996) used retrospective questionnaires to trace out the types of practice that amateurs through Grandmasters engaged in from the year of their introduction to the game. Similar to findings for professional musicians (e.g., Ericsson et al., 1993) top-level players have spent thousands to tens of thousands of hours in solitary study and in playing in tournaments. Such practice has had some interesting byproducts in terms of acquired memory skill, as outlined in the famous Chase and Simon (1973) experiments. There is also strong evidence that the thousands of hours of staring at structured chess positions have modified the perceptual system of a chess player. As Chase and Simon (1973) pointed out, pattern recognition processes lie at the heart of skill in chess. Humans, unlike computers, examine only a tiny number of the branches in the exponentially expanding tree of possible chess moves when deliberating about their next move. Human players might examine between 10 and $10^2$ moves in a 3-min search episode (Charness, 1981). In that same time frame, top-flight computer programs will have examined between $10^6$ and $10^9$ moves.

Pattern recognition guides the selection of promising branches to explore. In line with the principle of moving from computation to recognition (minimize energy expenditure), eye-tracking studies reveal that expert chess players perceive important features of chess positions much more quickly and accurately than less-skilled players (Charness, Reingold, Pomplun, & Stampe, 2001; Reingold, Charness, Pomplun, & Stampe, 2001; Reingold, Charness, Schultetus, & Stampe, 2001). They possess a large visual span.

A formal examination of the potential for trade-off between knowledge and aging processes in the brain is given in Mireles and Charness (2002). They created a neural net simulation of memory for sequences of chess moves. The high-knowledge networks (greater initial training and knowledge) were differentially protected compared with low-knowledge networks when a variety of normative (slowing in learning rate, reduced signal-to-noise ratio) and nonnormative (lesioning) changes were made to simulate aging and disease effects. One way to interpret this beneficial effect of knowledge is in terms of brain reserve capacity, a hypothesis that has been productive in understanding dementia.

## Protective Effects of Occupations on the Brain During Dementia

Dementia affords an extreme form of *testing the limits* for the influence of occupation on mind. It has been noted for some time that education level is protective (a positive risk factor) for the diagnosis of Alzheimer's disease (e.g., Katzman, 1993).[1] However, the mechanism by which reserve capacity might function has not been delineated.

A notable attempt to look for clues in brain functioning is that by Stern et al. (1995), who showed that occupation could influence the course of a degenerative disease such as Alzheimer's disease. Using PET scans, Stern et al. (1995) showed that those diagnosed with Alzheimer's disease at similar levels of severity to other patients, but who came from occupations with more challenging cognitive demands (or physical demands), showed lower levels of parietal perfusion (a regional blood flow measure).

They interpreted this result as evidence for a reserve capacity having been built up by greater cognitive involvement at work. Namely, they argued that those people with lower perfusion scores were actually further along in the disease process, yet still scoring at the same level on dementia ratings and on the Mini-Mental State Examination as those less far along. Scarmeas et al. (2004) obtained similar findings for PET examination of different cortical areas sensitive to educational differences.

---

[1] Occupation and education may dissociate for providing reserve capacity to the brain. A study by Staff, Murray, Deary, and Whalley (2004) indicates that education level was more predictive of memory ability, whereas occupation level was a predictor of both memory ability and reasoning ability.

Although Stern et al. were puzzled as to why the physical demands of a job seemed to be protective in a way that was similar to the effects of cognitive demands, recent research has shown that aerobic exercise promotes positive brain changes in the same areas that are typically degraded by aging (Colcombe et al., 2003). The Colcombe et al. study provides another striking example of how environmental demands (exercise exertion) can directly influence the structure and function of the brain.

However, it is necessary to note that there are negative findings for the effects of occupation and education on dementia. Munoz, Ganapathy, Eliasziw, and Hachinski (2000) compared a large group of autopsy-diagnosed Alzheimer's patients with controls and failed to find educational differences between groups, but did find a marginal occupational difference. Because of the expense of brain imaging, most neuroimaging studies have small samples with concomitant risk of unreliability for generalization.

In summary, occupational exposure appears to be a potentially potent force in building up brain structures and functions that enable individuals to maintain performance even in the face of powerful brain disabling conditions such as dementia.

## CO-EVOLUTION OF BRAINS AND CULTURES

I end with some speculation about the multiplier effects mentioned earlier for the role of cultures on intellectual performance. Environments, particularly human engineered ones, can both support and encourage thinking. (Our educational system is predicated on this belief.) Thinking and associated psychomotor activity (string players), particularly of the type termed deliberate practice, leads to changes in brain function. The brains of our ancestors were probably not much different (volumewise) from ours. The demands that our cultural environments make on us have made us smarter (although perhaps not wiser). As an example, prior to the invention of the digital computer, there was no occupation known as programmer. Today, tens of thousands of people toil in a variety of formal educational programs acquiring expertise in programming. In the process, they program their brains to solve problems in various programming languages.

Although we typically use metabolically expensive processes such as search to solve problems for the first time, we often turn those solutions into knowledge products that enable us to respond more efficiently the next time the problem is encountered. We can then simply retrieve a solution rather than building it from scratch.

Cultures succeed to the extent that they can induce structures in the brains of their populations that help them excel in the occupations necessary for commerce. A sticking point for people is that they learn new chunks of information at a fixed and relatively slow rate for most rote learning tasks (Simon, 1974). Worse yet, for aging members of society, that learning rate slows to approximately half that for younger adults. As a result, skill at an occupation undoubtedly depends on the rate of change of knowledge necessary to perform well.

If conditions remain constant, prior investment in building specialized brain structures is sufficient to perform well. If circumstances change, more the rule than the exception in modern societies, workers must continually reprogram their brains to avoid obsolescence. An important challenge being faced by our species for the very first time in its relatively short history is the long lives of many of its members. Until the appearance of universal pension schemes about a half-century ago in industrialized nations, most people worked until they died. Now, a previously nonnormative event, retirement, has become normative. The cost of maintaining a large fraction of a culture's population in a state of retirement is rising. Developed nations are beginning to grapple with a number of potential solutions, the most equitable probably being a longer work life given increases in both longevity and healthy longevity. However, the very recent pressures of international competition make it imperative to keep all the workforce functioning at very high levels of productivity. As economists have long noted, productivity increases depend heavily on investment in tools and processes to equip human capital to perform work tasks with greater efficiency.

Will aging workforces be able to keep up with the training and technology adoption requirements (e.g., Hunt, 1995)? Barring neuroscience breakthroughs that can directly enhance the functioning of neural structures with chemical interventions, aging individuals face ever-slowing learning processes. Faced with this diminishing learning rate, older adults will undoubtedly have to rely heavily on smart digital (and human) assistants. So, the future progress of cultures with aging populations may well depend on the abilities of designers to adapt technology artifacts to human use, particularly to use by older adults (Fisk, Rogers, Charness, Czaja, & Sharit, 2004; see Chapter 16).

Such technological interventions hold the promise of providing strong environmental support to free an older worker's diminishing physical and mental resources. However, as is evident in the effect of a sedentary lifestyle on physical functioning, there is undoubtedly a fine line between providing needed support while maintaining the level of challenge necessary to encourage continuing development.

NEW DIRECTIONS TO CONSIDER

Although I have reviewed some salient examples of biocultural co-construction of the brain from the perspective of occupations, we still have a long way to go to elucidate the mechanisms. To pursue the relationship of occupations to brain functioning more directly, we need progress on a number of fronts. First, the O*NET project needs to make further progress on its classification task. Having better validated indicators of job requirements, such as mental (educational), physical, and social demands for occupations, will enable more sensitive tests of the effects of occupational demands on brain development.

Second, more in-depth estimates of time spent on occupational activities should be solicited in addition to the frequency information gathered by O*NET (daily, weekly, monthly, yearly, never). Perhaps surveys could be developed similar to those that examine deliberate practice (e.g., Charness et al., 1996) and bolstered by observational studies.

Third, following the example of the recent work on mnemonists, it is evident that both structural MRI and fMRI data are needed to assess both types of changes in the brain in parallel.

Fourth, it would be useful to assess the durability of brain structures and functions when people stop practicing a particular activity. It is well known that muscles deteriorate quite quickly when they are kept inactive (e.g., when a limb is in a cast, or when an astronaut is in zero gravity and does not exercise). What happens over time to specialized areas of cerebral cortex under enforced inactivity? It would be very useful to trace brain correlates of practice and cessation of practice across time.

Finally, better measures of regional and whole cortical metabolic activity need to be developed to assess hypotheses about metabolic cost for brain functioning. However, the future seems particularly bright given the technological progress in brain imaging. Such advances promise to provide much more detailed information about the role of occupations in brain development.

### References

Atherton, M., Zhuang, J., Bart, W. M., Hu, X., & He, S. (2003). A functional MRI study of high-level cognition: I. The game of chess. *Cognitive Brain Research, 16,* 26–31.

Baltes, P. B. (1979). Life-span developmental psychology: Some converging observations on history and theory. In P. B. Baltes & O. G. Brim, Jr. (Eds.), *Life-span development and behavior* (Vol. 2, pp. 255–279). New York: Academic Press.

Cabeza, R. (2002). Hemispheric asymmetry reduction in older adults: The HAROLD model. *Psychology and Aging, 17,* 85–100.

Campitelli, G. (2003). *Cognitive and neuronal bases of expertise.* Unpublished doctoral dissertation, University of Nottingham, Nottingham, UK.

Charness, N. (1981). Search in chess: Age and skill differences. *Journal of Experimental Psychology: Human Perception and Performance, 7,* 467–476.

Charness, N., Krampe, R., & Mayr, U. (1996). The role of practice and coaching in entrepreneurial skill domains: An international comparison of life-span chess skill acquisition. In K. A. Ericsson (Ed.), *The road to excellence: The acquisition of* expert performance in the arts and sciences, sports and games (pp. 51–80). Mahwah, NJ: Erlbaum.

Charness, N., Reingold, E. M., Pomplun, M., & Stampe, D. M. (2001). The perceptual aspect of skilled performance in chess: Evidence from eye movements. *Memory and Cognition, 29,* 1146–1152.

Charness, N., Tuffiash, M., Krampe, R., Reingold, E. M., & Vasyukova, E. (2005). The role of deliberate practice in chess expertise. *Applied Cognitive Psychology, 19,* 151–165.

Chase, W. G., & Simon, H. A. (1973). Perception in chess. *Cognitive Psychology, 4,* 55–81.

Colcombe, S. J., Erickson, K. I., Raz, N., Webb, A. G., Cohen, N. J., McAuley, E., & Kramer, A. F. (2003). Aerobic fitness reduces brain tissue loss in aging humans. *Journal of Gerontology: Medical Sciences, 58A,* M176–M180.

de Groot, A. D. (1978). *Thought and choice in chess* (2nd ed.). The Hague: Mouton.

Dickens, W. T., & Flynn, J. R. (2001). Heritability estimates versus large environmental effects: The IQ paradox resolved. *Psychological Review, 108,* 346–369.

Elbert, T., Pantev, C., Wienbruch, C., Rockstroh, B., & Taub, E. (1995). Increased cortical representation of the fingers of the left hand in string players. *Science, 270,* 305–307.

Elo, A. E. (1965). Age changes in master chess performances. *Journal of Gerontology, 20,* 289–299.

Elo, A. E. (1986). *The rating of chessplayers, past and present* (2nd ed.). New York: Arco.

Ericsson, K. A., Chase, W. G., & Faloon, S. (1980). Acquisition of a memory skill. *Science, 208,* 1181–1182.

Ericsson, K. A., & Kintsch, W. (1995). Long-term working memory. *Psychological Review, 102,* 211–245.

Ericsson, K. A., Krampe, R. T., & Tesch-Römer, C. (1993). The role of deliberate practice in the acquisition of expert performance. *Psychological Review, 100,* 363–406.

Fisk, A. D., Rogers, W. A., Charness, N., Czaja, S. J., & Sharit, J. (2004). *Designing for older adults: Principles and creative human factors approaches.* London: Taylor & Francis.

Flynn, J. R. (1987). Massive gains in 14 nations: What IQ tests really measure. *Psychological Bulletin, 101,* 171–191.

Gauthier, I., & Tarr, M. J. (2002). Unraveling mechanisms for expert object recognition bridging brain activity and behavior. *Journal of Experimental Psychology: Human Perception and Performance, 28,* 431–446.

Hale, S., & Myerson, J. (1995). Fifty years older, fifty percent slower? Meta-analytic regression models and semantic context effects. *Aging and Cognition, 2,* 132–145.

Hunt, E. B. (1995). *Will we be smart enough? A cognitive analysis of the coming workforce.* New York: Russell Sage Foundation.

Isenmann, S., Kretz, A., & Cellerino, A. (2003). Molecular determinants of retinal ganglion cell development, survival, and regeneration. *Progress in Retinal and Eye Research, 22,* 483–543.

Katzman, R. (1993). Education and the prevalence of dementia and Alzheimer's disease. *Neurology, 43,* 13–20.

Laland, K. N., Odling-Smee, J., & Feldman, M. W. (2000). Niche construction, biological evolution, and cultural change. *Behavioral and Brain Sciences, 23*, 131–175.

Lemaire, P., & Siegler, R. S. (1995). Four aspects of strategic change: Contributions to children's learning of multiplication. *Journal of Experimental Psychology: General, 124*, 83–97.

Maguire, E. A., Frackowiak, R. S. J., & Frith, C. D. (1997). Recalling routes around London: Activation of the right hippocampus in taxi drivers. *Journal of Neuroscience, 17*, 7103–7110.

Maguire, E. A., Gadian, D. G., Johnsrude, I. S., Good, C. D., Ashburner, J., Frackowiak, R. S. J., & Frith, C. D. (2000). Navigation-related structural change in the hippocampi of taxi drivers. *Proceedings of the National Academy of Sciences (USA), 97*, 4398–4403.

Maguire, E. A., Valentine, E. R., Wilding, J. M., & Kapur, N. (2003). Routes to remembering: The brains behind superior memory. *Nature Neuroscience, 6*, 90–95.

Martin, S. J., Grimwood, P. D., & Morris, R. G. M. (2000). Synaptic plasticity and memory: An evaluation of the hypothesis. *Annual Review of Neuroscience, 23*, 649–711.

Mireles, D. E., & Charness, N. (2002). Computational explorations of the influence of structured knowledge on age-related cognitive decline. *Psychology and Aging, 17*, 245–259.

Munoz, D. G., Ganapathy, G. R., Eliasziw, M., & Hachinski, V. (2000). Educational attainment and socioeconomic status of patients with autopsy-confirmed Alzheimer disease. *Archives of Neurology, 57*, 85–89.

Newell, A. (1990). *Unified theories of cognition*. Cambridge, MA: Harvard University Press.

Noe, R. A., & Wilk, S. L. (1993). Investigation of the factors that influence employees' participation in developmental activities. *Journal of Applied Psychology, 78*, 291–302.

Pantev, C., Oostenveld, R., Engelien, A., Ross, B., Roberts, L. E., & Hoke, M. (1998). Increased auditory cortical representation in musicians. *Nature, 392*, 811–814.

Quartz, S. R., & Sejnowski, T. J. (1997). The neural basis of cognitive development: A constructivist manifesto. *Behavioral and Brain Sciences, 20*, 537–556.

Raz, N., Gunning-Dixon, F. M., Head, D., Dupuis, J. H., & Acker, J. D. (1998). Neuroanatomical correlates of cognitive aging: Evidence from structural magnetic resonance imaging. *Neuropsychology, 12*, 95–114.

Reingold, E. M., Charness, N., Pomplun, M., & Stampe, D. M. (2001). Visual span in expert chess players: Evidence from eye movements. *Psychological Science, 12*, 48–55.

Reingold, E. M., Charness, N., Schultetus, R. S., & Stampe, D. M. (2001). Perceptual automaticity in expert chess players: Parallel encoding of chess relations. *Psychonomic Bulletin and Review, 8*, 504–510.

Salthouse, T. A. (1996). The processing-speed theory of adult age differences in cognition. *Psychological Review, 103*, 403–428.

Scarmeas, N., Zarahn, E., Anderson, K. E., Honig, L. S., Park, A., Hilton, J., et al. (2004). Cognitive reserve-mediated modulation of positron emission tomographic activations during memory tasks in Alzheimer disease. *Archives of Neurology, 61*, 73–78.

Schooler, C., & Mulatu, M. S. (2001). The reciprocal effects of leisure time activities and intellectual functioning in older people: A longitudinal analysis. *Psychology and Aging, 16,* 466–482.

Schooler, C., Mulatu, M. S., & Oates, G. (1999). The continuing effects of substantively complex work on the intellectual functioning of older workers. *Psychology and Aging, 14,* 483–506.

Simon, H. A. (1974). How big is a chunk? *Science, 183,* 482–488.

Simon, H. A. (1981). *The sciences of the artificial* (2nd ed.). Cambridge, MA: MIT Press.

Sokoloff, L. (1989). Circulation and energy metabolism of the brain. In G. Siegel, B. Agranoff, R. W. Albers, & P. Molinoff (Eds.), *Basic neurochemistry* (4th ed., pp. 565–590). New York: Raven Press.

Staff, R. T., Murray, A. D., Deary, I. J., & Whalley, L. J. (2004). What provides cerebral reserve? *Brain, 127,* 1191–1199.

Stern, Y., Alexander, G. E., Prohovnik, I., Stricks, L., Link, B., Lennon, M. C., & Mayeux, R. (1995). Relationship between lifetime occupation and parietal flow: Implications for a reserve against Alzheimer's disease pathology. *Neurology, 45,* 55–60.

Tarr, M. J., & Gauthier, I. (2000). FFA: A flexible fusiform area for subordinate-level visual processing automatized by expertise. *Nature Neuroscience, 3,* 764–769.

United States Department of Labor. (1991). *Dictionary of occupational titles* (4th ed.). Washington, DC: U.S. Government Printing Office.

Vandenbergh, J. G. (2003). Prenatal hormone exposure and sexual variation. *American Scientist, 91,* 218–225.

# 15

# The Influence of Organized Violence and Terror on Brain and Mind: A Co-Constructive Perspective

Thomas Elbert, Brigitte Rockstroh, Iris-Tatjana Kolassa, Maggie Schauer, and Frank Neuner

> Genetic interventions make us better animals. Humans, we become, however, because of the ways that culture and our individual constructions exploit the brain and make it our servant.
>
> (Baltes & Singer, 2001, p. 72)

## ABSTRACT

*The human brain is formed by two interactive systems: the genetic-biological and the sociocultural systems. The brain, in turn, regulates behavior and thereby acts on the societal environment. This chapter examines how experience shapes the brain and describes the interaction of brain, behavior, and culture under conditions of extreme and traumatic stress as present in many of the world's war-torn regions. Traumatic events massively change the brain's structure and function. Within our model of biological-cultural interaction, we analyze how these experiences foster violent behavior and deal with the societal consequences of the traumatization of large parts of the population.*

## INTRODUCTION

In this day and age, humans are raised and live in a complex sociocultural environment with increased demands for the brain, the body, and the social structures to adapt. More information at increasingly complex levels has to be processed than ever before at an ever-increasing velocity and over an extended lifespan. This places high pressure on the individual and society to continuously adjust to new environmental conditions, resulting in a stream of continuous microstressors. At the same time, modern societies are becoming increasingly aware of the effects of macrostressors, including traumatic stress, which, although seemingly transient, may be changing the brain's processing machinery, resulting in characteristic behavioral, physiological, and psychological (mal)adaptations to environmental conditions and – when a whole community is affected – changes in the local culture. This in turn will impinge on all individuals in the community, even those not originally affected by the traumatic experience, because human behavior represents the co-constructive expression of biological-genetic and sociocultural conditions. Although recent neuroscientific advances have substantially improved our understanding of neuroplasticity – that is, the brain's extraordinary ability to change its structure and function in response to experience – less effort has been devoted to understanding mechanisms in relation to affect and distress. Furthermore, little is known on how changes on the level of the individual interact with those on a community level. Social stress and organized violence serve as good models for studying this interaction of adaptive alterations in individual and societal minds.

We currently witness a qualitative change in the way wars are waged and organized violence is exerted; in other words, a transformation in the "culture of violence" cannot be overlooked. Moreover, scientific methods are available to study how traumatic stressors change individuals and communities so we can expect increasing knowledge about how social stressors and related learning conditions shape the structure and function of both the brain and the "societal mind," including individual behavior and interactions on the community level.

The human brain constitutes the joint product or co-construction of two interactive systems of impact: the internal genetic-biological and the external sociocultural systems (Baltes, 1999). The social environment into which malleable individuals are born, together with their response to this environment – the way in which individuals live their lives – lead to the cultural determination of gene expression. In turn, individuals shape their sociocultural environment by imposing structure and function resulting from a history of genetic expression. Stressors exert a powerful influence on the brain, at the same time modifying brain structure, brain function, neuropsychological performance, and peripheral physiological responses. Extreme or continuous stress may drive the individual into an increasingly maladaptive state with the potential for mental disorders. Cultural settings can support only a limited number of such individuals before they become a driving force in cultural maladaptations.

This chapter extends the co-constructive perspective to effects of extreme social and traumatic stress (as, i.e., in organized violence) on the brain with its behavioral consequences. We first describe evidence on neuroplasticity in the brain and outline a theoretical model on how traumatic experiences change the brain on a structural and functional level. Then, we discuss characteristics of organized violence and "new wars" as conditions of traumatic stress to which large parts of the population are exposed in many war-torn regions around the globe, particularly in sub-Saharan Africa.

EXPERIENCE SHAPES THE BRAIN: NEURAL ADAPTATION
AND PLASTICITY

The brain is continuously modified by experience. The study of sensory representations in the cortex has provided an excellent model for studying how the brain's representations of the periphery are dynamically modified. Cortical representations mirror the spatial arrangement of the corresponding peripheral receptors in the form of cortical maps. Although genetically encoded programs control the connections of these maps from the periphery to the cortical destination, their organization ultimately depends on the efficacy of the synapses connecting the nerve cells within the network, which is affected by external input. For instance, two receptors of the same fingertip are more frequently activated simultaneously than two receptors in different digits. According to Hebb's learning model, synchronous stimulation should lead to connections between the representations of the same fingertip but to a separation from those of the other digits: representational zones are shaped by the temporal pattern of such coincident experience. An alteration in behaviorally relevant afferent input will trigger a reorganization of the map: the representation of a fingertip can be enlarged, representations of adjacent fingers can invade its territory, or the representation of two fingers can get fused. Using magnetic source imaging, we have demonstrated that skilled string instrument players – a category for which both cultural and psychological preconditions are necessary – have larger representational zones of their left hand in their cerebral cortex compared with the brains of people who do not engage in such extensive practice (Elbert, Pantev, Wienbruch, Rockstroh, & Taub, 1995). Using the same culturally determined quasiexperimental set-up, structural magnetic resonance imaging reveals that the change in function is intertwined with structural alterations (the depth of the left hemispheric central sulcus) that extend into the macroscopic range. Moreover, the musician's cerebral cortex not only exemplifies adaptation (or, in some cases, maladaptation; Elbert et al., 1998) to somatosensory requirements, but also differs from "normal" cortex in many regions (e.g., Pantev et al., 1998) and probably also in other respects that are not (yet) accessible to our observations.

Reorganization varies with perceptual correlates of superior performance – an adaptive advantage of cortical plasticity. Adaptive cortical plasticity can also be observed in persons with disabilities – as in blind individuals who are forced by their disability to rely on nonvisual modalities, including hearing, for information about their external environment.

Sensory input via nonvisual avenues thus gains greater behavioral relevance and becomes a focus of greater attention to enable effective interaction with the world. For instance, when attention is directed to peripheral auditory space, localization of sounds is better in blind than in sighted people (e.g., Lessard, Pare, Lepore, & Lassonde, 1998). Individuals who lost their sight at an early age may outperform sighted persons in nonvisual tasks, including speech perception (e.g., Muchnik, Efrati, Nemeth, Malin, & Hildesheimer, 1991), verbal memory (e.g., Röder, Rösler, & Neville, 2001), and musical abilities (e.g., Gougoux et al., 2004). Behaviorally relevant stimulation over extended periods has been found to produce a substantial enlargement in the representational zones of the involved portions of the tonotopic system in animals and humans (Elbert et al., 2002). In addition, there is cross-modal plasticity in the blind, such that tactile and auditory (e.g., Gougoux, Zatorre, Lassonde, Voss, & Lepore, 2005) stimuli come to be processed in the visual cortex. Obviously, environmental demands and individual experiences can dramatically remodel the brain's functional organization.

During "critical periods" of development, sensory stimulation without explicit behavioral significance is sufficient to alter the organization of the sensory cortex (e.g., Bao, Chang, Davis, Gobeske, & Merzenich, 2003). In contrast, functional reorganization in the adult cortex seems to be driven mainly by stimuli related to reinforcement; that is, it requires a behaviorally relevant context. The effects of reinforcement are mediated by cholinergic and dopaminergic pathways, which by themselves are subject to plastic alterations, as seen in psychosis. Although the model of the blind demonstrates that similar mechanisms also act beyond the representational cortex, additional mechanisms may come into play in associative or polymodal areas. Already at the level of the primary sensory cortex, context and top-down modulation driven by attention and motivation affect reorganization (e.g., Braun et al., 2002).

Plastic alterations are not necessarily adaptive. Stressful life experiences during "critical periods" may affect brain organization in harmful ways. Childhood and adolescence are critical periods of cognitive and emotional development (e.g., Steinberg, 2005), as well as vulnerable phases for the development of the stress system (Charmandari, Kino, Souvatzoglou, & Chrousos, 2003). Because it is known that even a single traumatic experience can initiate a cascade of dynamic brain processes that may result in enhanced vulnerability to subsequent stressors (e.g., Neuner et al., 2004) or even in a breakdown of normal functioning, as seen in the pathologies of the trauma spectrum, children growing up in a culture of violence may be particularly affected. Here, we propose that violent and traumatic experiences, by altering the individual brain and mind (i.e., by modifying behavior), can induce a spiral of violence in which an increasing number of individuals influenced by traumatic experiences themselves commit crimes in the community. Thus, wartime strategies are increasingly characterized by mutual hate of ethnicities. Forcible displacement of civilians is used by both guerrilla and antiguerrilla forces in an attempt to unite one's own group through crimes against humanity. Wars are accompanied by systematic killings and ethnic cleansings, whole regions are left uninhabitable for the local people because towns are devastated, infrastructure ruined, and landmines make much of the land inaccessible.

## POSTTRAUMATIC STRESS DISORDER AS A MODEL OF TRAUMATIC STRESS EFFECTS ON THE BRAIN

In an attempt to understand the consequences of these atrocities on brain and mind, we have studied refugees in Germany and war victims in crises regions such as the Balkans (Neuner, Schauer, Roth, & Elbert, 2002), the West Nile (Karunakara et al., 2004; Neuner et al., 2004), Rwanda (e.g., Schaal & Elbert, in press), and Somalia (Odenwald et al., 2005). In these regions, we conducted diagnostic interviews and found high prevalence rates of posttraumatic stress disorder (PTSD) ranging from 15% to 50%.

An amazing finding was the ability of displaced persons from remote areas in Southern Sudan, who previously had almost no contact with the outside world and who were illiterate, to describe the classic symptoms of severely traumatized individuals as if taken from a psychiatric textbook. The core symptoms of PTSD are (1) reexperiencing symptoms that manifest at night in the form of nightmares and in the waking state as flashbacks and intrusive recollections that are so intense that the victim actually believes he or she is back amidst the atrocities; (2) an exaggerated startle response and a persistent hyperarousal, difficulties in calming down or falling asleep – these symptoms describe a readiness for fight or flight rather than a permanently enhanced autonomic activation; and (3) an active avoidance of places or thoughts associated with traumatic experiences and/or passive avoidance symptoms (i.e., numbing emotional responsiveness as a way to cope with unbearable feelings). In severe cases, this may include dissociative symptoms, for instance, feelings of detachment or estrangement from the external world (derealization) and of oneself (depersonalization), or even persecutory delusions.

Symptoms of the trauma spectrum and of PTSD, in particular, can be understood as a consequence of plastic changes in memory through stressful, traumatic experiences. Life experiences are stored in autobiographical memory. The autobiographical context memory has been called "cold memory" (Metcalve & Jacobs, 1996). It contains knowledge about life time periods and specific events. The sensory-perceptual representations of a traumatic event have been called "hot" or nondeclarative (implicit) memory. It comprises emotional and sensory memories of all modalities. Cold memories (e.g., on March 24 at 3:30, I was living on my farm in Djakovica and we had three cows) are usually connected with hot sensory memories (e.g., black-masked, dark night, shooting, burning smell), as well as with cognitive (e.g., I can't do anything), emotional (e.g., fear, sadness), and physiological elements (e.g., heart racing, fast breathing, sweating).

In individuals who are not affected by trauma or fear, hot memories are linked with autobiographic, declarative memories. However, in traumatized persons, sensory and emotional memories are activated by environmental stimuli without being related to autobiographic, declarative items (i.e., dates and places of autobiographical occurrences) – these autonomous hot memories form a fear network (Lang, 1979). An example of such a network is outlined in Figure 15.1. The activation of a single memory item (e.g., seeing a man in a uniform or feeling one's heartbeat) will cause the whole network to be activated. According to Hebbian learning, this will not only strengthen the interconnections between existing network units, but will also lead to an inclusion of additional network elements, namely,

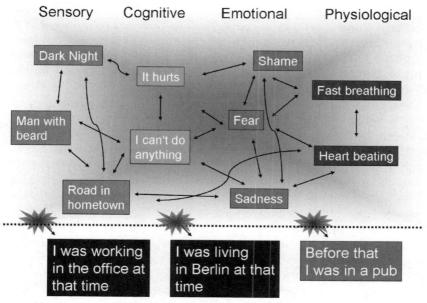

FIGURE 15.1. Example of a traumatic memory structure: the hot (nondeclarative) memory builds a fear network (upper part). With each additional traumatic experience, this fear network becomes more extended, while the connections to the specific cold autobiographic events (lower part) weaken further or even get lost ("fragmentation" of declarative and nondeclarative memory).

of those that are synchronously activated. Such an inclusion of additional nodes will be strongest during subsequent traumatic experiences or experiences with a strong emotional component that co-activate motivational and reward systems that enhance the brain's plasticity. As a consequence, the number of nondeclarative (hot) elements in the fear network and their interconnectivity will increase. At the same time, co-activation of declarative autobiographical memories becomes less likely because with an increasing number of experiences, the network contains more and more conflicting information. Typically, a person can only retrieve one context in which the fear network was previously activated (as we know that we cannot have been simultaneously at two places or create one imagery for two different time periods). As a result, hot and cold memory will separate, and only few connections of hot memory contents with declarative autobiographic memory will survive. This leads to a fragmentation of the autobiographic memory; that is, traumatized persons have difficulties in reconstructing dates and sequences of events associated with traumatic experiences. The described model assumes the fear network to be an example of plastic changes in the human brain in response to traumatic life events.

Studies on fear conditioning demonstrate that a single stressful or traumatic event can be sufficient to set up a fear network, but it will be connected to context. Repetitive traumatic experience will strengthen the fear, but the survivor begins to lose the context in which the fear occurred, rendering the victim vulnerable for mental disorders. Whenever the atrocities are multiple and repetitive, we find a linear relationship between the number of experienced traumata and the proportion of survivors with PTSD, with 100% traumatization in those who report some 25 or more fearful events (e.g., Neuner et al., 2004).

Memory is the ability to recall events from the past. However, it is a common mistake to restrict the function of memory to recollections of the past. What seems more likely is that the ability to envisage future scenarios was a driving force in the evolution of memory, and of episodic memory, in particular. Hebbian types of memory fit this explanation of memory well: every time a cell assembly is activated for "read-out," the content of the respective memory will not only be read, but also modified; that is, neurons of an activated cell assembly are not only activated, but will also modify their connections with each other. This activation modification occurs through both imagination and present experiences. Because each time a memory is activated, it is modified, a fear network, although originally formed by traumatic experience, may become connected to present conditions (e.g., when the survivor is forced to live under unsafe conditions). The resulting daily stress affects the neurohumoral axes that in turn exert their effects back on brain and mind. Thus, traumatic stress drives the organism to its limits.

## STRESS-INDUCED TILT OF NEUROHUMORAL AXES

Allostasis,[1] the adaptation of the internal milieu to meet perceived or anticipated threats in the environment, has evolved as a survival-securing response to escape acute danger. However, it may be an inappropriate response in the modern human. The same physiological responses (e.g., the supply of additional blood and oxygen to muscles) are still activated in the face of modern stressors, which can, however, neither be attacked nor escaped from by running away. Thus, prolonged stress turns adaptive allostasis into allostatic load. Permanently warding off stress turns the adaptive physiological responses into maladaptive diseases in the form of aches and pains, loss of appetite, or overeating. A chronically high allostatic load damages organs, including the brain (McEwen, 2004).

Central-peripheral circuits triggered by specific environmental cues that activate the fight–flight–freeze defense cascade strongly affect the dynamic storage of various elements of memory. The body's stress response is regulated by three systems (McEwen, 2004): first, the hippocampus and the hypothalamic-pituitary-adrenal (HPA) axis play a major role in the defense cascade and are involved in the feedback regulation of cortisol excretion. Second, the amygdala, the locus coeruleus, the adrenal gland, and the sympathetic nervous system are crucial in the stress-induced mobilization for fight or flight; they are involved in sharpening awareness in alarm situations and directing blood flow toward the brain and major muscles, and away from the surface of the skin in hands and feet, as well as away from digestive and reproductive organs. A third, less well-explored axis involves the vasopressin-oxytocin peptides (Heinrichs, Baumgartner, Kirschbaum, & Ehlert, 2003). When functioning properly, these systems secure survival in alarm situations. They also play a role in the stress-protective effects of positive social interactions. Dysregulations in these systems may be associated with clinical disorders. This happens, for instance, when neural representations of fearful past experiences activate the HPA axis permanently. The excreted stress hormones ultimately make their way back to the brain, affecting both behavior and health.

Two prime targets for stress hormones in the brain are the hippocampus and the amygdala. It is well established that acute elevations of adrenal stress hormones (catecholamines and glucocorticoids) enhance

---

[1] The body, including the brain, is able to deal with dangers in a flexible and adaptive way. In contrast to *homeostasis*, that is, the organism's ability to maintain a steady internal state, *allostasis* refers to the flexibility in the adjustment to stressors that range from Hans Selye's types of physical deprivation (cold, noise, deprivation of food, sleep, etc.) to the real or imagined fear-provoking situations that trigger an alarm response. The Greek word "allo," meaning "variable," is used by McEwen (2004) to emphasize the ability to choose various attack and defense mechanisms to counter negative impact.

memory consolidation of emotionally arousing, contextual (hippocampus-dependent) information in a dose-dependent manner in animals and humans (e.g., Buchanan & Lovallo, 2001). These enhancing effects of stress hormones are mediated by the basolateral nucleus of the amygdala. As the basolateral amygdala (BLA) projects to the hippocampal dentate gyrus, it may modulate hippocampus-dependent memory storage (e.g., Packard, Cahill, & McGaugh, 1994). Lesions of the BLA and the basomedial amygdala (BMA), but not the central or medial nuclei, attenuate hippocampal long-term potentiation (LTP) in the dentate gyrus (Ikegaya, Saito, & Abe, 1996b), whereas stimulation of the BLA and BMA facilitate LTP in the dentate gyrus of rats (Ikegaya, Saito, & Abe, 1996a). Thus, the amygdala seems to play an important role in mediating hippocampal neuroplasticity.

Although the memory-supporting effects of stress hormones are certainly adaptive when lasting memories of vital information (e.g., dangerous situations) have to be established, this mechanism may become maladaptive under conditions of extreme stress: persistent and intrusive memories of the traumatic event might be formed that promote the development of PTSD. Elevated glucocorticoid levels do not only enhance memory consolidation, but also impair memory retrieval (e.g., de Quervain, Roozendaal, Nitsch, McGaugh, & Hock, 2000). In addition, chronic glucocorticoid excess can lead to disturbances of synaptic plasticity, atrophy of dendritic branching, and an enhanced susceptibility to other neurotoxic insults (Sapolsky, 1999). Moreover, stress-related enhanced corticotrophin-releasing hormone secretion during "critical periods" of brain plasticity in childhood and adolescence enforces hippocampal volume loss, sensitization of hippocampal glucocorticoids receptors, and altered feedback properties of the HPA axis, which in turn promote endocrine hyperresponsivity to subsequent social stress. The seminal studies by Meaney and his group provide clear evidence that perinatal stress already changes the HPA axis, delays cognitive and emotional development, and may impair avoidance learning for the rest of the life (e.g., Meaney, Aitken, van Berkel, Bhatnagar, & Sapolsky, 1988). In addition, the medial prefrontal cortex, and here in particular the anterior cingulate cortex (ACC), are affected by stress. For these regions, high concentrations of mineralocorticoid and glucocorticoid receptors have been described, highlighting the pivotal role of these regions in mediating stress-induced changes in attention and (emotional) memory.

Thus, stressful experiences differentially activate a variety of responses designed by evolution to counter danger. The different chemical messengers may cause deficits in hippocampus-based learning and memory, and their effects on the amygdalae and the medial prefrontal and cingulate cortex may lead to an impaired inhibition of fear responses. A fragmentation of autobiographical memory due to a separation of emotional and declarative autobiographic memory contents is further promoted by these mechanisms. Repeated exposure to traumatic or chronic stress may lead to long-term dysregulations and impaired functioning of these systems, as well as symptoms of stress-related disorders such as hyperarousal, dissociation, flashbacks, avoidance, and depression. These symptoms in turn may promote maladaptive behaviors such as social withdrawal, inappropriate aggression, and self-sedation with drugs.

## FUNCTIONAL CHANGES OF THE BRAIN IN PTSD

How can we detect signs of a fear network in the brain? One would expect that stimuli specifically related to the individual traumatic experience are necessary to activate the fear network. However, contrary to expectations, it seems that emotionally arousing stimuli, not necessarily related to the traumatic event, suffice to activate the whole fear network. Junghöfer, Bradley, Elbert, and Lang (2001) introduced affective material into the rapid serial visual presentation (RSVP) paradigm: when presenting stimuli from the International Affective Picture System (IAPS) in fast succession (3 or 5 Hz), each emotional stimulus, presented for some 300 ms, should activate only one or more elements in a large fear network. Using this technique, Junghöfer et al. (2003) demonstrated that indeed many elements or nodes of the network will be activated, and the whole network will ignite. This stimulation proved capable of evoking affective processing and even provoked flashbacks in severely traumatized survivors of organized violence, including torture. (It should be noted that this was the case in individuals for whom flashbacks were so common that the one contingent on the RSVP did not add to their suffering, as they reported.) In both controls and traumatized individuals, the affective material activated the visual cortex and associated areas. However, only in traumatized survivors suffering from PTSD, the pre- and orbitofrontal areas and the cingulate gyrus were also activated (Junghöfer et al., 2003; the group difference is shown in Fig. 15.2). These data suggest that torture, like any other massive experience, dramatically alters the functional organization of the brain: an enlarged fear network is activated by any aversive material. Obviously, the (medial) prefrontal cortex (including the anterior cingulate) lost its ability to regulate these hyperresponsive fear structures, including the interplay between amygdala and frontal cortex.

## ABNORMAL BRAIN WAVES INDICATE PLASTIC CHANGES
## IN ARCHITECTURE AND FUNCTION OF NEURAL NETWORKS

Slow brain waves in the delta (0.5-4 Hz) and theta (4-7 Hz) frequency range, when focally generated and present during the waking state, do not appear in healthy individuals and thus signal altered cortical function (Rockstroh, Ray, Wienbruch, & Elbert, 2005). In psychiatric disorders, slow waves may

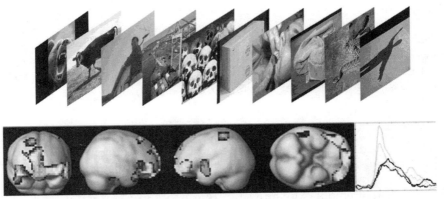

FIGURE 15.2. Event-related magnetic fields were recorded from 13 torture victims with a current diagnosis of PTSD and a group of 13 controls, matched for age, gender, and ethnic background. Aversive and neutral IAPS pictures (2 × 100 per affective condition) were presented for 333 ms each in an alternating fashion without ISI (upper row). The global activation in the time interval from 0 to 300 ms post stimulus onset is presented in the inset in the lower right. Grey lines represent PTSD patients, whereas black lines represent controls. Responses to aversive stimuli are marked by solid lines (upper curve of the black and grey lines, respectively), and responses to neutral ones are marked by dashed lines (lower curve of the black and grey lines, respectively). Inverse source analyses (L2-Minimum-Norm) were performed, and group differences were tested for an early 60- to 110-ms interval based on statistical parametric mapping. Sources were localized bilaterally in occipital and occipitoparietal areas with a right hemispheric dominance. Frontal difference activations were distinctly stronger in PTSD patients in both hemispheres (with right hemisphere dominance), as illustrated in the bottom row. (Data from Junghöfer et al., 2003.)

indicate dysfunctional neural networks, even when macroscopic structural lesions are not detectable. The regional distribution is disease specific. Indeed, the distribution of focal slow wave generators determined from the spontaneous magnetoencephalogram (by fitting single equivalent dipoles) differed in patients with PTSD from patients with other psychiatric diagnoses. When compared with the norm group of healthy controls, PTSD patients displayed high concentrations of abnormal brain waves in the pre- and orbitofrontal cortex, whereas depressed patients showed hypoactive regions, particularly in frontal areas (compare Figure 15.3 and 15.4). The "dysfunctional" significance of this brain activity is supported by its variation with successful therapeutic intervention in PTSD (Elbert et al., 2005). When mapping abnormal slow wave activity in 23 survivors of severe torture with a current diagnosis of PTSD, who had experienced multiple forms of psychological traumata (Schauer et al., 2005), the number of dissociative experiences was significantly and positively related to the density

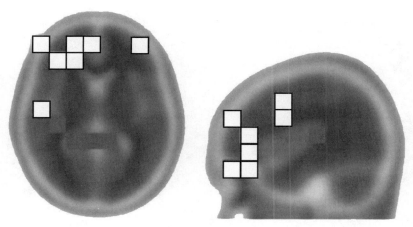

FIGURE 15.3. Example of abnormal neural generators in a PTSD patient scoring high in dissociative symptoms: white voxels depict deviations of more than 2 standard deviations from the norm (healthy controls). Dark grey indicates activity below normal. The patient shows a high density of focally generated slow waves in the left frontal region and the region of the anterior cingulate. During the recording session, the patient was fully awake and had less than average global power in the delta band (Schauer et al., 2005).

of abnormal slow wave generators in the left ventral region of the anterior cortical structures (correlations range from .4 to .65). Statistically partialing out the level of PTSD did not influence these relationships, suggesting that the level of dissociation contributes a separate component over and above PTSD symptoms to abnormal brain activity. This is theoretically consistent with DSM-IV not including dissociation as a PTSD criterion. Furthermore, the patient group showed significantly more abnormal slow waves in the left ventral region than a culturally matched control group without torture experience.

   Left frontal areas subserve language and executive function. However, more recently, neuroimaging studies showed the left ventral prefrontal cortex to also be involved in both verbal memory encoding and retrieval (Iidaka, Sadato, Yamada, & Yonekura, 2000). This might explain why dissociative individuals lack conscious, verbal access to certain previous traumatic experiences. It is a common experience in clinical practice that patients with PTSD have difficulties in verbalizing their traumatic experiences. The quality of emotional memories during reexperiencing symptoms is more emotional and sensory in nature, whereas feelings cannot be verbally expressed. A disruption of these frontal networks would explain why individuals experiencing intrusions and dissociative episodes are unable to actively retrieve and verbalize previous traumatic experiences. We assume that extreme traumatic stress such as torture initially

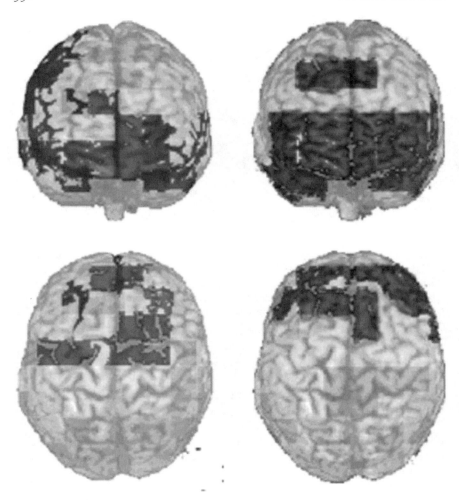

FIGURE 15.4. Mean regional distribution of abnormal slow waves for a group of 22 PTSD patients (left) and 15 depressive patients (right) relative to 25 normal controls. The top row offers a front view, whereas the bottom row shows the perspective from above. Voxels with significant differences to control groups are marked with white to indicate higher abnormal activity relative to controls, whereas dark shades indicate hypoactive areas. Mean z values are also shown. (Data from Rockstroh et al., 2005.)

prompts active or passive avoidance strategies in an attempt to reduce overwhelming fear, which may result in a permanent disruption of left frontal networks. The neural mechanisms of this disconnection may in part be explained by long-term depression as indicated previously, that is, by anti-Hebbian learning, as well as by the strengthening of inhibitory synapses.

This hypothesis of a functional disconnection of affective from language processing areas as a consequence of trauma-induced plastic changes in the brain's emotion and memory systems remains to be validated in future studies.

STRUCTURAL CEREBRAL CHANGES ASSOCIATED WITH PTSD

Several studies on PTSD patients with traumata resulting from combat, prolonged childhood abuse, rape, and traffic accidents have been conducted to analyze structural changes associated with PTSD. A meta-analysis of 14 studies of adult patients that met DSM criteria for PTSD, with a minimum patient sample size of $N = 10$, and including a well-matched control group was performed by Smith (2005). The studies were highly variable with respect to participant age, gender distribution, type and duration of trauma, severity of symptoms, duration of disorder, constitution of control groups, imaging parameters, and volumetric measurement methods. Nonetheless, tests of heterogeneity were only marginally significant, suggesting that most of the differences between individual studies in observed effect sizes were within the range of what might be expected from noise. On average (weighted by sample size), patients with PTSD had 12% smaller hippocampal volumes. These volume differences are similar in magnitude to those that have been reported in meta-analyses of patients suffering from depression. Whereas some studies suggest that the hippocampal atrophy might occur in response to exposure to exceptionally stressful events, Gilbertson et al. (2002) argued that they rather reflect preexisting differences that predispose an individual to development of PTSD under traumatic circumstances. To this end, Gilbertson et al. (2002) studied pairs of identical twins in which one member of each pair experienced combat in Vietnam, whereas the other stayed home. Combat veterans who developed PTSD had smaller hippocampi than combat veterans without PTSD. Furthermore, more severe PTSD was associated with an even smaller hippocampus. However, the crucial finding was that the stay-at-home siblings of PTSD combat veterans also had smaller hippocampi, and the hippocampal volume of the stay-at-home siblings was even equally predictive of the severity of the combat sibling's PTSD. Given that each stressful experience increases the vulnerability to develop PTSD (Neuner et al., 2004) and given that siblings share a history of traumatic stressors, it is likely that the resulting vulnerability is somehow reflected in the hippocampal size. Therefore, the results of Gilbertson et al. may not contradict the assumption that traumatic stress affects the morphology of the brain and that of the medial temporal lobe in particular. No knowledge exists as to whether hippocampal damage in PTSD is reversible through therapy because such studies were not controlled for temporal dynamics.

Based on the findings in rodents, one might expect structural changes in the amygdala of severely traumatized persons. However, no differences in amygdala size or volume between patients with PTSD and subjects without PTSD have been found (e.g., de Bellis et al., 2002).

The human ACC is implicated in evaluating the emotional significance of stimuli, in attentional function, and in detecting errors of performance (Cardinal, Parkinson, Hall, & Everitt, 2002). More recently, it has been suggested that the ACC "disambiguates" similar conditioned stimuli, depending on their association with reinforcement to prevent generalization between conditioned stimuli; that is, the ACC appears to discriminate similar stimuli (stimuli that share common elements) on the basis of their differential association with reinforcement. Some evidence for structural alterations in the ACC of traumatized patients exists. Rauch et al. (2003) found decreased volumes of the pregenual portion of the ACC (>25%) in combat nurses from the Vietnam War with PTSD compared with combat nurses without PTSD. The pregenual ACC, to which the results were specific, is believed to subserve affective function, whereas the dorsal ACC is believed to subserve cognitive motor functions. However, more research on structural (and functional) alterations of the ACC in traumatized individuals with PTSD is necessary.

In sum, structural, functional, and neuroendocrine changes can be observed in the brains of survivors of organized violence that can be linked to the (re)organization of memory. In threat situations when flight is impossible, fight is futile, and only freezing and fainting are left as response options in our evolutionary repertoire, the functioning of frontal and medial temporal lobe structures, which form the gateway to autobiographical memory, is altered: "hot" and "cold" memories lose their connection. We suggested that this disconnection of hot and cold memories, accompanied by an expanding fear network, explains flashbacks and the individual's entrapment in speechless terror and fear. Because the hot emotional memory is disconnected from autobiographical cold memory, the victim is unable to relate the proper autobiographical dates and places of occurrence to the flashback episodes. If one could restore this connection, the horror of the memories might be alleviated. Although the psychic scar inflicted to the mind cannot be undone, there are narrative approaches that can help alleviate PTSD symptoms. Reweaving hot memory contents back into cold memory networks can bring relief to the injured mind.

## VIOLENCE BREEDS VIOLENCE: CONSEQUENCES OF STRESS EFFECTS ON BEHAVIOR AND CULTURE

The previous sections summarized evidence on how brain and mind are affected by experiences of organized violence. A resulting question is how these changes, induced by stressful experiences preset the individual behavior with corresponding consequences for the society, including the way of dealing with violence. Therefore, in the second part of this chapter, we discuss the relationship between stress-induced changes and behavior on a societal level, with the theoretical model of stress effects on brain and mind serving as background to understand the cycle of violence.

The saying "violence breeds violence" was coined 40 years ago by Curtis (1963), who expressed the concern that "abused and neglected children would become tomorrow's murderers and perpetrators of other crimes of violence." The validity of this finding obviously cannot be assessed by direct experimental manipulations. However, converging evidence exists that experiencing violence – which, as we have seen, modifies brain and mind – is related to expressing violence: for instance, parents who were abused as children are more likely to abuse their own children. Rates of abuse double for parents who themselves grew up in violent environments compared with parents who did not. Prospective and retrospective studies on children who were abused or neglected disclose a high incidence of later delinquency. Children clinically referred to residential treatment with a history of abuse scored significantly higher on measures of reactive and verbal aggression than nonabused control children (Conner, Doerfler, Volungis, Steingard, & Melloni, 2003). Finally, a large proportion of homicide offenders come from unfavorable home environments and up to 80% of subjects within delinquent samples report witnessing violence in their childhood or adolescence.

It is important to note that effects are exerted from early on, that is, when plasticity for the brain and mind is greatest. Developmental studies indicate that abuse and neglect are related to aggression and later antisocial behavior in children as young as infants and toddlers. Thus, violent childhood experiences may leave their mark on brain and mind of the affected individuals, a vulnerability that interacts with future stressful experiences. Indeed, childhood experience seem to be an important factor in this dynamic interaction, as Van der Kolk and Fisler (1994) emphasized: "Abused children often fail to develop the capacity to express specific and differentiated emotions: Their difficulty putting feelings into words interferes with flexible response strategies and promotes acting out" (p. 145).

Traumatic stress, whether experienced in adulthood or earlier, furthers violent behavior. Although the "critical period" of stress system development suggests that childhood trauma should have more effects on the brain and behavior than adult trauma, evidence seems insufficient and studies are scarce until now. Our own studies with children in Ugandan refugee camps and survivors of the Rwandan genocide (Schaal & Elbert, in press) are designed to provide further evidence.

Many studies addressing consequences of traumatic experiences in war veterans found increased impulsive aggression toward intimate partners and unknown persons (e.g., Byrne & Riggs, 1996). Similarly, high rates of traumatic experiences were found in a sample of juvenile delinquents (Abram et al., 1994). More than 90% of the sample ($N = 898$) had experienced one or more traumatic events; the most prominent event was witnessing violence. Approximately 11% of the sample even met criteria for PTSD in the past year. Thus, traumatic events seem to play an important role in individuals with violent or antisocial behavior. Similar results come from two studies of our group on forensic psychiatric patients (e.g., Saleptsi et al., 2004), which found higher than normal rates of PTSD among those patients. Similarly, Timmerman and Emmelkamp (2001) found sexual and emotional abuse to be significantly more prevalent among forensic patients than among prisoners. Using structural equation modeling, Orcutt, King, and King (2003) examined the impact of early life stressors, war-zone stressors, and PTSD symptom severity on partner's reports of recent male-perpetrated intimate partner violence among 376 Vietnam veteran couples. Results revealed a direct relationship of war-zone stressors (i.e., traumatic stress) and PTSD symptom severity with intimate partner violence. In addition, indirect effects (i.e., via PTSD) of stressful early life experiences, childhood antisocial behavior, and traumatic war-zone experiences were found on intimate partner violence. Thus, experiencing PTSD symptoms as a result of previous trauma appears to increase an individual's risk for perpetrating intimate partner violence.

Another example of the relation between stressful life experiences and subsequent violent behavior becomes obvious in the results of a study by Freeman, Roca, and Kimbrell (2003). War veterans with PTSD owned more than four times as many firearms as comparison groups of patients with schizophrenia or substance abuse, and they reported significantly higher levels of potentially dangerous firearm-related behaviors. Thus, experiencing violence that leads to trauma and PTSD lowers the threshold to exert violence. PTSD may increase the vulnerability for violence and impulsive aggression, in particular when confronted with stress. However, it seems important to note that although violent outbursts increase, organized violence does not.

## CULTURE OF ORGANIZED VIOLENCE: A BREEDING GROUND FOR TRAUMA SPECTRUM DISORDERS

In addition to trauma-related factors, cultural factors (i.e., society's attitude toward violence) also play a role in the prevalence and spread of violence. DeFronzo and Prochnow (2004) analyzed the rate of serial homicide across 50 states within the United States and found that 34% to 45% of the interstate variation in rates of serial killer activity could be accounted for by dimensions of local culture, with higher rates of violence being found in states supporting game hunting, military training, and a local culture supporting punitive violence.

Organized violence comprises war, torture, and other severe human rights violations that wound the psyche and cause mental illnesses. Three types of organized violence can be distinguished (see Neuner, 2003). The first type is the permanent state-sponsored persecution that is present in all dictatorships, and even in some countries that are considered democracies. This harassment includes different forms of violence such as torture, extralegal executions, and disappearances. The second type is the massive violence committed against people in an interstate or civil war. The third type of organized violence is characterized by violence committed by terror organizations. All three types aim to systematically augment anxiety and depression in the population and to mentally destroy at least some part of the population by inducing trauma spectrum disorders.

"New wars" (Kaldor, 1999) involve conditions of particular traumatization of large groups of people. The public view of wars is dominated by knowledge about the twentieth century's world wars. However, currently, wars fought between two or more fighting countries are the exception rather than the rule. In 2001, more than nine out of ten wars (91%) were intrastate conflicts or civil wars (Schreiber, 2002). Although foreign armies may participate in the fighting, these wars do not originate from conflicts between nations but arise within a country. There are two different reasons for civil wars: currently, in about half of the intrastate conflicts, a rebel army fights for the autonomy or secession of a region. In the other half of the wars, rebels aim to overthrow the ruling regime. Kaldor (1999) introduced the term "new war" to describe these currently dominant ways of warfare, with prominent characteristics such as (Neuner, 2003)

- *Irregular forces:* Fighting is dominated by irregular forces, including paramilitary units, rebel forces, mercenary troops, and foreign armies that intervene in civil wars on one side. The majority of fighters on all sides of the conflicts have limited military training. Because many characteristics of regular armies, such as uniforms and regular salaries, are not applicable to the majority of fighters, the clear separation between civilians and soldiers disappears. Forcibly recruited child soldiers belong to the usual repertoire of most forces in the new wars (Schreiber, 2002). Parties to the conflict are frequently led by powerful warlords who do not depend on governments. Because war offers them the opportunity to maintain power without oversight by regulating institutions, they have no immediate interest in a termination of war. Consequently, many wars are extended by deliberately delaying peace negotiations and an unwillingness of both war parties to fight decisive battles against each other.
- *Justification by identities:* Conflicts are justified based on the parties' affiliation to different ethnic groups, cultures, or religions. Myths about

ancient rivalries and wars between the ethnic groups are used to moti-
vate the public for the war.

- *Civilian targets:* Because the best way to gain power in new wars is by
  controlling and frightening the civilian population and by displacing
  civilians, new warfare strategies include systematic atrocities, such as
  massacres and mass rapes, to frighten civilians and to make regions
  uninhabitable for the group to be expelled. Another reason for the prevalence of atrocities in current wars is the assumption that they help unite
  the group committing the atrocities. Once a person has participated
  in committing war crimes, it is almost impossible to leave the group
  because the perpetrator will always be rejected by others. Easily available small weapons are sufficient for this type of warfare.
- *Economic factors:* In a global economy, the war parties are usually not
  self-sufficient but obtain resources from supporting foreign countries
  and exile communities. Very often, the conflicts are fought to win or
  keep control over local resources such as diamonds, minerals, oil, and
  drugs.

In the new wars, more than 80% of casualties are civilians. The consequences of violence and the resulting traumatic stress severely impact the
daily lives of millions of war-affected people and of people who are on
the run because of fear and anxiety. As outlined in the next section, the
result is a high rate of trauma spectrum disorders in these populations
(e.g., Karunakara et al., 2004; Neuner et al., 2004; Schaal & Elbert, 2006),
and many people are affected by trauma in a subclinical fashion. Will these
victims fight back?

## CYCLE OF ORGANIZED VIOLENCE

The prevalence of PTSD in populations living in war regions varies with the
type and number of traumatic events experienced. In some cases, prevalence rates of more than 50% can be found; that is, more than half the
community suffers from this disabling condition, which impairs normal
family life and renders people unable to earn a living. A large-scale project
(Karunakara et al., 2004) screened 3,231 refugees in northern Uganda and
southern Sudan, revealing a surprisingly high prevalence of chronic mental illness. In one settlement with a count of approximately 12,000 refugees,
70% had experienced war, 78% had been threatened with a weapon, 61%
had been assaulted, and 49% had been abused or tortured. The prevalence
of disabling chronic mental illness in six camps ranged from 20% to 56%.
In one camp, more than half the population was unable to function due to
persistent mental health problems. These and other epidemiological findings demonstrate that communities at large are affected, not just a few
individuals.

How can we model this co-constructivism of individual and societal cycles of stress and violence? Beyond the fact that traumata and resulting trauma spectrum disorders are a consequence of violence, traumatic experiences can also cause domestic violence, as well as violent wars and conflicts, a circumstance that receives more and more consideration at a political level. Organizations providing psychosocial interventions in war-affected societies justify their interventions not only as a means of improving mental health care for individuals, but also by referring to sociopolitical factors. A common statement is that the treatment of "traumatized societies" is necessary to break the "cycle of trauma" (UNICEF, 2001). This reasoning is based on the assumption that traumatized individuals are more likely to become perpetrators themselves. Through treatment, one aims not only to reduce PTSD symptoms, but also to foster reconciliation and forgiveness. It remains to be empirically proven, whether this is the case. Although some investigations indicate that traumatized individuals are more likely to become perpetrators themselves (e.g., intimate partner violence, delinquent behavior), there is not enough evidence that confirms a "cycle of violence." The model of stress effects on the brain's structure and function with concomitant alterations of the mind (i.e., in memory, affect regulation, fear network, and PTSD symptoms) offers a platform to create and investigate hypotheses of the cycle of violence.

## OUTLOOK

Societal conflicts and civil war-affected communities provide a background for the study of the interaction of brain, mind, and culture. This interaction should be of utmost interest to scientific investigation, public health, and politics. Knowledge of the brain's ability to adapt and reorganize also helps one understand the enduring effects of social stress and trauma on brain systems involved in the regulation of affect and memory. Another challenge for future research is to apply this knowledge of stress/trauma-induced brain plasticity to the level of the society. Developing countries provide the most dramatic examples of "societal trauma." Although globalization contains a great deal of developmental chances for developing countries, sub-Saharan Africa has been cursed by a lack of stable political infrastructure and has thus been unable to participate in the opportunities offered by globalization, despite its wealth of natural resources.

In sub-Saharan Africa alone, more than ten countries are currently affected by civil wars. Many of these conflicts have lasted for decades. With few exceptions, most African countries have a recent history of armed conflicts and currently suffer from the consequences, in particular from the appalling degree of violence. The effects of these conflicts on politics, society, economy, and (mental) health last for decades and have been termed "development in reverse."

Currently, psychosocial services in conflict and postconflict settings offer no feasible guidelines on how to treat mental disturbances caused by traumatic experiences. Very little is known about the usefulness of psychiatric concepts and therapeutic approaches for survivors of severe violence who still live in stressful and potentially dangerous conditions such as refugee settlements. Furthermore, it is unpredictable how long-term development will be influenced by the common mental health problems in the aftermath of trauma, particularly if one considers the lack of access to high-quality treatment.

It has been argued that violence, conflict, and demoralization in these communities feed further violence, reinforcing a downward spiral. As pointed out, there is some evidence that, in particular, early traumatic experiences may foster interfamilial and intimate partner violence. However, there is no sufficient evidence to suggest that traumatic experiences promote organized violence on an individual or societal level. We are only beginning to understand the consequences of violence on the individual's brain, mind, and behavior, and how this impacts society. Perhaps some day we will also comprehend the roots of violence and how they can be counteracted – a great endeavor. As long as the underlying mechanisms of organized violence are not properly understood, we will have to focus on improving the therapeutic approaches for helping the victims.

ACKNOWLEDGMENTS

The research was supported by the Deutsche Forschungsgemeinschaft and the European Refugee Fund.

**References**

Abram, K. M., Teplin, L. A., Charles, D. R., Longworth, S. L., McClelland, G. M., & Dulcan, M. K. (1994). Posttraumatic stress disorder and trauma in youth in juvenile detention. *Archives of General Psychiatry, 61* (4), 403–410.
Baltes, P. (1999). Age and aging as incomplete architecture of human ontogenesis. *Zeitschrift für Gerontologie und Geriatrie, 32* (6), 433–448.
Baltes, P., & Singer, T. (2001). Plasticity and the aging mind: An exemplar of the bio-cultural orchestration of brain and behaviour. *European Review, 9*, 59–76.
Bao, S., Chang, E. F., Davis, J. D., Gobeske, K. T., & Merzenich, M. M. (2003). Progressive degradation and subsequent refinement of acoustic representations in the adult auditory cortex. *The Journal of Neuroscience, 23* (34), 10765–10775.
Braun, C., Haug, M., Wiech, K., Birbaumer, N., Elbert, T., & Roberts, L. (2002). Functional organization of primary somatosensory cortex depends on the focus of attention. *NeuroImage, 17*, 1451–1458.
Buchanan, T. W., & Lovallo, W. R. (2001). Enhanced memory for emotional material following stress-level cortisol treatment in humans. *Psychoneuroendocrinology, 26*, 307–317.

Byrne, C. A., & Riggs, D. S. (1996). The cycle of trauma: Relationship aggression in male Vietnam veterans with symptoms of posttraumatic stress disorder. *Violence and Victims, 11* (3), 213–225.

Cardinal, R. N., Parkinson, J. A., Hall, J., & Everitt, B. J. (2002). Emotion and motivation: The role of the amygdala, ventral striatum, and prefrontal cortex. *Neuroscience and Biobehavioral Reviews, 26,* 321–352.

Charmandari, E., Kino, T., Souvatzoglou, E., & Chrousos, G. P. (2003). Pediatric stress: Hormonal mediators and human development. *Hormone Research, 59* (4), 161–179.

Conner, D. F., Doerfler, L. A., Volungis, A. D., Steingard, R. J., & Melloni, R. H. (2003). Aggressive behavior in abused children. *Annals of the New York Academy of Sciences, 1008,* 79–90.

Curtis, G. C. (1963). Violence breeds violence – perhaps? *American Journal of Psychiatry, 120,* 386–387.

De Bellis, M. D., Keshavan, M. S., Shifflett, H., Iyengar, S., Beers, S. R., Hall, J., & Moritz, G. (2002). Brain structures in pediatric maltreatment-related posttraumatic stress disorder: A sociodemographically matched study. *Biological Psychiatry, 52* (11), 1066–1078.

DeFronzo, J., & Prochnow, J. (2004). Violent cultural factors and serial homicide by males. *Psychological Reports, 94* (1), 104–108.

De Quervain, D. J.-F., Roozendaal, B., Nitsch, R. M., McGaugh, J. L., & Hock, C. (2000). Acute cortisone administration impairs retrieval of long-term declarative memory in humans. *Nature Neuroscience, 3,* 313–314.

Elbert, T., Candia, V., Altenmüller, E., Rau, H., Sterr, A., Rockstroh, B., Pantev, C., & Taub, E. (1998). Alteration of digital representations in somatosensory cortex in focal hand dystonia. *Neuroreport, 16,* 3571–3575.

Elbert, T., Neuner, F., Schauer, M., Odenwald, M., Ruf, M., Wienbruch, C., & Rockstroh, B. (2005). *Successful psychotherapy modifies abnormal neural architecture in frontal cortex of traumatised patients.* Paper presented at the conference of the European Society for Traumatic Stress Studies, Stockholm.

Elbert, T., Pantev, C., Wienbruch, C., Rockstroh, B., & Taub, E. (1995). Increased use of the left hand in string players associated with increased cortical representation of the fingers. *Science, 270,* 305–307.

Elbert, T., Sterr, A., Rockstroh, B., Pantev, C., Müller, M. M., & Taub, E. (2002). Expansion of the tonotopic area in the auditory cortex of the blind. *The Journal of Neuroscience, 22,* 9941–9944.

Freeman, T. W., Roca, V., & Kimbrell, T. (2003). A survey of gun collection and use among three groups of veteran patients admitted to Veterans Affairs hospital treatment programs. *Southern Medical Journal, 96* (3), 240–243.

Gilbertson, M. W., Shenton, M. E., Ciszewski, A., Kasai, K., Lasko, N. B., Orr, S. P., & Pitman, R. K. (2002). Smaller hippocampal volume predicts pathologic vulnerability to psychological trauma. *Nature Neuroscience, 5* (11), 1242–1247.

Gougoux, F., Lepore, F., Lassonde, M., Voss, P., Zatorre, R. J., & Belin, P. (2004). Neuropsychology: Pitch discrimination in the early blind. *Nature, 430,* 309.

Gougoux, F., Zatorre, R. J., Lassonde, M., Voss, P., & Lepore, F. (2005). A functional neuroimaging study of sound localization: Visual cortex activity predicts performance in early-blind individuals. *PloS Biology, 3* (2), e27.

Heinrichs, M., Baumgartner, T., Kirschbaum, C., & Ehlert, U. (2003). Social support and oxytocin interact to suppress cortisol and subjective responses to psychosocial stress. *Biological Psychiatry, 54* (12), 1389–1398.

Iidaka, T., Sadato, N., Yamada, H., & Yonekura, Y. (2000). Functional asymmetry of human prefrontal cortex in verbal and non-verbal episodic memory as revealed by fMRI. *Cognitive Brain Research, 9,* 73–83.

Ikegaya, Y., Saito, H., & Abe, K. (1996a). Dentate gyrus field potentials evoked by stimulation of the basolateral amygdaloid nucleus in anesthetized rats. *Brain Research, 718* (1–2), 53–60.

Ikegaya, Y., Saito, H., & Abe, K. (1996b). The basomedial and basolateral amygdaloid nuclei contribute to the induction of long-term potentiation in the dentate gyrus in vivo. *The European Journal of Neurosciences, 8* (9), 1833–1839.

Junghöfer, M., Bradley, M., Elbert, T., & Lang, P. (2001). Fleeting images: A new look at early emotion discrimination. *Psychophysiology, 38,* 175–178.

Junghöfer, M., Schauer, M., Neuner, F., Odenwald, M., Rockstroh, B., & Elbert, T. (2003). Enhanced fear-network in torture survivors activated by RVSP of aversive material can be monitored by MEG. *Psychophysiology, 40* (Suppl), 51.

Kaldor, M. (1999). *New and old wars: Organized violence in a global era.* London: Blackwell.

Karunakara, U. K., Neuner, F., Schauer, M., Singh, K., Hill, K., Elbert, T., & Burnha, G. (2004). Traumatic events and symptoms of post-traumatic stress disorder amongst Sudanese nationals, refugees and Ugandans in the West Nile. *African Health Sciences, 4* (2), 83–93.

Lang, P. (1979). Presidential address, 1978: A bio-informational theory of emotional imagery. *Psychophysiology, 16* (6), 495–512.

Lessard, N., Pare, M., Lepore, F., & Lassonde, M. (1998). Early-blind human subjects localize sound sources better than sighted subjects. *Nature, 392,* 811–814.

McEwen, B. (2004). Protection and damage from acute and chronic stress. *Annals of the New York Academy of Sciences, 1032,* 1–7.

Meaney, M., Aitken, D., van Berkel, C., Bhatnagar, C., & Sapolsky, R. (1988). Effects of neonatal handling on age-related impairments associated with the hippocampus. *Science, 239,* 766–770.

Metcalve, J., & Jacobs, W. (1996). A "hot-system/cool-system" view of memory under stress. *PTSD Research Quarterly, 7,* 1–3.

Muchnik, C., Efrati, M., Nemeth, E., Malin, M., & Hildesheimer, M. (1991). Central auditory skills in blind and sighted subjects. *Scandinavian Audiology, 20,* 19–23.

Neuner, F. (2003). *Epidemiology and treatment of posttraumatic stress disorder in West-Nile populations of Sudan and Uganda.* Ph.D. dissertation, University of Konstanz, Konstanz, Germany. Available: www.ub.uni-konstanz.de/kops/volltexte/2003/1082/pdf/dissNeuner.pdf.

Neuner, F., Schauer, M., Karunakara, U., Klaschik, C., Robert, C., & Elbert, T. (2004). Psychological trauma and evidence for enhanced vulnerability for PTSD through previous trauma in West Nile refugees. *BMC Psychiatry, 4* (1), 34.

Neuner, F., Schauer, M., Roth, W. T., & Elbert, T. (2002). Testimony therapy as an acute intervention in a Macedonian refugee camp: Two case reports. *Behavioral and Cognitive Psychotherapy, 30,* 205–209.

Odenwald, M., Neuner, F., Schauer, M., Elbert, T., Catani, C., Lingenfelder, B., Hinkel, H., Hafner, H., & Rockstroh, B. (2005). Khat use as risk factor for psychotic disorders: A cross-sectional and case-control study in Somalia. *BMC Medicine, 3* (1), 5.

Orcutt, H. K., King, L. A., & King, D. W. (2003). Male-perpetrated violence among Vietnam veteran couples: Relationships with veteran's early life characteristics, trauma history, and PTSD symptomatology. *Journal of Trauma and Stress, 16* (4), 381–390.

Packard, M. G., Cahill, L., & McGaugh, J. L. (1994). Amygdala modulation of hippocampal-dependent and caudate nucleus-dependent memory processes. *Proceedings of the National Academy of Sciences (USA), 91,* 8477–8481.

Pantev, C., Oostenveld, R., Engelien, A., Ross, B., Roberts, L. E., & Hoke, M. (1998). Increased auditory cortical representation in musicians. *Nature, 392,* 811–814.

Rauch, S. L., Shin, L. M., Segal, E., Pitman, R. K., Carson, M. A., McMullin, K., Whalen, P. J., & Makris, N. (2003). Selectively reduced regional cortical volumes in post-traumatic stress disorder. *Neuroreport, 14,* 913–916.

Rockstroh, B., Ray, W., Wienbruch, C., & Elbert, T. (2005). *Identification of dysfunctional cortical network architecture and communication: Abnormal slow wave activity mapping (ASWAM) in neurological and psychiatric disorders.* Manuscript submitted for publication.

Röder, B., Rösler, F., & Neville, H. J. (2001). Auditory memory in congenitally blind adults: A behavioural-electrophysiological investigation. *Cognitive Brain Research, 11,* 289–303.

Saleptsi, E., Bichescu, D., Rockstroh, B., Neuner, F., Schauer, M., Studer, K., Hoffmann, K., & Elbert, T. (2004). Association between psychiatric diagnoses and negative and positive childhood experiences during the different developmental periods. *BMC Psychiatry, 4,* 40.

Sapolsky, R. M. (1999). Glucocorticoids, stress, and their adverse neurological effects: Relevance to aging. *Experimental Gerontology, 34,* 721–732.

Schaal, S., & Elbert, T. (in press). Ten years after the genocide: Trauma confrontation and posttraumatic stress in Rwandan adolescents. *Journal of Traumatic Stress.*

Schauer, M., Ray, W. J., Odenwald, M., Neuner, F., Ruf, M., Rockstroh, B., & Elbert, T. (2005). *Decoupling neural networks from reality: Dissociative experiences modify the neural architecture in left frontal cortex.* Paper presented at the conference of the European Society for Traumatic Stress Studies, Stockholm.

Schreiber, W. (2002). *Das Kriegsgeschehen 2001.* Opladen: Leske + Budrich.

Smith, M. (2005). Bilateral hippocampal volume reduction in adults with post traumatic stress disorder: A meta-analysis of structural MRI studies. *Hippocampus, 15* (6), 798–807.

Steinberg, L. (2005). Cognitive and affective development in adolescence. *Trends in Cognitive Sciences, 9,* 69–74.

Timmerman, I. G., & Emmelkamp, P. M. (2001). The relationship between traumatic experiences, dissociation, and borderline personality pathology among male forensic patients and prisoners. *Journal of Personality Disorders, 15* (2), 136–149.

UNICEF. (2001). *The state of the world's children 2001.* New York: UNICEF.

Van der Kolk, B. A., & Fisler, R. E. (1994). Childhood abuse and neglect and loss of self-regulation. *Bulletin of the Menninger Clinic, 58* (2), 145–168.

# 16

## Co-Constructing Human Engineering Technologies in Old Age: Lifespan Psychology as a Conceptual Foundation

Ulman Lindenberger and Martin Lövdén

ABSTRACT

*Human engineering technologies highlight the bioculturally co-constructed nature of human ontogeny. Based on concepts from lifespan psychology, we propose three criteria for evaluating human engineering technologies in old age: marginal gain for the individual, person specificity and adaptability, and conjoint consideration of distal and proximal frames of evaluation. Informed by research on expert memory performance and negative adult age differences in sensory, motor, and cognitive functioning, we propose strategies for incorporating these criteria into the design of human engineering technologies. We expect that intelligent human engineering technologies will alter the aging of future generations by reducing cognitive resource demands through personalized external cuing structures.*

INTRODUCTION

Recent years have witnessed increasing efforts at improving and expanding human engineering technologies for diverse segments of the adult and elderly population (Charness & Schaie, 2003; Kautz, Etzioni, Fox, & Weld, 2004; LoPresti, Mihailidis, & Kirsch, 2004). In this chapter, we discuss the potential of human engineering technologies to counteract negative adult age changes in sensory/sensorimotor and cognitive domains. We devote special attention to intelligent human engineering technology (IHET), that is, to assistive devices and environments apt to learn from, control, supervise, and regulate behavior (Kautz et al., 2004; Patterson, Liao, Fox, & Kautz, 2003).

Human behavior enmeshed in assistive technology is not fundamentally different from any other form of human behavior. At the same time, the unprecedented capacity of IHET to adapt to, predict, supervise, assist, and eventually control human behavior sets it apart from less adaptive assistive devices such as canes or reading glasses. It is likely that future cohorts of aging individuals will delegate control over certain aspects of everyday functioning to IHET, while continuing to exert more direct forms of control in others. In this manner, IHET highlights and radicalizes the dialectic tension between environmental and personal control, and forces us to take notice of the societally constructed nature of human agency and self-determination (cf. Prinz, 2004).

Biocultural lifespan co-constructivism (Baltes, Lindenberger, & Staudinger, 2006; Li, 2003; see Chapter 1) highlights both the malleable and the invariant aspects of different age periods in human ontogeny. By reducing, circumventing, or postponing normative losses in functional integrity and the onset of age-associated pathologies, cultural evolution has transformed old age from an exceptional into a normative period of life. However, cultural evolution has not succeeded in abolishing the increasing vulnerability and frailty inherent with advancing old age. Hence, the precariousness of old age, and of very old age in particular, continues to be a motor of cultural innovation for each subsequent generation.

In this chapter, we scrutinize human engineering technologies from the perspectives of lifespan psychology (Baltes et al., 2006); and research on expert memory performance (Ericsson, 1985; Mäntylä, 1986). We draw on the selection, optimization, and compensation (SOC) model of successful development proposed by Baltes and Baltes (1990; Freund & Baltes, 2000) to gauge the developmental benefits of human engineering technologies. We then provide an overview of negative adult age changes in sensory, sensorimotor, and cognitive dimensions of behavior, and propose two strategies for the design of human engineering technologies. First, we suggest that IHET may be used to reduce the cognitive demands of sensory/ sensorimotor aspects of behavior, thereby resulting in a net release of cognitive resources that can then be invested into genuinely cognitive task requirements or activities. Second, informed by findings on expert memory performance, we propose that IHET can directly reduce cognitive resource demands through personalized external cuing structures. In conclusion, we stress the need to arrive at a conceptual foundation for human engineering technologies in old age, and argue that lifespan psychology can serve as an organizing force in this endeavor.

## SELECTION, OPTIMIZATION, AND COMPENSATION AS AN EVALUATIVE FRAMEWORK

The SOC model was originally developed to address the nature of successful lifespan development (cf. Baltes & Baltes, 1990). This model may provide guidelines for assessing the capacity of human engineering technologies to promote desirable and avoid or ameliorate undesirable developmental pathways and outcomes. Successful development is defined as the conjoint maximization of gains (desirable goals or outcomes) and the minimization of losses (avoidance of undesirable goals or outcomes). The nature of what constitutes gains and losses, as well as the dynamics between them, are conditioned by cultural, ontogenetic, and person-related factors. Thus, a desirable developmental outcome achieved through SOC mechanisms may become dysfunctional later in ontogenetic time or in a different context. Moreover, what constitutes a gain and what constitutes a loss depends on the methods and concepts used to measure and define desirable developmental outcomes (Baltes & Baltes, 1990; Freund & Baltes, 2000). For instance, subjective criteria such as personal well-being may yield different results than objective criteria such as everyday competence.

Within the SOC framework, selection refers to focusing one's resources on a subset of potentially available options, thereby giving development its direction. Development inevitably requires selection because a large number of potential developmental trajectories is transformed into those chosen and those dismissed. Optimization reflects the growth aspect of development. It encompasses the search for beneficial environments, and refers to the acquisition, refinement, and coordinated application of resources directed at the achievement of higher functional levels. Compensation addresses the regulation of loss in development. It involves efforts to maintain a given level of functioning despite decline in, or loss of, previously available resources, either by replacing dysfunctional means to reach a desirable goal with alternative processes, or by changing the goal itself.

When resources are scarce, selection, optimization, and compensation are particularly important for promoting success in development. For instance, with advancing adult age, depleting cognitive resources need to be channeled economically, and SOC theory helps describe and evaluate the effectiveness of these channeling attempts. Assistive technology should serve the goal of minimizing losses and maximizing gains by enhancing the efficiency of SOC mechanisms. Thus, criteria for the developmental utility of human engineering technology in old age can be defined in relation to SOC mechanisms. We specify three such criteria (Fig. 16.1). First, *net resource release* (marginal resource gain) denotes that the costs associated with the use of human engineering technologies must be lower than the gains produced by other changes in task characteristics. Second, *person specificity* mandates that human engineering technologies should adapt themselves to the knowledge structure, habits, and preferences of the individual user. Third, the notion of *proximal versus distal frames of evaluation* helps remind us that a critical assessment of human engineering technologies requires attention to both short- and long-term effects.

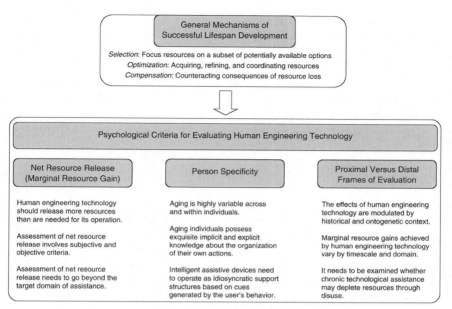

FIGURE 16.1. Toward a conceptual foundation for evaluating the developmental benefits of human engineering technology in adulthood and old age.

## Net Resource Release (Marginal Resource Gain)

Human engineering technology usually comes at a resource cost because its operation requires an investment of physical and mental resources. Its use is adaptive only if this cost is lower than the payoff associated with other changes in processing (cf. Dixon & Bäckman, 1995). Whenever the use of human engineering technology requires fewer resources than it releases, the marginal gain associated with selecting assistive technology is positive. This point is analogous to the definition of successful aging in terms of maximization of gains and minimization of losses.

In this context, objective and subjective (user-perceived) facets of marginal gain need to be set apart. An older individual's perception of marginal gain is more likely to determine usage of human engineering technologies than a cost–benefit ratio assessed in some objective manner. Furthermore, both objective and perceived marginal gain are influenced by the effects of human engineering technologies on individuals' total functioning or life space, which includes not only targeted domains (e.g., cognitive competence and sensory/sensorimotor functioning), but also all other relevant domains (e.g., affective and social dimensions). Comprehensive assessments of net resource release (marginal resource gain) need to consider all of them.

In sum, human engineering technology falls short of its central objective if its use does not result in marginal resource gains. To enhance the likelihood of such an outcome, its design has to incorporate knowledge about negative adult age changes. Psychologists need to specify under what conditions behavior with technological assistance is in fact less resource demanding than behavior without. In addition, the evaluation of net resource release has to be based on a broad set of objective and subjective indicators that go beyond the target activity or functional domain.

**Person Specificity**

Cognitive and sensorimotor functioning are variable within and across individuals (Li, Aggen, Nesselroade, & Baltes, 2001). Moreover, average age trends do not apply to all members of the aging population (Baltes & Mayer, 1999; Lövdén & Lindenberger, 2005). Using knowledge about the average aging individual provides little more than a viable starting point for the development and use of human engineering technology in general and IHET in particular. To be successful, IHET must fine-tune itself to the idiosyncrasies of the individual's behavior, that is, to his or her specific competencies, habits, and preferences. As we argue in this chapter, this process of fine-tuning critically involves the evolution of a cuing structure that matches the structure of the individual's action space.

From modeling and human engineering perspectives, the "average aging individual" can provide the starting values, or default parameters, of IHET. The technology then needs to capture the regularities in a given individual's behavior, and needs to react or adapt to the user's fluctuations and long-term changes in competencies (Kautz et al., 2004). Given the sizeable variability in behavioral competence within the elderly population (e.g., Lindenberger & Baltes, 1997), adaptation to individual users is a precondition for enhancing the marginal gains of IHET.

**Proximal Versus Distal Frames of Evaluation**

The effects of human engineering technologies are modulated by historical and ontogenetic context (cf. Baltes et al., 2006). Hence, potential benefits of human engineering technology vary across historical and ontogenetic time. Historically, prior lifespan exposure to the same or related technologies is likely to influence the marginal gain of human engineering technology in old age through positive or negative transfer. For instance, today's generation of middle-age adults will make different use of mobile phones than many members of today's generation of individuals older than 80. Also, within individuals, short- and long-term benefits may not always be congruent. For instance, the use of modern global positioning system (GPS)-based spatial navigation aids may have positive short-term effects on way-finding behavior. However, to the extent that the use of such aids reinforces route learning strategies at the cost of strategies that achieve spatial integration, long-term and transfer effects may actually be negative. Just as any other form of intervention, then, human engineering technologies, especially of the intelligent kind, alter the action space of an individual, and need to be evaluated on multiple time scales and dimensions.

## AVERAGE AGING LOSSES IN BODILY AND COGNITIVE RESOURCES

This section provides a selective overview of functional domains that are particularly relevant for theory-guided design of human engineering technology. Specifically, we focus on age-associated declines in cognitive, sensory, and motor domains during adulthood and old age, and on the ways in which age changes in these domains interact with each other in the course of goal-directed action. The overview is confined to normal (healthy) aging, and is targeted to aspects deemed critical for the theory-guided design of human engineering technology. The material covered is therefore selective and cannot do justice to the multidirectional nature of cognitive lifespan development.

## Cognition

### *Cognitive Control*
A central task of IHET is to regulate behavior. Therefore, age changes in individuals' abilities to exert cognitive control are at the very heart of IHET design for the elderly. In most situations, the behavior of humans is not directly controlled by external stimuli, rather it is guided by internal representations of goals and the means to achieve them. Cognitive (or executive) control refers to such mechanisms of top-down regulation of perception, action, and thought (Miller & Cohen, 2001). Aging-induced difficulties in implementing control mechanisms differ widely by task, context, and person. When tasks are clearly structured and distracting stimuli are absent, demands on cognitive control tend to be low, and adult age differences tend to be small. Conversely, when multiple tasks need to be coordinated, when tasks conflict with perceptual input (e.g., when top-down and bottom-up activation are discordant), or both, demands on cognitive control are high, and adult age differences tend to be large. Typical examples for situations that impose high demands on cognitive control include multitasking (Mayr, Kliegl, & Krampe, 1996), the selection and shifting between tasks under conditions of high stimulus ambiguity (Kray & Lindenberger, 2000), and the suppression of strong stimulus-driven action tendencies (Salthouse & Meinz, 1995).

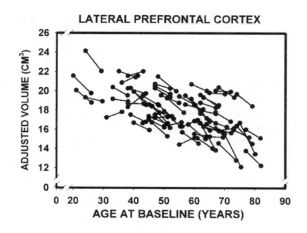

LATERAL PREFRONTAL CORTEX

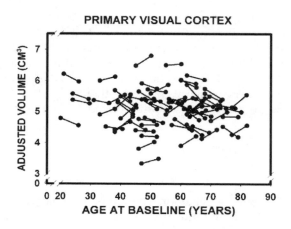

PRIMARY VISUAL CORTEX

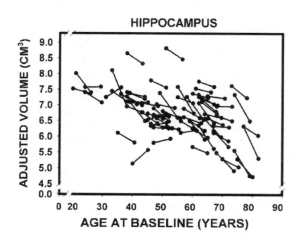

HIPPOCAMPUS

*Working Memory*

Similar to the notion of cognitive control, working memory denotes the ability to preserve information in one or more short-term stores while transforming the same or some other information (Just, Carpenter, & Keller, 1996). Working memory clearly serves an important function for cognitive control because it allows individuals to coordinate various goals when working on complex or multiple tasks. One way to study adult age differences in working memory is to vary the relative importance of temporary storage and processing (i.e., information transformation) demands within or across tasks. Generally, this research has demonstrated that negative age differences during adulthood are more pronounced when demands on processing are increased (Mayr et al., 1996). In other words, age differences are especially pronounced for tasks that put high demands on the simultaneous coordination of various pieces of incoming information, stored information, or both. Differential susceptibility to coordinative demands may also help explain why lifespan age differences in marker tests of fluid intelligence such as Raven's matrices tend to persist even when participants are given unlimited amounts of time to solve the items.

The prefrontal cortex plays a central role in cognitive control and working memory (Miller & Cohen, 2001). The behavioral evidence on particularly pronounced adult age differences in cognitive control is matched by evidence suggesting that the prefrontal cortex and the functionally connected basal ganglia show greater and earlier signs of decline than most other areas of the brain. In a comprehensive review of the neuroanatomical literature, Raz (2000) reported average cross-sectional reductions in brain weight and volume of about 2% per decade during adulthood, which were more pronounced for anterior parts of the brain. Figure 16.2 shows results from a recent longitudinal study that reinforced these findings (Raz et al., 2005). It depicts longitudinal declines in adjusted volumes of the lateral prefrontal and primary visual cortices, as well as of the hippocampus. Clearly, decrease in the prefrontal cortex is more pronounced than in the hippocampus and, especially, more pronounced than in the visual cortex, in which decrease is virtually absent.

*Binding*

Closely related to losses in cognitive control efficiency and working memory, growing evidence suggests that binding mechanisms are

---

FIGURE 16.2. Longitudinal changes in volumes of the lateral prefrontal cortex, primary visual cortex, and hippocampus as a function of baseline age. (Adapted from Raz, N., Lindenberger, U., Rodrigue, K. M., Kennedy, K. M., Head, D., Williamson, A., et al. (2005). Regional brain changes in aging healthy adults: General trends, individual differences, and modifiers. *Cerebral Cortex*, by permission of Oxford University Press.)

disproportionately impaired in old age. Binding serves to associate elements during perception, working memory, and memory (e.g., Murre,
Wolters, & Raffone, in press). Synchronous and co-active binding mechanisms structure perceptual input and are at the basis of working memory. Interactive binding allows highly specific interpretations to become
active during encoding and enables cue-driven selective activation of memory items during recall. Associative binding allows for long-term storage.
Murre et al. (in press) argued that a cascade of binding mechanisms may
be imagined at different levels, in which bound episodes, scenes, events,
and entities reflect the structure of experience.

Various binding mechanisms decline during adulthood and old age
(e.g., Chalfonte & Johnson, 1996; Craik, in press; Li, Naveh-Benjamin, &
Lindenberger, 2005). For example, when young and older adults study
pairs of words, age-based decrements are more pronounced for recognition
of pairs than for recognition of individual words (Naveh-Benjamin, 2000).
Similarly, adult age differences in episodic memory performance increase
as a function of between-list similarity, probably reflecting older adults'
disproportionate deficits in binding memory items with their encoding
contexts (Kliegl & Lindenberger, 1993). Importantly, age changes in binding extend to operations that link incoming information to preexisting
schemas and knowledge structures (e.g., Craik, 1983, in press).

According to Murre et al. (in press), human versatility in coping with
continuously changing environments and demands reflects the brain's
capacity to store coherent patterns of input and output in long-term memory, and its capacity to control the processing of input by selecting and
maintaining task-relevant information in working memory. Thus, the various time scales of binding continuously interact: what is transiently bound
in working memory partly determines what is temporarily and eventually
permanently bound in long-term memory, and what is permanently bound
biases transient binding in working memory. With advancing adult age,
this intricate interplay of binding processes operating at different time
scales and resolutions during perception, encoding, memory consolidation, and retrieval becomes ever more fragile and error prone. New bind-
ings are less easily established, and previous binding events are less easily
reinstantiated by appropriate cues.

The notions of cognitive control, working memory, and binding overlap
in content and scope. For instance, working memory serves a function in
cognitive control, and synchronous binding mechanisms probably form
the basis of working memory. Taken together, the presence of pronounced
age-related decrements in these functions and mechanisms underscore the
potential utility of IHET in old age. In a situation in which top-down control
and binding mechanisms deteriorate, IHET offers the opportunity to help
individuals organize their behavior through the external provision of task-
relevant cues and information.

## Sensory and Motor Functioning

### Vision

Vision declines with age (e.g., Baltes & Lindenberger, 1997; Lindenberger & Baltes, 1994; Marsiske et al., 1999; cf. Hawthorn, 2000, for a review focused on implications for assistive technology). During middle adulthood, many individuals start to notice problems with adjusting focus for near vision. Likewise, visual acuity, the ability to see details, begins to decline. Further- more, declines in contrast sensitivity and reduced sensitivity to color are noted. With advancing age, adults also become more susceptible to glare and adapt more slowly to shifts in brightness. Over and above continued decline in visual acuity, visual field reductions emerge during early old age (e.g., after age 60). Thus, relative to young adults, peripheral stimuli need to be presented for longer times, with greater contrast, or moved toward the center of the visual field to be detected. Age-related decline in vision extends beyond the peripheral stages of perception, for exam- ple, the ability to identify figures embedded into other figures and the capacity to recognize fragmented objects deteriorate as well (Salthouse & Prill, 1988).

### Hearing

Based on World Health Organization criteria, about 20% of individuals ages 40 to 50 years have some form of hearing impairment. This percentage increases to 75% (Marsiske et al., 1999; cf. Hawthorn, 2000) for adults ages 70 to 80 years. Tone detection is generally impaired, with sounds at high pitch being affected earlier and more strongly than others. Older adults often miss sounds that peak at frequencies over 2,500 Hz. Although this finding is well established, technical appliances often use high-pitch sounds to alert their users. For example, telephone bells and smoke alarms often have intensity peaks around 4,000 Hz. In many languages, conso- nants are high pitched, which results in parts of speech being unavailable to the older listener. Estimates suggest that most individuals older than 80 years of age miss about 25% of the words in a conversation, having to guess or infer their meaning (Feldman & Reger, 1967). Aggravated by con- comitant declines in selective attention, background noise is an ubiquitous problem for older individuals.

### Posture and Gait

The high prevalence of falls in the elderly population is the most dramatic symptom for the increasing difficulties of aging individuals to avoid mal- adaptive postural sway while standing or walking (Marsiske et al., 1999). The maintenance of postural stability while standing or walking requires the continuous coordination and integration of visual, proprioceptive, and vestibular sensory information in several areas of the brain, including the cerebellum, brainstem, basal ganglia, and sensorimotor cortex (Woollacott & Jensen, 1996), as well as the execution of balancing movements by the limb and trunk muscles, which receive impulses from the spinal cord and peripheral nerves. Normal aging appears to negatively affect all stages of the postural control system, resulting in less reliable sensory information, less accurate integration, and less effective postural control (Brown & Woollacott, 1998).

### Interactions Between Sensory/Sensorimotor and Cognitive Aging

A growing body of literature has explored the hypothesis that sensory and sensorimotor performance of older adults should be compromised more than that of younger adults when cognitive demands are increased relative to a baseline condition. Such a result would be consistent with the idea that sensory and sensorimotor systems are increasingly in need of control and supervision as we age. In general, the available evidence supports this view (for a summary, see Li & Lindenberger, 2002). In addition to revealing more peripheral changes in sensory and motor domains, age-comparative analyses have demonstrated that cognitive control processes contribute to age differences in maintaining a stable upright stance (Teasdale et al., 1992). Studies in the domain of walking report similar results (e.g., Li, Lindenberger, Freund, & Baltes, 2001; Lindenberger, Marsiske, & Baltes, 2000).

To examine the effects of cognitive load on sensory processing, Sekuler, Bennett, and Mamelak (2000) assessed adults ages 15 to 84 years on a measure of peripheral visual processing, the useful field-of-view test. The useful field of view was tested either alone or concurrently with a centrally presented letter identification task. Whereas performance on the central task showed little effect of divided attention, error rates on the useful field-of-view test increased disproportionately when the central letter identification task was performed concurrently. This finding suggests that older adults' diminished useful field of view primarily reflects age-associated decrements in cognitive (e.g., attentional) resources.

Other studies have examined interactions between cognitive load and sensorimotor performance rather than sensory performance. Again, the general expectation was that cognitive load would hinder balance or locomotion in older adults more than in young adults. Research from the fields of kinesiology and rehabilitation medicine adopted the dual task paradigm from cognitive psychology to examine how specific aspects of walking (Chen et al., 1996) or balance control (Brown, Shumway-Cook, & Woollacott, 1999) are compromised by adding a concurrent cognitive task. For example, Brown et al. (1999) tested balance recovery by measuring center of mass before and after perturbations on a moving platform. Under dual task conditions, participants engaged in a concurrent counting backward task. Whereas young and older adults demonstrated similar counting speeds before perturbations, older adults were differentially slowed in counting speed during the recovery period.

In the field of cognitive aging, a growing interest in the relationship between cognitive and sensorimotor aging has prompted sensorimotor dual task research that emphasizes cognitive issues such as reduced attentional capacity (Lindenberger et al., 2000). In contrast to earlier studies, this literature has also examined more complex cognitive tasks such as walking while talking (Kemper, Herman, & Lian, 2003) or walking while memorizing words using mental imagery (Li, Lindenberger et al., 2001; Lindenberger et al., 2000).

In the walking and memorizing study carried out by Lindenberger et al. (2000), young and older adults were trained to perform a memorizing task while walking quickly and accurately. On several measures of memory and walking, older adults showed a greater drop in performance under dual task conditions than young adults. Li, Lindenberger et al. (2001) replicated and extended these results by incorporating more extensive training of each task and individualized manipulations of task difficulty. Older adults were able to maintain high levels of walking performance but showed significant effects of divided attention in the cognitive domain. In addition to demonstrating a strong relationship between cognitive and sensorimotor ability, the findings also relate to the issue of task priority because older adults appeared to be protecting walking performance at the expense of cognitive performance.

Cross-sectional correlational evidence extending into very old age is also suggestive of connections among cognitive, sensory, and sensorimotor aging (see Li & Lindenberger, 2002, for review). Associations across domains appear to increase with age (Baltes & Lindenberger, 1997; Lindenberger & Baltes, 1994). To the extent that mean age trends and interindividual differences around mean age trends reflect similar mechanisms, these findings suggest that at least some of the mechanisms underlying age changes in sensory and intellectual abilities are functionally and perhaps causally related. Recent longitudinal analyses of sensory and intellectual changes in old and very old age lend more direct support to this interpretation (Ghisletta & Lindenberger, 2004).

CO-CONSTRUCTING ENVIRONMENTAL SUPPORT IN OLD AGE

## Strategies for Human Engineering Technologies in Old Age: A Preliminary Resumé

Two broad classes of change processes are occurring simultaneously in the course of later adulthood and old age, probably in part for related reasons. First, the functional integrity and automaticity of sensory and motor systems is deteriorating, with the important consequence that sensory and motor aspects of behavior are increasingly in need of cognitive resources. Second, cognitive resources such as executive control operations, working memory, and binding mechanisms also decline with advancing age. In combination, these two classes of changes result in increasing demands on decreasing resources, and constitute the quandary of behavioral aging (e.g., Lindenberger et al., 2000). A key purpose of assistive technology in old age is to attenuate the adverse effects of this quandary on development in later adulthood, old age, and very old age. Evidently, progress toward this goal requires the integrated consideration of sensory, motor, and cognitive changes. Specifically, designers of human engineering technology need to be aware of the reciprocal and increasingly tight interactions among motor, sensory, and cognitive aspects of behavior with advancing age.

Initially, we specified three criteria for evaluating the effectiveness of human engineering technologies in old age (Fig. 16.1). Net resource release (marginal resource gain) prescribes that the resource costs associated with the use of human engineering technologies must be lower than the resource release produced by other changes in task characteristics. Person specificity mandates that human engineering technologies ought to adapt themselves to the knowledge structure, habits, and preferences of the individual user. It also underscores that the criteria needed to judge the effectiveness of human engineering technologies should not be restricted to objective measures within the target domain but need to include subjective criteria, as well as the total life space of the individual. Third, the notion of proximal versus distal frames of evaluation helps remind us that a critical assessment of human engineering technologies requires attention to both short- and long-term effects.

With these three criteria in mind, and after having defined the quandary of behavioral aging in terms of increasing demands on decreasing cognitive resources, we are now in a position to formulate strategies for the effective implementation of human engineering technologies in old age. Emphasizing either the sensory/sensorimotor or the cognitive constituents of the quandary, two complementary and interconnected strategies come to mind. The first strategy approaches the quandary from the sensory/sensorimotor side: it attempts to free up cognitive resources by reducing the cognitive demands of sensory or sensorimotor aspects of performance. The second strategy attempts to provide individuals with adaptive external cuing structures that directly alleviate the effects of reduced cognitive control, working memory, and binding capabilities on cognitive performance. To be effective, the latter strategy needs to incorporate knowledge about the structure of the task, the task environment, and the person into an artifact that supports goal-oriented action in an adaptive and flexible manner.

The sensory/sensorimotor strategy, which aims at reducing cognitive resource demands by facilitating sensory and sensorimotor aspects of behavior, is generally less difficult to implement than the cognitive strategy. Therefore, past design recommendations have favored this approach (e.g., Hawthorn, 2000). Typical examples include the reduction of background noise, or glare-free, high-contrast, and well-lit workplaces. Assistive technology of this kind is often consistent with task-appropriate environments in general, and does not mandate any person- or task-specific adaptive capabilities. Other forms of human engineering technology targeting our sensory and bodily functions, such as glasses or canes, are person specific but, once adopted, require relatively little flexibility within persons (unless long-term changes in bodily functions need to be accommodated).

Note, however, that assistive technology aimed at our senses also can be quite complicated. For instance, many older adults experience the use of hearing aids with various nonautomated amplification modes for different auditory environments as cumbersome. In our terminology, the marginal resource gain of these aids is negative because the potential gain (i.e., less attention-demanding hearing) is outweighed by the resource demands associated with the operation of the aid. More recent hearing aids automatically adapt their amplification strategy to the auditory scene and are more likely to result in a net release of cognitive resources.

## Enhancing Cognition by Providing Sensorimotor Support: Sample Case of Spatial Navigation

Attempts at enhancing cognition by providing basic forms of sensory or sensorimotor support that require little cognitive investment can be surprisingly effective. A recent example from our own laboratory illustrates this claim. Lövdén, Schellenbach, Grossman-Hutter, Krüger, and Lindenberger (2005) projected virtual, maze-like museums in front of a treadmill. Young and older men were asked to perform a way-finding task in each of these virtual museums while walking on the treadmill. The task was to navigate from the entrance of the museum to its bistro twice in a row without error (i.e., without taking wrong turns at intersections). In the sensorimotor support condition, participants were allowed to hold on to a handrail. In the no support condition, participants were asked to walk freely on the treadmill. Young adults' navigation performance was not affected by walking support. However, in line with the predictions, older adults showed better navigation learning when holding on to the handrail (Fig. 16.3). It took older adults considerably less time and less walking distance to learn their way through a virtual museum when gait control was aided by handrail support.

These results indicate that supporting stability of gait in old age can have a beneficial effect on spatial navigation performance and demonstrate, once

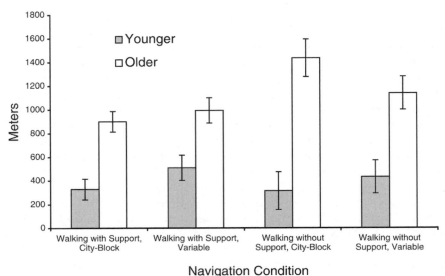

Navigation Condition

FIGURE 16.3. Adult age differences in way finding (spatial navigation) are modulated by sensorimotor demands. Bars display the mean distance covered to criterion
(± standard error) as a function of age group (young vs. older adults), topography
of the virtual environment (variable vs. city block), and walking demand (with or
without support). (Adapted from Lövdén et al., 2005.)

again, the close connection between sensorimotor and cognitive aspects of
behavior in old age. In older adults, support for walking not only improves
postural control, but also frees up attentional resources that can then be
invested into navigation-related processing. Based on this close coupling
between sensorimotor and spatial aspects of locomotion, we predict that
spatial navigation support should increase walking stability among older
adults.

## Intelligent Human Engineering Technology as Adaptive and Personalized Cuing Structures

We now turn to the second assistive strategy, which aims at reducing cognitive resource demands through genuinely cognitive rather than sensory
or sensorimotor intervention. Here, we highlight research on expertise
(Krampe & Baltes, 2003), particularly research on skilled memory performance (e.g., Ericsson, 1985; Mäntylä, 1986).

IHET sometimes invokes the impression that elderly users, and IHET
users in general, are expected to adapt their ways of thinking and acting
to technological requirements. We want to propagate the opposite position. In line with the SOC model of successful lifespan development, we

conceive of older individuals as experts in leading their lives and pursuing their personal goals, and as people who own a rich behavioral repertoire and body of knowledge in accordance with their preferences, habits, and specializations. As "experts about themselves," aging individuals possess exquisite knowledge, both implicit and explicit, about the ways in which their actions are organized in time and space. At the same time, due to decrements in cognitive control, working memory, and binding mechanisms, they experience difficulties in implementing their own knowledge in the course of action, especially under difficult conditions and in declarative manners – when they are tired, when distracting goals are present, when multiple goals are pursued simultaneously, when integration across different levels of generality or contexts is required, and when their sensory and sensorimotor systems are taxed and in need of additional attention. According to our interpretation, the key purpose of IHET in such instances is to act as an external cuing structure that keeps older individuals on the track of their own goal-directed actions.

## Mnemonic Devices and Expert Knowledge

Knowledge about the effectiveness of cuing structures in supporting goal-directed action is not new. In psychological research, cuing structures have been studied extensively in the context of exceptional memory performance (e.g., Ericsson, 1985). This work therefore provides a good point of departure for exploring the role of cuing structures in IHET design. Mnemonic devices always contain a series of overlearned cues, or "pegs." In one particular mnemonic strategy, the Method of Loci (Bower, 1970), these pegs or cues consist of an invariant sequence of well-known locations. When memorizing a series of items, one associates each to-be-learned item with one element of the cuing structure. In the Method of Loci, one forms interactive images or thoughts that connect each of the to-be-learned items with one of the locations from the landmark sequence. At retrieval, the cuing structure (e.g., the locations) prompts the retrieval of newly learned items in serial order. As this example illustrates, a mnemonic device acts as a cuing structure during encoding and recall by integrating new information to a knowledge base in long-term memory.

Of course, cues as organizers of action and thought are not confined to mnemonic devices. Rather, the invention of mnemonic devices, which dates back to Ancient Greece and Rome, speaks to the power of cuing structures as organizers of thought and action, which in turn reflects the ubiquitous interplay of various binding mechanisms in learning and memory (Murre et al., in press). Thus, any well-organized body of knowledge simultaneously constitutes a cuing structure (Ericsson, 1985). For this reason, individuals inevitably show superior memory performance in their domains of expertise, whether it is bridge (e.g.,

Charness, 1979) or an area of professional specialization (Krampe & Baltes, 2003).

## Determinants of Cue Effectiveness: Compatibility and Distinctiveness

What determines the effectiveness with which cues facilitate access to goal-relevant information? Two aspects, compatibility and distinctiveness, are central (e.g., Mäntylä, 1986). Cues are said to be compatible when they contain or point to attributes that are functionally related to the task-relevant memory episode or action tendency. For instance, a stop signal effectively cues the action of stopping one's car because it has been firmly associated with this action during prior learning episodes. Note that this cue is likely to be compatible for all individuals whose learning history includes driving experience. However, the compatibility of other cues may vary widely from person to person because the corresponding learning histories are less uniform. Conceptually, the notion of cue compatibility is consistent with the principle of encoding specificity (Tulving & Thompson, 1973).

In addition to being compatible, cues should also be distinctive; that is, they should activate the specific action required without co-activating a large number of competing actions. Again, cue distinctiveness may not be invariant across persons and contexts (e.g., Hunt & Einstein, 1981). Depending on context and knowledge, cues that are distinct for one person may be ambiguous for another. The recent proliferation of ring tones speaks to the speed with which distinctiveness of cues can be gained (and lost).

When individuals generate their own cues, either explicitly or as implicit residues of successful behavior and action, these cues are likely to match their knowledge, habits, and preferences. Such cues should therefore show superior compatibility and distinctiveness compared with cues generated by other people. Mäntylä (1986) tested this hypothesis by asking college students to define their own retrieval cues by generating properties or features for each to-be-remembered word presented at the encoding phase. In his second experiment, one group of participants generated, on 3 consecutive days, one property to a total of 504 words. A second study group generated three properties to each word. During unexpected recall tests administered repeatedly at different retention intervals (immediate, 1 day, 2 days, and 7 days), participants in these two groups were given both their own properties and those generated by someone else as retrieval cues. In addition, participants in a no study condition were not presented with the to-be-remembered items. Instead, they were given 504 single properties or sets of three properties that the participants in the study condition had previously generated and were asked to generate the study words based on these properties.

The outcome of this experiment was quite spectacular. Self-generated properties presented as cues resulted in exceptionally high levels of recall. For instance, after 7 days, participants recalled on average 327 of the 504 words when given three self-generated properties as cues; immediately after study, they recalled 459 of the 504 words. Also, self-generated retrieval cues were far more effective than those generated by someone else. The difference in immediate recall between self-generated properties and properties generated by others was more than 35% when three properties were presented, and nearly 50% when only one property was presented as a cue.

The data also showed that participants were more likely to forget self-generated retrieval cues than those generated by someone else. Mean recall performance decreased as a function of retention interval by approximately 30% when the participants were presented with their own properties. When someone else's properties were presented as cues, a smaller decrease in performance was observed. These data indicate that self-generated properties are powerful cues but that their effectiveness depends on contextual factors. Finally, when one or three properties were presented as cues without any preceding study phase, the mean proportions of correctly generated target words were 5% and 17% for one and three properties, respectively. Thus, the high degrees of recall obtained in the self-generated cue conditions clearly resulted from retention and not from any general cuing power of the properties per se.

In subsequent studies, it was found that self-generated cues also boost recall performance in older adults (Bäckman & Mäntylä, 1988); however, the effect was less pronounced than in young adults. The observed age difference probably reflects age-based increments in intraperson context variability, less idiosyncratic processing of older adults at encoding, and less efficient binding mechanisms (Bäckman & Mäntylä, 1988; cf. Craik, in press; Li & Lindenberger, 1999; Li et al., 2005). Still, when compared with other forms of cuing, self-generated cues are extraordinarily effective in late adulthood and old age.

To summarize, effective cues are compatible and distinct. Self-generated cues excel on both dimensions and permit exceptionally high levels of recall performance. By analogy, compatibility and distinctiveness of expertise-related cues (e.g., chessboard configurations) are predictably high in experts because their personalized knowledge system is consistent with the rules and history of the expertise domain (e.g., chess).

## Toward the Design of Person-Oriented Assistive Technology

Older adults have difficulties in accessing, and operating with, details, but they show less or no decline when processing general or gist-like information, probably due to impaired binding mechanisms. In addition, executive processes that help regulate and coordinate goal-directed action also function less reliably, and the ability to simultaneously process and retain events in working memory is reduced. In this situation, a key purpose of IHET is to provide an adaptive cuing structure. This structure orients the aging individual in time and space by providing prompts that connect properties in the environment to the action goals of the individual. Cues are helpful when they prompt the appropriate action at the right point in time. Relevant research on memory functioning indicates that compatibility and distinctiveness contribute to cue efficiency, and that self-generated cues excel in both regards.

In agreement with these considerations, IHET designers are asked to adapt the properties of assistive devices to aging individuals' needs and competencies (e.g., Charness & Schaie, 2003). To approximate this goal, some systems require explicit input and manual reprogramming from the user of the assistive device (e.g., LoPresti et al., 2004). This, in turn, greatly reduces the net cognitive resource release assisted with the operation of such devices, at least during the initial phases of IHET customizing.

However, adapting IHET to the individual user can also be accomplished in a different, technologically more demanding but psychologically more promising manner. Put simply, the assistive device or the instrumented environment itself, rather than the user, can be charged with the task of learning the user's habits and preferences. Work on several systems of this kind is in progress (e.g., Kautz et al., 2004). For example, a wide range of sensors, such as GPS and motion detectors, can monitor aspects of an individual's location and environment (e.g., ubiquitous computing; cf. Patterson et al., 2003). Based on pattern recognition and machine learning algorithms, IHET extracts the individual's patterns of behavior and deviations from the individual's normal daily routines. It assists the user by prompting for action and providing action-relevant information, and further customizes its cuing structure in response to the user's reactions.

We envision the functioning of IHET as a multilayered, ontogenetically adaptive process of individualization. Initially, when knowledge about the individual user is absent, IHET will operate on the basis of a default model (e.g., the "average user"). Explicit offline information about the user's cognitive, sensory, and sensorimotor abilities, as well as his or her preferences and habits, may be entered to modify these default parameters. More important, however, is an extended period of "acculturation" that permits IHET to learn the regularities and contingencies that permeate the life of the individual user.

## Individualized IHET: An Imaginary Case Study

To render our vision of individualized IHET more concrete, we end this chapter with an illustrative and admittedly fictitious case study. Ms. Miller, a 90-year-old widow, lives in her own apartment in a small town in Europe.

Her core family consists of two daughters and their families. Ms. Miller is mentally fit and physically healthy, and has no intention of giving up her apartment; being able to live in her own home matters much to her. On the occasion of her ninetieth birthday, she receives a handheld electronic device from one of her daughters. At first sight, the device looks like a mobile phone and, in fact, can be used as such. Ms. Miller has been using mobile phones for several years, and she immediately starts using the handheld for this purpose, taking it with her on all errands.

In addition to serving as a mobile phone, the new handheld also has other capabilities: it is equipped with GPS, a large and well-lit short message service display, a piezoelectric movement sensor, an infrared receiver/transmitter, and, most important, with machine learning capabilities. At home, it is electronically connected to the stationary telephone, and registers all incoming and outgoing calls.

Initially, Ms. Miller does not make active use of these additional functions; for her, the device is just a new and somewhat clumsy mobile phone. However, most of these additional functions are operating from the very first day. Due to its machine learning capabilities, the handheld is extracting regularities in Ms. Miller's life. For instance, it will register (1) that Ms. Miller calls the younger of her daughters about every other day in the afternoon; (2) that she calls the other daughter each day early in the morning; (3) that she walks to the cemetery once a week to visit the grave of her late husband; (4) that she goes to the hairdresser every Saturday morning; (5) that she goes to church every Sunday morning; (6) that she receives a phone call from one of her two granddaughters living in another European country every other month; and (7) that she moves the device before 9 AM every day.

With advancing age, Ms. Miller's cognitive abilities eventually begin to decline. At age 94, she tends to forget planned actions and is more easily distracted than before. In this situation, the handheld slowly begins to assume its role as a personalized cuing device that assists Ms. Miller with her everyday activities. At first, Ms. Miller is somewhat annoyed by the messages from the handheld that remind her of things she may want to do by making remarks such as "Good time to call your daughter Anna!" or "What about the hairdresser?" However, she eventually gets used to these kinds of prompts. She also notices that her relatives are impressed by her persisting independence and competence. The device continues to take notice of enduring changes in daily routines and adapts to them. For instance, the visit to the cemetery is now taking place every other week.

Ms. Miller has also begun to make use of the shopping aid component of the device. Before leaving her apartment for shopping, she sits down at the kitchen table, and registers her shopping items on the handheld with a voice key. She then goes to the shopping mall equipped with infrared sensors matching those of the handheld device. The sensors make contact with Ms. Miller's handheld, register her shopping list, and suggest a shopping route, navigating Ms. Miller through the mall from shop to shop by giving directions on the display of her handheld. When Ms. Miller has reached a shop, the handheld prompts her with the shopping items that are available at this location. If an item is sold out, the handheld redirects Ms. Miller to another store in the mall that may also carry that item and reconfigures the shopping route accordingly. In this manner, the handheld keeps track of the shopping list and navigates Ms. Miller through the mall until all her shopping needs are satisfied.

One morning, Ms. Miller feels sick and is not able to get out of bed. At 9:00 AM, the piezoelectric sensor notes that the handheld has not yet been moved and starts ringing. Ms. Miller cannot respond because the handheld is too far away. At 9:20 AM, the handheld automatically calls the hospital, and an ambulance arrives in time to provide medical treatment.[1]

CONCLUSION AND OUTLOOK

In this chapter, we critically examined human engineering technologies from the perspective of lifespan theory and biocultural co-constructivism. Our aim was neither to review the latest technological developments nor to provide descriptions of relevant hardware and software (but see Kautz et al., 2004; LoPresti et al., 2004; Patterson et al., 2003). Instead, we wanted to propose genuinely psychological guidelines that provide a conceptual foundation for the development of assisted technology in old age. In our judgment, such a psychological foundation is badly needed. Perhaps the most palpable desiderata of IHET design reflect insufficient attention to psychological laws and findings rather than technological shortcomings. For example, based on the theoretical framework presented in this chapter, we predict that individuals suffering from dementia will profit most if IHET is introduced into their lives prior to, rather than after, the onset of the disease.

Our evaluation of human engineering technology in old age was based on lifespan theory (Baltes et al., 2006); findings about age-associated decrements in sensory, motor, and cognitive functions; and general laws of learning, memory, and expert performance. Informed by the SOC model of successful lifespan development, we established three criteria for IHET design: net resource release, person specificity, and proximal versus distal frames of evaluation (Fig. 16.1). We argued that IHET design needs to consider determinants of cue effectiveness, the increasing need of sensory

---

[1] All technological components described in this imaginary case study, including the shopping assistant (Krüger et al., 2004), are available. However, to the best of our knowledge, a device of this kind has not yet been developed.

and sensorimotor functions for cognitive control, and the idiosyncratic habits and preferences of aging individuals.

In future research on IHET, the issue of proximal versus distal evaluation merits special attention. The initial operation of a new assistive device may impose additional resource demands, thereby violating the criterion of net resource release. After a few weeks, most elements of skill involved in using the device may have become automatized, and the resource balance may eventually become positive. However, after a few years, chronic net resource release may induce reactive resource depletion because certain skills and abilities that would have been practiced and trained without the device have not been used anymore. In short, too much technological assistance may be harmful. Finding the right balance between "environmental support" and "self-initiated processing" (Craik, 1983, in press) to arrive at support that adaptively avoids undershooting the maximum manageable difficulty will become a central element for the design and evaluation of IHET. For instance, spatial navigation aids may have positive effects on individuals' way-finding success. However, to the extent that the use of such aids installs route learning strategies and disuse of cognitive processes involved in spatial integration, long-term and transfer effects may be negative. In light of mind-tickling findings relating increased size of the brain structures (posterior hippocampus) functionally involved in spatial integration to exposure to environments with high demands on navigational skill (London taxi drivers; Maguire et al., 2000), one might predict that disuse induced by technological interventions could negatively affect the human brain. In other words, just as the specific needs of the growing population of aging individuals impose demands on society in general, and engineers and industry in particular, to construct supportive environments, these environments may eventually reshape the architecture of the aging brain.

ACKNOWLEDGMENTS

The authors want to thank Alexandra M. Freund, Antonio Krüger, Karen Z. H. Li, Baska Lindenberger, Michael Schellenbach, and Hubert Zimmer for helpful discussions.

### References

Bäckman, L., & Mäntylä, T. (1988). Effectiveness of self-generated cues in younger and older adults: The role of retention interval. *International Journal of Aging and Human Development, 26,* 241–248.

Baltes, P. B., & Baltes, M. M. (1990). Psychological perspectives on successful aging: The model of selective optimization with compensation. In P. B. Baltes & M. M. Baltes (Eds.), *Succcessful aging: Perspectives from the behavioral sciences* (pp. 1–34). New York: Cambridge University Press.

372                                  *Ulman Lindenberger and Martin Lövdén*

Baltes, P. B., & Lindenberger, U. (1997). Emergence of a powerful connection between sensory and cognitive functions across the adult life span: A new window to the study of cognitive aging? *Psychology and Aging, 12,* 12–21.

Baltes, P. B., Lindenberger, U., & Staudinger, U. M. (2006). Lifespan theory in developmental psychology. In R. M. Lerner (Ed.), *Theoretical models of human development: Vol. 1. Handbook of child psychology* (6th ed., pp. 569–664). New York: Wiley.

Baltes, P. B., & Mayer, K. U. (Eds.). (1999). *The Berlin Aging Study: Aging from 70 to 100.* New York: Cambridge University Press.

Bower, G. H. (1970). Analysis of a mnemonic device. *American Scientist, 58,* 496–510.

Brown, L. A., Shumway-Cook, A., & Woollacott, M. H. (1999). Attentional demands and postural recovery: The effects of aging. *Journal of Gerontology: Medical Sciences, 54,* 165–171.

Brown, L. A., & Woollacott, M. H. (1998). The effects of aging on the control of posture and locomotion in healthy older adults: An emphasis on cognition. *Psychologische Beiträge, 40,* 27–43.

Chalfonte, B. L., & Johnson, M. K. (1996). Feature memory and binding in young and old adults. *Memory and Cognition, 24,* 403–416.

Charness, N. (1979). Components of skill in bridge. *Canadian Journal of Psychology, 33,* 1–16.

Charness, N., & Schaie, K. W. (Eds.). (2003). *Impact of technology on successful aging.* New York: Springer.

Chen, H- C., Schultz, A. B., Ashton-Miller, J. A., Giordani, B., Alexander, N. B., & Guire, K. E. (1996). Stepping over obstacles: Dividing attention impairs performance of old more than young adults. *Journals of Gerontology: Medical Sciences, 51,* M116–M122.

Craik, F. I. M. (1983). On the transfer of information from temporary to permanent memory. *Philosophical Transactions of the Royal Society of London, B302,* 341–359.

Craik, F. I. M. (in press). Remembering items and their contexts: Effects of aging and divided attention. In H. D. Zimmer, A. Mecklinger, & U. Lindenberger (Eds.), *Binding in human memory: A neurocognitive perspective.* Oxford, UK: Oxford University Press.

Dixon, R. A., & Bäckman, L. (Eds.). (1995). *Compensating for psychological deficits and declines: Managing losses and promoting gains.* Mahwah, NJ: Erlbaum.

Ericsson, K. A. (1985). Memory skill. *Canadian Journal of Psychology, 39,* 188–231.

Feldman, R. M., & Reger, S. N. (1967). Relations among hearing, reaction time, and age. *Journal of Speech and Hearing Research, 10,* 479–495.

Freund, A. M., & Baltes, P. B. (2000). The orchestration of selection, optimization, and compensation: An action-theoretical conceptualization of a theory of developmental regulation. In W. J. Perrig & A. Grob (Eds.), *Control of human behavior, mental processes, and consciousness* (pp. 35–58). Mahwah, NJ: Erlbaum.

Ghisletta, P., & Lindenberger, U. (2005). *Exploring structural dynamics within and between sensory and intellectual functioning in old and very old age: Longitudinal evidence from the Berlin Aging Study. Intelligence, 33,* 555–587.

Hawthorn, D. (2000). Possible implications of aging for interface designers. *Interacting with Computers, 12,* 507–528.

Hunt, R. R., & Einstein, G. O. (1981). Relational and item-specific information in memory. *Journal of Verbal Learning and Verbal Behavior, 20,* 497–514.

Just, M. A., Carpenter, P. A., & Keller, T. A. (1996). The capacity theory of comprehension: New frontiers of evidence and arguments. *Psychological Review, 103*, 773–780.

Kautz, H., Etzioni, O., Fox, D., & Weld, D. (2004). *Foundations of assisted cognition systems* (Technical Report CSE-02-AC-01). Seattle: Department of Computer Science and Engineering, University of Washington.

Kemper, S., Herman, R. E., & Lian, C. H. T. (2003). The costs of doing two things at once for young and older adults: Talking while walking, finger tapping, and ignoring noise or speech. *Psychology and Aging, 18*, 181–192.

Kliegl, R., & Lindenberger, U. (1993). Modeling intrusions and correct recall in episodic memory: Adult age differences in encoding of list context. *Journal of Experimental Psychology: Learning, Memory, and Cognition, 19*, 617–637.

Krampe, R. T., & Baltes, P. B. (2003). Intelligence as adaptive resource development and resource allocation: A new look through the lenses of SOC and expertise. In R. J. Sternberg & E. L. Grigorenko (Eds.), *Perspectives on the psychology of abilities, competencies, and expertise* (pp. 31–69). New York: Cambridge University Press.

Kray, J., & Lindenberger, U. (2000). Adult age differences in task switching. *Psychology and Aging, 15*, 126–147.

Krüger, A., Butz, A., Müller, C., Stahl, C., Wasinger, R., Steinberg, K.-E., & Dirschl, A. (2004). The connected user interface: Realizing a personal situated navigation service. In N. Jardim Nunes & C. Rich (Eds.), *Proceedings of the International Conference on Intelligent User Interfaces (IUI 2004)* (pp.161–168). New York: ACM Press.

Li, K. Z. H., & Lindenberger, U. (2002). Relations between aging sensory/sensorimotor and cognitive functions. *Neuroscience and Biobehavioral Reviews, 26*, 777–783.

Li, K. Z. H., Lindenberger, U., Freund, A. M., & Baltes, P. B. (2001). Walking while memorizing: Age-related differences in compensatory behavior. *Psychological Science, 12*, 230–237.

Li, S.-C. (2003). Biocultural orchestration of developmental plasticity across levels: The interplay of biology and culture in shaping the mind and behavior across the life span. *Psychological Bulletin, 129*, 171–194.

Li, S.-C., Aggen, S., Nesselroade, J. R., & Baltes, P. B. (2001). Short-term fluctuations in elderly people's sensorimotor functioning predict text and spatial memory performance. *Gerontology, 47*, 100–116.

Li, S.-C., & Lindenberger, U. (1999). Cross-level unification: A computational exploration of the link between deterioration of neurotransmitter systems and dedifferentiation of cognitive abilities in old age. In L.-G. Nilsson & H. J. Markowitsch (Eds.), *Cognitive neuroscience of memory* (pp. 103–146). Seattle: Hogrefe & Huber.

Li, S.-C., Naveh-Benjamin, M., & Lindenberger, U. (2005). Aging neuromodulation impairs associative binding: A neurocomputational account. *Psychological Science, 16*, 445–450.

Lindenberger, U., & Baltes, P. B. (1994). Sensory functioning and intelligence in old age: A strong connection. *Psychology and Aging, 9*, 339–355.

Lindenberger, U., & Baltes, P. B. (1997). Intellectual functioning in old and very old age: Cross-sectional results from the Berlin Aging Study. *Psychology and Aging, 12*, 410–432.

Lindenberger, U., Marsiske, M., & Baltes, P. B. (2000). Memorizing while walking: Increase in dual-task costs from young adulthood to old age. *Psychology and Aging, 15*, 417–436.

LoPresti, E. F., Mihailidis, A., & Kirsch, N. (2004). Assistive technology for cognitive rehabilitation: State of the art. *Neuropsychological Rehabilitation, 14*, 5–39.

Lövdén, M., & Lindenberger, U. (2005). Development of intellectual abilities in old age: From age gradients to individuals. In O. Wilhelm & R. W. Engle (Eds.), *Handbook of Understanding* (pp. 203–221). Thousand Oaks, CA: Sage.

Lövdén, M., Schellenbach, M., Grossman-Hutter, B., Krüger, A., & Lindenberger, U. (2005). Environmental topography and postural control demands shape aging-associated decrements in spatial navigation performance. *Psychology and Aging, 20*(4), 683–694.

Maguire, E. A., Gadian, D. G., Johnsrude, I. S., Good, C. D., Ashburner, J., Frackowiak, R. S. J., & Frith, C. D. (2000). Navigation-related structural change in the hippocampi of taxi drivers. *Proceedings of the National Academy of Sciences (USA), 97*, 4398–4403.

Mäntylä, T. (1986). Optimizing cue effectiveness: Recall of 500 and 600 incidentally learned words. *Journal of Experimental Psychology: Learning, Memory, and Cognition, 12*, 66–71.

Marsiske, M., Delius, J., Maas, I., Lindenberger, U., Scherer, H., & Tesch-Römer, C. (1999). Sensory systems in old age. In P. B. Baltes & K. U. Mayer (Eds.), *The Berlin Aging Study: Aging from 70 to 100* (pp. 360–383). New York: Cambridge University Press.

Mayr, U., Kliegl, R., & Krampe, R. T. (1996). Sequential and coordinative processing dynamics in figural transformations across the life span. *Cognition, 59*, 61–90.

Miller, E. K., & Cohen, J. D. (2001). An integrative theory of prefontal cortex function. *Annual Review of Neuroscience, 24*, 167–202.

Murre, J. M. J., Wolters, G., & Raffone, A. (in press). Binding in working memory and long-term memory: Towards an integrated model. In H. D. Zimmer, A. Mecklinger, & U. Lindenberger (Eds.), *Binding in human memory: A neurocognitive perspective.* Oxford, UK: Oxford University Press.

Naveh-Benjamin, M. (2000). Adult age differences in memory performance: Tests of an associative deficit hypothesis. *Journal of Experimental Psychology: Learning, Memory, and Cognition, 26*, 1170–1187.

Patterson, P., Liao, L., Fox, D., & Kautz, H. (2003). Inferring high level behavior from low level sensors. In A. K. Dey, A. Schmidt, & J. F. McCarthy (Eds.), *Proceedings of the Fifth Annual Conference on Ubiquitous Computing (UbiComp 2003)* (pp. 73–89). Berlin: Springer-Verlag.

Prinz, W. (2004). Kritik des freien Willens: Bemerkungen über eine soziale Institution [Critique of free will: Some remarks on a social institution]. *Psychologische Rundschau, 55*, 198–206.

Raz, N. (2000). Aging of the brain and its impact on cognitive performance: Integration of structural and functional findings. In F. I. M. Craik & T. A. Salthouse (Eds.), *The handbook of aging and cognition* (2nd ed., pp. 1–90). Mahwah, NJ: Erlbaum.

Raz, N., Lindenberger, U., Rodrigue, K. M., Kennedy, K. M., Head, D., Williamson, A., et al. (2005). Regional brain changes in aging healthy adults: General trends, individual differences, and modifiers. *Cerebral Cortex.*

Salthouse, T. A., & Meinz, E. J. (1995). Aging, inhibition, working memory, and speed. *Journals of Gerontology: Psychological Sciences, 50B*, P297–P306.

Salthouse, T. A., & Prill, K. A. (1988). Effects of aging on perceptual closure. *American Journal of Psychology, 101*, 217–238.

Sekuler, A. B., Bennett, P. J., & Mamelak, M. (2000). Effects of aging on the useful field of view. *Experimental Aging Research, 26*, 103–120.

Teasdale, N., Bard, C., Dadouchi, F., Fleury, M., Larue, J., & Stelmach, G. E. (1992). Posture and elderly persons: Evidence for deficits in the central integrative mechanisms. In G. E. Stelmach & J. Requin (Eds.), *Tutorials in motor behavior II* (pp. 917–931). Amsterdam: North-Holland.

Tulving, E., & Thompson, D. M. (1973). Encoding specificity and retrieval processes in episodic memory. *Psychological Review, 80*, 352–373.

Woollacott, M. H., & Jensen, J. L. (1996). Posture and locomotion. In H. Heuer & S. W. Keele (Eds.), *Handbook of perception and action: Vol. 2. Motor skills* (pp. 333–403). London: Academic Press.

# PART SEVEN

# EPILOGUE

# 17

# Letters on Nature and Nurture

## Onur Güntürkün

ABSTRACT

*Humans and most other animals have a dual origin. One of these origins is defined by the genetic background that assembles brains, thereby implanting prewired expectations about the sensory and causal regularities of the world in which we are born. The second origin is the organized system of experiences that provides a plethora of feedback and instructions that slowly shape the brain into its final status. In humans, these experiences start especially early to modify the newborn brain and provide an unusually variable tapestry. For decades, scientists have tried to disentangle the impact of nature and nurture, and have proposed mental territories that are mostly governed by one or the other. Here, I argue that genetic predispositions and environmentally dependent learning processes interact continuously at every neural and mental entity, from cortical development to social customs. Not a single territory of our mind is outside the scope of this interaction.*

## PRELUDE

Scientific inquiries into the interaction of biology and culture usually study a certain developmental span, an important event, or a neural, affective, or cognitive system to set a stage on which the details of biocultural co-constructivism can be outlined. This approach necessarily takes a narrow focus but provides great depth and insight into the interactive mechanisms. This book provides many outstanding examples of this kind of approach. As fruitful as this strategy is, there is also the need for a further perspective showing that biology and culture not only interact at the selected focus area, but also at every single entity that constitutes the human mind. It is difficult to couch such a broad picture without being too long or too shallow. I have therefore tried to express this view by a letter exchange between

379

two fictive scientists, Hakan and Maxim, who attended the meeting on biocultural co-constructivism at Dölln-Schorfheide and who continue the debate they began there on the terrace. Hakan is leaning more toward the cultural side, whereas Maxim feels close to biology-driven arguments. Via their letter exchange, they explore the vast territory from genes to culture that is constantly co-constructed by nature and nurture.

THE DIALOGUE

Melun, August 22, 2003
Dear Maxim,
It was a great pleasure to meet you at the conference. After getting home, I had a long discussion with my wife, Meltem, about some of your arguments. She was impressed by your biology-prone reasoning and has now tried to convince me that the basic wiring programs of the brain proceed with little environmental feedback. After having Aylin (she is now 2 months old), all questions about the forces that shape the emergence of personality in our little daughter are obviously hotly debated between Meltem and me.

Although I must admit that you provided strong data on genetic determinism during the conference, I'm still reluctant to accept that they are able to explain most of the even basic details that make us human. For example, in passing, you said: "You aren't taught to see! You develop vision by yourself." I don't believe that, and I'm pretty confident that I have excellent arguments on my side. I think that the genetic program is far too limited to have a chance to determine the fate of the brain. It merely defines a few rules. The details of wiring depend on subsequent sensory input that shapes the nervous system into its adult form.

Let's start the most simple way – by counting genes in the human genome. Latest estimates from the Human Genome Project suggest that there might be 24,500 or even fewer protein-coding genes. This number is constantly dwindling from previous estimates of around 100,000. Yes, we meanwhile know that some genes code for more than one protein, but we also know that more than 3,000 genes of our limited gene number are probably pseudogenes, ones that code for nothing due to some aberration of their DNA. This lower estimate came as a shock to many scientists because counting genes was viewed as a way of quantifying genetic complexity. With far less than 30,000, the human gene count would be only a little bit greater than that of the simple roundworm *Caenorhabditis elegans*, which has about 20,000 genes. By the same token, humans appear only four times as complex as the bacterium *Pseudomonas aeruginosa* (Claverie, 2001). So, our gene content does not appear to be directly related to our intuitive perception of organismal complexity. But, the situation is even worse: the genome projects of animals such as dogs, cows, and chickens, and others such as puffer fish, show a large overlap of sequences, with humans and chimpanzees sharing 98.8% of their DNA sequences (Pääbo, 2003). So, the genetic degrees of freedom to construct those aspects that make us specifically human are getting smaller and smaller (Chapter 4).

Now, let us as an extreme argument assume that all human genes exclusively code for our brain – an assumption that is of course vastly exaggerated (estimates assume about half of our genome to be coding for the brain). The human neocortex hosts about $21 \times 10^9$ neurons (Pakkenberg & Gundersen, 1997). This is easily surpassed by the number of granular cells in our cerebellum, $11 \times 10^{10}$ (Andersen, Gundersen, & Pakkenberg, 2003). If we only concentrate on neocortical neurons and use rather conservative estimates of the number of synapses per cell, we may assume that we have more than $20 \times 10^{13}$ synapses in our cortex (Schüz & Palm, 1989). Thus, the gene-to-synapse relation is about 1:1,000,000,000 – and that's only for neocortex.

In school, I learned the saying of Pythagoras that numbers set a limit to the limitless and that they constitute the true nature of things. According to this logic, these simple calculations show that it is beyond the possibilities of the genome to control the detailed wirings of our brain. The only thing our genome can do is to define some rules and then lean back to let life mold the brain into its final shape. Therefore, my friend, we have to learn to see. We are blind without nurture, and we go on shaping our brain through each of our mental abilities, from mere perceiving to reading and thinking (Chapter 8). I will try to convince you by bravely stepping into your own turf: I now talk about the ontogeny of seeing.

As you know, preventing mammals from seeing after birth for several months renders them largely blind. Our visual system does not have the capacity to wire itself in a functional way without meaningful (patterned) input (Chapter 3). Just a few hours of seeing can, however, outweigh or protect against much longer periods of deprivation and permits the development of normal visual acuity in both eyes (Mitchell, Kind, Sengpiel, & Murphy, 2003). This seems to be, by the way, different for insects. Praying mantis that use stereoscopic vision to strike their prey do not need binocular experience to integrate the input of both eyes (Mathis, Eschbach, & Rossel, 1992). Thus, the complexity of an organism (I simply assume that we are more complex than the praying mantis; as you know, I'm hopelessly anthropocentric) determines the degree to which instructions from outside the organism are needed to wire the brain. Providing kittens with a striped environment of only one orientation tunes their visual system and subsequently their behavioral repertoire to this orientation only (Blakemore & Cooper, 1970). This need for an outside "instructor" is so important that, in mammals, the outside world is imported to prenatal life by synchronous bursts of retinal activity, creating virtual patterns to instruct the developing embryonic visual system (Meister, Wong, Baylor, & Shatz, 1991). This whole field has meanwhile moved to experiments where sensory systems are rewired such that they synapse in the territory of other modalities. It can be shown that they are functional in their new destiny; thus, animals start seeing with their auditory system (Chapter 5). The reverse – superior hearing and language processing within areas outside the classic auditory system – can be shown in congenitally blind subjects (Röder et al., 1999; Chapter 6).

So, what do these stories mean? My conclusion is that during biological evolution, the project to construct a human (or any other complex organism) was faced with the serious bottleneck of a genetic code that was too scarce to be useful for a true genetic determinism of the brain. Therefore, genetic codes had to be used to determine a rather small set of rules that subsequently guide the ontogeny of the nervous system by exploiting the regularities of the sensory input. As a result, environmental instructions creep into our brains very early and at every neural level to shape its structure. By this mechanism, we are adapted to the very specific world in which we live and we are tuned to the regularities that we experience. Yes, we have to learn to see. Our brains are instructed and wired by the world around us. It was important for me to clarify this matter. I'd be delighted to hear what you think.

Hakan

Odense, September 11, 2003
Dear Hakan,
Yes, you are right that experience-dependent factors play an important role in shaping the juvenile brain. You are also probably right that I underestimate some of their impact. But I guess that you also underestimate the power of nature. As you will see, genetic factors are far more important than you assume.

First, you cited Blakemore and Cooper (1970) to underline your point that environmental information is used by the juvenile visual system to tune its orientation properties. This classic study has been meanwhile repeated with modern techniques and shows some very interesting additional facts (Sengpiel, Stawinski, & Bonhoeffer, 1999). If the visual cortex of kittens reared in a striped environment is analyzed using optical imaging, it is indeed evident that twice as much surface area is devoted to the experienced orientation as compared with the orthogonal one. However, the analysis also shows the existence of many neurons responding to orientations that were never seen by the kitten. Cortical orientation maps are therefore remarkably rigid in the sense that orientations that were never experienced by the animal occupy a relatively large portion of the cortical territory. In addition, other studies show that orientation-selective neurons are present within the visual cortex of optically deprived young kittens at the time of natural eye opening. These animals evinced quite normal maps of orientation preference. In light of this evidence, it seems unlikely that the role of experience is to give a *tabula rasa* its final shape. Instead, visual experience seems to have an instructive role, whereby only those neurons whose initial (and thus genetically prewired) response range include the specific orientation seen after eye opening shift their preferences toward this experienced orientation. Obviously, there is a considerable intrinsic component in determining the layout of orientation preference maps. Environmental factors can modify these properties to some extent, but they do not create them.

This conclusion fits perfectly into the frame of newer studies that analyze the properties of the brain before experience begins. For instance, ocular dominance columns of the visual cortex are present in ferrets before visual experience begins and do not even require the presence of eyes for their initial establishment (Crowley & Katz, 1999). Although there is no dispute that activity-dependent processes are able to shape the system (this activity can be endogenous and therefore not necessarily externally driven) and that these processes are often necessary to stabilize a certain pattern, your assumption that "environmental instructions creep into our brain very early and at every neural level to shape its structure" is certainly misleading: the system already starts with a quite sophisticated initial shape.

In addition, our new understanding of plasticity in the brains of adult individuals shows that the principles of ontogenetic neural alterations according to environmental stimuli proceed in a similar way (Chapter 14). Even neurogenesis, once believed to be a hallmark of very young brains, is now known to also characterize the adult brain and possibly to continue until the end of life (Chapter 4).

There is also good evidence that the initial parcellation of cortex is regulated by molecular determinants that are independent of external influences and thus intrinsic to the developing cortex. Even factors that regulate structural borders and later cortical connectivity seem to be determined at an embryonic time point before the arrival of thalamic axons. Thus, genes that control the initial arealization of the neocortex also affect the whole connectivity of the system (Sur & Leamey, 2001).

Now, I come back to your argument that gene number is simply insufficient to code for wiring details. This view completely underestimates the power exerted by local molecular factors, which are able to pattern the brain. It is likely that you don't need too much genetic determinism to set up sufficient molecular rules to let the developing neurons find their own way. For example, cadherins (a group of cell adhesion molecules) provide a local code that regulates the binding of functional neural structures distributed across the embryonic modules. These modules represent histogenetic fields in which neurons are born and aggregate in distinct cell groups. Different subsets of these aggregates become selectively connected by nerve fiber tracts and, finally, by synapses, thus forming the neural circuits of the functional systems in the central nervous system (CNS). Cadherin-mediated adhesive specificity may thus provide a molecular code for early embryonic CNS regionalization, from major embryonic subdivisions down to the level of individual synapses (Redies, 2000).

There is one more point where innateness strikes back, and that's with regard to time. I argue that the orchestration of the time-dependent influence of experience is under genetic control. To make this point clear, I briefly remind you of the mechanisms that guide imprinting. When young chicks are exposed to a visually conspicuous object, they approach it, learn its characteristics, and form a social attachment to it. In natural conditions, the object is usually the hen, but it need not to be; a wide range of objects will do, although those that resemble a hen are more effective than others. This latter point shows that a predisposition already exists but can be overridden by experience. Imprinting in chicks narrows the range of objects the animal will approach. Given a choice between a stimulus to which it was exposed, say, a rotating red box, and a different object like a rotating blue cylinder, a chick will prefer the training stimulus and will actively avoid the blue cylinder, which it has not previously seen. The sensitive period is normally rather short but can be extended if no object for imprinting occurs. Thus, the young organism is experience expectant, but its genes define a sharp time window for experience to occur. Even more interesting is that an imprinting episode early in life is able to influence sexual preferences during adolescence (Bischof, 1983). You might argue that imprinting is a mechanism that occurs only in a few species and has no relation to humans. I see it differently. Imprinting is just the extreme form of a genetically determined time window for certain experiences. All vocal learners (including us) operate with sensitive periods (White, 2001). I will send you copies of a report by Singh (1964), who described the inability of two young girls found in the Indian jungle to learn to speak because they had spent their early years with a pack of wolves. Slowly, after years, they learned to scream or to moan when trying to focus the attention of the nurses to some problems they recognized, but all this was signal-based communication – not speech. The time window had been closed, and the young women were trapped without language (Chapter 7).

In summary, I argue that genetic factors structure most details of the brain before experience occurs. Environmental input is subsequently only able to modify the innate pattern to some extent and within limits. Genes even impose system-specific time limits for experience to be incorporated. Thus, culture comes too late to shape us to an important extent, and the time frames of cultural influence are under innate control.

Best regards,
Maxim

Melun, September 21, 2003

Dear Maxim,

I must admit that I wasn't aware how prestructured our brain is before external input begins to arrive. But don't you think that some of these studies nevertheless overestimate the impact of innateness? I give you an example.

Humans and a few other animals display a left–right difference in motor control that we call handedness in primates and "pawedness" or "footedness" in the case of cats, dogs, mice, parrots, and so on. The decisive contribution of genetics in handedness has been supported by a large number of studies in families of twins and adopted individuals (Corballis, 1997). Presently, there are several genetic models on the market that show interesting associations between handedness and, for example, the direction of scalp hair-whorl (Klar, 2003). I guess no environmentalist dares to argue that the direction of hair-whorl can be influenced by culture. Nonetheless, it is possible that the final determinant of several aspects of behavior derive from the environment. These arguments come from studies with birds, where the factors controlling the ontogenetic events that resulted in the establishment of cerebral asymmetries of the visual system could be clarified.

Birds such as chickens and pigeons show a left hemispheric superiority in processing detailed features of visual objects. As a result of this cerebral asymmetry, they display a right-eye superiority in pattern discrimination tasks (Güntürkün, 2002). The onset of this lateralization starts before hatching. Avian embryos keep their head turned so the right eye is exposed to light, which is shining through the translucent shell, while the left eye is occluded by the body. Because brooding parents regularly turn their eggs and often leave their nests for short time periods, the embryo's right eye has a high probability of being stimulated by light before hatching. This, indeed, is the trigger for the development of visual lateralization because dark incubation of chicken and pigeon eggs prevents the establishment of visual lateralization in visual discriminations, and merely 2 hours of light exposure with 400 lux within the last days before hatching suffice to establish visual lateralization in dark-incubated chicken eggs (Rogers, 1982). It is even possible to reverse the direction of the asymmetry by occluding the right eye and exposing the left to light (Rogers, 1996).

Now, why do avian embryos turn their head to the right? All vertebrates, including humans, exhibit a left–right (LR) asymmetry in the position of their visceral organs, as in the case of the heart which invariantly loops to the right side. Experiments with chickens have revealed the genetic mechanisms that determine the embryological events leading to this asymmetry (Ramsdell & Yost, 1998). During normal embryonic development, chains of interdependent genetic factors result in a rightward looping of the heart, a counterclockwise looping of the gut, and finally in a slight torsion of the embryo with the forehead pointing to the right. This last point is just what is needed to induce visual lateralization. Now, look at this – while the right turn of the head is under genetic control, the induction of visual asymmetry is not. If no light shines on the egg, the animal will hatch with a symmetric brain. Thus, everything looks as if it is genetically determined, but when it comes to shaping the asymmetries of the brain, an environmental input is needed that interacts with the asymmetric head position of the embryo to lateralize the brain.

Conditions in humans may be similar. The rightward spinal torsion is also true for the human embryo, which has a preference for sucking on its right thumb, partly due to an embryonic right turn of its head (Hepper, Shahidullah, & White, 1991). Most newborns still have a preference for a right turn of their heads when in a supine position, and this preference seems to correlate with subsequent handedness (Michel & Harkins, 1986). The preference for right turns of the head still prevails in adult humans, making it possible that this constant bias molds cerebral asymmetries of the developing brain in humans as it does in birds (Güntürkün, 2003).

Taken together, important aspects of brain organization can derive from an interaction of nature and nurture, although they look strictly genetically determined at the first glance. I'm pretty sure that more discoveries like that are ahead of us.

I hope I could convince you.

Hakan

Odense, October 3, 2003

Dear Hakan,

Your story with the asymmetric birds is a good one. I must admit that it's a nice example for the intricacies of biological and environmental interactions. However, these kinds of examples can also be found in the opposite. Just think of the last twist on posttraumatic stress disorder (PTSD) and hippocampal volume that you might also have read about in the scientific press.

As you know, animal research has provided evidence that exposure to severe stress can damage the hippocampus and, thus, the integrity of declarative memory. Such studies point to a neurotoxic role for corticosteroids, elevated levels of which probably damage hippocampal neurons (Sapolsky, Uno, Rebert, & Finch, 1990). The same probably holds for humans and might explain why, in the psychiatric condition of PTSD, the hippocampus is significantly smaller (Stein, Koverola, Hanna, Torchia, & McClarty, 1997). PTSD is a constellation of disabling behavioral and emotional symptoms that occur in some individuals who have experienced severe psychological trauma such as combat, sexual abuse, or natural disaster. These results raise the possibility that psychological trauma may induce neurological damage in humans. The logic would be that humans who experienced severe stress would survive conditions where parts of their hippocampus would be destroyed. Subsequently, they would suffer from memory deficits, including lapses for the events that caused the hippocampal damage. Recently, Gilbertson et al. (2002) turned this whole logic upside down.

In their study, they examined samples of male monozygotic twin pairs in which one twin was a Vietnam combat veteran and his identical co-twin had no combat exposure. In some twin pairs, the combat-exposed brother developed chronic PTSD, whereas in other twin pairs the combat veteran never developed PTSD. Consistent with previous reports, Gilbertson et al. (2002) also found smaller hippocampal volume in trauma-exposed persons diagnosed with PTSD. The key finding, however, was that the identical twins who were not themselves exposed to combat showed hippocampal volumes that were comparable to their combat-exposed brothers. These noncombat twins had significantly smaller hippocampi than those of combat veterans without PTSD and their noncombat-exposed twins. These data indicate that smaller hippocampi in PTSD represent a preexisting, familial vulnerability factor rather than the neurotoxic-induced product of trauma exposure per se. Thus, what used to be seen as an effect of an environmental factor affecting the brain now has to be seen as a predisposition that is associated with a higher risk for developing PTSD under stressful conditions. Isn't that great?

In summary, some conditions look environmentally induced but aren't. You are right that, however, some effects look genetically determined but are in fact induced by external input. So, we are even. But of course our discussion here is not to have the last word but to better understand what aspects of our biology and what aspects of our environment are responsible for creating us in the way we exist. I would go so far as to say that each single psychological entity of a person is, to at least some extent, influenced by his or her genetics. This may sound dogmatic, but dogmata aren't bad if they are correct.

Maxim

Melun, October 14, 2003
Dear Maxim,
No doubt, both genes and culture form us. But your last dogmatic statement implies a way of thinking that is widespread but incomplete. You assume that information always flows from genes through substrate to behavior: genes → brain → behavior. But the interaction is both ways: genes ←→ brain ←→ behavior. Perceiving and attending to some environmental stimuli (e.g., a novel smell) is accompanied by neuronal interactions that can induce the activation of immediate-early genes (IEGs; Montag-Sallaz, Welzl, Kuhl, Montag, & Schachner, 1999). IEGs are genes that show a rapid and transient expression immediately after resting cells are stimulated by extracellular signals such as hormones and neurotransmitters. Meanwhile many IEGs have been described and named with cryptic terms such as

jun, c-fos, arg 3.1, ZENK, CREB, and so on. These genes, once activated, can both activate and repress further gene expression that then controls structural changes of brain tissue. The important point is that the environment controls gene expression. Genes are then the dependent variable. The study of Jarvis, Scharff, Grossman, Ramos, and Nottebohm (1998) is a nice illustration of this link. These scientists studied singing zebra finches that were either singing for courtship in front of a female or alone and therefore just for themselves. They could show that ZENK expression in the song system of these birds showed different patterns for singing for a female or singing alone. Thus, although the song was the same, the internal state of the animals was different, and thus this internal state had the power to drive different brain areas to express IEGs.

If internal states are able to drive the differential expression of IEGs, we should expect psychological states to affect hormone levels. Therefore, I now argue for the reversal of the usual causal contingencies. First, you have a specific thought, and then you induce IE expressions, because your thought is, for your brain, equivalent to an (external) stimulus. Finally, your IEGs induce the production of gene products like hormones, for example. Finally, elevated levels of hormones can alter the shape of your body (possibly everything from synapses to hair growth). Recently, some interesting examples for this chain of events were reported. For example, the consistently better performance seen by teams in various sporting contexts when playing at home is referred to as the "home advantage." Neave and Wolfson (2003) showed that salivary testosterone levels in soccer players were significantly higher before a home game than before an away game. Perceived rivalry of the opposing team was important because testosterone levels were higher before playing an "extreme" rival than a "moderate" rival. Similarly, Salvador, Suay, Gonzalez-Bono, and Serrano (2003) studied anticipatory hormonal and psychological responses of judo players mentally preparing for an official competition and found that this increased both testosterone and cortisol levels. Elevated hormone levels in turn predicted a better outcome in the competition. Thus, psychological conditions affect hormone release that can subsequently improve success in sports. It is important to note that an increase of testosterone does not depend on physical exercise. Gladue, Boechler, and McCaul (1989) asked volunteers to participate in a computer game against another person. The winner was, unknown to the participants, predetermined by the scientists. Nevertheless, testosterone levels were significantly increased in winners. So, the psychological experience of winning against somebody else activates testosterone release.

Similarly, Born, Hansen, Marshall, Molle, and Fehm (1999) showed that your expectation of having to wake up at a certain time in the morning regulates your timely increase in adrenocorticotropin release before the expected time of waking. A sadder story is that of Elzinga, Schmal,

Vermetten, van Dyck, and Bremner (2003), who showed that female PTSD patients that were victims of childhood abuse have drastically increased cortisol levels when confronted with verbal reminders of their trauma. In principle, these elevated cortisol levels can damage the hippocampus of these women.

I think the best study of this whole field is one that was published anonymously. I was told about this experiment but couldn't yet get a hold of a copy. I hope the person who told me about this publication got the details straight. The story is so good that it ought to be true. It's a little paper published by an anonymous ethologist who spent years on a remote island, banding birds, observing animals, and so on. Every 2 weeks, a small vessel took him to a larger island where he would look for female company. After awhile, he recognized that his beard was growing faster in the days before his free weekend. Because he had a lot of time and all necessary instruments at hand, he started to weigh the remains of the beard he shaved every morning. Indeed, a few days before his trip to the inhabited island, his beard started to grow much faster. He recognized the possibly relevant link: first, there were his thoughts about his sexual plans for the weekend. Second, these thoughts changed his hormonal levels, possibly via an activation of IEGs. Third, because androgens stimulate hair follicles in the beard, his elevated levels of testosterone caused his beard to grow faster.

I must say this story is one of my favorites, and I will definitely try to track this paper down. So, my conclusion is that our thoughts and our environment can be seen as an independent variable with respect to genes. The interaction of genes and cultures is therefore a symmetric one.

All the best,
Hakan

Odense, October 28, 2003
Dear Hakan,
Your story of the ethologist's beard growing is my wife Irina's favorite story. She talks about it at every party! I really hope that the story is true.

I am in bit of a hurry because the deadline for the book chapter on bio-cultural co-constructivism is approaching. So, my response will be rather short this time. Yes, you are right that the interaction of genes and culture is reciprocal, but don't forget that your genes limit the entire mental machinery with which you deal with the world around you. It's your genome that specifies how your synapses and all molecular mechanisms that are associated with synaptic plasticity work. Synapses are highly complex little machines with hundreds of variations of their receptors, G proteins, and so on, that ultimately define your speed of thought and the efficacy of short- and long-term synaptic change. Thus, your mental speed and the ease with which you memorize new information are defined by your synapses – and so, ultimately, by your genome (Chapter 11).

Although axonal conductance speed doesn't correlate with intelligence (Reed & Jensen, 1991), the latencies and amplitudes of sensory-evoked potentials (Tan, Akgun, Komsuoglu, & Telatar, 1993) and of various event-related potentials (ERPs) do (Robaey, Cansino, Dugas, & Renault, 1995). The relationship is such that elevated IQ scores correlate with higher amplitudes and shorter latencies. Although there are still many open questions, there is, in general, good support for the synaptic speed theory of intelligence. I have to admit that the physiological measures explain only a small part of the IQ variance; however, because they represent averages of neural activity over major portions of the brain, a higher resolution is probably difficult to expect.

A study by Wright et al. (2001) might be interesting for you to read in this respect. I can send you the pdf if your library doesn't have the journal. These authors investigated what proportion of the variance in the amplitude and latency of the P300 (an ERP that is elicited by unpredictable, unlikely, or highly significant stimuli and that provides an electrophysiological index of the attention and working-memory demands of a task) could be attributed to genetic factors. To this end, they analyzed the P300-data in 335 adolescent twin pairs and 48 siblings, and showed that additive genetic factors accounted for most of the variance in P300 amplitude. Approximately one-third of the genetic variation at frontal sites was mediated by a common genetic factor that also influenced the genetic variation at parietal and central sites. Genetic covariance in P300 latency across sites was substantial, with a large part of the variance found at parietal, central, and frontal sites attributed to a common genetic factor. It is very interesting to see to what extent a physiological measure that covaries with behavioral IQ is genetically associated.

My conclusion is simple. We are like fish swimming in a bowl. Within our little world, we learn and change by the things we encounter. We may dream that we define our horizon by our own mental power, unlimited by our heritage, but in fact we swim within the tiny limits of our own genetic bowl. Sounds pessimistic, but if I don't switch back now to my book chapter, I will have much more reason for pessimism, I guess. Is yours ready?

All the best,
Maxim


Melun, November 5, 2003
Dear Maxim,
I think you got me wrong. I didn't mean that genes do not bind our IQ. The nature–nurture story with respect to the intelligence problem is so old, boring, and solved that I wonder why the media still go on debating it. I also follow to some extent the new data on the physiological correlates of IQ and don't have any problems with them. After all, the genetic contribution

to intelligence obviously has to manifest itself in some brain measures. The ERP data and IQ correlations therefore fit nicely (Chapter 13).

No, my point is different. I will give you an example. I am an atheist, whereas Meltem is Muslim. Surely, neither of these conditions is genetically wired. Meltem and I discuss our ways of interpreting life, and we both have our arguments. Our views have changed over time and possibly will go on changing. These changes reflect the mental impact of new encounters, arguments, and experiences. Obviously, we reflect about these arguments in our brains, and obviously, our brains are wired to some extent by genetic information. We also hear and read new arguments about religion with our sensory organs, which have a genetic blueprint laid down in each of our cells. We think about what we hear and read by using synapses that are genetically tuned. Likewise, we remember old arguments by using memory mechanisms that have a genetic background, and so on, but still the *content* of our thinking is culture. Pure culture. Culture without a single grain of gene. This kind of culture defines most of what we do and what we are. We might be limited in the speed and extent of grasping the essence of complex problems through a mixture of nature and nurture. Our brains may be tuned to the sounds of our language by properties defined early in childhood. Thus, we may have a hard time distinguishing some sounds in Thai or other languages (Chapter 7). All these aspects are secondary, however. Of principle importance for our daily life is only the content, the message as such. You are not going to tell me that the content of our culture is naturebound, are you?

Did you finish the chapter before deadline? I usually do not care too much about deadlines.

Hakan

Odense, November 18, 2003
Dear Hakan,
I have bad news for you. I think our culture is also a mixture of nature and nurture. I will start my arguments with a classical one. I will talk about incest.

Incest is forbidden by law or represents at least a social taboo in more or less all societies. It is obvious that incest over several generations reduces genetic variance and increases the likelihood of alleles with negative consequences becoming homozygotic. All facilities producing inbred animals for research fight with sophisticated mating programs against the adverse effects of inbreeding. The prevention of incest thus makes biological sense. The universality of the incest taboo across all human cultures therefore renders a biological origin of incest aversion likely. Consequently, different authors have already argued for an evolutionary origin of the incest taboo (Lévi-Strauss, 1984). But how, you will ask, should the translation from biology to culture work? Yanai and McClearn (1972) were probably the first to really show that mice reared with their relatives until weaning avoided them as sexual partners, whereas those that were reared in foster families did not. Thus, learning some cues about the mice that are present during early childhood makes them unattractive as sexual partners. Possibly, the situation in humans is similar for brother–sister incest. In northern Taiwan, a now vanished tradition involved the introduction of the bride in her future husband's home as an infant. Bride and groom were then raised as members of the same family. The name of this kind of bride was Sim-Pua (little sister). By all criteria (increase of divorces, lack of children, likelihood of the male living with a mistress or the female having a lover), Sim-Pua marriages turned out to be the least successful in comparison to other forms of marriages that involved two young adults coming together (Wolf, 1995).

A similar condition was reported by Shepher (1983) for the kibbutz in Israel. Here, babies from different families live from birth on in small groups called kvutza that function like families with many children. Kibbutzim have an ideological background; parents who have their children living in a kibbutz share a similar ideology. They would possibly favor their children choosing a spouse from the kibbutz, but this rarely, if ever, happens, at least for the children growing up within a kvutza. Shepher (1983) was able to gather quite convincing data that for children of the opposite gender, living together for their first 6 years in a kvutza seemed to considerably reduce sexual attraction, although nobody would object and thus there were no taboos to overcome. The incest taboo thus possibly works in us similarly to the way it does in other animals. We learn the individual characteristics of other children who grow up with us within a family. Years later, these characteristics make them unattractive as sexual partners. Because humans usually grow up with their brothers and sisters, incest is prevented by this simple mechanism.

If the incest taboo is rooted biologically, it is easy to see why more or less all cultures have made a taboo out of it. Although some authors (discussed in Lévi-Strauss, 1984) ask why you need a law against something that is already prevented by nature, these modern intellectuals ignore how primitive, village-level social constructions work. There, at the fundament of human social cultural evolution, social taboos result not only out of the harmful, but also out of the unusual. Only because of that were minorities such as left handers seen as something sinful in most societies. The only reason for their status as outcasts was their statistical rareness. The rareness of incest is therefore possibly one of the main reasons it became a social taboo. With the advent of script, social taboos were possibly transformed into laws and have survived until today. Presently, we are living in a time when scrutinizing laws according to their internal logic, consistency, and compatibility with liberal thinking may sweep away the judicial basis of some of our more ancient social customs.

Incest is just one aspect of a much larger picture. During the last 100,000 years, biological evolution has slowly been transformed into cultural evolution (Chapter 2). If you look carefully, you will see that most *topoi* of today's culture are fully compatible with their sociobiological origin. I can almost hear you protesting, but I will explain what I mean exactly. I will start with the Ten Commandments. I don't know if they were also incorporated into Islam. As a child I had to learn them, but now, I have to admit, I only remember two of them (you should neither kill your neighbor nor cast an eye at his wife ... ). Looking them up after all these years from my old books, I was amazed to what extent they were compatible with my thesis.

1. You shall have no other gods before Me.
2. You shall not make yourself a carved image.
3. You shall not take the name of the Lord your God in vain.
4. Remember the Sabbath day, to keep it holy.
5. Honor your father and your mother.
6. You shall not murder.
7. You shall not commit adultery.
8. You shall not steal.
9. You shall not bear false witness against your neighbor.
10. You shall not covet your neighbor's wife.

Although the first four are more related to the social techniques of keeping a faith in power, the last six are beautifully compatible with the sociobiological mechanisms governing interactions within a small group of interrelated primates for whom the human specialty of large-scale social cooperation has evolved (Fehr & Fischbacher, 2003). Yes, I know, many more complex interpretations can be put forward for the Ten Commandments, but clear-cut cases such as incest and more mixed cases such as religious rules all point to a sociobiological carpet on which our culture is standing. There-fore, I truly doubt that the content (yes, my friend, the content; not the synapses that transport it) of our thoughts, discussions, and dreams today is free of our biological past. I even go a step further and argue that most of our songs, plays, and fairy tales are instantly understandable to every-body, from young to old, because they evoke emotional constructions that are innate to *Homo sapiens* (Chapter 10).

Just reading a beginner's book such as "The Selfish Gene" by Richard Dawkins (1989) suffices to understand why in "Sleeping Beauty" a male prince has to undertake so much nonsense to kiss the young maiden. It is also instantly understandable that Cinderella has to be young and beau-tiful (but otherwise can be poor), whereas the prince simply goes with being the prince, and so captures social power in his wake. Everybody understands the motives of Cinderella's stepmother who tries to knot the ties between her own (genetically related) daughters and the prince. Did you know that there are more than 3,000 versions of the Cinderella myth? Almost every world culture has one. She's known as "Yeh Shen" in China, "The Burnt Face Girl" to the Mik'maq tribe, "Tattercoats" in England, and "Marouckla" to the Slavs. Reading studies on human mating preferences against the backdrop of evolutionary science (Buss, 2003) makes clear why the (stepmother) Queen ordered Snow White to be killed when the magic mirror said: "O Lady Queen, though fair ye be, Snow White is fairer far to see."

So, to be specific, my point is not that all social constructions and belief systems are one-to-one biologically constructed, but that they (1) are either directly rooted in biological mechanisms that describe more or less the same behavior (incest is an example of that), or (2) have a biological underpinning that delivers the general emotional or social context on which the social construction can blossom (Cinderella and other tales, operas, and movies are examples).

You said that the religious (non)beliefs you and Meltem have didn't have a grain of biology. I doubt it. The details of religions might be pure cultural heritage, but as long as religions reduce anxiety by (seemingly) increasing the predictability of life, as long as they provide fairy tales that strike a sociobiological chord in all of us, and as long as they produce a hierarchy of social power that could once be translated directly into reproductive success (yes, I know Catholicism is a remarkable exception, but mainly in more recent times), religions will have a fabric of social and biological threads that are inextricably intertwined. In this respect, religions follow the same patterns as most other social constructions.

All the best,
Maxim

Melun, November 28, 2003
My dear friend,
About 3 months ago, I ignited our letter exchange on nature and nurture by commenting on a sentence that you said in passing. This morning, I had time to read all our letters again, one by one. I think I could convince you that experience-related factors shape each aspect of our brain, but you have likewise convinced me that our biology has "crept" into the most inner details of my existence. Thus, I have to accept that our little daughter was born with prewired expectations about the physical and social realities of the world. Equally, I know that the experiences she is going to make will shape everything she is, that is, her whole psychological and physical existence.

You said that as scientists it is our duty to see and paint the larger picture. I agree. But we should draw with little brushes on a huge canvas. We should see the grand parts and the tiny details. Presently, I can only see outlines, maybe here and there a few detailed strokes. We discussed many battlefields: cortical development, intelligence, cerebral asymmetries, gene numbers, imprinting, incest, and even religion. Wherever we looked, we saw nature and nurture to be present. In some areas, the cultural side dominated, whereas in others, the biological side took precedence. But not a single territory of our mind seemed to be outside the scope of the interaction of biology and culture.

Is this really all we can say? Or are new discoveries ahead of us?

All the best,

Hakan

### References

Andersen, B. B., Gundersen, H. J., & Pakkenberg, B. (2003). Aging of the human cerebellum: A stereological study. *Journal of Comparative Neurology, 466,* 356–365.

Bischof, H.-J. (1983). Imprinting and cortical plasticity: A comparative review. *Neuroscience and Biobehavioral Reviews, 7,* 213–225.

Blakemore, C., & Cooper, G. F. (1970). Development of the brain depends on the visual environment. *Nature, 228,* 477–478.

Born, J., Hansen, K., Marshall, L., Molle, M., & Fehm, H. L. (1999). Timing the end of nocturnal sleep. *Nature, 397,* 29–30.

Buss, D. (2003). *Evolutionary psychology: The new science of the mind* (2nd ed.). Boston: Pearson Allyn & Bacon.

Claverie, J.-M. (2001). Gene number: What if there are only 30,000 human genes? *Science, 291,* 1255–1257.

Corballis, M. C. (1997). The genetics and evolution of handedness. *Psychological Review, 105,* 714–777.

Crowley, J. C., & Katz, L. C. (1999). Development of ocular dominance columns in the absence of retinal input. *Nature Neuroscience, 2,* 1125–1130.

Dawkins, R. (1989). *The selfish gene* (2nd ed.). Oxford, UK: Oxford University Press.

Elzinga, B. M., Schmal, C. G., Vermetten, E., van Dyck, R., & Bremner, J. D. (2003). Higher cortisol levels following exposure to traumatic reminders in abuse-related PTSD. *Neuropsychopharmacology, 28,* 1656–1665.

Fehr, E., & Fischbacher, U. (2003). The nature of human altruism. *Nature, 425,* 785–791.

Gilbertson, M. W., Shenton, M. E., Ciszewski, A., Kasai, K., Lasko, N. B., Orr, S. P., & Pitman, R. K. (2002). Smaller hippocampal volume predicts pathologic vulnerability to psychological trauma. *Nature Neuroscience, 5,* 1242–1247.

Gladue, B. A., Boechler, M., & McCaul, K. D. (1989). Hormonal responses to competition in human males. *Aggressive Behavior, 15,* 409–422.

Güntürkün, O. (2002). Hemispheric asymmetry in the visual system of birds. In K. Hugdahl & R. J. Davidson (Eds.), *Brain asymmetry* (2nd ed., pp. 3–36). Cambridge, MA: MIT Press.

Güntürkün, O. (2003). Human behaviour: Adult persistence of head turning asymmetry. *Nature, 421,* 711.

Hepper, P. G., Shahidullah, S., & White, R. (1991). Handedness in the human fetus. *Neuropsychologia, 29,* 1107–1111.

Jarvis, E. D., Scharff, C., Grossman, M. R., Ramos, J. A., & Nottebohm, F. (1998). For whom the bird sings: Context-dependent gene expression. *Neuron, 21*, 775–788.

Klar, A. J. S. (2003). Human handedness and scalp hair-whorl direction develop from a common genetic mechanism. *Genetics, 165*, 269–276.

Lévi-Strauss, C. (1984). *Die elementaren Strukturen der Verwandtschaft [The elemental structures of relatedness]*. Frankfurt a.M.: Suhrkamp.

Mathis, U., Eschbach, S., & Rossel, S. (1992). Functional binocular vision is not dependent on visual experience in the praying mantis. *Visual Neuroscience, 9* (2), 199–203.

Meister, M., Wong, R. O., Baylor, D. A., & Shatz, C. J. (1991). Synchronous bursts of action potentials in ganglion cells of the developing mammalian retina. *Science, 252*, 939–943.

Michel, G. F., & Harkins, D. A. (1986). Postural and lateral asymmetries in the ontogeny of handedness during infancy. *Developmental Psychobiology, 19*, 247–258.

Mitchell, D. E., Kind, P. C., Sengpiel, F., & Murphy, K. (2003). Brief daily periods of binocular vision prevent deprivation-induced acuity loss. *Current Biology, 13*, 1704–1708.

Montag-Sallaz, M., Welzl, H., Kuhl, D., Montag, D., & Schachner, M. (1999). Novelty-induced increased expression of immediate early-genes c-fos and arg 3.1 in the mouse brain. *Journal of Neurobiology, 38*, 234–246.

Neave, N., & Wolfson, S. (2003). Testosterone, territoriality, and the "home advantage." *Physiology and Behavior, 78*, 269–275.

Pääbo, S. (2003). The mosaic that is our genome. *Nature, 421*, 409–412.

Pakkenberg, B., & Gundersen, H. J. (1997). Neocortical neuron number in humans: Effect of sex and age. *Journal of Comparative Neurology, 384*, 312–320.

Ramsdell, A. F., & Yost, H. J. (1998). Molecular mechanisms of vertebrate left–right development. *Trends in Genetics, 14*, 459–465.

Redies, C. (2000). Cadherins in the central nervous system. *Progress in Neurobiology, 61*, 611–648.

Reed, T. E., & Jensen, A. R. (1991). Arm nerve conduction velocity (NCV), brain NCV, reaction time, and intelligence. *Intelligence, 15*, 33–47.

Robaey, P., Cansino, S., Dugas, M., & Renault, B. (1995). A comparative study of ERP correlates of psychometric and Piagetian intelligence measures in normal and hyperactive children. *Electroencephalography and Clinical Neurophysiology, 96*, 56–75.

Röder, B., Teder-Sälejärvi, W., Sterr, A., Rösler, F., Hillyard, S. A., & Neville, H. J. (1999). Improved auditory spatial tuning in blind humans. *Nature, 400*, 162–166.

Rogers, L. J. (1982). Light experience and asymmetry of brain function in chickens. *Nature, 297*, 223–225.

Rogers, L. (1996). Behavioral, structural and neurochemical asymmetries in the avian brain: A model system for studying visual development and processing. *Neuroscience and Biobehavioral Reviews, 20*, 487–503.

Salvador, A., Suay, F., Gonzalez-Bono, E., & Serrano, M. A. (2003). Anticipatory cortisol, testosterone and psychological responses to judo competition in young men. *Psychoneuroendocrinology, 28*, 364–375.

Sapolsky, R. M., Uno, H., Rebert, C. S., & Finch, C. E. (1990). Hippocampal damage associated with prolonged glucocorticoid exposure in primates. *Journal of Neuroscience, 10,* 2897–2902.

Schüz, A., & Palm, G. (1989). Density of neurons and synapses in the cerebral cortex of the mouse. *Journal of Comparative Neurology, 286,* 442–455.

Sengpiel, F., Stawinski, P., & Bonhoeffer, T. (1999). Influence of experience on orientation maps in cat visual cortex. *Nature Neuroscience, 2,* 727–732.

Shepher, J. (1983). *Incest: A biosocial view.* New York: Academic Press.

Singh, J. A. L. (1964). *Die "Wolfskinder" von Midnapore* [The wolf-children of Midnapore]. Heidelberg: Quelle & Meyer.

Stein, M. B., Koverola, C., Hanna, C., Torchia, M. G., & McClarty, B. (1997). Hippocampal volume in women victimized by childhood sexual abuse. *Psychological Medicine, 27,* 951–959.

Sur, M., & Leamey, C. A. (2001). Development and plasticity of cortical areas and networks. *Nature Reviews Neuroscience, 2,* 251–261.

Tan, Ü., Akgun, A., Komsuoglu, S., & Telatar, M. (1993). Inverse relationship between nonverbal intelligence and the parameters of pattern reversal visual evoked potentials in left-handed male subjects: Importance of right brain and testosterone. *International Journal of Neuroscience, 71,* 189–200.

White, S. A. (2001). Learning to communicate. *Current Opinion in Neurobiology, 11,* 510–520.

Wolf, A. P. (1995). *Sexual attraction and childhood association: A Chinese brief for Edward Westermarck.* Stanford, CA: Stanford University Press.

Wright, M. J., Hansell, N. K., Geffen, G. M., Geffen, L. B., Smith, G. A., & Martin, N. G. (2001). Genetic influence on the variance in P3 amplitude and latency. *Behavioral Genetics, 31,* 555–565.

Yanai, J., & McClearn, G. E. (1972). Assortative mating in mice and the incest taboo. *Nature, 238,* 281–282.

# Author Index

Abadzi, H., 280
ABC Research Group, 13
Abdi, H., 69
Abe, K., 334
Abram, K. M., 346
Abutalebi, J., 172
Acker, J. D., 243, 315
Adams, M. M., 48
Adolfson, R., 252
Adolphs, R., 53, 213
Aggen, S., 354, 373
Aguirre, G. K., 173, 188, 189
Ahern, F., 252
Aitken, D., 334
Akgun, A., 390
Albert, M. S., 243, 244, 262
Alborn, A. M., 82, 88
Alegria, J., 286
Alexander, G. E., 253, 319, 325
Alexander, M. P., 189
Alexander, N. B., 360
Alho, K., 48, 120, 137, 179, 181
Allik, J., 48, 179, 181
Allison, T., 189
Almkvist, O., 250
Alpermann, A., 170
Alpert, N., 173
Alsop, D. C., 188, 189
Altenmüller, E. O., 222, 225, 226, 347
Alter, K., 165
Altman, J., 83, 84
Amaral, L. A. N., 15
Amedi, A., 149
Amunts, K., 225, 233

Andersen, A. H., 253
Andersen, B. B., 381
Andersen, R. A., 137
Anderson, A. W., 186
Anderson, C. A., 193
Anderson, D. J., 85
Anderson, K. E., 253, 324
Anderson, N. D., 251
Anderson, S. W., 181, 189, 191
Andersson, J. L. R., 245, 246
Ando, S., 48
Andres, D., 262
Andrews, P. W., 218
Angelergues, R., 192
Angrilli, A., 170
Aoki, K., 45
Arai, T., 191
Arbuckle, T. Y., 262
Ardal, S., 173
Ardila, A., 280, 286
Arguin, M., 188
Arno, P., 120
Arvidsson, A., 87
Asada, T., 52
Aschersleben, G., 15, 274
Ashburner, J., 48, 52, 99, 184, 324, 374
Ashton-Miller, J. A., 360
Askelöf, S., 281, 299, 304
Assmann, A., 8, 10, 12
Atherton, M., 317
Avison, M. J., 253
Awh, E., 266
Ayari, M., 227
Aziz-Sultan, A., 139

Bachevalier, J., 69
Bach-y-Rita, P., 120
Bäckman, L., 26, 242, 243, 245, 250, 252, 253, 260, 353, 367
Baddeley, A., 286, 302
Ball, K., 250
Baltes, M. M., 27, 351, 352
Baltes, P. B., 5, 6, 11, 15, 21, 26, 27, 28, 30, 31, 32, 35, 43, 46, 261, 263, 270, 272, 274, 308, 326, 327, 351, 352, 374
Banaji, M. R., 209, 210, 215
Bandura, A., 206
Bandy, D., 253
Bangert, M. W., 226
Bannon, M. J., 242
Bao, S., 329
Barad, V., 274
Barbaro, N. M., 88
Barch, D. M., 251
Bard, C., 375
Barkow, J. H., 34
Barnea, A., 84
Barnes, L. L., 98, 247
Barnett, W. S., 73
Barry, C., 191
Barss, A., 170, 179, 181
Barton, D., 290
Bart, W. M., 317
Bassuk, S. S., 247
Basun, H., 241, 249
Battaglia, F., 103
Baumgartner, T., 333
Bavelier, D., 48, 50, 118, 134, 136, 137, 166, 226
Baylor, D. A., 381
Beaulieu, C., 113
Beauvois, M. F., 189, 190
Bechara, A., 203, 204, 213
Beer, R. D., 15
Beers, S. R., 347
BEIP Core Group, 75, 76, 81
Beja-Pereira, A., 45
Belger, A., 189
Belichenko, P. V., 113
Belin, P., 347
Bellugi, U., 165, 166
Beltrami, M., 299
Bench, C., 253
Bennett, D. A., 247
Bennett, E. L., 96
Bennett, P. J., 360
Bentin, S., 170

Berardi, N., 114, 130, 153
Berch, D. B., 250
Berger, J. S., 266
Berkman, L. F., 247, 262
Bernatzky, G., 221, 232
Bernhard, T., 98
Berntson, G. G., 53
Berscheid, E., 46
Bertelson, P., 286
Bertorelle, G., 45
Besson, M., 170
Bettinardi, V., 71, 181
Bhatnagar, C., 334
Bialystok, E., 272
Bichescu, D., 349
Bickford, P. C., 274
Bielinski, D., 274
Bienias, J. L., 98, 247
Bien, S., 120
Biernat, M., 209
Binder, J. R., 187
Birbaumer, N., 346
Bischof, H.-J., 384
Bittar, R. G., 126
Björk-Eriksson, T., 82, 88
Bjorklund, A., 82
Bjorklund, D. F., 50
Black, J. E., 5, 22, 41, 46, 67, 72, 88, 153
Blakemore, C., 113, 381, 382
Blin, J., 120
Bliss, T. V. P., 40
Blonder, L. X., 253
Blood, A. J., 232
Bloom, F. E., 61
BoBo, L., 209
Boechler, M., 388
Bogdahn, U., 99
Boire, D., 121, 123, 127
Bol, A., 120
Bonhoeffer, T., 382
Bookheimer, S., 164
Born, J., 388
Bornkessel, I., 171
Bornstein, M. H., 46
Boss, B. D., 101
Bouchard, P., 116
Bourgeois, J.-P., 153
Bower, G. H., 365
Bradley, D. G., 45
Bradley, M. M., 210, 335
Brady, S. A., 286

Brandon, E. P., 98
Brandtstädter, J., 12
Braun, C., 346
Braver, T. S., 251
Bremner, J. D., 389
Brent, H. P., 69
Bronchti, G., 119
Bronfenbrenner, U., 5, 12, 34, 43
Brown, C. M., 169, 170, 171
Brown, L. A., 360, 372
Brown, S., 221
Brown, T. T., 52
Brown, W. D., 188
Brunswick, N., 51, 304
Bub, D. N., 188
Buchanan, T. W., 334
Buchel, C., 203
Buckner, R. L., 248, 250, 253, 267
Bucy, P. C., 201
Bülau, P., 165
Bullmore, E., 249
Burke, W., 118
Burnha, G., 330, 348
Busch, V., 99
Bushnell, M. C., 127
Buss, D., 394
Butterworth, B., 193
Butz, A., 370, 373
Byrne, C. A., 341

Cabeza, R., 47, 48, 52, 164, 243, 246, 251,
    267, 311
Cacioppo, J. T., 53
Cahill, L., 334
Calder, A. J., 213
Calford, M. B., 118
Cameron, H. A., 84, 103
Cameron, R. F., 299
Campbell, G., 66
Campitelli, G., 317
Camras, L. A., 70
Candia, V., 347
Canli, T., 213
Canossa de Tolipan, L., 299
Cansino, S., 390
Caplan, D., 173
Cappa, S. F., 51, 172, 280
Caramazza, A., 188, 191
Cardinal, R. N., 340
Carlier, E., 119
Carlson, E., 76
Carmo, I., 299

Carpenter, P. A., 357
Carrasco, M., 213
Carson, M. A., 349
Carstensen, L. L., 257, 260, 273
Carter, C. S., 251
Carterette, E. C., 227
Carver, L. J., 53
Cary, L., 286, 288, 290, 293
Casanova, C., 121, 123, 127
Caselli, R. J., 253
Caspi, A., 15
Castellanos, F. X., 303
Castro-Caldas, A., 281, 305
Castro, M. J., 299
Castro, S., 170
Catani, C., 330
Cavaleiro, M., 299
Cavallis-Sforza, L. L., 34
Ceci, S. J., 5, 43
Cellerino, A., 310
Celnik, P., 120
Cepeda, N. J., 274
Ceponiene, R., 48, 179, 181
Chalfonte, B. L., 358
Chalmers, D. J., 34
Chance, J. E., 69
Chang, E. F., 329
Changeux, J.-P., 43, 47
Chan, G. L. Y., 242
Chanoine, E., 304
Charles, D. R., 346
Charles, S. T., 257, 273
Charmandari, E., 329
Charness, N., 318, 319, 321, 322, 350,
    366, 368
Chase, W. G., 317, 318
Chen, H.-C., 360
Chen, K. W., 253
Cheour, M., 48, 181
Chino, Y. M., 118
Choi, I., 35, 42, 46
Chomsky, N., 162, 280
Christie, B. R., 154, 261
Chrousos, G. P., 329
Chun, M. M., 185
Churchill, J. D., 99, 261, 273
Chwilla, D. J., 179
Ciccarelli, L., 170
Cicchetti, D., 35
Cipolotti, L., 192, 193
Ciszewski, A., 347, 395
Clark, A., 19, 34, 35, 44

Clark, D. A., 49
Claverie, J.-M., 380
Cobb, N., 150
Cohen, D. M., 261
Cohen, J. D., 251, 355, 374
Cohen, L., 71, 188, 192
Cohen, L. G., 120, 139
Cohen, N. J., 48, 49, 99, 251, 272, 274, 323
Cohen, Y. E., 137
Colcombe, S. J., 48, 49, 99, 247, 261, 272, 273, 274, 323
Cole, M., 5, 12, 35, 42, 45
Collignon, R., 192
Collingridge, G. L., 40
Collins, W. A., 46
Collin, T., 87
Conner, D. F., 341
Convit, A., 252
Cooke, D. F., 141
Cook, M., 206
Cooper, G. F., 113, 381, 382
Coppens, P., 293, 303
Coq, J. O., 113
Corballis, M. C., 385
Corina, D. P., 165, 166
Corkin, S., 212
Cornoldi, C., 146
Corwell, B., 120
Coslett, H. B., 187
Cosmides, L., 34
Cotman, C. W., 9, 10, 88
Coulson, S., 170, 171, 179
Cowan, W. M., 84, 91, 101
Cowey, A., 125
Craik, F. I. M., 258, 272, 358, 367, 371
Crandall, C. S., 209
Crespo, D., 84, 91
Crist, R. E., 147
Crowley, J. C., 383
Cruts, M., 252
Csibra, G., 181
Cuckle, P., 303
Cuddy, L. L., 226
Cunningham, W. A., 209, 215
Curran, T., 144
Currier, R. D., 299
Curtis, G. C., 341
Curtis, J. W., 72, 73
Cuthbert, B. N., 210
Cycowicz, Y. M., 144, 150
Cynader, M., 113
Czaja, S. J., 321

Dabholkar, A. S., 135, 144, 153
Dabringhaus, A., 233
Dadouchi, F., 375
Dalby, M., 125
Damasio, A. R., 181, 185, 189, 191, 213
Damasio, H., 181, 185, 189, 191, 213
Dambrosia, J., 120
Dame, A., 252
Dannefer, D., 10, 12, 28
Darlington, R., 72
Darwin, C. R., 220
Das, G. D., 83
Davidson, M., 206
Davis, J. D., 329
Davis, M., 202, 203, 206, 210, 211, 215
Dawkins, R., 393
Day, M., 100
Deary, I. J., 319
De Bastiani, P., 191
De Bellis, M. D., 340, 347
De Beni, R., 146
Deffenbacher, K. A., 69
DeFries, J. C., 195
DeFronzo, J., 342
de Groot, A. D., 317
de Haan, M., 47, 63, 69, 72
Dehaene-Lambertz, G., 177, 188, 301
Dehaene, S., 71, 181, 188, 192, 301
Deiber, M. P., 120
Dejerine, J., 187, 188
de Leon, M., 252
Delgado, M. R., 203, 215
Delius, J., 360, 374
Démonet, J.-F, 304
Demuth, L., 143, 154
Denes, G., 193
Denisova, N. A., 274
Dennett, D. C., 218
De Quervain, D. J.-F., 334
Derouesne, J., 189, 190
Desanti, S., 252
D'Esposito, M., 173, 188, 189, 243, 266
Detre, J. A., 188, 189
Deutsch, A., 170, 226
Deutsch, D., 226
De Vincenzi, M., 170
De Volder, A. G., 120
Díaz-Guilera, A., 15
Dickens, W. T., 315
Dickinson-Anson, H., 103
Dietrich, E., 19
DiGirolamo, G. J., 270, 274

Ding, Y. S., 242
Dirschl, A., 370, 373
Di Stefano, M., 116, 118
Dixon, R. A., 26, 250, 252, 260, 353
Dobko, T., 242
Doerfler, L. A., 341
Dolan, R. J., 203, 216
Dolson, M., 226
Donald, M. W., 173
Dosch, H. G., 235
Dostie, D., 71
Draganski, B., 99
Dreher, B., 118
D'Sa, C., 103
Duffy, S., 42
Dugas, M., 390
Dulawa, S., 103
Dulcan, M. K., 346
Duman, R. S., 103
Dumoulin, S. O., 126
Dunbar, R. I. M., 17, 45, 49
Duncan, G. H., 127
Dunton, B. C., 209
Dupoux, E., 71, 181
Dupuis, J. H., 315
Durham, W. H., 5, 9, 11, 13, 29, 34

Ebendal, T., 41
EFA Global Monitoring Report Team, 280
Efrati, M., 329
Ehlert, U., 333
Ehninger, D., 99
Ehrlich, P., 5, 7, 9, 14, 34
Eimas, P. D., 177
Eimer, M., 138, 139, 144
Einstein, G. O., 366
Elbert, T., 48, 51, 162, 184, 222, 225, 233, 316, 328, 336, 344, 349
Eliasziw, M., 320
Ellmore, T. M., 249
Elo, A. E., 318
Elzinga, B. M., 388
Emmelkamp, P. M., 342
Engelien, A., 162, 235, 324, 349
Enghild, J., 253
England, P. R., 45
English, T., 213
Erickson, K. I., 48, 49, 99, 247, 261, 272, 320
Ericsson, K., 247
Ericsson, K. A., 222, 245, 310, 317, 318, 351, 364, 365
Eriksson, P. S., 82, 88

Eschbach, S., 381
Esposito, G., 249
Esteves, F., 212
Etzioni, O., 350, 373
Evans, A. C., 71, 172, 299
Evans, D. A., 98, 247
Everitt, B. J., 340

Fagan, J. F., 69
Faísca, L., 304, 305
Faith Berman, K., 249
Fallah, M., 82
Falls, W. A., 203, 212
Faloon, S., 317
Falz, L., 120
Farah, M. J., 173, 188, 189
Farde, L., 242, 250
Farkas, T., 119
Farran, D. C., 73
Faubert, J., 125, 126
Fazio, F., 51, 304
Fazio, R. H., 209
Feher, O., 118
Fehm, H. L., 388
Fehr, E., 393
Feldman, M. W., 5, 7, 9, 14, 34, 45, 311
Feldman, R. M., 359
Fendrich, R., 127
Fernandes, L., 294
Fiebach, C. J., 181
Fiez, J. A., 173
Finch, C. E., 261, 386
Findling, R., 50, 65
Finlay, B. L., 46
Fischbacher, U., 393
Fischer, H., 214
Fischer, R. S., 189, 195
Fisher, S. E., 195
Fisk, A. D., 321
Fisler, R. E., 341
Fleury, M., 375
Flykt, A., 212
Flynn, J., 247
Flynn, J. R., 315
Fodor, J., 185
Fonteneau, E., 170
Forster, K., 170, 181
Fortin, A., 125, 127
Fowler, J. S., 242
Fox, D., 350, 374
Fox, N. A., 75
Fox, P. T., 188

Frackowiak, R. S. J., 48, 52, 99, 184, 188, 268, 316, 371, 374
Francis, D. D., 66
Fratiglioni, L., 247
Freeman, T. W., 342
Freistone, S. E., 149
Freund, A. M., 351, 352, 360, 373
Friederici, A. D., 162, 165, 175, 176, 181
Friedman, D., 144
Friedman, L. F., 241
Friedman, R., 189
Frisch, S., 170, 171
Friston, K. J., 188, 203
Frith, C. D., 48, 52, 184, 216, 316, 324, 374
Frost, D. O., 121, 123
Frysinger, R. C., 202
Fuchs, E., 82
Funayama, E. S., 206, 215
Furey, M. L., 186

Gaab, N., 226
Gabrielsson, A., 231
Gadian, D. G., 48, 52, 99, 184, 324, 374
Gage, F. H., 48, 85, 87, 92, 98, 102, 103, 154, 261
Gallagher, M., 202
Galles, N. S., 71, 181
Gallistel, C. R., 193
Galvez, R., 99, 261, 273
Ganapathy, G. R., 320
Gandour, J., 165
Gangestad, S. W., 218
Garcia, C., 286
Garcia-Lara, J., 120
Gärdenfors, P., 34
Garrett, M., 170, 179, 181
Gaser, C., 99, 225
Gast, D., 103
Gatenby, J. C., 203, 206, 215
Gathercole, S., 287, 302
Gauna, K., 71
Gauthier, I., 186, 310
Gauvain, M., 45, 74
Gazzaniga, M. S., 127
Geffen, G. M., 397
Geffen, L. B., 397
Gehlen, A., 13, 27, 256
Gelman, R., 193
Gerull, F. C., 206
Geschwind, N., 188
Ghisletta, P., 361
Gibson, E., 170

Giedd, J. N., 299, 303
Gigerenzer, G., 13
Giguere, J. F., 121, 123
Gilbert, C. D., 147
Gilbert, J. H., 177
Gilbertson, M. W., 339, 347, 387, 395
Gingras, G., 123
Ginovart, N., 250
Giordani, B., 360
Gjedde, A., 125
Gladue, B. A., 388
Glass, T. A., 247
Gobbini, M. I., 186
Gobeske, K. T., 329
Goldberger, A. L., 15
Goldblum, M.-C., 285
Gold, D., 262
Goldman-Rakic, P. S., 153
Goldman, S. A., 84
Goldman, W. P., 247, 251
Goldstein, A. G., 69
Goldstein, K., 192
Gondan, M., 137
Gonzalez-Bono, E., 388
Good, C. D., 48, 52, 99, 184, 324, 374
Goodman, R. A., 191
Goody, J., 281
Gore, J. C., 186, 203, 206, 215
Gottesman, I. I., 219
Gottlieb, G., 5, 9, 10, 17, 34, 43, 47, 135, 219
Gougoux, F., 329, 347
Gould, E., 66, 82, 84
Gould, S. J., 219
Gout, A., 177
Grady, C. L., 267
Grafman, J., 120
Grandin, C., 120
Grant, E. A., 251
Grant, J., 280, 303
Graziano, M. S., 141
Greenfield, S., 5, 28, 32, 34
Greenough, W. T., 5, 22, 41, 46, 67, 72, 88, 99, 153, 261, 262
Greenwald, A. G., 209
Grillon, C., 206, 215
Grimwood, P. D., 315
Grodzinsky, Y., 165
Groh, J. M., 143
Groothusen, J., 180
Gross, C., 103
Gross, C. G., 47, 66, 82
Grossman-Hutter, B., 363, 374

Grossman, M. R., 388
Grow, J. G., 70
Guerreiro, M., 282, 283, 286, 294, 305
Guillemot, J. P., 116, 118
Guire, K. E., 360
Gundersen, H. J., 381
Gunnar, M. R., 74
Gunning-Dixon, F. M., 244, 315
Gunter, T. C., 162, 180
Güntürkün, O., 385, 386
Gupta, N., 88
Gur, R. C., 242
Gutchess, A. H., 262
Guthrie, D., 76
Gutschalk, A., 235

Ha, B., 127
Habeck, C. G., 253
Habib, R., 243, 249
Hachinski, V., 320
Haerer, A. F., 299
Hafner, H., 330
Hagen, E. H., 10, 24
Hagoort, P., 169, 170, 180
Hahne, A., 170, 171, 175, 176 180
Hahn, K., 228
Hale, S., 312
Halldin, C., 250
Hallett, M., 120, 139
Hall, J., 340, 347
Hall, M., 287
Hamann, S., 212, 213
Hamilton, M. E., 290
Hamilton, R. H., 48
Hammerstein, P., 10, 24
Hanley, J. R., 191
Hanna, C., 386
Hansell, N. K., 397
Hansen, K., 388
Hanson, D. R., 219
Harkins, D. A., 386
Harris, A., 170
Hart, A. J., 214
Haselton, J. R., 202
Hasher, L., 258, 259
Haug, M., 346
Hauser, M. D., 221
Hawkley, L. C., 53
Hawthorn, D., 359, 363
Haxby, J. V., 186
Head, D., 243, 315
Hebb, D. O., 41, 72, 96, 114, 328, 331, 332, 338

Hecaen, H., 192
Heckhausen, J., 12
Hedden, T., 262
Heffner, H. E., 119
Heffner, R. S., 119
Heicklen-Klein, A. J., 119
Heil, P., 119
Heinrichs, M., 333
Helmers, K. F., 250
Henaff, M. A., 188
Hennighausen, E., 140, 147
Henriksson, B. G., 41
Henthorn, T., 226
Hepper, P. G., 386
Herbin, M., 127
Herman, R. E., 361
Hertz-Pannier, L., 301
He, S., 317
Hess, A., 119
Hickok, G., 165, 166
Hildesheimer, M., 329
Hill, J., 70
Hill, K., 330, 344
Hill, R. D., 252
Hillyard, S. A., 139, 140, 169, 170, 396
Hilton, J., 253, 324
Hinds, J. W., 84
Hinkel, H., 330
Hirakata, M., 52
Hirsch, J., 50, 172, 181
Hock, C., 334
Hofer, S. M., 252
Hoffman, K., 349
Hoffrage, U., 215, 219
Hogarth, P., 193
Hoke, M., 162, 235, 324, 349
Holcomb, P. J., 169, 170
Holden, J. E., 242
Holmes, B. D., 213
Hommel, B., 15, 274
Honey, G., 249
Honig, L. S., 253, 324
Horwitz, B., 139
Hötting, K., 137, 139
Houillier, S., 192
Howard, D., 188
Howard, R., 242, 253
Howieson, D., 243, 252
Hsieh, L., 165
Huang, Y., 225, 235
Hubel, D. H., 114, 115
Hugdahl, K., 205

Huizenga, H. M., 15
Hull, T., 144, 145, 146
Hulse, S. H., 226
Humphrey, K., 177
Hunt, E. B., 321
Hunt, R. R., 366
Huotilainen, M., 181
Huron, D., 221
Hutchins, G. D., 165
Huttenlocher, P. R., 135, 144, 153
Hu, X., 317
Hygge, S., 207

Iacoboni, M., 299
Ibanez, V., 120
Igarashi, M., 48
Iidaka, T., 337
Iivonen, A., 181
Ikegaya, Y., 334
Imabayashi, E., 52
Ingvar, M., 253, 281, 283, 286, 298, 299, 305
Insel, T. R., 67
Isaacowitz, D. M., 257, 264, 273
Isenmann, S., 310
Ishai, A., 186
Iyengar, S., 347
Izraeli, R., 119

Jablonka, E., 5, 6, 9, 10, 11, 13, 29, 34
Jackson, J. R., 209
Jacobs, B. L., 103
Jacobs, W., 330
James, W., 135
Jäncke, L., 222, 225, 235
Jann, O. C., 45
Jarvis, E. D., 388
Jensen, A. R., 390
Jensen, J. L., 360
Jezzard, P., 48
Jobe, J. B., 250
Job, R., 170
Joffe, T. H., 50
Johannes, S., 170
Johanssen, P., 125
Johansson, B., 241
Johansson, B. B., 113
Johnson, D. E., 75
Johnson, J. S., 71
Johnson, M., 6
Johnson, M. H., 47, 72, 177
Johnson, M. K., 358
Johnsrude, I. S., 48, 52, 99, 184, 324, 374

Jones, D. K., 252
Jones, M. C., 280, 303
Jones, S., 252
Jones, T. A., 67, 153
Jonides, J., 259, 266, 275
Joseph, J. A., 261, 274
Julin, P., 249
Junghöfer, M., 335, 336, 348
Juslin, P. N., 231
Just, M. A., 357

Kaan, E., 170
Kaas, J. H., 184
Kaczmarek, K. A., 120
Kahn, D. M., 112, 119
Kahn, H. J., 192
Kahn, R. L., 240
Kaldor, M., 343
Kanwisher, N., 185
Kaplan, M. S., 84
Kapp, B. S., 202
Kapur, N., 245, 252, 316
Kapur, S., 267
Karmiloff-Smith, A., 35, 52, 177, 280, 290, 303
Karni, A., 48, 166
Karnos, T., 252
Karunakara, U., 330, 344, 348
Kasai, K., 347, 395
Katanoda, K., 189
Katan, S. A., 149
Katoh, A., 52
Katz, L. C., 130, 383
Katzman, R., 319
Kaube, H., 216
Kaufman, J. C., 220
Kautz, H., 350, 354, 368, 370, 373, 374
Kawamura, T., 42
Kaye, J. A., 243, 251, 252
Kay, J., 187, 188
Kaysen, D., 303
Keenan, J. M., 193
Keir, R., 206
Keller, T. A., 357
Kelso, S., 18
Kempermann, G., 48, 92, 95, 97, 98, 99, 101, 102, 103
Kemper, S., 361
Kempe, V., 181
Kendall, R. A., 227
Kennedy, K. M., 243, 357, 374
Kenny, P. A., 135
Kensinger, E. A., 212

Keshavan, M. S., 340, 347
Keys, B. A., 251
Kiebel, S., 165
Killiany, R. J., 243, 244
Kimbrell, T., 342
Kim, K. H. S., 50, 172, 181
Kind, P. C., 114, 381
Kindy, M. S., 253
King, D. W., 342
King, J., 170, 179
King, L. A., 342
Kingsbury, M. A., 46
Kino, T., 329
Kinsbourne, M., 188
Kintsch, W., 317
Kirby, G. S., 249
Kirik, D., 87
Kirk, K., 165, 166
Kirschbaum, C., 333
Kirsch, N., 350, 374
Kistler, D. J., 70
Kitayama, S., 42
Klar, A. J. S., 385
Klaschik, C., 348
Klein, D., 172, 181
Klein, R., 272
Kliegl, R., 46, 260, 355, 357, 358, 374
Klingberg, T., 249, 287
Kluender, K. R., 173
Kluver, H., 201
Knudsen, E. I., 139, 153
Koay, G., 119
Kobajashi, S., 48
Koelsch, S., 162, 225
Koeppe, R. A., 275
Koga, S., 75, 76
Koga, S. F. M., 75
Kohlmetz, C., 225
Kokaia, Z., 87
Kolb, B., 123
Kolinsky, R., 288
Komiya, Y., 48
Komsuoglu, S., 390
Koverola, C., 386
Kraemer, H. C., 241
Kramer, A. F., 48, 49, 99, 247, 251, 271, 323
Krampe, R. T., 222, 310, 318, 322, 355, 357, 364, 366, 369
Kray, J., 355
Kretz, A., 310
Kronenberg, G., 103
Krubitzer, L., 112, 119

Krüger, A., 363, 370, 374
Kryscio, R. J., 253
Kuhl, D., 387
Kuhl, P. K., 70
Kuhn, H. G., 48, 92, 95, 96, 97, 102, 103
Kujala, T., 120, 137
Kunej, D., 218
Kunwar, S., 88
Kupers, R., 120, 123
Kutas, M., 169, 171, 179

LaBar, K. S., 214
Labouvie, G. V., 26
Lakoff, G., 6
Laland, K. N., 34, 45, 311
Lalwani, A., 166
Lamb, M. J., 5, 6, 9, 10, 11, 13, 29, 34
Lambon Ralph, M. A., 285
Lambourn, D., 6
Lamish, M., 119
Lang, P. J., 210, 331, 335
Langston, R., 100
Långström, B., 250
Larsen, J. T., 42
Larsson, A., 253
Larue, J., 375
Lasko, N. B., 347, 395
Lassonde, M., 329, 347
Launer, L. J., 244
Lawrence, D. M., 150
Lawrence, J. A., 10, 12
Lawson, D., 170
Lazar, I., 72
Leamey, C. A., 383
Leary, D. E., 6
Leavitt, B., 87
Leclercq, C., 192
Lecours, A. R., 293, 299, 303
LeDoux, J. E., 200, 202, 203, 214, 215
Lee, K. M., 50, 172, 181
Lehericy, S., 188
Lehtokoski, A., 48, 179, 181
Lemaire, P., 317
Lennes, M., 179, 181
Lennon, M. C., 325
Leote, F., 299
Lepore, F., 116, 118, 329, 347
Lerner, R. M., 4, 7, 9, 10, 12
Lessard, N., 329
Lettman, N. A., 46
Leveck, M. D., 250
Levelt, W. J. M., 283

Levin, A. V., 69
Lévi-Strauss, C., 391, 392
Levitin, D. J., 226
Levitt, P., 63
Lewandowsky, M., 192
Lewis, T. L., 68, 149
Lewkowicz, D. J., 136
Lewontin, R. C., 219
Lian, C. H. T., 361
Liao, L., 374
Lickliter, R., 5, 9, 10, 136
Li, K. Z. H., 261, 272, 274, 360, 367, 373
Lindenberger, U., 5, 6, 9, 12, 15, 21, 26, 32,
    35, 46, 52, 249, 259, 260, 272, 274, 351, 354,
    364, 367, 370, 374
Lind, J., 241, 253
Lindvall, O., 82, 87
Lingenfelder, B., 330
Ling, S., 213
Link, B., 325
Lipsitt, L. P., 5, 9
Lipsitz, L. A., 15
Li, S.-C., 6, 15, 20, 28, 35, 44, 48, 52, 249, 259,
    270, 274, 351, 354, 373
Liu, H. M., 70
Locantore, J. K., 251
Lo, D. C., 130
Logan, J. M., 248, 267
Lomber, S. G., 129
Long, C., 249
Longworth, S. L., 346
Lönnberg, P., 242
Loosen, F., 228
LoPresti, E. F., 350, 368, 370, 374
Lovallo, W. R., 334
Lövdén, M., 354, 364, 374
Luce, M., 173
Luciana, M., 72
Lugar, H. M., 52
Luikart, G., 45
Lupien, S. J., 252
Lusignolo, T. M., 262
Lustig, C., 266, 267, 269, 270
Luuk, A., 48, 177, 179, 181
Lyckman, A. W., 121

Maas, I., 359, 360, 374
MacDonald, D., 299
Macklis, J., 87
Maffei, L., 114, 130, 153
Magavi, S., 87
Magnusson, D., 4, 5, 9, 43

Maguire, E. A., 48, 52, 99, 252, 324, 374
Mahy, J., 192
Maitland, S. B., 239, 240, 252
Mak, E., 242
Malach, R., 149
Malin, M., 329
Malloy, T. E., 146
Mamelak, M., 360
Mäntylä, T., 351, 364, 366, 367
Marchand, S., 127
Marchant, B., 146
Marcoen, A., 245
Marjamäki, P., 242
Markakis, E. A., 87
Markham, R., 145
Markman, A. B., 19
Markus, H. S., 252
Marshall, J., 125
Marshall, L., 388
Marshall, P., 75
Marshuetz, C., 255, 260, 275
Marsiske, M., 250, 362, 374
Martin, A., 274
Martin, N. G., 397
Martino, S., 70
Martin, S. J., 315
Martin, W. D., 67
Marzi, C. A., 126
Mason, H., 144, 146
Mather, M., 213
Mathis, U., 381
Matsuda, H., 52
Matthews, D., 218
Matute de Duran, E., 285
Matzke, M., 170
Maurer, D., 68, 135, 136, 149
Mauricio, M., 241
May, A., 99
Mayer, K. U., 12, 354
Mayeux, R., 325
Mayr, U., 318, 322, 355, 357, 374
Maytan, M., 247
McAdams, S., 227
McAllister, A. K., 130
McAuley, E., 48, 49, 99, 251, 261, 274, 323
McBurney, S. L., 165, 166
McCarthy, G., 189
McCaul, K. D., 388
McClarty, B., 386
McClearn, G. E., 241, 391
McClelland, G. M., 342, 346
McConahay, J. P., 210

McCrory, E., 51, 280, 304
McDermott, J., 185, 221
McEwen, B. S., 84, 333
McEwen, J. J., 274
McGaugh, J. L., 334
McGhee, J. L., 209
McInerney, S. C., 214
McIntosh, A. R., 246
McKay, R. D., 103
McKeel, D. W., 251
McMullin, K., 349
Meaney, M., 334
Mehler, J., 71, 299
Meinz, E. J., 355
Meister, M., 381
Melchner, L. von, 123
Melloni, R. H., 341
Mendes de Leon, C. F., 98, 247
Mendonça, A., 288, 289, 291, 304
Mendonça, S., 283, 291, 304
Menoncello, L., 51, 280
Merker, B., 221
Merzenich, M. M., 184, 329
Metcalve, J., 330
Meuter, R., 173
Meyer, E., 172
Meyer, G., 48
Michel, C., 120
Michel, F., 188
Michel, G. F., 386
Miezin, F. M., 52
Mihailidis, A., 350, 368, 374
Mikels, J. A., 255, 260, 264, 273, 275
Milham, M. P., 270, 274
Millar, S., 140
Miller, A. C., 265, 275
Miller, E. K., 355, 357, 374
Miller, G., 221
Mills, D., 50, 170
Milner, B., 172
Mineka, S., 206
Mireles, D. E., 319
Miserendino, M. J., 203, 212
Mitchell, D. E., 381
Mitra, P. P., 50
Miyamoto, Y., 42
Moberg, P. J., 242
Mobley, L. A., 171
Mohammed, A. H., 41
Mohr, J. P., 187
Molenaar, P. C. M., 15
Molle, M., 388

Monk, C. S., 63, 144, 149
Montag, D., 387
Montag-Sallaz, M., 387
Moore, M. M., 243, 252
Morais, J., 280, 281, 283, 286, 288
Moreira, A. A., 15
Morin, C., 127
Moritz, G., 347
Morris, J., 203
Morris, J. C., 247, 248, 251, 267
Morris, R. G., 100, 244
Morris, R. G. M., 40, 315
Muchnik, C., 329
Mueller, J., 173
Mulatu, M. S., 29, 42, 313, 314, 318
Mulder, G., 170, 180
Muldrew, S., 173
Müller, C., 370, 373
Mûller, M. M., 347
Müller, S. P., 165
Munoz, D. G., 320
Münte, T. F., 170, 222, 225
Murphy, G. M., Jr., 241
Murphy, K., 381
Murray, A. D., 319
Murray, H., 72
Murre, J. M. J., 358, 365, 374
Musso, M., 165
Myerson, J., 312

Näätänen, R., 48, 120, 137, 179, 181
Naccache, L., 188
Nager, W., 225
Nair, N. P. V., 252
Nakamura, H., 48
Naveh-Benjamin, M., 358, 367
Nearing, K., 203, 208, 215
Neave, N., 388
Nelson, C. A., 5, 47, 53, 63, 65, 67, 69, 70, 72, 73, 75, 76, 144, 149, 150, 153
Nelson, J. K., 266, 268, 275
Nelson, K., 46
Nelson, N. D., 150
Nemeth, E., 329
Nesselroade, J. R., 5, 15, 35, 354, 373
Neuner, F., 329, 330, 332, 335, 337, 339, 342, 344, 349
Neville, H. J., 48, 50, 118, 120, 134, 136, 137, 139, 140, 146, 148, 149, 152, 153, 166, 169, 174, 175, 181, 226, 329, 382, 396
Newell, A., 317
Newport, E. L., 71

Nicol, J. L., 170, 179, 181
Niederhausen, B., 137
Nikeiski, E. J., 71
Nilsson, L.-G., 146, 150, 151, 239, 242, 244, 246, 249
Nisbett, R. E., 35, 42, 46, 262
Nishikawa, M., 52
Nitsch, R. M., 334
Nobre, A., 189
Noe, R. A., 314
Nordberg, A., 250
Nordborg, C., 82, 88
Norenzayan, A., 35, 42, 46
Nosek, B. A., 209
Nottebohm, F., 84, 388
Nyberg. L., 164, 239, 243, 250, 252, 253, 267

Oates, G., 29, 313, 318
Ochsner, K., 213
O'Connor, K. J., 206, 215
Odenwald, M., 330, 335, 349
Odling-Smee, F. J., 34, 45, 311
O'Doherty, J., 216
O'Hara, R., 241
Ohashi, Y., 48
Ohman, A., 205, 207, 212
Ohnishi, T., 52
Ojemann, G. A., 192
Olausson, H., 127
Olesen, P. J., 249, 287
Olsson, A., 206, 208
Olsson, T., 41
Oostenveld, R., 162, 224, 235, 316, 324, 349
Orcutt, H. K., 342
Orr, S. P., 347, 395
Osborne, D., 253
Osterhout, L., 170, 171, 180
O'Sullivan, M., 244, 252
O'Toole, A. J., 69
Otsuka, A., 191
Otsuki, M., 191

Pääbo, S., 381
Packard, M. G., 334
Pakkenberg, B., 381
Pallas, S. L., 123
Palmer, T. D., 87, 154
Palm, G., 381
Panksepp, J., 221, 232
Pantev, C., 48, 51, 162, 184, 222, 224, 225, 233, 235, 316, 324, 328, 349

Papagno, C., 286, 302
Papez, J. W., 202
Pare, M., 329
Parente, M. A., 293, 299, 303
Park, A., 253, 324
Park, D. C., 255, 260, 262, 267
Parker, S. W., 75, 76
Parkinson, J. A., 340
Pascalis, O., 47, 69
Pascual-Leone, A., 48, 120, 222
Patterson, K. E., 187, 188, 285
Patterson, P., 368, 370, 374
Paulesu, E., 51, 71, 181, 304
Paus, T., 126
Pavlov, Ivan, 200, 213
Payne, B. R., 129
Peacker, S. M., 287
Pedersen, N. L., 252
Pellegrini, A. D., 50
Peng, K., 35, 42, 46
Penolazzi, B., 170
Perani, D., 71, 172, 181
Perfilieva, E., 82, 88
Pericak-Vance, M., 253
Peritz, G., 192
Persson, J., 241, 246, 252, 253, 268, 275
Pestell, S. J., 191
Petersen, S. E., 52, 188
Peterson, D. A., 82, 88
Peterson, G. M., 101
Peters, S., 191
Petersson, K. M., 241, 252, 281, 298, 299, 304, 305
Petitto, L. A., 71
Pfeifer, E., 170, 176, 179
Phelps, E. A., 203, 204, 206, 208, 215
Piaget, J., 72, 135
Pianka, P., 149
Pickering, S. J., 287
Pietrini, P., 186
Pinel, P., 192
Pitman, R. K., 347, 349, 395
Pizzorusso, T., 114, 130, 153
Polk, T. A., 188, 189, 193, 255, 260, 275
Pollak, S. D., 70
Pomplun, M., 319
Port, R., 15
Postle, B. R., 266
Praag, H., 103
Price, J. L., 251
Prill, K. A., 359
Pring, L., 149

Prinz, W., 15, 274, 351
Prochnow, J., 342
Prohovnik, I., 325
Proust, Marcel, 19
Ptito, A., 127
Ptito, M., 116, 121, 123, 127
Puce, A., 189
Pujol, R., 119

Quartz, S. R., 5, 9, 17, 35, 46, 310
Quessy, S., 116, 118
Quinones-Hinojosa, A., 88

Radeau, M., 170
Raffone, A., 374
Raichle, M. E., 188
Rajapakse, J. C., 303
Rakic, P., 153
Ramey, C. T., 73
Ramey, S. L., 73
Ramos, J. A., 388
Rampon, C., 113
Ramsdell, A. F., 385
Ranganath, C., 243
Rapee, R. M., 206
Rapp, B. C., 188
Ratto, G. M., 114, 130
Rauch, S. L., 173, 214, 340
Rau, H., 347
Rauschecker, J. P., 120, 139, 166, 230
Ravid, D., 281
Ray, W. J., 335, 336, 338
Raz, N., 48, 49, 149, 243, 244, 251, 257, 315, 323, 374
Rebert, C. S., 386
Rebillard, G., 119
Rebillard, M., 119
Redies, C., 384
Reed, C. L., 193
Reed, L., 249
Reed, T. E., 390
Reese, H., 5, 9
Reeves, A. J., 82
Reeves, S., 253
Reger, S. N., 359
Reiman, E. M., 253
Reineck, R., 250
Reingold, E. M., 318, 319
Reis, A.,
Reis, H. T., 46
Relkin, N. R., 50, 172, 180
Renault, B., 390

Reuter-Lorenz, P. A., 47, 48, 52, 245, 255, 270, 274, 275
Reynolds, B. A., 84
Ribeiro, C., 299
Ribordy, S. C., 70
Riggs, D. S., 341
Rijntjes, M., 165
Rinne, J. O., 242
Rivera-Gaxiola, M., 177, 181
Robaey, P., 390
Robert, C., 329, 332, 339, 344
Roberts, B. W., 15
Roberts, L. E., 162, 224, 316, 328, 329
Robins Wahlin, T.-B., 250
Roca, V., 342
Rockland, C., 213
Rockstroh, B., 48, 51, 162, 184, 225, 233, 316, 328, 349
Röder, B., 120, 123, 140, 142, 143, 146, 152, 154, 329, 382
Rodrigue, K. M., 243, 357, 374
Rogers, L., 385
Rogers, L. J., 385
Rogers, W. A., 321
Rönnberg, J., 146, 150, 151
Rönnlund, M., 253
Roozendaal, B., 334
Rosas, P., 286
Rosenzweig, M. R., 40, 41, 96
Roses, A. D., 253
Rösler, F., 120, 123, 140, 142, 143, 151, 154, 329, 382, 396
Ross, B., 162, 235, 324, 349
Ross, D., 206
Rosselli, M., 286
Rossel, S., 381
Rossor, M. N., 192
Ross, S. A., 206
Roth, W. T., 330
Rowe, J. W., 240
Royce, J., 73
Rubin, E. H., 251
Ruf, M., 336, 347, 349
Rugg, M. D., 146
Rumsey, J. M., 303
Rupp, A., 235
Rüschemeyer, S.-A., 173, 181
Russo, F. A., 226

Sadato, N., 120, 337
Saddy, D., 170
Sadka, R., 119

Safar, F., 87
Saffran, E. M., 187
Saito, H., 334
Saito, S., 48
Saleptsi, E., 342, 349
Salthouse, T. A., 258, 309, 355, 359
Salvador, A., 388
Salvesen, G. S., 253
Sanai, N., 88
Sandblom, J., 245, 246, 252
Sanders, A. L., 248, 267
Sanders, M. D., 125
Santarelli, L., 103
Sapolsky, R. M., 334, 386
Saunders, A. M., 241, 253
Saxe, M., 103
Scalf, P., 99, 274
Scarmeas, N., 247, 253, 319, 324
Schaal, S., 330, 341, 344
Schachner, M., 387
Schacter, D. L., 144
Schaie, K. W., 10, 30, 258, 350, 368
Scharff, C., 388
Schauer, M., 329, 330, 332, 335, 337, 339, 344, 347, 349
Scheich, H., 119
Schellenbach, M., 363, 364, 374
Scherer, H., 360, 374
Scherg, M., 235
Schicke, T., 143, 154
Schinder, A. F., 154
Schlaggar, B. L., 52
Schlaug, G., 200, 213, 225, 226, 233, 235
Schleicher, A., 223, 225, 233
Schlesewsky, M., 170, 171
Schmal, C. G., 388
Schmechel, D., 241, 253
Schmitt, F. A., 253
Schneider, J. A., 98, 247
Schneider, P., 224, 235
Schönberger, J., 231
Schooler, C., 29, 42, 313, 314, 318
Schouten, J. L., 186
Schreiber, W., 343
Schröger, E., 162, 225
Schuierer, G., 99
Schultetus, R. S., 319
Schultz, A. B., 360
Schulzer, M., 242
Schulz, S. C., 50, 65
Schumacher, E. H., 266
Schuman, H., 209

Schüz, A., 381
Schwartz, J. L., 209
Scott, L., 69
Seckl, J. R., 41
Seeman, T. E., 262
Segal, E., 349
Sejnowski, T. J., 5, 9, 17, 46, 261, 310
Sekuler, A. B., 360
Sengpiel, F., 114, 381, 382
Serrano, M. A., 388
Settersten, R. A., Jr., 10, 12, 28
Seymour, B., 216
Shahidullah, S., 386
Shallice, T., 190, 251
Sharit, J., 321
Shatz, C. J., 381
Shenton, M. E., 347, 395
Shepher, J., 392
Shifflett, H., 347
Shiner, R. L., 15
Shin, L. M., 214, 349
Shukitt-Hale, B., 274
Shumway-Cook, A., 360, 372
Siegler, R. S., 317
Sigman, M., 147
Sikström, S., 11, 249
Silva, C. G., 283, 286, 288, 290, 293, 294
Simon, H. A., 311, 317, 318, 321
Sims, K., 280, 303
Singer, T., 6, 10, 21, 46, 326
Singer, W., 5, 7, 34
Singer, Y., 216
Singh, J. A. L., 384
Singh, K., 330, 348
Skudlarski, P., 186
Sloboda, J. A., 231
Small, B. J., 241, 247
Smith, C. D., 241, 253
Smith, E. E., 259, 266, 274, 275
Smith, G. A., 390, 397
Smith, J., 260
Smith, L., 18
Smith, M., 339
Smyke, A. T., 75, 76
Snipper, A., 73
Snyder, A. Z., 188, 248, 267
Söderlund, H., 244
Soderström, S., 41
Sokoloff, L., 309
Soma, Y., 191
Souvatzoglou, E., 329

Spacarelli, S., 70
Sparks, D. L., 143
Specht, H. J., 235
Spelke, E., 192
Spence, C., 142, 143, 154
Spencer, D. D., 203, 214
Stadelmann, E., 192
Staff, R. T., 319
Stahl, C., 370, 373
Stallcup, M., 188, 189
Stampe, D. M., 319
Stanczak, L., 267, 275
Stanescu, R., 192
Stanfield, B. B., 84, 91
Staudinger, U. M., 5, 6, 12, 15, 21, 28, 32, 35,
    351, 372
Stawinski, P., 382
Steeh, C., 209
Steele, K. M., 224
Stefani, R., 70
Stein, B. E., 136, 143
Steinberg, K.-E., 370, 373
Steinberg, L., 329
Steingard, R. J., 341
Steinhauer, K., 176
Stein, M. B., 386
Steinmetz, H., 223, 233, 235
Stelmach, G. E., 375
Sternberg, R. J., 6, 7, 12, 30, 31, 35,
    220
Stern, P., 260
Stern, Y., 247, 319, 320, 325
Sterr, A., 139, 140, 347, 396
Stigsdotter Neely, A., 252
Stock, O., 120
Storandt, M., 251
Stowe, L. A., 180
Stricks, L., 319, 325
Strittmatter, W. J., 241, 253
Stromswold, K., 173
Studer, K., 349
Stuss, D. T., 243
Suay, F., 388
Suckling, J., 249
Sugishita, M., 189
Summers, P. E., 252
Surget, A., 103
Sur, M., 121, 123, 383
Swain, R. A., 99, 273
Swihart, T., 252
Sylvester, C.-Y. C., 266, 268, 269
Szegda, K., 66

Takeuchi, A. H., 226
Tal, J., 46
Tamis-LeMonda, C. S., 46
Tanapat, P., 82
Tan, Ü., 390
Tarr, M. J., 186, 310
Tarshish, C., 252
Taub, E., 48, 51, 162, 184, 222, 233, 316, 328,
    347
Taylor, C. S., 141
Taylor, S. F., 255, 275
Teasdale, N., 360, 375
Teder-Sälejärvi, W., 139, 140, 396
Tees, R. C., 177
Telatar, M., 390
Teplin, L. A., 346
Tervaniemi, M., 162, 225
Tesch-Römer, C., 222, 318, 323, 374
Tetens, J. N., 10, 43
Thelen, E., 18
Theoret, H., 127
Thomas, K. M., 63
Thomas, M., 52
Thompson, D. M., 366
Thompson, P. M., 299, 305
Thompson-Schill, S. L., 173
Tian, B., 139
Timmerman, I. G., 342
Todd, P. M., 13
Toga, A. W., 299
Tolchinsky, L., 281
Toldi, J., 118, 119
Tomaiuolo, F., 126
Tomasello, M., 5, 9, 12, 14, 34, 35, 42
Toni, N., 154
Tooby, J., 34
Torchia, M. G., 386
Torres, F., 120
Tramontin, A. D., 88
Tranel, D., 213
Trice, J. E., 84
Tsao, F. M., 70
Tsien, J. Z., 113
Tsivkin, S., 192
Tsuji, S., 191
Tuffiash, M., 318
Tulving, E., 243, 366
Turkewitz, G., 135
Turk, I., 218
Turner, A. L., 69
Turner, R., 48
Tyler, M. E., 120

Ungerleider, L. G., 48
UNICEF, 345
United States Department of Labor, 312
Uno, H., 386

Vaituzis, A. C., 303
Valentin, D., 69
Valentine, E. R., 245, 252, 316
Valentine, J., 72
Valsiner, J., 10, 12
van Berkel, C., 334
van Broeckhoven, C., 252
Vandenbergh, J. G., 310
Van der Kolk, B. A., 341
Vandermeer, J., 34
van Dyck, R., 389
van Gelder, T., 15
Van Hoesen, G. W., 185
Van Horn, J. D., 249
Van Lancker, D., 165
Van Praag, H., 98, 154, 261
Varney, N. R., 280
Vasyukova, E., 318
Venneri, A., 191
Veraart, C., 120
Verhaeghe, A., 290, 293
Verhaeghen, P., 245
Vermetten, E., 389
Vespignani, F., 170
Visscher, K. M., 52
Viswanathan, M., 272
Vitouch, O., 215, 219, 221, 223, 225, 226, 228
Vogler, G. P., 241
Volgyi, B., 119
Volkow, N. D., 242
Volungis, A. D., 341
Voss, P., 329, 347
Vouloumanos, A., 70
Vygotsky, L. S., 280

Wahlin, Å., 247, 252
Wahlsten, D, 5, 9, 10
Wahlund, L.-O., 249
Wais, P., 213
Wallace, C. S., 67, 72, 136, 143
Wallace, M. T., 136, 143
Wallin, N. L., 221
Wang, G.-J., 242
Wang, H. X., 247
Wang, S. S. H., 50
Wang, Y., 242
Ward, N. S., 268

Warrington, E. D., 125
Warrington, E. K., 187, 188, 192, 193
Wasinger, R., 370, 373
Webb, A. G., 48, 49, 251, 323
Webb, S. J., 63, 144, 149
Weber-Fox, C., 174, 175
Weeks, R., 139
Weiller, C., 165, 188
Weinzapfel, B., 165
Weiskrantz, L., 125, 201
Weissman, D. H., 85, 274
Weissman, I. L., 85
Weiss, S., 84
Weld, D., 350, 373
Welsh, K. M., 275
Welzl, H., 387
Werker, J. F., 70, 177
Wessinger, C. M., 127, 139
Westerberg, H., 249, 287
Whalen, P. J., 211, 213, 214, 349
Whalley, L. J., 319
Wheeler, M. A., 243
Whishaw, I. Q., 123
Whitaker, H. A., 192
White, R., 386
White, S. A., 384
White, T., 65
Whitfield, K., 252
Whitfield, S., 213
Whitty, C. J., 242
Whorf, B., 50
Wiech, K., 346
Wienbruch, C., 48, 51, 162, 184, 222, 233, 316, 328, 349
Wiesel, T. N., 114, 115
Wilding, J. M., 245, 252, 316
Wilk, S. L., 314
Willhoite, A. R., 87
Williams, C. J., 209
Williams, K., 72
Williams, S. C. R., 252
Williamson, A., 357, 374
Willis, S. L., 26, 255, 272
Wilson, R. S., 98, 247
Winblad, B., 247, 250
Windell, D. L., 226
Wise, R., 188
Wiskott, L., 101
Wolf, A. P., 392
Wolff, J. R., 118
Wolfson, S., 388
Wollberg, Z., 119

Wolters, G., 358, 374
Wong, D., 165
Wong, R. O., 381
Woods, R. P., 299
Woollacott, M. H., 360, 372
Woolley, C. S., 84
Wright, M. J., 390, 397
Wyver, S. R., 145

Xerri, C., 113

Yamada, H., 337
Yanai, J., 391
Yesavage, J. A., 241
Yonekura, Y., 337
Yoshikawa, K., 189

Yost, H. J., 385
Young, A. W., 213

Zacks, R. T., 258, 259
Zaidel, E., 299
Zarahn, E., 253, 324
Zatorre, R. J., 71, 172, 226, 232, 329, 347
Zdrahal-Urbanek, J., 221
Zeanah, C. H., 75, 76
Zeki, S., 123
Zelaya, F., 249
Zeng, J., 208
Zhuang, J., 317
Zigler, E., 72
Zilles, K., 233
Zohary, E., 149

# Subject Index

Abecedarian program, 73
absolute pitch. *See* AP
acalculia, 192
"activity-dependent synaptic plasticity and memory hypothesis," 40
*Adagio*, 231
adult neurogenesis. *See* neurogenesis, adult
adulthood, late
  IHET in, 361–363
  net source release in, 362
  person specificity in, 362
  proximal v. distal frames in, 362
aerobic fitness
  aging and, 261
  cognition and, 247, 248
aging. *See also* aging, cognitive
  adult neurogenesis and, 102–104
  aerobic fitness and, 261
  amygdala and, 213
  bilingualism and, 272
  brain and, effects on, 249, 258, 357
  cerebral blood flow and, 309
  chemical imbalances in, 260
  cognitive, 26, 257–260
  cognitive compensation and, 244–246
  hearing and, 359
  lifespan development for, 318–319
  memory and, 32, 151, 239–241
  plasticity in, 260–263
  posture and, effects on, 359–360
  sensorimotor functioning and, 359–360
  short-term memory and, 239
  signal-to-noise relation modulations and, 249, 258
  spatial navigation and, 364

  verb generation tasks and, 268
  vision loss and, 359
aging, cognitive, 26, 257–260
  HAROLD model for, 311
  information processing and, 259
  inhibitory processing declines in, 259
  intelligence testing and, 258
  sensory/sensorimotor functioning and, 360–361
allostasis, 333
  homeostasis v., 333
Alzheimer's disease, 98, 319
  hippocampal structure and, 100
*Amadeus*, 231
amblyopia, 116
American Sign Language. *See* ASL
amygdala, 202
  aging effects on, 213
  damage of, 210
  differential activation of, 205
  emotional learning and, 206, 211
  fear conditioning and, 201, 202–203
  hippocampal damage and, 204
  Klüver-Bucy syndrome and, 202
  in limbic system, 202
  stress regulation by, 333
AP (absolute pitch)
  early learning for, 226
  musicality and, 226–227
  perceptual learning and, 226
aphasia
  factors for, in brain development, 299
  in sign languages, 166
APOE (apolipoproteins), 241–242
apolipoproteins. *See* APOE

416

apoptosis, during brain development, 310
arithmetic, 192–195
    acalculia, 192
    number-related words, 194
ASL (American Sign Language), 166
attention, 212
auditory systems
    aging's effects on, 359
    localization of, during blindness, 139, 143
    loss, WHO criteria for, 359
autobiographic memory, 331

BAs (Brodmann's areas), 164
behavioral plasticity. *See* plasticity, behavioral
BEIP (Bucharest Early Intervention Project), 22, 74
    FCG as part of, 74
    IG as part of, 74
    NIG as part of, 75
    procedures/measures for, 75–76
bilingualism
    activation patterns and, 172–173
    aging and, 272
    brain development and, 172–176
    ELAN in, 175
    electrophysiological components for, 173–176
    *N400* components in, 174
    *P600* components in, 175
binding mechanisms
    associative, 358
    within IHET, 357, 358
    interactive, 358
    synchronous/co-active, 358
biocultural co-construction hypothesis, 14–19, 33–34, 61–62, 256
    brain development and, 43–49
    change as factor in, 14–15
    CNS and, 15–16
    cross-level dynamic framework for, 44
    CRUNCH and, 256
    experience as factor in, 63
    formalization of, 16
    language evolution within, 49–50
    musicality and, 229
    SST and, 257
    temporal windows in, 15

biocultural constructivism, 9, 11. *See also* biocultural co-construction hypothesis
    collaboration within, 8, 33–34
    developmental, 3–4, 20
    interactionism and, 7–9
    reciprocal modification within, 8
biological evolution. *See* evolution, biological
blindness
    auditory localization during, 139, 143
    Braille method and, 119
    congenital, 119
    cortical, 125
    ERPs grand means for, 148–153
    fMRI and, 120
    memory and, 144–152
    PET measurements for, 120, 121
    processing levels during, 146–149, 152
    recognition scores during (memory), 146–151
    sensory system development with, 135–137
    studies on, 119–120
    transcranial magnetic stimulation, 120
"blindsight," 125
    hemispherectomies and, 125
block design tasks, 246
"blooming buzzing confusion," 135
Braille method, 119
brain (adult). *See also* brain development
    aging and, 249, 258, 357
    IAT activation of, 211
    MRT studies on, 99
    neuronal development in, 88–92
    occupations and, 308
    PTSD influence on, 335–339
    structural changes to, from memory, 243–244
    structures of, 186
brain development, 4, 63–66, 310–311
    anatomical views for, 64
    aphasia and, factors for, 299
    apoptosis during, 310
    arithmetic and, 192–195
    behavioral plasticity and, 45–46
    bilingualism and, 172–176
    co-construction hypothesis and, 43–49
    cognitive development as part of, 71–76
    corpus callosum, 299
    cortical organization in, 112
    critical periods of, 134

brain development (*cont.*)
  encephalization and, 49, 50
  evolutionary plasticity and, 45
  experience as influence on, 66–68, 72, 76,
    77
  glial cells in, 95
  heredity and, 195
  language activation patterns and,
    164–169, 174, 177–178
  language development as part of, 70–71
  musical biographies and, 218
  nature-nurture theories and, 111–112
  neural specialization as part of,
    183–185
  neuronal plasticity and, 134
  occupational influences on, 308, 311–312,
    315–318
  plasticity in, 94–95, 328–330
  PTSD's influence on, 335, 339–340
  quantitative effects during, 184
  reading and, 187–189
  retirement's influence on, 314
  RF size and, 184
  social-emotional development as part of,
    74–75
  timeline for, 65
  visual system development as part of,
    68–70
  writing and, 189–191
brain imaging methods, 163–164. *See also*
    fMRI; PET
  fMRI, 27, 30, 120, 163
  PET, 120, 121, 163
brain plasticity, 94–95
  activity-dependent regulation of, 102
Brodmann's areas. *See* BAs
Bucharest Early Intervention Project. *See*
    BEIP

cadherins, 383
  CNS and, 384
"Candle in the Wind," 232
cells
  glial, 95
  precursor, 87, 89
  progenitor, 90–91
  stem, 85–88, 90–91
central nervous system. *See* CNS
chess playing, 317, 318–319
  pattern recognition in, 318–319
child development
  abuse as factor during, 341

environmental enrichment during, 72–73,
    74
  IQ development during, 73
  language development in, 50
  sensory systems during, 136
"chill and thrills," 231
Chrystallins, 93
*Cinderella* myths, 394
classical conditioning, 200. *See also* fear
    conditioning
  CR as part of, 200
  CS as part of, 200
  fear, 201–204
  UCS as part of, 200
CNS (central nervous system), 134
  cadherins and, 384
  co-construction hypothesis and, 15–16
  sensory system development and,
    135–137
co-evolution, 8. *See also* evolution, biological
cognition
  aerobic fitness as factor for, 247,
    248
  aging and, 26, 257–260
  cognitive reserve hypothesis, 247
  IHET and, 355–358
  lifestyle factors for, 246–248
  SEM for, 298
  social disengagement and, 247, 262
  substance abuse and, 246
cognitive aging. *See* aging, cognitive
cognitive development, 71–76
cognitive reserve hypothesis, 247
"cold memory," 330
  "hot" and, 332
compensation, in lifespan development, 31,
    352
compensation-related utilization of neural
    circuits hypothesis. *See* CRUNCH
complex environment paradigms. *See*
    environment paradigms, complex
*Concerto for Clarinet and Orchestra*, 229
conditioned response. *See* CR
conditioned stimuli. *See* CS
congenital blindness, 119
congenital strabismus, 116
  amblyopia from, 116
  in felines, 117
constructivism. *See also* biocultural
    constructivism
  biological, 9
  interactionism and, 8

corpus callosum, 299, 301
cortical blindness, 125
cortical lesions, 123–129
    by area, 125
cortical orientation maps, 382
CR (conditioned response), 200
*Critique of Pure Reason* (Kant), 220
CRUNCH (compensation-related utilization
        of neural circuits hypothesis), 256,
        265–270
    empirical bases of, 266–270
    overactivation regions in, 267, 269, 270
    PET for, 267
CS (conditioned stimuli), 200
cues, 366–367. *See also* cuing structures,
        personalized
    compatibility for, 366
    distinctive, 366
    self-generated, 367
cuing structures, personalized
    for IHET, 364–365
    mnemonic devices as, 365
cultural biases. *See also* race biases
    fear conditioning and, 208–212
    IAT and, 209
    MRS of, 210
    race, 209, 211
cultural development. *See* sociocultural
        development

"deliberate practice," 222
dementia
    Mini-Mental State Examinations for,
        319
    occupational effects on, 319–320
dendrites, 91
dentate gyrus, 88, 97, 101
    lipotuscin in, 103
depression, hippocampus and, 103–104
depth perception, 68
*Dictionary of Occupational Titles* (US
        Department of Labor), 312
difference according to memory effect. *See*
        DM
DM (difference according to memory)
    effect, 146–151

early learning, for AP, 226
early left-anterior negativity. *See* ELAN
education, 279. *See also* learning
        development
    as cultural transmission, 279

fluency and, 295
    preadaptations and, 280
ELAN (early left-anterior negativity)
    in bilingualism, 175
    in language development, 170
emotional learning, amygdala and, 206, 211
emotional science, 231
encephalization, brain development and,
        49, 50
environment paradigms, complex, 41–43
environmental enrichment
    Abecedarian program, 73
    behavioral development and, 261
    during early child development, 72–73, 74
    Head Start program, 72
    housing, 41–43, 113
    paradigms for, 97
EP (evolutionary psychology), 218
epigenetic inheritance, 10
"episodic" memory, 100, 148–153
ERPs (event-related potentials)
    grand means (blindness), 148–153
    grand means (tones), 138
    for language development, 50, 177
    long-term memory and, 146–149, 152
    spatial functions and, 137, 138
event-related potentials. *See* ERPs
"evo-devo" movement, 219
evolution, biological, 218–220. *See also*
        co-evolution
    behavioral plasticity and, 219
    co-evolution within, 8
    developmental qualitative innovation in,
        8
    environmental effects on, 311
    EP and, 218
    "evo-devo" movement and, 219
    genetic coding and, 218
    *Homo plasticus*, 219
    musicality and, 220–229
    "selection pressure rules" in, 218
    sexual dimorphism and, 221
    spandrels in, 219
evolutionary plasticity. *See* plasticity,
        evolutionary
evolutionary psychology. *See* EP
exaptations. *See* spandrels
experience
    in biocultural co-construction hypothesis,
        63
    brain development and, influence on,
        66–68, 72, 76

experience (*cont.*)
  brain function domains and, 77
  in child development, 76
  "cold memory" and, 330
  face perception from, 69
  Hebb-Williams maze and, 72
  LTD and, 130
  LTP and, 130
  molecular basis of, 130–131
  neuronal plasticity and, 153
  neurotrophins and, 130
  plasticity and, 41, 67
  timing/duration effects of, 77
expertise, neuronal plasticity and,
    51–52
extinction learning, race biases and, 211
eye misalignment, visual system
    development and, 116–118

face perception, 69–70
  experience as factor for, 69
fear conditioning, 201–204
  amygdala and, 201, 202–203
  cultural bias and, 208–212
  instructed, 205, 206
  through observation, 206–207
  social learning and, 204–208
  stress and, 332
fear networks, from "hot memory," 331
fluency
  education influence on, 295
  semantic, 293–295
  verbal, 294
fluid intelligence, 258
Flynn effect, IQ and, 30, 315
fMRI (functional magnetic resonance
    imaging), 163
  for blindness, 120
  for memory tasks, 27, 30
free recall tasks, 246
functional magnetic resonance imaging.
    *See* fMRI
fusiform face area, 186

gene expression, 17
  genomes and, 219
  genomic sequencing and, 93–94
  immediate-early, 387
  nature-nurture theories and, 92–94
  neuronal plasticity and, 153
  proteomes and, 93, 219
genetic coding, evolution and, 218
genetic plasticity. *See* plasticity, genetic

genetics, memory and, 241–242
genomes, 219
  Human Genome Project, 380
glial cells, 95
*Gran Partita*, 231
graphemic codes, 190

habituation, 136
haptic sense, 140
HAROLD (hemispheric asymmetry
    reduction in older adults) model, 311
Head Start program, 72
hearing. *See also* auditory systems
  aging and, 359
  loss, WHO estimates, 359
Hebb-Williams maze, 72
hemispherectomies, 125–129
  "blindsight" and, 125
  in primates, 128
  RGC depletion and, 127
hemispheric asymmetry reduction in older
    adults model. *See* HAROLD
heredity, brain development and, 195
"Hey Jude," 232
hippocampus, 89. *See also* dentate gyrus
  adult neurogenesis and, 84, 87, 88, 90
  Alzheimer's disease and, 100
  amygdala and, 204
  dentate gyrus as part of, 88, 97, 101
  depression and, 103–104
  memory and, 101, 243
  PTSD and, 386
  stress regulation by, 333
homeostasis
  allostasis v., 333
*Homo plasticus*, 219
*Homo sapiens*
  cultural development and, 27
  musicality and, 217
hormones, 388
  stress, 333
"hot memory," 330
  autobiographic memories as part of, 331
  "cold" and, 332
  fear networks from, 331
HPA (hypothalamic-pituitary-adrenal) axis,
    stress regulation by, 333
Human Genome Project, 380
hypothalamic-pituitary-adrenal axis. *See*
    HPA

"I Want To Hold Your Hand," 232
"I Will Always Love You," 231

"I Will Survive," 232
IAPS (International Affective Picture
    System), 335
IAT (Implicit Association Test), 209
  brain activation during, 211
IFG (inferior frontal gyrus), language
    development and, 164
IHET (intelligent human engineering
    technology), 350
  behavior regulation under, 355
  binding mechanisms within, 357,
    358
  cognition and, 355–358
  conceptual foundation for, 353
  cuing structures for, personalized,
    364–365
  individualized, 368–370
  in late adulthood, 361–363
  net resource release as part of, 352,
    353–354
  person specificity as part of, 352,
    354
  person-oriented assisted technology and,
    367–368
  proximal v. distal evaluation as part of,
    352, 354–355
  working memory and, 357
illiteracy
  object naming and, 283–285
  phrase type errors and, 291, 292
  pseudoword processing and, 289
  rates, in Portugal, 282
  semantic strategies for, 288–289
  sentence context and, 289–293
  word "clitization" and, 290
ILPG (intrasulcal length of the precentral
    gyrus), 223
Implicit Association Test. See IAT
incest, 391–393
inferior frontal gyrus. See IFG
inheritance, 11. See also epigenetic
    inheritance
  epigenetic, 10
instructed fear conditioning, 205, 206
  observation v., 207–208
intelligence. See also IQ
  cognitive aging and, 258
  cultural effects on, 320–321
  fluid, 258
  *Metaphors of the Mind: Conceptions of the
    Nature of Intelligence*, 6
intelligent human engineering technology.
    See IHET

interactionism
  biocultural constructivism and, 7–9
  constructivism and, 8
  emergent properties of, 8
  plasticity and, 9
International Affective Picture System. See
    IAPS
intrasulcal length of the precentral gyrus.
    See ILPG
IQ (intelligence quotient)
  child development and, 73
  Flynn effect and, 30, 315
*Italian Concerto*, 51
"It's Now or Never," 232

JNDs (just noticeable differences), for
    sensory systems, 142

Klüver-Bucy syndrome, 202

LAN (left anterior negativity), in language
    development, 170
language development, 70–71, 280. See also
    bilingualism
  BAs and, 164
  in childhood, 50
  in co-construction hypothesis, 49–50
  as cultural construct, 161
  culture-specific environments and, 50–51
  ELAN in, 170
  ERP data for, 50, 177
  IFG and, 164
  LAN in, 170
  MMN as part of, 177
  *N400* components in, 169–170
  neural representations of, 163
  *P600* components in, 170
  second language acquisition and, 71
  semantic anomalies in, 169
  semantic violations in, 167
  social group size and, 49
  speech perception as part of, 70–71
  STG and, 164
  syntactic processing in, 170
  syntactic violations in, 166, 167
languages. See also language development
  ASL, 166
  brain activation patterns across, 164–169,
    174, 177–178
  electrophysiological components across,
    169–172
  sign, 165
  social learning and, 204

learning development. *See also* arithmetic; learning disorders; learning theories; reading; writing
  adult neurogenesis and, 99–102
  emotional, 206, 211
learning disorders
  acalculia, 192
  pure alexia, 187, 188
  pure dysgraphia, 189
learning theories
  early learning, 226
  emotional learning, 206, 211
  extinction learning, 211
  perceptual learning, 226
  social learning, 204–208
left-anterior negativity. *See* LAN
lifespan development. *See also* biocultural co-construction hypothesis
  for aging, 318–319
  compensation as part of, 31, 352
  cortical plasticity and, 47–49
  optimization as part of, 31, 352
  selection as part of, 31, 310, 352
limbic system, 202
literacy, 281. *See also* illiteracy
  brain structure and, 299–301
  pseudowords and, 295
  semantic fluency and, 293–295
  study comparisons, 295–301
  study populations, Portugal, 282
long-term depression. *See* LTD
long-term memory. *See* memory, long-term
long-term potentiation. *See* LTP
LTD (long-term depression)
  experience and, 130
  NMDA receptors and, 130
LTP (long-term potentiation)
  experience and, 130
  NMDA receptors and, 130

magnetic resonance tomography. *See* MRT
magnetoencephalography. *See* MEG
MEG (magnetoencephalography), 222
memory, 144–152. *See also* memory, long-term; memory, short-term; memory, working
  aging and, 32, 151, 240
  APOE expression and, 241–242
  autobiographic, 331
  blindness and, 144–152
  block design tasks for, 246
  brain changes and, structural, 243–244

  "cold," 330
  "episodic," 100, 148–153
  false manipulation of, 146–150
  fMRI for, 27, 30
  free recall tasks for, 246
  genetic influences for, 241–242
  hippocampal role in, 101, 243
  "hot," 330
  long-term functions, 146–152
  neurotransmission systems and, 242–243
  nigrostriatal dopamine system and, 242, 243
  phonological processing and, 285–288
  retrieval monitoring as part of, 144
  short-term functions, 144–146
  source, 144
  structure of, 99–100
  "superior memorizers" for, 245
  for voices, 147, 152
  "wild associations" and, 100
  Wisconsin Card Sorting Test for, 244
  working, 212, 287–288, 357
memory, long-term, 212
  DM effect and, 146–151
  ERPs and, 146–149, 152
  false alarm rates and (testing), 147, 153
  functions, 146–152
  hits and (testing), 147, 152
  old/new effect and, 146–150
  recognition, 146–149, 151
memory, short-term, 286–287
  aging's influence on, 239
  digit span tasks and, 286
  functions of, 144–146
  spatial span tasks and, 286
memory, working, 212
  IHET and, 357
  prefrontal cortex role in, 357, 358
  pseudoword processing in, 287–288
metalinguistic awareness
  reading and, 280, 286
metaphors, 6–7
*Metaphors in the History of Psychology* (Leary), 6
*Metaphors of the Mind: Conceptions of the Nature of Intelligence* (Sternberg), 6
*Metaphors We Live By* (Johnson/Lakoff), 6
Method of Loci, 316, 365
Mini-Mental State Examinations, 319
mismatch negativity. *See* MMN

MMN (mismatch negativity)
  in language development, 177
  in musicality, 225
mnemonic devices, 365–366. *See also*
    "superior memorizers"
  as cuing structure, 365
  Method of Loci, 316, 365
Modern Racism Scale. *See* MRS
modularity, 185–187
  fusiform face area, 186
"Mozart effect," 224
MRS (Modern Racism Scale), 210
MRT (magnetic resonance tomography),
    brain studies (adult), 99
multipotency, 85
"Music: The Mathematics of Feelings," 230
musicality. *See also* AP
  aesthetic experiences of, 229–232
  age as factor for, 223
  AP and, 226–227
  biocultural co-construction hypothesis
      and, 229
  brain development and, 218
  "chill and thrills" and, 231
  chromatic modulations and, 228
  "deliberate practice" approach to, 222
  equal-tempered preferences as part of,
      228
  evolution theories of, 220–229
  *Homo sapiens* and, 217
  MMN in, 225
  "Mozart effect," 224
  multiple origins of, 232
  *N100* component in, 225
  natural v. sexual selection and, 220
  perception and, 224–226, 230
  performance and, 222–224
  plasticity and, 226–227
  scale systems and, 227–229
  tuning systems and, 227
  "Youth Radar" survey for, 221
musicians, ILPG in, 223

*N100* component, 225
*N400* components
  in bilingualism, 174
  in language development, 169–170
nature-nurture theories. *See also* brain
    plasticity
  adult neurogenesis and, 95–99
  brain development and, 111–112
  developmental scholars and, 5

genes and, 92–94
  rearing conditions as part of, 112–114
  visual deprivation as part of, 114–116
"nervenkitt," 95
net source release
  in IHET, 352, 353–354
  in late adulthood, 362
"neural constructivism," 46
neurites, 91
  dendrites and, 91
neurobiology, plasticity as part of, 10
neurodegenerative disorders
  Alzheimer's disease, 98
  Parkinson's disease, 98
neurogenesis, adult, 82–83
  aging and, 102–104
  cell identification in, 83
  hippocampus and, 84, 87, 88, 90
  learning development and, 99–102
  nature-nurture theories and,
      95–99
  neurons in, 85
  olfactory system and, 87, 88
  precursor cells in, 87, 89
  stem cells in, 85–88
neurohumoral axes, stress and, 333–335
neuronal plasticity. *See* plasticity, neuronal
neurons, 85
  neurites as part of, 91
  structural processes of, 91
neurosciences. *See also* brain development
  cultural, 262
  development of, 4
  education requirements for, 62
  neurobiology, 10
neurotransmission systems
  memory and, 242–243
  PET for, 242
  single photon emission tomography for,
      242
neurotrophins, 130
"new wars," 343
  civilian targets during, 344
  economic factors for, 344
  identity justification as part of,
      343–344
  irregular forces as part of, 343
"niche construction," 45
nigrostriatal dopamine system, memory
    and, 242, 243
NMDA (N-d-methylaspartate) receptors,
    LTP/LTD and, 130

object naming, illiteracy and, influence on, 283–285
observation
  acquisition phase of, 207
  fear conditioning through, 206–207
  instruction v., 207–208
  test phase of, 207
Occupational Information Network. *See* O*NET
occupations
  brain development and, 308, 311–312, 315–318
  complexity of, 313–315
  demands of, 312–313
  dementia and, effects on, 319–320
  *Dictionary of Occupational Titles*, 312
  lifespan development for, 308–312
  O*NET review for, 312
ocular dominance
  thalmic retinal projections and, 115
  visual deprivation and, 114
old age. *See* adulthood, late
olfactory system, adult neurogenesis and, 87, 88
O*NET (Occupational Information Network), 312, 322
ontogenesis, 11
optimization, in lifespan development, 31, 352
organized violence. *See* violence, organized

P600 components
  in bilingualism, 175
  in language development, 170
pair matching, 136
parenting studies, behavioral plasticity and, 46
Parkinson's disease, 98
pattern recognition, 68–69
  in chess playing, 318–319
perception, 213
  musicality and, 224–226, 230
"perception of rule-based invariance," 147, 153
perceptual learning, 226
person specificity, 354
  in IHET, 352, 354
  in late adulthood, 362
personalized cuing structures. *See* cuing structures, personalized
person-oriented assisted technology, 367–368

PET (positron emission tomography), 120, 163
  blindness studies and, 120, 121
  for CRUNCH, 267
  for neurotransmission systems, 242
*Philadelphia*, 231
phonological processing
  memory and, 285–288
  phonological loop, 286
plasticity. *See also* brain development; brain plasticity; experience; lifespan development; plasticity, behavioral; plasticity, cortical; plasticity, evolutionary; plasticity, genetic; plasticity, memory; plasticity, neuronal; plasticity, societal
  activity patterns and, 17
  in aging, 260–263
  behavioral, 12, 45–46
  in brain development, 94–95, 328–330
  as concept, 9–14
  cortical, 47–49
  environmental modification-induced, 112–116
  evolutionary, 45
  experience-dependent, 41, 67
  genetic, 47
  interactionism and, 9
  memory, 246
  neurobiology and, 10
  neuronal, 12, 17, 46
  peripheral manipulation-induced, 116–120
  reciprocal modifiability and, 9
  societal, 12, 20
  sociocultural influences on, 42
plasticity, behavioral, 12, 45–46
  evolution and, 219
  parenting studies and, 46
  sociocultural influences and, 45
plasticity, cortical, 47–49
  lifespan development and, 48
plasticity, evolutionary
  brain development and, 45
  "niche construction" and, 45
plasticity, genetic, 47
plasticity, memory, 246
plasticity, neuronal, 12, 17, 46
  brain development and, 134
  experience-dependent, 153
  experience-expectant, 153

expertise and, 51–52
gene-driven, 153
maladaptive effects of, 53
"neural constructivism," 46
"perception of rule-based invariance"
and, 147, 153
plasticity, societal, 12, 20
sociocultural sciences and, 12–13
Portugal
illiteracy rates in, 282
literacy studies in, 282
positron emission tomography.
*See* PET
posttraumatic stress disorder. *See* PTSD
posture, aging's effects on, 359–360
preadaptations, 280
precursor cells, 87, 89
progenitor cells, 90–91
precursor cells and, 90
proteomes, 93, 219
proximal v. distal frames, 354–355
in IHET, 352, 354–355
in late adulthood, 362
pseudoword processing
illiteracy and, 289
literacy group studies and, 295
in working memory, 287–288
PsycINFO database, 307
PTSD (posttraumatic stress disorder),
330–332, 386
brain structure and, 335,
339–340
brain waves during, 335–339
core symptoms of, 330
hippocampus and, 386
"hot memory" and, 330
IAPS and, 335
RSVP paradigm in, 335
twins and, 387
Vietnam War during, 340
in women, 389
pure alexia, 187, 188
pure dysgraphia, 189

race biases, 209, 211
extinction learning and, 211
rapid serial visual presentation paradigm.
*See* RSVP
reading, 187–189
metalinguistic awareness and, 280,
286
pure alexia and, 187, 188

rearing conditions
dark, 112
in nature-nurture theories, 112–114
single orientation, 113–114
receptive fields. *See* RFs
*A la recherché du temps perdu* (A
Remembrance of Things Past) (Proust),
19
reciprocal modifiability, 9
retina
lesions, 118
retinofugal projections and, 121–123
RFs in, 118
retinal ganglion cells. *See* RGCs
retirement, brain development and, 314
RFs (receptive fields)
brain development and, size factors, 184
in retina, 118
spatiotemporal discrimination and, 141
RGCs (retinal ganglion cells), depletion of,
127
"Rock Around the Clock," 232
RSVP (rapid serial visual presentation)
paradigm, in PTSD, 335

scale systems, 227–229
schizophrenia, 104
selection
in lifespan development, 31, 310, 352
natural v. sexual, in musicality, 220
sexual, 221
selective attention, 137–140
*The Selfish Gene* (Dawkins), 393
SEM (structural equation modeling), for
cognition, 298
semantic anomalies, in language
development, 169
semantic fluency, 293–295
hierarchical cluster analysis of, 296
semantic strategies, for illiteracy, 288–289
semantic violations, in language
development, 167
sensory systems. *See also* visual system
development
"blooming buzzing confusion" and,
135
during child development, 136
development of, during blindness,
135–137
habituation and, 136
JNDs for, 142
pair matching for, 136

sensory/sensorimotor functioning, 32
    aging and, 359–360
    cognitive aging and, 360–361
    hearing, 359
    vision, 359
sexual dimorphism, 221
sign languages, 165
    aphasia in, 166
    ASL, 166
    lateralization processing of, 166
single photon emission tomography, for
        neurotransmission systems, 242
*Sleeping Beauty*, 393
SOC (selection, optimization,
        compensation), 263–264, 351–355. *See
        also* selection
    biological vulnerability and, 263
    cultural learning's influence on, 263
social learning
    fear conditioning and, 204–208
    language as, 204
societal plasticity. *See* plasticity, societal
sociocultural development
    behavioral plasticity and, 45
    *Homo sapiens* and, 27
    influences on, 42
sociocultural sciences, societal plasticity
        and, 12–13
socioemotional selectivity theory. *See* SST
spandrels, 219
spatial functions, 137–144
    bimodal stimuli and, 137
    ERP and, 137, 138
    haptic sense, 140
    imagery, 140–141
    navigation, 32, 363–364
    spatio-temporal discrimination,
        141–144
spatial navigation, 32
    age differences in, 364
    sample cases of, 363–364
spatio-temporal discrimination
    RFs and, 141
    ventriloquist illusion and, 141
speech perception, 70–71
*Der Spiegel*, 230
SST (socioemotional selectivity theory), 257,
        264
    future time perspective and, 264
stem cells, 87
    in adult neurogenesis, 85–88
    embryonic, 85

multipotency for, 85
progenitor cells from, 90–91
STG (superior temporal gyrus), language
        development and, 164
stress, 326–327. *See also* PTSD
    allostasis and, 333
    amygdala and, 333
    fear conditioning and, 332
    hippocampus and, 333
    hormones, 333
    HPA axis and, 333
    neurohumoral axes and, 333–335
    perinatal, 334
    PTSD, 330–332
    torture as, 337
    vasopressin-oxytocin peptides and,
        333
structural equation modeling. *See* SEM
substance abuse, 246
"superior memorizers," 245
superior temporal gyrus. *See* STG
syntactic processing, 170
syntactic violations, in language
        development, 166, 167

temporal windows, in co-construction
        hypothesis, 15
"tongue display unit," 120
transcranial magnetic stimulation,
        120
tuning systems, 227
*Twelve Monkeys*, 231
twins, PTSD and, 387

UCS (unconditioned stimuli), 200

vasopressin-oxytocin peptides, stress
        regulation by, 333
verb generation tasks, 268
Vietnam War, PTSD during, 340
violence
    cycles of, 344–345
    organized, 327, 342–344
    state-sponsored, 343
    "violence breeds violence," 31,
        340–342
    war as, 343
"violence breeds violence," 31, 340–342. *See
        also* PTSD
vision, aging and, 359
visual deprivation, 114–116, 118–119
    effects of, 115

monocular, 136
ocular dominance and, 114
visual system development. *See also*
  ocular dominance; spatial functions;
  vision
  behavior and, guided, 124
  blindness, 119–120
  "blindsight" and, 125
  brain development and, 68–70
  cell properties, 122
  congenital strabismus, 116
  depth perception as part of, 68
  eye misalignment and, 116–118
  face perception as part of, 69–70
  pattern perception as part of, 68–69
  retinal lesions and, effects on, 118
  retinofugal projections and, 121–123
  spatial functions in, 137–144
voices, memory for, 147, 152
*Voyagers* (spacecrafts), 217

*Walking* (Bernhard), 98
wars. *See also* "new wars"
  in Vietnam, PTSD effects of, 340
  as violence, 343
*Well-Tempered Clavier*, 217
WHO (World Health Organization), hearing
  loss estimates, 359
"wild associations," 100
Wisconsin Card Sorting Test,
    244
women, PTSD in, 389
writing, 189–191, 280
  allographic stage of, 190
  graphemic codes for, 190
  graphomotor stage of, 191
  lexical dysgraphics and, 190
  literacy and, 281
  pure dysgraphia and, 189

"Youth Radar" survey, 221